COMPETITIVE STRATEGIC MANAGEMENT

ROBERT BOYDEN LAMB, Editor
New York University

PRENTICE-HALL, INC., ENGLEWOOD CLIFFS, NJ 07632

Library of Congress Cataloging in Publication Data
Main entry under title:

Competitive strategic management.

   Bibliography: p.

   1. Corporate Planning–Addresses, essays, lectures.
I. Lamb, Robert
HD30.28.C648 1984   658.4'012   84-4781
ISBN 0-13-154972-3

To my son

Robert Kenneth Wittman Lamb

Editorial/production supervision and interior design: Eve Mossman
Cover design: Lundgren Graphics, Ltd.
Manufacturing buyer: Ed O'Dougherty

Printed in the United States of America

10 9 8 7 6 5 4 3 2

ISBN 0-13-154972-3   01

Prentice-Hall International, Inc., *London*
Prentice-Hall of Australia Pty. Limited, *Sydney*
Editora Prentice-Hall do Brasil, Ltda., *Rio de Janeiro*
Prentice-Hall Canada Inc., *Toronto*
Prentice-Hall of India Private Limited, *New Delhi*
Prentice-Hall of Japan, Inc., *Tokyo*
Prentice-Hall of Southeast Asia Pte. Ltd., *Singapore*
Whitehall Books Limited, *Wellington, New Zealand*

Contents

Preface

STRATEGIC ANALYSIS

Strategic analysis is still in its infancy. For roughly three decades there have been landmark studies of business strategy and structure, product life cycles, experience curves and learning curves, portfolio theories, growth share matrices, and various theories of business scenario formulations.

All of these separate and related analytical techniques are still being refined today. However, in addition, a concerted effort is being made by both corporate strategy management practitioners and strategy management consulting firms, as well as by research organizations and professors of business management, to search for entirely new strategic analysis techniques.

Included in this book are several new methods of strategic analysis. Walker Lewis and his associates in strategic planning in Washington, D.C., have developed a strategic evaluation technique based on shareholder value of investors' stock. David Hertz and Howard Thomas have further refined their earlier work on strategic risk analysis during turbulent times. Richard Rumelt has taken the bull by the horns and set out to create a full-scale strategic theory of the firm. McKinsey and Company has been exploring the strategic analysis ramifications of its formulation of an underlying theory of economic value. Another very large scale multi-industry, multicompany investigation into strategic analysis has been the PIMS research. Brad Gale and Ben Branch, by working with the extensive PIMS research into actual strategies of over one thousand corporations for the past fifteen years, have sought to develop an ROI benchmark for strategic performance.

Finally, a large portion of strategic analysis techniques remains focused on long-range planning as well as short-range and mid-range investigations of internal corporate organizational behavior changes. These studies have been extended enormously in the past decade by studies of issue analysis and of stakeholder analysis, along with some studies of business environmental threats and opportunities including interventions by various domestic and foreign governments, unions, social-interest groups, and demographic pressures.

Robert Boyden Lamb
New York University

Introduction

ROBERT BOYDEN LAMB

Strategic management is the prime focus of top corporate leaders today.

The reason why strategic management has become so vitally important is that there has been an enormous increase in business complexity and uncertainty. The time is past when chief executives or managers could simply guess about future plans. They cannot continue managing, budgeting, hiring, purchasing, and financing the way they always did. It is not enough to rely on hunches and guesswork and gut feel anymore because there are far too many pitfalls and problems and aggressive competitors who are already using strategic planning.

Strategic management starts by rethinking: What business should we be in? How are we now positioned to compete in that business versus others? What strengths and weaknesses and range of resources do we possess versus those of our present competitors or our potential competitors if we were to branch out to certain new businesses and new markets? In short, strategic management goes far beyond simply developing a strategic plan once and for all time. Strategic management is an ongoing process that assesses the business and the industries in which the company is involved; assesses its competitors and sets goals and strategies to meet all existing and potential competitors; and then reassesses each strategy annually or quarterly to determine how it has been implemented and whether it has succeeded or needs replacement by a new strategy to meet changed circumstances, new technology, new competitors, a new economic environment, or a new social, financial, or political environment.

Strategic management techniques today focus on how top businesspeople can accurately evaluate their own and their competitors' strengths and weaknesses; that is, they focus on the gathering of strategic information and its assessment. But strategic management also requires step-by-step analysis of how corporations can evaluate *each* product market, *each* new technology, *each* new cost change among their factors of production, along with financing, in order to reassess *their own* market position continually and choose appropriate goals. Each of these areas has received extensive attention from strategic mangement specialists.

There are now a number of quite different, but very detailed, techniques by which corporations can conduct their strategic self-evaluation. Basic portfolio analysis of each separate business in which the company is involved is the most common technique. Next is the formulation of detailed growth share matrices to examine, control, and reposition the growth potential of each separate business the company owns to decide which businesses or products to feed and expand and which to sell off or starve and which to simply milk as "cash cows."

For some strategic management theorists the best technique for self-analysis consists of building different scenarios of potential futures. For others the best method is strategic issue analysis or strategic scanning of the company's environment to anticipate future threats, pressures, opportunities, and change. Alternatively, some experts contend that the proper technique for a company's strategic self-analysis is to do an assessment of industry structure and its strategy constraints. Others recommend a careful study of the strategic groups within each of the industries in which the company competes to see which strategy works the best.

The most advanced and most comprehensive method of strategic industry analysis today focuses upon fluid "strategic arenas" in which different new industries are emerging and thereby obscuring and undermining traditional industries. "Strategic Industrial Morphology" is a final new technique for cross-industry strategic analysis.

Another basic approach to corporate self-analysis involves assessing the stage in the product life cycle—namely, development, growth, maturity, and decline of different products that the company sells. Still another approach consists of evaluating the intrinsic strengths or weaknesses in the *compatibility* of a company's functions, goals, products: their interdependence, mutual vulnerability, concentration, synergy—or ability to produce a higher financial return together than separately.

And for still other experts the strategic process must involve *all* these techniques together. But the critical problems of strategy formulation are that the very concept of corporate goals is becoming confused, not clarified, by this multiplicity of strategy techniques.

In short, is a company's strategic goal single, multiple, or combined, or is it an optimization of several different and conflicting or partially incompatible goals?

For example, is the strategic goal of a corporation strictly financial—i.e., bottom line, total profit, or return on equity, or return on investment, return on sales? Or is it some mix of these different objectives? In contrast, is the goal an operational strategic end such as production or distribution efficiency, or is the goal not profit maximization but growth? To expand the total volume of sales? Or growth of the total business assets? Or the achievement of lower cost? For some companies the strategic goal may be an intangible, such as achieving the top image of product quality or industry leadership in prestige. Or the goal may be internally relative, such as lowering last year's overhead costs. Or it may be industry relative, such as achieving constantly increasing profit margins, or capturing the industry's largest market share, or becoming the cheapest cost producer. For other companies the strategic goal is the carving out of a specific market niche in one product or one region of the country.

Alternatively, the company's strategic goal may be to diversify its businesses or products so that it is far less vulnerable to failure in an economic recession due to excessive concentration in one product or one business.

STRATEGY IMPLEMENTATION

Implementation of a corporate strategy involves the laying out of steps or stages of strategic change and development. Next a strategic implementation requires not only establishing a specific plan but also setting out a method of strategic funds programming in order to finance each stage of the corporation's strategic change and also a strategic focus for materials, resources, production, distribution, marketing, and control. Next the staffing or human resources strategy must be organized to ensure that the right executives, staff, and type of labor force are hired for, or focused on, carrying out each chosen strategy and specifically directed toward each of the parts of that strategy in sequence.

The few strategy implementation books and articles that have appeared have concentrated primarily on laying out and contrasting each of those steps or stages followed by actual companies today. This has been useful and in this book, for example, William Rothschild of General Electric explains how GE redesigns and carries out its strategic plan each year. These stages of strategy implementation will obviously vary in different companies and in different industries and sometimes between different products, but most corporate programs of strategy implementation include the same basic phases and stages in development and similar schedules of progress and similar hard choices for the allocation of material, financial, and human resources.

But perhaps the most important, and least well-understood, part of strategy implementation is the political infighting, coalition-building and power brokering involved in many corporate strategy implementation success stories and strategy failures. The politics of the strategy implementation process are absolutely central.

Strategy implementation will usually be divided into (1) a design fit stage; (2) a planning stage; (3) a reorganization stage, or restructuring of the current businesses; (4) an acquisition stage involving new businesses, new products, new technology, or new personnel; and (5) a stage for a progressive creation and development of a timetable of future strategic self-examination and yearly future planning stages. There is finally a stage of strategic evaluation and control to monitor and assess how well and whether this company's whole strategic formulation process made sense or actually failed to achieve any strategic goal that was set by the plan in the first place.

In contrast to strategic goal setting and strategy formulation, which have received considerable attention in books and articles and reports by corporations and professional management consultants and professors of management, strategy implementation has suffered from a lack of attention. Unpleasant and difficult and quite critical problems have arisen in strategy implementation because it has not yet received the necessary attention of top management in some companies, nor strong analysis by professors and consultants.

This situation is now changing and by 1990 will no doubt have improved. But in the meantime, in anticipation of this great need for more-detailed information on strategic implementation, we have devoted a disproportionate number of articles in this book to this area of strategic stages of implementation and human resource strategy because they have not been provided in previous work. In short, these articles will help you determine how you can fully implement a strategy in a step-by-step fashion. They will also make you aware of the key pitfalls and problems of strategy implementation, along with the relevant warning signals.

HUMAN RESOURCES STRATEGY

In this book we have included eight articles focusing on different aspects of *human resources strategy* because this is among the most important yet least understood reasons for corporate strategy failures today.

In short, human resources strategy is perhaps *the* crucial part of implementing strategic management systems—not the stage of goal setting, nor strategy formulation, nor funding priorities. Too many companies have failed to carry out their chosen strategy (1) because they put the wrong people in charge; (2) because these managers were offered contradictory plans, confused priorities, or improper rewards; (3) because the chief executive failed to lend sufficient weight to the strategic plan; or (4) because this executive did not indicate what should be the key goal; nor (5) did he or she spell out the proper financial and personnel rewards for managers, staff, and work force who were responsible for carrying out the strategy. The result? Chaos, confusion, resentment, backbiting, and unproductive divisions and waste of management's time in endless meetings that lead nowhere and reports that sit on the shelf and are not implemented.

Although there are countless books and articles on employee productivity, employee motivation, and personnel planning, very few publications have concentrated on how to implement human resources strategy successfully. Until recently, few managers or planners realized that there was a crucial link between strategy planning and human resources, and their inability to see this link was one of the reasons for the failure of many strategy implementations.

First, the type of manager chosen for a division, a product, or a project must be matched with the type of strategy that is to be implemented. All too frequently there is no match at all; indeed the managers and staff and work force are usually antagonistic to the strategy and subconsciously tend to sabotage or work at cross-purposes to the strategic long-range goals by continually opting for short-term profit in order to ensure that they obtain their raises or bonuses.

In some cases the strategy is never given a chance to work because all the financial incentives for the employees remain fixed in the old pre-strategic-management mold. By matching the type of manager's skills to the type of strategy chosen for his or her division, and especially by matching the manager's talents to the specific stage of the product life cycle involved in that profit center, a company should be better able to coordinate its strategy. For example, the stage of new-product development or the growth stage of a product may require a different type of manager and different type of team of employees than a product that is being phased out or sold off.

Second, paying for strategic performance is a key strategic management decision that involves designing the company's salary, bonus, reward, and promotion structure in such a way as to justify employee and management efforts to meet the long-term strategic goals, schedules, and stages of development. Simple as that sounds, however, it has proved to be the major stumbling block in the implementation of many corporations' strategic management systems. This reward structure must be clear and well understood so that the short-term profit maximization does not overwhelm or undermine the long-term strategy.

Third, the employee and management tasks, meetings, reports, and problems in carrying out the planning cycle and monitoring of the strategy are so time consuming that unfortunately a number of managements have frequently found that such strategy-monitoring tasks are self-defeating. Strategic planning and implementation are not easy and usually require complex assessments, evaluations, and coordination of whole networks of resources and ranges of functions from production, distribution, marketing, and financial departments and the coordination of a whole range of schedules and setting of new and different priorities for individuals at all levels of the corporation.

Above all, what this means is that the *strategy must make sense to all of those carrying it out.* The strategic management system must not simply result in confusion. Clear direction must exist to answer the competing claims of competing priorities. And in every organization there always are real or perceived competing claims on resources, money, time, initiative, or political clout. All the managers involved in the strategy, therefore, must be able to understand it and explain it to their staff of workers in order to have any chance whatever of successfully carrying it out.

This strategy coordination and rationalization is especially vital because today's corporations are increasingly moving toward matrix management, which is the complex interrelation of project teams of managers from all the different divisions to get specific top-priority tasks done immediately instead of working slowly through the separated bureaucratic functional divisions of a company.

Strategy implementation today in corporations with such a matrix form of management requires that all the different, quite separate, functional divisions coordinate these ad hoc teams on the spot and thereby draw from many specialists in all different areas as needed. Such teams form clusters to accomplish special projects or to produce key products, and thus strategic management systems in companies with matrix management systems are not and cannot be simply keyed to functions, or to single product markets, or to single goals, because these project teams must regroup in different ways with different members for different projects.

This matrix system is too complex to succeed by itself in fulfilling the strategy of the corporation unless a very conscious effort is made not only to tie the evaluation of the employee and his or her department together to measures of the overall strategies but also to make sure that the top overriding corporate strategy goals underlie the type of human and managerial organization that the company adopts—not vice versa.

Next the strategic-planning department or other strategic management groups in corporations frequently suffer because planning behavior is seen as lowly staff work and not as work for top-line management. Strategy is also seen as designing charts and paper pushing and unrealistic hopes for the future instead of being focused on tomorrow's immediate bottom-line profits. In other words, strategy is sometimes dismissed as unrealisitic. Also, strategic planning too often suffers from a pervasive corporate attitude that it is inconsequential: a playing with numbers out into the future, but not results-oriented to today or tomorrow. Hence some critics charge that there is no real way to evaluate and pay for or to stimulate strategic management activity except in a totally arbitrary fashion because the concrete results of a strategic change will not be known for perhaps years.

Then there is a concern among old-line traditional managers that this strategy management and strategy-planning business is dominated by whiz kids who don't know how to manage people or a budget or teams of production facilities. Strategic management planners also frequently represent a direct threat to the established ways of doing things. They *are* a real threat professionally, managerially, and in terms of finances, resources, and product markets because they are sometimes perceived as having excessive power to change things, but all too frequently they do not know enough about the businesses that they are changing or shifting or evaluating in order to ensure that their strategic changes are for the better. Indeed, some strategic management changes may well inevitably be for the worse. This is beause it is not short-term evaluation that counts in strategy but long-term changes, so that in the short term the company and the division and the product mix might well lose money.

Also there is the problem that foreign management methods—especially in Japan and Germany—have begun to make U.S. managers seriously doubt their own production experience, be skeptical of their own employee-management methods, and question their own basis of judgment. In short, American managers now wonder whether it is old carrots and old sticks that lead to productivity, or whether it is a totally different philosophy of employee-management cooperative planning that is needed to try to eliminate the age-old antagonistic relationship that exists in U.S. corporations.

In other words, human resources strategy inside the United States is crucial today specifically because it must confront very different practices abroad among our foreign competitors. And it is also crucial because the productivity of

U.S. workers has been steadily slipping while productivity in other countries has been steadily rising. Thus it is obvious that one of the key reasons for the need for strategic management today is to examine ways to make the same potential total corporate resources—especially human resources—stretch further to become more productive and efficient.

MERGERS—ACQUISITIONS AND DIVESTITURE STRATEGY

Mergers and acquisition strategy have been the major strategic forms of U.S. corporate growth during the past forty years. Acquisitions were usually considered less risky, much quicker, and even cheaper for a company than trying to develop from scratch a variety of new products or divisions internally in order to expand and diversify.

The result has been an inordinate pressure on top management to think strategically primarily (or sometimes exclusively) in terms of buying whatever growth business it lacked instead of even attempting to develop its own new business internally. In his article Harold Geneen, chief executive of ITT, analyzes that strategy of growth by acquisition, showing the arguments both for it and against it.

However, most of those unrelated business acquisitions that took place over the past forty years were often failures essentially because the acquiring management knew nothing about managing the newly acquired unrelated business or, for a variety of reasons, was unsuited to making a success of that newly acquired product mix. In short, these waves of unrelated acquisitions resulted in substantially lower and often negative returns. They also resulted in a lower rate of growth in our national GNP, than had these same companies spent these same sums to develop fledgling new business internally.

Looking back over this period of four decades, we see that there were overwhelming legal-governmental antitrust constraints that literally shaped this wave of unrelated mergers and acquisitions instead of the purchase of closely related businesses in a horizontal or vertical merger that was, or would have been, blocked or outlawed on the basis of this diminishing of competition, or restraining of trade, or leading to monopolies or oligopolistic power. Harold Geneen, Michael Porter, and A. Michael Spence focus on this key strategic phenomenon of critical regulatory constraints.

The primary strategic outcome of this legal-governmental set of constraints has been that corporations have made countless mergers with and acquisitions of unrelated businesses with little or no synergy and little or no shared experience, shared costs, shared supplies or production facilities, or shared markets. Almost inevitably, then, those acquirers who still lacked in-depth understanding of and skill at running or managing these acquisitions five or ten years later found their acquisitions largely unprofitable. Hence many of those unrelated mergers and acquisitions have been divested or put up for sale. Divestiture strategy has become a critical factor in strategic management practice today. Determining what businesses to sell, when to sell, how to sell, and especially how to manage the business up until the corporation sells to maximize its profit or minimize its loss have been topics investigated by various experts. Kathryn Harrigan has perhaps done the most work in this area and spells it out in her article on the strategic exit decision.

NEW TECHNOLOGY STRATEGY

New technology strategy is in part a distinct focus of its own. But the introduction of all types of new technology into each phase of a business is inextricably bound to the questions of human resources strategy and employee management planning. In other words, strategic decisions about new technology will in most cases directly affect and be affected by funding, as well as allocation and priorities assigned to the company's human resources.

Today we as a nation are finally beginning to realize that only a strategic focus on new high technology, new materials technology, new communications technology, new production technology, new distribution technology, and so forth, will offer the possibility for increased long-term productivity and true growth potential to enable American corporations to remain competitive internationally.

The key problems today in new technology strategy implementation include designing a corporate organization capable of using, adapting, appraising, and devising new technology instead of stifling it. Introducing new technology leads corporations to question their old ways and to question how they should refocus their managerial time, internal political force, span of control, type of direction, and bureaucratization of the work force.

New technology that is devised and adopted by a corporation, however, can also (1) eliminate vast numbers of workers, (2) exhaust a corporation's capital expansion, and (3) destroy a corporation's traditional character. Many negative consequences of a new technology are difficult to predict. New technology puts enormous strains not only on a corporation's strategic ability to change and be flexible but also on a corporation's strategic resources—financial, human, material, etc.

For many corporations the key strategic question involved in fast-changing industries is whether to attempt to be the technological leader. Should they assume the substantial research and development expense, resource commitment, and risk of failure? Or, instead, adopt a role as technological follower in the industry and let other companies lead, hoping to capitalize on their experimental mistakes by capturing this market later—when it may be too late. In short, what are the risks and rewards of adopting a technological pre-emtive strategy versus a technological predator strategy? What are the chances of a company's leapfrogging the technology of competitors? Can it successfully establish a new experience curve for the industry? Alternatively, what is the likelihood of failure with the new technology; either to make it work, or to gain sufficient market acceptance in a period brief enough to ensure its financial viability. What is this technology's life-span and how soon will it be eclipsed? Other crucial issues involve ensuring the company's ability to afford the lengthy delays and inevitable cost-overruns in adopting a new technology as well as to cope with internal corporate organizational resistance to all the shifts and sacrifices.

Perhaps most important, new technology must be completely integrated into a corporation's overall strategy, not simply added on as an afterthought to a ready-made ongoing organization. Corporate strategic managers must seek out, develop, and make use of the whole range of all types of new technology, such as new materials and CAD–CAM computer-aided design and computer-aided manufacture, robotics, and genetic engineering, which have each received the greatest publicity to date. But strategic planners must also anticipate the whole range of new technology that can involve new chemicals, plastics, textiles, metals, fibers, and energy sources, as well as new distribution channels, new communication networks, new information-gathering techniques, and new methods of product development.

It is toward this larger objective of encompassing the strategic management implications of all new technology that we have included articles on (1) how to design the innovative organization, (2) how to use the new technology that a company develops or acquires, and (3) how to analyze the importance of new technology for strategic planning itself and for achieving strategy goals, strategy formulation, and strategy implementation. New technology is also important for monitoring and evaluating and controlling strategy. In short, these new technologies represent not only new materials and tools but new integral parts of the strategic management process itself.

PART ONE
STRATEGIC GOALS AND STRATEGY
FORMULATION

1

On Corporate Strategy

BRUCE D. HENDERSON
The Boston Consulting Group, Inc.

From *Henderson on Corporate Strategy* (Cambridge, Mass.: Abt Associates, Inc., 1979), pp. 3–44.
Reprinted by permission.

BUSINESS STRATEGY TODAY

Since the beginning of business, all firms have had plans and all firms have followed some kind of strategy. Characteristically, both the plans and the strategy have been intuitive or traditonal. However, the increasing pace of change is forcing management to make their strategies explicit and often to change them. Strategy as such is getting more and more attention.

There are many ways of thinking about strategy development. In a static sense it can be thought of in terms of strengths and weaknesses. By using military parallel, it is possible to think of it in terms of concentration of strength against competitors' weaknesses. However, the military analogy has only a limited application to business because business is a continuing process, not just a battle, a campaign, or even a war to be won and finished.

More useful concepts of corporate strategy relate the firm to its competitors in terms of a competitive system in equilibrium. Any really useful strategy must include a means of upsetting the competitive equilibrium and re-establishing it again on a more favorable basis. This is why strategy is more than a posture or a pattern; it is a dynamic concept involving sequence, timing, and competitive reaction.

Mathematics has made a contribution to strategy, particularly in terms of decision theory and risk evaluation. However, there are broad problems of strategy in which the critical factor depends upon perceptions, attitudes, and business brinkmanship. Strategy is far more than an application of logic. In any given business it is usually the reaction or initiative of a few key competitors who determine the stability of the competitive situation. Assessment and use of competitors' behavioral characteristics often require the exercise of business brinkmanship.

Any approach to strategy quickly encounters a conflict between corporate objectives and corporate capabilities. Attempting the impossible is not good strategy; it is just a waste of resources. On the other hand, setting inadequate objectives is obviously self-defeating. However, setting the proper objectives depends upon prejudgment of the potential success of the strategy used. Yet, you cannot determine the strategy until you know the objectives. Strategy development is thus a reiterative process requiring art as well as science.

Some of the frustrations we have just mentioned may account for the fact that many corporate strategies are traditional and intuitive rather than logical and tightly reasoned. But there *are* concepts and techniques which are of great value in approximating the opportunities of a corporation and speeding up the process of strategy development.

One of these concepts, for example, involves market segmentation. This has its military parallel in terms of isolating the battlefield. There are also some parallels with the duelist's choice of weapons, although in business it is the challenger who has the choice.

A market can be viewed in many different ways, and a product can be used in many different ways. Each time the product-market pairing is varied, the relative competitive strength is varied too. Many businessmen do not recognize that a key element in strategy is choosing the competitor whom you wish to challenge as well as choosing the market segment and product characteristics with which you will compete.

Business has only financial objectives in the final analysis. Judicious use of financial insight can be a major strategic weapon. It is easy to demonstrate that in some industries superior financial policies can be the equivalent of twenty, thirty, forty percent or greater differential in selling price. The financial equivalent of that price/cost differential can permit price reductions of that magnitude and still achieve the same results in profit, growth, and return to stockholders with the same underlying cost structure. Strategic use of this kind of potential differential is heavily dependent on effective risk analysis and on accurate determination of the true cost of capital. To be effective, this approach to strategy must be based on system analysis, not factor evaluation.

It is interesting to observe that many companies make intuitive decisions which are often correct, even though they are in direct contradiction to the logic of the policies they state. This reflects the highly intuitive character of such policies. For example, many companies state that they will not undertake any investments in which the before tax return on assets is less than, say, twenty percent. Yet, they will make investments in certain kinds of projects with far less return than this. Company consumer finance operations are a typical example. This paradox has a sound basis even though it is unstated. But it need not be so implicit. There are ways of equating risk, return, and cost of capital. These relations can be used in such a way that competitive advantages will, in fact, be optimized.

Over the past several years the fast pace of some industries, such as electronics, aerospace, and certain kinds of chemicals, has dramatized the need for industrial economic concepts. It is now beginning to appear that technology and economics can be related in a quantitative fashion in a dynamic model. It is possible to approximate the effect of interaction between competitors when technical progress is a major factor. For example, it now seems practical to place an approximate price tag on the value of a change in market share and evaluate the return on investment, even for a fast-moving, rapidly growing technical product.

Many of these newer concepts produce real problems of internal organization. In a dynamic economy, all of the factors of technology, finance, marketing, and competitive economics are interrelated. Optimizing functions instead of the whole company is far from adequate to produce superior corporate performance. Such organizational concepts leave only the chief executive in a position to think in terms of the corporation as a whole.

Complex corporations have tried in many ways to broaden the scope of the chief executive in dealing with such complexities. Many of these approaches were well suited to a slower paced economy and nonintegrated operations. The profit center concept was one such approach.

Unfortunately, the profit center concept emphasizes short-term consequences, which are often transient, rather than shifts in competitive equilibrium over time. Even worse, it is disfunctional when it optimizes the profit center instead of the corporation as a whole.

Innovations in organization have also become necessary. The computer has provided some assistance, and specialized staff has been useful in many cases. However, it is becoming increasingly necessary to find a more effective organizational arrangement for dealing with corporate strategy on a continuing basis. Many companies do need to relate separate businesses. Each business may be facing major policy choices which are of far-reaching significance to the future of each such business. Yet each business must be related to the company as a whole and its objectives too.

The accelerating rate of change is producing a business world in which customary managerial habits and organization are increasingly inadequate. Experience was an adequate guide when changes could be made in small increments. But intuitive and experience-based management philosophies are grossly inadequate when decisions are strategic and have major irreversible consequences. Supersonic airliners, antimissile missile systems, and a common computer language, for example, are producing such obvious problems that the management alternatives are being discussed in the public press. Fortunately, the state of the art in strategy development is itself changing at an accelerating rate.

Stategy concepts need to be explicit in order to be executed in a coordinated fashion in complex organizations. But concepts are the very thing that have been missing from strategy discussions in businesses in the past. Now, more than ever before, the rewards for a conceptual model of the business appear to by pyramiding. Those managers who can conceptualize their strategy and make it explicit in terms of a system of competition will dominate their businesses in the future.

There are an increasing number of conceptual models of business relationships. Many of these can be quantified enough to at least establish the sensitivity of the various factors and to determine the stability or instability of the various relationships.

The fact that these concepts can be quantified also means that they can be programmed for a computer. This now offers the opportunity for economically and quickly exploring a range of combinations and alternatives that was utterly impossible a short while ago. Perhaps more important, this machine-man interface is vastly accelerating the learning process by which a manager acquires a complete grasp of complex relationships. The combination of new concepts plus new techniques promises a major acceleration in the development of explicit strategies.

Strategy development for business is only in its infancy. It is still very much an intuitive art, although both concepts and techniques are available to change this art into something closer to a logical, explicit, and orderly analysis.

Strategy is something quite different from administrative skills. Unfortunately, the two are typically grouped together under the heading of "Management."

One prediction seems safe: explicit and sophisticated approaches to strategy are emerging. The rewards for developing a superior business strategy are great. The state of the art can be expected to move extremely fast in the immediate future.

THE STRATEGIC PERSPECTIVE:

Growth and Equilibrium

In most firms strategy tends to be intuitive and based upon traditonal patterns of behavior which have been successful in the past. In growth industries or in a changing environment, this kind of strategy is rarely adequate. In any company a significant improvement in performance over time usually depends upon a change in strategy if previous operations have been competently managed.

A significant change in strategy is always a momentous and difficult process. It requires a complete rethinking of the organizations's objectives, resources, and competitive relationships. The change itself requires a reorientation of values at every level in the organization if the change is to be implemented effectively. Good corporate strategy needs to be explicitly stated and the objectives need to be widely understood even if the underlying reasoning is not revealed.

When the growth rate exceeds the cost of capital, the competitive relationships become inherently unstable. Aggressive competition then produces revolution instead of evolution in competitive relationships.

A growth situation is fundamentally different, in its strategy requirements, from a normal competitive relationship. All large businessess were once small. At some time in their growth they passed through a high growth rate period. What made for success then is not necessarily appropriate later.

A business should be regarded as a system in equilibrium. An effective corporate strategy is a predetermined sequence for the allocation of resources in such a fashion that the equilibrium will be shifted to a more favorable relationship.

To examine equilibrium in this sense requires system analysis of financial, technoeconomic, brinkmanship, and organizational factors, in addition to the effects of accelerated growth rate.

Financial Strategies

Astute use of financial resources can often produce competitive advantages equal to many years of normal growth. It is easy to demonstrate that in some industries financial policies can produce the equivalent of a ten, twenty, thirty percent or more differential in costs relative to otherwise equivalent competitors.

There is a convincing amount of evidence that in growth industries this particular kind of financial leverage can be reconverted directly into an essentially permanent differential in product cost, as well as a differential in market participation.

Failure to use corporate assets aggressively not only makes a company vulnerable in its markets but, equally important, can cause the company to be raided, the purchase funded in fact with the company's own money.

Aside from financial strategies of competition, there are often major opportunities for achieving corporate goals through financial engineering. When market, tax, or book values are not congruent, there is usually an opportunity to arbitrate the difference and convert it into a strategic advantage.

Market Strategies

Market strategies are all based upon segmentation and concentration of resources. A market can be viewed in many different ways, and each time the market-product pairing is varied, the relative competitive capability is changed also.

Segmentation implicitly means identifying competitors, and their resources relative to yours, for each relevant market-product pairing. Successful market strategies in effect segment the total market in a way that minimizes competitors' strengths while maximizing yours. The parallel in military strategy is "isolating the battlefield." Control Data's spectacular success in entering the computer market against IBM is a classic example of astute segmentation. Most dramatically successful business strategies are based on market segmentation and concentration of resources in that segment.

Technoeconomic Product Strategies

There is an impressive array of evidence that cost, price, margin, market share, and accumulated experience are directly related in a characteristic pattern. This pattern can be used in a predictive fashion to see what would normally be expected to happen if individual competitors chose various alternatives in their own strategy. These consequences involve the combined effects of technology, scale, organizational effectiveness, financial constraints, and market elasticity.

It is possible to demonstrate that, at various stages of product development, the critical strategy element shifts from technical lead, to financial resources, to organizational policy coordination, and finally to market share.

It is also possible to demonstrate that competitive equilibrium is highly unstable under certain conditions, conditionally unstable under others, and finally the equilibrium is almost certain to become essentially stable.

Brinkmanship Strategies

It is not usually recognized that competitive equilibrium must be the result of voluntary self-restraint by all competitors. If this were not true, then unlimited competition would exhaust the resources of successive competitors until only one survived. This does not happen because individual competitors become convinced that their best interests are served by not pushing competition beyond a certain point. Sometimes this point is determined by the lack of incremental reward, even if the competition is successful. More commonly, self-restraint is imposed by expectations about competitive reactions.

It follows that appraisal of probable competitive reaction is critical to predicting the consequences of any strategy. It also follows that anything which influences competitive decision making can be of great importance. All improvements in market share, for example, depend upon convincing competitors that it will not be worthwhile to invest in serving a larger market.

Business brinkmanship is based on the recognition that (1) competition has a psychological and emotional side; (2) it is absolutely necessary to understand the irrational content and emotional biases of competitors' behavior; and (3) indeed, success in business is often linked with the ability to predict and capitalize on the response of competitors to your strategic actions.

Strategy and Organization

Different kinds of organization are required to implement different kinds of strategy. There must be tradeoffs between degree of coordination, speed of response, dependability of behavior, and amount and kind of information available. The vast difference between military organization and that of a university derives from more than tradition and cultural background. The differences reflect very real requirements for effective specialization of decision making in dissimilar environments requiring dissimilar deployment and control of resources.

For the corporation with multiple products and multiple profit centers or administrative units, organizational form automatically limits potential strategies.

Business Strategy
on an International Scale

Competition across national boundaries is becoming increasingly significant. This is both a major opportunity and a major added threat. In effect, the business chess game becomes three-dimensional. This added dimension has its own special characteristics. Unless these are understood in terms of long-term equilibrium, they can provide very unpleasant surprises.

The producer with the largest home market has some significant strategic advantages if other things are equal. Capitalizing on this advantage usually requires quite different strategies, however, from those which were successful in that home market.

THE FUNDAMENTAL RULE OF STRATEGY

"Induce your competitors not to invest in those products, markets, and services where you expect to invest the most." That is the fundamental rule of strategy.

Competitors determine your market share. Competitors determine your price. Competitors determine your return on investment. They do this by their investments.

If your competitors invest much more rapidly than the market grows, there is almost no way for anyone to make a profit. If competitors for any reason avoid investment in a given business, then there is no real limit on the market share or price level of those who are willing to invest in advance to supply the market.

After periods of inflation, it is usually unnecessary to dissuade competitors from investing. This is particularly true if inflation has been followed by depression. Inflation is always followed by "stagflation" before prosperity returns. In periods such as 1976, competitors do not invest. They have been persuaded. The problem changes to convincing yourself to invest in the face of apparently far from adequate returns.

Inflation makes the return on new investment seem correspondingly low compared to the return on capacity bought at preinflation prices.

Inflation makes the required minimum return higher by the amount of inflation itself just to finance the inflation.

The recession following inflation makes the need for added capacity seem distant.

The liquidity squeeze that ends inflation makes new debt to both finance inflation and add capacity seem like double jeopardy.

Inflation persuades all, or nearly all, competitors to underinvest.

Yet failure to invest at a rate equal to physical market growth plus inflation plus depreciation will inevitably lead to shortages. Shortages lead to higher prices. Prices must inevitably rise until the apparent return induces enough investment to relieve the shortage. It must be this way sooner or later.

Those who have additional existing capacity during a period of shortage and extended delivery are inevitably able to achieve a market share equivalent to their then available capacity.

If an increase in market share is achieved, it can and should result in a proportionate reduction in cost due to the experience curve effect. Increased market share times increased cost differential leads to an exponential increase in profit multiplied by the added margin required to induce others also to invest in added capacity. Thus, for those with the foresight, resources, and wisdom to invest in capacity before others are willing to do so, the rewards can be high.

The obvious risk-free place to invest is in those product-market areas where you are already the leader and low-cost competitor. The risk must be less for you than for those who have higher costs. The profitable company is rare indeed which does not make most of its profit in those few product-market sectors in which it is the acknowledged leader or very close to being the leader.

Those products and markets where someone else is the clear-cut leader are impregnable if the leader has acheived his cost potential, is well managed, and well financed. However, such leaders are often overtaken and passed by higher cost competitors when such leaders optimize short-term performance instead of long-term competitive advantage.

If you have the will and the resources to invest, then periods following high inflation, recession, and liquidity squeeze are periods of major opportunity. These are the periods in which it is not necessary to discourage investment by competitors—they have already been discouraged.

Unless you believe that inflation is permanently over and will not need to be financed, unless you believe that industry growth has stopped and no more capacity will be needed, unless you believe that prices will never rise enough to justify further investment, then it should be obvious that investing in capacity before it is needed will be handsomely rewarded. You will be severely punished if you wait to invest until you are already out of capacity while your competitors did not wait.

However it is done and whatever the business climate, the fundamental rule of strategy remains the same. You must directly or indirectly induce your competitors to refrain from investment in those areas which you find the most attractive for investment. It has been done many times before. If it had not, you would not see high-cost, low-share challengers take away the market share of entrenched, low-cost leaders.

BUSINESS STRATEGY CONCEPTS

Spectacular business successes are usually new ways of doing business in familiar markets with familiar products. These are the true strategic victories, won by using corporate resources to substantially outperform a competitor with superior strength.

The concept of superior performance without superior resources is usually identified with trying harder. Yet most companies seem to work very hard to produce only minor differentials in performance.

The underlying principle of a good strategy is simple: "Concentrate your strength against your competitor's relative weakness." This principle has a major corollary in a dynamic competitive environment: concentration of effort will inevitably produce a counter-concentration by competition; therefore, timing and sequence are critical. A major attack should never be launched against a competent, well-entrenched competitor without first eliminating his ability or willingness to respond in kind.

There are many prerequisites to a successful strategy:

The characteristics of the competition must be known in detail, including characteristic attitudes and behavior.

The environment in which competition will take place must be equally well understood.

Your own relative strengths must be accurately and objectively appraised.

The strategic concept must not be based on the obvious exercise of known strengths. If it is, you don't need a strategy, just a plan.

It must be possible to achieve stability if the strategy succeeds.

Your own organization must not be misled by your efforts to outmaneuver competition. Strategic goals must be very explicit.

Once the strategic framework has been designed, the tactics of attack must be selected. Concentration of resources can be achieved in several ways:

Choose the most vulnerable market segment.

Choose products or markets which require response rates beyond a competitor's ability.

Choose products or markets which require capital that a competitor is unwilling to commit.

Recognize the commercial potential of new technology early.

Exploit managerial differences in style, method, or system, such as overhead rate, distribution channels, market image, or flexibility.

The value of the initiative depends on when and how the competiton responds. Therefore, an effective strategy must choose the best initiative and also dissuade competition from responding. This is a fundamental strategic concept that is often neglected. Strategic success almost always depends upon the competitor's decision not to compete. Therefore, ability to influence the competitor's decision is critical. It is necessary to win in the mind of the competition.

Diversion and dissuasion fall into classic categories:

Appear to be unworthy of attention. Quickly cut off a part of the market which is too small to justify a major response. Repeat.

Appear to be unbeatable. Convince competitors that if they follow your lead and practices, they will gain nothing since you will equal or better any market actions they take.

Avoid attention. Be secretive. Do not let competitors know about new products, policies, or capabilities until it is too late for them to respond effectively.

Redirect attention. Focus competitive attention on the major volume areas of company sales, not on the high-potential areas.

Attract attention but discredit significance. Overstate and overpublicize the potentials of new products or policies.

Appear to be irrational. Take actions which seem emotional or implusive but which make competitive investment unattractive.

These and other patterns have exact counterparts in military behavior. In business as in war, the lessons of experience teach the same thing:

> . . . We can at least crystallize the lessons into two simple maxims—one negative, the other positive. The first is that, in the face of the overwhelming evidence of history, no general is justified in launching his troops in a direct attack upon an enemy firmly in position. The second, that instead of seeking to upset the enemy's equilibrium by one's attack, it must be upset before a real attack is, or can be, successfully launched.
>
> Liddell Hart, *Strategy*

A GUIDELINE FOR BUSINESS STRATEGY

Any businessman who can answer certain basic questions better than his competitors has a major strategic advantage. Most of these questions are asked constantly, in one form or another, in virtually every company:

> What are my competitors' costs?
>
> Why do I make money on one product but lose money on an equally good one?
>
> How shall I price this new product?
>
> How much is more market share worth for a given product? Alternatively, what are *all* the costs of losing market share?
>
> Should I lower prices? When? By how much?
>
> How much capacity shall I add? When?
>
> What will prices be next year? Five years from now?
>
> Why have my prices broken so sharply? When will the decline stop?

All these issues are part of a single fundamental question: why does one competitor outperform another (assuming comparable management skills and resources)? Are there basic rules for success?

There do indeed appear to be rules for success, and they relate to the impact of accumulated experience on competitors' costs, industry prices, and the interrelations between the two.

Prices

It is a matter of nearly everyone's experience that the price of a new product declines after its initial introduction and as the product becomes more widely produced and commonly available. In recent years, the rate of new product growth in some markets has been so high that it has been easy to observe the price decline during the early life of many new products. With some, such as semiconductor devices, the postintroduction decline has been so rapid that it has been the subject of considerable attention in the industry.

It is not commonly recognized that price declines follow a remarkably consistent pattern and that the pattern appears to apply to a wide range of products. The characteristic pattern is one in which the price declines by a constant percentage with each doubling of the total number of units produced by the entire industry.

This kind of decline has previously been observed in the labor cost element of various products. In describing the decline in the hours of labor required to produce a product, it has become customary to speak of a "learning curve." Hirschmann[1] recently reviewed many aspects of the learning curve and pointed out its importance as a tool of operating management. Texas Instruments Corporation[2] has used its knowledge of this relationship in the semiconductors market to set management objectives.

Costs

If prices decline according to a set pattern, then *costs* of successful producers must behave in a similar manner. Costs declining more slowly would eventually exceed prices. Costs declining more rapidly, by steadily increasing profits, would attract more competition and capacity, with a resulting pressure for price declines.

The key phenomenon, then, is the decline of unit cost made possible by increased experience, even though most (but not all) of our observed data relate the decline of *unit price* to increased experience.

There is a natural reluctance to accept the possibility that costs can always be reduced. Although Hirschmann's paper argues this point effectively, it is worth emphasizing the reasons for its plausibility. For example, we are accustomed to an annual and substantial increase in national manufacturing produc-

[1]Winfred B. Hirschmann, "Profit from the Learning Curve," *Harvard Business Review,* January–February 1964, pp. 125–39.

[2]"Texas Instruments: All Systems Go," *Duns Review,* January 1967, p. 25 et seq.

tivity measured in terms of real output per man-hour. Why should this occur year after year?

Some of the improvements may be due to the fact that operatives have learned to perform their production tasks more effectively. Some of the improvement may be caused by the adoption of better methods, scheduling, and work organization. Some may be ascribed to improved tools and capital investments. Even so, a major cause of increases in productivity is technological change, which periodically provides a new basis to which the traditional improvements can be applied.

Implications for Business Strategy

The implications of such cost behavior are profound indeed. The concepts of competition, return on investment, public policy, and corporate strategy are all affected.

The most important implication, by far, is that competitive relationships are not stable. If gains in market share (and thus accumulated experience) produce lower costs *relative to competition,* then this can be converted into further increases in market share. This, of course, suggests a significant influence on corporate strategy potentials.

If costs, prices, volume, and relative earning power over time can be quantitively related to each other, then we have a powerful tool for evaluating strategy alternatives. This, in fact, seems to be the potential which cost/volume and price/volume slopes offer and is a compelling reason to understand the characteristic behavior thoroughly.

In a sense, this insight is not basically different from the well-known learning curve phenomenon. However, the implications are far more profound than the mere prediction of labor costs. It appears that the basic relationship applies to the full range of costs, including development, capital, distribution, and overhead, as well as labor costs. Furthermore, the characteristic relationships among competitors seem to be determined by these patterns.

If this concept is valid, then we can predict the conditions under which relationships among competitors will stabilize.

CONSTRUCTION OF A BUSINESS STRATEGY

Most companies feel they are in a highly competitive business. Most companies regard their competitors as the principal obstacle to either higher profits or faster growth. This is natural and proper. The question is how to compete.

Strategy is the manner of using resources which is expected to provide superior results in spite of a competitor's otherwise equal or superior capabilities.

Games have been classified as: (1) games of chance, (2) games of skill, and (3) games of strategy. For the purpose of this discussion, assume that chance and skill are equally distributed. How can a business firm develop a superior strategy?

We can assume that each firm is relatively free to choose its businesses. This choice can be expressed in terms of product line, market segments, geographical coverage, or other elements. However, the choice of business also determines the competition. Therefore, freedom to choose the business means freedom to choose who the competitors will be.

Firms are never identical. They have different histories and traditions, different resources, different reputations, different management styles, and often different objectives. These differences may be either strengths or weaknesses, depending upon the strategy chosen. We can assume that such differences exist, and that they are important to the choice of strategy.

We can also assume that neither your own nor your competitor's objectives are simple or obvious. There are many tradeoffs between near-term and long-term profits; growth and profits; growth in assets and growth in reported profits; stability and growth; dividends and growth; and stockholders, employees, creditors, and others. It is reasonable to assume that these differences will result in different goals for different competitors.

It is also safe to assume that the future will produce a substantial amount of change in technology, markets, and competitors. Any strategy must take this change into account.

Based upon these assumptions, the starting point for strategy development should be:

1. definition of the business area involved
2. identification of the significant competitors in that business area
3. identification of the differences between you and the significant competitors
4. forecast of the changes in the environment which can affect the competition
5. identification of your own objectives and any known differences between them and those of competitors

These are all obvious factors, but they should be made explicit since a change in one requires a re-examination of the entire sequence.

The difficult part of constructing a strategy is the development of the strategy concept. Any strategy of value requires that you follow a different course from your competitors; or initiate action which will not be effective for the competitor if he attempts to emulate you; or follow a course which will have quite different, and more favorable, consequences for you than for your competitor.

The essential element of successful strategy is that it derives its success from the differences between competitors, with a consequent difference in their behavior. Ordinarily, this means that any corporate policy and plan which is typical of the industry is doomed to mediocrity. Where this is not so, it should be possible to demonstrate that all *other* competitors are at a distinct disadvantage.

Strategy development, then, consists of conceiving of ways and means to emphasize the value of the differences between you and your competitors. The normal procedure includes the following sequence:

1. Start with the present business as it now is.

2. Forecast what will happen to its environment in general over a reasonable period of years. This includes markets, technology, industry volume, and competitive behavior.

3. Predict what your performance will be over this period if you continue with no significant change in your policies or methods of operation.

4. If this is fully satisfactory, then stop there, since you do not need to develop any further to achieve satisfaction. If the prediction is not fully satisfying, then continue.

5. Appraise the significant strengths and weaknesses that you have in comparison to your more important competitors. This appraisal should include any factors which may become important (finance, marketing ability, technology, costs, organization, morale, reputation, management depth, etc).

6. Evaluate the differences between your policies and strategies and those of your major competitors.

7. Attempt to conceive of some variation in policy or strategy which would improve your competitive posture in the future.

8. Appraise the proposed alternate strategy in terms of possible risks, competitive response, and potential payout. Evaluate in terms of minimum acceptable corporate performance.

9. If this is satisfactory, then stop strategy development and concentrate on planning the implementation.

10. If a satisfactory result has not been found in the previous stages, then broaden the definition of the present business and repeat the cycle above. Ordinarily, redefinition of the business means looking at other products you can supply to a market which you know and understand. Sometimes it means supplying existing products to a different market. Less frequently, it means applying technical or financial abilities to new products and new markets simultaneously.

11. The process of broadening the definition of the business to provide a wide horizon can be continued until one of the following occurs:
    a. The knowledge of the new area becomes so thin that a choice of the sector to study becomes intuitive or based upon obviously inadequate judgment.

b.   The cost of studying the new area becomes prohibitively expensive because of lack of related experience.

c.   It becomes clear that the prospects of finding a competitive opportunity are remote.

12.   If the existing business is not satisfactory and no attempt to broaden it offers satisfactory prospects, then only two alternatives exist:

a.   Lower the performance expectations.

b.   Reverse the process and attempt to find an orderly method of disin-
vestment.

The critical element in strategy development is the development of a concept. This is an inherently intuitive and cut-and-dry process, even though first-
class staff research is an absolutely essential prerequisite to success.

Thus, the process of constructing a business strategy tends to be a continuous cycle. It cannot be otherwise. Strategy development is an art, not a science.

CORPORATE STYLE
AND CORPORATE STRATEGY

Strategy Dynamics

The strategies required for growth are utterly different from those required
to maximize profit in a static business. Many of the usual controls and measures
of performance are misleading and sometimes dysfunctional.

For static businesses and products, the near-term cash payouts represent a
large portion of the present value, even though the profitability may continue
forever. By contrast, virtually the entire present value of growth products depends upon volume, profit margin, and cash throwoff after growth has subsided.

This produces an apparent paradox. Static products appear highly profitable but present no investment potential. Growth products offer a very high investment return but depress profits and are not self-financing. Conventional
management control measurement obscures the very large strategy opportunity
that is implicit in these relationships.

Financial Strategy

All business strategies can be cast in financial terms since return on equity
investment is the common denominator. Fundamentally, this is the value of cash
put in compared with the value of cash returned later.

The short-term performance measurements can become inverted where
there is a dynamic factor in apparent investment return because of growth. Less
debt can become more risky than more debt. Lower prices can produce a higher
return on investment than higher prices. Many financial measurements which

are useful and valid in steady-state or static situations are strategic traps in growth situations.

These financial misperceptions can be converted into very potent competitive strategies. The conventional management controls can prevent competitors from reacting to aggressive strategies or perceiving the missed opportunities.

Experience Cost and Price Policy

Much of the dynamic character of growth products results from the influence of growth on costs. Rate of growth can be directly related to rate of decline in costs by Experience Curve Theory, which states that differences in growth rate will result in progressively greater differences in cost. Characteristically, this cost difference is translated back into continued differences in growth rate. The result, of course, is a continuing shift in relative ability to compete.

Shifts in competitive capability are almost always reflected in either price behavior or shifts in market share penetration. However, different competitors have different attitudes toward price level and growth rate. These differences are fundamental consequences of market and production economies, as well as corporate history. Because this is true, it is possible both to explain and to predict characteristic price behavior. Experience Curve Theory provides a full integration of the relationships among growth, market share, cost, price, and competitive stability. Competitors' attitudes are the only significant unknown variable. Good businessmen should know their competitors.

Computers and Strategy

Successful and experienced businessmen have an intuitive feel for many strategic relationships. Unfortunately even intuitive genius has severe limitations in practice. In the absence of a conceptual base, it is impossible to communicate or teach the basis for decision. Alternatives cannot be explored by discussion or logic. Optimization is impractical because sensitivity cannot be checked. This leads inevitably to strategy conservatism or unacceptable risks in spite of insight and intuitive genius.

However, even when these concepts are made explicit and are well understood, they are still complex in terms of calculation and analysis. Before the advent of computers, many of these relationships were too difficult to calculate in any practical fashion. They were used either intuitively or not at all.

Modern computers provide the necessary means to translate concepts into simulations and models. With computers, many things can be explored which would otherwise be merely a matter of conjecture or opinion. This kind of process underlies the dramatic improvement in inventory utilization in the last decade. However, simulation can be applied to strategy models of the business concepts as easily as it can to inventory models or decision rules.

The really significant application of the computer is in policy formulation. If the concepts and relationships are made explicit, it is possible to use computers to simulate the reaction of the business to policy changes. Only in this way is it possible to optimize the differences in policies over time for the different products that constitute a modern diversified business. A similar process has been used for years to teach captains of jetliners how to adjust to the differences among similar aircraft of great complexity and cost. The rewards for business strategy simulation are far greater than those for jet aircraft flight simulation.

Acquisitions and Strategy

Evaluation of strategy alternatives often points to the need for more change in corporate resource application. Acquisitions are often a useful way to cause an instant recapitalization of the company, an instant increase in debt capacity, or an instant opening of major investment opportunities. Often, acquisitions provide one time instant increases in *reported* earning. Yet, by itself, acquisition can merely convert a mediocre company into a larger, less manageable, equally mediocre company. The real payoffs in acquisitions come from sequential fitting of companies into a strategic plan which requires specific elements at specific times. Acquisitions are a means to an end, not an end in themselves. Evaluation of true synergy is possible only in the context of a strategy concept.

Organization and Strategy

Business optimization has profound implications for business organization as well as for policy formulation. During the fifties, there was a near fad of decentralization and line-staff organization. This was a natural attempt to deal with increasing complexity, size, and diversity by mixing specialization and dispersion of authority.

Yet, present concepts of business dynamics demonstrate dramatically that there are no independent parts of any corporation if it has any reason for being a single corporation. Operations must be decentralized as a practical matter. They are too complex and too diverse. Simultaneously, the choice of objectives, the coordination of action, and the implementation must be conceived, evaluated, optimized, planned, and programmed centrally. The individual units of a corporation are no more independent profit centers than the ships in a navy are independent of each other's behavior.

Management Style
and Strategy

The conclusion seems inescapable that the combination of dynamic business concepts, growth potential, and computers requires a basically different management style for competitive success than the traditional approaches of the past. There are multiple examples of companies who grow into giant, diversified corporations from humble beginnings, far outstripping their more traditional competitors. Perhaps they take far greater risks in their growth period, but they seem to more than compensate by their greater relative strength when they succeed. Yet, it takes a concept of the business as an integrated dynamic whole in equilibrium with its competitive environment to be able to evaluate alternate risks versus rewards. That evaluation, of course, is the essence of business policy, investment, and management.

INTUITIVE STRATEGY

Strategy formulation does not come easily even for the experienced executive. The seasoned executive has many years of trial and error behind him in his adminsitrative skills. He has learned from many mistakes; he has been conditioned. He knows what happens if he does something different. None of this applies to strategy.

Strategy cannot be changed very often. It is, by definition, the essentially irretrievable commitment of resources. Consequently, few executives ever see strategy changed. It is almost never possible to know what alternative strategies would have accomplished. In any case, strategy decisions are not visible except to senior executives. Real exposure to strategy considerations does not begin until near the peak of an executive's career.

Neither experience nor intuition is of much help in strategy formulation even if both are vital to implementation. Systematic analysis of competitive equilibrium is the only technique that works. This kind of analysis is not a normal executive skill or requirement. It is also a way of thinking that is difficult to learn.

The multidivision corporation with multiple products and numerous overlapping competitors is a particularly complex strategy problem because it has so many alternatives open. The usual solution is to break the problem down to manageable size by dividing the company into profit centers and treating each as if it were an independent operation.

However, profit centers offer no genuine solution to this complexity. Profit center optimization is certain to be suboptimization for the corporation as a whole. The results are almost sure to fall far short of the company's potential.

Profit centers are not and cannot be independent; they share common financial resources. As a consequence, the actions of one profit center automatically place constraints on the others. Furthermore, each profit center has differing opportunities to use the common resources. The activities of each profit center have quite differing effects on common competitors.

The whole competitive system must be optimized at once in order to improve performance. Competitors, too, are always very much a part of the system, and their reactions must be integrated in the analysis. Strategy and performance can be optimized only if the whole system is fully understood.

Most significant multidivision companies can be more profitable, grow faster, and simultaneously lower prices even if their operating efficiency is unchanged. Corporate performance is a function of corporate strategy and control as a whole, not the sum of individual profit centers or product strategies.

Product portfolio strategy is the real basis for competitive superiority among multidivision, multiproduct companies. All product markets should not be treated alike. Some products should supply investment opportunities; others should supply the funds to invest. Current profitability is not the measure of performance, value, or of appropriate management objectives.

> Some products are highly profitable but have no future except to generate cash. They are not an investment opportunity now.
>
> Others are very unprofitable now but can be richly rewarding if the appropriate investment is made soon enough.
>
> Some products are profitable now, but the real payoffs will come later if position is merely maintained.
>
> Other products appear profitable but in fact will be cash traps forever.

Choices of this kind are not made well by intuition. Nor are most companies equipped to make them using a systems approach.

Each product in the multidivision portfolio has a different role, a different use, and requires a different objective. The use of identical goals and common objectives for all profit centers is a certain and guaranteed way to insure inferior performance.

The utility of each product in a company's portfolio cannot be determined except with reference to the product portfolio of the significant competitors. The match between product portfolios in business can be as critical as the match between the cards held in a poker game. In both cases, the proper use of superiority can result in the winner taking all. In both cases it is perceived relative strength that really matters.

Strategy is more complex than the profit center concept implies. A profit center is not an independent company. It does not have the same constraints as a separate company. Nor does the independent company have the same investment opportunities it would have as part of a balanced multidivision, multiproduct company.

Operating and administrative units of a multiproduct company should have objectives that are considerably more complex than those implied by reported profit. No operating unit of a multidivision company can set its own objectives properly until the corporate strategy has defined the corporate priorities.

Cash flow control is the integrating feedback loop that supplies the information to permit the multiproduct company to optimize its performance. Cash flow control disregards the artificial classifications of expense and capital investments. Strategy based on cash flow analysis focuses on the ultimate measure of performance: "How fast is cash input compounded?" Every other factor is included in that single number if the cash is traced until it becomes cash output.

The opportunity for the multidivision company is often very great. It has the ability to concentrate its resources where they will be the most productive. But such concentration requires a strategy specifically designed to outperform specific competitors on specific products in a specific sequence. Such strategy is not a position or posture. It is a sequence of moves.

Real success for the multiproduct company requires a company-wide coordination of sequence and timing in the deployment of resources. Failure to do this is the underlying reason why many multiproduct companies perform no better than a portfolio of unrelated investments. Success for the multidivision business depends upon organization around a strategy, not vice versa.

In the absence of an overall corporate strategy, the multidivision corporation is handicapped. It has higher overhead. It has less flexibility. It has no advantage of importance except financial reserves. This lack of strategy is formalized in the conventional profit center organizational form. Typical profit center control guarantees suboptimum objectives and performance.

A multidivision company without an overall strategy is not even as good as the sum of its parts. It is merely a portfolio of nonliquid, nontradable investments, with added overhead and constraints. Such closed-end investments properly sell at a discount from the sum of the parts. Intuition alone is an inadequate substitute for an integrated strategy.

BRINKMANSHIP IN BUSINESS

A businessman often convinces himself that he is completely logical in his behavior when in fact the critical factor is his emotional bias compared to the emotional bias of his opposition. Unfortunately, some businessmen and students perceive competition as some kind of impersonal, objective, colorless affair, with a company competing against the field as a golfer competes in medal play. A better case can be made that business competition is a major battle in which there are many contenders, each of whom must be dealt with individually. Victory, if achieved, is more often won in the mind of a competitor than in the economic arena.

I shall emphasize two points. The first is that the management of a company must persuade each competitor voluntarily to stop short of a maximum effort to acquire customers and profits. The second point is that persuasion depends on emotional and intuitive factors rather than on analysis or deduction.

The negotiator's skill lies in being as arbitrary as necessary to obtain the best possible compromise without actually destroying the basis for voluntary mutual cooperation of self-restraint. There are some common-sense rules for success in such an endeavor:

1. Be sure that your rival is fully aware of what he can gain if he cooperates and what it will cost him if he does not.

2. Avoid any action which will arouse your competitor's emotions, since it is essential that he behave in a logical, reasonable fashion.

3. Convince your opponent that you are emotionally dedicated to your position and are completely convinced that it is reasonable.

It is worth emphasizing that your competitor is under the maximum handicap if he acts in a completely rational, objective, and logical fashion. For then he will cooperate as long as he thinks he can benefit. In fact, if he is completely logical, he will not forgo the profit of cooperation as long as there is *any* net benefit.

Friendly Competitors

It may strike most businessmen as strange to talk about cooperation with competitors. But it is hard to visualize a situation in which it would be worthwhile to pursue competition to the utter destruction of a competitor. In every case there is a greater advantage to reducing the competition on the condition that the competitor does likewise. Such mutual restraint is cooperation, whether recognized as such or not.

Without cooperation on the part of competitors, there can be no stability. We see this most clearly in international relationships during times of peace. There are constant encroachments and aggressive acts. And the eventual consequence is always either voluntarily imposed self-restraint or mutual destruction. Thus, international diplomacy has only one purpose: to stabilize cooperation between independent nations on the most favorable basis possible. Diplomacy can be described as the art of being stubborn, arbitrary, and unreasonable without arousing emotional responses.

Businessmen should notice the similarity between economic competition and the peacetime behavior of nations. The object in both cases is to achieve a voluntary, cooperative restraint on the part of otherwise aggressive competitors. Complete elimination of competition is almost inconceivable. The goal of the hottest economic war is an agreement for coexistence, not annihilation. The competition and mutual encroachment do not stop; they go on forever. But they do so under some measure of mutual restraint.

"Cold War" Tactics

A breakdown in negotiations is inevitable if both parties persist in arbitrary positions which are incompatible. Yet there are major areas in business where some degree of arbitrary behavior is essential for protecting a company's self-interest. In effect, a type of brinkmanship is necessary. The term was coined to describe cold war international diplomacy, but it describes a normal pattern in business, too.

In a confrontation between parties who are in part competitors and in part cooperators, deciding what to accept is essentially emotional or arbitrary. Deciding what is attainable requires an evaluation of the other party's degree of intransigence. The purpose is to convince him that you are arbitrary and emotionally committed while trying to discover what he would really accept in settlement. The competitor known to be coldly logical is at a great disadvantage. Logically, he can afford to compromise until there is no advantage left in cooperation. If, instead, he is emotional, irrational, and arbitrary, he has a great advantage.

Conclusion

The heart of business strategy for a company is to promote attitudes on the part of its competitors that will cause them either to restrain themselves or to act in a fashion which management deems advantageous. In diplomacy and military strategy the key to success is very much the same.

The most easily recognized way of enforcing cooperation is to exhibit obvious willingness to use irresistible or overwhelming force. This requires little strategic skill, but there is the problem of convincing the competing organization that the force will be used without actually resorting to it (which would be expensive and inconvenient).

In industry, however, the available force is usually not overwhelming, although one company may be able to inflict major punishment on another. In the classic case, each party can inflict such punishment on the other. If there were open conflict, then both parties would lose. If they cooperate, both parties are better off, but not necessarily equally so—particularly if one is trying to change the status quo.

When each party can punish the other, the prospects of agreement depend on three things:

1. each party's willingness to accept the risk of punishment
2. each party's belief that the other party is willing to accept the risk of punishment
3. the degree of rationality in the behavior of each party

If these conclusions are correct, what can we deduce about how advantages are gained and lost in business competition?

First, management's unwillingness to accept the risk of punishment is almost certain to produce either the punishment or progressively more onerous conditions for cooperation—provided the competition recognized the attitude.

Second, beliefs about a competitor's future behavior or response are all that determine competitive cooperation. In other words, it is the judgment not of actual capability but of probable use of capability that counts.

Third, the less rational or less predictable the behavior of a competitor appears to be, the greater the advantage he possesses in establishing a favorable competitive balance. This advantage is limited only by his need to avoid forcing his competitors into an untenable position or creating an emotional antagonism that will lead them to be unreasonable and irrational (as he is).

Rules for the Strategist

If I were asked to distill the conditions and forces described into advice for the business-strategist, I would suggest five rules:

1. You must know as accurately as possible just what your competition has at stake in his contact with you. It is not what you gain or lose, but what he gains or loses that sets the limit on his ability to compromise with you.
2. The less the competition knows about your stakes, the less advantage he has. Without a reference point, he does not even know whether you are being unreasonable.
3. It is absolutely essential to know the character, attitudes, motives, and habitual behavior of a competitor if you wish to have a negotiating advantage.
4. The more arbitrary your demands are, the better your relative competitive position—provided you do not arouse an emotional reaction.
5. The less arbitrary you seem, the more arbitrary you can in fact be.

These rules make up the art of business brinkmanship. They are guidelines for winning a strategic victory in the minds of competitors. Once this victory has been won, it can be converted into a competitive victory in terms of sales volume, costs, and profits.

THE NONLOGICAL STRATEGY

The goal of strategy in business, diplomacy, and war is to produce a stable-relationship favorable to you with the consent of your competitors. By definition, restraint by a competitor is cooperation. Such cooperation from a competitor must seem to be profitable to him. *Any competition which does not eventually eliminate a competitor requires his cooperation to stabilize the situation.* The agreement is usually that of tacit nonaggression; the alternative is death for all but one competitor. A stable competitive situation requires an agreement between competing parties to maintain self-restraint. Such agreement cannot be arrived at by logic. It must be achieved by an emotional balance of forces. This is why it is necessary to appear irrational to competitors. For the same reason, you must seem unreasonable and arbitrary in negotiations with customers and suppliers.

Competition and cooperation go hand in hand in all real-life situations. Otherwise, conflict could only end in extermination of the competitor. There is a point in all situations of conflict where both parties gain more or lose less from peace than they can hope to gain from any foreseeable victory. Beyond that point cooperation is more profitable than conflict. But how will the benefits be shared?

In negotiated conflict situations, the participant who is coldly logical is at a great disadvantage. Logically, he can afford to compromise until there is no advantage left in cooperation. The negotiator/competitor whose behavior is irrational or arbitrary has a great advantage if he can depend upon his opponent being logical and unemotional. The arbitrary or irrational competitor can demand far more than a reasonable share and yet his logical opponent can still gain by compromise rather than breaking off the cooperation.

Absence of monopoly in business requires voluntary restraint of competition. At some point there must be tacit agreement not to compete. Unless this restraint of trade were acceptable to all competitors, the resulting aggression would inevitably eliminate the less efficient competitors leaving only one. Antitrust laws represent a formal attempt to limit competition. All antimonopoly and fair trade laws constitute restraint of competition.

Utter destruction of a competitor is almost never profitable unless the competitor is unwilling to accept peace. In our daily social contacts, in our international affairs, and in our business affairs, we have far more ability to damage those around us than we ever dare use. Others have the same power to damage us. The implied agreement to restrain our potential aggression is all that stands between us and eventual elimination of one by the other. Both war and diplomacy are mechanisms for establishing or maintaining this self-imposed restraint on all competitors. The conflict continues, but within the implied area of cooperative agreement.

There is a definite limit to the range within which competitors can expect to achieve an equilibrium or negotiate a shift in equilibrium even by implication. Arbitrary, uncooperative, or aggressive attitudes will produce equally emotional reactions. These emotional reactions are in turn the basis for nonlogical and arbitrary responses. Thus, nonlogical behavior is self-limiting.

This is why the art of diplomacy can be described as the ability to be unreasonable without arousing resentment. It is worth remembering that the objective of diplomacy is to induce cooperation on terms that are relatively more favorable to you than to your protagonist without actual force being used.

More business victories are won in the minds of competitors than in the laboratory, the factory, or the marketplace. The competitor's conviction that you are emotional, dogmatic, or otherwise nonlogical in your business strategy can be a great asset. This conviction on his part can result in an acceptance of your actions without retaliation, which would otherwise be unthinkable. More important, the anticipation of nonlogical or unrestrained reactions on your part can inhibit his competitive aggression.

PREVENTING STRATEGY
OBSOLESCENCE

There is nothing new about long-range planning, corporate strategy, or corporate development. Only the emphasis is new. By one means or another, all companies in the past have adjusted to changes in competition, markets, and technology. All companies to some degree have always had plans for improving their situation.

A few companies have been very successful, and their success rapidly brought them fame and profits. Others have had equally spectacular difficulties. For most companies, however, life has consisted of working very hard to produce small differences in performance. Yet in even the most static industries, the perspective of history reveals that different strategies eventually produce quite different consequences.

Corporate success for any company must be the result of superior use of that company's distinguishing characteristics. Yet few companies attempt to examine the strategy which brought them success in the past. Moreover, success reinforces the organization's belief in the essential correctness of past methods, philosophy, and competitive posture. So long as the underlying competitve conditions and relationships continue to hold, the corporate success may also continue. But in time these conditions must change.

This is why strategies become obsolete and inappropriate in a changing world. It is a matter of common observation that more companies seem to fall prey to creeping decline than to identifiable or specific mistakes by management in decision making.

While a persuasive case can be made that intuitive leadership was responsible for the early success of most businesses, an almost equally persuasive case can be made that this intuitive strategy cannot be extended indefinitely if:

> the organization becomes large
>
> the management generations increase
>
> the initial environment changes substantially

The first major policy question about strategy, then, is whether an intuitive or implicit corporate strategy, defined only by the cumulative evidence of past decisions, is adequate, or whether it is necessary to have a strategy that is: (1) derived from analysis, (2) explicitly stated, (3) supported by consensus, and (4) modified by methodical reviews.

In the absence of an explicit strategy, the adaptation to changing conditions is almost certain to be deferred until past successful strategies are clearly failing. Intuitive and implied strategy adjustments are apt to be too late, too slow, and even inappropriate to cope with rapid change in a complex organization.

In complex, large-scale organizations the decision making is neceesarily so diffuse that direction cannot be changed by means of individual decisions without chaos. It must be changed by changing explicit goals and approach methods (strategy) or by changing people.

The natural course of inquiry would seem to start with the present strategy, the present resources, the present competition, and the present environment. The natural pursuit of insight would seem to require an ever widening field of exploration and analysis. But for the starting point to be useful for comparison, it must be explicit:

Why has the company succeeded against this competition in this environment?

Is there a consistent pattern which constitutes a strategy?

What are the critical factors for the strategy to succeed?

Is there a reasonable possibility of any of these factors being significantly affected by either changes in the environment or competitive action?

Only in this fashion can the projection of past success into the future be validated.

Experience repeatedly demonstrates that conditions change and competitors take the initiative. Not only does new technology provide new means, but the whole market is constantly changing in character. Therefore, an extension of past strategy is essentially a negative course. No matter how well chosen it may be, the fact remains that sooner or later it will become inappropriate.

Still, successful strategy revision in an organization is a difficult task. The very lack of explicitness about past and current strategy and the reasons for its success can be an obstacle to accepting the need for change. High morale carries with it the implicit assumption that personal competence rather than strategic leverage is the underlying cause for superior performance. In the absence of an explicit analysis and acceptance of the strategies of the past, it is almost a foregone conclusion that any effort to change them will be regarded as an attack against those who administered them.

Underlying the entire problem of strategy formulation are pervasive difficulties of definitions, semantics, and symbols for conceptual thinking. In most business situations, there are severe constraints on the issues which may be raised. Ordinarily, decisions are made within a framework of precedent, policy, organizational responsibility, and assumptions about the purpose and nature of the business. Even the most important decisions involving capital expenditure and new product introduction are made within these bounds. The direction and character of the business are usually assumed to be unchanged. For this reason, many important strategic assumptions are accepted without question.

Another fundamental difficulty in strategic planning is that there is no inherent limit to the freedom of choice. Yet the universe is too large to explore.

There is an inescapable necessity to limit the area of study to manageable proportions. But how and where? How far into the unknown must exploration go to be a reasonable investment of time and effort? When and how should this review of strategic plans take place?

As we examine these questions, it becomes clear that the role of the chief executive is far more comprehensive in the area of strategic planning than it is in the operation of the business. Whereas operating responsibilities can be delegated, strategic planning cannot. Operations can be managed by means of precedents and controls, but strategic planning requires that all decisions be treated as exceptions. Most important of all is the fact that the intuitive character of these decisions permits only the chief executive to take the initiative. For this reason, only the chief executive is within his authority in calling for a definition of strategy or in initiating a fundamental change in corporate behavior.

STRATEGIC SECTORS

A strategic sector is one in which you can obtain a competitive advantage and exploit it. Strategic sectors are defined entirely in terms of competitive differences. Strategic sector analysis performs the same function as cost effectiveness analysis. Cost effectiveness analysis optimizes value versus cost. Strategic sector analysis optimizes margin relative to competition.

Strategic sector analysis, like cost effectiveness analysis, ignores the adminsitrative unit until the objective and its feasibility have been evaluated. The resources and the program component are assigned as necessary to adminsitrative units in order to accomplish the mission.

Strategic sectors cut across profit centers, strategic business units, groups, divisions, departments, markets, and all other administrative units. The boundary of a strategic sector is defined by the maximum rate of change of relative competitive margin as you cross that boundary.

Strategic sectors exist because the same product can be made in many variations and supplied with many related services. Each feature and each service has a cost. But the value added by such increments varies from customer to customer. It affects product design, manufacturing capability, and distribution practices. Every change in these factors affects both cost and value simultaneously.

Design requires a focus on the strategic sector to be served. Yet every compromise of that focus either adds cost or reduces value.

Manufacture also requires a focus on the strategic sector to be served. Compromises and variety produce the same consequences on cost and value. No job shop can match the cost of a full-scale, focused factory operation.

A given strategic sector can rarely use more than one distribution channel. Since different channels have different costs and provide different services, they appeal to different customers. Therefore, customers of one channel tend to be in a different strategic sector than those served by other channels. Competitors who try to serve both strategic sectors at the same price are handicapped by a too high price in one sector and a too high cost in the other sector.

Profit centers and strategic business units are self-defeating in terms of profit unless the whole company is the profit center. GM can be the most profitable competitor because the whole company is the business unit while internal adminsitrative units are tailored to focus on value added in strategic sectors in which they can be the largest factor.

Profit centers originated when companies became too big and complex to be managed by individual function. Decentralization, however, led to suboptimization and loss of internal financial mobility that is critical to strategic concentration.

Strategic business units were devised to reverse the effects of overfragmentation into profit centers. So-called SBUs attempted to aggregate all the strategy decisions in an adminstrative unit. However, the critical factor, cash flow, cannot be delegated to any SBU. If it were, then the parent would merely be a lock box holding company without strategic options as a company except divestment or acquisition.

Strategic sectors are the key to strategy because each sector's frame of reference is competition. The largest competitor in an industry can be unprofitable if the individual strategic sectors are dominated by smaller competitors. Thus, market share in the strategic sector is what determines profitability, not size of company.

THE STRATEGY REVIEW

Few companies question their strategy when all operations are profitable and successful. Success itself is the justification for continuation of the practices, policies, and patterns which brought about that success. There appears to be no need for strategy review.

When a company is in difficulty, strategy is subordinated to operations. The near-term problems of current profitability are given the highest priority. The time horizon contracts, and management performance is measured by this year's profits. There is no time for strategy review; the cost and effort appear to be an unwarranted luxury.

It would almost seem as if there is no appropriate time for a critical reappraisal of corporate strategy. Yet it is obvious that periodically the basic practices of the company must change to deal with changing conditions and competitive capabilities. If this does not happen, then the company becomes the prisoner of its own past success. It is unable to change course until unsatisfactory results make it obvious to everyone that the strategy should have been changed long before.

This pattern suggests that the success of the present must be fully understood before constructive changes can be made. It is a fact that random changes in any complex system almost invariably degrade the system performance

The pattern also suggests that constant change in an orderly and purposeful fashion is necessary. The environment and the competition are constantly evolving, even if the company is not. These external changes will degrade performance unless the whole system is adjusted to accommodate to and take advantage of such change. The question is: "When should this review of the system as a whole occur and how can it be done?"

A strategy review is a very demanding and time-consuming task; it requires a reassessment of all underlying assumptions, and reconstruction and evaluation of all interlocking relationships. In effect, a strategy review is a system equilibrium analysis. Such analysis is a major undertaking.

Under ordinary circumstances, a company can hardly afford to question most of the characteristic policies which it follows. Too much of this kind of introspection would paralyze the ability of management to carry on everyday operations. However, at its best a strategy review does not occur as a separate event which happens periodically and is otherwise forgotten. Ideally, it is an iterative process, a sequence of theory formulation, analysis, validation, reformulation, reanalysis, and re-evaluation. If it happens this way, the critical underlying assumptions receive the attention that is required to appreciate fully their far-ranging significance. Day-by-day feedback is evaluated and checks and balances of the system are observed. The system itself is tuned. From this process a gradual evolution and upgrading can and does occur. This is probably how most strategies for an on-going business evolve. It *is* an evolution.

The process is probably primarily intuitive for most people. In this form, it has one characteristic weakness. Except under real stress, it is all too easy to be satisfied with superficial explanations and easy rationalizations. There is no pressure to analyze deeply or re-examine the underlying fundamentals.

Characteristically, intuitive insights can tolerate great inconsistencies and ambiguities no matter how brilliant or important. Fortunately, the communication and implementation of the conclusions require verbalization and discussion. This is a critical part of the rationalization of intuitive insight. Further, it leads to the exploration and testing of the whole system of relationships, not just a single facet of a relationship. This validation of various perspectives is one of the major contributions of group discussion, regardless of the decision-making process itself.

At their best, explication and reformulation lead to a full consensus of members of the organization in regard to company goals and methods. This means that the strategy becomes a part of the corporate culture. The organization is improved because the internal policies become part of the everyday knowledge of every member of the organization.

At its worst, strategy review founders on one of two extremes. At one extreme, no consensus is reached; the organization never accepts the goals; the required policies are modified beyond recognition in implementation. At the other extreme, complete acceptance of the strategy is reinforced by its success until the strategy becomes sanctified, such that questioning the strategy and its underlying assumptions becomes an attack on the organization itself.

Clearly, strategy must be under constant review; this is a demanding process in which objectivity and thoroughness are extremely difficult to achieve. Obviously, it requires a high degree of executive skill to encourage and manage the process of strategy review. This is more the art of management than the science.

A test of the mastery of this art is possible. A specific written review of strategy is a revealing exercise, as well as a record of the perspective and reasoning at a given point of time. Such a written analysis also has the great advantage of providing the focus for the discussion and depth understanding which leads to both consensus and further improvement. Discussion and communication may be far more valuable than any tangible end product.

A truly effective strategy review will answer these questions to the general satisfaction of the organization:

Where do we put our priorities in allocating our resources in money and effort?

What are the major policies that we choose to implement the strategy?

What are the products and markets in which we choose to compete?

What critical assumptions are we making about the competition and the environment?

Exactly what do we expect to do differently or better than our competitors to be successful?

Not many companies make their strategies explicit. Not many even question their strategies in any formal fashion until they are in some difficulty. This may be changing. Explicit strategies have always been normal in areas where events characteristically move fast, such as in war and politics. Events are moving rapidly now in business, too.

An effort to review corporate strategy formally and make it specific is likely to be very frustrating and reveal considerable confusion on the subject. It can also be very much worth the effort.

BUSINESS THINKING

Business thinking starts with an intuitive choice of assumptions. Its progress as analysis is intertwined with intuition. The final choice is always intuitive. If that were not true, all problems of almost any kind would be solved by mathematicians with nonquantitive data.

The final choice in all business decisions, is of course, intuitive. It must be. Otherwise, it is not a decision, just a conclusion—a printout.

The tradeoff between subjective nonquantifiable values is by definition a subjective and intuitive choice. Intuition can be awesome in its value at times. It is known as good judgment in everyday affairs. Intuition is in fact the subconscious integration of all the experiences, conditioning, and knowledge of a lifetime, including the emotional and cultural biases of that lifetime.

But intuition alone is never enough; in fact, alone it can be disastrously wrong. Analysis, too, can be disastrously wrong. Analysis depends upon keeping the required data within manageable proportions. It also means keeping the nonquantifiable data to a minimum. Thus, analysis, by its very nature, requires initial oversimplification and an intuitive choice of initial assumptions, as well as exclusion of certain data. All of these choices are intuitive. A mistake in any one can be fatal to the analysis.

A complex problem entails a nearly infinite combination of facts and relationships. Business in particular is affected by everything, including the past, the nonlogical, and the unknowable. This complexity is compounded by multiple objectives to serve multiple constituencies, many of whose objectives must be traded off. In the face of such complexity, problem solving requires an orderly, systematic approach in order to even hope to optimize the final decision.

When the results of analysis and intuition coincide, there is little gained except confidence. When the analysis reaches conclusions that are counterintuitive, then more rigorous analysis and re-examination of underlying assumptions are always called for. The expansion of the frame of reference and the increased rigor of analysis may be fruitful.

But in nearly all problem solving there is a universe of alternative choices, most of which must be discarded without more than cursory attention. To do otherwise is to incur costs beyond the value of any solution and defer the decision to beyond the time horizon. A frame of reference is needed to screen the intuitive selection of assumptions and the relevance of data, methodology, and implicit value judgments. That frame of reference is the concept.

Conceptual thinking is the skeleton or the framework on which all the other choices are sorted out. A concept is by its nature an oversimplification. Yet its fundamental relationships are so powerful and important that they will tend to override all except the most extreme exceptions. Such exceptions are usually obvious in their importance. A concept defines a system of interactions in terms of the relative values that produce equilibrium of the system. Consequently, a concept defines the initial assumptions, the data required, and the relationships among the data inputs. In this way it permits analysis of the consequences of change in input data.

Concepts are simple in statement but complex in practice. Outputs are almost always part of the input by means of feedback. The feedback itself is consequently a subsystem interconnected with other subsystems.

Theoretically, conceptual business systems can be solved by a series of simultaneous equations. In practice, computer simulation is the only practical way to deal with characteristic multiple inputs, feedback loops, and higher order effects in a reasonable time, at reasonable cost, and with all the underlying assumptions made explicit. Pure mathematics becomes far too ponderous.

Concepts are developed in hard science and business alike from an approximation of the scientific method. They start with a generalization of an observed pattern of experience. A concept is stated first as a hypothesis, then postulated as a theory, then defined as a decision rule. It is validated by its ability to predict. Such decision rules are often crystallized as policies. Rarely does a business concept permit sufficient proof to be called a "law," except facetiously.

Intuition disguised as status, seniority, and rank is the underlying normative mode of all business decisions. It could not be otherwise. Too many choices must be made too often. Data is expensive to collect, and is often of uncertain quality of relevance. Analysis is laborious and often far too expensive, even if only superficial.

Yet two kinds of decisions justify rigorous and painstaking analysis, guided by intuition derived from accumulated experience. The irrevocable commitment of major reserves of resources deserves such treatment. So do the major policies which guide and control the implementation of such commitments.

All rigorous analysis is inherently an iterative process. It starts with an intuitive choice and ends with an intuitive decision. The first definition of a problem must be intuitive in order to be recognized as a problem at all. The final decision is also intuitive; otherwise, there is no choice and therefore no need for decision.

Between the beginning and ending points, the rigorous process must take place. The sequence is analysis, problem redefinition, reanalysis, and then even more rigorous problem redefinition, and so forth until the law of diminishing returns dictates a halt—intuitively.

The methodology and sequence of business thinking can be stated or at least approximated as follows:

State the problem as clearly and fully as possible.

Search for and identify the basic concepts that relate to the perceived critical elements.

Define the data inputs this conceptual reference will require. Check off and identify any major factors which are not implicitly included in the conceptual base.

Redefine the problem and broaden the concept as necessary to include any such required inputs.

Gather the data and analyze the problem.

Find out to which data inputs the analysis is sensitive. Reexamine the range of options with respect to those factors and the resulting range of outputs.

Based on the insights developed by the analysis, redefine the problem and repeat the process.

Reiterate until there is a consensus that the possible incremental improvement in insight is no longer worth the incremental costs. That consensus will be intuitive. It must be, since there is no way to know the value of the unknown.

It is a matter of common observation that much of the value of a rigorous and objective examination of a problem will be found in one of three areas:

First, the previously accepted underlying assumptions may prove to be invalid or inadequate as the problem definition is changed.

Second, the interaction among component functions may have been neglected, resulting in suboptimization by function.

Third, a previously unknown, unaccepted, or misunderstood conceptual framework may be postulated which both permits prediction of the consequence of change and partially explains these consequences.

It is also a matter of common observation that the wisest of intuitive judgments comes after full exploration of and consensus on the nature of the problem by peers with equivalent but diverse experience.

Finally, it is generally recognized that implementation of the optimum decision will prove difficult if that discussion and consensus have not been continued long enough to make the relationship between the overall objective and the specific action seem clear to all who must interpret and implement the required policies. Otherwise, the intuition of those who do the implementation will be used to redefine the policies which emerged from analysis. This is one reason why planned organizational change is so difficult, and random drift is so common.

Here are some fundamental procedural suggestions. Define the problem and hypothesize the approach to a solution intuitively before wasting time on data collection and analysis. Do the first analysis lightly. Then, and only then, redefine the problem more rigorously and reanalyze in depth. (Don't go to the library and read all the books before you know what you want to learn.) Use mixed project research teams composed of some people with finely honed intuitions from experience and others with highly developed analytical skills but too little experience to know what cannot be done. Perhaps in this way you can achieve the best of both analysis and intuition in combination and offset the weaknesses of each.

2

Managing Strategies Incrementally

JAMES BRIAN QUINN
Dartmouth College

When sophisticated large organizations make significant changes in strategy, the approaches they use frequently bear little resemblance to the rational-analytical systems so often touted in the planning literature. Such systems are rarely the source of overall corporate strategies. Instead the processes used to generate major strategies are typically fragmented and evolutionary with a high degree of intuitive content. Although one usually finds imbedded in these fragments some very refined pieces of formal analysis, overall strategies tend to *emerge* as a series of conscious internal decisions blend and interact with changing external events to slowly mutate key managers' broad *consensus* about what *patterns* of action make sense for the future. Following are some further conclusions from a multiyear study of how major organizations actually do change their strategies.[1]

Normative: Not "Antiplanning"

In my sample, managers purposely guided important actions *incrementally* toward strategies embodying many of the structural principles of elegant formal strategies. In these concerns the approach was neither "antiplanning" nor an abrogation of the hard intellectual thought processes required for formal strategic analyses. In fact formal planning was usually an essential building block in the step-by-step process executives used to develop overall strategies. But for good reasons, they relied on much more evolutionary practices than this model usually imples.[2] Their approach might at first seem to be disjointed or muddling.[3] But on closer analysis the rationale behind their incremental approach to strategy formulation was so powerful that it perhaps provides a normative model for most strategic decisions. Why and how do effective executives manage in this mode?

[1]THE STUDY: From diverse industries a sample of some ten multibillion dollar companies was selected. Each had recently undergone major strategic changes. Important participants were asked how the overall strategy and each of its important components had come about. With each company's help I tried to document all statements as carefully as possible from both primary and secondary sources. These materials were integrated and published in a series of detailed case studies which make up the data base I refer to here. Participating companies were: General Mills, Inc., and Pillsbury Company (consumable products); Exxon Corporation and Continental Group (basic processes); Xerox Corporation and Pilkington Brothers Ltd. (advanced technology); and General Motors Corporation, Chrysler Corporation, and Volvo AB (consumer durables). The study has been published in J. B. Quinn, *Strategies for Change: Logical Incrementalism* (Homewood, Ill.: Dow Jones/Irwin. 1980)

[2]For a rigorous presentation of the formal model, see M. L. Mace, "The President and Corporate Planning," *Harvard Business Review,* January–February 1965, pp. 49–62; W. D. Guth, "Formulating Organizational Objectives and Strategy: A Systematic Approach," *Journal of Business Policy,* Autumn 1971, pp. 24–31; K. J. Cohen and R. M. Cyert, "Strategy: Formulation, Implementation, and Monitoring," *Journal of Business,* July 1973, pp. 349–67; G. J. Skibbins, "Top Management Goal Appraisal," *International Management,* July 1974, pp. 41–42; F. Goronzy and E. Gray, "Factors in Corporate Growth," *Management International Review,* No. 4–5, (1974), 75–90; and W. E. Rothschild, *Putting It All Together: A Guide to Strategic Thinking* (New York: AMACOM, 1976).

[3]C. E. Lindblom, "The Science of 'Muddling Through,' " *Public Administration Review,* Spring 1959, pp. 79–88, is the classic statement of this approach.

From Broad to Specific

Strategy deals with the unknowable.[4] In the beginning it is literally impossible to predict all the important events and forces that might possibly shape the future of the enterprise—much less the total effect of their interactions.[5] The best executives can do is to forecast the forces *most likely* to impinge on the company's future and the probable nature and range of their potential impacts.[6] From these they can define broadly and flexibly what they would like to do—i.e., their *vision* of success.[7] Then successful strategists try to build a *resource base* and a *posture* that is so strong and flexible that the enterprise can survive and prosper toward its vision despite all but the most devastating events. They consciously seek a market/technological/product scope within which their concerns can be "preeminent" despite their resource limits.[8] Then when possible, they place some "side bets": (a) to decrease the risk of catastrophic failure or (b) to offer the company added future options.[9]

However, instead of seeking ultimate specificity in their overall strategies, executives in my study accepted much ambiguity.[10] They initially worked out in their own minds—and shared with selected colleagues—only a few integrating concepts, principles, or philosophies that would help rationalize and guide the company's overall movements. They proceeded step by step from the early generalities toward later specifics,[11] clarifying the strategy incrementally as events permitted or dictated. In early stages they consciously avoided overprecise statements that might impair the flexibility or imagination needed to exploit new in-

[4]H. I. Ansoff *Corporate Strategy: An Analytic Approach to Business Policy for Growth and Expansion* (New York: McGraw-Hill, 1965).

[5]Statistically the problem is as follows. With a very large number of powerful forces determining ultimate outcomes, the probability that any particular combination of forces will occur leading to a specific forecastable outcome approaches zero.

[6]See in H. Klein, "Environmental Analysis and Forecasting," ed. W. R. King, "The Importance of Strategic Issues," *Journal of Business Strategy,* Winter 1981.

[7]R. Pascale and A. Athos, in *The Art of Japanese Management* (Cambridge, Mass.: Harvard University, 1981), suggest that the thing that distinguishes the most successfully managed U. S. companies most is that they have defined this "superordinate goal" and it has become a portion of the value system influencing all major divisions on a day-to-day basis.

[8]B. Henderson, in *The Concept of Strategy,* (Boston, Mass.: Boston Consulting Group, 1981) describes this process in Social Darwinist terms that—as in the biological analogue—successful companies are those that assume the specific differentiating characteristics necessary to outperform all others in their selected niches.

[9]J. L. Bower, "Planning within the Firm," *American Economic Review,* May 1970, pp. 186–94, notes that executives place such diversifying side bets to reduce their personal risk as well as corporate risk. Ansoff, in *Corporate Strategy* details the need for internal and external flexibilities.

[10]H. E. Wrapp, "Good Managers Don't Make Policy Decisions," *Harvard Business Review,* September–October, pp. 91–99, also notes this phenomenon.

[11]A. Newell and H. A. Simon, in *Human Problem Solving* (Englewood Cliffs, N. J.: Prentice Hall, 1972) note that when faced with complex constructional decisions, executives tend to break them down into subdecisions to which more routinized or understood decision procedures can be applied.

formation or opportunities.[12] They constantly reassessed the future, found new congruencies as events unfurled, and blended the organization's skills and resources into new balances of concentration and risk dispersion as external forces and internal potentials intersected to suggest better—but never perfect—alignments. The process was dynamic with neither a real beginning nor end.

In the hands of skillful executives incrementalism is not merely reactive, as some have suggested.[13] Incrementalism can be a purposeful, powerful management technique for integrating the analytical, behavioral, political, and timing aspects of strategy formulation.

WHY INCREMENTALISM

There are five basic reasons for using careful incrementalism in strategy formulation. It helps executives

1. Improve the quality of information available for strategic decisions
2. Deal with the different lead times and sequencing problems involved in major decisions
3. Stimulate flexibility, creativity, and opportunism in pursuing desired goals
4. Overcome political and emotional barriers to change
5. Create the personal and organizational commitment needed to implement strategies effectively

Specific examples will demonstrate how incrementalism contributes in various common and difficult strategic situations.

Precipitating Events

No matter how carefully executives plan, external events—over which they have essentially no control—can precipitate urgent, piecemeal, interim decisions with critical long-term strategic consequences.[14] Early decisions made under stress can create new thrusts, precedents, or opportunities that are difficult to reverse later. Recognizing this, top executives often consciously try to deal with precipitating events in an incremental fashion. Early commitments are kept formative, tentative, and subject to later review. In some cases, neither the

---

[12]For the complete rationale behind this, see J. B. Quinn, "Strategic Goals: Process and Politics," *Sloan Management Review,* Fall 1977.

[13]H. I. Ansoff, "The Concept of Strategic Management," *Journal of Business Policy,* Summer 1972, pp. 2–7.

[14]Guth, "Formulating Organizational Objectives and Strategy," pp. 24–31, also notes this phenomenon.

company nor the external players can understand the full implications of alternative actions. All want to test assumptions and have a chance to learn from and adapt to the others' responses:[15]

> When I was in the office of Esso France's president, our discussions were interrupted several times by announcements that the country was being shut down by political turmoil and that various activist groups had taken over one or another of Esso's facilities. Instead of ending our conversation to take some action, the president quietly said, "Right now we must merely find out what is going on. Then we must wait until the situation clarifies enough to know what to do." It took several days to clarify the demands of the activists, to understand the forces at play, and to participate effectively in coalitions. Haste could have set in motion forces which permanently damaged the French company's strategic position.

Further information has a value. And effective executives consciously try to keep their options open until they can better understand how later events may affect their enterprise, their various constituencies, and their power bases. Logic dictates that critical decisions should be made as late as possible consistent with the information available.[16] This usually means incrementally. But crisis decisions do not provide the sole—or central—rationale for incrementalism in strategy formulation. Other aspects of strategy do.

Technology Development

Although one can—and should—lay out the broad goals and a planned framework for R & D activities, the precise directions in which R & D may project the company can only be understood step by step as scientists uncover new phenomena, amplify discoveries, reduce concepts to practice, build prototypes, and interact with potential users.[17] Throughout this process a wise management will maintain its options and proceed incrementally from broad visions toward final specific positioning strategies.[18] The latter pattern is often significantly affected by where breakthroughs occur, their timing, and relative economic potentials, none of which can be accurately predicted when the program begins.

> For example: Pilkington's entire worldwide strategy would have been markedly changed if its float glass program had not had a bit of luck at a crucial moment. When a pouring spout on its experimental glass facility broke, the accident led to

---

[15]R. Normann, *Management for Growth,* trans. N. Adler, (New York: John Wiley, 1977) provides an excellent discussion of such interaction learning processes.

[16]J. Marschak, "Toward an Economic Theory of Organization and Information," in *Decision Processes,* ed. R. M. Thrall, C. H. Coombs, and R. L. Davis (New York: John Wiley, 1954).

[17]See J. B. Quinn, "Long Range Planning of Industrial Research," *Harvard Business Review,* July–August 1961.

[18]In "Technological Innovation, Entrepreneurship, and Strategy," *Sloan Management Review,* Spring 1979, I develop this rationale in depth.

solution of the final bottleneck in the revolutionary new process which then dominated the industry for 20 years.[19] On the other hand, if Pilkington's fiberglass programs had been relatively more successful earlier, the company's whole strategy might well have shifted in other directions.

Similarly today, Genentech must see which of its genetically engineered products and processes can be reduced to practice first and which will perform safely and effectively in life systems before it defines much of its eventual strategy. Even now it appears that Genentech's early positioning may be in animal disease prevention, not in the glamorous human health areas it first envisioned.

Recognizing the need for flexibility in technical strategies, the U. S. Defense Department and companies like IBM and Xerox have developed "phased program planning" systems. They make concrete decisions only on the current phase of a project. Then they consciously try to introduce data from further technical findings and user interactions[20] into the program as long as possible until truly fixed commitments must be made for plants, components, or major facilities. This added information often positions the new technology differently and more effectively than earlier formal analyses suggested—with important consequences for strategy.

Acquisition/Diversification Programs

Acquisition/diversification strategies also require an incremental approach for maximum effectiveness. Formal analyses can lay out broad goals for such programs, define the criteria candidate companies must meet, set priorities for the search, build needed resource and organizational flexibilities, and anticipate potential problems in integrating new units into the enterprise.[21] But so much depends on the availability, sequencing, conditions of purchase, and specific management characteristics of the individual companies acquired that successful acquisition programs must proceed flexibly and opportunistically, interactively reshaping initial visions and strategies as concrete potentials emerge.[22] This is especially important for large single acquisitions where each new unit markedly changes the company's overall strategic capabilities.

[19] J. B. Quinn, Pilkington Brothers Ltd., copyrighted © case, 1977, Amos Tuck School of Business Administration, Dartmouth College.

[20] E. Von Hipple, "The Dominant Role of the User in Semiconductor and Electronic Process Innovation," *IEEE Transactions,* May 2, 1977, first suggests that a significant portion of all innovation is actually user induced. His later publication develops this in depth.

[21] M. L. Mace and G. G. Montgomery, *Management Problems of Corporate Acquistions,* Division of Research, Graduate School of Business Administration, Harvard University, 1962, laid out the classic pattern for this approach.

[22] R. F. Vancil and P. Lorange, "Strategic Planning in Diversified Companies," *Harvard Business Review,* January–February 1975, pp. 81–90, also note that formal strategic planning is inappropriate beyond setting broad goals and guidelines for acquisition planning.

For example, Continental Group would have a very different strategic posture today if it had purchased Peabody Coal instead of Richmond Insurance. Yet both would have made viable "fourth legs" for Continental's business at the time of their consideration. And the acquisition of one might have preempted the other.[23] Similarly, Seagram's unsuccessful billion dollar attempts to acquire St. Joe Minerals and CONOCO will probably lead to a completely different future strategic posture than it once anticipated. Yet such divergent results are common hazards of acquisition strategies.

Even in acquiring smaller companies the final impact of a diversification program will be determined by whether and when specific candidates become available[24]—always a somewhat random process. Some of the most successful acquisitions come "over the transom"—as Steak and Ale did for Pillsbury[25]—to a flexibly prepared company. One can rarely completely foresee how such acquisitions will fit and blend into a new strategy until at least the key pieces are known and in place.

For example: General Mills very carefully laid out the criteria for its early 1970's acquisitions in the classic manner. Its intention was: (1) to expand in food-related fields, (2) to develop new growth centers based on its skills at marketing to the homemaker. The consensus was that the majority of resources should go to food-related areas. Almost the exact opposite occurred. Because of external factors beyond its control the company had a good selection of candidates in non-foods areas and few in foods. By 1973 General Mills had diversified into a wide array of new areas from toys, to creative crafts, to fine clothing with high impact on its total posture.[26]

In addition to handling such sequencing and timing considerations, incremental processes also assist in achieving the crucial psychological and power shifts that so significantly affect a program's overall directions and consequences. Properly used they step by step help to create the broad conceptual consensus, risk-taking attitudes, and adaptive dynamics critical to success. Most important among these processes are: (1) generating the initial psychological commitment to diversify outside of familiar fields, (2) building a sufficient "comfort factor" about risk taking for key managers to actually commit resources to new areas, (3) consciously realigning the enterprise's resources and organization structure so it can move opportunistically, (4) empowering an "activist" whose career depends upon the success of the diversification program (5) shortening

[23]*Continental Group,* copyrighted case © 1981, J. B. Quinn, Dartmouth College, Hanover, N. H.

[24]J. G. March et al., *Ambiguity and Choice in Organizations,* (Bergen, Norway: Universitetsforlaget, 1976) also documents how the sequence in which key decisions are made can affect final strategic outcomes.

[25]*Pillsbury Company,* copyrighted case © 1980, J. B. Quinn, Dartmouth College, Hanover, N. H.

[26]*General Mills, Inc.* copyrighted case © 1978, J. B. Quinn and M. Jelinek, Dartmouth College, Hanover, N.H.

lines of communication from the activist to the highest decision authorities, (6) overcoming political resistance to redirecting funds, and (7) actively changing the company's past ethos as new attitudes, potentials, and power centers emerge.[27]

Each of these processes can effect the timing and direction of the strategy as much as any formal analysis. Each has it own timing imperatives. And each interacts with other decision processes and the random appearance of acquisition candidates to redirect initially planned actions, time scales, and results in unexpected ways. Complexities are so great that few diversification programs end up as initially envisioned. Experienced managers recognize this and manage their acquisition programs incrementally, reshaping their broad early visions flexibly, step by step, as new opportunities, acquired competencies, and executive personalities merge to create new potential patterns for success. Until these patterns are clear, acquisition goals are kept general and are rarely explicitly announced.

> As George Wiessman, chief architect of Philip Morris's successful acquisition program said: "We don't announce growth goals in new areas because we don't want to get trapped into doing something stupid. We might be tempted to acquire a company when we shouldn't. Or we might hang on to an operation we really should sell off. Public statements can sometimes generate powerful expectations— internally and externally—that can pressure you to do the wrong thing."

Major Reorganizations

Macro organizational changes tend to be associated with most major corporate strategy shifts.[28] Like most other important strategic decisions, these moves are also typically handled incrementally *and* outside the formal planning process. Why?

Their effects on personal or power relationships preclude discussion in the open forums and reports of formal planning. Top executives have to think through the new roles, capabilities, and probable individual reactions of the many principals affected. They may have to wait for the promotion or retirement of a valued colleague before making a particular desired change. Then they frequently have to bring in, train, or test new people for substanital periods before they can staff key posts with confidence. As individual's potentials, perfor-

---

[27]My cases on *Continental Group, General Mills, Inc.,* and *Pillsbury Company,* © *op. cit.,* detail the incremental interaction of rational analytical, political, and psychological confidence-building processes in acquisition programs. Normann, *Management for Growth,* describes and models how this interactive learning process adjusts both goal perceptions and the relevancy of options incrementally as new information and psychological commitments develop.

[28]A. D. Chandler, *Strategy and Structure: Chapters in the History of the Industrial Enterprise* (Cambridge, Mass.: M. I. T. Press, 1962); and D. R. Daniel, "Reorganizing for Results," *Harvard Business Review,* November–December 1966, pp. 96–104.

mance, personal drives, and relationships to other team members develop, top managers may substantially modify key elements in their original organization concept as well as the overall corporate strategy.[29]

> For example, at General Mills Charles Bell brought in a new team of outside professional managers under General Rawlings. This team redefined the company's problems and opportunities in ways the prior management could not have foreseen. Over a period of time they divested many divisions which had been the core of the old business. These divestitures released funds for acquisitions in new areas, thus automatically increasing the visibility and power of the new controllership-financial group brought in by Rawlings. But with fewer large divisions competing for funds, the Consumer Foods Group also rapidly grew in importance. This ultimately led to the choice of the Consumer Foods head, James McFarland, for the corporation's next CEO—and set the direction of General Mills future strategy.[30]

Successful reorganizations—other than those made in crises—tend to proceed opportunistically, step by step, selectively moving people and unit structures toward a broadly conceived organizational goal which is constantly modified and rarely articulated in detail until the most important psychological and structural pieces finally fit together. An overall concept of "decentralization," "SBUs," or "global product units" may prevail throughout. But if adequate allowance is made for testing, flexibility, and feedback, the final formulation may bear little likeness to initial conceptions. And the outcome is usually an improvement.

Government–External Relations Strategies

Government–external relations strategies also require incremental formulation. Such strategies typically deal with very large scale forces, most beyond the company's direct control. Data tend to be very soft, often can only be subjectively sensed, and may be costly or impossible to quantify. The way outside individuals or groups will respond to a particular stimulus is difficult to predict. These forces can be very powerful relative to the company. And their potential attack modes can be so diverse that it is physically impossible to lay out probabilistic decision diagrams that have much meaning. Bizarre actions of outsiders can determine final outcomes. Results are unpredictable and error costs extreme. Hence the most rational seeming and best-intended strategies can be con-

---

[29]The Pilkington experience was typical. Despite careful planning, the reorganization strategy overdecentralized and the "polo" at the center had to be recorrected. The addition of professional managers, while necessary, unintentionally changed the values of the company and encouraged: the use of more formal plans and controls, isolation of workers from owners, the willingness of workers to strike, the nature of reward systems, and so on. Pilkington Bros. Ltd. case, *op. cit.*

[30]*General Mills, Inc.* case, op. cit.

verted into disasters unless they are interactively developed and tested. For example:

> In the 1960's General Motors found that technical discussions of cost vs. benefit tradeoffs were useless against demagogic slogans like "smog kills" or "GM is the worst polluter in the world." Despite assisting in the basic studies that defined automotive exhausts as a major causative factor in smog, GM publicly resisted some early attempts to impose effluent standards as "beyond the state of the art." Then later, after successfully completing the costly and risky ($100 million) development of the catalytic converter, GM had its earlier concerns thrown in its face as "foot dragging" or "lying" about technical potentials. As one executive said, "You were damned if you did and damned if you didn't"
> Only after prolonged interactions with regulators, legislators, and public interest groups did GM truly understand the needs and pressure potentials of its opponents. Area by area it experimented with better ways to communicate with various interests. Only then could it identify effective patterns to mold into its overall corporate strategy.[31]

Other Strategies

Other strategies—such as those for divestitures, capital access, international relations, and human resources development—are so sensitive that they too are usually determined in subsystems outside the forums of formal planning. The timing imperatives of each subsystem—or strategic area—tend to drive its decisions out of synchronization with the others. Consequently just as managers move forward incrementally within each strategic area, they also must proceed incrementally toward a total strategy.[32] They constantly try—both intuitively and analytically—to integrate their actions into a cohesive pattern as they go along. But rarely do all the pieces fit neatly and totally in detail at any specific instant, especially at the moment annual plans are due.

Formal-Planning Increments Too

In most cases formal planning itself should be a part of the incremental process. Most sophisticated managements purposely design their plans to be "living" or "ever green." They are best thought of as frameworks to guide and provide consistency for future decisions made incrementally. To act otherwise is to deny that further information has a value. Properly developed, such systems

---

[31]J. B. Quinn, *General Motors Corporation: The Downsizing Decision,* copyrighted case © 1978, Amos Tuck School, Dartmouth College, Hanover, N. H.

[32]J. G. March and H. A. Simon, "Cognitive Limits on Rationality," in *Organizations* rote 10 supra; and C. E. Lindblom, *The Policy-Making Process* (Englewood Cliffs, N. J.: Prentice-Hall, 1968), note that the incremental manager is a shrewd, resourceful problem solver, wrestling bravely with a universe he is wise enough to know is too big for him.

are very useful—indeed essential—as components of the strategic process. They teach managers about the future and extend the time horizon of detailed plans. They serve as important vehicles for involving lower-level managers and forcing negotiations on goals and program balances throughout the organization. In the planning guidelines issued from the top and in the commitment patterns they eventually set forth, they systematize and confirm incrementally made strategic decisions. Annual planning provides a critical interface between strategic and tactical commitments. It is the *sine qua non* of all decentralization and sensible management control.[33]

But in my sample, annual planning was rarely the source point for major new strategies—and certainly not for overall corporate strategies. These evolved from the kinds of incremental processes described above.

Formulation and Implementation Blur

In large organizations overall strategies rarely burst forth full blown from even the best strategic studies.[34] Even MacArthur's brilliant "island hopping" strategy was slowly synthesized from a series of studies, political interactions, tests, and early failures.[35] Executives tend to adopt only a piece of a given study's total recommendations and leave other key elements to be defined as new information becomes available, politics permit, or specific opportunities or thrusts crystallize. Overall strategies *emerge* organically as executives link together and create order out of a series of partially overlapping processes and interacting decisions that may span many years.[36] Such incrementalism is a conscious adaptation to the psychological and informational problems of getting an everchanging group of people with diverse talents and interests to work effectively together in a continually dynamic environment.

The lines between strategy formulation and implementation constantly blur. Some parts of a major strategy will be in early awareness-building stages, other parts in analytical stages, others in experimental phases, others in unpredictable flux or crisis situations, and still others in introduction or implementa-

[33]These benefits are a bit different from the usual lists assessed for planning (W. B. Schaffir, "What Have We Learned about Corporate Planning?" *Management Review*, August 1973, pp. 19–26), but they were repeatedly confirmed by top executives—rather than planners. They are amplified in *ibid.*, Chap. 5.

[34]Note that this study deals with corporate strategy changes in very large organizations. H. Mintzberg, "Strategy Making in Three Modes," *California Management Review*, Winter 1973, pp. 44–53, and others have noted different forms of strategy formulation in somewhat smaller companies.

[35]See W. Manchester, *American Caesar: Douglas MacArthur 1880–1964* (Boston: Little, Brown, 1978).

[36]R. M. Cyert and J. G. March,, in *A Behavioral Theory of the Firm* (Englewood Cliffs, N.J.: Prentice-Hall, 1963), p. 123, note this learning-feedback-adaptiveness of goals and feasible alternatives over time as organizational learning.

tion modes that require later modification. Partial implementation of large-scale strategies must be underway even as other formulation efforts go forward. Thoughtful executives treat each step in the formulation process as an integral part of implementation. They see that key people are informed, involved, and committed in developing their particular phases of the strategy. They build existing momentums into the strategy, wherever possible. And they constantly try to see that essential interim decisions—like facilities, technology, or personnel selections—help implant or flexibly support intuitively perceived strategic thrusts that may not yet be worked out in detail. Because of such dynamics it may be misleading to think that in large organizations one can realistically first formulate a detailed overall strategy, announce it, and then proceed to implement it. Much more subtle, interrelated, continous, evolutionary processes tend to dominate strategy development in these circumstances.

MANAGING INCREMENTALISM

How can one proactively manage strategy formulation in this mode? One executive provided perhaps the most articulate short statement of the overall approach:

> Typically you start with a general concern, vaguely felt. Next, you roll an issue around in your mind until you think you have a conclusion that makes sense for the company. Then you go out and sort of post the idea without being too wedded to its details. You then start hearing the arguments pro and con, and some very good refinements of the idea usually emerge. Then you pull the idea in and put some resources together to study it so it can be put forward as more of a formal presentation. You wait for "stimuli occurrences" or "crises," and launch pieces of the idea to help in these situations. But they lead toward your ultimate aim. You know where you want to get. You'd like to get there in six months. But it may take three years, or you may not get there at all. And when you do get there, you don't know whether it was originally your own idea—or somebody else had reached the same conclusion before you and just got you on board for it. You never know.[37]

Because of differences in organizational form, management style, and the content of individual decisions, no single paradigm holds for all strategic decisions.[38] But my study suggests that executives tend to utilize somewhat similar incremental processes as they manage complex strategy shifts. A few glimpses follow.

Leading the formal information system is a conscious part of such strategic management. Rarely do the earliest signals for strategic change come from the

[37]*Xerox Corporation,* copyrighted case © 1979, J. B. Quinn, Amos Tuck School, Dartmouth College, Hanover, N. H.

[38]In my *Strategies for Change,* I cite from different paradigms, each of which makes significant contributions.

company's formal horizon scanning,[39] planning, or reporting systems. Instead, initial sensing of needs for major strategic changes is often described as "something you feel uneasy about," "inconsistencies," or "anomalies"[40] between the enterprise's current posture and some general perception of its future environment.[41] Effective managers purposely establish multiple credible internal and external sources to obtain objective information about their enterprise and its environments.[42] They consciously use these networks to short-circuit all the careful screens their organizations build up "to tell the top only what it wants to hear."[43] They actively search beyond their organization's formal information systems, deeming the latter to be too historical, tradition oriented, or extrapolative to pinpoint needed basic changes in time.[44]

To avoid their own natural biases, executives who are aggressively seeking new potential opportunities or threats make sure their networks include people who look at the world quite differently from the dominating culture of the enterprise. Some companies have structured "devil's advocates" into their planning processes for this purpose. Others have undertaken "aggressor company" exercises to simulate how intelligent aggressors could best attack their patents, markets, or desired future positions. Still others—like Xerox—have commissioned groups of known independent thinkers to make special studies, with the extensive help of outside consultants and authorities, to ensure top managers view changing environments analytically and creatively.

Amplifying understanding is often an essential diagnostic process that can simultaneously improve the quality of information, generate involvement and commitment of key people, and deal with some of the political and psychological resistance to new ideas.[45] Sometimes the initial pressing symptom of a problem

---

[39]Virtually all my sample companies had elaborate planning and horizon scanning systems of the sorts suggested in Guth, "Formulating Organizational Objectives and Strategy," pp. 24–31; and F. J. Aguilar, *Scanning the Business Environment* (New York: Macmillan, 1967).

[40]Normann, in *Management for Growth*, p. 19, also discusses various types of "misfits" between the organization and its environment as a basis for identifying problems.

[41]H. Mintzberg, D. Raisinghani, and A. Theoret, in "The Structure of 'Unstructured' Decision Processes," *Administrative Science Quarterly,* June 1976, pp. 246–75, confirm this early vagueness and ambiguity in problem form and identification.

[42]Wrapp "Good Managers Don't Make Policy Decisions."

[43]For a classic view of how these screens operate, see C. Argyris, "Double Loop Learning in Organizations," *Harvard Business Review,* September–October 1977, pp. 115–25.

[44]E. E. Carter, in "The Behavioral Theory of the Firm and Top-Level Corporate Decisions," *Administrative Science Quarterly,* December 1971, pp. 413–28, describes active search processes by executives to define new problems, not just to respond to problems as Cyert and March suggest. H. Mintzberg, in *Nature of Managerial Work* (Englewood Cliffs, N. J.: Prentice-Hall, 1980), p. 78, also describes this informal scanning activity.

[45]This stage corresponds to Mintzberg's "diagnostic routine." See Mintzberg, Raisinghani, and Theoret, "Structure of 'Unstructured' Decision Processes," pp. 246–75.

(demogogues attacking the auto industry) evolves under investigation to something more basic (a changing public expectation about auto performance). In
other cases executives may quickly perceive the broad dimensions of needed
changes but want more organizational support before initiating changes. They
want to have a few colleagues become more knowledgeable about an issue and
help them think through its ramifications.[46] And they may want to avoid being
the prime supporter of a losing idea or having the organization attack or slavish-
ly adapt "the boss's solution" and have to change it as more evidence becomes
available. Even though executives may not have in mind specific solutions to
emerging problems, they can proactively guide action in intuitively desired directions by defining the issues that staffs investigate, selecting the people who
make the investigations, and controlling the reporting process. They may not
terminate this phase of investigation until they have identified potential proponents and opponents of various positions and are sure that enough people will
"get on board" to make a solution work.

Building organizational awareness may be essential when key players do
not have enough information or psychological stimulation to change their past
action patterns voluntarily or to investigate options creatively. At early stages,
successful change managers seem to consciously generate and consider a broad
array of alternatives.[47] While tapping the "collective wit" of the organization,
they try to build awareness and concern about new issues. They assemble objective data to argue against preconceived ideas or blindly followed past practices.
Yet they want to avoid prematurely threatening power centers that might kill
important changes before potential supporters really know what is at stake and
can bring broader interests to bear. At this stage, management processes are
rarely directive. Instead they are likely to involve studying, challenging, questioning, listening, talking to creative people outside ordinary decision channels,
generating options, but purposely avoiding irreversible commitments.[48] For example:

> In the early 1970's there was a glut in world oil supplies. Nevertheless, GM's Chief
> Economist began to project an increased U. S. dependency on foreign oil and high-
> er future prices. These concerns led the Board in 1972 to create an *ad hoc* energy
> task force of key executives under David Collier. The group's report in May 1973
> "created a good deal of discussion around the company" in the months before the
> oil embargo hit. "We were trying to get other people to think about the issue," said
> Richard Gerstenberg, then chairman of GM. These discussions provided an impor-

---

[46]As a member of the top-management coalition begins to sponsor a proposal, a process of "uncer-
tainity absorption" takes place; see March and Simon, *Organizations*. People begin to judge the com-
petency of the person who is sponsoring the idea rather than the evidence presented, and the individual's credibility and power suffer if he or she is wrong.

[47]Wrapp, in "Good Managers Don't Make Policy Decisions," also noted that this was true of top-
management search procedures.

[48]F. F. Gilmore, "Overcoming the Perils of Advocacy in Corporate Planning," *California Management Review,* Spring 1973, pp. 127–37.

tant backdrop for the crucial downsizing decisions made during the embargo period.

Building credibility/changing symbols may help managers signal the organization that certain types of changes are coming, even when specific solutions are not yet in hand. Knowing they cannot communicate directly with the thousands who must carry out a strategy, many executives purposely undertake a few highly visible symbolic actions which wordlessly convey complex messages they could never communicate as well—or as credibly—in verbal terms. Through word of mouth the informal grapevine can amplify signals of a pending change in ways no formal communication could.[49]

> In GM's downsizing decision, engineers said one of top management's early decisions affected the credibility of the whole weight-reduction program: "Initially, we proposed a program using a lot of aluminum and substitute materials to meet the new mass targets. But this would have meant a very high cost, and would have strained the suppliers' aluminum capacity. However, when we presented this program to management, they said, 'Okay, if necessary, we'll do it.' They didn't back down. We began to understand then that they were dead serious. Feeling that the company would spend the money was critical to the success of the entire mass reduction effort."

Organizations often need such symbolic moves—or decisions they regard as symbolic—to verify the intention of a new strategy or to build credibility behind one in its initial stages. Without such actions people may interpret even forceful verbiage as mere rhetoric and delay their commitment to new thrusts.

Legitimizing new viewpoints often involves planned delays. Top managers may purposely create discussion forums or allow slack time for their organizations to talk through threatening issues, work out the implications of new solutions, or gain an improved information base that permits new options to be evaluated objectively in comparison with more familiar alternatives. Because of familiarity, solutions that arise out of executives' prior experience are perceived as having lower risks (or potential costs) than newer alternatives that are more attractive when viewed objectively. In many cases, strategic concepts that are at first strongly resisted can gain acceptance and positive commitment simply by the passage of time and open discussion of new information—when executives do not exacerbate hostility by pushing them too fast from the top.[50] Many top executives, planners, and change agents consciously arrange for such "gestation periods" and find that the concept itself is frequently made more effective by the resulting feedback and acceptance.

---

[49]E. Rhenman, in *Organization Theory for Long-Range Planning* (New York: John Wiley, 1973), p. 63, notes a similar phenomenon.

[50]R. M. Cyert, W. R. Dill, and J. G. March, in "The Role of Expectations in Business Decision Making," *Administrative Science Quarterly,* December 1958, pp. 307–40, point out the perils of top-management advocacy because existing polities may unconsciously bias information to support views they value.

When William Spoor took over as CEO at Pillsbury, one of the biggest issues he faced was whether to stay in or get out of the Pillsbury Farms' chicken business. Management was deeply split on the question. Spoor asked all key protagonists for position papers and purposely commissioned two papers on each side for the Board. He invited consultants' views and visited Ralston Purina, which had undergone a similar divestiture. He got an estimate from Lehman Brothers as to the division's value. All this went to the Board which debated the issue for months. A key event occurred when Lehman found a potential European buyer at a good price. Finally, when the vote was taken only one person—Pillsbury Farms' original champion—voted for retention.

Tactical shifts and partial solutions are typical steps in developing a new overall strategic posture. Early problem resolutions are likely to be partial, tentative, or experimental.[51] Beginning moves are often handled as mere tactical adjustments in the enterprise's existing posture. As such they encounter little opposition. Executives can often obtain agreement to a series of small programs when a broad objective change would encounter too much opposition. Such programs allow the guiding executive to maintain the enterprise's ongoing strengths while shifting momentum—at the margin—toward new needs.[52] At this stage, top executives themselves may not yet comprehend the full nature or extent of the strategic shifts they are beginning.[53] They can still experiment with partial new approaches without risking the viability of the total enterprise. Yet their broad early steps can still legitimately lead to a variety of different success scenarios.[54]

Following the Collier report, when the oil embargo hit in fall 1973, General Motors responded at first by merely increasing production of its existing small cars. Then as the crisis deepened, it added another partial solution, the subcompact "T car"—the Chevette—and accelerated the Seville's development cycle. As economy appeared more salable, executives set an initial target of removing 400 pounds from big-car bodies by 1977. Then as fuel economy pressures persisted and engineering feasibilities offered greater confidence, this target was tightened further to 800–1,000 pounds (3 miles per gallon). No step by itself shifted the company's total strategic posture until the full downsizing of all lines was agreed upon. But each partial solution built confidence and commitment toward a new direction.

As events unfurl, the solutions to several initially unrelated problems tend to flow together into a new synthesis. When possible, strategic logic (risk mini-

---

[51]March et al., *Ambiguity and Choice in Organizations.*

[52]This is part of the process of "uncertainty avoidance" as noted by Cyert and March in *Behavioral Theory of the Firm.*

[53]An initial consensus on goals by the dominant coalition is by no means a common element in the strategic decision process. See E. E. Carter, "A Behavioral Theory Approach to Firm Investment and Acquisition Decisions," (unpublished doctoral dissertation, Graduate School of Industrial Administration, Carnegie-Mellon University, 1970).

[54]Mintzberg, Raisinghani, and Theoret, in "Structure of 'Unstructured' Decision Processes," liken the process to a decision tree where decisions at each node become more narrow, with failure at any mode recycling back to the broader tree trunk.

mization) dictates starting broad initiatives that can be flexibly guided in any of several possible desirable directions.[55]

Broadening political support for emerging new thrusts is frequently an essential and consciously proactive step in major strategy changes. Committees, task forces, or retreats tend to be favored mechanisms. By selecting such groups' chairmen, membership, timing, and agenda, the guiding executive can largely influence and predict a desired outcome, yet nudge other executives toward a consensus.[56] The careful executive, of course, still maintains complete control over these "advisory" processes through his various influence and veto potentials. In addition to facilitating smooth implementation, many managers report that interactive consensus building also improves the quality of the strategic decisions themselves and helps achieve positive and innovative assistance when things would otherwise go wrong.

> Shortly after he became CEO of General Mills, James MacFarland took his 35 top people on a three-day retreat to discuss "how to move a good company to greatness." He wanted the views of others in defining greatness and their active participation in achieving it. Working in groups of 6 to 8, the management team defined what the characteristics of a great company were from various points of view, what General Mills' shortcomings were, and what main thrusts were needed to overcome these. Over time, these broad visions, goals, and programs were converted into charters for various divisions and groups. They became the initial guidelines for the company's very successful and flexible development over the next decade.

Overcoming opposition is almost always necessary at some stage. Careful executives realize that they must deal with the support the preceding strategy had. They try not to unnecessarily alienate managers from the earlier era—whose talents they may need in future ventures—through a frontal assault on old approaches. Instead they persuade individuals toward new concepts whenever possible,[57] co-opt or neutralize serious opposition if necessary,[58] or move through zones of indifference[59] where early changes will not be disastrously op-

---

[55]Wrapp, in "Good Managers Don't Make Policy Decisions," notes that a conditioning process which may stretch over months or years is necessary to prepare the organization for radical departures from what it is already striving to attain.

[56]Properly guided these do not become the "garbage can" of ideas some have suggested. March et al., *Ambiguity and Choice in Organizations.*

[57]I was impressed by the number of times executives would create and participate in different forums to expose and discuss new ideas, rather than ram them through from the top.

[58]L. Sayles, *Managerial Behavior: Administration in Complex Organizations* (New York: McGraw-Hill, 1964) provides an excellent overview of the processes involved.

[59]Cyert and March, in *Behavioral Theory of the Firm;* and J. G. March, in "Business Decision Making," *Readings in Managerial Psychology,* ed. H. J. Leavitt and L. R. Pondy (Chicago: University of Chicago Press, 1965), both note the need of executives for coalition behavior to reduce the organizational conflict due to differing interests and goal preferences in large organizations. C. I. Barnard, in *The Functions of the Executive* (Cambridge, Mass.: Harvard University Press, 1938), provides perhaps the first reference to the concept of the "zone of indifference."

posed. Under the best circumstances, they find "no lose" situations that activate all important players positively toward new common goals.

> After the "Goodness to Greatness" conference described above, General Mills had two major strategic thrusts: (1) to expand internally and through acquisitions in food-related areas and (2) to acquire new growth centers based on General Mills' marketing skills. Neither of the two critical power centers—the more traditional product groups nor the strong finance/acquisition group—was foreclosed from participation and active involvement in the new strategy. In fact, both were stimulated to support it for their own future benefit.

Successful executives tend to honor legitimate differences in views concerning even major directions and note that initial opponents often thoughtfully shape new strategies in more effective directions. Some may become active supporters as new information emerges to change their views. But consensus is not always possible. Strong-minded executives sometimes disagree to the point where they must be moved to positions of less influence or stimulated to leave. And timing can dictate very firm top-level direction at key junctures.

> Mr. Bruce Smart, Chairman and CEO of Continental Group, once noted "We had a devil of a time getting the can business in the U. S. to recognize its maturity, because this was perceived by its management to be an unacceptable solution. . . . This created a number of battles between New York corporate headquarters and the Chicago metals headquarters over what was a proper direction for that business. The upshot of this was that you do what you have to do as a manager. If you can't change the guy's opinion, you change the guy. It ended all the trauma and put the thing on a new path strategically."

Consciously structured flexibility is essential to deal with the many "unknowables" in the total environment. One cannot possibly predict the precise form or timing of all important threats and opportunities the firm may encounter. Logic dictates therefore that managers purposely design flexibility into their organizations and have resources ready to deploy incrementally as events demand. This requires (1) proactive horizon scanning to identify the general range, scale, and impact of the opportunities and threats the firm is most likely to encounter; (2) creating sufficient resource buffers—or slacks—to respond as events actually do unfurl; (3) developing and positioning "champions" who will be motivated to take advantage of specific opportunities as they occur; and (4) shortening decision lines between such persons and the top for rapid system response. These—rather than precapsuled (and shelved) programs to respond to stimuli that never occur quite as expected—are the keys to real contingency planning.

The concept of resource buffers perhaps requires some amplification. A few examples will suggest their strategic nature:

> Exxon set up its Exploration Group to purposely undertake the higher risks and longer-term investments necessary to search for oil in new areas, and thus to reduce the potential impact on Exxon if there were sudden unpredictable changes in

the availability of Middle East oil. Instead of hoarding cash, Pillsbury and General Mills sold off unprofitable businesses and cleaned up their financial statements to improve their access to external capital sources for acquisitions. Such access in essence provided the protection of a cash buffer without its investment. IBM's large R & D facility and its project team approach to development assured that it had a pool of people it could quickly shift among various projects to exploit interesting new technologies opportunistically as they developed.

With such flexible patterns designed into the strategy, the enterprise is proactively ready to move on those thrusts that by their very nature may have to evolve incrementally.

Trial balloons and systematic waiting are often the next steps for prepared strategists. As Roosevelt awaited a critical event like Pearl Harbor, the strategists may have to wait patiently for the proper option or precipitating event to appear.

The availability of desired acquisitions or real estate may depend upon a death, divorce, fiscal crisis, management change, or erratic economic break.[60] Technological advances may await new knowledge, inventions, or lucky accidents. Or planned market entries may not be wise until new legislation, trade agreements, or competitive shakeouts occur. Very often the optimum strategy depends on the timing and sequence of such random events. For example, the timing and nature of SDS Inc.'s availability was a proximate cause of both the date and the results of this first Xerox entry into computers.

Executives may also consciously launch trial concepts like Mr. McColough's "Architecture of Information" or Mr. Spoor's "Super Box" in order to attract options and concrete proposals. Usually these trial balloons are phrased in very broad contextual terms. Without making a commitment to any specific solution, the executive activates the organization's creative abilities.[61] This approach keeps the manager's own options open until substantive alternatives can be evaluated against each other and against concrete current realities. And it prevents practical line managers from rejecting desirable strategic shifts because they are forced to compare "paper options" against what they see as well-defined, urgent, needs.

Creating pockets of commitment may be necessary for entirely new strategic thrusts. The executive may encourage exploratory projects, to test options, create necessary skills or technologies, or build commitment for several possible options deep within the organization. Initial projects may be kept small, partial, or ad hoc, not forming a comprehensive program or seeming to be integrated into a cohesive strategy. At this stage guiding executives may merely provide broad goals, a proper climate, and flexible resource support, without being iden-

[60]Cyert and March, in *Behavioral Theory of the Firm,* also note that not only do organizations seek alternatives but also "alternatives seek organizations," as when finders, scientists, bankers, and others bring in new solutions.

[61]This is a variant of P. O. Soelberg's "trap search" in "Unprogrammed Decision Making," *Industrial Management Review,* Spring 1967, pp. 19–29.

tified with specific projects.[62] In this way they can avoid escalating attention to any one solution too soon or losing personal credibility if it fails. But they can stimulate those options that lead in desired directions, set higher hurdles for those that do not, or quietly have them killed some levels below to maintain the executives' own flexibility. Executives can then keep their own options open, control premature momentum, openly back only winners, and select the right moment to blend several successful thrusts into a broader program or concept.[63] They can delay their own final decisions on a total thrust until the last moment, thus obtaining the best possible match-up between the company's capabilities, psychological commitments, and changing market needs.

> For years IBM has made the technical "shoot out" a portion of its style in managing development programs. They allow various teams to work independently on alternate approaches to a desired solution. Then they have the teams demonstrate their approach in a prototype competition. Top management maintains the right of ultimate choice. But the winning team is already committed to its approach and ready to champion it in the organization. Such parallel development improves each team's motivation to invent and progress, enhances the quality of information used to critique each approach, creates genuine options, and allows final choices to be made as near the marketplace as possible. By increasing the effectiveness of decisions, the efficiency of development improves despite the apparent cost of parallel development. Similar techniques have been used by Bell Laboratories, Pilkington, United Technology, and other successful technical groups.

Crystallizing focus at critical points in the process is of course vital. Sometimes executives will state a few key goals at an early stage to generate action or cohesion in a difficult or crisis situation. But for reasons noted, guiding executives often purposely keep early goal statements vague and commitments broad and tentative.[64] Then as they develop information or consensus on desirable thrusts, they may use their prestige or power to push or crystallize a particular formulation. Despite adhering to the rhetoric of specific goal setting, most executives in my study were careful not to state many new strategic objectives in concrete terms until they had carefully built consensus among key players.[65] To do otherwise might inadvertently centralize their organizations, preempt interesting options, provide a common focus for otherwise fragmented opposition, or

---

[62]In a sense this approach counters the concept (Mintzberg, Raisinghani, and Theoret, "Structure of 'Unstructured' Decision Processes") that only one fully developed, custom-made solution comes forward—unless one considers that only one option survives the final selection or that incomplete developmental systems do not amount to a full option.

[63]Witte, in "Field Research on Complex Decision-Making Processes—The Phase Theorem," International Studies of Management and Organization, Summer 1972, pp. 156–82, notes a number—up to 51—of specific decisions in observed strategic processes which had to be blended in a several-year series to attain the final strategic outcome.

[64]For a more complete development see Quinn, "Strategic Goals: Process and Politics."

[65]In fact, E. A. Locke, in "Toward a Theory of Task Motivation and Incentives," *Organizational Behavior and Human Performance,* 3 (1968), 157–89, suggests that assigned goals have effect only to the extent that they are accepted and internalized by the subordinate.

cause the organization to undertake undesirable actions just to carry out a stated commitment. Because the net direction of an organization's goals ultimately reflects a negotiated balance among the imperatives felt by the dominant executive coalition[66] and the most important power centers and stakeholders in the enterprise,[67] the last thing an executive wants is to weaken his or her position by creating an unintended countercoalition. When to crystallize viewpoints and when to maintain open options is one of the true arts of strategic management.

> For example, the principal stockholder in a $200 million drilling company wanted the company to grow relatively rapidly by selective acquisitions. But when its Board representative presented a detailed plan outlining proposed areas for growth and diversification, the proposal was stymied. Other Board members—based on limited experience—took a rigid stance on one specific aspect of the plan, acquisition of "service companies" supporting the line. No progress was made until the principal stockholder went back and sold the Board on an idea they all could accept, growth through acquisition. As Board members became comfortable with this broad concept it became possible later to reintroduce the idea of "service companies" and allay the Board's fears with a specific example.

Formalizing commitment is the final step in formulation. As partial consensus emerges, the guiding executive may crystallize events by stating a few broad goals in more specific terms for internal consumption. Finally when sufficient general acceptance exists and the timing is right, the decision may appear in more public pronouncements. For example, as General Mills divested several of its major "old line" divisions its annual reports began to state these as moves "to concentrate on the company's strengths" and "to intensify General Mills efforts in the convenience foods field," statements that it would have been unwise or impolitic to make until many of the actual divestitures had taken place and a new management coalition and consensus had emerged.

As each major new thrust comes into focus, guiding executives ensure that some individual or individuals feel responsible for its execution. Plans are locked into programs or budgets, and control and reward systems are aligned to reflect intended strategic emphases.[68] Since so much has been written on this subject, I will avoid details here. However, if a particular thrust is entirely new to the enterprise, top executives often want more than mere accountability for its success—they want genuine commitment from its leaders.[69] They generally seek to

[66]C. Perrow, in "The Analysis of Goals in Complex Organizations," *American Sociological Review,* February 1961, pp. 854–66, stresses the central power of a dominant coalition which negotiates key goal relationships among itself and uses its combined power to enforce these as organization goals.

[67]P. Georgiou, in "The Goal Paradigm and Notes Towards a Counter Paradigm," *Administrative Science Quarterly,* September 1973, pp. 291–310, suggests a wider negotiation involving lower-level task groups as well.

[68]Cohen and Cyert, "Strategy: Formulation, Implementation, and Monitoring," pp. 349–67.

[69]A. Zaleznik, in "Power and Politics in Organizational Life," *Harvard Business Review,* May–June 1970, notes that confusing compliance with commitment is one of the most common and difficult problems of strategic implementation. He notes that often organizational commitment may override personal interest if the former is carefully developed.

find or empower a "champion" with a psychological or career commitment to the venture and make potential rewards appropriately higher.

Continuing dynamics and eroding consensus must immediately follow initial implementation. Otherwise old crusades become the new conventional wisdom and the organization fails to prepare itself for new concerns and concepts. In trying to build commitment, executives often surround themselves with people who see the world in the same way. They can rapidly become systematic screens against new views. Once the organization has arrived at its new consensus, guiding executives must rapidly move to ensure that this too does not become inflexible. The most effective executives therefore purposely continue the change process, constantly introducing new faces and stimuli at the top. They consciously begin to mutate the very strategic thrusts they might have just created—a very difficult but essential psychological and management task. Thus strategy formulation in successful large orgranizations becomes a continuously evolving, political, consensus-building process with neither a finite beginning nor end.

Not a Linear Process

While the generation of a strategy generally flows in the sequence of processes presented, the stages are by no means orderly or discrete. It would be improper to assume that any executive consciously manages the process through all its phases linearly. Although executives do manage individual steps proactively, any single decision might well involve numerous loops back to earlier stages as unexpected issues were encountered.[70] Similarly, decision times might become extremely compressed and require short circuiting leaps forward if major crises suddenly appear and options precipitously narrow. Each major portion of a strategy is likely to be in a different phase of its development—from initial awareness toward ultimate commitment—at any given moment. The strategy's ultimate development involves a series of nested partial decisions (in each strategic area) interacting with other partial decisions in all other areas and with the total resource base available. Pfiffner has aptly described the process as "like fermentation in biochemistry, rather than an industrial assembly line."[71] In fact the validity of a strategy lies not in whether it is maintained intact, but in its capacity to adopt successfully to unknowable realities, reshape itself, and ultimately use resources most effectively toward selected goals.

The real integration of all the components in a total enterprise's strategy takes place primarily in the minds of individual top executives. Some portions of the strategy may be seen the same by all. But each executive may legitimately

---

[70]For a more complete development, see J. B. Quinn, "Strategic Change: Logical Incrementalism," *Sloan Management Review,* Fall 1978.

[71]J. M. Pfiffner, "Administrative Rationality," *Public Administration Review,* Summer 1960, likens the process more to the bubbling of fermentation than the linearity of a production line.

perceive the overall balance of goals and thrusts slightly differently.[72] Some differences may be openly expressed as issues to be resolved when new information becomes available. Others may remain unstated, hidden agendas to emerge at later dates. Still others may be masked by accepting so broad a statement of intention that many divergent views can be brought toward a seeming consensus—while a more specific statement might be divisive. In many cases it is even hard to discern the particular point in time when specific clear-cut decisions are made. Events often move almost imperceptibly from awareness, to concern, to experiments, to options, to momentums, to consensus, to formal reinforcement.

INTEGRATING THE STRATEGY

Nevertheless, the total pattern of actions—through incremental—does not remain piecemeal in well-managed organizations. Effective executives constantly reassess the total organization, its capacities, and needs as related to environments. They seek new cohesive patterns that integrate interim decisions made in subordinate strategies. To coordinate these decisions cross-sectionally, wise managers use a variety of formal and informal techniques.

They see that the teams developing subordinate strategies have overlapping members. They require periodic briefings and reviews for higher-echelon groups to bring a total corporate view to bear and to learn from those with more-detailed knowledge. They use formal-planning techniques to interrelate and evaluate resources required, benefits sought, and risks undertaken. Some use highly developed scenario techniques or complex forecasting models to better understand basic relationships among specific subsystems, the total enterprise, and its critical environments. Others consciously create specialized staffs, "devil's advocates," or "contention teams" to make sure that all important aspects receive thorough evaluation. These techniques help in specific situations. But two other concepts lie at the core of most strategic integration.

Concentrating on a Few Key Thrusts

Strategic managers constantly seek to distill out a few (six to ten) "central themes" that draw the firm's diverse existing activities and new probes into common cause.[73] Once identified, these help maintain focus and consistency in the strategy. They make it easier to discuss and monitor intended directions. In ideal

[72]Mintzberg, Raisinghani, and Theoret, in "The Structure of 'Unstructured' Decision Processes," discuss some interesting aspects of these decision processes.

[73]D. J. Smalter and R. L. Ruggles, Jr., in "Six Business Lessons from the Pentagon," *Harvard Business Review,* March–April 1966, pp. 64–75, develop this form of missions planning in detail.

circumstances, these themes can be converted into a matrix of strategic "thrusts" or "missions" cutting across divisional plans and dominating other criteria used to rank divisional commitments.[74] Each division's plans have to show *enough* effort to accomplish its share of each thrust, even though this means overriding short-term present-value or rate-of-return rankings on projects within the division.[75] Texas Instruments and General Electric Company have provided some well-publicized formal models for doing this. Unfortunately, few companies seem able to implement such complex planning systems without generating voluminous paperwork, large planning bureaucracies, and undesirable rigidities in the plans themselves.

Formal planning serves many important motivational and communications purposes, as noted earlier. And careful professionalism in planning can pay high dividends. Still, the most effective planners do not rely primarily on annual planning processes to create overall strategies. In fact, they may well delegate those procedures to subordinates while they focus on other modes of intervention. In parallel with the concepts developed above, these are carefully orchestrated ad hoc efforts designed to (1) *teach* top managers about the future, (2) *sense* developing strategic needs early, (3) *build executive awareness* about options, (4) *broaden support* and comfort levels for action, (5) *crystallize* and communicate partial consensus as it emerges, (6) *stimulate* a few key executives' personal commitment toward new options, (7) *build attitudes,* communication channels, and resource buffers that make the organization more flexible toward change. Because these interventions take on so many forms, one can only suggest—not catalogue—a few interesting approaches here.

> Said the chief planner of a large chemical company: "For the price of one professional and his secretary, I can design for myself and a few key executives a biweekly series of seminars led by the very best people in the world. There's just no comparison between the potential impact of the two investments. And keeping my staff to minimum levels avoids political exposure."
>
> Said the vice-president of strategic planning of a large information products company: "I move when I know a top executive is about to make a speech or internal presentation where a reference about the future would be useful. I brief him or his speechwriters on potentially exciting developments or ideas I think may be ready for public exposure. Sometimes this is just a device to increase the executive's awareness of needs the company must respond to. Once an executive has spoken publicly about an issue, he is much more likely to feel he understands it and is committed to doing something about it. If I can get him to implicitly endorse a goal or a specific option in public, he will feel even more committed."

[74]Chapter 5 of my *Strategies for Change* develops this approach in some depth.

[75]Otherwise, as happens in many companies, strong divisions get their way without regard to the welfare of the whole. See J. Pfeffer, G. R. Salancik, and H. Leblebici, "The Effect of Uncertainty on the Use of Social Influence in Organizational Decision Making," *Administrative Science Quarterly,* June 1976, pp. 227–45.

Such "whispering in the ears of the gods" helps create awareness and set the hook of initial commitment. As a coalescing idea picks up momentum, planners often seek out its main sources of support and opposition and develop further processes to assess it or increase its psychological and potential viability.

> Said a very effective chief planner of a large consumer products company: "I may first have to build up a more adequate data base on the subject. Then I may arrange for some articulate proponents or neutral parties to prepare background papers on the topic with no recommended actions presented. As these endeavors accumulate weight and/or support, I may set up an informational meeting or two to inquire where we should go from here and what the prime concerns of opponents are. My office can often coordinate the accumulation of necessary data for the next stage of discussions. Finally, if necessary, I can arrange for a line executive to establish a carefully selected committee to look into the issue and come forward with recommendations. Or, if I can get a particular manager to sponsor the idea, it can be put forward as a trial balloon in his next formal plan."

All of these are legitimate interventions to help a new option over the hurdles of ignorance and suspicion it always encounters. As an idea gains momentum, planners can further stimulate its acceptance by having their staffs prepare special studies on it and by including inquiries about it in the instructions issued for drawing up long-range plans. Finally, as consensus emerges, the concept appears in assumptions, goals, and formal strategy statements of various groups. But this is the terminus of the strategy process. Not the essence of it.

Coalition Management

At the heart of all controlled strategy development lies coalition management. Top managers operate at a confluence of pressures from stockholders, environmentalists, government bodies, customers, suppliers, distributors, producing units, marketing groups, technologists, unions, special-issue activists, individual employees, ambitious executives, and so on, where knowledgeable people of good will can easily disagree on a proper balance of actions. In response to changing pressures and coalitions among these groups, the top-management team continously forms and reforms its own coalitions concerning specific decisions. These represent various members' different values and interests concerning the particular issue at hand and are sources of constant negotiations and implied bargains among the leadership group.[76]

Most major strategic moves tend to assist some interests—and executives' careers—at the expense of others. Consequently, each set of interests can serve as a check on the others and thus help maintain the breadth and balance of the overall strategy. To avoid significant errors some managements try to ensure

---

[76]Sayles, *Managerial Behavior: Administration in Complex Organizations,* pp. 207–17, provides an excellent view of the bargaining processes involved in coalition management.

that all important polities have representation or access at the top. And the guiding executive group may continuously adjust the number, power, or proximity of these access points as needed to maintain a desired balance and focus.[77] People selection and coalition management are the ultimate controls that top executives have in guiding and coordinating their companies' strategies. These must be managed with sophistication and care to achieve desired degrees of stimulation, objectivity, cohesion, and dynamism. Two quotations make the point well:

> One CEO said: "If good people share the same values, they will instinctively act together. We must know how people will respond intuitively when they are thousands of miles away. . . . We work hard and consciously to understand each other and where we are going. If we know these things and communicate openly, our actions will be sensible and cohesive. Yet we'll have the flexibility to deal with changing environments. These—and the choice of top-flight people—are our real controls for coordinating strategy development."

> Said Robert Hatfield, then the chairman of Continental Group: "How do you manage the strategic process? It all comes down to people: selecting people. First, you look for people with certain general characteristics. They have to be bright, energetic, flexible, with high integrity or they won't be adaptive and last in the long run. Among these, you look for the best people with the kinds of experience and interests likely to lead the company in directions you want it to go. But you have to be careful with this. You don't want just 'yes men' on the directions you believe in. You want people who can help you think out new approaches too. Finally, you purposely team people with somewhat different interests, skills, and management styles. You let them push and tug a bit to make sure different approaches get considered. And you do a lot of chatting and informal questioning to make sure you stay informed and can intervene if you have to."

CONCLUSIONS

In recent years there has been an increasing chorus of discontent concerning corporate strategic planning. Many managers are concerned that despite elaborate strategic-planning systems, costly staffs for this purpose, and major commitments of their own time, their most elaborate strategies get implemented poorly, if at all. These executives and their companies have generally fallen into the classic trap of thinking about strategy formulation and implementation as being separate sequential processes. They have relied on the awesome rationality of their formally derived strategies and the inherent power of their positions to cause their organizations to respond. When this does not occur, they become bewildered, if not frustrated and angry.

Instead, successful managers who operate logically and proactively in an incremental mode build the seeds of understanding, identity, and commitment into the very processes that create their strategies. Careful incrementalism al-

[77]Zaleznik, "Power and Politics in Organizational Life"; and Lindblom, "The Science of 'Muddling Through,' " develop this "watchdog thesis" well.

lows them to improve the quality of information used in decisions and deal with the practical politics of change—while they step by step build the organization's momentum toward the new strategy and the psychological motivation to carry it through. In large enterprises strategy formulation and implementation are largely overlapping, simultaneous, and continous functions. In their formulation processes, successful strategic managers generally create the awareness, concern, options, initial movement, personal identity, and organizational commitment that cause the strategy to be already flowing toward effective and flexible implementation before it is ever—if ever—announced in detail.

3

Researching the Formation of Strategies: The History of Canadian Lady, 1939–1976

HENRY MINTZBERG AND JAMES A. WATERS
McGill University

Our thanks to David Rappoport for data collection, to the Canadian Social Sciences and Humanities Research Council for its financial support, and to the executives of Canadian Lady, particularly Larry Nadler (president of the firm to the end of our study period), for their time and kind cooperation.

A major danger faced by the new field of Strategic Management is that prescription will get too far ahead of description. The urge to develop technique and prescribe procedure in the absence of in-depth knowledge about how strategies actually form may render much of that technique and procedure not just irrelevant but downright dysfunctional. This paper describes one approach to the study of strategy formation, based on what for most practitioners will be an unconventional view of the concept strategy. While we have used the approach for purposes of descriptive research, we also believe it has utility for organizations themselves, as a means to understand how their own strategies developed, what they are now, and how their current strategies might influence what they do in the future. Our research has taught us one very clear lesson: that no organization can deny its history in trying to formulate its strategies. Today's strategies—and tomorrow's—no matter how much they seek to alter direction, are very much rooted in yesterday's.

This research project began in 1971, under the title "Patterns in Strategy Formation," with the intention of developing a comprehensive understanding of how strategies form and are formulated in organizations. Viewing strategies as "patterns in streams of decisions," the focus was on tracking decision streams in organizations over long periods of time (several decades), inferring strategies as the consistencies in such streams and inferring periods of strategy development by considering the relationships among the different strategies, and then studying intensively the forces behind the appearance of the different periods.

An initial report described the results of the first two studies, of U. S. strategy in Vietnam (1950–73) and of Volkswagenwerk (1934–74).[1] Among other points noted in that paper was the key one that our view of strategy, which we refer to as *realized* strategy, when combined with the traditional view of the word as a plan or a set of guidelines, which we call *intended* strategy, yields three other basic views of strategy. As shown below, a *deliberate* strategy is one both intended and realized, an *unrealized* strategy is one intended but never realized, and an *emergent* strategy is one realized although never intended (which is not to say specifically unintended). This issue, of the deliberateness of strategy, became a central theme of the research, alongside two others: the interplay of environment, leadership, and organization; and the patterns of strategic change over time.

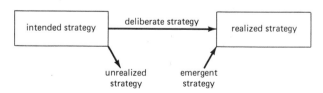

Subsequently this research became more systematic, with specific attempts to quantify decison streams where possible and to represent strategies in graphical or symbolic form. Studies have been undertaken of a large retail chain,[2] a mining company, an airline, a film-making agency, a small daily newspaper, a university, an architectural firm, and a garment manufacturer.

This paper presents the results of this last study, perhaps the simplest of those undertaken. We have a number of intentions in presenting it. First, we wish to illustrate the nature of the research approach, both for researchers and for practitioners who may wish to consider using it to better understand their own organizations. Second, we wish to promote a new concept of strategy, one that we think can change significantly how people think about the process of strategy making and thereby perhaps influence the direction taken by the field of Strategic Management. And third, we wish to give the reader the flavor of some of the theory that is emerging from our research. While there are a number of interesting findings characteristic of this particular firm, others are indicative of the broader set of results of this research project.

Each of our studies has proceeded in a number of steps, reflecting the inductive and intensive nature of the research. First we collect the basic data— chronologies of decisions and actions that shaped the organization's history, as well as related trends and events in the environment and figures available on the organization's performance. Then we infer strategies (patterns or consistencies) in these streams of decisions and actions, and label each and represent it in symbolic form. At this point we stack up all the strategies represented in symbolic form on a common time scale, and by scanning the result, infer major periods in the history of the company. The research then shifts to a more intensive investigation of each period, to try to understand especially what provoked major changes in strategies, how different strategies related to each other (e.g., which led and which lagged), what explains periods of continuity, how strategy related to structure, and so on. This step relies primarily on interviewing key actors of the period and on reading available records and in-depth reports about it. The final step is one of brainstorming, in which members of the research team sit down together to try to develop propositions and themes about the process of strategy formation, from an assessment of this study itself as well as a comparison with the results of studies of the other organizations. We are concerned about understanding how and why strategies change, what role timing plays in the process, what role judgment, bargaining, and analysis play in the process and what is the meaning of the word *planning* in strategy formation,[3] what relationship exists between strategy, structure, leadership, and environment, the conditions under which strategies emerge and under which they are deliberately formulated. One unique feature of this particular study is that the individual who was president of the firm for the last seven years of our study period joined the team for the brainstorming sessions. As a practitioner with strong conceptual in-

[2]H. Mintzberg and J. A. Waters, "Tracking Strategy in an Entrepreneurial Firm," *Academy of Management Journal,* 1982.

[3]See Mintzberg, "What Is Planning Anyway?"

terests—he holds an MBA from Harvard and has taught part-time in McGill's Faculty of Management for a number of years—his presence was most worthwhile.

Canadian Lady Inc., or more recently, Canadelle Inc., founded in 1939, has been primarily a manufacturer of women's undergarments, notably brassieres. To infer its strategies since its inception, we divided its decisions into seven functional areas: product lines, facilities (plants, warehouses, office), marketing, manufacturing technology, licensing, finance, and organizational structure. The strategies inferred, over thirty in number, were then combined to describe four major periods in the company's history. (Note that the history of the company is discussed up to 1976, although the diagrams of the strategies are shown to 1978.)

I. THE STRATEGIES
OF CANADIAN LADY

PRODUCT LINES

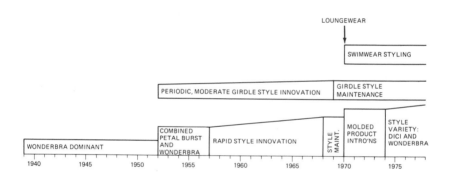

The company's products include brassieres, girdles, and swimwear, with very minor sales of such items as lingerie sets including panties, combination braslips, and shampoo for elastic products. The three major product strategies are described. With respect to brassieres, six differnt strategies were inferred:

1939–1952: Wonderbra
Dominant

The company began in 1939 with licenses to produce Lovable and Wonderbra brassieres in Canada. Lovable was a low-end brand which was not very successful, and the license was dropped around 1941. Wonderbra was a trademark for a brassiere product employing a diagonal slash strap which provided more comfort and freedom of movement for the user.

1952–1957: Combined Petal
Burst and Wonderbra

In anticipation of expiration of the Wonderbra patent and forthcoming negotiations with the patent owner, a U. S. firm, and in response to a new fashion trend—the pointed bust look—the company launched Petal Burst. This product, employing a spoke-stitched cup in combination with the diagonal slash strap, became an important part of the line, reaching 50 percent of brassiere sales by 1957.

1957–1968: Rapid Style
Innovation

The year 1957 marked the introduction of the first product design not covered by the diagonal slash patent. Over the next twelve years, a variety of new styles were introduced almost every year under such new brand names as Risque, Curve-V, Fleur de Lis, Petal Teen, Scandale, Young Wonder, and Wonder Bare. Also during this period, size ranges were extended for many lines and additional colors were introduced.

1969–1970: Style Maintenance

During these two years, the company engaged heavily in product and manufacturing work to produce a brassiere with a molded cup (discussed under "Manufacturing Technology"). While this experimentation was going on, very few style innovations were introduced (see also "Organization Structure"). Hence the strategy is labeled "Style Maintenance."

1970–1973: Molded Product
Introductions

Molded bras, with molding done by subcontractors, began to reach the market in 1970 under the Wonderbra brand name. Two styles were introduced, but while response was favorable, production difficulties prevented sales from becoming significant. In addition, the difficulty of working through outside subcontractors impeded design innovation (see "Manufacturing Technology") and no new styles were introduced in 1971.

The first in-house molded bra was introduced in 1972. The company also began to experiment with in-house production of the two styles that had been introduced earlier. During 1973 substantial improvement in the molding process was achieved, but no new products were introduced to the market. Except for the few introductions of molded Wonderbra products, there were few style innovations. During this transition period, similar garments were imported from France under the brand name of Pomone.

1974–1978+: Style Variety:
Dici and Wonderbra

In 1974 a new product line aimed at the younger consumer was introduced under the brand name of Dici. The younger consumer wanted a more natural, "less-bra" look. In keeping with this demand, Dici styles were all seamless and included both molded and non-molded stretch fabric designs. The brand name grew out of a packaging innovation (a cube, like dice, with holes in it so the customer could see and feel the product).

The brassiere business was consolidated into two major segments: Dici and Wonderbra. A variety of Dici styles were introduced with regularity as the product line came to represent a substantial portion of the business. At the same time, regular style innovation resumed in the Wonderbra line in both sewn styles and molded heavier fabrics. Regular style innovation continued through the end of the study period for both major lines.

(In 1978, after the study period, Dici Nova was introduced as a natural look product for the woman interested in high fashion. The line was expensive and appealed more to the Wonderbra age customer. It was also a response to the fact that the original Dici customers were now four years older.)

Over the study period, girdles represented a variable portion of the firm's business. At the high point, 1966, girdles were approximately one-third of the overall volume. At the end of the study period, the portion of total volume represented by girdles had fallen to approximately 5 percent. With respect to girdles, two different strategies were inferred:

1952–1968: Periodic,
Moderate Style Innovation

The first girdle product was "Winkie," which was copied from a U. S. product. This was followed by "Scandale" in 1957 (a French design licensed from U. S.) and "Oblique" in 1961 (licensed from U. S.). In 1964 all brands were consolidated under the umbrella brand of Wonderbra (e.g., "Oblique by Wonderbra"), and "Secret Service" by Wonderbra was introduced later in the year. Over the period, the firm also made moderate style innovations, but at a considerably slower pace than it did with brassieres.

1969–1978+: Style
Maintenance

With the advent of miniskirts and panty hose, the market for girdles dropped at a rate of approximately 30 percent per year, beginning in 1969. The firm serviced the existing market but introduced few new styles.

Following the introduction of "loungewear" in 1970, which met with a very poor response, the company introduced a line of swimwear to use the material that had been purchased for the ill-fated loungewear line. One strategy is identified for the swimwear business, as follows:

1970–1978+: Swimwear
Styling

The line of swimwear was marketed on the basis of fit—it was brassiere sized and sold through corset departments where clerks are trained to fit the customer. Once introduced, the firm followed industry practice of annual styling changes in color, fabric, and/or style. By the end of the study period, swimwear represented approximately 12 percent of total sales volume.

PLANT, WAREHOUSE,
AND OFFICE FACILITIES

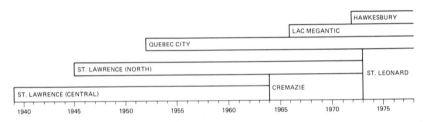

Decisions with respect to establishment and consolidation of plant, warehouse, and office facilities appear as events in the history of the firm. The overall strategy in this area might be described as "sporadic expansion in blocks," although we prefer to show specific detail.

The diagram depicts the expansion moves as follows:

1939: Total operations located at 4475 St. Lawrence Street, Montreal.

1945: Sewing and cutting operations moved to 9500 St. Lawrence while the office and finished goods warehouse remained at 4475 St. Lawrence; the move resulted in a net expansion of capacity.

1952: Additional sewing capacity in Quebec City, 248 kilometers from Montreal, because of labor scarcity and cost in Montreal. During the same year, warehouse moved from 4475 to 9500 St. Lawrence.

1964: 4475 St. Lawrence closed; offices and warehouse moved to Cremazie Blvd., resulting in a net expansion. Operations (and some warehouse) continued at 9500 St. Lawrence.

1966: Purchase of bankrupt lingerie plant in Lac Megantic, 193 kilometers from Montreal. Expansion was partly an opportunistic move in response to the availability of a plant all set up for sewing and the opportunity to get training grants and tax holiday of three years. Most importantly, this location permitted the hiring of locally available skilled workers, already trained to sew.

1972: Expanded by purchasing a plant in Hawkesbury, Ontario, 96 kilometers from Montreal. As with Lac Megantic, labor availability and government training grants were important considerations. Swimwear was produced here because labor regulations were more flexible regarding working hours and conditions than in Quebec where swimwear is classified as ladies' outerwear. This different classification would otherwise have required different working conditions in the same plant, causing confusion in operating practices.

1973: All Montreal operations consolidated in suburb of St. Leonard. This was not only a consolidation aimed at eliminating communication problems arising from fragmented locations but also an expansion of total operating space.

MARKETING

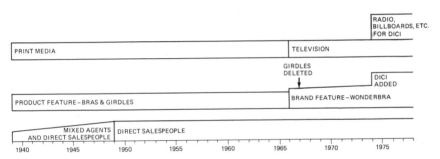

Three dimensions of marketing strategy are described. With respect to sales force decisions, two different strategies were employed.

1939–1949: Mixed Agents and Direct Salespeople

After starting with sales agents, the firm gradually switched to direct salespeople. One agent was retained in Ontario until his death in 1949.

1949–1979: Direct Salespeople

Since 1949, all selling has been done by company salespeople.

With respect to decisions about the content of advertising messages, three different strategies were employed:

1939–1965: Product
Feature—Bras and Girdles

Emphasis was on specific products and their features (e.g., Dream Lift, Oblique, Petal Burst, etc.).

1966–1974: Brand
Feature—Wonderbra

After a complete shift to TV advertising (discussed below), the decision was made to switch from a product emphasis to a brand emphasis. Ads attempted to build consumer awareness of the one brand name—Wonderbra. It was quickly discovered through research that women did not want to see girdles advertised on TV; girdles were seen as an armor against sex, while the reverse was true for bras. Thus, beginning in 1967, the content of advertising was focused exclusively on Wonderbra brand brassieres. The Wonderbra ads were based on fashion and emotional appeal (see discussion of "Product Lines"). The ads included a male in the picture, and the theme—"We care about the shape you're in" was used in one form or another from 1967 through the end of the study period.

1974–1978+: Brand
Feature—Wonderbra and Dici

With the addition of the Dici line, both brands were featured, but always in separate ads. Dici was aimed at a different market segment (see discussion of "Product Lines") and ads made a distinctly different appeal—no males—"It's like wearing no bra at all," or "Dici or nothing."

With respect to advertising media decisions, three strategies were inferred:

1939–1966: Print Media

All advertising took place in newspapers and magazines.

1966–1974: Television

After a change of advertising agency in 1966, the first TV commercials were shown in 1966. Following their success, most of the advertising budget was put into TV applications.

1974–1978+: Television
and Radio, Billboards, Subway Cars

Advertising for the mobile Dici consumer was on radio, billboards, and subway cars. Budget restrictions did not initially allow TV advertising of Dici;

moreover, there was some question about whether it would be as cost-effective for this market. Most of Wonderbra advertising continued on TV.

MANUFACTURING TECHNOLOGY

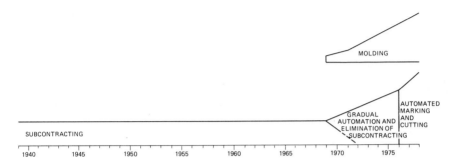

All of the company's products utilize various textiles and combinations of textiles. The company has never undertaken the production of basic textiles, so the basic manufacturing technology deals with the cutting, shaping, and sewing of yard goods. The manufacturing technology strategies are described as follows.

1939–1969: Subcontracting

In these years, substantial portions of the manufacturing process were contracted out to suppliers and subcontractors. Laminations (i.e., combinations of fabrics) were done by the textile manufacturers. Textiles were preslit by these manufacturers for binding tapes and straps.

In addition, shoulder and hook-and-eye straps were obtained through subcontractors, who employed homeworkers to sew these subassemblies. The final sewing, assembly, and packaging were done inhouse.

1969–1976: Gradual
Automation and Elimination
of Subcontracting

Following a study in 1969 of opportunities for vertical integration, an increasing portion of the manufacturing process was brought in-house and automated. The first step for the company was to purchase basic yard goods and do its own laminating and slitting. Research was undertaken, and machines were developed to make hook-and-eye tapes and to produce shoulder straps. By the end of the period, all this work was done in-house.

1976–1978+: Automated Marking and Cutting

A major increase in automation took place with the introduction in 1976 of the Camsco computer-assisted marker and the Gerber automated cutting machinery. Both of these machines produced substantial increaases in textile usage, efficiency, quality, reliability, and speed of production.

1969–1978+: Molding

This period covered the emergence of molding technology as an important element of manufacturing. At first this work was done by subcontractors. Because of high costs, quality-control problems, difficulties in introducing new designs, excessive lead-time requirements for the production of new products, and inability to control material waste, a program was undertaken to develop an in-house molding capability. After a two-year lead-in period (1969–1970), during which new fabric specifications were developed, proprietary molding machines were manufactured, and a mold-making shop was established, all molding was done in-house. This was the final step in eliminating reliance on subcontracting. Upward of 50 percent of brassiere production became molded.

LICENSING

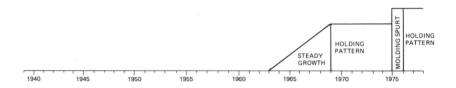

Licensing involves the selling, on a royalty basis, to other manufacturers of technological know-how, brand use, promotional aids (posters, ad copy, etc.), and, where applicable, patent rights.

Generally, a future licensee would import products from Canada for a few years and then begin domestic manufacturing. In a few cases, the period of importation was extended; in some cases, notably Switzerland, the "licensee" was primarily an importer and only engaged in limited manufacturing. While exact data are not available, exports independent of license arrangements were always a negligible portion of total sales. From 1963 to the end of the study period, net income from licensing represented between 2 and 6 percent of the company's total profits.

Three different strategies are identified over the study period, as follows.

1963–1969: Steady Growth

A new license arrangement was established in each year of this period except 1968. The licensees were in most of the major developed countries of Europe (England, Germany, Switzerland, Sweden, Italy, and the Benelux countries) and in South Africa. Two licensees were established in 1969, but one of these was minor and expired within a few years.

1969–1974: Holding Pattern

Over the next five years, only one license was established (Australia in 1971). This was a minor arrangement and expired within a few years. The license/export arrangements established in the previous period were maintained, though royalties began tapering off because no new-product innovations were made available to licensees.

1975: Molding License Spurt

In 1975, three licensees were established for the transfer of molding technology know-how. Two of these were for new countries (Mexico and the U. S. A.) and one was an addition to an existing license arrangement.

1976–1978+: Holding Pattern

Following the spurt in 1975, no subsequent licenses were established in the next few years, suggesting the start of a holding pattern.

FINANCE

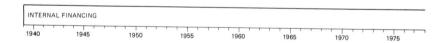

1939–1978+: Internal Financing

A constant strategy of internal financing was pursued over the study period. Only short-term borrowing was employed, and this never exceeded $1 million. Neither the formation of Reldan in 1947 nor the acquisition of the company in 1969 by Consolidated Foods resulted in long-term capital additions to the firm.

ORGANIZATION STRUCTURE

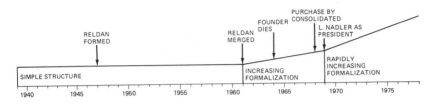

Three periods are identified in the evolution of organization structure over the study period.

1939–1961: Simple Structure

From 1939 to 1952, the firm was almost literally a one-man show. M. Nadler founded the firm, owned all the stock, and supervised all the details. However, his brother, D. Nadler, operated as an executive in the areas of advertising and sales.

In 1947 a new corporate unit called Reldan (Nadler spelled backwards) was created to provide a specific equity interest for D. Nadler after the war. Reldan was owned 50/50 by the Nadler brothers and was not completely separate from Canadian Lady. M. Nadler was president of both operations and made all the major decisions. From 1947 to 1952, sales of certain products (e.g., garter belts, strapless bras) were reported through Reldan, even though the two companies shared the same facilities (offices, manufacturing plant, warehouses, etc.). Beginning with the Winkie girdle in 1952, all girdle products were reported through Reldan.

L. Nadler, M. Nalder's son, joined the firm in 1955, working in various positions in sales and quality control. He went to Harvard Business School in 1959 but continued to take an active interest in the firm (e.g., with a classmate, he studied the firm as part of a course assignment).

1961–1969: Increasing Formalization

After graduating from Harvard, L. Nadler rejoined the firm full time in 1961 as secretary-treasurer. At his urging, the two firms were merged and D. Nadler received 25 percent of the resultant company, L. Nadler 10 percent, with M. Nadler retaining 65 percent.

L. Nadler brought with him many other ideas and desires for change. The firm began to hire MBA graduates in various positions as well as computer specialists, mathematicians, and accountants. Various clerical functions were automated during this period, including accounting and marketing reports, as well as routine credit decisions and product allocations among customers in times of shortage.

Upon the death of M. Nadler in 1964, D. Nadler became president and L. Nadler assumed the post of executive vice-president. The firm was purchased by Consolidated Foods, Inc., a U. S.-based conglomerate, in March 1968.

1969–1978+: Rapidly Increasing Formalization

In July 1969 L. Nadler became president of the company. Although he had been pushing for some time for a formalized long-range planning process for the company, the acquisition by Consolidated forced the development of this process.

A key change was the imposition of formal decision rules ensuring that new products would meet established profitability criteria. This was followed by the institution of a rule that a new stock-keeping unit (SKU—a specific product, size, color, package, etc.) be introduced only if an old SKU was dropped. This was done to arrest the proliferation of SKUs in brassieres.

Extensive budgets, market and environmental analyses, and capital investment plans began to be produced annually. An incentive compensation system for key executives was established. The formalization of work procedures and job specialization begun in the previous period continued but at a more rapid pace.

PERFORMANCE

Figure 1 presents combined annual net sales for Canadian Lady and Reldan over the study period. Missing data are represented by straight-line extrapolation between the years for which sales figures were available.

Figure 1   Annual Net Sales

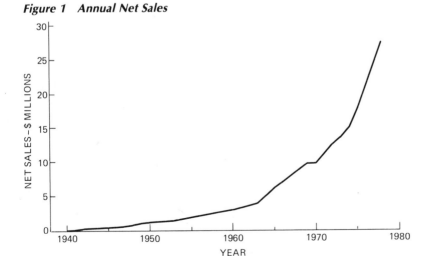

From 1939 through 1963, sales volume grew slowly with an average increase of approximately $160,000 per year over the period. From 1963 through 1978, sales volume grew much more rapidly, with an average increase of approximately $1.6 million per year over the period, or ten times the average annual sales increase during the previous twenty-four years. This sales growth was particularly rapid starting in 1975; for the three years from 1975 to 1978, the average sales growth was $3.2 million per year.

For the years 1972 to 1977, the following details of performance were available:

Year	Sales ($ Million)	Pretax Operating Profit %	Canadian Market Share %
1972	12.614	14.3	20.6
1973	13.422	15.3	19.1
1974	15.011	13.7	19.7
1975	18.039	14.6	21.6
1976	21.261	14.0	24.2
1977	24.900	12.3	26.8

Beyond the rapid sales growth, these data reveal the rapidly increasing share of the undergarment market. Over this six-year period, roughly three-quarters of sales volume was to customers in Quebec, Ontario, and the Maritime Provinces of Canada. The balance of sales was to Western provinces with minor exports.

II. PERIODS IN THE HISTORY
OF CANADIAN LADY

Our procedure is to combine all the graphical representations of the strategies on a single sheet with a common horizontal time scale, and then to scan the sheet to infer distinct periods in the history of strategy formation in the organizations. As noted in Figure 2, a reproduction of this sheet, the procedure resulted in four periods for Canadian Lady. From its inception, we could see no reason to introduce a new period until 1952. The figure shows only two seemingly minor changes before that year. In 1952, however, major changes occurred in product lines, and the Quebec City plant was opened. While a number of changes occurred in subsequent years, prior to 1968 these were spread out and none, in our view, signaled any major reorientation of the company. Thus we treat 1952 to 1968 as one consistent period. As is evident in Figure 2, this is clearly not true subsequently. The years 1968–1970 stand out for a number of major changes, notably in product line but also in manufacturing technology

Figure 2 Canadian Lady Strategy

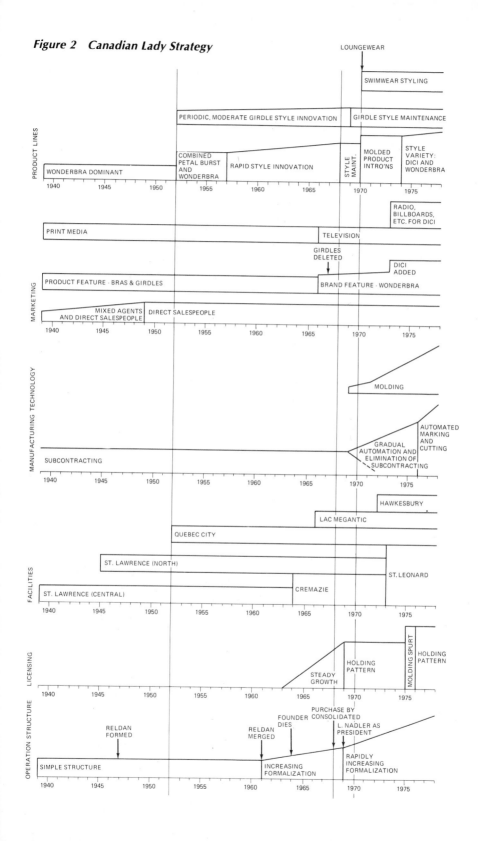

and some other areas. Subsequently, to the end of the study period, there was a steady stream of changes. But these, as we shall see, were manifestations of the reorientation of 1968–1970, and so we treat 1970 to 1976 as a single period. Our four periods are listed and labeled below and then each is discussed in turn, from a factual followed by a conceptual perspective.

1939–1952: Small, Simple, Focused Operations: Period of Making a Given Strategy Work

1952–1968: Becoming an Independent, Broad-Line Women's Undergarment Manufacturer: Period of Change in Thrust Followed by Growth

1968–1970: Rethinking the Business: Period of Reconception

1970–1976: Getting Settled in New Directions: Period of Elaborating the New Concepts

1939–1952: Small, Simple, Focused Operations: Period of Making a Given Strategy Work

Canadian Lady was started in 1939 when Moe Nadler, sensing an opportunity in a business he knew a little about, obtained an exclusive license from New York to manufacture and market Wonderbra brassieres in Canada. Despite his lack of knowledge (he had been in dress retailing), Nadler entered the business because, in the words of his son, "brassieres were stable" and they made money. The license covered patent rights to a unique shoulder strap design—diagonal slash—which permitted greater movement and comfort for the garment wearer. The license agreement also covered manufacturing know-how and marketing and promotional aids, including use of the Wonderbra trademark, with resulting benefits of associated national advertising in the United States.

Throughout this period the company remained small, with annual sales volume eventually reaching $1 million. The product line was primarily based on the diagonal slash feature brassiere in a variety of sizes, materials, and colors.

All internal operations were located at first in a 4,200-square-foot factory/warehouse at 4475 St. Lawrence Street in Montreal. In part because of its own size and in part because of limitations imposed by the war, the firm subcontracted the work of sewing the shoulder strap assemblies to women who worked in their own homes. Increasing volume and the release of some of the wartime constraints brought on an expansion of operations facilities, and additional factory/warehouse space was leased at 9500 St. Lawrence Street in 1945.

In 1947 a new corporate unit was formed called Reldan. It was differentiated from Canadian Lady only in terms of accounting records and was established to provide Moe Nadler's brother Dave with a specific equity interest in the firm.

Thus the period was spent in establishing the firm, utilizing the entry route of licensing. Toward the end of the period, however, the role of single-product licensee, dependent on an unresponsive licensor for product and marketing innovation, was beginning to chafe Mr. Nadler. He clearly had intentions for growth and, as we shall discuss below, was doing the design work that would facilitate his gaining of independence from the original licensor.

Conceptual interpretation. Our conceptual interpretation of this period is shown in Figure 3, with environmental factors on the left (in parallelograms), organizational and leadership factors on the right (in rounded rectangles and diamond shapes, respectively), and the strategies down the middle (in rectangles). What we have here is a fairly typical entrepreneurial beginning, with its resource limitations, giving rise to focus on a single product, limited financing, constrained operations, and simple structure. Atypical, perhaps, was the entrepreneur's lack of knowledge of the business, encouraging the licensing arrangement, and the wartime economy, imposing more stringent resource constraints than normal.

Figure 3   Establishment

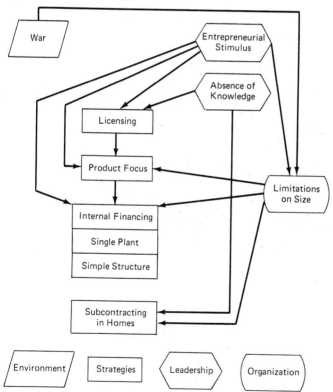

In terms of the strategies pursued, this was a period of stability, with signs of the changes to come appearing at the end. The strategies appear to be deliberate for the most part, although not particularly formalized (except, of course, for the licensing). They reflect the stability of the industry environment, the stage of development of the firm, and what we were told was an absence of stringent competition. The strategies were not particularly bold or unique (not what we have earlier called "gestalt strategy,"[4] although they did seem to be integrated around the basic status of the firm in these early years. The key strategy—concerning the one product—was clearly a copy of another strategy, and in that sense, it, and the strategies that resulted in part from it, could be considered given ones.

Thus we characterize the period as one of getting established—simply surviving, learning the business, building a base in it—and then, once this was done, beginning to consider how to break the initial bounds to become free of the initial constraints. The object of the company in these early years, then, was to make a given strategy work. The energies for most of the period were on operating matters, not strategic ones.

1952–1968: Becoming an Independent, Broad-Line Women's Undergarment Manufacturer: Period of Change in Thrust Followed by Growth

The Wonderbra patent was due to expire in 1952. In anticipation of this, and because of Moe Nadler's concern that the New York designer was not responding to a new-product trend—the pointed bust look introduced by Dior—the firm began work to design a new brassiere that would not use the Wonderbra technology. Maidenform, a major competitor in Canada, had a pointed bra product that was selling well, and Canadian Lady wanted a design with which it could compete.

As a result of this, a number of major shifts took place in Canadian Lady in 1952, all of which were to initiate a period that can be characterized as the flowering of an independent, broad-line women's undergarment manufacturer. With respect to the mainline brassiere business, the Petal Burst line, designed in-house, was launched in 1952 and was a major success. Petal Burst received the major advertising and promotional effort at the expense of Wonderbra, and by 1957 Petal Burst represented 50 percent of brassiere sales volume.

The Winkie girdle line was introduced in 1952 also. The line was copied from a U. S. product and was the firm's initial entry into the sizable girdle market, which was roughly the same size as the brassiere market. Girdle sales increased steadily until, by 1966, they represented approximately one-third of the

[4]H. Mintzberg, "Patterns in Strategy Formation," *Management Science,* 1978, pp. 934–48.

firm's total business volume. Girdle sales were reported through Reldan until 1962 when the accounting distinction was eliminated by merging the two companies.

Also in 1952, sewing operations were established in Quebec City. With this addition, total plant area increased by 10,000 square feet. The plant, located in Quebec City because of labor scarcity and cost in Montreal, represented an additional commitment to growth in the undergarment business.

After the launching of all these major changes, no shifts in strategy occurred until 1957. During the five-year period 1952 to 1957, negotiations continued with the Wonderbra licensor. The success of the Petal Burst line greatly strengthened the company's bargaining position. In 1957 these negotiations were concluded with Canadian Lady obtaining world rights to the Wonderbra know-how and name except for the United States, Africa, and Latin America.

Ironically the conclusion of these negotiations coincided with a decision not to limit product designs to the type covered by the diagonal slash patent. The firm had hired its first full-time designer in the early 1950s, and design innovation became a major route to growth. From 1957 to 1968 the product strategy was characterized by steady style innovation as new products and names were introduced almost every year.

With new products, new style variety, and new manufacturing capacity, annual sales volume grew from $1 million in 1952 to approximately $8.8 million in 1968. Significantly, the firm had established its independence from the original licensing arangement.

Increasing task specialization and formalization of procedures began to take place in the early 1960s following the return of Moe Nadler's son Larry to the company after completion of his MBA at Harvard. The resulting structure had sufficient vitality that the death of Moe Nadler in 1964 caused no immediate changes in the directions being pursued.

Production capacity was expanded twice, in 1964 and in 1966, to support the strong growth in business. Other evidence of the continuing transition to independence was the beginning of a foreign licensing program in 1963, which grew steadily to the end of the period. The original licensee operation was now the licensor of its own products and technology.

The advent of the overseas licensing program was stimulated by the strong success of a new product, known internally as Wonderbra 1350, one of the first lace brassieres that was not simple utilitarian but also emphasized fashion and sex appeal. On the domestic front, the success of this product and similar fashion products subsequently helped to increase the rate of sales growth over the period.

Perhaps the clearest symbol of the completion of the transformation to independent status was the shift in 1966 in advertising and promotional effort from a focus on product features to a focus on brand awareness. The company thus began to promote itself as a company, rather than promoting individual products.

A related change, the result of which gives a hint of the next period in the firm, was the move to television advertising in 1967. One-half of the 1967 TV budget was allocated to Wonderbra girdles, but in the words of Larry Nadler, "It was a big mistake." It was discovered that women did not like to see girdles on TV, so the TV budget was switched exclusively to brassieres six months into the year. Girdle sales continued at the same pace as before, and the company in fact introduced a new design in 1967. But the social reactions to the advertisement was a harbinger of changes to come.

Conceptual interpretation.   As shown in Figure 4, what particularly characterizes this period is a confluence of a few major changes in the environment—the running out of the patent coinciding with the appearance of Dior's pointed look, and the resultant rise of competition. All of this occurred together with the maturation of the firm and with the owners push for growth. In effect, conditions around and inside an organization can shift in global or "gestalt" ways to—that is, all at once, perhaps even suggesting their own form of integration (although later we shall see a much clearer example of such a shift). In this case, as implied in Figure 4, external changes and threats, internal developments, and managerial values all pointed in the same direction. Often, however,

Figure 4   Change in Thrust

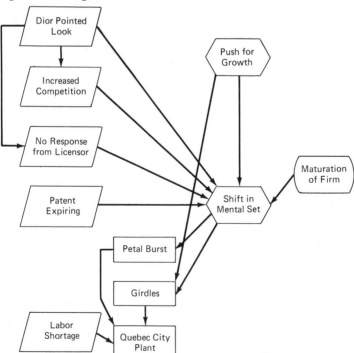

no matter how complementary, such changes require a tangible stimulus to evoke action. In this case, that stimulus was provided by the expiration of the patent—ostensibly a problem.

Such a gestalt shift can stimulate a change in mental set (or worldview, "Weltanschauung") on the part of responsive managers. That is what seems to have happened in this firm. From operating within a given strategy, the managers began to put that strategy itself into question—to rethink their concept of the business. This led to two major changes: (1) in the traditional product—their own brassiere, and (2) in market—the introduction of girdles. A third change resulted immediately—in plant capacity and location. And from this fairly sudden change in thrust followed extensive and sustained growth of the firm. The managers reverted to pursuing set strategies, the company thereby experiencing a long period of stability.

Again strategies of the period appeared to be deliberate—in part a kind of battle plan to deal with the licensor—but this time they were more original to the firm, although not particularly unique. They did, however, represent an opening up, a breaking away from earlier constraints, presumably associated with a sense of excitement. The stimulus that was a problem—how to deal with loss of patent protection—was turned into an opportunity. In these senses, strategic behavior of this period, compared with the last, can be described as being more proactive.

1968–1969: Rethinking the Business: Period of Reconception

A great deal changed beginning in 1968. For one thing, the head designer quit in 1968 and product style innovation in conventional lines dropped dramatically. New styles of sewn brassieres were introduced in 1968, but these were the products of previous work, and no new styles were introduced in 1969. The growth of licensing also came to an end in 1969, and in that year the firm was purchased by an American conglomerate, Consolidated Foods. This was done in order to convert the assets to cash value so that they could be divided between Moe Nadler's brother and son.

But the real changes were taking place in the environment. A sexual revolution of sorts was brewing. In sharp contrast to Dior's pointed look, women wished to appear more natural. "Bra burning" was a major symbol of the social upheaval of the times, and for a manufacturer of brassieres, the threat was obvious. The miniskirt dominated the fashion scene, which led to the development of panty hose, since the girdle became infeasible. Moreover, the girdle itself was threatened by the same social trend that was demanding increased freedom, comfort, and naturalness. As the executives of Canadian Lady put it, "the bottom fell out of the girdle business." Sales dropped by 30 percent per year, eventually stabilizing at about 5 percent of the firm's total business. Essentially it appeared that the whole environment—for years so receptive to the company's strategies—had suddenly turned rejective.

But in crisis loomed opportunity. New trends were emerging which offered hope for a management sensitive enough to perceive them and intuitive enough to synthesize their message. As Larry Nadler, who became president in 1969, described it, this was a time of confusion and groping, in which two key events led to a sudden crystallization of ideas, which gave birth to a major reconception of strategy.

At this time a French company was promoting a light, sexy, molded garment, called "Huit," with the theme "Just like not wearing a bra." Its target market was fifteen-to-twenty year-olds. Though expensive when it landed in Quebec, and not well fitting, the product sold well. Larry Nadler flew to France in an attempt to license the product for manufacturing in Canada. The French firm refused, but Nadler claimed that what he learned in "that one hour in their offices made the trip worthwhile." He learned that the no-bra movement was going to manifest itself primarily as a less-bra movement. What women seemed to want was a more natural look. He also found that the product was being target-marketed to younger people.

The second event, shortly after, was a trip to a sister firm in the Consolidated Foods group. There Larry Nadler realized the importance of market segmentation by age and life style. The company sponsored market research to better understand what women wanted from a brassiere. The results indicated that for the more mature customer, the brassiere was a cosmetic, which she wore to look and feel more attractive. The product had an important sex appeal dimension for these customers (see "Marketing"). Moreover, it was found that the Wonderbra brand had high recognition among these consumers. In contrast, the younger customer wanted to look and feel natural. The sex appeal dimension was considerably less important. Also, in the minds of these consumers, the Wonderbra brand name was associated with older women. Based on these distinctions, Larry Nadler became convinced that some major product line differentiation was required.

These two events led to major shift in strategy. Larry Nadler describes it as a kind of revelation—the confluence of different ideas to create a new mental set. In his words, "All of a sudden the idea forms." His groping had led to two new major concepts in the firm's strategy. On the marketing side was market segmentation, specifically the division of the market into older and younger customers. And on the technology and manufacturing side was the use of molding.

Canadian Lady initiated an intensive technology development program to produce its own molded brassiere, stimulated by the recent introduction of new fabrics. The firm introduced a molded garment out of Tricot under the Wonderbra name for older customers and a stretch garment of Lycra for the younger market. It might be noted that Canadian Lady was able to proceed with its development work without having to seek budget approval from its new parent firm. Canadian Lady was profitable, and the Consolidated Foods executive to whom it reported was occupied with other, less successful, divisions.

Another major change during the period was the development of a line of swimwear. The product was born from the ashes of a mistake. At the fall market in 1969, the company introduced a line of loungewear that "was a complete disaster"; nobody placed orders. Substantial amounts of specialized fabrics (colors and prints) had been purchased, and the company was faced with the prospect of a large write-off, even after canceling as many fabric shipments as possible. It was decided to experiment with the fabric to produce a line of bikini swimwear. The product was introduced in early 1970 and was greeted with success in the marketplace.

Finally, this period saw the start and acceleration of work to automate the manufacturing processes. A study of opportunities for vertical integration was completed in 1969, which led to an ongoing strategy to bring more and more of the manufacturing in-house.

Conceptual interpretation.   This was clearly a period of global change for the firm, of "organizational revolution," in which almost all of its strategies changed at once. (Remaining ones changed subsequently as a result, as we shall see.) In the short space of two to three years the company changed ownership and top management, saw the permanent downturn of one of its major product lines (girdles), began the experimentation required to respond to a major threat to its mainline business (brassieres), experienced a major product introduction failure (loungewear), successfully introduced another product as a result (swimwear), and established new strategies for automation and vertical integration.

Of particular interest here is the fact that the environment changed in global fashion, or perhaps more to the point, in gestalt fashion as well, as shown in Figure 5. That is, everything seemed to change all at once. It was as if the rug had been pulled out from under the firm.

How does an organization respond to such a gestalt shift in the environment? The pattern here is probably typical of effective management. A gestalt shift in situation elicits a gestalt shift in strategy. But not immediately. Managers used to a given conception of their world cannot just change overnight. As the chief executive of this organization described so clearly, the initial feeling was one of confusion, which stimulated a vigorous search for information, for every available scrap that might help explain what was happening, what opportunities might be available. Much as gestalt psychologists and scientists themselves have described the creative process,[5] the chief executive went through a period of preparation (informing himself), followed by incubation (the uncomfortable,

[5]G. Wallas, *The Art of Thought* (New York: Harcourt, Brace and World, 1926); and J. Hadamard, *Psychology of Invention in the Mathematical Field* (Princeton, N. J.: Princeton University Press, 1949).

Figure 5   Reconceptualization

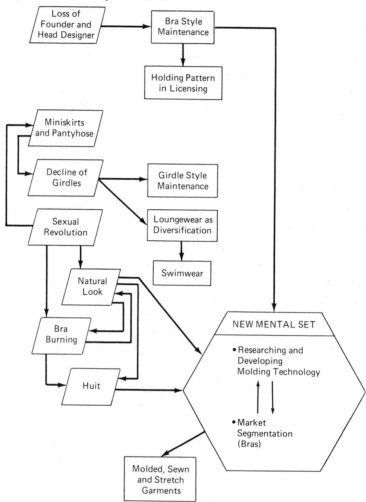

subconscious process of trying to put the disparate pieces together), to one of illumination (the sudden discovery, in this case two of them). The fourth stage, of verification, had its equivalent here too, as we shall see in the next period.

The illumination was the shift in mindset and worldview, as we noted, involving a reconception of the firm's markets and production technology. Segmenting the market in two may not seem like a great innovation in retrospect; but to a firm used to thinking one way for decades, the change must have been dramatic—it certainly had significant strategic consequences.

And once the reconception had taken place, the object was to follow its dictates—to work out the new technology (which was to take some time) and reach the new segments. In Larry Nadler's words, "Once the insight is there—

once you understand it—you know what to do about it and you go." In other words, the notion of reconception implies a high degree of deliberateness, although more in a general than a specific sense. The thrust was deliberate, but the details of it—the specific strategies—by having to be worked out, had an emergent quality to them. One could describe a deliberate umbrella under which specific orientations emerged. In fact the one move outside the umbrella—the diversification into loungewear—proved ineffective, and that was quickly pulled back in.

There is at least one major, if implicit, assumption in such an approach to strategy making—that the enviornment, no matter how sudden and dramatic its change, has become firmly established in a new direction. Much as an automobile turns from one highway on to another, so Canadian Lady proceeded as if the environment were again on a steady, if new, course. That proved to be a good assumption; had it not, the reconception could have proved dysfunctional, compared with a more adaptive mode of strategy making, with no deliberate thrust encompassing specific strategies.

The approach was largely entrepreneurial, in the sense that both the strategy-making process and the strategies themselves were very personalized, centering on one individual whose behavior seemed to be as much intuitive (as we are describing the processes of synthesis and illumination) as they were systematic or analytic. But once attention turned to developing the insight, and once the takeover by the parent firm was consolidated, the analytic component was to become more significant.

In our study of a highly entrepreneurial retail firm,[6] we discussed the "proactive reaction"—the turning of problems or crises into opportunities, oversolving them if you like. Here again, under entrepreneurial conditions we see this phenomenon. Bra burning became, not a cause for panic and diversification (as in the case of some competitors), but an opportunity to serve old markets in new ways. What might in contemporary terms of strategic management have been categorized as a "dog" was going to perform like a "star."

1970–1976: Getting Settled
in New Directions: Period
of Elaborating the New Concepts

Although the new directions were more or less identified during the 1968–1970 period, much more time would be required to establish them in an integrated way. For example, because some senior people in the company resisted the new concepts, the president formed two task forces of younger ones, bypassing the usual chain of command. Starting in 1970, one task force worked on molding technology and the other on marketing a new "young" brand.

As the task forces pushed their mandates, molded brassiere products, pro-

[6]Mintzberg and Waters, "Tracking Strategy."

duced by molding subcontractors, began to hit the market under the Wonderbra name. Quality-control problems existed (fit, durability), but good product acceptance encouraged continued effort. Some molded brassieres were imported from France to supplement the subcontracted production.

Meanwhile the marketing task force was being sabotaged by the regular organization. In order to minimize conflict and consolidate the innovations of the task forces, both were eventually merged into the organization as their work continued.

Eventually, out of this development effort came Dici, the new line for younger women, as well as molded Wonderbra products. Internal production began in 1973, although production problems continued as the Dici brand hit the market in 1974. These problems were eventually worked through, and by 1974 the firm was able to introduce a variety of styles once again in both molded and sewn brassieres. Success with Dici also produced a short burst of licensing activity in 1975.

Also during this settling-in period, the firm nurtured the fledgling swimwear line. In 1972 a plant was purchased in Ontario, and the swimwear was produced there. By the end of the study period, this line grew to account for about 10 percent of total company sales volume.

As part of this settling in, in 1973 all the Montreal operations—plant, warehouse and office—were consolidated in modern facilities in the suburb of St. Leonard. The plant incorporated the technological developments of the previous years and was highly automated. This automation reached its peak in 1975 with the installation of automated marking and cutting machinery. This equipment was the first of its kind in the garment industry in Canada and the first in the world in the brassiere business.

Finally, the company was also getting used to operating as a division of another company. This period saw the installation of annual budgets and business plans. Long-range plans for automation and market penetration were prepared, and small amounts of short-term funds were advanced by Consolidated. The increase in automation permitted increased sophistication in purchasing, production planning, and manufacturing, and it led to increases in the hiring of technical specialists and to the formalization of work procedures.

In summary, a great deal of energy went into the development of molded brassieres and into a marketing effort tailored to various segments. As these developments were successful, the technology and facilities fell into place so that by the end of the period, the company had emerged as a solidly established division of a major corporation. Sales for 1976 were $21 million, almost double what they had been at the start of the period, and the company seemed poised for a period of continuing growth.

Conceptual interpretation.   This period is very different from the last. It cannot be characterized as one of stability in strategy—as Figure 2 shows, there were changes in strategy throughout it, in parallel and on a piecemeal basis. Yet there was not the same groping. The general thrust had been determined; this was a period of elaboration—of pursuing the consequences of the new concepts. As noted earlier, the thrust was deliberate, with some specific strategies partially emergent, although once these were established, they became firmly deliberate as well. In simpler terms, once the firm had resolved certain specific problems—both technical and organizational—it then pursued the resulting strategies in explicit ways.

One can imagine the mood in the firm—of being up to date, if not on the cutting edge, of knowing what it wished to do, and of moving full-steam ahead to do it. The approach was clearly proactive. The concerns, however, were not conceptual, as in the previous period, but operational: how to solve technical problems, how to organize around a new strategic thrust. As the company's president remarked, "We were pushing the strength we had for all it was worth." As can be seen by comparing Figure 6 with Figure 5, whereas the previous period was driven by the environment, this period was driven by concepts—

Figure 6   Elaboration of New Concepts

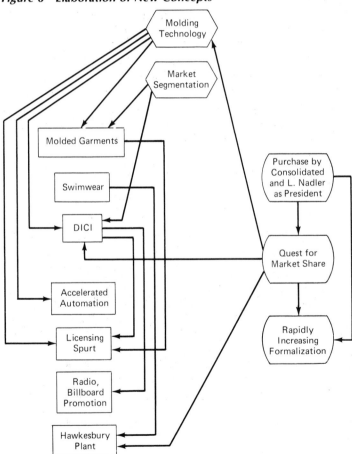

by the results of the previous period. Note that in the conceptual diagram for the period developed by Larry Nadler and the authors, no major environmental shifts appear. The environment naturally remained important, but all its major dimensions were now moving in a constant direction. The challenge was to operationalize efficiently what was proving to be the right concept.

Commensurate with greater attention to operating issues within the context of a given strategic thrust, behavior became much more analytic and decentralized, with more planning, the use of task forces, and so on. In effect, as the needs changed, so did the mode of behavior.

III. SOME CONCLUSIONS ABOUT STRATEGY FORMATION

Our purpose here is not to draw definitive conclusions, nor to be at all comprehensive about the issues we think need to be addressed in the realm of strategy formation. This is, after all, a report on the fourth of eleven studies of strategy formation, and it will be some time before we can draw our different conclusions together. What we wish to do is give the reader a flavor for the kinds of issues we are addressing, and the patterns that seem to be emerging in our own research, and try to develop some sense of what we think effective strategic management might be.

Our major interest is in the patterns of strategic change—how often different strategies change, in what interrelationships, and according to what forces. One conclusion that has appeared in all of our studies is reinforced here. Major shifts in strategic thrust happen only rarely, and they tend to be revolutionary rather than evolutionary. The fact of only two major shifts in thirty-seven years is not unusual. The implications of this for strategic management are, we believe, important (and evident), and we shall return to them shortly.

What is of special interest in this study is one particular pattern by which such shifts occur. Canadian Lady is, of course, the classic entrepreneurial firm in the process of formalizing and adopting more of what is called a "professional" style of management. Many firms subsequently undergo another transition, involving diversification followed by divisionalization.[7] But Canadian Lady did not. In fact, its president referred to the firm's good fortune in having its loungewear sortie nipped in the bud, thereby maintaining the focus of the management on its basic business. Commensurate with the entrepreneurial mode of strategy making that dominated during this study, we see an inclination toward the formation of deliberate strategies, or at least the quick perception of emergent patterns to make them deliberate, and what we called the "proactive reaction"—turning problems and crises into opportunities.

[7]B. R. Scott, "The Industrial State; Old Myths and New Realities," *Harvard Business Review,* March–April 1973, pp. 133–48.

The shifts we see in this firm are, we believe, characteristic of its entrepreneurial foundation, as well as of the fashion nature of its business. Twice in its history the firm exercised sudden and major changes in its strategic thrust, in both cases in response to rather sudden and global shifts in its environment. The two changes are similar in nature, but because the second was more pronounced on all counts and because we had access to its key actors, we concentrate our discussion on it.

The pattern seems clear enough. Coming out of a long period of stability in strategy, with an environment that had long been, if not munificent, then at least acquiescent, the firm finds that many of the important parameters have suddenly changed, all at once. Initially it is stunned, like the boxer who never saw the punch coming. But in time it adapts. Drawing on Lewin's notions, we can describe this adaptation in three stages: unfreezing, changing, and refreezing.[8]

The process of unfreezing is essentially one of overcoming the natural defense mechanisms to realize that the environment has in fact changed. Effective managers are supposed to scan their environments continually; indeed effective *strategic* managers are supposed to be especially in touch with changing trends. One danger of strategic management is that it may encourage managers to be *too* much in touch. Managers may be so busy managing strategic change—the big issues—that they may fail to do well what usually matters, namely to operate effectively with a given strategy. (Remember that Canadian Lady is not atypical in experiencing only two brief periods of major strategic change in thirty-seven years.) Or, equally dangerous (and perhaps more likely), is that the firm gives so much attention to strategic monitoring when nothing important is changing that when something finally does happen, the firm does not even notice it. The trick, of course, is to pick out the discontinuities that count. Many changes are temporary or simply unimportant. Some are consequential and a few, revolutionary. For Canadian Lady, the changes in 1968 were of the latter category.

The second step in unfreezing is to be willing to step into the void, so to speak, in order for the managers to shed their conventional notions of how the business is supposed to function (the industry recipe, as Grinyer and Spender have termed it[9]) and really open their minds to what is happening. Critical is the avoidance of premature closure—not to seize on a new thrust before it is clear what the signals really mean. This takes a special kind of management, one able to live with a good deal of uncertainty and discomfort. The president of this firm was able to articulate his feelings at the time: "There is a period of confusion before you know what to do about it. . . . You sleep on it . . . start looking for patterns . . . become an information hound, searching for [explanations] everywhere." This stage may be painful, but in our view it is critical to successful resolution.

[8]K. Lewin, *Field Theory in Social Science* (New York: Harper & Row, 1951).

[9]P. H. Grinyer and J-C Spender, *Turnaround—Managerial Recipes for Strategic Success* (Associated Business Press, 1979).

Strategic change of this magnitude seems to involve mindset before strategy and seems to be essentially conceptual in nature. In other words, the concepts of the strategy maker(s)—his or her Weltanschauung—must change before anything else can change. If this study gives any indication, then while problems and threats in the environment may provoke the unfreezing, it is opportunities that stimulate the process of change. With some idea of what *can* be done, the strategy maker(s) will begin to converge on a new concept of the business—a new strategic thrust. Our guess is that the experience here—of one or two basic driving ideas—is typical: Change in mindset is stimulated by a small number of key events, probably one critical incident in most cases. Continuous bombardment of facts, opinions, problems, and so on, may have had to prepare the mind for the change, but one simple insight probably creates the synthesis—brings all the disparate data together in one sudden "eureka"-type flash, like a supersaturated liquid that immediately freezes when disturbed slightly.

Once the mind is set, assuming it has read the new environment correctly and has not seized prematurely on trends that have not themselves stabilized, then the refreezing stage begins. Here the object is not to read the environment, at least not in a global sense, but, in effect, to block it out. This is no time for the monitoring precepts of strategic management. It is time to work out the consequences of the new strategic thrust. It has been claimed that obsession is an ingredient in effective organizations.[10] For the period of refreezing (not unfreezing or changing), we would certainly agree. This is not the time for questioning, but for pursuing the new orientation—the new mindset—with full vigor. When we asked the president how the post-1970 period differed from that of the two previous years, he commented: "Any idea is acceptable so long as it's . . ." He motioned with his hands in two parallel lines to indicate: so long as it is strictly within the bounds of the new concept. A management that was open and divergent in its thinking must now become convergent. We wonder how many executives fail in one or the other—remaining convergent when divergence becomes necessary, or failing to settle down to a convergent pattern after a period of divergence.

While unfreezing was a time of great discomfort, refreezing must be one of great excitement (at least for those who accept the reorientation). The organization now knows where it is going; the object of the exercise is to use all the skills at its command to get there. That is not to say that all is creative. Refreezing is characterized by an analytic mode of behavior, with heavy emphasis on formal evaluation, planning in the form of programming, and so on. Of course, not everyone accepts the reorientation; for them, the discomfort now begins, and this can spill over to the strategy maker(s) if considerable resistance arises. (At this point, it helps if the organization is small, as was Canadian Lady.)

The pattern we have been describing is one among a number that we sus-

[10]T. J. Peters, "A Style for All Seasons," *Executive* (Special Issue on Leadership, Cornell University, Summer 1980), pp. 12–16.

pect is common. It is an important one for the organization that experiences a sudden but permanent shift in its environment, as opposed to a gradual one, or is exposed to a more generally turbulent environment (i.e., one that does not stabilize). The process of adaptation that we have been describing is strongly intuitive and personal, at least in its early stages, in the sense that it depends on the synthesis created by a single mind (or a few that can work in concert). It is also a process characterized by design, the achievement of a unique strategy to cope with a new environment. This intuitive synthesis does not preclude analytical techniques. Analytical techniques certainly play a role in preparing for such processes and in pursuing their outcomes. However, the synthesis, the attainment of a new concept of the business, stands apart from those techniques. This process of adaptation by design stands in sharp contrast to approaches favored in the field of strategic management, which tend to emphasize selection from a portfolio of generic strategies based on formal analysis of specific parameters in the environment.

4

Marketing Strategy and the Science of Warfare

PHILIP KOTLER and RAVI SINGH ACHROL

Northwestern University

This article is a revised and significantly expanded version of Philip Kotler and Ravi Singh Achrol, "Marketing Warfare in the 1980's," *Journal of Business Strategy,* Vol. 1, No. 3 (Winter 1981), 30–41. It has been especially revised for *Competitive Strategic Management.* Reprinted by permission from Warren, Gorham and Lamont Inc., 210 South Street, Boston, Mass. All Rights Reserved. Copyright © 1981.

Marketing is merely a civilized form of warfare in which most battles are won with words, ideas, and disciplined thinking.

Albert W. Emery

As the decade of the 1980s unfolds, numerous signs point to an era of contined slow economic growth. Scarce resources, proliferation of technological resources across nations, sharply rising energy costs, economic slowdowns, trade barriers, political tensions, leveling off of population growth in the developed world, and other factors suggest that business prospects will become tougher in the years ahead. Companies will have to pursue their profitability through market share gains rather than market growth gains. The scene will move from normal marketing competition to marketing warfare. Successful marketers will devise "opponent"-centered strategies, not just customer-centered or distribution-centered strategies.

In moving from normal business competition to intensified business conflict, some companies adopt the old "rat-in-a-corner" psychology and bring all their firepower to bear in a free-for-all battle. The cigarette industry highlights this:

> The industry's stagnation is having a significant effect on marketing options: strategy is now geared to taking share away from competitors rather than expanding the total market. Brands are proliferating—55 have been introduced in the past three years, costing millions for advertising and crowding retail counters. To win customer approval, companies are fighting each other with point-of-purchase displays and discount coupons, tactics formerly shunned as unnecessary. Increasingly, only the financially strongest companies will survive.[1]

Such strategies may have their limited logic in an overpopulated industry, with equilibrium being restored through the painful process of an industry shakeout. It is a question of "hang in there and fight, and hope you will be one of the lucky survivors."

The purpose of this article is to develop the fundamentals of strategic action and show that more often than not, the science of competition, like the science of warfare, is a question of deft maneuver rather than brute force.

We will want to address the following issues:

In what ways do marketing and military situations resemble each other?

What are the objectives in war and in business?

What military strategies are available for market attack and what are their respective strengths and weaknesses?

What military strategies are available for market defense and what are their respective strengths and weaknesses?

[1]"Cigarette Sales Up—Maybe for the Last Time," *Business Week*, December 17, 1979, p. 54.

MILITARY SCIENCE
AND MARKETING COMPETITON

The increased focus of business on competitive strategy is leading business thinkers to examine military theory to see if this large body of thought contains principles and strategies that have been overlooked or insufficiently exploited. The classic works of Clausewitz, Liddell Hart, and other military theorists,[2] are being combed for ideas just as economic theory and psychosocial behavioral theories were combined in earlier times for possible applications to dynamic marketing competition.

Several signs of this stepped-up interest in the military metaphor have already appeared. One of the leading management-education firms, Advanced Management Research, has sponsored several successful one-day seminars bearing such titles as "Marketing Warfare" and "Attacking the Competition," and featuring topics such as "pre-battle preparation," "marketing weapons," "guerilla warfare," "attack formation." Their seminar brochure reads, "Perhaps the best book on marketing ever published is *On War* by the famous Prussian general and military theorist, Carl von Clausewitz." The well-known advertising agency of Ries Cappiello Colwell, Inc., which pioneered "positioning" thinking in marketing in the 1970s, is now making presentations to various companies on marketing warfare. And articles and books dealing with competitive strategy are on the increase.[3]

Business people often talk about their situations as if they were planning military campaigns. The reason is not that an undue number of American companies are run by former generals (although persons such as General Robert E. Wood headed Sears, and Lucius Clay headed Continental Can); but rather, the reason is the close resemblance between business and military situations. In both situations there are two or more "sides" with opposing interests. Each side is seeking to increase its power, almost always at the expense of the other.

Many examples can be cited of the warlike character of competitive business situations. In the mid-1950s Pepsi began its long and arduous uphill war to change from a "cheaper alternative to Coca-Cola" to a major competitor of Coke. Today it has bested Coke in the domestic take-home market and turned to mounting a challenge in overseas markets.[4] To understand what it took in ag-

---

[2]See Carl von Clausewitz, *On War* (London: Routledge & Kegan Paul), in 3 volumes; B. H. Liddell Hart, *Strategy* (New York: Praeger Publishers, 1967); J.F.C. Fuller, *The Conduct of War, 1789–1961* (London: Eyre and Spottiswoode, 1961); San Tsu, *The Art of War,* trans. Samuel B. Griffith (London: Oxford University Press, 1963).

[3]See Michael E. Porter, "How Competitive Forces Shape Strategy," *Harvard Business Review,* March–April 1979, pp. 137–45; Richard G. Hamermesh and Steven B. Silk, "How to Compete in Stagnant Industries," *Harvard Business Review,* September–October 1979, pp. 161–68; and Michael E. Porter, *Competitive Strategy* (New York: Free Press, 1980).

[4]"Corporate Culture," *Business Week,* October 27, 1980, p. 154.

gressiveness to achieve this stupendous turnaround, consider this early report on how Pepsi employees were grilled to think and act:

> Martial language has in recent years become a standard part of Pepsi rhetoric. Military terms drip from the lips of Pepsi executives and route men. They speak of "invading" Coke's markets, of developing new sales "weapons," of turning their salesmen into "shock troops." Overseas Pepsi even has a flying squad of salesmen they call their "Panzer Unit." One Pepsi official, with only a suggestion of a twinkle in his eye, says: "you ought to hear our sales-training courses. The men are taught to go out there and hate.[5]

British Airways' marketing programs have been based on military format for over ten years. Marketing operations worldwide are coordinated through the "war room" principle, advertising is seen as a form of heavy artillery, while its sales force is organized to operate as commando teams charged with securing specific objectives.[6]

Martial language and sentiments are familiar in many other business situations. We hear of "price wars," "border clashes," "skirmishes" among the major computer manufacturers, the "escalating arms budgets of soap companies," "guerilla warfare" by Purex against the soap giants, and the "sabotaging" and "spying" on test markets by competitors. A company's advertising is cast as its "propaganda arm," its salesmen as its "troops," and its marketing research is its "intelligence." There is talk about "confrontation," "brinkmanship," "super-weapons," "reprisals," and "psychological warfare."

The real question is whether the language of warfare in business is just descriptive, or whether its operational logic provides useful leverage in plotting competitive strategy. We feel there are unique insights to be had from military perspectives on conflict and strategy. In the first part of the paper, we will attempt to demonstrate that well-defined and conceptually consistent analogies can be drawn between military and marketing operations in the field. In the second half, we will describe and evaluate several models of attack and defense.

The Semantics of War and Marketing

We have suggested that martial language is becoming more commonplace in the marketing corridors of many business firms. The use of military language in business should not be treated as trivial. The language we use to describe our world has a profound influence on how we perceive it, and goes a long way to fashioning our attitudes, motivations, and ultimately the choice of our actions.

A cardinal principle of military science is that few advantages in weaponry

---

[5]Alvin Toffler, "The Competition That Refreshes," *Fortune,* May 1961.

[6]Personal communication.

and numbers can match the power of superior organization and morale of the fighting troops. To think and talk "war" provides marketers with the means for such organization and morale. When sales forces are organized around concepts such as panzer units and commando terms, when their operations are geared to moving in under barrages of advertising artillery, the choice of objectives, the team effort and motivation, and the allocation of supporting resources, cannot but help be influenced in more than trival ways.

The last decade has seen many giant U.S. corporations locked in fierce, and often frustrating, battle with their Japanese counterparts. Technological leadership, ample financial and managerial resources, and even a home-turf advantage, have not sufficed. Today many companies are turning to corporate "culture" and employee morale as major factors in the Japanese success story and thus the key for improving their own competitive efficiency.[7]

> "Culture implies values, such as aggressiveness, defensiveness, a nimbleness, that set a pattern for a company's activities, opinions, and actions." "A corporation's culture can be its major strength when it is consistent with its strategies."[8]

A corporate culture is admittedly much more than its language, but the flavor of cultures and their more subtle differences cannot be reflected and transmitted without unique languages and mannerisms of speech. Thus language is an important and integral part of consistent culture-strategy-organization meshes. Consider the all-out war raging in the beer industry these past five years (a detailed description of this illuminating case is provided in the Appendix).

Taking full advantage of its "first" in the light-beer revolution, Miller propelled itself from an also-ran seventh in the industry to powerful number 2, and publicly announced it was after number 1 Anheuser-Busch. Recently, one beer-industry analyst observed, "The war is already over, Anheuser-Busch will continue to maintain industry dominance." As *Newsweek* reported:

> A new cockiness at Miller played right into Anheuser-Busch's hands. Miller president John A. Murphy installed a rug with the Anheuser-Busch corporate seal under his desk—so that he could regularly stomp on it—and he publicly taunted the industry king. "It's not a question of if we pass them," he said in those days, "but when." Like an underdog football coach, Busch cleverly turned the remark against his rival. "Miller gave us the material we could post on the locker-room wall," says Long of A-B.[9]

Soon brewery and dock workers at A-B were wearing red T-shirts emblazoned "We are Miller killers." Language has a profound influence on the psychology

[7]See William G. Ouchi, *Theory Z* (Reading, Mass.: Addison-Wesley, 1981).

[8]"Corporate Culture," op. cit., p. 148.

[9]"The Battle of the Beers," *Newsweek,* March 9, 1981, p. 68.

and morale of competitive effort, and it also affects the organization and direction of competitive action. In mobilizing A-B to meet the Miller challenge, Busch put Long specifically in charge of the counterattack. The product-line and advertising were revamped. Those areas were targeted where A-B sales or potential were strongest, and "SWAT Squads" of employees in their twenties were sent in to work with wholesalers to increase market share.[10]

Of such effective mobilization and organization emerge the *potential* for successful strategic action. They cannot, however, ensure it. In addition, the company must select the appropriate strategy. A-B's successful defense was as much a consequence of selecting an appropriate strategy as it was of effective mobilization and organization. Thus, the principles of military science have much more to contribute to the design of marketing strategy than just a language of rhetoric.

Moving from Conventional
to Strategic Marketing

The 1960s were characterized by rapid economic growth and a phenomenal national affluence. Conventional marketing wisdom evolved in this environment. The emerging "marketing concept" held that companies would succeed if they finely analyzed the complex consumption patterns and needs and wants generated by affluence and the attendant culture of ostentation, and met them with appropriately differentiated products, prices, distribution, and promotion. Successful companies would be those practicing a *consumer-orientation,* and firms could grow by concentrating on customer desires without paying much attention to competitors. Competition usually amounted to no more than treading on another's toes, and indeed, the strategies of market segmentation and product differentiation are oriented to *reducing* the level of direct competition. *Niched* in target segments, the design of marketing strategy was a question of balancing the 4-Ps vis-à-vis these segments and changes in them. Recently a top executive at Mercedes-Benz said that his company still simply designs the best quality car for people who want quality and does not pay much attention to the cars of other companies.[11]

If the 1960s were the years of the "marketing concept" and consumer orientation, the 1970s might be loosely described as the decade of *distribution-orientation.* Successful firms will still be consumer-oriented and distribution-oriented, but they will also have to acquire a tough-mindedness about competition. Marketing success will require devising opponent-centered strategies, not just

[10]Ibid.

[11]Personal communication.

customer-centered strategies, since the only avenues to new segments and market growth are over the "body" of competitors, and not just their "toes."

Two other important factors—besides those associated with general economic sluggishness—are responsible for changing the quality and character of marketing competition. One is "commoditization," and the other is the increasingly "global" nature of markets and marketing ramifications.

What executives at Bic Corp. call "commoditization"[12] is in effect a return to standardization and the older "product" oriented styles of business strategy. When it can be successfully implemented, commoditization sharply reduces the opportunity for marketing concept inspired strategies of consumer segmentation and product differentiation.

The opportunity to commoditize has emerged because of (a) withdrawal by significant segments of consumers from highly personalized brand and status conscious consumption for certain product classes, and (b) because of a considerably standardized level of product quality available across-the-board of U.S. industry as a whole.

For example, Gillette's preeminence in the shaving products market has been based on a research staff of 200 that has determined that a man's beard grows an average of 15/1000 of an inch a day, and that in an average lifetime a man will spend 3,350 hours scraping 27½ feet of whiskers from his face. Its technology is unmatched and its product refinements pushed to the point that advantages in its razor blades over competitors' blades are visible only when 1/10,000 of an inch of the blade edges are magnified 50,000 times.[13]

In recent years, giant Gillette has been repeatedly and successfully challenged by little Bic Pen Corporation in three markets (disposable pens, disposable lighters, and most recently disposable razors). As one analyst put it, Bic "does not know and does not care how many hairs are in the average man's beard or how fast they grow," but its hollow plastic handled disposable razor at 19¾ cents has about half the disposable market.[14]

When increasing opportunities emerge for "commoditizing" products, the marketing concept inspired strategies of brand differentiation and loyalty are correspondingly attentuated. Also, the generally high standards of production quality in the U.S. today have contributed to the waning of the marketing concept. For a large number of products today, marketing theorists are talking of stochastic or random models of consumer preference and brand switching.[15]

When consumers grow less brand discriminating and their choices more random, the prescriptions that emerge from the marketing concept are no longer

---

[12]See "The War of the Razors," *Esquire,* February 1980, p. 29.

[13]Ibid.

[14]Ibid.

[15]Frank M. Bass, "The Theory of Stochastic Preference and Brand Switching," *Journal of Marketing Research,* XI (February 1974), p. 2.

as *standard* as they might have been.[16] When behavior can be viewed as stochastic, many of the military realities of firepower and dueling assume a far sharper applicability to the marketing situation. Marketing exchanges can then be conceptualized in terms of the two basic determinants of elementary combat: the "efficiency" of weapons and their numbers.

The earlier moves toward commoditized marketing were initiated largely by high-volume low-margin mass retailers, and even today they remain in the forefront (witness the rapid proliferation of "generic" and house brands priced below national brands). Among manufacturers, the Japanese must be pointed to as extremely successful practitioners of this strategy. Their initial footholds in world markets were largely obtained with cheaper "replica" type products of leading brands. On the other hand, it is only recently that U.S. manufacturers are more commonly targeting the mass markets. Curiously enough, the Japanese now have veered away toward more expensive, high quality, and more differentiated, product strategies. Indeed, while U.S. automakers scramble after the small, low-priced car market, at least one Japanese firm is known to be very carefully examining the Mercedes models!

The important understanding that emerges from all this is that in a changing, highly competitive, and largely nongrowing marketplace, the rules of the old game no longer always hold. The astonishing lunge to Dunkirk by massed German armor shook the very foundations of traditional military deployment and maneuver and the technique of war took a quantum leap from the trenches and barbed-wire "position-wars" of World War I (when advances were measured in yards) to the wide open field blitzkriegs of World War II. Analogously, in the post-WW II economic era, "marketing" as a philosophical and operational framework provided insightful business leaders the mobility and flexibility in market competition. But it was not the development of the tank per se (and analogously the recognition of consumer-orientation in business) that determined a new strategic reality. It was the method of its deployment—in mass, concentrated at the weakest point of the defense, and deployed to burst through and race deep into the defender's rear positions—that created the military havoc of the early WW II campaigns. Similarly, in an era of keen competition for scarce markets, it is not going to be the traditional marketing tools per se (which are avail-

[16]One of the key implications of the shift to a competition orientation is that some of the older philosophies of marketing, for a while considered archaic and supplanted forever by the apparently superior logic of the marketing concept, will stage a comeback. It was not long ago when textbooks referred to engineering/production-oriented and sales-oriented business approaches as the historical progression through which enlightened business practice emerged in the form of the marketing concept. Yet today it is appropriate to rethink whether these are not really business approaches relevant to particular environmental states, rather than marketing myopia of ill-trained managements, and to talk of them as *alternative* approaches to meeting business goals. The important point is that these need not be mutually exclusive, nor need sales or engineering orientations be necessarily inimical to consumer well-being. These issues have been developed in Ravi Singh Achrol and Philip Kotler, "The Marketing Concepts, Part II: Towards a Strategic Concept of Marketing" (Working Paper, Northwestern University, May 1981).

able to all) but how they are deployed and maneuvered that will determine competitive outcomes.

It appears that no matter how meticulously researched and planned the 4-Ps might be vis-à-vis the consumer, they no longer guarantee marketing success. The company must know not only all relevant details of consumer segments but also all relevant details of the opponent who will be confronted in fighting for some segment. The opponent must be attacked through his weaknesses, or alternatively, sufficiently superior resources must be marshalled to attack him head on. Thus the marketing mix can no longer be developed simply by studying the consumer segment. Indeed, the 4-Ps evolve from the particular strategy chosen to attack the competitor. Marketing success is then a function of choosing the correct strategy, given the competitor's dispositions in the market and his reserve resources.

Fundamental Differences Between Business and Military Conflict

Differences, if they are fundamental, limit the scope of the business and military analogy. It is as important to understand these limitations, as it is to appreciate the analogs.

1. Many wars are fought with the purpose of vanquishing, destroying, or capturing the enemy and his lands and resources. Business competition, on the other hand, is almost always carried on with more limited objectives. Many companies simply want modest improvements in market share, or even to maintain the status quo, rather than to destroy their competitors. A company, in fact, has to avoid actions whose purpose appears to be to weaken or destroy competition. The company can take normal steps to woo consumer preference for its products (improve product quality and service, improve communication and promotion, lower prices in a reasonable way in relation to costs, increase distribution, and so on) even when this hurts a competitor, as long as it does not hurt competition in a "predatory" fashion. That Miller Beer's aggressive marketing hurt Schlitz and that Texas Instrument's aggressive marketing hurt Rockwell were the consequence and not the aim of the policies that these aggressive companies adopted. Likewise, there are differences in *constraints*. Military engagements are fought with very few limits on weapons or tactics. "All is fair in love and war" goes the popular saying. In business, there are many more constraints on the weapons and tactics that companies can or are willing to use. Government has sought to define and prohibit discriminatory pricing, reciprocity, misrepresentation and deception, and predatory tactics.

2. There are differences in the *weapons*. Unique combat functions cannot necessarily be associated with particular marketing variables. Can advertising

be likened to the combat mobility and firepower of a formation of tanks? Can sales promotion assume the role of artillery support? Can salespeople be seen as infantry, or is the "occupation" function more appropriately likened to retail exposure and competition at the retail front? Such one-to-one correspondence is not completely appropriate, and less will be learned from military science about which combination of combat units is most appropriate for a limited tactical exercise than from the general models of strategic attack and defense.

3. There are differences in the *mechanism of victory*. Wars are won by one side inflicting such damage or fear on the other side that it breaks the other's will to resist. The enemy troops surrender or the enemy government capitulates. On the other hand, victory in a business war is decided mainly by the vote of a third party, namely consumers. That is why it is necessary to stress that competition orientation cannot be at the exclusion of consumer orientation, or even distribution or production orientation. Strategically, the distinction is often a question of *priority* and *emphasis* and seldom the exclusion of one for the other.

4. Probably the most fundamental difference in an operational sense is that marketing maneuvers cannot physically thwart the opponent. The most devastating impact of flank and in-depth maneuvering on the battlefield is the dislocation of the nerve center of enemy operations by cutting communications and administrative bases. In competition, this can never be duplicated, since it is virtually impossible to undermine the physical structure of competitors and isolate their various formations.

  Hence in marketing, the strategies of so-called "mobile" offense and defense must be approached with caution. At the heart of "mobile" strategy are the principles of *movement* and *surprise*. Movement lies in the physical sphere and is essentially oriented to exploiting the *line of least resistance*. Surprise is its psychological equivalent exploiting the *line of least expectation*. But both of these to be strategically effective require that they achieve a dislocation of the enemy's organization.

  In marketing what occurs is a dislocation of the opponent's *segment* structure or interface. While this is no trivial dislocation, the capacity of the opponent to riposte is far less affected than in a military situation. Consequently both the flanking opportunity or "gap," as well as the evolving situation once the gap has been penetrated, need to be very closely monitored. To begin with, the gap may not turn out significant enough to breach the market wide enough. Alternatively, the breach might effectively be blocked by an appropriate counteroffensive. In both these situations the strategic position would quickly degenerate into a "head on" frontal battle and unless sufficient resources are brought in, the maneuver will be unsuccessful.

  In sum, the concepts of maneuver, mobility, and the strategy of "indirect approach" are constrained and have to be approached with caution when operationalized in the business context.

Subject to the above four caveats, we proceed now to identify principles and operational models from military theory that might apply to the central strategic decisions business firms have to make—namely, determining competitive objectives, and developing strategy and tactics appropriate to the situation.

DETERMINING STRATEGIC OBJECTIVES

Military and Business Objectives

The issue of the "object of war" has a controversial history among military theorists. Clausewitz, the nineteenth century's greatest military theorist, saw war as an intrinsic and enduring characteristic of the relation among nations. Even peace, to his mind, was "the continuation of the war carried on by other means." The object of war is to vanquish the enemy by achieving an unconditional surrender which generally requires overwhelming him on the battlefield: "The destruction of the enemy's main forces on the battlefield constituted the only true aim in war." Although Clausewitz had a more subtle conception of war, this dictum, along with other loosely dropped phrases such as "blood is the price of victory," influenced the conduct of war for over a century before World War II. They led his less profound disciples such as Marshall Foch to confuse the means with the end.[17]

The twentieth century's greatest military theorist, Capt. Basil H. Liddell Hart (who was severely critical of Clausewitz), sets the contemporary position: "The 'object' in war is a *better state of peace,* even if only from your own point of view."[18]

Such a statement seems more compatible with the business milieu, since modern competitors rarely adopt the Clausewitzian objective of "total annihilation of the enemy." This is not to deny that competitors have the capacity to conduct themselves in this manner. Any large, well-resourced company could

[17]Marshal Ferdinand Foch was primarily responsible for indoctrinating the French Army to the dogmatic philosophy—*l'offensive brutale et à outrance.* As a consequence, World War I witnessed the senseless and bloody dissipation of French infantry in futile frontal charges against entrenched German machine guns and barbed wire. The Russians, even today, include "annihilation" as one of their nine fundamental principles of strategy.

[18]B. H. Liddell Hart, op. cit., p. 351. Liddell Hart was severely critical of Clausewitz: ". . . the universal adoption of the theory of unlimited war has gone far to wreck civilization. The teachings of Clausewitz, taken without understanding, largely influenced both the causation and character of World War I. Thereby it led on, all too logically, to World War II." (p. 357)

destroy a smaller company by slashing prices and causing losses both to its competitor and itself, until the competitor is forced out of business. And two large companies could slug it out until one of them surrenders or retreats. "Cutthroat competition" is the name given to this extreme state of business warfare, and it has characterized business competition in certain periods in certain industries (such as the oil industry and rubber industry). Cutthroat competition a la Clausewitz would be much more prevalent were it not for the antitrust laws starting with the Sherman Act (1890) and later the Clayton Act (1914). The legal sentiment has been that "unfair methods of competition in commerce are unlawful," "where the effect . . . may be to substantially lessen competition or tend to create a monopoly in any line of commerce." Indeed, were it not for antitrust laws, it could be argued that war, not peace, is the natural state of business.

Besides running afoul of antitrust legislation, companies that compete on the basis of wiping out competition might find in their very victory the seeds of ultimate defeat. While a unique advantage at a given time may afford it the brute force of wiping out competition, it is difficult to conceive of a single company differentiating its product line sufficiently to meet all segment variations. "Thinly spread" over the market, and complacent in its commanding position, it would offer an ideal target for the next clever and forceful competitor to come along and shatter its foundations.

Liddell Hart's doctrine that "the object in war is a better state of peace" may be a more appropriate guiding objective for business. Implicit in the doctrine is the principle of "limited objective" which reflects more faithfully the reality of business: "When the government appreciates that the enemy has the military superiority, either in general or in a particular theatre, it may wisely enjoin a strategy of limited aim."[19] When Bic attacks Gillette or Kodak attacks Polaroid, they are under no illusion that they can destroy their opponents. Rather, they are conducting limited warfare with limited objectives. The issue is largely what distribution of shares the two will implicitly settle for. When Kodak introduced its own version of the instant camera it may have aimed to achieve the dominant share, but Polaroid fought back and managed to contain Kodak's share at about 25 percent. Apparently, both of them now seem to be accepting this compromise division of strategic balance. Of course Kodak may mount another attack in the future to raise its share further—and this may be a breathing space fitting Clausewitz' view that peace is the continuation of war by other means. Finally, there is another interpretation of business seeking "a better state of peace." Each business seeks to groove itself in a part of the market where it identifies and develops a comparative advantage. When war breaks out, it is due to some competitor doing a poor job of serving its niched market segment, or some competitor trying to bring some new advantage to the market segment, or because environmental change is causing major shifts in the composition of segments.

[19]Ibid., p. 334.

Choosing the Strategic "Opponent"

The key military principle, the "principle of objective," holds that "every military operation must be directed toward a clearly defined, decisive, and attainable objective."

Deciding on the strategic objective, whether it is to crush the competitor, reduce the competitor's share, or contain the competitor to the present share, interacts with the question of *who* the competitor is. Unlike war, where for historical, geographic, or political reasons the enemy is "given," the business firm in most cases is able to *choose* its enemy. All markets are occupied by one or more firms that enjoy different competitive positions, strengths, and weaknesses. One firm is *the market leader,* having the largest market share. One or more other firms are *market challengers* in that they are large and willing to fight each other and the leader for territory. Still other firms are large but play the role of *market followers,* being content with their current positions in the market and not inclined to rock the boat. Lastly, several smaller firms are *market nichers* that serve market segments too small or isolated to attract the interest of the larger firms.

Basically, an aggressor firm has a choice of attacking three enemy targets:

1. It can attack a larger firm, say the market leader. This is a high risk but potentially high-payoff strategy and makes good sense if the leader is not a "true leader" and is not serving the market well. Thus Xerox attacked 3M in the paper copier market because it developed a better copying process (dry copying instead of wet copying).

2. The firm could define the enemy as firms of its own size when it feels its differential advantage is not enough to challenge superior resources, but enough to take on a less formidable opponent.

3. The firm could define its enemies as the smaller firms not doing a very economic job. Several of the major beer companies grew to their present size not by stealing each other's customers so much as by gobbling up the "small fry," namely local and regional brewers (also called a "guppy" strategy).

Identifying the most attractive target hinges on a careful assessment of "market coverage" gaps in each of these groups. The most powerful attack strategy in theory—the doctrine of "indirect approach"—is based on the principle of exploiting the weaknesses of the opponent and using this wedge to turn the flank and expose the rear to his "strengths."

Assessing the *structural mesh* of an industry amounts to mapping out the strategic terrain—the natural barriers, enemy dispositions, and fortifications across terrain features, possible lines of advance, and so on. The most important structural parameters are:[20]

Level of consumer need satisfaction—the greater the degree of felt satisfaction in the segment, the easier it is for the occupant to defend it.

Stability of technology, distribution, supply—instability in these parameters creates fissures in the market which are not often readily perceived. These provide a line of approach that can generate good strategic surprise and depth.

In weighing the leader as a potential target the "terrain" to examine closely is consumer satisfaction. If a substantial area is unserved, it offers a great strategic opportunity. Miller's campaign in the beer market was so successful because it pivoted initially on discovering the "lite" beer segment. The other alternative indirect strategy is to out-innovate the leader across the whole segment. This is obviously an unusual gap to look for given that most market leaders are also innovation leaders. Besides, the incremental technological advantage needed is likely to be considerable in the face of strong leader brand loyalty. However, history is replete with examples of leaders who led too long and grew complacent.

In considering competitors of the attacker's own size, both consumer satisfaction and innovation potential need to be examined minutely. The aggressor can also consider a frontal attack strategy if the enemy's resources are limited.

The "guppy strategy" can usually be followed at will by any large company. In most cases, however, it is seldom worth expending the time and energy in competing with market nichers. Acquisition is a far easier and painless process. In both instances the strategic constraints reside in the attacker's legal position vis-à-vis antitrust law.

Thus choosing the enemy and choosing the objective interact. If the attacking company goes after the market leader, its objective may be to gain a certain share. If it goes after a small local company, its objective may be to drive that company out of existence. The important principle remains: "Every military operation must be directed toward a clearly defined, decisive, and attainable objective."

Grand Strategy

Just as "tactics is an application of strategy on a lower plane, so strategy is an application on a lower plane of 'grand strategy.' "[21] When we think of strate-

---

[20]These and other factors are developed in greater detail in Philip Kotler, Karl Hellman, and Han Samzelius, "Strategies for Market Leaders" (Working Paper, Northwestern University, March 1980).

[21]Liddell Hart, op. cit.

gic objectives interacting with grand strategy we are raising both a time dimension and a geographical dimension.

The time dimension reminds us that the choice of a competitive objective should not be determined by short-run considerations. Just as in warfare the larger strategy is composed of a *sequence* of strategic objectives, so in business the choice of an opponent, product/brand, or segment should be based on a long-term plan.

While large attackers have the resources to pursue a single strategic objective over the attack period, smaller attackers must adopt a carefully sequenced strategy. The initial objectives should be those of least importance and commitment to the opponent. This forestalls any massive retaliation and allows the attacker to expand his resource base enough to withstand the retaliation when it comes. Two classic cases are worth mentioning.

The first is little Bic vs. mighty Gillette. Anybody attacking Gillette in the razor blade market could expect immediate and massive retaliation. Bic chose instead to attack the cheap pen market in 1958, and today has 60 percent of that market to Gillette's 20. In 1974 Bic moved into the disposable lighters market to emerge with a 52 percent share against Gillette's 30 percent. In 1976 Bic opened its offensive in the disposable razors market and currently each has about half of the disposable market.[22]

Geographical sequencing is illustrated by Vlasic Foods which used a "guppy" attack strategy to displace Heinz from market leadership of the U.S. pickle market. Vlasic, a small Detroit "regional" in the late 1960s, slowly bought up other regionals. It retained the acquired firms' products tailored to regional tastes (thus avoiding any direct market confrontation) until it had adequate market coverage to employ TV advertising and heavy in-store promotions and go national. By 1978 Vlasic held 26 percent of the market to Heinz's 10 percent.[23]

There are further geographic dimensions to grand strategy. Japan's economic victories are based in part on its corporations pursuing global market shares. The impact of such *global* shares becomes evident when we compare U.S. and European motorcycle production facilities of 20–50 thousand units per year to Japanese facilities producing from 300 thousand to 2 million units per year. It is not with the *"percentages"* of Japanese *"imports"* that the U.S. manufacturers are competing but with the marketing, financial, technological, and managerial skills and resources of Japanese organizations working in a global environment. The Japanese derive their competitive strength and base of operations from the entire theatre they are maneuvering in. Givens succinctly sums up the sequential strategy used by Japanese companies:

> The pattern has been fairly predictable. The Japanese get into an industry by importing the technology. They protect that industry during the initial phases, until

[22]"The War of the Razors," op. cit.

[23]See Roberto Buaron, "How to Win the Market-Share Game? Try Changing the Rules," *Management Review,* January 1981.

they have achieved competitive cost positions. They begin exporting into third-world countries, *to which most of our producers are largely indifferent.* By that means, they achieve additional global market share, which enables them to bring costs down further and then come at us head-on in our own domestic markets. *And once that cycle has been completed, they repeat it at a higher level of technology.*[24]

Concentration vs. Dispersion

The question of deciding the strategic objective can be reduced to the alternatives depicted in Exhibit 1. One dimension involves the choice of going after market leaders, challengers, followers, or nichers. A second dimension involves the long-run question of whether a single or multiple objective is to be pursued, and if multiple, whether these will be attacked sequentially or simultaneously. And third, the degree of concentration-dispersion to be achieved.

In general, going after a market leader involves a more concentrated objective than pursuing nichers, and targeting simultaneous objectives involves more dispersal than single or sequenced objectives. However, there is a further level of concentration-dispersion involved in strategic decision making, viz., the concentration-dispersal of marketing resources. Having decided who the enemy is, the question remains where the attack against him is to be launched. Should the attack be concentrated on a single product attribute or many? Should resources primarily be devoted to advertising and promotion or should they be dispersed on a sales force as well as distribution offensive and a price attack?

At the heart of effective strategy is the principle of "mass," i.e., concentra-

[24]William L. Givens and William V. Rapp, "What It Takes to Meet the Japanese Challenge," *Fortune,* June 18, 1979, p. 104. The authors perceive the next target industry the Japanese will go all out to achieve worldwide supremacy in is the computer industry in particular and microprocessor technology in general, as these are obviously the key, strategic resources for the 1980s and beyond.

Exhibit 1   The Strategic Gameboard

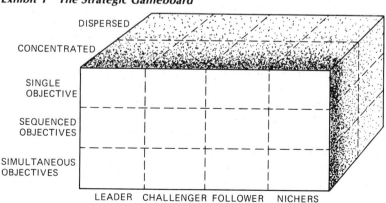

tion of strength at the appropriate point. However, every principle of war carries a dual principle that demands a well-calculated compromise:

> "Effective concentration can only be obtained when the opposing forces are dispersed; and, usually, in order to ensure this, one's own forces must be widely distributed. Thus by an outward paradox, true concentration is the product of calculated dispersion."
>
> The duality axiom also stresses the strategic importance of "alternative objectives":
>
> "For if the enemy is certain as to your point of *aim* he has the best possible chance of guarding himself—and blunting your weapon. If on the other hand, you take a line that threatens alternative objectives, you distract his mind and forces."[25]

Thus in some marketing situations a certain amount of calculated dispersion may be more effective than concentration, and the ability to switch to alternative objective without radically revising the marketing plan must also be built into the strategy. When the U.S. auto industry is launching an all-out attack on the small car, the Japanese may consider dispersing a little and attacking the luxury sedan market.

Not long ago, marketing observers chided traditional watchmakers for failing to assess the changes in consumer behavior and staying with their traditional high-margin jewelry outlets while new competitors penetrated mass distribution outlets with lower-priced watches. A whole decade passed before famous U.S. watchmakers like Waltham, Gruen, Elgin, and Hamilton attempted to enter the mass market for watches. They were too late. And while they were switching, Seiko stepped in and snapped up these traditional channels anticipating a void would result with the exodus. Today Seiko is the undisputed leader in the $6-billion world watch industry. And as the leader, the company practices a highly dispersed preemptive defense strategy marketing some 2,300 models worldwide.[26]

Clearly sometimes it pays to concentrate, sometimes to disperse, and at all times the company must be ready to switch objectives and strategies as the situation changes. The appropriate strategy is a question of the situation existing at any given time, and whether the strategy calls for concentration or dispersion is a question of the strategic model implicit in the appropriate strategy.

CHOOSING THE ATTACK STRATEGY

In this section, we will describe the five attack strategies illustrated in Exhibit 2: (1) frontal attack; (2) flanking attack; (3) encirclement attack; (4) bypass attack; and (5) guerilla attack.

[25]Liddell Hart, op. cit., p. 343.

[26]See "Seiko's Smash," *Business Week,* June 5, 1978.

Exhibit 2   Five Attack Strategies

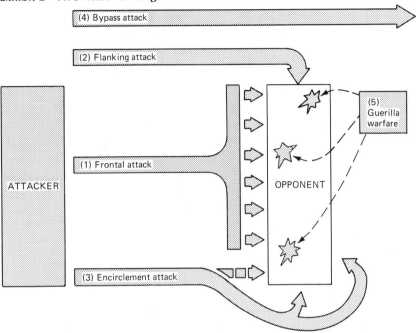

Frontal Attack

An aggressor is said to launch a frontal (or "head-on") attack when it masses its forces right up against those of its opponent. Essentially the aggressor is attacking the opponent's strengths rather than weaknesses. The outcome depends on who has the greater strength and endurance. In a pure frontal attack, the attacker matches product for product, advertising for advertising, price for price, and so on. Recently the second-placed razor blade manufacturer in Brazil decided to go after Gillette, the market leader. Management was asked if they were offering the consumer a better blade. "No," was the reply. "A lower price?" "No." "Then how do you expect to take share away from Gillette?" they were asked. "Will power," was the reply. Needless to say, their offensive failed.

For a pure frontal attack to succeed, the aggressor needs a strength advantage over the competitor. The "principle of force" says that the side with the greater manpower (resources) will win the engagement. This is modified if the defender has greater firing efficiency through enjoying a terrain advantage (such as holding a mountain top). The military dogma is that a successful frontal attack against a well-entrenched opponent or one controlling the "high ground" requires a 3:1 advantage in combat firepower. If the aggressor has a smaller force or poorer fire-power than the defender, a frontal attack amounts to a suicide mission and makes no sense. RCA, GE, and Xerox learned this the hard way when they launched frontal attacks on IBM, overlooking its superior defensive position.[27]

As an example of a successful pure frontal attack and the resources it required, consider S. C. Johnson & Son's entry into the shampoo market.[28] In 1977, with "almost Japanese-like thoroughness," S. C. Johnson raided Colgate and others for experienced executives. Then it blitzed the market with a $14 million promotion that included 30 million sample bottles of its new hair conditioner, Agree. That about equaled the industry's total promotion on hair conditioners. It grabbed 15 percent of the market in its first year, wrestled from such giants as P&G, Revlon, and Johnson and Johnson (by 1979 share was 20 percent). Then in 1978 it blasted the shampoo market, reportedly spending $30 million in marketing costs in the summer of that year. It ended up with a 6 percent share when it had originally hoped for about 2 percent.

As an alternative to a pure frontal attack, the aggressor may launch a *modified* frontal attack, the most common being to cut its price vis-à-vis the opponent's. Such attacks can take two forms. The more usual ploy is to match the leader's offer on other counts and beat it on price. This can work if

1. the market leader does not retaliate by cutting price too, and
2. a. the market is successfully convinced that the aggressor's product is equal or almost equal in quality, or
   b. the price differential is substantial enough that buyers are willing to forgo some quality.

The rapid proliferation of "generic," "no-brand" products in canned foods and basic household goods provides an excellent example of condition (2b). Helene Curtis is a master practitioner of the somewhat risky strategy implicit in (2a).[29] Curtis makes no bones about its approach—producing *budget* imitations of leading high-priced brands and promoting them with blatant comparative advertising campaigns: "We do what theirs does for less than half the price," is the message. In 1972 Curtis had a meager 1 percent share of the shampoo market for its five Suave shampoos. Its new strategy was launched in 1973. By 1976 it had overtaken Procter & Gamble's Head & Shoulders and Johnson & Johnson's Baby Shampoo to lead the market in volume, which hit 16 percent in 1979.

In "me-too" or "copycat" frontal assault, the firm spends little on R&D (Helene Curtis allocates only 1 percent to R&D). The other form of price-ag-

---

[27]See "RCA Goes Head-to-Head with IBM," *Fortune,* October 1970; and "The 250 Million Dollar Disaster That Hit RCA," *Business Week,* September 25, 1971.

[28]See "Stopping the Greasies," *Forbes,* July 9, 1979, p. 121.

[29]"A 'Me-Too' Strategy That Paid Off," *Fortune,* August 27, 1979, p. 86.

gressive strategy is where the attacker invests heavily in research, and trading on hugh volumes to achieve lower production costs, attacks competitors on a price basis. Texas Instruments has brilliantly executed this strategy, investing heavily in R&D and moving rapidly down the *experience curve*. The Japanese, too, launch frontal attacks on the basis of cost-related price cutting. This is one of the most viable bases upon which a *sustained* frontal attack can be founded.

Conceptually a frontal assault in marketing means that the attacker is not offering anything *tangibly* different from that offered by the competitor. Existing segment structures are not changed but almost torn away from those who currently occupy them. On the other hand, marketing strategies that deliver tangible new benefits or *perceptions* of such benefits, operate to alter the existing segment structure. Such strategies are conceptually identified as equivalent to flanking and envelopment strategies in the military theatre.

Flanking Attack

The "principles" of modern warfare can be summarized in the statement —*concentration of strength against weakness.*[30] The aggressor searches for the enemy's weak spots ("blindsides") and concentrates the mass of his resources at the points to exploit the path of least resistance. The corollary to this is the "turning" maneuver. Turning is accomplished by an attack around the flank of the enemy's main positions and is directed at his rear. The "psychology" of an army is as vulnerable to a menace to its back as that of a man, and turning unbalances a defender. An army on a battlefield is deployed to be strongest where it expects the enemy to attack, but it is usually difficult to secure the flanks completely. Flanking attacks always make sense, but are particularly attractive to the aggressor possessing fewer resources than the opponent. If he cannot overwhelm the opponent with his strength, he can outmaneuver him with subterfuge.

A flanking attack can be directed against a competitor along two strategic dimensions—*geographical* and *segmental.* A geographical attack consists of the aggressor spotting areas in the country or the world in which the opponent is not performing at high levels. For example, some of IBM's rivals chose to set up strong branches in medium and smaller-size cities which are relatively neglected by IBM. According to a Honeywell field sales manager:

- Out in the rural areas, we are relatively better off than in the cities. We have been quite successful in these areas because our sales force does not meet the ten-plus to one ratio it hits in the cities where IBM concentrates its people. Thus, ours must be a concentration game.[31]

[30]Liddell Hart, op. cit., p. 347.

[31]Quoted in "Honeywell Information Systems" (case available from the Intercollegiate Case Clearing House, Soldiers Field, Boston, 1975), pp. 7–8.

The other, and potentially more powerful, flanking strategy is to spot uncovered market needs not being served by the leaders:

- German and Japanese automakers chose not to compete with American automakers by producing large flashy gas-guzzling automobiles even though these were supposedly the preference of American buyers. Instead, they recognized an unserved consumer segment who wanted small, fuel-efficient cars. They moved vigorously to fill this hole in the market and to their satisfaction and Detroit's surprise, American taste for smaller fuel-efficient cars grew to be a substantial part of the market.
- "Discovering," so to speak, the "light" beer segment, Miller Brewing Company pivoted on this unserved gap in the market and vigorously developed it into a huge breach across the whole industry's front and propelled itself from seventh place in the industry to a very close second in five years.

A flanking attack is a strategy of identifying shifts in market segments— which are causing gaps to develop that are not being served by the industry's product mix—and rushing in to fill these gaps and develop them into strong segments. Instead of a bloody battle between two or more companies trying to serve the same market, flanking leads to a fuller coverage of the varied needs of the whole market. Flanking is in the best tradition of modern marketing philosophy, which holds that the purpose of marketing is to "discover needs and serve them." Flanking attacks have a higher probability of being successful than frontal attacks. In general, the strategy of indirect approach has overwhelming support from history as the most effective and economic form of offense. In his penetrating analysis of the thirty most important conflicts of the world from the Greek wars up to World War I (which embraced more than 280 campaigns), Liddell Hart concluded that in only six campaigns did decisive results follow strategies of direct head-on assault.[32]

We have characterized the flank attack as hinging on gaps in the geographic or segment coverage of the opponent. Of course gaps may exist elsewhere in the business system. There may be gaps in procurement, production, service, distribution efficiency, etc. Such gaps generate opportunity for economic efficiencies. For our purposes, the important distinction is between gaps that generate increased economic efficiency vs. gaps that affect the existing segment structure of the market. The former, by and large, generate the bases for *modified* frontal attack strategies, while the latter carry the potential for flanking maneuvers.

Encirclement Attack

The pure flanking maneuver was defined as pivoting on a gap in the existing market coverage of the enemy. The encirclement maneuver attempts to *disperse* this coverage so that the enemy's segment differentiation, and therefore

[32]Liddell Hart, op. cit., p. 161.

brand loyalty, is diluted and a more fluid front is created which can be pierced at a number of points.

Encirclement (also called envelopment) involves launching a multiple offensive against the enemy on several fronts so that the enemy must protect his front, sides, and rear simultaneously. The strategy makes sense where the aggressor has superior resources and can execute the encirclement swiftly enough to break the opponent's will to resist.

In military envelopment, the aggressor cuts through weak points in the enemy's front and then turns around in a "pincering" maneuver to trap the enemy's formations within. In business envelopment, the aggressor is trying to create *segment-diffusion.* A clasic way to accomplish this is to *bracket* the opponent's brand along some product attribute. Thus, the company may offer a premium product at a higher price to act as one arm of the pincer, and a regular quality product at a lower price to act as the other arm. Diffusion can be attempted along any product dimension—design, functional features, even lifestyle "image"—the important requirement being that the attribute be of significance to a substantial part of the opponent's consumer segment.

An example of a classic bracketing maneuver (employed defensively) is Heublein's strategy in defending its Smirnoff vodka against an attack from Wolfschmidt in the 1960s. Wolfschmidt, aiming to diffuse Smirnoff's brand image, priced its vodka at a dollar less a bottle and claimed an equivalent quality. After considering all frontal counteroffensive alternatives, Heublein rejected them as detrimental to its profits and came up with a brilliant pincering maneuver. It *raised* the price of Smirnoff by one dollar, effectively preventing segment diffusion, and introduced two new brands to meet Wolfschmidt head on (a same price brand) and on the other flank (a lower price brand).

An aggressor can attempt to encircle an opponent on· many marketing fronts simultanously. This is what Hunt attempted, albeit unsuccessfully, in its grand envelopment offensive on Heinz. In 1963, Hunt, with a 19 percent share of the ketchup market, launched a major encirclement attack on Heinz's 27 percent market share. Hunt rolled out a number of marketing attacks simultaneously. It introduced two new flavor brands of ketchup (pizza and hickory) to disrupt the consumers' traditional taste preference for Heniz and also to capture more retail shelf space. It lowered its price to 70 percent of Heinz's price, offered heavy trade allowances to retailers, and raised its advertising budget to over twice the level of Heinz. Hunt was willing to lose money if it could ultimately attract enough brand switchers. Unfortunately, the strategy failed. Not enough Heinz users tried the Hunt brand, and of those that did, most returned to the Heinz brand.

The Hunt debacle underscores our core proposition that segmentation opportunity is fundamental to choosing the axis for an indirect approach. If the opportunity does not exist through segment gaps, or cannot be created by segment diffusion tactics, then what is an indirect attack in the mind of the aggressor peters out into a plain frontal attack in the marketplace. As such, it would require the 3:1 advantage in combat firepower to succeed.

Bypass Attack

Years ago, the president of Lever Brothers (who liked to refer to his weekly meetings of the marketing committee as his "general staff meetings") said of his chief competitor: "What we did was to quit trying to meet Procter & Gamble head on. We just stopped wearing ourselves out in a frontal battle we could never win, and started going around them."[33]

The bypass is the most indirect of assault strategies and eschews any belligerent move directed against the enemy's existing segment span. Conceptually, the bypass hinges on a much more global, or at least macro, conception of competition than enemy A and his territory Z. The bypass is analogous to peacetime political "warfare" ("cold war") in which allied pacts, so to speak, are created against the prospect of future hostilities in the core confrontation zone. The company bypasses the arch enemy and attacks easier markets so as to broaden its resource base. This offers two lines of approach—diversifying into unrelated products, and/or diversifying into new geographical markets for existing products.

Consider, for example, Colgate's impressive turnaround.[34] Colgate almost always lost to P&G in its U.S. battles. In heavy-duty detergents, P&G's Tide routed Colgate's Fab by almost 5:1. In dishwashing liquids, P&G had almost twice Colgate's share. In soaps, too, Colgate trailed far behind. When David Foster took over the $1.3 billion company in 1971, Colgate had the reputation of a stodgy soap and detergent marketer. By 1979 he had transformed Colgate into a $4.3 billion conglomerate, capable of challenging P&G if necessary. Foster recognized that any head-on battle with P&G was futile: "They outgunned us 3 to 1 at the store level," said Foster, "and had three research people to our one." Foster's strategy was simple—maintain Colgate's lead abroad and bypass P&G at home by diversifying into markets sans P&G. A string of acquisitions followed in textiles and hospital products, cosmetics, and a range of sporting goods and food products. The outcome: whereas in 1971 Colgate was underdog to P&G in about half of its business, by 1976, in three-fourths of its business, Colgate was either comfortably placed against P&G, or didn't face it at all.

Product or geographic diversification provide the bases of by-pass strategies in marketing. But in the larger business context the strategies of peacetime political warfare extended to maneuvers involving location, mergers, and joint enterprises. A classic case in point is the response of Japanese electronics companies to being forced to reduce color TV exports to the U.S. by 30 percent from the 1976 level. Resorting to some classic bypass strategies, the Japanese were able to reduce the agreement to what one industry analyst called a "sham."

[33]Quoted in Ferdinand Mauser, *Modern Marketing Management: An Integrated Approach* (New York: McGraw-Hill, 1961), p. 61.

[34]See "The Changing of the Guard," *Fortune,* September 24, 1979; and "How to be Happy Though No. Two," *Forbes,* July 15, 1976, p. 36.

While Zenith, RCA, and other U.S. firms were rushing to set up plants in low labor-cost Far Eastern countries, Japan's Sony quietly set up a big production facility at San Diego. As Sony's chairman said, "I always travel in the opposite direction." Other Japanese firms too were busily entrenching themselves in depth. Matsushita acquired Motorola's Chicago plant in 1974. Sanyo bought 75 percent of troubled Warwick Electronics, and General Television and Hitachi went in for a joint venture. So in 1977 when the export agreement was reached Japanese production *in the U.S.* jumped from 750,000 units to 1.2 million, nearly swamping out any effect of the agreement.[35]

Guerrilla Warfare

Guerrilla warfare, another attack option, consists of making small, intermittent attacks on different territories of the opponent, with the aim of harassing and demoralizing the opponent and eventually securing concessions. The military rationale is stated below:

> The more usual reason for adopting a strategy of limited aim is that of awaiting a change in the balance of force—a change often sought and achieved by draining the enemy's force, weakening him by pricks instead of risking blows. The essential condition of such a strategy is that the drain on him should be disproportionately greater than on oneself. The object may be sought by raiding his supplies; by local attacks which annihilate or inflict disproportionate loss on parts of his force; by bringing him into unprofitable attacks; by causing an excessively wide distribution of his force; and, not least, by exhausting his moral and physical energy.[36]

The guerrilla attacker will use both conventional and unconventional means to harass the opponent. In the business world, these would include selective price cuts, supply interferences, executive raids, intense promotional bursts, and assorted legal actions against the opponent.

The last, legal action, is becoming one of the most effective ways to harass the other side. Many firms find it worthwhile to search the opponent's legal conduct for possible violations of antitrust law, for trademark infringement, or deceptive trade practices. As an example, a Seattle-based beer distributor who had been supplying beer to Alaska by ship was upset when the Oetker Group of West Germany obtained 75 percent tax credit for ten years from the Alaska legislature to establish beer production in Alaska. The Seattle distributor slapped a lawsuit on Oetker charging the tax incentive was unconstitutional. Oetker eventually won in the courts, but four years of delay crippled its hope of capitalizing on the oil-pipeline construction boom. After operating just thirty months, Oetker closed its Anchorage brewery.[37]

[35]See "The TV-Set Competition That Won't Go Away," *Business Week,* May 8, 1978, p. 86; and "Technology versus Tariffs," *Forbes,* April 15, 1977, p. 27.

[36]Liddell Hart op. cit., p. 335.

[37]"Alaska Chills a German Beer," *Business Week,* April 23, 1979, p. 42.

Normally guerrilla warfare is practiced by a smaller firm against a larger one. Not able to mount a frontal or even effective flanking attack, the smaller firm launches a barrage of short promotional and price attacks in random corners of the larger opponent's market in a manner calculated to gradually weaken the latter's market hold. Even here, the attacker has to decide between launching a few major attacks or a continuous stream of minor attacks. Military dogma holds that a continuous stream of minor attacks usually creates a more cumulative impact, disorganization, and confusion in the enemy than a few major ones. In line with this, the attacker would find it more effective to attack the small, isolated, weakly defended markets rather than major stronghold markets like New York, Chicago, or Los Angeles, where the defender is better entrenched and more willing to retaliate quickly and decisively.

It would be a mistake to think of a guerrilla campaign as a "low-cost" alternative available to financially weak challengers. Conducting a continuous guerrilla campaign can be expensive, although probably less expensive than a frontal, encirclement, or even flanking attack. Furthermore, guerrilla war is more a preparation for war than a war in itself. Ultimately it must be backed by a stronger attack if the aggressor hopes to "beat" the opponent. Hence, in terms of resources, guerrilla warfare is not necessarily a cheap operation.

Further Attack Considerations

Numerous other factors impinge upon the conduct of offensive operations. For example, the *weather* has provided critical tactical cover or opportunity in many military campaigns. Both the Germans and Napoleon lost critical momentum in their drive on Moscow because of severe winter weather. The Battle of the Bulge, which delivered a stunning shock to the Allies in the closing phases of World War II, was timed by the Germans to coincide with forecasted bad weather so as to nullify Allied supremacy in the skies.

The marketplace has many "climatic" features: economic upswings and downswings, capital market fluctuations, changing consumer sentiments (from optimistic behavior to conservative spending), changing trade sentiments, supply stringencies, etc.[38] All of these affect some companies' competitive capacities more than others, and provide leverage for offensive action to those better positioned in relation to the "weather."

A particularly opportune weather condition is provided for the smaller attacker when his larger opponent is embroiled in a major battle in some other market. This is akin to *opening a new front* on the defender. For many years, the Swiss watch industry has been reeling under the massive blows dealt to it all over the world by Japanese companies. A number of Swiss firms integrated to

---

[38]Conceptually, *weather* conditions should be distinguished from terrain features. The former refer to short-run cyclical movements while the latter to more permanent changes and structural characteristics of the market.

fight the unrelenting Japanese onslaught. One of these, the Longines Watch Co., has taken advantage of the Japanese preoccupation with mass world markets to open a new front right in Japan's backyard. In 1977, the biggest market for Longines watches (which are priced at $150 to $50,000) was Japan, where they sell in a "prestige" segment.[39]

Other tactical principles such as *feigning* (misleading the opponent as to one's intentions) and *surprise* (attacking very suddenly and/or in an unexpected way) are also critical considerations in the design of military campaigns, and provide "grist" to the business planner. However, our focus here has been to develop the general framework of strategtic action rather than look into operational details and tactical considerations.

We turn now to consideration of the other hemisphere of strategic action—viz., defense.

CHOOSING THE DEFENSE STRATEGY

We have seen that strategic business competition can be cast in a scenario that closely resemblies the field of military offense. Are similar models of defensive action available? The answer is yes, although the strategic issues will often appear as *reflections* of offensive action. This is because the successful defense, more often than not, hinges on the offensive component of defense strategy. The available strategies are dictated by the specific nature of the opponent's attack.

Consider the alternatives available against frontal attack. Pure frontal assaults of the nature of short-run promotional or price blitzes can be thwarted by a head-on counterattack. Such slugging matches usually die down with only minor adjustments in market share. The really ominous threat is posed by cost-oriented "commoditization" and experience-curve pricers, and short-run countermeasures are likely to be ineffective against them.

The fundamental principle of "concentration in mass" at the attacker's weakest point is again probably the best defensive strategy. The weakest point for price challengers is usually their weak innovations capacity (because of scarce research dollars). Successful market leaders, such as IBM, Xerox, and Hewlett-Packard, have fought off price cutters by following a high innovations counterstrategy. Their objective is to innovate consistently and at a level that their products remain differentiated enough to command a premium. Consider Hewlett-Packard: "The fundamental tenet on which they have built the company . . . is that rather than compete on price, H-P must concentrate on developing products so advanced that customers are willing to pay a premium for them."[40]

---

[39]"Seiko's Smash," op. cit., p. 89.

[40]"Hewlett Packard: Where Slower Growth Is Smarter Management," *Business Week,* June 9, 1975, p. 50.

So in the mid 70s when competitors were slashing prices to boost sales and cutting back on research budgets to buoy earnings, Hewlett-Packard raised prices by 10 percent and increased R&D expenditure by 20 percent to $80 million annually.

An "innovations" defense strategy is not without high risk and seems at least more feasible in high technology markets where product differentiation has a sharper visibility than in soft consumer goods. But even in high technology segments the risks are immense in an increasingly faster paced innovations environment that allows the pioneer less and less of lead time. To beat experience curve pricers demands a very high commitment to R&D and no short measures are likely to suffice for long. Hewlett-Packard, along with Bell Laboratories, is

Exhibit 3   Models of Strategic Defense (i)

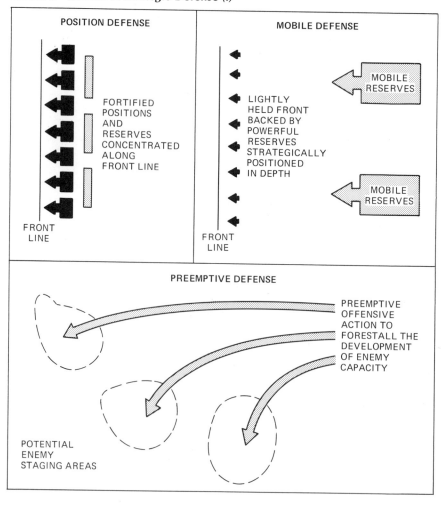

Exhibit 4   Models of Strategic Defense (ii)

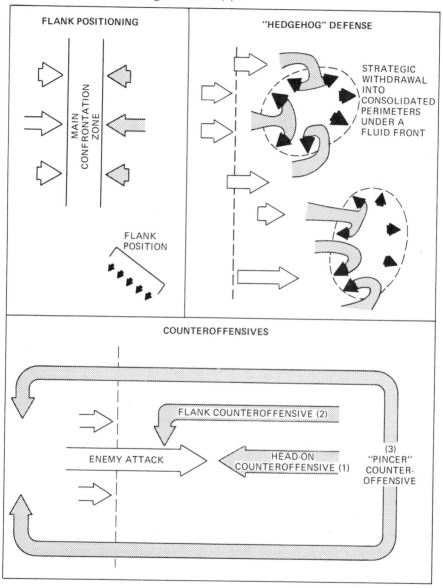

reputed to skim the cream of the crop of bright young engineers and supports them in a very rewarding environment.

Taking another example, what defenses does an opponent have against guerrilla campaigns? The defender has a whole range of possible retorts, from simply fortifying its defenses so that it is less attackable (spending more on promoting brand differentiation and consumer loyalty), to meeting the attacker in each territory with return fire, to sniping at the attacker's other territories (which is to fight guerrilla warfare with guerrilla warfare), to launching a major attack on the guerrilla's home base to discipline or destroy him.

So the questions of defensive and offensive action reflect upon one another and actually draw upon the same body of operational principles. However, from a conceptual point of view, defense strategy can be modeled separately. Six models of defensive deployment are illustrated in Exhibits 3 and 4 discussed below.

Position Defense
("The Fortified Frontline")

The traditional concept of defense is closely tied to a *psychology* of "fortification." The French Maginot-line, the German Siegfried-line, and most recently the Israeli Barlev-line on the Suez, are twentieth century versions of the "fort" of the Middle Ages. Like almost all the great forts of history, these extensive, supposedly impregnable, fortified frontlines all failed in the hour of peril. Static fortlike defense, like frontal attack, is the riskiest strategy in the military theatre, primarily because of its *inherent inflexibility.*

How do we interpret static defense in the business world? The appropriate analogy is with the *marketing myopia* of "product provincialism."[41] Typically, fortification imples an *obsessive* commitment to existing products, the existing organization, and "traditional" ways of doing business. Most of the company's resources are channelled into just improving the "existing" system. Typically, such firms are heavily production and financially oriented, and their marketing emphasis is on cultivating their existing customers and promoting their loyalty.

Such firms are often successful over some period of time, but because of "inbreeding" and inherent inflexibility they run into serious problems when environments change. The marketing concept for many years has sought to demolish the myth of the invincible product and taught marketers to think in terms of underlying *generic* needs and product life cycles. No amount of fortification would have protected the horse carriage against the advent of the automobile. Later, Henry Ford's myopic obsession with the Model-T brought an enviably healthy company to the brink of financial ruin. And only recently, Facit in Europe came to grief when they blindly held on to the mechanical cash register and supported it with all their financial and marketing resources in the face of a massive attack from the new, more efficient, electronic registers.

Changes in technology, life styles, and even usage situations alter the "fit" between products and underlying generic needs of customers. Back in the 1950s steel-wool scouring pads were a major product for cleaning kitchen utensils. But two major developments have radically altered that. Technological advances in another field introduced the nonstick teflon-coated utensil, radically altering the

---

[41]Terms from Theodore Levitt, "Marketing Myopia," *Harvard Business Review,* July–August 1960, pp. 45–56.

usage situation for scouring pads. At the same time, new plastic devices were developed with good abrasive properties but which would not scratch utensils nor rust like steel-wool. All this led to a major adjustment of the product alternatives available to fit the generic needs of the market.

Fortification makes organizations insensitive to the signals of environmental change and fosters a lethargy to adapt. Even such death-defying brands as Coca-Cola and Bayer Aspirin cannot be relied upon by their companies as the main source of future growth and profitability. Coca-Cola today, in spite of producing nearly half the soft drinks of the world, has aggressively moved into the wine market, has acquired fruit drink companies, and has diversified into desalinization equipment manufacture and plastics.[42] Clearly, even market leaders would be foolish to base their long-term defense on putting all their resources into building fortifications around their current major products.

Mobile Defense ("Defense in Depth")

In military doctrine, the "mobile" defense is generally considered far superior to position defense. The need for generating some "mobility" to America's nuclear deterence is the critical purpose behind the plan for "shuttling" the MX missile. Having one's formations mobile, and deployed in some depth to the front line, provides the strategic counter to an enemy attacker capitalizing too much on the principle of surprise and "turning" maneuvers. One can allow the enemy's offensive to "develop" without risking the threat of one's main formations being cut off, and then counterattack at the most appropriate time and place.

In business, the ingredients for generating strategic "depth" are all those approaches that (a) reduce the chances of being radically surprised, and (b) enhance the firm's capacity to respond if surprised. What these requirements call for are:

1. openness to environmental information,
2. the ability to weather an unexpected and telling blow on some front without risking the company's total retaliatory capacity, and
3. the flexibility in current systems to turn them around and operate in very different ways.

The functions of marketing research and intelligence are the traditional avenues for information absorption into the organization. However, the efficacy of "intelligence" activities in guarding against strategic surprise is severely limited by the fact that in business, unlike in war, the "enemy" is not *given*. Moreover, the type of information which is collected, processed, and attended to by the or-

---

[42]"The Strategy That Refreshes?" *Forbes,* November 27, 1978, p. 81.

ganization is biased by the short-term needs and existing beliefs and values of organizational decision-makers. As Ansoff observes about the recent "petroleum crisis":

> ... large and important firms were suddenly confronted with a major discontinuity, although advance forecasts of Arab action were not only publicly available, but on the day of the surprise were to be found on the desks of some of the surprised managers.[43]

Thus environmental "openness" calls for more than marketing research and intelligence. The company needs proper organizational "structures" that channel information search in the right directions and reduce the filters and biases affecting the utilization of available information. It needs *organizational depth.*

Central to the idea of organizational depth is the concept of "fit" between the organization and its environment.[44] Such fit demands primarily that the degree of organizational centralization-differentiation correspond to the level of heterogeneity, complexity, and uncertainty in the environment. Secondarily, but no less important, the organization's internal systems must be fine-tuned to reflect and support the structural fit so that coordination and synergy are maximized. Critical internal systems are the *lateral* relations and communications system, the reward and evaluations system, and corporate *cultures*, executive role-models, and top-management involvement.[45]

Organizational structures and the levels of in-built flexibility and differentiation of systems and processes are also directly concerned with the company's ability to turn around and adapt to new ways of doing things.

Protecting the company's capacity to retaliate involves two different capacities, the technological capacity to meet some new breakthrough, and the resource capacity to generate sufficient funds to counterattack even when some product or market has been devastated by a surprise attack. The dimension of strategic depth corresponding to the former is *technological depth.* Corresponding to the latter are the dimensions of *geographic depth* and *product-mix depth.*

Technological depth refers to the company's innovation activity on two fronts—namely, *market broadening* and *market diversification.*

Market broadening is the "defense-in-depth" solution advocated by Theodore Levitt in his widely acclaimed article "Marketing Myopia."[46] Levitt calls

[43]H. Igor Ansoff, "Managing Surprise and Discontinuity: Strategic Response to Weak Signals" in *Strategy + Structure = Performance,* ed. Hans B. Thorelli (Bloomington: Indiana University Press, 1977), pp. 53–82.

[44]See Jay R. Galbraith, *Organization Design* (Reading, Mass.: Addison-Wesley, 1977).

[45]These concepts are further developed in a marketing concept context in Ravi Singh Achrol and Philip Kotler, Working Paper, op. cit.

[46]Levitt, op. cit.

upon a company to shift its focus from the current product to the underlying generic need and get involved in R&D across the whole range of technology associated with that need. Thus "petroleum" companies are asked to recast themselves into "energy" companies. Implicitly, this would demand dipping their research fingers into the oil, coal, nuclear, hydro-electricity, and chemical industries. It would seem that, carried too far, such market broadening strategies could be disastrous. In a strategic sense, they fault two fundamental principles—the principle of the *objective* ("clearly defined and attainable") and the principle of *mass*. The objective of being in the energy business is too broad—the energy business is not a single need but a whole range of needs (heating, lighting, propelling, etc.). Furthermore, too much broadening would dilute the company's mass in the competitive theatre today, and survival today surely must take precedence over the grand battles imagined for some tomorrow. The error of marketing myopia would be replaced by *marketing hyperopia* (a condition where vision is better for distant than for near objects).

Reasonable broadening, however, makes sense. Armstrong-Cork exemplifies a successful market broadening strategy by redefining its domain from "floor covering" to "decorative room covering" (including walls and ceilings). By recoganizing the customer's need to create a pleasant interior through various covering materials, Armstrong-Cork expanded into neighboring businesses that were synergistically balanced for growth and defense.

The other alternative to generating technological depth is diversification into unrelated technologies. The multidivision corporation is such a common feature today that it seems almost the only route to growth and competitive strength. In a strategic sense, market diversification is the defense analogue to the bypass attack. Thus Colgate and Lever not only bypassed P&G in their offensive posture but simultaneously built a defensive depth from which to draw resources in future counterattacks or challenges that they may need to launch in the confrontation zone with P&G.

In conclusion, the concepts of mobile defense and strategic depth in business that safeguard a company's core resources and competitiveness from the consequences of strategic surprise, pertain to proper strategic orientation along dimensions of geographic, product-mix, technological, and organizational depth. In planning its long-run defense, a company must carefully consider its strengths and weaknesses in each of these areas.

Preemptive Defense
("Offensive-Defense")

Offense as a form of preemptive defense assumes that prevention is better than cure. It assumes that war and not peace is the natural state of business. As such, a model of "offensive-defense" would include all the attack strategies considered earlier, as well as some of the defensive bases discussed here.

For example, a company could launch a flank or envelopment attack against a competitor whose market share is approaching some criterion mark. When Chrysler's market share began rising from 12 to 18 percent some years ago, one rival marketing executive was overheard to say, "If they [Chrysler] go to 20 percent, it will be over our dead bodies."[47]

Or a company could practice a sort of sustained guerrilla action across the market—hitting a competitor here, another there—and keep everyone off-balance at the tactical theatre. Or the offensive-defense could assume the proportions of a *grand* market envelopment as practiced by Seiko, or the sustained frontal barrage of the Texas Instruments' type.

Consider Seiko's high-pressure, preemptive marketing strategy. For several years it has been acquiring distribution in every major watch outlet and overwhelming its competitors and consumers with an enormous variety of constantly changing product models. In the U.S. it offers some 400 models, but its marketing clout is backed by some 2,300 models it makes and sells worldwide. "They hit the mark on fashion, features, user preferences, and everything else that might motivate the consumer," says an admiring vice-president of a U.S. competitor.[48]

Sustained high-pressure strategies aim at retaining the initiative at all times and keeping the competition always on the defensive. It is clear that such strategies must rely heavily on strategic "depth" to their innovations capacity, and consequently, companies adopting them must trade on huge volumes to support the level of R&D demanded.

The question facing the defender is how *broad* a preemptive offensive stance can any firm realistically hope to sustain across a diverse market. Moreover, too broad a stance may carry the danger of dissipation of critical mass.

Companies fortunate enough to enjoy high levels of market assets—high brand loyalty, technological leadership, and so on—would probably find it disadvantageous to pursue a broad preemptive strategy. They have the capacity to weather some punishment and may even prefer to entice the opponents into expensive and costly attacks that will not pay off (hopefully) in the long run. Heinz let Hunt carry out its massive attack in the ketchup market without much counteroffensive, and in the end this proved very costly to Hunt. Standing firm in the face of an attack calls, however, for great confidence in the ultimate superiority of the company's market offer.

"Flank-Positioning" Defense

The flanking "position" is established by a defender as a hedge against some probable but uncertain eventuality, or as a defensive corner overlooking a weak front. As in the military theatre, a flanking position is of little value if it is so lightly held that an enemy could pin it down with a small force while its main

---

[47] "If the Big Three's a Crowd, Blame Chrysler," *Newsweek*, May 20, 1968, p. 84.

[48] "Seiko's Smash," op. cit.

formations swing past unmolested. Hence a careful assessment of any potential threat must be made and, if warranted, a relatively serious commitment made to flanking the threat. Companies should avoid throwing up all sorts of flank positions which amount to no more than dabbling about in various markets.

Many instances of "flank positioning" are to be found in the business world. The strategic stance taken by Chicago-based Jewel Food Stores is instructive of a head-on counteroffensive along a chosen axis supported by strong flank positions in other sensitive markets. Jewel believes that the supermarket will continue to remain dominant in food retailing. Jewel's counteroffense consists of strengthening its assortments "fit" via-à-vis changing life-style parameters of its consumer segment. The fast-food boom has been met by a wide assortment of instant and frozen meals, the discount food challenge by promoting generic lines, and its various supermarkets are being tailored to suit local demands for assortments such as fresh bakery products and ethnic foods.

However, it is taking no chances with some institutional developments in other fields. It has set up the Jewel-T division, which is a network of "box" discount stores patterned after pioneer Aldi. Watching a sudden turnaround in the competitive position of "independents" in 1977, Jewel's Star Market division in New England promptly began moving into franchising the following year. To hedge the "combo" store challenge it integrated a large number of its supermarkets with its Osco Drug Stores using both side-by-side and fully integrated designs.

The Jewel case is illustrative of exceptionally strong flank positioning, so much so that it treads pretty close to being a multiple envelopment offense. But the company believes firmly in the furture of its Jewel, Eisner, Star, and Buttrey supermaket chains and is promoting them aggressively. In most other cases, firms would probably flank position with much lighter resources—though our emphasis is that the position be strong *enough* to deter attack.

An example of a lightly positioned flank deterrent would be Pfizer's warning to the industry that it would build more capacity and lower its prices if competitors start to build a plant. Obviously, such a deterrent would not thwart a large, aggressive competitor, but would probably suffice under a working "price-umbrella" or "peace plan" *implicitly* policed by a powerful leader.

The "Counteroffensive" in Defense

A defender can respond to an attack by mobilizing his reserves and counterattacking the opponent. He has the strategic choice of (1) meeting the attacker's spearhead head on, or (2) maneuvering against the flank of the salient, or (3) launching a *pincer* movement threatening to cut off the attacking formations from their base of operation.

When Oxy-5 blitzed the acne medications market with an extremely powerful promotional attack, competitors, including market leader Clearasil, retaliated with stepped-up counter promotions of their own. Sometimes erosion of market share is so rapid that such a head-on counterattack may be necessitated. But a defender enjoying some strategic depth can often weather the initial attack and riposte with an effective counterstroke at the opportune moment. In many situations it may be worth some minor setbacks to allow the offensive to develop fully before countering. This may seem a dangerous stratgey of wait-and-see, but there are sound reasons for not barrelling into a counteroffensive.

The principal argument is that a flank attack is successful against a well-entrenched defender only when it pivots on some significant gap in market coverage. The market leader often needs time to study the nature of this previously unknown gap to figure out an effective response. This is precisely what Anheuser-Busch did in defending against Miller's massive Lite beer offense. Unlike Schlitz, which barrelled into the counteroffensive in a year, Anheuser waited two years. Its two-pronged "pincering" counteroffensive evolved from a careful analysis of the light beer market. It assessed that light beer drinkers were not purely calorie/weight conscious drinkers, and that light beer had strong appeals also in terms of its less "filling" characteristics and being in tune with a larger trend of health consciousness in the U.S. A-B's *Natural* Light emerged from such a concept, and its Michelob Light from other analyses of the "taste" factor and sociological factors. Presently it appears A-B has been remarkably successful in its counteroffensive.

Schlitz did find a gap in the flank of Miller's offensive—viz., in the "taste" factor—but it failed to exploit this gap vigorously and effectively enough. A-B on the other hand found another gap—viz., appeal in terms of less filling characteristics. It thus achieved a much more effective "pincering" counteroffensive.

The strategies open to a challenger vs. defender differ in that the challenger must zero in on one brand to get maximum concentration of mass. For the defender the best counterattack is a *sequenced* flank and double envelopment aimed at *dissipating* the uniqueness of the challenger's product and diffusing his segment. Note that sequencing the double envelopment retains concentration of mass for the defender as well as avoids the danger of diffusing the campaign's own image clarity as might happen in a simultaneous envelopment.

"Hedgehog" Defense ("Strategic Withdrawal")

Strategic withdrawal is a move to consolidate one's competitive strength in the market, and concentrate mass at pivotal positions for counterattack. When Hitler found his army bogged down and stretched across an enormous Russian front and facing a perilous winter and impossible supply situation, he ordered his armies to withdraw into large circular defensive formations which were supplied mostly by air.

The *strategic* withdrawal has parallels in business. The hedgehog pattern of withdrawing into consolidated positions along the front line fits the marketing operation of *countersegmentation.*[49]

The fashionable marketing doctrines of "product differentiation" and "market segmentation" have resulted in an enormous proliferation of brands and highly fragmented markets. In the slow-growth 1980s, an increasing opportunity lies in either eliminating or fusing these fragmented segments. This opinion is shared by seventy chief marketing executives of *Fortune's "500"* who responded to a questionnaire study. Westinghouse's refrigerator models have been cut from 40 to the 30 that accounted for 85 percent of sales. General Motors has standardized its auto engines and offers fewer options. Campbell Soup, Heinz, General Mills, Del Monte, Georgia-Pacific, Studebaker-Worthington, Gable Industries, and APL Corp. are among those that have significantly pruned their product lines in recent years.[50]

The firm defending itself by pulling into hedgehog strongholds should position these against the weakest fronts of their main competitor. In free-for-all, industry-wide marketing warfare, such as faced by the cigarette industry today, the major victors may well be those that go against the tide of brand proliferation and concentrate their marketing resources behind a few well-positioned brands.

CONCLUSION

The use of the military metaphor in business is becoming so prevalent today that it surely must reflect some striving on the part of managements to come to grips with a new environmental reality. But there is danger, as in the early stages of the marketing concept, that the emerging logic will be swamped in a protracted deluge of semantics and rhetoric.

Corporate strategy consultants in USA share what *Fortune* calls a "somewhat dirty little secret: most believe that over 90 percent of American companies, their clients included, have so far proved incapable of developing and executing meaningful corporate strategies."[51]

The program is that while many of the available techniques provide useful analytical frameworks and decision criteria, the contexts of these decisions are narrowly defined and are tactical more than strategic in nature. The development of a strategic framework for thinking about competitive options is a prerequisite to the effective utilization of tactical decisions techniques.

The business world in the West is currently undergoing an astonishing

[49]See Alan J. Resnik, Peter B. B. Turney, and J. Barry Mason, "Marketers Turn to Countersegmentation," *Harvard Business Review,* September–October 1979, p. 100.

[50]Ibid.

[51]"Playing by the Rules of the Corporate Strategy Game," *Fortune,* September 24, 1979, p. 110.

metamorphosis. Market share and rank have become almost obsessive concerns in the executive suite. That these parameters are closely correlated to company profitability has become almost a dogma.[52] Market share has assumed such a pivotal role that many companies are willing to abandon markets if they cannot be assured of anything less than number one, two, or three *rank* in the market, and even investor circles are coming around to employing such decision criteria. All this is fueling a vicious cycle. The strong are growing stronger in their markets and others are looking elsewhere to develop their strengths.

With the strong getting stronger, and the weak dropping out or becoming incidental, the strategic balances quickly start assuming the nature of *deterrence* power in the market. For the "others," the "elsewhere" is increasingly a global opportunity, albeit not many American companies think effectively in terms of global strategies as the Japanese did. But we feel it is in this global context that the competitive strengths and weaknesses of a company will be tested tomorrow. All said, we believe that geopolitical thinking and strategic deterrence are likely to be key conceptual hinges on which future strategic thought in business will turn.

APPENDIX
THE BEER WARS: AN ANATOMY
OF MARKETING WARFARE

In 1970, Miller Brewing Company, a subsidiary of Philip Morris, Inc., occupied seventh place in the industry with a meager 4.2 percent share. Early in 1975 Miller launched a powerful offensive the reverberations of which continue to rock the industry, which has dwindled from 92 brewers to 41 in the past decade. Miller found and attacked a gap in the industry flank. Pivoting on its newly discovered "light" beer segment, it supported the breakthrough with an $11 million advertising blitz (the largest in beer marketing history), a packaging innovation ("pony" size bottles), and strong retail promotion. Today Miller is a strong No. 2 in the industry with a 21 percent share of the market, and the No. 1 spot is its declared objective.

A year after Miller opened its offensive, Schlitz, hurting most, rallied to the counteroffensive. Attempting to break the flank of Miller's deep salient, it introduced its own light beer, matched Miller's *ad* dollars, and pivoted its counterflank on a "taste" positioning ("It took Schlitz to bring the taste to light").

In a marketing sense Miller had borne the brunt of the challenge of breaking psychological resistance to light beers as "sissy products." It successfully used a "macho" image campaign to appeal directly to the hard core of the beer

---

[52]See Robert D. Buzzell, Bradley T. Gale, and Ralph G. M. Sultan, "Market Share—A Key to Profitability," *Harvard Business Review,* January–February 1975, p. 97; and "Corporate Strategists Giving New Emphasis to Market Share, Rank," *Wall Street Journal,* February 3, 1978.

market, viz., the male blue-collar worker. But research indicated that the very high trier-rejector rate was because of a *perceived* sacrifice in taste.

Thus Schlitz did have an appropriate counterstrategy. However, analysts feel its campaign was less than effective, and that Schiltz's gain of 20 percent of the light beer market was due to synergy with the parent brand. The important lesson is that in a battle between opponents matched in combat capacity and strategic depth, the flank, once pierced, must be exploited vigorously while the main body of the defender is held down in position. This means that Schlitz needed to more than match Miller if it were to hold Miller down and still support the flank momentum. One anlayst observed that the Schlitz campaign created low product awareness, low advertising awareness, and *low registration of the product's major benefit—good taste.*

In contrast, when market-leader Anheuser-Busch entered the light beer foray two years after the debut of Miller Lite, it executed a classic envelopment, driving home on a very strong flank attack and following through with a double envelopment. Anheuser-Busch launched Natural Lite with an $11 million campaign attempting to outflank Miller and Schlitz in the blue-collar market, and then followed through with Michelob Lite which pincered in on the white-collar side of the market.

Anheuser's two-pronged assault evolved from a careful assessment of the whole market, and the results support our argument that a well-positioned defender might do better to wait a while and see before counterattacking (though A-B appears to have come perilously close to waiting too long). A-B's research revealed two important characteristics of the "lite" market:

1. Light beer drinkers were not purely calorie/weight conscious drinkers. Consumers actually preferred its lighter, milder, smoother taste. They liked the less "filling" character of the beer, and its freedom from side effects. Most important, Anheuser felt the appeal of light beers was a part of a larger trend of health and personal care consciousness among U.S. consumers.

   Natural Light emerged from such a concept and was brewed with all natural ingredients, with natural carbonation, and without enzymes or additives. In eight months it captured the No. 2 position in the "light" market from Schlitz.

2. Anheuser's second onslaught, Michelob Light, attacked the "taste" deficiency from an angle different from Schlitz's. All brands of light in the market had fewer than 100 calories, and a void existed between that and the 150 calorie regular beers. Furthermore, management felt that the growth potential of its premium label Michelob was being hindered by the light beers in general and that the segment of young, upscale, white-collar beer drinkers was beginning to show up with light beer in situations where they would normally have had Michelob.

Into this void was launched Michelob Light, "The one light beer with a few more calories but a lot more taste." Despite being priced as a premium beer, in seven months the brand had taken fourth place in the light market. In all, A-B had snared 23 percent of the light beer market by 1979.

Anheuser's defense seems to have paid off and certainly the momentum of Miller's offensive has been slowed. In 1979 Miller's sales *growth* dropped to 14.5 from 29.1 percent, while A-B fell from 13.7 to 11.1 percent. In 1980 A-B widened its sales lead over Miller for the first time in several years, its sales rising by 8.5 percent to Miller's 4 percent. A-B continues to pursue its pincering counter-strategy—"The plan is to bracket and pinion each Miller entry in a particular category with two flanking Anheuser products." But as one industry analyst observed early in 1981, "The war is already over, Anheuser-Busch will continue to maintain industry dominance."

A-B employed other sound military principles to maximize the momentum of its counteroffensive. It whipped up the morale of its "troops," identifying Miller as the aggressor. A-B's top executives met with each of its 14,000 employees at a series of dinners and made much of Miller's publicly proclaimed objective to capture A-B's No. 1 position and the fact that Miller president John A. Murphy had installed a rug with the A-B corporate seal under his desk so that he could regularly stomp on it. Busch put President Long especially in charge of the counterattack. A-B targeted areas where its sales were strongest or had the greatest potential (conversely, areas where Miller was weakest), and sent in "SWAT Squads" of employees in their twenties to work with distributors. All this was supported with a revamped and heavy promotional barrage.

The beer wars also involved subversive guerrilla actions. When Schlitz launched its counteroffensive, Miller attempted to thwart its momentum by a flurry of legal challenges. Likewise, when Miller turned in 1977 to pinning down Anheuser with a direct frontal attack on Michelob with its premium label Lowenbrau, Anheuser protested angrily to the Federal Trade Commission that Miller was using deceptive packaging and advertising to mislead consumers into believing they were buying an imported beer when in fact the domestic brand was significantly different in brewing process and ingredients from the 600-year-old German Lowenbrau.

The publicity surrounding this has obviously had effect. Despite a $15.6 million advertising outlay on Lowenbrau in 1979, sales were only 1 million barrels compared with 8.3 million for Michelob supported by $15.1 million in advertising. Note that Miller's outflanking maneuver in this instance consisted of generating an "import" image to diffuse Michelob's segment. Once this was thwarted, the battle reduced to a frontal confrontation which would have called for much heavier odds.

The wars continue to rage even if the first encounter between Miller and A-B might have currently eased off. Battered sidelines are moving in with aggressive counterstrategies. The theme of Olympia's (seventh largest in the market) recent national distributors' conference was "Our field, our time," a paraphrase of Clausewitz's dictum—"Never engage the enemy on his field, at his time, in a manner of his choosing." Olympia's new marketing strategy, unveiled at the conference, is attempting the multiple envelopment with brand proliferation and heavy promotional support as its cornerstones.

From a strategic point of view it is apparent that the strategic plane is rapidly changing in the beer market. Such proliferation strategies will diffuse segments so much that competition will be reduced to slugging frontal attacks and Olympia's pincers may never materialize as effective thrusts against the enemies' flanks. It will be interesting to study the aftermath.

REFERENCES

1. "A-B Aims to Win by Segmenting Light Beer," *Marketing News*, December 29, 1978.
2. "The Battle of the Beers," *Newsweek*, September 4, 1978.
3. "Anheuser's Plan to Flatten Miller's Head," *Business Week*, April 21, 1980.
4. "Olympia Mapping Strategy for Brewery Battlefield," *Chicago Tribune*, April 6, 1980, Sec. 5, p. 3
5. "The Battle of the Beers," *Newsweek*, March 9, 1981.

5

Industrial Organization, Corporate Strategy and Structure

RICHARD E. CAVES
Harvard University

The author is indebted for comments and suggestions to Alfred D. Chandler, Jr.; Herman Daems; Sharon Oster; Michael E. Porter; and Oliver E. Williamson.

Let us start with a sketch of the relationships to be surveyed in this paper. The large firm sells[1] in product markets having structural features that constrain its behavior and define its options. "Market structure" refers to certain stable attributes of the market that influence the firm's conduct in the marketplace. Significant elements of market structure include the number and size distribution of sellers and buyers, height of barriers to entry and exit, extent and character of product differentiation, extent and character of international competition (if the market is defined no more broadly than the nation), and certain parameters of demand (elasticity, growth rate). The firm holds tangible or intangible semi-fixed assets or skills. The top managers' perceptions of the market structure and the firm's strengths and weaknesses jointly determine their choice of *corporate strategy* (its long-run plan for profit maximization) and *organizational structure* (the internal allocation of tasks, decision rules, and procedures for appraisal and reward, selected for the best pursuit of that strategy). Both corporate strategy and organizational structure influence the economic performance of the firm and the market in which it sells.[2]

These relations between the firm and its market environment lie at the intersection between industrial organization, as a branch of economics, and the study of organizational behavior and administration. My intention is not to survey literature familiar to economists but to synthesize and report research undertaken from other disciplinary bases. One of my objectives is to report some interesting findings about the causes and consequences of market structure, arising from the firm's strategic choice and structural adaptation. The other goal is to present some promising opportunities for theoretical and empirical research flushed out by scholars in other disciplines. I shall cover a literature from business history on the evolution of the large multidivisional company as a response to changing technologies and market opportunities, studies from business policy that view the same relation in cross-section, and analyses from organizational behavior and sociology of the influence of technology, uncertainty, and competition on organizational structure. The first two literatures are treated together in the first part of this paper because they share a common conceptual foundation. The third receives separate treatment. Economists' contributions, both theoretical and empirical, are noted where appropriate, but my emphasis is on wares imported from other disciplines.[3]

[1] The discussion in this paper will relate to the firm primarily in its capacity as a seller, although in principle the analysis should be symmetrical between the selling and buying sides of the market.

[2] By the economic performance of the firm we mean its efficiency (measured by the divergence of its input-output relation from the best attainable), its profitability relative to comparable competitors, or some other operational test of efficiency. However, our inquiry is ultimately motivated by a concern with market performance, an aggregation over the performance characteristics of firms in the market.

[3] It should be stressed that the literature of business policy covers a great wealth of case studies and experience distilled by practitioners into a body of normative instruction for business students and advice for business executives. This survey makes no attempt to synthesize that material. It is concerned only with positive or explanatory models and evidence that has taken the form of systematic cross-section studies. Coverage of the case-study material would no doubt enrich the conclusions reported below.

I. THE POSITIVE ECONOMICS
OF CORPORATE STATEGY

A. Corporate Strategy
and Organizational Structure:
Concepts and Theoretical Framework

The unifying concept of corporate strategy first emerged in the study of business decision-making to provide business managers with a simple and operational method for devising a long-term plan to assure the maximal attainment of the firm's objectives.[4] The firm rests on contractual relations that unite and coordinate various fixed assets or factors, some of them physical, others consisting of human skills, knowledge, and experience—some of them shared collectively by the managerial hierarchy. These factors are assumed to be semipermanently tied to the firm by recontracting costs and, perhaps, market imperfections.[5] An implication is that the firm does its long-run planning taking fixed factors as given, so that its maximization process becomes one of maximizing quasi-rents to these fixed factors. Another implication of these heterogeneous fixed assets is that a firm can succeed (i.e., forge a viable combination of fixed inputs) in a given market by possessing superior assets of any of several types. Equally successful market rivals thus may employ quite different bundles of fixed asset qualities (strengths and weaknesses).

These properties of corporate strategies and their formation hold several implications for the market environment in which strategy is to be employed. The standard model of perfect competition assumes these fixed factors away, and so the concept of corporate strategy applies to market environments that would be described as imperfectly competitive. Because the strategy model implies that competing firms earn different efficiency rents and that they can serve the same market by means of quite different input combinations, we expect that the products they offer to the market are multidimensional and heterogeneous, and that a firm's strategic strengths and weaknesses can be evaluated meaningfully only with respect to identified rivals. The strategy model hence has an affinity for a market structure of differentiated oligopoly.

---

[4]Important textbook statements are Kenneth R. Andrews (1971) and H. Igor Ansoff (1965). When we translate this process into economic terminology we shall assume that the goal is long-run profit maximization (maximum present market value of the firm). The authors surveyed in this section seldom tie their analysis to any goal that precise. They often imply that avoidance of risk (especially risk of bankruptcy) motivates the firm, and there are occasional suggestions of growth maximization. No important issues discussed below will turn on the exact ingredients in the objective function of the firm's managers or owners.

[5]Furthermore, at least some of them are simply not traded on open markets that permit capitalizing their differential qualities into their contract prices. Thus rents that the firm can earn are not entirely passed along to the unique fixed factors responsible for them. The strategy model does not itself explain why firms should be organized around long-term contractual coalitions. Given that they are, it explains how their shared objectives are pursued.

Strategic choice is a general process (as defined in the business literature). However, only a few major types of strategic decisions have been studied systematically—those committing the firm to multimarket activities through diversification, vertical integration, and geographic market expansion (multiregional or multinational production).[6] Insight seems to come from less general models that explain why firms extend administrative links across activities in different markets and thereby displace arm's-length contracts, the economic use of proprietary information, etc. Although multimarket activity is clearly a central strategic choice, other strategic choices can probably be identified empirically and analyzed theoretically.[7]

The other key concept is that of organizational structure, the arrangements whereby the firm motivates, coordinates, appraises, and rewards the inputs and resources that belong to its coalition.[8] The choice of these arrangements also can be conceived as an optimizing decision, and some theoretical aspects of the allocations involved are considered in *Section II* of this survey. For now, we can view the selection of organizational structure more narrowly as a process of choosing arrangements that maximize the value of the firm's chosen strategy, given the fixed assets that warrant that strategic choice. Oliver E. Williamson (1970) has formalized Alfred D. Chandler's analysis of the properties of two key prototype structures—the functional and the multidivisional—and the relation of their respective advantages to the firm's strategic alternatives. The functionally specialized firm subdivides its activities into departments, each of which undertakes a distinctive function—production, finance, marketing, etc. Their heads report to a chief coordinator whose responsibilities must include the continuous reconciliation of the subgoals set for these departments. The multidivisional firm makes its primary organizational breakdown into divisions assigned different tasks or having responsibility for serving different markets. Each division contains an appropriate set of functional departments. The top coordinator appraises the performance of divisional profit or cost centers, characteristically using return-on-investment criteria, and concentrates chiefly on formulating long-run plans and making a consonant allocation of resources among the divisions.

A departmental organization in a functional firm can achieve economies of specialization and scale and reduce the number of communication channels

---

[6]Paul H. Rubin (1973) and Michael S. Proctor (1976) deal with the expansion of the firm holding fixed assets that cannot be costlessly divested in the short run. An important antecedent is Edith T. Penrose (1959).

[7]For an attempt, see Derek F. Abell.

[8]The term "structure" will be employed here because it has become conventional, although it is in some way unfortunate. It suggests—quite properly—the firm's organization chart, but it does not adequately invoke the control apparatus by which the firm keeps its records, appraises and evaluates the performance of its various inputs and activities, or motivates and rewards its employees. The breadth of the concept should be kept in mind, especially because most empirical research has addressed the organization-chart aspects of structure.

needed among members of the firm. However, diversification and geographic expansion by the firm (with or without departmental proliferation) inject problems that are potentially solvable by switching to a multidivisional (henceforth MD) form. One problem arises from the mere expansion of the organization's size. Given the supervisor's span of control, enlargement of the number of primary operatives requires a predictable increase in the number of supervisory levels; more vertical levels mean greater "control loss" as messages get garbled while passing up or down the hierarchy, and the top coordination level experiences increased problems with "bounded rationality"—its ability to absorb and act promptly upon all relevant information (Williamson, 1970, chap. 2).

Another problem arises if the firm's growth enlarges the number of activities it undertakes. If so, each functional department may come to carry on heterogenous activities, even if additional departments are created. Redundant communication channels are retained within functional departments, and channels between them are inefficiently used. The top coordinator's task multiplies in complexity, especially because performance criteria cannot easily be applied to the individual activities in the firm's portfolio. The MD form offers a potential solution to either or both problems.

The preceding analysis follows Williamson and others in explaining why firms may switch from the functional to the MD form as their activities grow larger and more complex. Although some writers tend to conclude that the MD firm has all the advantages, the Williamson model really implies that the rational choice between the two depends on the firm's circumstances (1975, pp. 148–50). With the firm's activity set held constant, adoption of the MD form presumptively costs the firm the resources needed to add a new top layer of coordination. It gains the efficiency of being able to use better performance criteria, and it may gain from reductions in control loss, the deletion of redundant communication channels as the functional departments undergo reorganizational, and economies in the use of specialized resources as the top coordinator's elite staff is formed.

The elements of bounded rationality, control loss, and the avoidance of redundant communication channels carry many specific implications for the design of organizational structures that minimize adminstrative cost or maximize the expected value of a corporate strategy (James D. Thompson, 1967; Jay W. Lorsch and Stephen A. Allen, III, 1973, chap. 8). Most of these implications have emerged from empirical investigations rather than being derived from abstract premises. Consequently the next sections focus on historical evolution and cross-sectional analysis.

B. Historical Evolution

The development of the American economy in the past two centuries has brought great changes in technology, market structure, and the organization of companies, and these sweeping changes reveal starkly the power of the market environment to alter business strategy and structure. The major systematic insights stem from Alfred D. Chandler's two books *Strategy and Structure* (1962) and *The Visible Hand* (1977).[9] The former—as original conceptually as it was historically—concentrated on the changing strategies of a small group of large companies and analyzed their groping efforts to devise new organizational structures to pursue these strategies more effectively. *The Visible Hand* takes a longer perspective on the changing opportunities for business enterprise wrought by changes in technology and market organization from the late eighteenth century down to the present, but with emphasis on the nineteenth century. It stresses the connection between the market's constraints and opportunities and the frontier of companies' strategic choices—the opportunities seized by the frontrunners and later disseminated to other competitors and industries. The following analytical summary can only hint at the richness of Chandler's analysis.

Early in the nation's development the small sizes of markets, the slow pace of transportation media, and the primitive technology for transmitting information denied any reward for the productive coordination of economic activity through the large enterprise. Slow communications, whether between or within firms, forced a decentralized trading company to employ a "trusted agent" at each trading point; it could not decentralize decision-making beyond equity participants in the firm. The restricted opportunities for hedging limited the size of the firm, as did small markets, costly transportation, and the lack of large-scale power sources. The firm had little to gain from sophisticated accounting systems (costs mattered less for trading profits than did skill in acting quickly on limited market information) or closely coordinated logistics (because of the slow pace of transportation) (Chandler, 1977, chaps. 1,2). As a result, in 1840 there were no middle managers in the United States and, correspondingly little scope for strategic choice and sophisticated organization.

Strategic choices leading to large-scale organization first became possible with the rise of modern modes of transportation and communication—the railroad and the telegraph. Chandler concentrates on the railroad enterprises themselves, especially the Pennsylvania (1977, chap. 3). First the consideration of safety, then the organization's sheer volume of transactions and size of its capital requirements impelled an integrated, hierarchical organization. From the railroad's efforts to deal efficiently with its complex task emerged many mainstay features of modern business organization—financial accounting, the line staff distinction, and data flows permitting the comparative appraisal of performance. Functional, departmentalized organization evolved, as indeed did geographic divisions, and eventually the multidivisional form for managing the many properties acquired by some major railroads. Chandler contrasts this organization evolved by "managerial" railroads such as the Pennsylvania with the very differ-

---

[9]Chandler draws on a wide variety of historical materials, including numerous company histories. We shall not attempt to extend our survey to the level of these company histories. (See Bernard Alford, 1976).

ent structures of independent companies with interlocking directorates and a central financial office employed in the railroad empires dominated by financiers, such as the New York Central system. The lesser effectiveness of this latter system for long-term planning and coordination was shown in the greater centralization that their managers imposed on these networks as internal reorganizations took place (1977, pp. 175–85).

Fast modes of transportation and communication gave rise to strategic options that led to national and multimarket firms in the manufacturing and distribution sectors. Successful firms could now establish branded goods, build national distribution systems, and develop multiproduct lines. Which industries seized these strategies also depended on changing technology; Chandler finds that the firms venturing to integrate forward into distribution were employing new large-scale technologies whose production outran the firm's previous distribution capacity (1977, chap. 9). He attributes the resulting large size of firms and enduring high levels of seller concentration not so much to the new capital- and energy-intensive technologies (except in primary metals) as to the resultant vertical integration into marketing and distribution systems (1977, pp. 364–67). Integrated distribution systems in turn tended to have excess capacity and hence to promote the broadening of product lines,[10] so that integration and diversification ultimately proved complementary. While some firms successfully chose these strategies of large-scale integration, others opted for a strategy of horizontal merger to attain monopoly profits or stem the erosion of local monopolies. Chandler argues that merger strategies failed unless the combining firms genuinely consolidated and adopted a strategy of vertical integration (1977, chap. 10). One wonders, though, whether the failures lost out through oversight or because integration in some industries failed to offer either real or pecuniary economies. This problem—whether strategic choice is determinate or involves entrepreneurial free will—turns up repeatedly in the literature surveyed in this paper.

If much of Chandler's *The Visible Hand* traces the effect of changing technology and market structures on firms' opportunity sets, his *Strategy and Structure* (1962) shows how the resulting innovations in corporate strategy subsequently induced changes in business organization. Companies whose success brought them to prominence in the national market for their principal product followed the lead of the early railroads and communication companies, employing a functional organization to minimize costs. Eventually, however, the continued expansion of companies in geographic or product space made their functional departments too heterogenous for maximal effectiveness, and the

---

[10]Chandler (1977, pp. 307, 326); Thomas Horst (1974, chap. 2). This analysis yields other conclusions of great interest for industrial organization. First, specific motives for displacing arm's-length distribution systems can be observed: effecting product differentiation, guaranteeing service on new and complex machinery, reducing uncertainty and delay in cash flows associated with the thinner stream of information flowing from arm's-length distributors. Second, the analysis reveals a great deal about the genesis of entry barriers, conveying the impression that barriers we now tend to blame on advertising originally stemmed from scale economies in intergrated distribution systems.

multidivisional form was adopted. Chandler's case studies reveal that this form evolved independently in four major companies, emerging not full-blown but as a piecemeal adaptation to recurrent problems (1962, chaps. 2–5). The timing of the change, if not its ultimate fact, often depended on a perceived threat that made clear the hazards of continuing with the old organization. Although the MD organization itself serves to decentralize operating authority while centralizing the planning and coordination roles, these companies in some cases went through periods of tighter centralization when the weaknesses of previous organizational structures showed up (e.g., excessive inventory accumulation in the 1921 recession).

Foreign direct investment resembles integration and diversification in carrying the firm into multimarket activity (Peter Buckley and Mark Casson, 1976, chap. 2) and so it should receive parallel treatment. Mira Wilkins identifies the developments in market organizations and public policy that brought the multinational companies into being (1970). Some companies chose a strategy of foreign production when foreign agents handling export sales failed to provide adequate servicing or to differentiate the product effectively. Others became multinational when foreign acquisitions were made to quell a price war or cement a nonaggression pact with foreign competitors. Still others were pushed into foreign production by foreign tariffs or patent laws, which made exports unprofitable. Horst's study of the food-processing firm notes the stronger propensity to foreign investment by the "marketers"—firms skilled in the promotion of branded goods—than by the "distributors"—firms whose domestic strategies had emphasized the low-cost distribution of undifferentiated goods through geographically integrated distribution systems (1974, chap. 3). Clearly the former strategy would travel to distant lands more effectively than the latter. Overall, the forces that caused or facilitated multinational status correspond well to those uncovered by Chandler.

C. Cross-Section Evidence

Chandler's penetrating insights were picked up by other students of business organization who applied them to cross sections of leading nonfinancial corporations in several industrial countries. Besides testing in cross section Chandler's hypothesis that strategic options determine organizational structures, these studies reveal the channels by which innovations in business organization spread internationally, and the social and economic forces that spur or retard them. Other systematic empirical studies have probed the association between strategy and business structure, and its implications for market performance.

John H. McArthur and Bruce R. Scott explored the reliance on strategic planning of a small cross-section of French enterprises and tested (with negative results) for a relation between major strategic moves and the choice of appropriate organization structures (1969, chap. 5). Leonard Wrigley showed that the strategies employed by large manufacturing firms can be classified systematically (1970), and that strategy and structure are aligned as Chandler's work suggested. Wrigley's classification of strategies, the basis for most subsequent work, turned on the degree of diversification of the company and the relation between its diversified activities and its basic business. Wrigley (1970) and later Richard P. Rumelt (1974, chap. 1) emphasized the subject and company-specific character of the definition of basic business and the bonds that link it to the company's other businesses. That is, firms can make their businesses cohere in a variety of ways and two firms' basic businesses might consist of sets of activities partly overlapping each other, integrated to equal degrees but in different ways. When he defined basic businesses in this non-mechanistic fashion, Wrigley found that large companies were not distributed continuously in their degree of diversification. He distinguished first between single-product and dominant-product firms, with non-basic businesses in the latter accounting for no more than one-fifth of sales. At that threshold he found a break in the distribution: if a company's diversified activities account for as much as 20 percent of sales, it had usually gone on to raise the diversified percentage of its sales to 40 percent or more. Companies with 40 percent or more diversified sales were classified into "related product" and "unrelated product" groups. An unrelated-product firm's diversifying activities carry it primarily into technologies and markets that are not shared with its basic business, whereas related-product firms exhibit one of many linkages to the basic business (similar products, processes, or markets; complementary products; jointly supplied products; common technology; common markets but new technology; or application of common research results).

Rumelt (1974, chap. 1) supplied subheadings to Wrigley's categories in order to identify the process by which basic and peripheral businesses are linked. He subdivided the "related" and "dominant" groups into companies whose diversification was either "constrained" (stayed in businesses necessarily and directly related to the basic business) or "linked" (businesses entered were initially unrelated, but the firm devised ways to tie them to its basic business). The "dominant" category also contains a subcategory for vertically integrated dominant firms. The "unrelated" group is subdivided into "unrelated-passive" and "acquisitive conglomerates" (the latter are fast-growing and thin in their top management). Rumelt's addition of these strategic linkages nicely complements Wrigley's finding that large companies were not distributed continuously in their degree of diversification.

Indeed, Wrigley's key hypothesis was that multidivisional structures would be chosen more frequently by the companies whose strategies involved greater diversification, and this pattern was strongly apparent (1970, chap. 3). None of the single-product firms in the *Fortune* 500 list were MD, while 64 percent of the dominant-product group, 95 percent of the related-product firms, and all of the unrelated-product firms, and all of the unrelated product companies were MD. This finding replicated Chandler's strategy-structure relation in cross-section and indirectly confirmed that companies' strategies could be classified on a comparable basis. Still to be answered were questions of how promptly companies adapted their structures to strategic changes, and whether the strategy-structure association could be replicated for other countries. These questions were pursued in a series of studies by Rumelt (1974) on the United States, Derek F. Channon (1973) on the United Kingdom, Gareth P. Dyas and Heinz T. Thanheiser (1976) on France and Germany, Robert J. Pavan (1972) on Italy, and Wrigley (1976) on Canada.[11] TABLE 1 summarizes their key results. The studies cover different numbers of firms, but the sample sizes are desirably correlated with the sizes of the countries and thus with their total numbers of firms; that is, roughly the same proportions of the largest nonfinancial companies is covered for each. Two principal conclusions emerge:

1. As Chandler's historical research implied, the strategies of leading companies have run toward increased diversification in all of the countries. Some companies move down the categories from single-product to unrelated-product passing through all the intermediate stages, but others make discrete jumps in classification. Moves to a less diversified strategy are uncommon although not unknown. Diversified strategies emerged first in the United States, then spread gradually to other countries. The authors suggest various factors that help to explain why diversification came no sooner to Europe. Legal access to horizontal mergers reduced the incentive to diversify in order to avert risks to the basic business, and managerial preoccupation with maintaining collusive arrangements in the basic business reduced the firm's capacity to extend its activities to other markets.[12] Similarly, operation in a regulatory and bureaucratic environment such as France tended to tie down executives to mediating with public officials on operating questions and distract their attention from questions of long-range planning (Dyas and Thanheiser, 1976, pp. 242–44). Heavier tasks of reconstruction after World War II also concentrated managerial resources on production problems in the basic business and delayed diversification.

2. A diffusion of the MD structure apparently took place during 1950–70, so that in all countries the match of structure to strategy was appreciably closer in 1970 than in 1950. The lag in structural adaptation to strategy is clear in each study, but the research designs do not focus cleanly on the average duration of the lag or on what factors explain why firms in some situations might delay longer than those otherwise situated. On this issue only a few hints appear. Channon (1973, p. 75) and Pavan (1972, p. IV–50) observe that the lag has often been long and to some degree extended by the adoption of a holding company structure that permitted diversification to continue but without central strategic control. Dyas and Thanheiser (1976, p. 115 and chap. 15) confirm this for France and Germany and put the average lag in adopting MD structure behind

---

[11]These studies were directed by Professor Bruce Scott. Data are also available on Japan, for 1972 only. Ken'ichi Imai reports that 2.4 percent of 124 leading firms were single-product, 22.6 percent dominant-product, 33.1 percent related-product, and 41.9 percent unrelated-product (1978, p. 51).

[12]Channon (1973, p. 90); Pavan (1972, chap. 6, p. VII–46); Dyas and Thanheiser (1976, p. 249–50).

Table 1 Strategic and Structural Choices of Leading Nonfinancial Companies in Five Industrial Countries, 1950–1970 [a]

Country	Year	No. of Companies		Strategic Classification Single	Dominant	Related	Unrelated
United States	1949	500[b]	% dist.	34	35	27	3
			% MD	5	20	44	100
	1969	500[b]	% dist.	6	29	45	19
			% MD	24	62	90	98
United Kingdom	1950	92	% dist.	34	40	24	2
			% MD	6	11	32	0
	1970	100	% dist.	6	34	54	6
			% MD	17	73	79	50
France	1950	100	% dist.	42	21	33	4
			% MD	5	0	12	0
	1970	100	% dist.	16	32	42	10
			% MD	19	59	64	50
Germany	1950–	99	% dist.	34	26	32	7
	1955		% MD	0	8	9	0
	1970	100	% dist.	22	22	38	18
			% MD	9	45	88	56
Italy	1950	84	% dist.	30	24	43	4
			% MD	0	0	14	33
	1970	100	% dist.	10	33	52	5
			% MD	0	45	58	60

Sources: Rumelt (1974, pp. 51, 71); Channon (1973, Table III-2); Dyas (1972, p. 168); Thanheiser (1972, Table V-3); Pavan (1972, Table IV-3). Figures for Canada from Wrigley (1976, p. 23) are omitted from the table because they are available only for 1961–72 and because they are not classified by organization. The percentages of Wrigley's 86 companies in the four strategic categories are respectively 31, 29, 36, and 3 for 1961; 12, 38, 44, and 6 for 1972.

[a] The line labeled "% dist." indicates the percentage distribution of companies among the four strategic categories. The line labeled "% MD" indicates the proportion of companies in each category that are multidivisional.

[b] Rumelt's procedure is based on a sample taken from the largest 500 companies for each year (1974, Appendix A).

diversification around 15 to 20 years for the median firm (1976, pp. 73, 195). In both the United Kingdom and Italy it appears that family ownership status delayed both diversification and the subsequent adoption of the MD structure.[13]

The international spread of MD structures, like that of diversified strategies, shows a lag, which again suggests the innovative role of U.S. companies. In the European countries, foreign-controlled enterprises were in the van of local enterprises in adopting the MD structure.[14] One suspects this conclusion slightly because the structural (and strategic) classification of a company in these studies is based not on the organization chart of the subsidiary itself but on that of its foreign parent. However, the role of American consulting firms, teaching materials, and personal contacts was evident (Dyas and Thanheiser, 1976, pp. 112-13). Also, Lawrence G. Franko found that the European multinationals that were quickest to abandon an informal "mother-daughter" control mechanism were those with the largest and most successful operations in the United States (1976, chap. 8). Pavan found a demonstration effect flowing from the two large Italian state-owned companies, I.R.I. and E.N.I. (1972, p. IV-30).

The cross-section studies document a linkage between strategy and organization, but they examine only the most aggregated traits of business organization. The vintage can be fortified somewhat by turning to research on the organization of firm's multinational activities, which complicate the choice between functional and MD organization. John M. Stopford and Louis T. Wells point out that the risk (initially, at least) and specialized knowledge associated with international operations demand an internal organization different from that optimal for a strategy of diversification (1972, chaps. 2, 5). Companies manage their first foreign ventures through an international division that is viewed as highly risky and hence is cordoned off from the domestic organization (often functional, at that time). As the domestic organization gravitates to product divisions, tensions result because the domestic divisions have little incentive to share their intangibles and other assets with the international division. The larger and more diversified foreign operations become, the more likely is the firm to grope for some "global structure"—international area divisions, global product divisions, or some combination of the two.[15]

Franko's study of the viability of multinational joint ventures also sheds light on the strategy-structure relation (1971). Broadly speaking, the multinational firms tolerant of joint ventures are the diversified MD enterprises. Conversely, a more specialized and functionally organized company frequently

---

[13]Channon (1973, p. 76); Pavan (1972, p. IV-54).

[14]Channon (1973, p. 69); Dyas and Thanheiser (1976, pp. 65, 66, 112-13); Pavan (1972, chap. 4).

[15]Franko's study of European multinationals (1976, chap. 8) shows that their sequence of organizational development differed because of their heritage of less competitive domestic markets. The international division was generally skipped, and the MD organization adopted internationally and at home at about the same time. His evidence suggests that the adaptation of structure to strategy was hastened by the more competitive environment that these firms faced in their foreign operations.

clings to a core technology—an intangible asset that cannot easily be shared with another enterprise on a contractual basis. The functional organization finds its access to information impaired by a joint venture and fears for the damage to its goodwill asset if its various markets around the world are interdependent.

Finally, the strategy-to-structure mapping has been checked in studies that investigate whether the locus of decision-making varies with structure as it should if structures are utilized so as to maximize the value of the strategies with which they are associated. Jesse W. Markham, following the lead of previous case studies, collected information from 202 diversified companies and from 173 firms acquired by these companies. He examined the levels at which various decisions are taken—divisional profit center or. corporate headquarters (1973, chap. 4). Capital-expenditure decisions were always centralized, but the centralization of pricing, advertising, and research and development decisions declined as the acquiring company's overall diversification increased. Stephen A. Allen argues that the category of multidivisional companies can be further subdivided according to the degree of divisional self-containment, the elaborateness and complexity of interdivisional coordinating devices, and the fineness of the company's divisionalization (1978). He offered some evidence that this subdivision is operational and that firms change their subcategory membership in explicable ways. Richard F. Vancil showed that the degree to which a company decentralizes functions to its divisions varies with its strategic choices (1979); broadly, the more diversified the strategy, the more functions are decentralized.

These studies demonstrate the adaptation of business organization to strategy, but they do not explain the genesis of the whole process—the environmental forces that control the choice of corporate strategy. Because the Wrigley-Rumelt classification of strategies is obviously correlated with diversification—even if not coterminous with it—one expects the causal forces of market structure to resemble those assigned to corporate diversification. That expectation holds, but the determinants of corporate strategy and structure do reveal something more.

Chandler analyzed the association between large companies' organizational structures and the market structures of their basic business (1962, chap. 7)—a reduced-form relation with the intermediary choice of corporate strategy solved out. He examined the 70 largest U.S. manufacturing enterprises in 1948, adducing a generous list of environmental traits associated with the choice between functional and MD organization. Some are simply the traits that cause firms to diversify their product lines. More interesting are the factors that specifically discourage such diversification because they imply scale diseconomies in top-level management coordination; if the firm's main activity is monolithic and imposes a heavy task of managerial coordination, it seems to have no entrepreneurial forces "left over" to swing into diversified activities that would lead to a MD structure. Chandler finds that the following factors discourage MD organization:

1. Customers and products that are few in number, making strategic decisions simple enough that top management needs no insulation from day-to-day

concerns in order to handle them effectively. Producer-good firms hence tend to eschew MD organization unless their customers are quite numerous and/or their production facilities geographically decentralized (e.g., metal containers).

2. Vertically related production processes that require intricate temporal coordination and hence a heavy volume of top-level tactical decisions. Backward vertical integration thus is negatively related to MD organization, whereas forward integration from manufacturing into distribution or the fabrication of heterogeneous final products encourages the MD structure. The pattern is consistent with the general proposition that materials become more heterogeneous as they pass through successive stages of fabrication.

3. Large absolute scales of efficient production and high capital requirements. If a firm must be "very large" and raise giant quantities of capital to carry out its base activity efficiently, it neither diversifies much nor becomes MD.[16] Diseconomies of scale in top-level coordination are suggested by this pattern.

4. The output of a production process can be heterogeneous without mandating a MD organization as long as the process itself remains fully integrated. Petroleum refiners, for example, have tended to retain functional organizations and to go MD through geographic rather than product-line divisions. The presence of a large amount of custom production promotes functional organization even though the output is heterogeneous.

MD organization, on the other hand, is encouraged by the standard causes of diversification—heavy investments in marketing and distribution systems, extensive resort to research activities or use of skilled technical personnel whose capacities can be spread to other activities, high levels of risk or cyclical instability in the base activity that promotes diversification through risk-spreading.

The subsequent country studies followed Chandler in confining themselves to an impressive review of the market-structure correlates of companies' organizational choices, but shifted their focus from the relation between market structure and corporate strategy. The patterns seem consistent with what Chandler found—both as to the specific industrial sectors associated with high and low diversification and the common structural traits attributed to these sectors. Channon argues that high concentration and the sheltering effect of entry barriers deter diversification (1973, pp. 90–91, 131), and Pavan notes that falling tariff barriers pose a competitive threat that promotes it (1972, p. VII–2). The European studies agree that family control discourages diversification because its maintenance tends to limit the firm's access to both financial and managerial resources.[17]

A statistical study of 125 Canadian companies by Caves, Michael E. Por-

---

[16]This pattern was noted among American companies by Rumelt (1974, pp. 131–35), among British companies by Channon (1973, pp. 68, 77), and among French ones by Dyas and Thanheiser (1976, pp. 207–10).

[17]Channon (1973, pp. 75–76); Dyas and Thanheiser (1976, pp. 78–79, 202); Pavan (1972, p. IV–54, chaps. 5, 7).

ter, and Michael Spence tested the association of strategic choice with many characteristics of the firm and its base industry, confirming statistically a number of the relations already observed (1980, chap. 12). For example, the related-product firms' base industries exhibit significantly higher levels of research outlays, labor skills, and professional and technical employment than the base industries of other firms. In addition, their analysis brings out the influence of differences in the riskiness of the firm's base industry. Single-product firms in Canada are notably free of competitive threats; compared with other strategic groups, their base industries show less exposure to international competition and penetration by multinational companies, more regional fragmentation, and more product differentiation.

We can note one recent development in the adaptation of organizational structure to market structure—the matrix organization recently surveyed by Stanley M. Davis and Paul R. Lawrence (1977) and not yet sanctified by systematic empirical study. The functional organization's main virtue is minimizing cost; the MD organization's is optimizing the firm's response to changing environmental demands (especially market conditions). The matrix organization tries for the best of both worlds by employing more than one organizational stratum, e.g., one in terms of functional departments and one in terms of product markets. The key consequence of matrix organizations is that some middle managers (e.g., plant managers) will have to answer to two bosses, and the bosses must thrash out conflicting demands or jointly supervised facilities as they appear. Although the matrix organization flies in the face of wisdom reaching back to Biblical injunction, Davis and Lawrence argue that it maximizes profits for companies that (1) must manage more than one key dimension of activity that can strongly affect the firm's performance (e.g., attaining technical efficiency and discerning the needs of particular customers) and (2) face a heavy load of information processing (because events are uncertain, the organization's task is complicated, and interdependencies among its parts are strong) (1977, chap. 2).[18] The matrix organization is especially promising where scale economies in production must be reconciled with fragmented and diverse product markets. This kind of organization was first identified in such sectors as aeronautics and appears to some degree in many multinational companies. Matrices can take several dimensions, and neither the incidence of the form nor its chief "objective" structural determinants have yet been charted. Indeed, one wonders whether the matrix form can be clearly distinguished from MD organizations with interdivisional coordinating devices.

---

[18]This case for the matrix organization indicates a key point in the business literature on MD organization that is not stressed by economists who have written on it. If the firm possesses substantial fixed factors that cannot be costlessly divested in the short run and faces a constantly varying set of market opportunities, it pays to allocate resources to forecasting those opportunities and optimizing the reallocation, refurbishing, expansion, or divestment of the fixed assets. The MD organization reallocates top-management resources to that purpose. The matrix organization can, among other things, diffuse that adaptation machinery downward through the organization.

The final link in the chain of relationships runs from the firm's organizational structure to its market behavior. The principal study to document this link directly is Joseph L. Bower's comparative analysis of investment projects undertaken by a single large MD firm (1970a). Bower holds that a company's top management approves or rejects projects but has little direct influence on how they get defined or on which ones are pushed through the firm's lower levels of decision-making to become claimants for top-executive approval. The plans cast up at these crucial early stages depend on how problems are perceived by persons who can propose investment projects as their solutions and whether middle managers find their interests served by providing "impetus"—putting their reputations on the line to support the project. Definition and impetus in turn depend on the "situational context" of these lower-level decision-makers. Context consists of organizational structure, meaning not only the organization-chart assignment of responsibilities and powers but also the organization's system of measuring and rewarding performance; it also includes an incrustation of history and random events. Middle managers given responsibility for a certain portion of the firm's activities will define problems in terms of their department's assigned goals and formulate solutions in terms of the instruments within their experience.[19] Top management cannot keep the character and composition of the projects that rise for their approval from being colored by structural context. However, top management *can* influence that structural context by means of the organization chart it establishes (and the power relations embodied in it) and the measurement/reward system it employs. In their nature Bower's cases cannot document the effect on market competition and performance of the coloration of investment projects. But since these projects determine the long-run context of a company's behavior in its markets, this influence seems impossible to dispute.

Bower contrasts his analysis with that of Richard M. Cyert and James G. March (1963). Although this survey cannot give recognition to the Carnegie-Mellon group's impressive body of work on organizational structure and behavior, we must note some of its limitations pointed out by Bower in relation to the topic discussed. One is that it places great emphasis on the cognitive process of problem solving, which is supposed to proceed mechanistically from the perception of job-defined discrepancies. Bower argues that the cognitive process "merely describes how a project gets defined" and that the surrounding contextual forces permit a mechanistic definition "only when there is no intervention from higher levels with more aggregate viewpoints" (1970a, pp. 67–68). He also objects that the Carnegie model neglects the role of impetus and that its analysis of power relations among decision centers within a business organization loses sight of the fact that the relative weight swung by different decision-makers itself is determined by organizational choices made by the firm's top decision-makers.

[19]This much of the analysis is anticipated by Yair Aharoni's study of the foreign investment decision process (1966, esp. chap. 6).

Studies of the relation between a business's strategy or organization and its market behavior have not gone beyond individual case studies. Michael S. Hunt stresses that differences in the market behavior of firms in the major home application industry could be explained by differing strategic choices (1972). Indirect but compelling evidence of the importance of strategic choice for market behavior appears in cross-industrial statistical studies, which show that industries seem typically to contain firms following diverse strategies (Porter, 1979) and that the more heterogeneous the strategic-group structure of an industry, the less fully is oligopolistic mutual dependence recognized (Howard H. Newman, 1978).

D. Normative Issues

The circuit of relations among market structure, corporate strategy and organization, and market behavior raises several normative issues about the efficiency of firms and the performance of markets. The most central of these concerns the choice of strategy and structure. The development of diversified strategies and MD structures was evidently an innovative response to changes in market opportunities. Although the strategies facilitated by the MD corporation may have their drawbacks in that they raise entry barriers to new competitors—an issue not dealt with in this paper—this invention clearly substituted organizational for market allocation of resources in many settings where society's resources could thereby be used more effectively. Given the distribution of corporate strategies and structures that we now observe in modern industrial countries, has this boundary between administration and the market been optimally located?

Business administration specialists have approached this question obliquely via the proposition that some one strategy or structure might be intrinsically better than any other. Bruce R. Scott, in particular, argues that MD structures are intrinsically more efficient than functional ones (1973) and that the normative problems of John Kenneth Galbraith's *New Industrial State* (1967)—information impacted in the technostructure, non-profit maximizing motivation, etc.—are strictly those of the functionally organized company. Does this mean that any group of activities that the firm can encompass are better organized in MD than functional form? that merging five functionally organized companies into a five-division MD enterprise will automatically reform allocations among the subtended functional departments? Scott seems to offer an unsupported affirmative answer. Rumelt clearly recognized that strategy should be matched to the opportunities inherent in the firm's environment (1974). His first attempt to control for the firm's opportunities was not successful (1974); subsequently he developed a procedure of comparing each firm's actual profit rate to a synthetic profit rate that is a weighted average of aggregate profits for the industries in which this firm operates, using its own distribution of activities for weights (1977). The best-performing firms, on this test, are the single-business firms, and the poorest performers the unrelated-product group. *Without* controlling for industry mix, the best-performing firms would be those related-product firms that link all their activities around a common core skill; but they do not significantly outperform their competitors, on average. Rumelt's findings suggest the hypothesis that a firm doing very well in its base activity carries on with more of the same, whereas less successful enterprises seek their fortunes elsewhere (with results depending on the transferability of their talents).

Caves, Porter, and Spence employ a different approach designed to test the effect of *optimal* strategic choice on performance (1980, chap. 12). Using many characteristics of firms' base industries, they develop a model that yields an estimate of the probability that a given firm should be in each of the four strategic categories (set out in TABLE 1). They then regress a measure of each firm's profits on numerous control variables and on the probability that it should have chosen the strategy that it in fact employs. They indeed find a significant positive influence of the probability of correct choice for dominant-product and related-product firms (unrelated-product firms were too few and had to be dropped). The positive regression coefficient for the single-product group is not significant, however, suggesting that the single-product group includes both "mature" single-product firms and adolescents that will grow into other strategies.

Just as correct strategic choice should improve economic performance, so should an organizational structure that is correct given the strategy that the firm has chosen to follow. Two recent studies test this hypothesis. In both cases the control for strategy is an indirect one, provided by restricting the sample and/or including controls for differences in the firm's opportunities. Both classify organizational structures not just as functional or multidivisional, but in a more elaborate classification derived from Williamson and Narottam Bhargava that includes holding companies, firms in transition to MD organization, and "corrupt" MD forms in which top management is still preoccupied with operating problems (1972).[20] Peter S. Steer and John R. Cable conclude that the functional organizations perform best when the firm is based in a process industry or an uncertain environment, but otherwise a MD form is preferred (1978). Henry Ogden Armour and David J. Teece structured their analysis of oil companies to emphasize the diffusion of the MD innovation throughout the industry (1978). They find that during the 1955–68 period MD firms were significantly more profitable, but by 1969 MD had been adopted wherever appropriate, and the difference in profits had disappeared.

Other studies using different approaches have found that firms' profits are impaired—and the social allocation of resources worsened—if organizational structure is improperly matched to strategy or if the elements of the structure are improperly combined. Joan Woodward (1965), discussed below, seems to

---

[20]This classification itself incorporates performance judgments directly, and so a test of profitability in relation to these organization structures must take this potential circularity into account. Both studies mentioned in the text deal adequately with the problem.

have innovated the systematic empirical testing of the hypothesis that a firm performs better if its structure matches the requisites of its environment. Stopford and Wells found evidence that firms whose overseas operations are organizationally mismatched to their domestic structures earn lower profits abroad than those with consistent structures (1972, pp. 79–80). An elaborate study by Jay W. Lorsch and Stephen A. Allen turns on the proposition that the firm that has rationally chosen a multidivisional or a functional (vertically integrated) structure must then optimize the inputs needed to coordinate and integrate its divisions (1973). They find that the less successful diversified companies in their small sample undertook too much coordination; the less successful vertically integrated companies too little; but they recognize that the errors could just as easily have gone the other direction. Finally, K.R. Srinivasa Murthy finds that the incentive structure of the firm's executive compensation must accord with its strategic choice (1974). He investigates how tightly the top executive's compensation is keyed to the firm's short-run performance (return to book equity, growth in earnings per share). If most disturbances faced by the firm are exogenous, as for a vertically integrated dominant-product firm, there is little point to inflicting risk on the president by tying his salary to swings in the firm's fate. On the other hand, the incentive value of profit-leveraged compensation can be realized in a related-product or unrelated-product firm where the top executive's primary role is long-range planning. The 53 companies sampled by Murthy generally match the hypothesized pattern, but the match is clearly better for the more profitable ones. Interestingly, the overall level of top-executive compensation does not vary with strategy.

Doubts have been voiced about the vaunted effectiveness of the MD organization, echoing the more general concerns heard from economists about the efficiency of the large, highly diversified company.[21] Dennis C. Mueller argues that the large MD firm becomes ripe for growth-maximizing managerial behavior (1972), and Henry G. Grabowski and Mueller found suggestive statistical evidence that the mature company (judged by age of the company and of its principal products) experienced a lower incremental return on its investments than did younger companies (1975). Also, Bower (1970b) and the European studies stress that a holding company is a poor approximation to an MD structure and unlikely to impose rational allocation of resources upon its controlled firms as would a MD company on its component divisions.

These studies of strategy, structure, and performance nearly all agree on two propositions: (1) correctly matching strategy to opportunities and structure to strategy increases a firm's profits and presumably increases the efficiency with which society's resources are used; (2) certain strategies and structures have dif-

---

[21]We note the considerable number of papers by economists who sought to determine whether corporations that have engaged in extensive conglomerate expansion are more or less profitable as a result; for a survey, see Peter O. Steiner (1975, chap. 8). Many of these papers pay little attention to the opportunity set of the diversifying firm and the very subtle problem of finding an appropriate control group of comparison.

fused as innovations, with large firms progressively moving toward choices that make the best of their opportunities.

II. TECHNOLOGY
AND ORGANIZATIONAL DESIGN

Running parallel to the analysis of corporate strategy and structure is an independent line of inquiry, carried out by students of industrial sociology and organizational behavior, into the relation between the technology of a production unit and certain detailed features of its organization chart. Corporate strategy is invisible in this literature, as indeed are the broad organizational divisions of the enterprise. The hypotheses developed and tested deal with the relation between market structure and organizational structure. But the spotlight now shines on details farther down the organization chart—how the span of control of each supervisor, the number of supervisory hierarchies, and the flexibility of these hierarchical arrangements respond to differing tasks of the organization. This literature hence addresses the production function of organizational design: how the organization's structure is best adapted to performing a given task in a given market environment. It complements the strategy-structure literature described above while sharing a common form of hypothesis: market structure determines organizational structure, which in turn affects market behavior and performance.

A. Economic Theory

This organizational production function has received some attention in economic theory. Although the theoretical contributions are empirically more tantalizing than informative, they should be juxtaposed with the evidence if only to promote future integrative efforts. A staple of the literature of public administration is a model that relates the span of control (s, number of employees supervised by each supervisor) and the number of hierarchical levels (k) to an organization's total number of employees (n). Thus, $n = (s^k - 1)/(s - 1)$. If s is taken as given, the formula explains how k must vary with n. Certain questions naturally occur to an economist who contemplates this model:

    1. Why should the span of control not be considered a policy variable, to be optimized for the technical and market environment of each organization? Not much economic theory addresses optimal spans of control directly, but a good deal is indirectly relevant. Harvey Leibenstein has elaborately investigated the behavior of employees performing under incomplete (output cannot be specified) employment contracts (1976, chaps. 6–10). Armen A. Alchian and Harold Demsetz emphasize the productivity of supervision for monitoring contracts and curbing the opportunism that would otherwise limit human participation in efficient cooperation endeavors (1972). It is also pointed out by Williamson, Mi-

chael L. Wachter, and Jeffrey E. Harris that many jobs are idiosyncratic (1975); their content cannot be determined in advance through a complete contract, nor are spot contracts viable, and so a supervisory relationship becomes the efficient choice. These considerations are closely related to the optimal structuring of the employment contract, e.g., the combination of piece-work and straight-time rates to be offered (Joseph E. Stiglitz, 1975). The interrelation between organizational structure and compensation has been developed by James A. Mirrlees on the assumption that risk-averse individuals behave to maximize individual utility and not some goal of the firm (1976). Spans of control turn out to depend on supervisors' levels of risk aversion (constant, increasing, or decreasing) and to be determined jointly with the structure of compensation. The model is extended to multiple levels of hierarchy.

2. How does the optimal span of control relate to the flow of information within the organization? The theory of teams investigates the case in which members of a coalition share common preferences but have access to diverse information (see Jakob Marschak and Roy Radner[1972]). Certain conclusions follow about the optimal amount of information to be shared and about efficient coordinating devices for sharing information or decentralizing decisions.

3. How does the multiplication of hierarchical levels, as an organization grows, affect the organization's efficient overall size? Williamson shows formally how control loss and bounded rationality within a hierarchical organization can limit its efficient size (1967). Without any limitation placed on the firm's size by factor supplies, technology, or market demand, size is nonetheless limited by the inefficiency of expanding levels of hierarchy because (by assumption) those farther up in the hierarchy are paid more, and the control loss occurring at each hierarchical level is cumulative (that is, not offset by adding higher levels). Mirrlees's model similarly implies a limitation on firm size (1976). Guillermo A. Calvo and Stanislaw Wellisz (1978) drop Williamson's assumption about the relation between pay and hierarchical position and instead allow employees at each level to optimize effort (and thus determine their pay) contingent on the process by which they are supervised. Whether or not the optimal size of the firm is bounded depends on the nature of that process.

B. Technology and Organization: Empirical Evidence

These theoretical contributions are striking and insightful, but they do not easily yield testable hypotheses about the structures of actual organizations. Therefore we pick up the inductive empirical literature that started two decades ago from the insight that optimal organization is not a constant, but rather a set of parameters that depend on the organization's tasks, the stability of its environment, etc. Tom Burns and G. M. Stalker dramatized the issue by contrasting firms in a highly dynamic industry (electronics) with those in a stable environment (textile machinery) (1961). The latter firms chose a "mechanistic" system of management, with well-defined responsibilities and specialist functions laid down from the top. Electronics firms employed an "organic" approach with ill-defined hierarchies and responsibilities and little stable content to any individual's job. In an organic firm, changes coming from any direction generally modify (and are expected to modify) everybody's responsibilities. When something disturbs a mechanistic firm, it characteristically creates a new group to deal with the problem and leaves other responsibilities unchanged. Similarly, William R. Dill argued in an influential case study that the delegation of authority in a managerial hierarchy depends on the structure of the firm's environment, access to information about that environment, and managerial perceptions about the meaning of the information (1958).

These insights came together into a systematic line of research with the publication of Joan Woodward's *Industrial Organization: Behaviour and Control* (1965) (see also, 1970). Woodward's study of one hundred firms and plants in the southeast-Essex area began from the hypothesis that successful firms (successful relative to their competitors) share common organizational traits that will reveal the vaunted universal best organization. But she found that the best-performing firms were quite diverse organizationally, as were the worst-performing. Then began the search for a correlation between the unit's organization and its technology or task. The initial hypothesis was transformed: the best-performing units are those using organizational structures most appropriate to their tasks.

Woodward's procedure for detecting links between technology and organization was largely ad hoc but contains threads of a model. She eventually arrived at a taxonomy of production systems dichotomized between assembly and process technology; the former is divided into small-batch or custom production, large batch, and mass production; the latter is divided into batch and continuous-flow production. As we move from customized assembly to continuous-flow processes, the decision-making autonomy best delegated to the primary operatives diminishes and the optimal span of control changes at various levels of the organization. The span for top management widens as the pacing of production becomes more built into the technology, but the span of control of middle management shrinks as technology grows more complex. On balance, Woodward concludes that the ratio of managerial to total personnel increases along her scale, with the size of the organization held constant (1965, chap. 4).

The mechanistic-organic distinction of Burns and Stalker does not change monotonically along Woodward's typology, however. The largest spans of control for first-line supervisors come in the large-batch and mass-assembly firms, where relationships with operatives are least informal and intimate. The line/ staff distinction is most fully developed here, and these firms find it easiest to produce an organization chart. Fluid, organic management systems appear at the ends of Woodward's spectrum, where either the heterogeneity of the output or the complexity of the technology is great (Woodward, 1965, pp. 60–65; Tom Kynaston Reeves and Barry A. Turner, 1972).

Woodward tests her hypothesis about performance by cross-classifying firms by technology and degree of success (1965, pp. 68–72). The highly successful tend to cluster tightly around the organizational characteristics best suited to their technologies; the poor performers are more dispersed.[22] Thus, technology appears to determine the optimal structure of an organization.

Woodward's insights have generated a large literature that refines and retests her propositions and seeks to place some of them alongside competing hypotheses. This body of material makes somewhat frustrating reading for an economist. On the one hand, the authors deserve great credit for attempting to explain features of economic organization that have suffered almost total neglect from professional economists. On the other hand, the authors are addressing problems of optimizing behavior by the firm, although they are largely unfamiliar with the methods devised by economic theory for dealing with the firm's decisions. As a result, parameters determined outside the firm are treated as decision variables and vice versa, and many asserted results become unacceptable. Empirically, some bizarre samples are drawn that mix branch plants with independent firms, service establishments with manufacturing companies, and government departments with profit-seeking enterprises.[23] I shall report what conclusions seem sound from these studies and forego cirticism except in a few strategic cases.

Some studies replicate Woodward's analysis or propose direct extensions or modifications of it. William L. Zwerman (1970) repeated Woodward's procedure using a sample of 55 firms in the Minneapolis–St. Paul area, drawn once again from a wide range of manufacturing industries. Like many subsequent studies, Zwerman shrinks Woodward's typology of production structures somewhat—in this case to small batch, large batch or mass production, and process technologies. He confirms most of her results while employing somewhat improved controls for other variables that might affect them. Her association of mechanistic management with large-batch and mass-production technologies is confirmed and shown to survive after control for the size of the organization and any divorce of ownership from management of the enterprise. There is no relation between the mechanistic/organic management distinction and company size except for some suggestion of a mechanistic tilt for firms employing more than one thousand. Owner-controlled firms lean toward organic management, but there is no tendency for management-controlled firms to choose a mechanistic style.[24] Zwerman confirmed Woodward's finding that top-management spans

---

[22]Woodward supports this proposition only with charts for selected organizational traits, so the robustness of the finding is hard to judge.

[23]A particularly unfortunate victim is the ambitious series of studies by the University of Aston group; for a critique, see Howard E. Aldrich (1972).

[24]Zwerman (1970, chap. 3). Zwerman hypothesized that the controlling owner would choose a narrower span of control at the top in order to maximize his knowledge and control of his subordinates, and confirmed this in his sample (1970, chap. 5). Because owner-control tends to diminish along the technology scale, however, the respective influence on control spans of technology and owner-management is not clear (either for Zwerman or Woodward, who did not address the implications of an ownership-control split).

of control enlarge as we proceed from unit or small-batch to process technologies, but her nonmonotonic relation for first-line supervisors (broader spans for mass assembly technologies) was not confirmed. Zwerman found (1970, chap. 4), as did Woodward, that the proportion of supervisory personnel and the number of levels of management hierarchy both rise as we move along the technology scale. Zwerman finds some support for the hypothesis that successful firms have chosen better suited organizational arrangements than have other firms; it is not clear, though, that he follows Woodward in defining success relative to competitors in the firm's chief industry.

Woodward's model leaves little room for a nation's cultural and legal institutions to affect the firm's organization, and Zwerman's replication on U.S. firms of her findings for a U.K. population supports this negative implication. Charles J. McMillan *et al.* addressed this issue directly by drawing two transnational samples (U.K.–Canada, U.K.–U.S.) of firms or plants matched by base industry and size (1973). They found no difference in the extent of functional specialization, formalization of role definitions in the managerial hierarchy, or the autonomy of decision-making at various levels. The only difference was more formal documentation—more things get written down—in North American firms. J. H. K. Inkson *et al.* undertook a similar study that reached the same conclusion (1970).

Woodward's election of technology types as key determinants of organization has met general acceptance, but not all have agreed with her specific predictions. Edward Harvey argues that technology types should run from the specific (unitary, turning out a fixed menu of product) to the diffuse (heterogeneous, producing a variable and/or changing mix of products) (1968). Specific and unitary technologies should require more levels of authority, a higher ratio of managers and supervisors to total personnel (Woodward would agree with these propositions), more specialization of subunits, and more formal definition of roles and procedures (Woodward would disagree with the last, for process industries). Cross-tabulations of the organizational traits of the 43 firms sampled by Harvey seem to conform to his amended technology scale, although no formal tests of significance are used. A composite score on the four aspects of organization mentioned above is strongly related to the technology scale but unrelated to the sizes of the sampled firms. Harvey's technology scale is somewhat unsatisfying because it assumes that the static variability of a firm's output mix is highly correlated with the dynamic turnover of new products—an assumption one expects to hold for the industries Harvey chose but not necessarily for all samples. Robert T. Keller, John W. Slocum, and Gerald I. Susman (1974) sought to resolve the key empirical difference between Woodward and Harvey on whether continuous-process firms run to organic or mechanistic management. Among a sample of continuous-process firms, they found organic management to be associated with successful firms, but no association between the turnover of products and factors indicating organic management (lack of impersonal hierarchy, presence of group decision-making, lack of formal rules for decision-making). Thus, they support Woodward against Harvey. Ample room remains for further work because all these studies are less than rigorous in their hypotheses and open to some criticism on their controls for the size and industry mix of the sampled firms.

An example of the microtheoretical structure needed in this literature is supplied by William G. Ouchi, who proposes that the alignment of organizational structures to the technological situation depends on how managers meter their employees' activities (1977). Methods of control vary, depending on whether or not the activity's output is measurable and whether management has specific knowledge of the transformation process. With management informed on the transformation process but unable to measure the output, control rests on monitoring the behavior of the primary operators. In the opposite situation output norms can be set. Where management lacks both kinds of information, it rationally buys high-quality inputs and hopes for the best.[25] Ouchi tested these propositions on data for a sample of department stores. A store with more horizontal subdivision of departments or more vertical levels of hierarchy should resort more to output-related controls because direct observation of behavior (i.e., the transformation process) becomes more costly. This prediction is not fully supported, but among groups of employees Ouchi does find that output measures are used where the transformation process is less well known and that training of employees (as a form of behavior control) and managers' access to output measures are inversely related.

An issue discussed more extensively than fruitfully in this literature is the relative influence of size and technology on business organization. The trouble is immediately apparent to an economist: Given input prices, any technology has its own well-defined scale-economy characteristics, which will surely influence the sizes of establishments using it (if not determine them entirely). Because size and technology are collinear, the researcher must either go after their joint influence or use a fine hand in sampling to hold one constant while letting the other vary. Before Woodward, analysts of organizations had presumed a relation between the size of a functional organization and the height and breadth of its best managerial hierarchy, and many empirical studies of the relation had been carried out.[26] Post-Woodward researchers have found that her relation between technology and organization tends to weaken or disappear in any heterogeneous sample of establishments (or whatever) that vary widely in size of unit, and the authors of the Aston studies (e.g., D. S. Pugh et al. [1969]) generally conclude that Woodward's findings hold for only small establishments or enterprises. This

---

[25]Ouchi's research comes closer than most of this literature to addressing issues raised in the economic theory of agency and hierarchy (1977). Also see Ouchi's extension of this analysis to multiple levels of hierarchy (1978).

[26]See John R. Kimberly's critical survey, which concludes rhetorically, "Does size determine structure? Does structure determine size? Or, perhaps more fundamentally, are these even the right questions to ask?" (1976).

conclusion was not supported by one of the better size-*vs.*-technology studies, Peter M. Blau *et al.* (1976), who observe correctly that Woodward's technology scale is really a list of categories and not a monotonic ordering. Organizational variables—horizontal subdivision of the organization, number of vertical hierarchies, extent of functional specialization, width of spans of control, etc.—are all correlated with size (for a sample of 110 New Jersey manufacturing plants), but none shows any relation to a linearized score based on Woodward's technology scale except for the smaller plants. With the nonmonotonic character of her scale recognized, however, most of her conclusions come through.[27] It is regrettable that the authors of these studies have tended to see technology and scale as competitive rather than additive explanations of organizational structure. No samples have been drawn to isolate size variations for a given technology (or industry) or technology differences for a given size of unit.

A more fruitful line of research has tested Max Weber's proposition that organizations can pursue coherent purposes either by centralizing authority (controlling the substance of decisions as they get made) or by structuring the activities of persons within the hierarchy (prescribing decision rules through specialization, standardization, formalization, or high vertical spans of control). The prediction translates comfortably into economic analysis of the organization of firms; the proportion of these control techniques should evidently depend on the nature and frequency of events requiring decisions. The Aston study has not confirmed a trade-off between centralization and formalization; however, that study's scoring system, when applied to a sample of units varying widely in their independence of higher authority, could not be expected to produce satisfactory results. John Child (1972) replicated the Aston procedures on a carefully selected sample of companies in Britain and tended to support Weber's hypothesis.

C. Effect of Competition

The studies reported so far deal mainly with the "production set" for organizing a firm or division—how to find the most effective organization, given the technology of the unit's activity. Its organizational structure can also be affected by the market processes surrounding the unit, and the influence of competition and uncertainty have both received a good deal of attention.

The central hypotheses in Jeffrey Pfeffer and Huseyin Leblebici (1973) flow from the economic argument that a competitive environment requires tighter coordination and more shipshape use of the firm's resources, while in its absence the additional profits can be taken partly in the utility derived from organizational slack. Thus, a competitive firm should choose less horizontal sepa-

---

[27]An interesting incidental result of Blau *et al.* is that the introduction of computers affects organization in a way similar to the use of process technology, raising average skill levels and narrowing the spans of first-level supervisors (1976); but it does not have the effect sometimes predicted of reducing the horizontal subdivision and number of vertical hierarchies in the organization.

ration into departments and more hierarchical layers of supervisors. It should demand more frequent reporting and specify decision-making procedures more fully in advance. It should restrict the resources under discretionary control of department heads and depend more on oral communication (writing it down takes too long). Pfeffer and Leblebici (1973) recognize that these hypotheses interact with Woodward's; diverse and changing technologies are a countervailing force for decentralization and horizontal differentiation, so some parts of her technology-structure relation should be more evident in less competitive environments. For a sample of small manufacturing firms (for which size is uncorrelated with the extent of competition), they find competition (measured from the chief executive's perception—a worrisome practice) indeed to be positively related to advance specification of decision procedures, proportion of oral communication, and review of performance. The interaction with Woodward's hypotheses also emerges clearly. For example, department heads' ceilings on discretionary spending are positively and significantly correlated with the number of product and process changes only in noncompetitive environments; the same holds for the horizontal decentralization of the company and the absence of advance specification of decision procedures.[28]

Pfeffer's and Leblebici's finding that competition is inimical to written communication and performance review accords with a study by Pradip N. Khandwalla, which posits that sophisticated formal management controls may not pay their way where quick competitive response is necessary (1973a). The intensity of competition (price, product, marketing) rated subjectively by executives is correlated with measures of the delegation of authority and the use of sophisticated controls in nine decision areas, and with a measure of the selectivity of delegation and control usage. The use of controls actually shows a significant positive relation to competition overall, but this turns out to ride on product competition alone (their relation to the intensity of price competition is negative and insignificant), and product competition similarly encourages the delegation of authority (which has an insignificant negative relation to price competition). The selectivity with which controls are used is positively and significantly related to the intensity of competition (all dimensions) and positively but not significantly related to the selectivity of delegation. Thus, the speedy and selective response necessary to compete in product dimensions turns out to qualify Khandwalla's hypothesis, but generally it gains strong support. Broadly similar results emerge from a paper by Jack L. Simonetti and F. Glenn Boseman, who conclude from a study of Italian and Mexican companies that firms in competitive markets perform better if they employ more decentralized decision-mak-

---

[28]Contrary to Pfeffer and Leblebici, Johannes M. Pennings treats competition as an incentive for relatively loose control (1975; 1976). His sample of branch brokerage offices of a single company seems to confirm this. However, one wonders whether, within a company, the causation might not be reversed; the better performing offices are given a longer leash by top management.

ing structures, whereas this trait is unrelated to the performance of firms in non-competitive markets (1975).[29]

Another arresting analysis of competition and organization emerges from Michael A. DuBick's study of 72 newspapers (1978). The differentiation of their organizational structures (number of departments, unevenness of department sizes) is positively related to the intensity of competition (a two-firm concentration ratio), after account is taken of their sizes and various aspects of the differentiation of their urban environments. Competition induces a significant increase in the number of departments; also, the organizations of newspapers in competitive markets respond more sensitively to the degrees of differentiation found in their environments than do those of noncompetitive papers.

The firm's autonomy or competitive vulnerability should influence a very different aspect of its organization—the composition of its board of directors. Pfeffer argues a co-optation hypothesis: when the firm is beholden to an external power center which it can neither absorb nor be absorbed by, it awards a "say" on the board of directors (1972). Firms with larger capital requirements should have more outside directors and more representatives of financial institutions. Firms based in regional industries should appoint more outside directors affiliated with local power centers. The total number of directors should increase with needs for external funds and the presence of regulation as well as with the firm's size (because the bigger and more diversified firm has a wider range of impacts on the community). A sample of 80 large nonfinancial companies provides confirmation for essentially all of these hypotheses (not everything is quite significant statistically), and firms using the "wrong" proportion of inside directors (i.e., deviants from the regression plane) tend to be less profitable.[30]

D. Effect of Environmental Uncertainty

Although the effect of uncertainty on organization had been recognized in the organic-mechanistic distinction of Tom Burns and G. M. Stalker (1961), Paul R. Lawrence and Jay W. Lorsch advanced the analysis greatly with their specific and subtle treatment of uncertainty's effects on an organization's differentiation and integration (1967). Whereas Woodward emphasized uncertainty in the production department (1965), Lawrence and Lorsch are concerned with un-

---

[29]Simonetti and Boseman compile not only an index of economic performance (profits, growth of sales) but also one of behavioral performance that chiefly registers employee's contentment. Contentment always increases with decentralization, but economic performance does not. For a similar but less satisfactory study see Anant R. Negandhi and Bernard C. Riemann (1973).

[30]Michael Patrick Allen suggests (and confirms) that directoral interlocks grew less localized over a 35-year period in which the average large company surely found itself subject to more national than localized disturbances and threats (1974). Otherwise, Allen's empirical conclusions diverge somewhat from Pfeffer's.

certainties facing all departments (production, sales, research, etc.) and in particular the problems of integrating these departments when uncertainty levels differ considerably among them. Empirically, they compare better-performing with worse-performing firms in a given industry as well as the organization of better-performing firms in different industries. The more that uncertainty levels faced by a firm's departments differ, the more differentiated those departments' organizational traits should be (formality of organization, goal orientation, time horizons, style of personal interaction, etc.). Lawrence and Lorsch find that the better-performing firms have matched the organizational traits of each department more effectively to the demands of its environment[31] and also attuned the relative importance of their departments better to the importance (for the firm's objectives) of uncertainty stemming from various environmental corners (1967, chap. 2).[32] The more differentiated are departments, however, the more resources must be devoted to integrating their efforts to the performance of their joint task; the better performing organizations also distinguished themselves in seeming to allocate the right amount of resources to the integrating function.[33]

The research design developed by Lawrence and Lorsch (1967) for the functionally organized firm was applied by Lorsch and Allen (1973) to the multidivisional firm. Once more, they find that the companies performing better have suited the structures of their division more aptly to the uncertainties of their environments. Given the differentiation (defined as before) of the divisions of the MD firm, the conclusion again emerges that the commitment of resources to integrative effort must be optimized. The conclusions of the two studies parallel each other quite extensively and lead the authors to a rich "contingency theory of complex organizations" (1973, chap. 8), i.e., that optimal organization depends in a complex but predictable way on the firm's market environment. Nontheless, I am not convinced that the problem of differentiation *vs.* integration translates from the functional to the MD organization as simply as Lorsch and Allen imply. In the MD organization, the fineness with which activities are divided among divisions is itself a policy variable—one that should be optimized jointly with the differentiation of those divisions and the integrating effort ap-

---

[31]The same conclusion seems to emerge from Khandwalla (1973b), although the conceptual basis of his study is rather murky.

[32]Lawrence's and Lorsch's measure of environmental uncertainty (subjectively, from top-managers' responses to a questionnaire) has been criticized by W. Kirk Downey, Don Hellriegel, and John W. Slocum for its low correlation with objective measures of short-term uncertainty (e.g., number of competitors, volatility of price or sales) (1975). It is not clear which group is closer to the ideal concept of the *ex ante* probability distribution of outcomes.

[33]Lawrence and Lorsch give some evidence of the resources committed to integration, but their measure of "integration" is *ex post* contentment of managers with the achieved state of coordination. Integration in this sense does not vary among better performing companies in different industries, although differentiation differs substantially. For a study that identifies a specific resource commitment to integration, see Anders Edström and Jay R. Galbraith (1977).

plied in coordinating them, in order to maximize the value of the firm's strategy. The findings of Lorsch and Allen imply that integrative effort should be optimized for any given degree of differentiation of divisions, but the joint decision variable—degree of subdivision—does not receive parallel attention.

Lawrence and Lorsch show that uncertainty affects not only the differentiation of the organization's departments but also the structure of those departments and the character of the devices used to integrate them (1967). Pennings drew a blank in his attempt to associate external uncertainty with the absence of bureaucracy in brokerage-house offices (1975). He explains that failure (1977) on lines consistent with Lawrence and Lorsch—that the firm may respond to uncertainty not by adopting a more flexible organization (as Burns and Stalker [1961] had suggested) but by creating organizational buffers to fend it off.

III. CONCLUSIONS

The goals of this paper, mainly positive and methodological, are best stated in terms of the structuralist paradigm of industrial organization. We have been concerned with the way in which the firm's rational selection of a corporate strategy and an internal organizational structure responds to the market structure surrounding it and with the effect of those choices on the firm's behavior, and hence on the structure and performance of markets. Although economists have made important contributions to our knowledge of these relations, this survey has concentrated on evidence from other fields—business history, business policy, and organizational behavior.

Two symmetrical types of conclusions result. First, economists have something to learn from this literature. For example, there is strong evidence to support the following propositions: The structures of markets have been affected by the organizational options open to firms. The productivity with which resources are used depends on whether or not firms make the best choices of strategy and business organization, given the market and technological environments in which they operate. Innovations in business organization have arisen in the United States and diffused through the industrial world. They have enlarged the feasible scope of the corporation but have not liberated it from diseconomies in the top-level coordination of diffuse activities. Diversification is not, in the long run, a continuous process because organizational choices are discrete. Economists' vague suspicion that competition is the enemy of sloth can be specifically documented in the effect of competition (and environmental uncertainty) on the decision-making structures and control devices used by firms.

The second conclusion is that economists have something to offer in this line of research. I shall not let professional modesty blur an important conclusion: well-trained professional economists could have carried out many of the research projects cited in this paper more proficiently than did their authors, who were less effectively equipped by their own disciplines.[34] If one accepts the weak postulate that the firm is a purposive organization maximizing some objective function, it follows that its strategic and structural choice represents a constrained optimization problem. My reading is that students of business organization with disciplinary bases outside of economics would accept that proposition but have lacked the tools to follow its blueprint. Constrained-maximization problems are mother's milk to the well-trained economist. However, economists' preconceptions have steered them away from business strategy and organization as an area of research. Business organization involves in essence selecting the right point on a production function, but "production function" for the economist evokes only the harmonies of labor, capital, and land. Business organization is concerned with assigning responsibilities to persons and evaluating and rewarding their performance—matters that turn on individuals' optimizing behavior. The ingenuity lavished on individual optimizing behavior in marriage, procreation, and church attendance has not been matched by attention to persons' adaptation to an organizational hierarchy.

There are many opportunities for the logical extension of economic research into the questions covered in this survey, and they range widely from pure theory, to empirical and statistical research. Here are a few tentative suggestions:

1. The standard taxonomy of corporate strategies has proved fruitful, but is certainly incomplete. For instance, the alternative strategies available to firms directly competing in a given market often seem to differ in many ways other than the extent of their diversification and vertical integration. We must determine what other families of strategic choices are widely represented in industrial markets, what conditions lead firms to select them, and what consequences they hold for firm's organization and market behavior.

2. Industrial organization economists have only begun to incorporate strategic choice into their analyses of market structure, conduct, and performance. The central hypothesis considered to date is that the more heterogeneous are the strategies chosen by an industry's oligopolistic members, the less effectively monopolistic will be the bargain they reach. The quality of performance associated with particular strategies could be investigated more effectively, and the performance dimensions should reach beyond allocative efficiency, the sole one addressed so far.

3. Even more incomplete is the taxonomy of organizational structures. The prototypes of personal, functional, and multidivisional organization do not

[34]The shortcomings include both errors and omissions. In business administration, the field of business policy has downplayed the influence of market environment on the firm's strategic choices and has sometimes fostered the delusive notion that a "best strategy" does not depend sensitively on the firm's market opportunity set. Students of organizational behavior have recognized the dependence of optimal organization on the environment ("contingency" in their parlance). But they have dealt too casually with the theoretical complexities of optimizing organizational structures, have treated the firm's objectives unclearly, and have embraced research designs that lack controls for differing opportunity sets and objectives.

necessarily exhaust the possible alternatives. And the structural options for organizing and transmitting information, or appraising and rewarding performance have hardly been identified as prototypes, let alone tested for their optimal selection. Economic theorists have recently made some arresting contributions in this area; can theory and evidence be brought closer together?

4. There lurks in the literature on organizational behavior an unfamiliar but fundamentally economic notion of an organizational production function. The "output" is the ability to reallocate the firm's complement of fixed factors (especially its personnel, contractually committed and with fixed endowments of skills) in response to unexpected disturbances. "More output" means faster adjustment to a new optimal configuration of activities, following an unexpected change. The inputs are resources devoted to collecting and analyzing information, coordinating agents to whom different tasks are assigned, etc. Can theorists clarify this concept of resources committed to a capacity to adapt to disturbances and indicate the specific kinds of optimization that it implies?

REFERENCES

1. ABELL, DEREK F. *Defining the business: The starting point of strategic planning.* Englewood Cliffs, N.J.: Prentice-Hall, 1980

2. AHARONI, YAIR. *The foreign investment decision process.* Boston: Division of Research, Graduate School of Business Administration, Harvard University, 1966.

3. ALCHIAN, ARMEN A. and DEMSETZ, HAROLD. "Production, Information Costs, and Economic Organization," *Amer. Econ. Rev.,* Dec. 1972, *62*(5), pp. 777–95.

4. ALDRICH, HOWARD E. "Technology and Organizational Structure: A Reexamination of the Findings of the Aston Group," *Admin. Science Q.,* March 1972, *17*(1), pp. 26–43.

5. ALFORD, BERNARD W. E. "The Chandler Thesis—Some General Observations," In HANNAH, LESLIE, ed. (1976), pp. 52–70.

6. ALLEN, MICHAEL PATRICK. "The Structure of Interorganizational Elite Corporation: Interlocking Corporate Directorates," *Amer. Soc. Rev.,* June 1974, *39*(3), pp. 393–406.

7. ALLEN, STEPHEN A. "Organizational Choices and General Management Influence Networks in Divisionalized Companies," *Acad. Management J.,* Sept. 1978, *21*(3), pp. 341–65.

8. ANDREWS, KENNETH R. *The concept of corporate strategy.* Homewood, Ill.: Dow Jones-Irwin, 1971.

9. ANSOFF, H. ICOR. *Corporate strategy: An analytic approach to business policy for growth and expansion.* New York: McGraw-Hill, 1965.

10. ARMOUR, HENRY OGDEN and TEECE, DAVID J. "Organizational Struc-

ture and Economic Performance: A Test of the Multidivisional Hypothesis," *Bell J. Econ.,* Spring 1978, *9*(1), pp. 106–22.

11. BLAU, PETER M., et al. "Technology and Organization in Manufacturing," *Admin. Science Quart.,* March 1976, *21*(1), pp. 20–40.

12. BOWER, JOSEPH L. *Managing the resource allocation process: A study of corporate planning and investment.* Boston: Division of Research, Graduate School of Business Administration, Harvard University, 1970a.

13. ———. "Planning within the Firm," *Amer. Econ. Rev.,* May 1970[b], *60*(2), pp. 186–94.

14. BUCKLEY, PETER J. and CASSON, MARK. *The future of the multinational enterprise.* New York: Holmes and Meier, 1976.

15. BURNS, TOM and STALKER, G.M. *The management of innovation.* London: Tavistock, 1961.

16. CALVO, GUILLERMO A. and WELLISZ, STANISLAW. "Supervision, Loss of Control, and the Optimum Size of the Firm," *J. Polit. Econ.,* Oct. 1978, *86*(5), pp. 943–52.

17. CAVES, RICHARD E.; PORTER, MICHAEL E. and SPENCE, MICHAEL. *Competition in the open economy: A model applied to Canada.* Cambridge: Harvard University Press, 1980.

18. CHANDLER, ALFRED D., JR. *Strategy and structure: Chapters in the history of the industrial enterprise.* Cambridge: M.I.T. Press, 1962.

19. ———. *The visible hand: The managerial revolution in American business.* Cambridge: Harvard University Press, Belknap Press, 1977.

20. CHANNON, DEREK F. *The strategy and structure of British enterprise.* Boston: Division of Research, Graduate School of Business Administration, Harvard University, 1973.

21. CHILD, JOHN. "Organization Structure and Strategies of Control: A Replication of the Aston Study," *Admin. Science Quart.,* June 1972, *17*(2), pp. 163–77.

22. CYERT, RICHARD M. and MARCH, JAMES G. *A behavioral theory of the firm.* Englewood Cliffs, N.J.: Prentice-Hall, 1963.

23. DAVIS, STANLEY M. and LAWRENCE, PAUL R. *Matrix.* Reading, Mass.: Addison-Wesley, 1977.

24. DILL, WILLIAM R. "Environment as an Influence on Managerial Autonomy," *Admin. Science Quart.,* 1958, *2*, pp. 409–43.

25. DOWNEY, W. KIRK; HELLRIEGEL, DON and SLOCUM, JOHN W., JR. "Environmental Uncertainty: The Construct and Its Applications," *Admin. Science Quart.,* Dec. 1975, *20*(4), pp. 613–29.

26. DUBICK, MICHAEL A. "The Organizational Structure of Newspapers in Relation to Their Metropolitan Environments," *Admin. Science Quart.,* Sept. 1978, *23*(3), pp. 418–33.

27. DYAS, GARETH P. *The strategy and structure of French industrial enterprise.* Unpublished D.B.A. thesis, Graduate School of Business Administration, Harvard University, 1972.

28. ———. and THANHEISER, HEINZ T. *The emerging European enterprise: Strategy and structure in French and German industry.* London: Macmillan, 1976.

29. EDSTRÖM, ANDERS and GALBRAITH, JAY R. "Transfer of Managers as a Coordination and Control Strategy in Multinational Organizations," *Admin. Science Quart.,* June 1977, *22*(2) pp. 248–63.

30. FRANKO, LAWRENCE G. *Joint venture survival in multinational corporations.* New York: Praeger, 1971.

31. ———. *The European multinationals: A renewed challenge to American and British big business.* Stamford, Conn.: Greylock, 1976.

32. GALBRAITH, JOHN KENNETH. *The new industrial state.* Second edition. Boston: Houghton Mifflin, [1967] 1971.

33. GRABOWSKI, HENRY G. and MUELLER, DENNIS C. "Life-Cycle Effects on Corporate Returns on Retentions," *Rev. Econ. Statist.,* Nov. 1975, *57*(4), pp. 400–409.

34. HANNAH, LESLIE, ed. *Management strategy and businesses development: An historical and comparative study.* London: Macmillan, 1976.

35. HARVEY, EDWARD. "Technolgy and the Structure of Organizations," *Amer. Soc. Rev.,* April 1968, *33*(2), pp. 247–59.

36. HORST, THOMAS. *At home abroad: A study of the domestic and foreign operations of the American food-processing industry.* Cambridge, Mass: Ballinger, 1974.

37. HUNT, MICHAEL S. *Competition in the major home appliance industry, 1960–1970.* Unpublished Ph.D. dissertation, Harvard University, 1972.

38. IMAI, KEN'ICHI. "Japan's Industrial Organization," *Japanese Econ. Studies,* Spring–Summer 1978, *6*(3–4), pp. 3–67.

39. INKSON, J. H. K., et al. "A Comparison of Organization Structure and Managerial Roles: Ohio, U.S.A., and the Midlands, England," *J. Management Stud.,* Oct. 1970, *7*(3), pp. 347–63.

40. KELLER, ROBERT T.; SLOCUM, JOHN W., JR. and SUSMAN, GERALD I. "Uncertainty and Type of Management System in Continuous Process Organizations," *Acad. Management J.,* March 1974, *17*(1), pp. 56–68.

41. KHANDWALLA, PRADIP N. "Effect of Competition on the Structure of Top Management Control," *Acad. Management J.,* June 1973[a], *16*(2), pp. 285–95.

42. ———. "Viable and Effective Organizational Designs of Firms," *Acad. Management J.,* Sept. 1973[b], *16*(3), pp. 481–95.

43. KIMBERLY, JOHN R. "Organizational Size and the Structuralist Perspective: A Review, Critique and Proposal," *Admin. Science Quart.,* Dec. 1976, *21*(4), pp. 571–97.

44. KYNASTON REEVES, TOM and TURNER, BARRY A. "A Theory of Organization and Behavior in Batch Production Factories," *Admin. Science Quart.,* March 1972, *17*(1), pp. 81–98.

45. LAWRENCE, PAUL R. and LORSCH, JAY W. *Organization and environ-*

ment: *Managing differentiation and integration.* Boston: Division of Research, Graduate School of Business Administration, Harvard University, 1967.

46. LEIBENSTEIN, HARVEY. *Beyond economic man: A new foundation for microeconomics.* Cambridge: Harvard University Press, 1976.

47. LORSCH, JAY W. and ALLEN, STEPHEN A., III. *Managing diversity and interdependence: An organizational study of multidivisional firms.* Boston: Division of Research, Graduate School of Business Administration, Harvard University, 1973.

48. MARKHAM, JESSE W. *Conglomerate enterprise and public policy.* Boston: Division of Research, Graduate School of Business Administration, Harvard University, 1973.

49. MARSCHAK, JAKOB and RADNER, ROY. *Economic theory of teams.* Cowles Foundation Monograph No. 22. New Haven: Yale University Press, 1972.

50. MCARTHUR, JOHN H. and SCOTT, BRUCE R. *Industrial planning in France.* Boston: Division of Research, Graduate School of Business Administration, Harvard University, 1969.

51. MCMILLAN, CHARLES J., et al. "The Structure of Work Organization across Societies," *Acad. Management J.,* Dec., 1973, *16*(4), pp. 555–69.

52. MIRRLEES, JAMES A. "The Optimal Structure of Incentives and Authority within an Organization," *Bell J. Econ.,* Spring 1976, *7*(1), pp. 105–31.

53. MUELLER, DENNIS C., "A Life Cycle Theory of the Firm," *J. Ind. Econ.,* July 1972, *20*(3), pp. 199–219.

54. MURTHY, K. R. SRINIVASA. *Corporate strategy and top executive compensation.* Boston: Division of Research, Graduate School of Business Administration, Harvard University, 1974.

55. NEGANDHI, ANANT R. and REIMANN, BERNARD C. "Correlates of Decentralization: Closed and Open Systems Perspective," *Acad. Management J.,* Dec. 1973, *16*(4), pp. 570–82.

56. NEWMAN, HOWARD H. "Strategic Groups and the Structure-Performance Relationship," *Rev. Econ. Statist.,* August 1978, *60*(3), pp. 417–27.

57. OUCHI, WILLIAM G. "The Relationship between Organizational Structure and Organizational Control," *Admin. Science Quart.,* March 1977, *22*(1), pp. 95–113.

58. ———. "The Transmission of Control through Organizational Hierarchy," *Acad. Management J.,* June, 1978, *21*(2), pp. 173–92.

59. PAVAN, ROBERT J. *The strategy and structure of Italian enterprise.* Unpublished D.B.A. thesis, Graduate School of Business Administration, Harvard University, 1972.

60. PENNINGS, JOHANNES M. "The Relevance of the Structural-Contingency Model for Organizational Effectiveness," *Admin. Science Quart.,* Sept. 1975, *20*(3), pp. 393–410.

61. ———. "Dimensions of Organizational Influence and Their Effectiveness Correlates." *Admin. Science Quart.,* Dec. 1976, *21*(4), pp. 688–99.

62. ———. "Structural Correlates of the Environment," in *Strategy +
structure = performance: The strategic planning imperative.* Edited by
HANS B. THORELLI. Bloomington: University of Indiana Press, 1977, pp.
260–76.

63. PENROSE, EDITH T. *The theory of the growth of the firm.* Oxford: Basil
Blackwell, 1959.

64. PFEFFER, JEFFREY. "Size and Composition of Corporate Boards of Directors: The Organization and Its Environment," *Admin. Science Quart.,*
June 1972, *17*(2), pp. 218–28.

65. ——— and LEBLEBICI, HUSEYIN. "The Effect of Competition on Some
Dimensions of Organizational Structure," *Social Forces,* Dec. 1973. *52*(2),
pp. 268–79.

66. ——— and SALANCIK, GERALD R. *The external control of organizations:
A resource dependence perspective.* New York: Harper & Row, 1978.

67. PORTER, MICHAEL E. "The Structure within Industries and Companies'
Performance," *Rev. Econ. Statist.,* May 1979, *61*(2), pp. 214–27.

68. PROCTOR, MICHAEL S. "Production, Investment, and Idle Capacity,"
Southern Econ. J., July 1976, *43*(1), pp. 855–63.

69. PUGH, D. S., et al. "The Context of Organization Structures," *Admin. Science Quart.,* March 1969, *14*(1), pp. 91–114.

70. RUBIN, PAUL H. "The Expansion of Firms," *J. Polit. Econ.,* July–August
1973, *81*(4), pp. 936–49.

71. RUMELT, RICHARD P. *Strategy, structure, and economic performance.* Boston: Division of Research, Graduate School of Business Administration,
Harvard University, 1974.

72. ———. "Diversity and Profitability," Paper MGL-51, Managerial Studies
Center, Graduate School of Management, University of California, Los
Angeles, 1977.

73. SCOTT, BRUCE R. "The Industrial State: Old Myths and New Realities,"
Harvard Bus. Rev., March–April 1973, *51*(2), pp. 133–48.

74. SIMONETTI, JACK L. and BOSEMAN, F. GLENN. "The Impact of Market
Competition on Organization Structure and Effectiveness: A Cross-Cul-
tural Study." *Acad. Management J.,* Sept. 1975, *18*(3), pp. 631–38.

75. STEER, PETER S. and CABLE, JOHN R. "Internal Organization and Profit:
An Empirical Analysis of Large U.K. Companies," *J. Ind. Econ.,* Sept.
1978, *27*(1), pp. 13–30.

76. STEINER, PETER O. *Mergers: Motives, effects, policies.* Ann Arbor: University of Michigan Press, 1975.

77. STIGLITZ, JOSEPH E. "Incentives, Risk, and Information: Notes Towards a
Theory of Hierarchy," *Bell J. Econ.,* Autumn 1975, *6*(2), pp. 552–79.

78. STOPFORD, JOHN M. and WELLS, LOUIS T., JR. *Managing the multinational enterprise: Organization of the firm and ownership of the subsidiaries.*
New York: Basic Books, 1972.

79. THANHEISER, HEINZ T. *Strategy and structure of German industrial enter-*

prise. Unpublished D.B.A. thesis, Graduate School of Business Administration, Harvard University, 1972.

80. THOMPSON, JAMES D. *Organizations in action: Social science bases of administrative theory.* New York: McGraw-Hill, 1967.

81. VANCIL, RICHARD F. *Decentralization: Managerial ambiguity by design.* New York: Dow Jones-Irwin, 1979.

82. WILKINS, MIRA. *The emergence of multinational enterprise American business abroad from the colonial era to 1914.* Cambridge: Harvard University Press, 1970.

83. WILLIAMSON, OLIVER E. "Hierarchical Control and Optimum Firm Size," *J. Polit. Econ.,* April 1967, *75*(2), pp. 123–38.

84. ———. *Corporate control and business behavior.* Englewood Cliffs, N.J.: Prentice-Hall, 1970.

85. ———. *Markets and hierarchies.* New York: Free Press, 1975.

86. ——— and BHARGAVA, NAROTTAM. *"Assessing and Classifying the Internal Structure and Control Apparatus of the Modern Corporation"* in *Market structure and corporate behavior.* Edited by KEITH COWLING. London: Gray-Mills, 1972, pp. 125–49.

87. ———; WACHTER, MICHAEL L. and HARRIS, JEFFREY E. "Understanding the Employment Relation: The Analysis of Idiosyncratic Exchange," *Bell J. Econ.,* Spring 1975, *6*(1), pp. 250–78.

88. WOODWARD, JOAN. *Industrial organization: Theory and practice.* London: Oxford University Press, 1965.

89. ———, ed. *Industrial organization: Behavior and control.* London: Oxford University Press, 1970.

90. WRIGLEY, LEONARD, *Divisional autonomy and diversification.* Unpublished D.B.A. thesis, Harvard Business School, 1970.

91. ———. "Conglomerate Growth in Canada," brief prepared for Royal Commission on Corporate Concentration. Mimeographed. London, Ontario: School of Business Administration, University of Western Ontario, 1976.

92. ZWERMAN, WILLIAM L. *New perspectives on organization theory.* Contributions in Sociology, No. 1. Westport, Conn.: Greenwood, 1970.

6

Evaluating and Choosing Among Policy/Strategy Alternatives

**GEORGE A. STEINER, JOHN B. MINER,
AND EDMUND R. GRAY**
University of California at Los Angeles

Reprinted by permission of Macmillan Publishing Company from *Management Policy and Strategy,*
2nd ed., Chapter 9, George A. Steiner, John B. Miner, and Edmund R. Gray. Copyright © 1982 by
Macmillan Publishing Company.

INTRODUCTION

In recent years there has grown up a body of literature concerning this process called "decision theory" [Harrison, 1981]. Decision theory itself is not new. The "economic man" concept of the economist, for instance, was for generations the core of normative economic decision making. However, today's decision theory has broadened considerably beyond this narrow range. Some writers refer to the process as policy science [Dror, 1971]. Others speak of policy analysis [Wildavsky, 1979]. The words decision theory are used more often among management scholars, and policy analysis or science among those studying public policy decision making. They are both, however, referring to the same phenomenon—the making of strategic decisions in organizations.

It should be noted here that decision theory falls today into two broad classifications—normative and descriptive. Most relevant current research is of the normative type, and most of that is concerned with quantitative optimization models in monetary terms. One reason for the slow growth of research about decision making is that the real world is a very messy place. The processes are extremely difficult to unravel and trace, and universal generalizations of cogency are difficult to discover. This is truer the higher in an organization's hierarchy one probes and, generally, the more significant the decision is to the organization.

The purposes of this chapter are to examine the conceptual and operational processes of evaluation and choice of dominant policies and strategies; to illustrate the variety of disciplines focused on the strategic decision-making process; to illustrate the types of tools available for analysis, their strengths and weaknesses; and to present major overall tests for strategy evaluation and choice. . . .

SOME MAJOR CHARACTERISTICS OF THE OPERATIONAL STRATEGIC DECISION-MAKING PROCESS

Evaluation Does Not Always Follow Identification

It is worthwhile to point out that, when managers individually or in their planning processes identify alternative policies and strategies, the conceptual process of decision making calls for evaluation and choice. This does not always happen. Many managers fail to see that the end result of strategic planning is current decisions not just "plans." Some of the reasons why they do not leap to decisions once they have identified policies and strategies are as follows.

Decision-making is risky. A major decision demands that executives take a stand. If they are wrong, their careers may be at stake. Making major decisions requires courage, and executives may prefer the safety of no decision.

Strategic decision making is fundamentally a creative process that is difficult. It demands a type of thinking and breadth of knowledge that many executives who have arrived at top management levels have neglected as they rose in the ranks because they devoted themselves to solving short-range problems in their narrow functional areas of expertise.

Most major strategic decisions are controversial and demand leadership to implement. How many times has one heard in corporations a statement such as this: "We ought to get out of that business." But nothing is done. Leadership is needed to decide to act and see that action is taken.

Finally, the promotion and evaluation systems in many corporations work against the making of significant decisions. Managers that show the best short-run profit results tend to be promoted rapidly, which means that they may not be obliged to live with the medium- and long-range impacts of their decisions [Salveson, 1974]. As Gerstner notes [1972:9] "... incentive compensation is often tied either to short-term earnings performance or to stock-price movements, neither of which has anything to do with strategic success."

The Uniqueness of the Process

The decision-making process for the most significant decisions made by top executives will vary from organization to organization. Each process is unique because involved in the decision making will be managerial value systems and judgments; internal political forces; interpersonnel relationships; and individual managerial skills, capabilities, motivations, and values. In no two organizations will these be identical. Furthermore, major strategic decisions tend to be, but may not always be, unique to each organization.

The Decision-Making Process
Is Very Complex

One of the authors had an opportunity to make major policy decisions in government organizations and concluded, after careful consideration, that even immediately following a top policy decision he could not reconstruct the detailed processes by means of which the decision was made. The forces, events, information flows, and thought processes were much too complex. Former White House Press Secretary Moyers undoubtedly felt the same way in responding to an inquiry about how a particular decision had been made. He said: "You begin with the general principle that the process of decision making is inscrutable. No man knows how a decision is ultimately shaped. It's usually impossible even to know at what point a decision is made" [Los Angeles Times, January 23, 1966:1]. Efforts to describe the decision-making process from which major decisions have come underscore this point [Allison, 1971; Hitch, 1966; Bryan, 1964; and Bailey, 1950]. Mintzberg and his students studied 25 decision-making processes in companies over a five-year period of time and concluded that descriptions of the 25 decision processes suggest

> ... a strategic decision process is characterized by novelty, complexity, and open-endedness, by the fact that the organization usually begins with little understanding of the decision situation it faces or the route to its solution, and only a vague idea of what the solution might be and how it will be evaluated when it is developed. Only by groping through a recursive, discontinuous process involving many difficult steps and a host of dynamic factors over a considerable period of time is a final choice made. This is not the decision making under *uncertainty* of the textbook, where alternatives are given even if their consequences are not, but decision making under *ambiguity,* where almost nothing is given or easily determined" [Mintzberg, Raisinghani and Théorêt 1976:250–251].

The Interdisciplinary Framework of Decision Making

There is no simple analytical model upon which basis strategic choices are made. Figure 1 is presented to show that at least six classifications of phenomena

Figure 1   An interdisciplinary framework of decision making. [Adapted from Harrison, 1975, p. 41.]

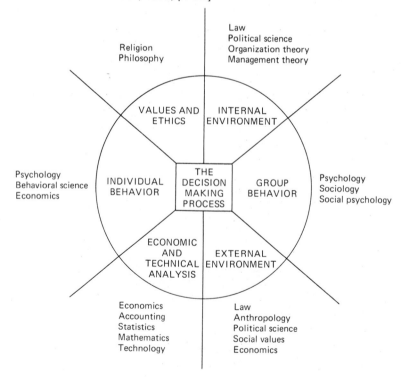

can have significant influence on strategic decision making in organizations. This diagram also shows that a large number of disciplines relate to the detailed forces in the phenomenon classes. The decision-making process is obviously complicated by the fact that different disciplines apply to different strategic problems. The student of strategic decision making must understand that there are no neat formulas to determine how much of each discipline will apply to a particular problem nor how much weight a decision maker should give the discipline.

The Decision-Making Process
Is Iterative and Fluid

Major policy/strategy decisions are typically made only after long discussions among managers and staffs, reevaluations, checking and double checking, and jumping from one point in a conceptual decision-making process to another. This is undoubtedly what Marion Folsom, a top executive in business and government, had in mind when he said, "Decisions generally are the result of a long series of discussions by both line and staff people after the staff has collected the pertinent material. It is often hard to pinpoint the exact stage at which a decision is reached. More often than not, the decision comes about naturally during discussions, when the consensus seems to be reached among those whose judgment and opinion the executive seeks" [Folsom, 1962:4].

From company to company, and within the same company, the decision process is constantly changing. It alters with subject matter but also because of different individual and group involvements in the process.

Although there may be a certain amount of formality to a planning process in a company, there can be and usually are informal communication and decision processes also at work. Grinyer and Norburn [1974:86] in their study of British corporations concluded that ". . . those involved in the real process of strategic decision making recognized that it is ultimately a political process in which power and influence of individuals change with the nature of the challenges to the company, with changing personal relationships, and with other factors like the health of top managers . . . informal political processes constitute the system by which decisions are really made." They go on to conclude that ". . . financially more successful companies tended to use more informal channels of communication . . ." [Grinyer and Norburn, 1974:86].

Dominance of Nonquantifiable
Element in Decision Making

Much of the literature of decision making emphasizes quantitative decision measures, and quantitative models and techniques to reach conclusions. This includes such measures as return on investment, maximization of output per unit of input, least cost, and profit maximation. For any major decision a manager will have available enormous quantities of factual information. Despite this quantitative emphasis in decision making, the facts are, as observed by Greiner, Leitch, and Barnes [1970], that informed managers rely much more on qualitative than quantitative criteria in appraising performance, even when quantitative information is available and in use. Former Secretary of Defense McNamara validated this conclusion for a large and complex decision, that of the TFX airplane, in testimony before the Congress, as follows:

> Fundamentally, we are dealing with a question of judgment. Granted there are specific technical facts and calculations involved; in the final analysis, judgment is what is at issue. . . . In this case we are faced with a situation in which judgments are pyramided upon judgments. . . . There is only one way I know to minimize the compounding error . . . and that way is to apply the judgment of the decision maker not only to the final recommendation but also to the underlying recommendations and factors [*TFX Contract Investigation,* 1963:387].

This conclusion of the Secretary is even more significant given the fact that, for the first time in the history of the Department of Defense, he had established in the Office of the Secretary a large and distinguished staff of mathematicians and quantitative science experts specifically to help him make such decisions.

Why is the preceding statement true? Fundamentally, it is because the "right" type of quantifiable information is not available; what is available is not convincing or creditable; but, more importantly, there are overriding considerations in decision making with which quantitative data cannot deal. Many major decisions must be made by managers that cannot be proven to be correct or incorrect by quantitative methods. An outstanding illustration is the definition of an organization's mission and purpose.

One of the most fateful strategic decisions a chief executive will make is to answer the question: "What is our business?" As Drucker [1974:79] points out, there never is one right answer and the answer, when derived, is seldom if ever the result of logical conclusions drawn from a set of "facts." The evaluation of alternatives and final choice is made solely on the basis of judgment.

No other strategic decision is as important as this one. This is so because . . . the mission establishes the lines of business and markets in which the firm will engage and the purposes will establish the main policies and standards of conduct for all employees both for economic and ethical activities. This is the foundation for determining specific objectives, resource priorities, strategies, plans, work assignments, organizational structure, and managerial tasks [Abell, 1980].

Strategies and policies may also be determined at lower levels, which spring from a manager's judgment rather than any set of facts that lead to the decision. For instance, irrespective of financial conditions an executive may decide from among one of the following strategies: invest for future growth, manage for earnings, or manage for immediate cash. Each of these choices will have a different impact on such decision areas as market share, pricing, promotion, existing product line, and new products. Kirchhoff's studies [1980] show that if a manager values short-run ROI over long-run ROI the strategies he chooses will differ considerably than vice versa.

Conceptual Versus Operational Models

The preceding discussion makes quite clear the fact that the strategic decision-making process in practice is by no means standardized. The literature on decision-making is filled with conceptual models. Virtually every writer on the subject has created his or her conceptual model. (See Lang, Dittrich, and White [1978] for a comparison of many models.) The simplest ones usually follow a few fundamental steps, such as: (1) recognize the need for decision making, (2) consider and analyze alternatives, (3) select an alternative or strategy to attain a goal, (4) communicate and implement the decision, and (5) evaluate and review. The more complex conceptual models are variations on details in these basic steps.

Despite the vast differences in steps in strategic decision making in industry our empirical observations, as well as scholarly studies, reveal that there are patterns of decision making that have broad application to and are used in practice. Mintzberg's empirical research suggested to him a basic framework that described unstructured, strategic decision processes [Mintzberg, Raisinghani, and Théorêt, 1976]. Quinn [1977] interviewed 100 top managers and found that, in practice, executives followed a sequence of steps in strategic decision making, which he called "logical incrementalism." First, Quinn said, they recognized a need for change. Second, they sought to encourage the organization to acknowledge this need by commissioning study groups, staff members, or consultants to examine problems, options, contingencies, or opportunities posed by the sensed need. Third, they tried to broaden support through unstructured discussions, probing of positions, definition of differences of opinion, encouraging concepts favored by the chief executive, discouraging ideas not favored by top management, and so on. Fourth, they created pockets of commitment by building necessary skills or technologies within the organization, testing options, and taking opportunities to make decisions to build support. Fifth, they established a clear focus either by creating an *ad hoc* committee to formulate a position or by expressing specific ends that top management desired. Sixth, they obtained real commitment by assigning someone who would champion the goal and be accountable for its accomplishment. This last step can be expanded, for example, by including specific commitments in budgets and by making short-range operating plans. Finally, the chief executive must insure that the organization is capable of responding to new opportunities and threats; in other words, that once a decision is made, the firm will not become locked in a fixed position. Quinn concludes:

> ... most strategic decisions in large enterprises emerge as continuous, evolving political consensus-building processes with no precise beginning or end. Managing

the generation and evolution of this consensus is one of the true arts of management, calling for the best practices of both behavioral and decision scientists [Quinn, 1980:205].

Strategic Decisions Are Made Throughout Organizations

In virtually all normative models of strategic decision making the final choices are made by top management of organizations. In fact, strategic decisions are made at different levels in organizations [Hofer and Schendel, 1978; Lorange and Vancil, 1977]. Kinnunen offers eight hypotheses in this connection which are worthy of thought and research for confirmation

1. CEOs in large divisionalized corporations tend to ratify strategic investment proposals sent to them by managers heading operating units.

2. Executives heading fairly autonomous operating units in large divisionalized corporations are the primary formulators of company strategy.

3. Operating units in large divisionalized corporations develop strategy for their business, and the strategy of the corporation is the sum of the strategies of the operating units.

4. As one proceeds from large divisionalized corporations to corporations of smaller size (as indicated by sales) and complexity (as indicated by product diversity), the CEO will do more formulating and less ratifying until the point is reached where the CEO is the chief strategist of the corporation.

5. Clear articulation of strategy from the CEO to various operating units is seldom a characteristic of the formulation process in large divisionalized corporations.

6. CEOs of large divisionalized corporations ratify strategic investment proposals because they have chosen to approve rather than dictate the strategic direction of individual operating units.

7. The absence of a clear articulation of strategy by the CEO forces executives heading operating units to choose the direction they feel is best for the unit they govern.

8. Whether or not strategic investment proposals from operating executives are ratified (as opposed to being thoroughly examined for appropriateness with total company objectives) will depend on the competence of executives of the operating units as viewed by the CEO [Kinnunen, 1976:9–12].

These hypotheses add additional insights into our discussion of the strategy formulation processes. It must be remembered, however, that even in highly decentralized companies there are certain strategies that are distinctly the prerogative of the CEO. . . .

RATIONALITY IN THE DECISION-MAKING PROCESS

Types of Rationality

In theory, managers are the most successful stewards of their organizations when they make rational decisions either upon the basis of intuition, logical evaluation of facts, or both. But, when is a decision rational? In the simplest of terms, a decision is rational when it effectively and efficiently assures the achievement of aims for which the means are selected. If a man is cold and wants to get warm, it is rational for him to get close to a fire. If a man is in business, it is rational to satisfy consumer wants at a profit.

Such simple concepts get complicated in organizational life. When Consolidated Edison of New York passed its dividend in 1974 for the first time in decades, the action was considered to be rational by management but the stockholders did not think so. The fact is that many individuals and groups are interested in every action a manager takes. Each has different aspirations, needs, and interests and views rationality in different ways. Even top managers of a business often disagree upon the rationality of a decision.

This suggests that rationality may be defined as the best selection of means to achieve an objective that is acceptable to the value system of the evaluator. The test of which means is best is, of course, determined by the same value system. For example, if the evaluator is a stockholder, his system of values may establish maximum rate of return on his investment as the desired objective. He can determine over time whether his objective has been met, but he will find it difficult to determine whether any particular decision is rational since its influence on the rate of return may be obscure. Suppose, for instance, management decided to maximize stockholder investment by building a new productive facility but the investment turned sour because a competitor got to the market first. Was the decision rational?

Different disciplines also look upon rationality in diverse terms. Rational action to the economist is that which maximizes profit. Chester Barnard [1968] defined rational decisions as being those which assured the communication, coordination, and motivation necessary to weld the organization into a cooperative effort to reach common ends. Quantitative scientists think of rational decision making as that which optimizes output per unit of input. Behavioral scientists look upon decision making as being rational when it meets certain human psychological needs. Environmentalists look at decisions in terms of impact on environment.

Simon suggests one way to avoid, or to clarify, complexities in determining whether a decision is rational or not is to think of different types of rationality. He says:

> . . . a decision may be called "objectively" rational if *in fact* it is the correct behavior for maximizing given values in a given situation. It is "subjectively" rational if

it maximizes attainment relative to the actual knowledge of the subject. It is "consciously" rational to the degree that the adjustment of means to ends is a conscious process. It is "deliberately" rational to the degree that the adjustment of means to ends has been deliberately brought about (by the individual or by the organization). A decision is "organizationally" rational if it is oriented to the organization's goals; it is "personally" rational if it is oriented to the individual's goals [Simon, 1976:76–77].

It is obvious that there is no universal standard for judging rationality of managerial decisions. What is rational depends upon the evaluator. Much is to be said, however, for determining the rationality of managerial decisions in terms of the decision makers' own frame of reference [March and Simon, 1958]. Of course, frames of reference vary among individuals and organizations, as will be shown shortly.

Theories of rational behavior, rooted in classical economic theory, use the concept "comprehensive rationality." According to it a goal is established and rationality involves the choice of best alternatives, taking into account probabilities and utilities. Such choice requires knowledge of all possible alternatives, complete assessment of probabilities and consequences of each, evaluation of each set of consequences in achieving the objective, and choice of those alternatives that optimize goal achievement. Because a decision maker cannot comprehend all that this process would require, he forms simplified models of the real world and uses them to make decisions. Simon calls this "bounded rationality" [1976]. Theoretically, this process is not likely to produce as rational a decision as the first, but in practice it probably does and is much easier.

Organizational Models and Rationality

One's theory of the organization has much to do with his rational behavior. Until the publication of *Organizations* by March and Simon [1958] and later *A Behavioral Theory of the Firm* by Cyert and March [1963], classical economic theory dominated organizational theory. A core concept of classical economic theory is that firms operate rationally when they seek to maximize profits under conditions of comprehensive rationality. Cyert, Simon, and March, on the other hand, view organizations as coalitions of participants with different motivations and limited ability to solve all problems simultaneously. Goals are formed in light of such constraints and achieved through a bargaining process.

The most complete description and differentiation of major organizational models, especially with respect to decision making, is that of Allison [1971]. He explains the differences between what he calls "The Rational Actor," "Organizational Process," and "Governmental Politics" models. The first is patterned after the classical economic model, the second sees organizations as composed of different organizational units that have their own ways of doing things, and the third views organizations as institutions that get things done through political processes. The third encompasses the Cyert, Simon, and March model.

In sum, rational behavior as perceived from inside and from outside an organization depends upon the model that best explains the functioning of the organization.

Rationality of Profit Maximization

Central in decision making in "rational" business organizations is the goal to achieve profit maximization. Any decision is irrational in classical economic theory that does not serve to achieve this result. Hence, in economic theory, profit maximization is the goal of the firm.

There are many who challenge this notion of maximization. Anthony [1960] suggests the more usual objective is satisfactory return on capital employed. Alchian [1950] says the objective of firms is "realized positive profits." Steiner [1969b; 1971] says the goal is "required and steadily rising profits," and Simon [1976], whose phrase has been most widely used, says it is "satisfactory profits."

Others challenge the idea that profit maximization is *the* goal of a firm. Mason [1958] quotes Keynes as saying the general stability and reputation of an institution is a higher goal. Baumol [1967] maintains that sales, subject to a profit constraint, is the objective. Clark [1961] says firms have many objectives, a fact that is amply clear from what has been said previously in this book.

Transition Comment

As noted, much more will be said about the theory and practice of decision making. This discussion at this point is designed as a frame of reference in building a bridge between scholarly research and actual practice. It dramatises the role of these two approaches in identifying policies/strategies, analyzing and evaluating policies/strategies, and making of a final choice. Again, this is not a sequential but an iterative and continuous process.

ANALYTICAL TOOLS FOR EVALUATING POLICY/STRATEGY

The palette of analytical techniques for helping managers to decide upon policies/strategies is indeed rich. . . . Our purpose in this section is to help the reader get a feel for the richness of the palette of analytical tools available for evaluation; to look at the strengths and weaknesses of some of the tools, . . . and to relate the use of analytical tools to managerial requirements and responsibilities.

The Spectrum
of Analytical Tools

The many tools available for evaluation may be divided into four major categories. First are older nonquantitative techniques. Included here, for illustrative purposes would be individual creativity, judgment, hunches, intuition and reliance on experience. Also in this category would be such techniques as brainstorming, project teams, and Delphi.

Second are older quantitative methods. In this class would be accounting systems and models in the accounting systems, such as balance sheets, profit and loss statements, cash flows, accounting ratio analysis, break-even analysis, budgets, cost control models, and so on. Quantitative forecasting methods are numerous, such as trend extrapolation, correlation analysis, econometric models, input-out analysis, and multiple regression analysis. Another class in this area would be tracking models, such as milestone charts, decision trees, and critical path models like PERT/Time.

Third are new computer based models. Included here are newer mathematical techniques and the adaptation of older techniques to computers. Computer-based simulation models are the most extensively used models in strategic planning today. The most popular ones are financial models [Naylor, 1979]. Older techniques of forecasting, such as correlation analysis, are frequently used in computer-based models to project future trends. PIMS is a new computer-based model and is fundamentally a correlation analysis. Cost-experience curves can also be classified here, since they frequently involve computer modeling. Most of the computer-based models are deterministic as distinct from probabilistic. A major exception is risk analysis as developed by Hertz [1969].

Finally, there are various complex techniques that combine many different tools. In mind, for example, are elaborate cost-benefit analyses, social science research, formal strategic planning systems, and program budgeting.

This short classification by no means exhausts the list of analytical tools available in formulating policy/strategy. As brief as it is, however, it should make clear the wide range of available tools. Each tool has its own strengths and weaknesses and relevance to particular policy/strategy problems. This, too, is a very large subject, and space limitations permit only illustrations of the point.

Strengths and Weaknesses
of Selected Techniques

Intuition. As was mentioned before but it is worth repeating: There is no more powerful method to evaluate and choose the best policies/strategies. However, as far as we know there is no record of any individual who depended upon this technique with an infallible record.

The accounting system.   There are few if any more important analytical tools for policy/strategy analysis in industry than found in the typical accounting system of a company. Ratio analysis, for example, is a powerful tool of analysis with predictive value. . . . In a longitudinal study of 221 firms and 48 financial ratios, Pinches, Eubank, and Mingo [1975] identified the following as having the highest predictive value: earnings before interest and taxes/total assets, net income/total assets, earnings before interest and taxes/sales, net worth/sales, sales/working capital, debt/total capital, and debt/total assets.

Observe, however, that accounting data can be manipulated in many ways to produce a variety of results, all within standard accounting principles and practices. William Casey when chairman of the Securities and Exchange Commission lamented:

> The public has lost more money through the use of permissible variations in accounting to exaggerate earnings and growth than through the whole catalogue of things which we have made impermissible [Quoted in Andrews, 1973].

Even with consistent and well-understood accounting practices, accounting ratios must be used very carefully. Reservations even about the widely used and powerful return-on-investment ratios have been raised [Dearden, 1969]. Weston [1972], however, says ROI has powerful applicability at all levels of decision making.

The portfolio matrix.   This is, of course, a powerful tool for identifying strategies as well as evaluating them. . . . The matrix must be used with great care, however, if errors in strategy are to be avoided. Managers must not assume that because a product lands in one of the squares on the matrix that the decision about strategy is made. For example, if a product falls in the upper left corner—strong market position and strong industry attractiveness—it is not a foregone conclusion that the strategy should be "invest for growth." Even for a product in such an enviable position, careful analysis of its situation might lead to the conclusion that the company should sell the product or phase it out of its line.

Location of a product on the matrix can be influenced by manipulation or judgment. For example, forecasts of market growth rates can be manipulated by managers. Managers may also define a market to achieve a desired location of a product on the matrix. For example, what is the market for General Foods' Country Time brand of lemonade powdered soft drink? Is it the cold refreshment beverage market? Is it the lemonade soft drink market? Is it the powdered soft drink (PSD) market? Is it the sugar-sweetened PSD market? Or, is it the presweetened PSD market for canister products? The market share of this product will vary from 2 to 51 per cent depending on the operating manager's selection of market served [Palesy, 1980].

The product life cycle (PLC).   The PLC is a simple and powerful analytical tool but it does have significant limitations in policy/strategy formulation. Dhalla and Yuspeth [1976] have admonished managers to "forget the product life cycle." Their position is that simplistic use of the PLC has led managers to take actions that have been contrary to the best interests of their companies. They certainly are correct in underscoring the fact that, actually, the PLC is a very complicated phenomenon. Hofer [1975], for example, has observed that the PLC must be examined and defined in more specific contexts and with more variables than a simple sales and profit curve. Variables that he has in mind include purchase frequency, nature of the buyer's needs, rate of technological change, the ratio of distribution costs to value added, price elasticity of demand, marginal plant size, and so on. Note also that there are many different PLCs. Shin and Wall [1979] have identified nine different life cycle curves. It should not be forgotten, too, that the PLC depends very much upon management decisions. Its shape, direction, and time span can be influenced by strategic decisions.

Pims.   There is no question about the fact . . . that PIMS is a potent model for formulating strategy/policy. But, it too, has weaknesses that must be understood if the technique is to be used effectively. Anderson and Paine [1978] and Naylor [1978] have set forth the major limitations of PIMS. Gale [1978] replied to Naylor's criticisms. Space limitations prevent any full analysis of PIMS's shortcomings. But, to illustrate, the quantitative correlations of PIMS must not be taken without reservations for there is high potential for management controllability among the many independent variables used by PIMS. For example, PIMS says that high R&D plus high marketing depress ROI. Hewlett-Packard did not find this to be true. Also, although there is general acceptance to the PIMS conclusion that high market share and profitability are closely related, there are also significant exceptions. High market share has sometimes been unprofitable [Fruhan, 1972]. On the other hand, Burroughs Corporation, Crown Cork & Seal Co., Inc., and Union Camp Corporation do not enjoy dominant market shares in their industries and yet they are highly profitable [Hammermesh, Anderson, and Harris, 1978]. As a correlation analysis of past activity PIMS deals with the past, not the future. Those relationships of the past that resulted in one conclusion can change in the future and bring a far different conclusion. Despite these and other limitations of PIMS, the data are valuable in policy/strategy formulation; however, they are not substitutes for careful managerial analysis and creativity.

The learning curve.   Here, as in the preceding discussion, the relationship between cost and output is a powerful analytical tool; however, it has serious shortcomings if used without careful analysis. Like the PLC there are many variables that affect the relationship, and many of them are controllable by management. An increase in productivity, for example, can be produced by the introduction of new capital investment. However, if the investment is too great

Figure 2   *Relationship between enterprise's development phase and forecasting techniques at policy strategic planning level. Source: Don LeBell, and O. J. Krasner, "Selecting Environmental Forecasting Techniques from Business Planning Requirements."* The Academy of Management Review, **July 1977:379.**)

Maturity Phase \ Forecasting Techniques	Single-Variable Extrapolation	Theoretical Limit Envelope	Dynamic Models	Mapping	Multivariable Interaction Analysis	Unstructured Expert Opinion	Structured Expert Opinion	Structured Inexpert Opinion	Unstructured Inexpert Speculation
Product Technology									
Capital Resources									
Production and Distribution									
Marketing									
Competition									
Socio-Political									
Diversification									

Legend: □ Appropriate   ▤ Moderately or occasionally appropriate   ▦ Inappropriate

and results in excess capacity, the net impact may be a cost increase. For an analysis of major limits to the learning curve see Abernathy and Wayne [1974].

Forecasting.   There are a vast number of forecasting techniques available for policy/strategy analysis. Each has its own strengths and weaknesses. Space limitations prevent any analysis of the uses of different techniques, but the point is illustrated in Figure 2. This chart shows that different techniques have different applicabilities for different subjects of analysis in policy/strategy formulation.

The Manager Is His Own Best Analytical Technique

The preceding illustrations of strengths and weaknesses of selected analytical tools makes clear that thought must be given to when and where each technique is applicable and how much of it is appropriate. Decisions such as these should be made by managers not staff specialists. Staff specialists can and should advise managers, but the decisions are for the managers. A biographer of Winston Churchill observed on this point:

> He was always deeply interested in techniques of all kinds and listened avidly to experts and professionals, imbibing all they told him with a rare accuracy and grasp. But he never fell a victim to the black magic of specialist infallibility. It was the task of specialists and experts to supply the weights and measures: it was for him to assess them and to reach conclusions [Carter 1965:36]

In developing the needed assessment capabilities of diverse disciplines focused on the policy/strategy-formulation process the manager becomes his own best analytical tool.

KEY QUESTIONS TO TEST STRATEGIES/POLICIES

Tilles [1963] first suggested a set of overarching tests for strategies, an evaluation approach that we think is most significant. Following are our seven major overarching criteria, following Tilles, with comments and illustrative questions. It is our view that if questions such as these are forthrightly asked and answered, the result will be the formulation of superior strategies and assurance of their implementation. The history of business, on the other hand, is filled with instances where a company failed to ask and answer one or another of these questions and, as a result, disappeared.

Is the Strategy Consistent with Environment?

If it is to perform well, a firm must adapt to its [total] environment. . . . The policies/strategies of a firm must reflect not only the current but the evolving elements in the environment, which open up major opportunities and pose potentially lethal threats. For example, . . . the strategies of a firm must make it competitive for survival. Also, . . . a large, exposed company that ignores changing social values will create difficult problems for itself. The current plight of the automobile companies is witness to the truth of this observation. Illustrative of the questions that suggest themselves in this category are the following:

> Is your strategy acceptable to the major constituents of your company?
>
> Is your strategy in consonance with your competitive environment?
>
> Do you really have an honest and accurate appraisal of your competition? Are you underestimating your competiton?

Does your strategy leave you vulnerable to the power of one major customer?

Does your strategy give you a dominant competitive edge?

Is your strategy vulnerable to a successful strategic counterattack by competitors?

Are the forecasts upon which your strategy is based really creditable?

Does your strategy follow that of a strong competitor?

Does your strategy pit you against a powerful competitor?

Is your market share (present and/or prospective) sufficient to be competitive and make an acceptable profit?

If your strategy seeks an enlarged market share is it likely to be questioned by the Antitrust Division of the Department of Justice or the Federal Trade Commission?

Is it possible that other federal government agencies will prevent your achieving the objectives sought by your strategy?

Is your strategy in conformance with moral and ethical codes of conduct applicable to your company?

Is the Strategy Consistent with Your Internal Policies, Styles of Management, Philosophy, and Operating Procedures?

A living organization is a composite of policies, procedures, values, work habits, aspirations of people, communications, interpersonal linkages, and so on. Obviously, the better policies/strategies are in congruence with the most effective workings of this mechanism the more likely they are to be successful. No strategy will succeed, for instance, if it is contrary to the strongly held values of top management. Mighty General Motors Corporation found out at Lordstown that it had to be concerned with worker attitudes. Some questions that arise in this classification are:

Does the strategy/policy really fit management's values, philosophy, know-how, personality, and sense of social responsibility?

Is your strategy identifiable and understood by all those in the company with a need to know?

Is your strategy consistent with the internal strengths, objectives, and policies of your organization?

Is the strategy under evaluation divided into appropriate substrategies that interrelate properly?

Does the strategy under review conflict with other strategies in your company?

Does the strategy under review exploit your strengths and avoid your major weaknesses?

Is your organizational structure consistent with your strategy?

Does your policy/strategy make the greatest overall contribution to the performance of your company?

Is the strategy likely to produce a minimum of new administrative problems for your organization?

Is the Policy/Strategy Appropriate in Light of Your Resources?

Resources are those tangible and intangible assets a company has that are important contributors to its viability and success. This, of course, includes a wide range of assets from money to managerial competence and employee loyalty. A few illustrative questions in three classes of assets follow:

Money

Do you have sufficient capital, or can you get it, to see the strategy through to successful implementation?

What will be the financial consequences associated with the allocation of capital to this strategy? What other projects may be denied funding? Are the financial substrategies associated with this funding acceptable?

Physical Facilities

Is your strategy appropriate with respect to existing and prospective physical plant? Will the strategy utilize plant capacity? Is equipment obsolete for the proper implementation of the strategy?

Managerial and Employee Resources

Are there identifiable and committed managers to implement the strategy?

Do we have the necessary skills among both managers and employees to make the strategy successful?

Are the Risks in Pursuing the Strategy Acceptable?

There are all types of risks associated with strategic decisions. The spectrum ranges from no risk, which might be the case where a company decides to stick with its current products rather than diversify, to a situation where the very survival of the company may be at stake. Broadly speaking, a policy/strategy is a higher risk where amounts of capital involved are great, the payout period is long, and the uncertainty of outcome is significant, than just the reverse. But there are other risks, such as, for example, a risk that skilled managers and workers may not be acquired in time to perform as required to make the strategy/ policy successful. Appropriate questions in this area would include:

Has the strategy/policy been tested with appropriate analysis, such as return on investment, sensitivity analysis, the firm's ability and willingness to bear specific risks, etc.?

Does your strategy balance the acceptance of minimum risk with the maximum profit potential consistent with your company's resources and prospects?

Do you have too much and too large a proportion of your capital and management tied into this strategy?

Is this payback period acceptable in light of potential environmental change?

Does the strategy take you too far from your current products and markets?

Does the Strategy Fit Product
Life Cycle and Market Strength/
Market Attractiveness Situation

Is the strategy appropriate for the present and prospective position in the market strength/attractiveness matrix?

Have you considered all the characteristics in the matrix that are pertinent to evaluating properly your strategy?

Is your strategy in consonance with your product life cycle as it exists and/or as you have the power to make it?

Are you rushing a revolutionary product to the market?

If your strategy is to fill a niche not now filled in the market, have you inquired about the niche remaining open to you long enough to return your capital investment plus a required profit?

Can Your Strategy Be
Implemented Efficiently
and Effectively?

Many of the questions raised previously pertain to implementation of policy/strategy, but the subject is so important that it deserves separation. The ability of a company to implement a policy/strategy involves a great many conditions. A strategy is not implementable, of course, if sufficient capital is available to make it work, or if managers and employees are indifferent to its success. It will not work if there are absent the necessary coordination and control mechanisms to assure that strategic plans are indeed fulfilled. Probably the most neglected area in scholarly treatment of policy/strategy rests in the implementation of it. A few illustrative questions in this area are:

Overall, can the strategy be implemented in an efficient and effective fashion?

Is there a commitment, a system of communications and control, a managerial and employee capability, that will help to assure the proper implementation of the strategy?

Is the timing of implementation appropriate in light of what is known about market conditions, competition, etc.?

Are There Other Important Considerations?

This final grouping is, of course, a catchall to identify other pertinent considerations not dealt with in the preceding classes. A few questions here could be

Have you tried to identify the major forces inside and outside the organization that will be most influential in insuring the success of the strategy and/or in raising problems of implementation? Have you given them the proper evaluation?

Are all the important assumptions realistic upon which your strategy/policy is based?

Has the strategy been tested with appropriate analytical tools?

Has the strategy been tested with appropriate criteria such as past, present, and prospective economic, political, and social trends?

This is indeed a formidable list of questions. Not every question will be most relevant in every situation. So, managers have the responsibility for determining which is the most pertinent question. Any one might turn out to be the core question. For instance, Rolls Royce could answer affirmatively most all of these questions but it failed to ask this one: Are you rushing a revolutionary product to the market? It did indeed rush the RB-211 jet engine designed for Lockheed's L-1011 to the market. Technical problems and enormous cost overruns pushed the company into bankruptcy in 1971. For any particular situation questions other than those posed or narrower versions of those raised above may be more appropriate.

There is no implication here that every one of the preceding, or other, questions must be answered in depth. In many cases, merely to ask a question will quickly yield an acceptable quick response. For others, of course, a good bit of rigorous analysis will be appropriate.

A CONCLUDING OBSERVATION

Alfred Sloan in his book *My Years With General Motors* said, "No company ever stops changing. Change will come for better or worse. I also hope I have not left an impression that the organization runs itself automatically. An organization does not make decisions; its function is to provide a framework, based upon established criteria within which decisions can be fashioned in an orderly manner. Individuals make the decisions and take the responsibility for them. . . . The task of management is not to apply a formula but to decide issues on a case-by-case basis. No fixed, inflexible rule can ever be substituted for exercise of sound business judgment in the decision-making process" [Sloan, 1964:443].

Clearly, at the strategic decision-making level each case is unique. Yet, there are underlying approaches to identifying preferred strategies, to evaluating the strategies, and to making the final choices. Research is no more than ankle deep in the search for tested theories applicable to this process.

QUESTIONS

Discussion Guides
on Chapter Content

1. Why does not policy/strategy evaluation always follow identification?

2. Discuss the complexity of decision making in a firm.

3. Identify a major strategic decision of a company of which you are aware and hypothesize about the many different disciplines that probably influenced the decision.

4. How do conceptual and operational models of decision making differ?

5. Do you think it would be correct to say that the higher in an organization a decision is made, and the more important the decision, the less likelihood the decision will be made upon the basis of quantitative analysis and/or a single discipline? Explain.

6. Where in an organization are policy/strategy decisions made?

7. "Any important decision in an organization is irrational to someone." Do you agree or disagree? Explain.

8. Economic theory asserts that profit maximization is a completely rational goal of an enterprise, but there are many scholars who say that profit maximization as the single goal of an operating firm is irrational. Where do you stand and why?

9. Comment on the outstanding strengths and weaknesses of these analytical tools for formulating policy/strategy: a company's accounting system, the portfolio matrix, the product life cycle, PIMS, the learning curve, and major forecasting techniques.

10. The authors have set forth in this chapter seven overarching questions, with a number of subquestions, as criteria for testing and evaluating policies/strategies. Do you think this is a valuable list? Explain. Pick out one of the questions and explain in detail why it might have great power in determining whether a manager chooses the right or wrong strategy.

REFERENCES

1. ABELL, DEREK F.: *Defining the Business: The Starting Point of Strategic Planning.* Englewood Cliffs, N.J., Prentice-Hall, 1980.
2. ABERNATHY, WILLIAM J., and KENNETH WAYNE: "Limits of the Learning Curve." *Harvard Business Review,* September–October 1974.
3. ALCHIAN, ARMEN A.: "Uncertainty, Evolution, and Economic Theory." *Journal of Political Economy,* June 1950.
4. ALLISON, GRAHAM T.: *Essence of Decision: Explaining the Cuban Missle Crisis.* Boston, Little, Brown, 1971.
5. ANDERSON, CARL R., and FRANK T. PAINE: "PIMS: A Reexamination." *Academy of Management Review,* July 1978.
6. ANDREWS, FREDERICK: "Abe Briloff Tees Off on Creativity in Accounting." *Wall Street Journal,* March 13, 1973.
7. ANTHONY, ROBERT N.: "The Trouble with Profit Maximization." *Harvard Business Review,* November–December 1960.
8. BAILEY, STEPHEN K.: *Congress Makes a Law.* New York, Columbia University Press, 1950.
9. BARNARD, CHESTER I.: *The Functions of the Executive.* Cambridge, MA, Harvard University Press, 1968.
10. BAUMOL, WILLIAM J.: *Business Behavior, Values and Growth.* New York, Harcourt, Brace and World, 1967.
11. BRYAN, STANLEY E.: "TFX—A Case in Policy Level Decision Making." *Academy of Management Journal,* March 1964.
12. CARTER, VIOLET BONHAM: *Winston Churchill: An Intimate Portrait.* New York, Harcourt, Brace, 1965.
13. CLARK JOHN M.: *Competition as a Dynamic Process.* Washington, D.C., The Brookings Institution, 1961.
14. CYERT, RICHARD M., and JAMES G. MARCH: *A Behavioral Theory of the Firm.* Englewood Cliffs, N.J., Prentice-Hall, 1963.
15. DEARDEN, JOHN: "The Case Against ROI Control." *Harvard Business Review,* May–June 1969.
16. DHALLA, NARIMAN K., and SONIA YUSPEH "Forget the Product Life Cycle Concept." *Harvard Business Review,* January–February 1976.
17. DROR, YEHEZKEL: *Ventures in Policy Sciences.* New York, American Elsevier Publishing, 1971.

18. DRUCKER, PETER F.: *Management: Tasks, Responsibilities, Practices.* New York, Harper and Row, 1974.
19. FOLSOM, MARION B.: *Executive Decision Making.* New York, McGraw-Hill, 1962.
20. FRUHAN, WILLIAM E., JR.: "Pyrrhic Victories in Fights for Market Share." *Harvard Business Review,* September–October 1972.
21. GALE, BRADLEY T.: "Cross-Sectional Analysis." *Planning Review,* March 1978.
22. GERSTNER, LOUIS V.: "Can Strategic Planning Pay Off?" *Business Horizons,* December 1972.
23. GREINER, LARRY E., D. PAUL LEITCH, and LOUIS B. BARNES: "Putting Judgment Back Into Decisions." *Harvard Business Review,* March–April 1970.
24. GRINYER, PETER H., and DAVID NORBURN: "Strategic Planning in 21 U.K. Companies." *Long Range Planning,* August 1974.
25. HAMMERMESH, R. G., M. J. ANDERSON, JR., and J. E. HARRIS: "Strategies for Low Market Share Business." *Harvard Business Review,* May–June 1978.
26. HARRISON, E. FRANK: *The Managerial Decision-Making Process.* 2nd Ed. Boston, Houghton Mifflin, 1981.
27. HERTZ, DAVID B.: *New Power for Management.* New York, McGraw-Hill, 1969.
28. HITCH, CHARLES J.: *Decision-Making for Defense.* Berkeley and Los Angeles, University of California Press, 1966.
29. HOFER, CHARLES W.: "Toward a Contingency Theory of Business Strategy." *Academy of Management Journal,* December 1975.
30. HOFER, CHARLES W., and DAN SCHENDEL: *Strategy Formulation: Analytical Concepts.* St. Paul, MN, West, 1978.
31. KINNUNEN, RAYMOND M.: "Hypotheses Related to Strategy Formulation in Large Divisionalized Companies." *Academy of Management Review,* October 1976.
32. KIRCHOFF, BRUCE A.: "Empirical Assessment of the Strategy/Tactics Dilemma." *Academy of Management Proceedings,* August 1980.
33. LANG, JAMES R., JOHN E. DITTRICH, and SAM E. WHITE: "Managerial Problem Solving Models: A Review and Proposal." *Academy of Management Review,* October 1978.
34. LeBELL, DON, and O. J. KRASNER: "Selecting Environmental Forecasting Techniques from Business Planning Requirements." *Academy of Management Review,* July 1977.
35. LORANGE, PETER, and RICHARD F. VANCIL: *Strategic Planning Systems.* Englewood Cliffs, N.J., Prentice-Hall, 1977.
36. MARCH, JAMES G., and HERBERT A. SIMON: *Organizations.* New York, Wiley, 1958.

37. MASON, EDWARD S.: "The Apologetics of 'Managerialism.'" *Journal of Business,* January 1958

38. MINTZBERG, HENRY, DURU RAISINGHAMI, and ANDRÉ THÉORÊT: "The Structure of 'Unstructured' Decision Process." *Administrative Science Quarterly,* June 1976.

39. NAYLOR, THOMAS H.: "PIMS: Through a Different Looking Glass." *Planning Review,* March 1978.

40. NAYLOR, THOMAS H.: *Corporate Planning Models.* Reading, MA, Addison-Wesley, 1970.

41. PALESY, STEVEN R.: "Motivating Line Management Using the Planning Process." *Planning Review,* March 1980.

42. PINCHES, GEORGE E., ARTHUR A. EUBANK, and KENT A. MINGO: "The Hierarchical Classification of Financial Ratios." *Journal of Business Research,* October 1975.

43. QUINN, JAMES BRIAN: "Strategic Goals: Process and Politics." *Sloan Management Review,* Fall 1977.

44. QUINN, JAMES BRIAN: *Strategies for Change: Logical Incrementalism.* Homewood, IL, Irwin, 1980.

45. SALVESON, MELVIN E.: "The Management of Strategy." *Long Range Planning,* February 1974.

46. SHIN, BONG-GON P., and JERRY L. WALL: "An Investigation of Product Life Cycle Curvatures: Their Frequency and Their Occurrence by Industry." College of Business, Western Illinois University. Working paper, 1979.

47. SIMON, HERBERT A.: *Administrative Behavior: A Study of Decision-Making Processes in Administrative Organization.* New York, Free Press, 1976.

48. SLOAN, ALFRED P., JR.: *My Years with General Motors.* New York, Doubleday and Company, 1964.

49. STEINER, GEORGE A.: *Top Management Planning.* New York, Macmillan, 1969.

50. STEINER, GEORGE A.: *Comprehensive Managerial Planning.* Oxford, OH, Planning Executives Institute, 1971.

51. *TFX Contract Investigation.* Hearings Before the Permanent Subcommittee on Investigation of the Committee on Government Operations, U.S. Senate, 88th Congress. Washington, D.C., U.S. Government Printing Office, 1963.

52. TILLES, SEYMOUR: "How to Evaluate Corporate Strategy." *Harvard Business Review,* July–August 1963.

53. WESTON, J. FRED: "ROI Planning and Control." *Business Horizons,* August 1972.

54. WILDAVSKY, AARON: *Speaking Truth to Power: The Art and Craft of Policy Analysis.* Boston, Little, Brown, 1979.

PART TWO
STRATEGY IMPLEMENTATION

7

How to Ensure the Continued Growth of Strategic Planning

WILLIAM E. ROTHSCHILD

General Electric Company

As a concept and management practice, strategic planning continues to grow in popularity and acceptance. In fact, during the decade of the 1970s, this approach to planning moved from the embryonic to the rapid-growth stage; but the real issue is whether it will continue to grow in popularity, level off, or even decline.

Its continued growth will depend on meeting four success factors. Before examining these factors, however, let us review the characteristics of growth situations and how these pertain to strategic planning today.

During the growth phase of concept development, there are almost always a number of different techniques competing for the user's application; and there are always strong advocates for each of these techniques. So it has been with strategic planning; a number of techniques have been developed and advocated as the best approaches available for assisting in the making of strategic decisions. These techniques have been developed by consulting firms, educators, and practitioners. Moreover, each of the major consulting firms has moved aggressively to increase its share of the strategic planning consultant business, as well as to further the development of that market. Likewise, new specialty firms have grown and have been given birth to still other small specialty firms. And both the generalist national/international firms and the specialists have tried to differentiate their offerings and demonstrate unique skills by creating new analytical approaches or using new information systems models and techniques—each advocating its brand or approach and some even making claims that have not been supported by fact. The result has been an increasing number of techniques and approaches from which the manager can select.

During the same period, there has also been a significant increase in the number of books, articles, and seminars devoted to strategic planning. Thus, major magazines, like *Business Week, Forbes,* and *Fortune,* have developed continuing columns or articles on corporate strategies. Similarly, articles have appeared in *Harvard Business Review* and the *Wall Street Journal* extolling and evaluating the merits of various types of strategic planning techniques. Moreover, as the popularity of the subject has increased, there have been a growing number of courses, seminars, and workshops sponsored by national organizations like *Business Week,* Conference Board, and universities and associations, including the American Management Association and the North American Society for Corporate Planning. The result: a vast volume of papers, including a number of confusing, conflicting Ph.D. dissertations.

Increased communications and education have also resulted in the growth of corporate planning and strategic planning organizations within business, nonprofit and governmental institutions. Over 300 companies increased the size of their planning staffs by 30 percent in the past two years, and these same firms expect to increase their staffs by an additional 16 percent in the next two years. This, in turn, has resulted in the creation of a number of recruiting and placement consultants who have specialized in the search and placement of strategic and corporate planners. The result: increased expectations on the part of management that something magic and dynamic will soon occur.

Moreover, as strategic planning has grown, it has begun to develop its own vocabulary and terminology. Thus, the terms "business unit" and "strategic business unit" (SBU) have become as commonplace as "division" or "group." In addition, we now hear about environmental forecasts, planning matrices, the use of futurists, strategic thinking, strategic management, and so on. The result: the need to learn a new vocabulary, which all too often merely renames something quite old.

All of these characteristics are typical of any growth area. Taken in total, however, they clearly indicate that strategic planning is truly "in." Its "disciples" also predict that it will continue to grow and that over the long term it will become an increasingly important management technique.

Strategic planning is a valuable management tool, and it will continue to increase in application and value if four major conditions are satisfied. If they are not, strategic planning will follow the course of past fads, like MBO, long-range planning, and participative management.

THE SUCCESS FACTORS

These four critical success conditions are:

Top management commitment to and practice of strategic planning precepts.

The establishment of well-defined SBUs within an organization, based on sound segmentation concepts.

The training and development of all levels of middle and top management in the use of strategic planning techniques and concepts.

The development of strategic control systems to determine whether SBU strategies are being implemented as proposed and approved.

HOW TOP MANAGEMENT FOSTERS SUCCESS

Developing Commitment

Top management often preaches and promotes but fails to practice the concepts that are popular at any given time. This has happened over and over again and can be the kiss of death to any technique or concept. Thus, for strategic planning to continue to grow, the top managers of corporations, nonprofit institutions, small businesses, or government agencies must be willing to become strategic thinkers who have long-range vision of their organizations and who are willing to at least consider some short-term sacrifice for the long term. They may still decide to focus on the near term, but at least they will do so with an understanding of the long-term implications of their decisions. They must also be willing to make strategic planning a way of life. This means they must personally commit time to reviewing and studying strategic plans, as well as the evaluations of these plans by others in the organization. It also means there must be a willingness by top management to critique and provide feedback on such plans and to take actions based on them when required.

Assuring Follow-Through

To do all of this requires a management system and schedule to assure that plans are written, reviews made, and meetings held: otherwise, such activities will inevitably be sacrificed to "fight day-to-day fires." Moreover, such meetings must be planned to assure they are efficient and combine both formal and informal discussions. Further, all these sessions must be decision-oriented so that when lower-level management leave these meetings, they will know whether or not the strategy is approved so that they can then either reverse it or proceed with implementation. Also, the questioning during such meetings must focus on the strategy to be reviewed and not degenerate into a short-term budget review—unless, of course, that is the issue being discussed. And even then, part of the discussion should focus on how the long range can build on the short range.

HOW EXECUTIVE COMMITMENT
WORKS AT GENERAL ELECTRIC

Perhaps the best way to illustrate all of these points is to describe one of the more successful systems—that of the General Electric Company. GE's success has come first and foremost because of the commitment and involvement of the executive office. In this regard, the executive office prepares and commits itself to a planning schedule. This is not an easy task since the schedule must meet the requirements of several key individuals while still permitting time for other management responsibilities. Once the schedule is established, however, it is followed closely, although some changes do occur for competitive and other reasons. (See Exhibit 1.)

During the month of January, a management meeting focuses on the key corporate and SBU planning challenges for the coming year, the macroenvironmental forecasts prepared by corporate staff, and major questions of corporate strategy and direction. The output of this meeting then serves as a background for the various SBU plans, which are developed in the February through May period, reviewed by sector-level management in June, and submitted to corporate management by July.

In July, a strategy review meeting allows each of GE's sectors to describe its planning situations, the responses it proposes to the planning challenges identified earlier, and the impact its proposed plans will have on GE as a whole.

Exhibit 1 GE's Annual Planning Cycle

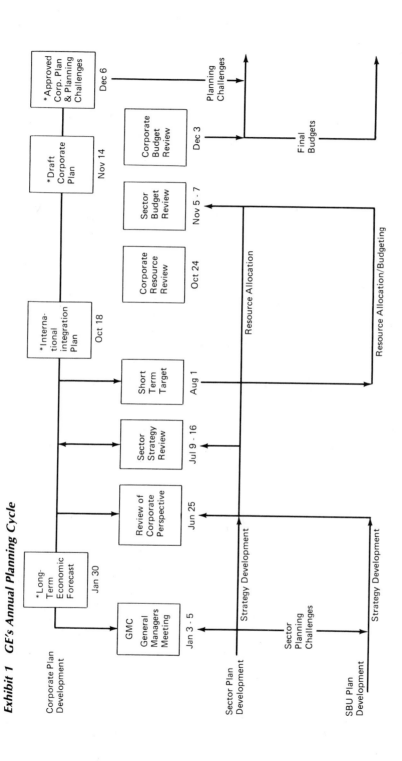

These meetings then lead to a preliminary budget review in August, after which the corporate planning staff integrates the requirements and implications of all of these plans for the corporation. In October, the various resource staffs then identify key planning issues based on a review of these strategies and resource plans, as well as an assessment of corporate capabilities, competitive challenge, and environmental changes. During November, all of these factors are incorporated into a tentative corporate plan. In December, the budgets and challenges associated with this plan are approved and the cycle is repeated. In sum, the cycle begins with a macrolook at the world, moves to specific business strategies, identifies both the short- and long-term financial results of these strategies, specifies the major planning challenges to be met, and finally produces an approved budget for the coming year. Moreover, since each of these sessions involves the chairman, vice-chairmen, and senior vice-presidents of planning, finance, legal affairs, human resources, technology, and production, there is a continuing dialogue and coupling of short- and long-term actions and plans. One further indication of the commitment of top management to this system is the fact that sessions are rarely cancelled, nor are they permitted to be too lengthy for effective decision making, or allowed to degenerate into short-range problem-solving or complaint sessions.

SBU DESIGNATION IS CRUCIAL

The term "strategic business unit" or "business unit" has become very popular but is often misapplied in practice. The purpose of such a designation is to determine where in the organization strategic planning should be done.

Unfortunately, many SBUs in many organizations are not truly strategic planning centers, but rather are cost or resource centers. As a result, they are forced to submit strategic plans but have trouble doing so because of their character. This has resulted in confusion, conflict, and negative rather than positive results both for the SBUs themselves and for the organizations of which they are a part.

What Makes an SBU?

Consequently; it will be useful to review the criteria that should be met before an organizational component is classified as an SBU.

- First of all, an SBU must serve an external, rather than an internal, market; that is, it must have a set of external customers and not merely serve as an internal supplier or opportunistic external supplier.
- Second, it should have a clear set of external competitors, which it is trying to equal or surpass.
- Third, it should have control over its own destiny. This means that it must be able to decide for itself what products to offer, how and when to go to

market, and where to obtain its supplies, components, or even products. This does not mean that it cannot use pooled resources such as a common manufacturing plant, or a combined sales force, or even corporate R&D. The key is choice. It must be able to choose, and not merely be the victim of someone else's decisions. It must have options from which it may select the alternative(s) that best achieves the corporate and its business objectives.

- Fourth, its performance must be measurable in terms of profit and loss; that is, it must be a true profit center.

No organization is a pure SBU, but most SBUs should meet most of these criteria and all must meet the third one.

An SBU or Not?
Three Examples

To illustrate these points more thoroughly, let us consider three examples: the woodlands operations of a forest product company, a wholly owned distributing organization, and an internal component supplier.

The woodlands operations of a forest product company could be either a strategic business unit or a cost center. If its prime purpose is to supply pulp to the company's own converters and it does not have the discretion as to whether it supplies the pulp or not and/or if it must sell to the converters at cost, then it is not an SBU but rather a cost center. If, however, it is geared to serve both internal and external converters and has a choice of whom to serve and what to charge, it is an SBU. Obviously, the choice in any company should be based on total system profitability and not merely on what is good for the woodlands operation, but once a decision is made it should be implemented strongly and consistently.

A wholly owned distributor could also be either a cost center or a strategic business unit. Thus, if it is primarily geared to serve the distribution needs of other components of the company and/or if its prime reason for existence is that it is the lowest-cost way to reach the market, then it is a cost center and should be treated and planned for accordingly. However, if it is permitted to decide on the goods it will distribute and can carry competing brands, price competitively, and do what is necessary to compete profitably, then it is an SBU.

Some companies have internal component suppliers that make motors, wire and cable, and integrated circuits. Most such units are set up to assure supply or to provide lower-cost components. At some point, however, they may gain the capacity to serve both internal and external needs. In such instances, the question of whether the component supplier is an SBU or cost center depends on the emphasis it puts on these markets and the freedom it has to go its own way. If it can set its own direction and sells primarily to outside markets, it is an SBU. If it sells primarily to internal markets on a cost or cost-plus basis, it is a cost center. But what if it sells 60 percent to outside, but is expected to be a supplier of last resort on a cost-plus basis? Or suppose it sells 60 percent inside, but can set its own prices and can refuse internal orders. In such situations, the decision is never perfectly clear since each option has its advantages and disadvantages. Nevertheless, it is almost always better to make a clear choice one way or the other rather than to try to be both an internal captive supplier and strategic planning center simultaneously.

HOW TO TRAIN MANAGEMENT FOR STRATEGIC PLANNING

Once SBUs have been designated and the corporate planning system and planning schedule have been developed, it is vital that all corporate, group, SBU, and top financial managers and planners be properly trained. This training should acquaint these managers with the relevant strategic planning concepts and techniques, and it should be adapted to fit the existing corporate systems and culture. Normally, such training consists of a blend of classroom lectures, guidebooks, periodic seminars, and even personal consulting. For example, when General Electric installed its current strategic planning system in the early 1970s, every general manager at the department level and above, as well as all the planners at their levels, was required to attend one or more strategic planning seminars. These seminars ranged from three and one-half days for general management to two weeks for planners. They enabled the participants to learn by doing, i.e., to apply concept and techniques to a simulated business and present their strategic recommendations for dealing with this situation. They were also exposed to professional consultants, academics, and internal specialists, and told how to get continuing help if they wanted it. Thus, even though the workshop was only an introduction to strategic planning, it served as a means to let the participants experiment with new behavior and challenge their existing thought processes. Perhaps most important of all, however, was the fact that it indicated that the company was serious about and committed to applying strategic planning approaches in the future.

SETTING UP STRATEGIC CONTROL SYSTEMS

Even if a corporation has a well-designed strategic planning system, has defined its SBUs properly, and has a well-trained management team, its strategic planning efforts will come to nil unless it assures that each of its SBUs is implementing its approved strategy. This comes down to two questions:

- Are the necessary resources being allocated to the SBU to permit it to achieve its strategic objectives and investment strategies?

- Are the day-to-day action programs of the business consistent with its overall business strategy?

Unfortunately, top management cannot assume that these allocations and programs are consistent, since SBU management may achieve short-term results at the expense of the long term or may achieve them with a different strategy than the one approved. Consequently, if a corporation wishes to allow a maximum of creativity but also desires to have a corporate thrust and direction, strategy reviews and controls are critical.

Resources vs. Investment Priorities

The first step to resolve the question of where and how much to invest is to determine the corporate investment priorities. This can be done in a variety of ways, including:

- The selection of the businesses or potential opportunities with the highest ROI or ROS. This is a hurdle rate approach.
- The evaluation of each business in terms of its market growth rate and relative share position. This is advocated by Boston Consulting Group and provides a means of identifying cash generators and cash users.
- Use of the product life cycle, and investing as required.
- Use of attractiveness/competitive position screen, which measures the relative attractiveness of the various markets, technologies, competitive climates, profitablility, and economic requirements of the firm's various businesses, as well as the relative ability of these businesses to market, produce, design, and manage.

Each approach has its advantages and disadvantages. Each also provides somewhat different insights.

The critical element in each approach is the effective segmentation of the organization into SBUs. The end result of each is simply a classification of the organization's different businesses (SBUs) in some priority order with respect to the likelihood that investments in them will meet the organization's overall objectives.

Using the Attractiveness/ Competitive Position Screen

For instance, in the attractiveness/competitive position approach (which the author prefers), there are four levels of investment priority, as indicated in Exhibit 2.

Exhibit 2   Attractiveness/Competitive Position Screen

Attractiveness

		High	Medium	Low
Competitive Position	Strong	I	II	III
	Average	II	III	IV
	Weak	III	IV	IV

The top priority businesses for corporate investment are those with high attractiveness and strong position. Second priority is given to those with medium attractiveness and strong position or average strength and high attractiveness, and so on.

Such classifications enable a company to determine where to invest its limited resources or where to cut back if resources become limited.

Coordinating Allocations with Priority

Once such a prioritization is made—which usually requires a number of iterations between corporate and SBU business management—the next step is to assure that both corporate and business resource allocations are consistent with this prioritization. This always requires corporate effort and attention, even in single-industry, centrally controlled companies. It is particularly difficult in multi-industry, decentralized companies, however.

In order to make such determinations, one must have a means of deciding what allocations are required for each category of business. To do this, one should compare each business' expenditures for plant and equipment, marketing, engineering, working capital, and salaried employment over the past six years with those it projects will be needed for the next three years in terms of both real dollars and as a percent of sales. Such an analysis permits the identification of those businesses whose plans are significantly more aggressive than those of the past as well as those that are projecting significantly decreased resource needs. Put differently, for each business in the company, the degree of change in its investment aggressiveness should be related to its own past, since arbitrary allocations, such as a 5 percent expenditure for sales programs, may be high for some businesses but low for others.

In some instances, it may also be useful to make such comparisons with the investment patterns and plans of one's competitors. Furthermore, all of these comparisons may be misleading if the strategic character of the business has

Exhibit 3   Investment Priority Category

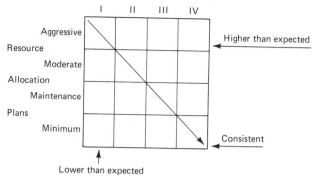

changed. In general, however, one would expect that the high-priority businesses would have needs that are the same as or higher than those of the past so they can continue to grow and defend their positions. Likewise, one would expect most lower-priority businesses, many of which should be following gradual harvest strategies, to be decreasing their investment expenditures relative to the past.

Based on this type of analysis, each business can be plotted on a matrix like that in Exhibit 3, which compares their investment priority with their resource allocation plans. The four cells along the diagonal represent businesses whose resource allocation plans are consistent with their investment priorities. Those above the diagonal represent businesses that are planning to spend more than their investment priority would indicate is appropriate, whereas those below the diagonal indicate lower than expected investment. This provides a quick way to identify businesses whose spending patterns seem suspect. Once these businesses are identified, however, further reviews must be conducted to determine the reasons for the discrepancy. If these are sound, then the planned allocation should be permitted. However, if the reasoning is faulty, the business should normally be asked to replan and reassess its resource allocation.

Are Allocations Adequate?

An example may help to clarify these points. Consider the case of a business that has been evaluated to be highly attractive and strongly positioned, i.e., a Priority I business. During the past five-year period, it has spent 5.5 percent of its sales, which has totaled over $5 million a year, on plant and equipment. However, its projection is to reduce this expenditure to 3 percent and $3.5 million a year during the next three years. In addition, it has projected that programmed expenditures will hold at 4 percent and around $4.7 million, working capital turnover will increase, and salaried employment will decline. In short, this "growth" business appears to be on a hold/defend strategy, i.e., its allocations are not consistent with its Priority I investment category.

The issue is: why? Is this business suboptimizing its position, or are its allocations realistic? One possibility might be that its past expenditures for plant and equipment were designed to provide more than ample capacity for the future, which would explain the decline in expenditures for the next three years. Likewise, the decline in salaried employment may be the result of increased office automation and computerized design. If so, the business might be quite justified in the expenditure and employee decreases it has forecast, although further checks of the investment intensity of the business and competitor plans might be made.

On the other hand, if no such explanations were forthcoming, it would tend to indicate that the planned allocations are inadequate and that there should be management action to correct the situation or to reclassify the business from Category I to Category II or III if its long-term strategic position really has been changed.

DO PROGRAMS FIT STRATEGIES?

In addition to this type of analysis, there is also a need to evaluate whether the type of functional strategic action programs planned by the business fits its investment and management strategies. This means that functional specialists must assess whether the planned engineering, manufacturing, marketing, and financial programs will lead to the successful execution of the SBU's planned business strategy. In this regard, Exhibit 4 illustrates the differences in the type of programs required to implement two different business strategies. For instance, if one wishes to grow via product innovation, one's engineering programs should strive for leadership, differentiation, and proprietary position. By contrast, if one wishes to defend via promotion, one's engineering programs should stress the ability to quickly meet competitor's innovations with standardized products that one has adapted and/or licensed from others. Similar differences arise in each of the other functional areas for these two different business strategies. Moreover, there are many additional business strategies one could follow, each of which has its own pattern of functional action programs. To assure strategic success, however, it is essential to make such consistency checks before implementing any strategy.

The corporate staff should do this type of detailed strategic program review. Thus, the corporate technologists should evaluate the nature and type of technical programs; and if there is a variance from the strategies of the programs being implemented, they should probe the reason for it. If the reason is sound, no further action is required. Those variations that cannot be explained, though, should be evaluated further to determine whether the business strategy is inappropriate or the functional strategy needs adjusting and this information communicated to the appropriate line managers. Similar reviews of production, human resources, and marketing programs should be conducted by the corporate staff in these areas.

Exhibit 4   Suggested Implementation Strategies for Two Different Investment and Management Strategies

Investment Strategy/ Management Strategy	Growth via Product Innovation	Defense via Promotion
	Engineering Implementation Strategies	
Scope	Full scope from basic research to design	Limited scope—primarily design or specification
Position	Leader	Quick or reluctant follower
Response	Rapidly differentiated, possibly customized	Standardized at own pace or to meet competition
Funding	Internal—preferred; External—only if you can protect	Any way that you can
Exclusivity	Proprietary, protectable	Adaptation or licensed from someone else
Facilities	Corporate, specialized—total commitment	Business generalized; customer responsive
	Manufacturing Implementation Strategies	
Facilities	Small, close to market, self-owned	Large, generalized, owned or leased
Capacity	As much as possible, without sacrificing innovation and quality	"Loan Leveling," constantly high utilization
Flexibility	High—using either people or easy-to-reprogram computers	Moderate to low
Sufficiency	Flexibility—not critical	Sufficiency is critical
Productivity	Do not emphasize cost too soon	Ability to be "least-cost" for contingency response
Logistics	Some concern about incoming traffic	Critical—to assure proper response
	Marketing Implementation Strategies	
Product Management	Lead, limited scope initially, differentiate	Reluctant follower, full scope and standardized
Distribution	Specialized, service, exclusive long-term commitment	Generalized, non-service, multiple brand, low-medium commitment
Sales	Highly qualified trained, knowledgeable, applications, training, owned-salary and some commission	Not experts, some training, order takers, commission
Service	Strong for sales Bundled Trained, skilled	For profit Unbundled
Intelligence	Customer focused Future Primary	Competitively focused Avoid surprises Secondary
Readiness	Rapid/anticipatory Controlled	Meet competition Intermediaries

Continued

Exhibit 4   (Continued)

Investment Strategy/ Management Strategy	Growth via Product Innovation	Defense via Promotion
Promotion	Strong pull Aggressive Above average	Strong Aggressive Above average
Pricing	High Controlled Perceived value Terms if necessary	Meet competition Cost/margin Compatible terms

Judgment rather than consistency is the key, however, because there are some circumstances in which the "consistent" action will not work. For example, product innovation growth strategies normally call for "value pricing," that is, for pricing a product on the basis of its high real value rather than on the basis of its manufacturing costs. Moreover, such high prices are normally required to generate the funds needed to support innovation. In some instances, though, this type of pricing will not work because of the aggressiveness of competition. Thus, if a competitor wishes to gain share, has an equally effective though less innovative product, and is willing to accept short-term losses to improve his long-term position, value pricing, although preferred, will probably not work and management would be ill advised to try it. Furthermore, in such instances, it may even be necessary to modify the strategy of product innovation if over the long term customers are unwilling to pay for the extra value of such innovations through either higher prices or increased share.

The specifics of such review are not the critical factor, however, since there are a number of different ways to check for such business strategy/functional action plan consistencies, just as there are a number of different ways to develop SBU investment priorities. What is critical is that some type of strategic review and control system be established not only to ensure the overall integrity of the strategic planning process but also to ensure that what is planned is what in fact occurs.

CONCLUSION

Growth will happen only if strategic planning is:

- Applied properly with explicit CEO commitment and involvement;
- Used at the appropriate organizational level by true SBUs; and
- Accompanied by the proper reviews and controls.

8

From Strategic Planning to Strategic Performance: Closing the Achievement Gap

JOHN D.C. ROACH
Booz·Allen & Hamilton Inc.

Most companies have made significant progress in the last 10 to 15 years in improving their strategic planning capabilities. Clear, concise methods have been developed for analyzing and evaluating market segments, business performance, pricing and cost structures. Creative, even elegant, methods have been devised for displaying the results of these strategic analyses to top management.

Few today would argue the value—in theory at least—of the strategic approach to business planning. Reginald Jones, former chairman of General Electric, described that value well in a recent interview:

> More and more, strategic planning is no longer just a buzz phrase or a paperwork exercise. At GE, we entered the 1970s getting 80 percent of our earnings from electrical equipment. By 1979, that was down to 47 percent. If you take this longer-term strategic approach, it will get you more capital investment, increased productivity, and take you out of dying industries and into ones that are growing.

Unfortunately, GE's successful experience appears to be more the exception than the rule. Much more typical, we have found, are the results of a survey conducted for a recent *Business Week* conference, in which 80 percent of the 145 participating firms indicated that they were dissatisfied with the poor results of their strategic planning.

Why the "achievement gap" between strategic planning and strategic performance? While the reasons undoubtedly vary from corporation to corporation, several appear to be most critical:

First, there is the inescapable fact that the global business environment is becoming increasingly complex. Political pressures, social needs, regulatory demands and rapid technological change are but a handful of the often cited challenges facing management today. Add to these the impact of global economics—international instability, a new wave of nationalism and critical resource shortages—and the result is a highly volatile strategic environment that differs dramatically from that of even 5 or 10 years ago. Consequently, the burden on strategic planners to anticipate rather than merely react to virtually unpredictable economic "dislocations" is greater than ever before.

A second reason for the "achievement gap" is the increasing sophistication of industry competitors' use of strategic planning. Previously, companies were able to achieve profit improvement through the use of strategy as an offensive weapon. Now that strategic planning techniques are so widely employed, there is a need for a second wave of capability in their use.

The third reason for the questionable payoff from strategic planning stems directly from the planning process itself. Although valuable data may be gathered from historical business analysis, the identification of successful formulas in other industries and the use of broad strategic concepts, generalized strategic approaches are exactly that: *generalizations.*

While they can provide a framework and a set of organizing principles for strategic planning, these techniques must be adapted and refined to meet the specific needs of an individual business. Strategic analysis based only on industry experiences or only on the rigid application of a single conceptual model or approach can lead, at best, to myopic business decisions and, at worst, to costly—even fatal—strategic errors.

It is also crucial that strategic planning techniques reflect the differing needs of manufacturing firms vs. high-technology firms, financial and service companies and other types of businesses. This need for an industry specific approach to strategy is perhaps most evident in the case of high-technology firms.

Traditionally, business portfolio analysis alone has provided the foundation for these firms' technology strategy. In our view this approach is dangerously inadequate and one-dimensional; it must be coupled with what we call a "technology portfolio" analysis. An analogue or complement to the business portfolio, this analysis defines a firm's relative product and process technologies in terms of technology positioning, competitive outlook, relative profit potential and emerging technologies. In tandem, the combined business/technology portfolio approach allows a firm to identify its major technology strengths and risks, assess its competitive position and evaluate its technology options from a strategic perspective.

Given the complexity of the volatile business environment of the 80s, the dangers of adopting a "one size fits all" strategic approach, and the difficulty of tailoring techniques to meet specific business needs, it is understandable that top management's frustration with strategic planning is high. Yet precisely because business issues are more complex and competition more fierce, the value of effective, opportunistic strategic analysis will increase dramatically in the next 10 years. Companies that haven't adopted sophisticated strategic plans will be compelled to do so if they're to survive in a slow-growth, inflationary global economy. Companies currently acknowledged as industry leaders will continue to outperform their competition only if they constantly upgrade their skills in strategic planning and execution.

Three critical areas of strategic planning that we believe top management must be concerned with in the immediate future are:

better business mix management—including more effective business segmentation, management of problem businesses and "growth through acquisition" strategies;

more creative and innovative planning—requiring responsive organization structures and effective technology management;

more effective implementation—involving the integration of strategic business analysis, planning and execution.

BETTER BUSINESS MIX MANAGEMENT

Virtually every company today is, in fact, comprised of a portfolio of businesses. Effective management of this portfolio or "business mix" is one of the key tools a company has at its command to improve its overall strategic performance. Basically, this involves allocating resources differently among component businesses within a carefully planned corporate strategic framework. Three factors contribute to the formulation of an effective strategic framework: strategic business segmentation, the handling of problem businesses, and the use of acquisitions to strengthen a firm's existing business mix.

Strategic Business Segmentation

A company's ability to identify and direct management attention and investment dollars to the most promising segments of its businesses—and gradually exit from or strengthen marginal ones—can mean the difference between outstanding or mediocre financial performance. For this reason, strategic business segmentation (SBS) will continue to be a critical tool for achieving superior financial performance throughout the 1980s.

While strategic options are usually very clear once the segment structure of a business has been analyzed, identifying the strategically relevant segment structure of that business is often an extremely complex task. One reason for the difficulty is that most companies take a purely product/market segmentation approach to analyzing their businesses, essentially organizing them along product lines and then matching products to markets (see Figure 1).

Figure 1: Product Market Segmentation

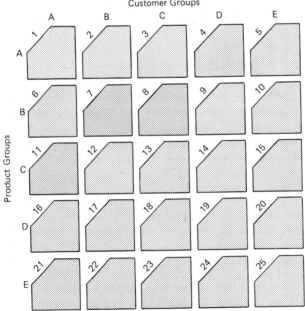

25 Distinct Product Market Segments

Figure 2: Strategic Business Segmentation

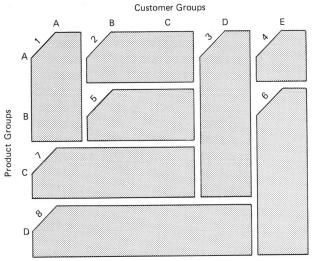

8 Distinct Strategic Business Segments

Strategic business segmentation is a more complicated process. Instead of merely identifying product/market relationships, it maps out those relationships and then regroups them along strategic lines by identifying sets of products and services that are designed, produced, marketed, distributed and serviced for relatively homogeneous groups of customers, users or intermediaries. Each cluster of product/marked elements with a high degree of commonality is approached as a distinct business component, driven by different economic forces and often requiring a different strategy (see Figure 2).

The ability of companies to identify and capitalize on underlying strategic business segments varies tremendously. As a result, many industries are characterized by one or several highly profitable leaders, a handful of small, more focused and perhaps equally profitable competitors; and a large number of firms in the middle with poor performance. This pattern is reflected in the often-observed industry profitability relationship known as the "V-Curve Effect" (see Figure 3).

The large firms on the V-curve tend to address the entire market, achieving cost advantages and high market share by realizing economies of sale. The small competitors reap high profits by focusing on some narrower segment of the business and by developing specialized approaches to production, marketing, and distribution for that segment.

Ironically, the medium-sized competitors at the trough of the V-curve are unable to realize any competitive advantage and often show the poorest performance. Trapped in a strategic "No Man's Land," they are too large to reap the benefits of more focused competition, yet too small to benefit from the economies of scale that their larger competitors enjoy.

Figure 3:   The V-Curve Effect:

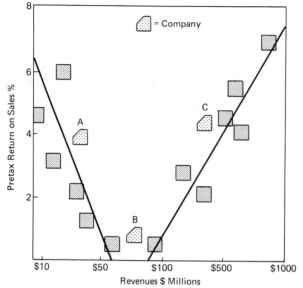

As illustrated, many industries are characterized by a small number
of highly profitable leaders, a handful of small, more focused and
perhaps equally profitable competitors, and a large number of firms
at the trough of the V-curve with poor performance.

Companies in a wide range of industries fall into one of the categories outlined here—each of which has its own set of strategic challenges. Industry leaders for instance, must be constantly concerned with maintaining their dominance because they are always in danger of being attacked by a school of
piranha-like competitors vying for their market position. Successful narrow-
segment-based firms are faced with the need to leverage their position without
losing the specialist strengths they have acquired.

Wherever a firm falls on the V-curve, concentrating on a practical strategic business segment can lead to superior performance if two conditions exist.
First, if the segment is sufficiently attractive in terms of size, probable growth
rate, and relative freedom from technical or government-triggered obsolescence.
Second, if the business segment provides a competitive barrier; that is, if some
aspect—technology, production process, distribution method or brand fran-
chise—results in the opportunity to establish and sustain a degree of competitive
advantage.

Strategic business segmentation is by no means an academic exercise; its
marketplace value can perhaps best be demonstrated by the following examples:

Company A, a large, narrow-segment-based firm, would like to improve
its performance by expanding into new markets or product lines, though one
outcome of an expansion move might be to dissipate the natural momentum of

its more narrowly focused historical approach. How can A expand its overall position without eroding the competitive advantage arising from its existing segment base? This may be the strategic dilemma faced, for example, by some firms in the computer industry, such as Amdahl Corporation, in large, mainframe computers, and Apple Computer, in small, at-home minicomputers.

Company C, on the other hand, is a small, broad-segment-based company. Improving its position by increasing its overall market share is extremely expensive and time consuming, and the ultimate payoff is uncertain. Improving performance by retrenching could prove equally difficult if smaller competitors have more focused, streamlined operations and compete in fundamentally different ways. Should Company C try to improve its poor performance and marginal competitive position by aggressive growth or retrenchment? How can if fend off competition from more focused companies, and simultaneously maintain or increase its relative advantage over other broadline competitors? These may be the strategic survival questions facing companies such as Chrysler.

Company B, caught in the middle, faces the most common of strategic dilemmas: should it expand, contract or divest?

These are the kinds of issues that emerge from effective strategic business segmentation. Essentially, it allows a firm to identify and leverage positions of strength, and to eliminate or offset operational weaknesses. Good strategic business segmentation is a complex and time-consuming process—and one that requires a combination of industry and technological expertise and creative, insightful, independent analysis.

In the 1980s, it is essential that companies accurately analyze the underlying strategic structure of each of their businesses, assess the competitive and investment implications of that structure, and finally, execute their strategies based on a sound business segmentation framework.

Management of Problem Businesses

Effective strategic segmentation can enable a firm to identify its problem businesses—the second element in effective portfolio management—and to analyze the strategic options available for either stabilizing or liquidating them.

Although straightforward divestment of unprofitable or marginal businesses may be the most desirable course of action, it may be increasingly difficult in the future for firms to exercise this option, for several reasons.

First, there are a number of emerging government restraints and social pressures that promise to make exiting a business almost prohibitive financially. These include stringent union agreements, very costly compensatory severance payments, and contingent liabilities associated with unfunded pension programs and other benefit plans.

Several European countries have adopted precedent-setting policies in this area that may have great impact on American business in the future. In Britain,

Belgium and Italy, for instance, it is tremendously costly to eliminate or cut back a failing business. It is equally unlikely that it will be bailed out by an acquisition-hungry one. The Montedison Group in Italy has lost a fortune in its efforts to institute labor and other cutbacks. BL (British Leyland) was able to lay off 20,000 to 30,000 workers only after great difficulty. British Steel Corporation, as a nationalized industry, has faced a doubly difficult challenge. Its struggle to initiate a six-month wage freeze and eliminate some 20,000 jobs is a classic example of the problems that face firms seeking to disengage themselves from marginal businesses and redirect their strategies.

The second reason that divestment is becoming more difficult is that companies are more sophisticated in their preliminary acquisitions planning. They have access to more accurate data on the nature of an acquisition candidate's problems and can use that information as negotiating leverage and to avoid paying historic premiums for those businesses.

Even if divestment appears to be the most attractive solution for strengthening a firm's business portfolio, today its feasibility as a business tool is questionable. There are so many businesses that currently fall into the "problem" category that the difficulties of widespread divestment are almost insurmount-

Figure 4:   Problem Business Proliferation

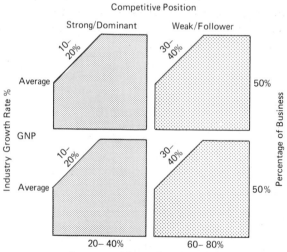

By definition, 50 percent of all businesses grow at a rate faster than GNP and 50 percent at a rate slower than GNP. On average, dominant competitors control 20 percent to 40 percent of the total market, with weaker competitors representing 60 percent to 80 percent. Defining a problem business as one with a weak position in a low-to-negative growth industry, between 30 percent and 40 percent of all businesses fall into the "problem" category.

able on a macroeconomic level. The potential impact of the situation is staggering in its magnitude. Defining a problem business as one with a weak relative competitive position in a low-growth industry, one finds that some 40 percent of all businesses nationwide can be labeled as "problem" ones (see Figure 4). On one hand, this vast pool of troubled enterprises undoubtedly offers attractive opportunities for synergy through acquisition. At the negative extreme, however, a collective divestment strategy could result in a giant swapping game in which one company sells its problem business to another one only to acquire a new set of problem businesses from a third company. The only beneficiaries in this type of churning environment would be the intermediaries that service the transactions.

It is almost impossible to imagine an international economy in which some 30 to 40 percent of all businesses are candidates for divestment year in and year out. Yet that appears to be the case today.

As a consequence, throughout the 1980s, more and more firms will be forced to manage rather than divest their problem businesses. At a minimum, firms will insist that problem operations remain in cash balance—a strategy employed by some European firms to ensure that problem businesses do not become drains on their overall portfolio.

Increasingly the need to control a problem business successfully will make effective strategic analysis and implementation more critical than ever and will involve:

- narrowing segment focus and improving performance through specialization;
- upsetting competitive equilibrium through the use of innovative techniques in marketing, product development, production and other areas; and
- better implementation through improved operations, organizational redesign and more effective executive compensation packages.

Growth Through Acquisition

The flip side of problem business management is growth through acquisition, an option that has surged in popularity recently. Entering a new business or expanding an existing operating base via a sound acquisition can often be a faster and lower risk—though not necessarily higher return—alternative than internal development.

In most cases, an acquisition is pursued in order to:

- improve the strategic position of an established business;
- take advantage of a cash-rich position with inadequate or unsuitable internal investment options; or

- upgrade or trade off a portfolio of businesses by capitalizing on a unique opportunity:

Numerous companies have grown successfully via acquisition. Philip Morris's acquisition of Miller Beer and White Consolidated's multiple acquisitions of Kelvinator, Frigidaire and Westinghouse are prime examples of successful matches in which the acquiring firms apparently developed very conscious pre-takeover strategies and post acquisition programs to integrate the newly acquired businesses into their existing operations.

In too many cases, however, an acquisition is seen as a panacea and merely deflects management attention from exploring internal investment options. As a result, numerous companies have made acquisitions for the wrong reasons at the wrong time, and with the wrong—if any—post-acquisition strategy. In one survey, in fact, some 50 percent of all managers involved in recent acquisitions said that the companies acquired had underperformed relative to both profit and growth expectations.

In analyzing recent acquisition trends, we have found that there are four nontraditional "strategic plays" for achieving superiority through acquisition:

- acquiring a company with underutilized financial strength;
- acquiring an underskilled company in a related industry;
- acquiring a company with underexploited physical assets; and
- acquiring an undervalued corporate portfolio.

INNOVATIVE PLANNING

Innovative planning is the second critical strategic action area demanding top management attention. Essentially this involves two related activities: first developing a planning process that encourages innovative ideas, techniques and products, and second, creating an innovative business strategy to implement them. In the 1980s, the need to generate growth and profitability through internal innovation is far greater than it has been in the past, because of the difficulties involved in divesting problem businesses and orchestrating successful acquisitions.

Nowhere is the demand for innovative ideas and strategy more forcefully expressed than at the top level of management. In a recent Booz·Allen survey on technology management, 86 percent of the 3,000 senior managers interviewed indicated that their current planning techniques were inadequate. Many in top management—even those in the fastest growing high-technology firms—refer with nostalgia to the dynamic start-up phase of their venture, when creativity and entrepreneurial spirit drove growth, an attitude they believe is impossible to recapture and sustain in today's business environment. As evidence, they contend that if today's rigorous financial criteria were applied to the new business ventures or products that turned their firms into high performers 10 or 20 years ago, most of them would have been "killed" before they left the drawing board.

Ironically, the widespread use of "sophisticated" planning techniques has often been cited as a key contributor to the decline of innovation. This argument has merit. There seems to be a widespread assumption, especially in U.S. firms, that the more complex a planning process is, the better its results.

One unfortunate byproduct of this attitude is that the planning process may become an end in itself: highly elaborate organizations are created whose only real product is paperwork. The tendency toward overplanning can also result in a dangerously conservative approach to technology innovation—especially when competing with the Japanese. Between 1960 and 1978 alone, the United States lost its marketplace position in 12 industries and gained ground in none, while the Japanese advanced in 8 industries and lost ground in none.

Effective strategic planning should eliminate organizational restraints, not multiply them, and contribute to innovation, not inhibit it. In the 1980s strategic planners face a unique challenge because innovation and new product development must be stimulated within the structure of the large, multinational corporate enterprise. A number of companies have proven that innovation and entrepreneurial drive *can* be institutionalized and fostered by a responsive organization structure. Celanese and IBM, for example, have established technology review boards to ensure that promising product ideas and new technologies receive adequate start-up support. Adopting another approach, Dow Chemical recently instituted an "innovation department" to streamline technology commercialization.

In analyzing the management and organizational style of technology leaders worldwide, a number of concrete methods for encouraging innovation have been identified:

- focus management attention on the goals of strategic planning rather than its process, i.e., concentrate on substance, not form;
- integrate into business strategy the analysis of emerging technologies and technology management, consumer trends and demographic shifts, regulatory impact and global economies;
- design totally new planning processes, review standards and acceptance criteria for technological advances and new business "thrusts" that may not conform completely to a firm's current corporate base;
- adopt a longer planning horizon to ensure that a promising business or technological development won't be cut off prematurely;
- ensure that overly stringent financial requirements aren't imposed during the start-up phase of a promising project;
- create special organizational "satellites," such as new venture groups whose mission is to pursue new ideas, free from the pressures of day-to-day operations;

- institute financial and career reward systems that encourage bold, innovative development programs.

STRATEGY IMPLEMENTATION

The third, and in Booz·Allen's experience, most neglected imperative demanding management action is strategy implementation. In our view, strategic planning, analysis and execution are all different phases of the same process—and are all equally vital to corporate performance. In the next five to ten years, as strategic planning reaches a higher level of sophistication, a corporation's ability to achieve competitive advantage in global markets will be directly tied to its success in implementing its chosen strategy.

There are a wide array of strategic tools for promoting effective implementation, including R&D allocations, operations planning, marketing, sales and advertising, pricing and distribution. In addition, organization structure, reward mechanisms, and information systems that measure performance against objectives are all valuable "levers" for inducing effective strategy execution. In particular, the value of a strategically linked incentive program that integrates strategy, organization structure and executive compensation is becoming apparent to many chief executives. More and more companies are realizing that together they constitute a "critical management triumvirate" that must be directed at the boardroom level.

Why consider them collectively and attach such importance to their impact? To improve corporate performance. Many companies with strong business strategies have failed to achieve superior financial success because their organization structure and reward system are inconsistent, or even in direct conflict, with their strategic objectives. A brief overview of these two topics seems appropriate here:

ORGANIZATION STRUCTURE
AND EXECUTIVE COMPENSATION

Ideally, a company's internal organization should be dictated by its overall corporate strategic direction and by the identification of the specific strategic missions and operating characteristics of its component businesses. In reality, however, it is equally important that the strategy itself—or at least the rate of its implementation—be tailored to existing management style, capabilities and organizational philosophy and structure.

As a result, the peace and sequence of major internal changes are as critical to their success as the process through which they are instituted. Alterations in strategy, top management or organizational structure are radical by definition. That is, they strike at the roots of a firm's operating style; its public, industry and self-image; and future competitive position. Given the sensitive and profound nature of changes in these areas, attempting to institute them by management fiat can be dangerous and disruptive, even when a sudden crisis or marketplace shift makes doing so a matter of survival, not choice. A carefully orchestrated shift that builds consensus from within the organization at all operating levels is far more likely to succeed—an approach that will be discussed in depth in a future issue of *Outlook*.

While executive compensation has always been viewed as an extremely important and sensitive issue, its direct link to both strategic objectives and organization planning has been largely unrecognized until recently. This has proven to be a costly oversight, and has too often contributed to the erosion of competitive advantage, loss of management talent and unrealized profit potential.

Far from being simply one more management incentive, the purpose of an executive compensation program is identical to that of business strategy itself: the achievement of competitive advantage. That goal is approached differently by each of the operations in a firm's business portfolio, because each is driven by different needs relative to market share, segment focus, new product development, technology innovation and competitive position. As a result, each business unit must have a compensation system designed to support the execution of its strategy. The top management of a mature, stable business must be rewarded and motivated differently from that of a newer, fast-growing, high-risk, but potentially high-profit operation.

Without such tailored compensation programs, the executive incentive system will reward steady-state, low-risk management and discourage risk-taking because it fails to recognize the different needs of management teams in different businesses and industries at different stages of development. . . .

STRATEGIC SUCCESS FACTORS

Closing the achievement gap between strategic planning and strategic performance requires concentration on better business mix management, more innovative planning and more effective implementation. To accomplish this, well-managed companies must:

- employ rigorous and creative analytical techniques to produce fresh, intriguing and practical insights into their business, its segment structure, and strategic options;
- combine extensive industry experience with in-depth knowledge of the technological forces that drive it;
- recognize implementation as an integral part of the strategic process; and
- develop an overall strategy, organization structure and compensation system that are mutually consistent and reinforcing.

Throughout the 1980s, individual companies and indeed, entire industries, will be affected as never before by world politics and economic developments. The next ten years will be an era of protracted battle for survival in global markets. Strategic planning will provide the blueprint for this worldwide competition, and management's margin for error—strategic and tactical—will be far smaller than before. The companies that emerge as leaders in the 1980s will be those able to transform the complex elements of strategic planning into competitive advantage. And the ones that move most quickly and forcefully will reap the greatest financial and strategic rewards.

9

Dispersed Positioning in Strategic Portfolio Analysis

H. IGOR ANSOFF

US International University, San Diego

WERNER KIRSCH AND PETER ROVENTA

University of Munich

Reprinted by permission from *Industrial Marketing Management,* Vol. II, No. 4, October 1982. Copyright © 1982, Elsevier Scientific Publishing Co., 52 Vanderbilt Ave., New York, N.Y.

INTRODUCTION

Since the Boston Consulting Group introduced the market growth–market share matrix, its applications have been broadened to more sophisticated forms of portfolio analysis: comparison of future prospects (including turbulence) with competitive position, analysis of strategic resources, risk analysis, synergy analysis, and, most recently, corporate capability analysis.[1,2]

All the applications suggested to date have been focused on enrichments of the *contents* of strategic analysis. In this paper we deal not with the content but with the *uncertainty* and *ignorance* that typically accompany all efforts to predict the future. As to contents, we will base our discussion on what has become known as the General Electric version of the matrix, which uses market attractiveness and relative competitive position as the two principal dimensions. However, everything we will have to say about the dispersed positioning of SBA[3] applies equally to analysis of other dimensions of the firm's future.

THE INFORMATION PROBLEM
IN PORTFOLIO ANALYSIS

Albach[4] has suggested that portfolio techniques are better suited to strategic analysis of turbulent environment than the earlier techniques (for example, gap analysis). But paradoxically, all applications of the portfolio techniques have to date been based on the assumption that the environment is not particularly turbulent, that it is "knowable" and fully predictable, and that management can expect its planners to produce information about trends, threats, and opportunities that is sufficiently rich and accurate to formulate precise and timely strategies. Typically, predictions of events and of strategy outcomes are reduced to single "most probable" estimates, and the chosen response strategies are not expected to be upset or modified, either by the turn of events or in the process of implementation. Because, under this view, the entries in the matrix are represented by a point, we will refer to this use of the single most probable estimate as the "point hypothesis" in strategic positioning.

Experience of the past fifteen to twenty years has shown that it is increas-

[1]H. Igor Ansoff (with James Leontiades), "Strategic Portfolio Management," *Journal of General Management*, Vol. 4, No. 1 (Autumn 1976).

[2]A survey is given, for example, in P. Roventa, *Portfolio-Analyse und Strategisches Management*, Planungs- und Organisationswissenschaftliche Schriften, München 1979.

[3]In today's use one finds two complementary concepts. The first is a *distinctive area of the firm's environment* (SBA) as defined above. The other is a *unit of the firm* that serves a distinctive environment (SBU). In our discussion we use the SBA concept.

[4]H. Albach, "Strategische Unternehmensplanung bei erhöhter Unsicherheit," *Zeitschrift für Betriebswirtschaft*, 1978, p. 702.

ingly difficult (and often impossible) to obtain information that is sufficiently rich and accurate to permit reliance on most probable estimates.[5] Today, in many cases, the most that an analyst can hope to do is to identify a range of probable future prospects in a strategic business area and a range within which the firm's future competitive position may lie. In an increasing number of cases, the information about the region determined by these two ranges is not only uncertain but also too vague to permit formulation of clear response strategies.[6] Under such an information regime, firms must increasingly build flexibility into their strategies, replace the arbitrary separation between planning and implementation by learning behavior, learn to detect weak signals of forthcoming events, and, on occasion, be prepared to deal with strategic surprises.[7] The information conveyed by a single point positioning is not adequate, either for alerting the management to the need for such flexible responses or for selecting the appropriate ones.

Thus reliance on the most probable "point hypothesis" is becoming dangerous. Management can no longer expect its planners to produce reliable "hard fact" forecasts. Managerial perceptions and judgment, the managerial vision made famous by the great entrepreneurs, must again become a part of the decision process. The historical sequential process of decision preparation by staff, followed by decision taking by line, is no longer a viable model for strategy formulation. New methods that permit the use of "soft" as well as "hard" data, and involve both staff and line in joint development of strategic action, must be developed. This paper is devoted to proposing and developing one such method.

The Current Approach in Positioning

Whatever its dimensions and content, the current use of portfolio analysis proceeds through typical steps. The first step is to circumscribe the strategic business areas,[8] product-market-technology combinations segmented in a way that subdivides the firm's environment into distinctive areas of opportunities, threats, trends, and turbulence.

Next the SRAs are positioned within the portfolio matrix. Determination of future prospects is based on forecasts, scenarios, environmental modeling, and so forth. The future competitive positioning is estimated through analysis of trends in the competitive structure, success variables, market shares, client groups, and so forth. The sources are not only publications and statistics but also

[5]H. Igor Ansoff, "The Changing Shape of the Strategic Problem," *Journal of General Management,* Vol. 4 (Summer 1979).

[6]H. Igor Ansoff, *Corporate Strategy* (New York: McGraw-Hill, 1965).

[7]H. Igor Ansoff, "Managing Strategic Surprise by Response to Weak Signals," *California Management Review,* Winter 1976.

[8]See footnote 3.

purely subjective estimates of reality. It is only in rare cases that this analytic approach will produce one single point placement in the matrix.

Therefore a subsequent attempt is made to converge on a commonly accepted point through group processes. As the planner of one firm has stated: "At the end of our discussion there is a good consensus on what's green, red or yellow."

In the language of probability theory, the process is aimed at obtaining a most probable estimate of the SBA position in the matrix through a combination of analysis and consensus building. Typically, both the analysis and the consensus process are a responsibility of the planning staff and/or of the external consultants. The results are presented to top management, which uses the scatter diagram to determine both the strategies for each SBA and the overall portfolio balance. This obviously does not mean that top management accepts the point positioning presented to it without critical discussion and rearrangement of the matrix. But it does not perceive position determination to be its major responsibility.

Criticism of the Point Hypothesis

Five criticisms can be made of the point hypothesis approach. The first is that managers are usually invited to accept or reject a positioning of the SBA proposed by the planners without a clear view of the underlying evaluation process that has led to the proposal, nor an opportunity to affect the process. If, instead of reacting to a proposed conclusion, managers involve themselves in the process of arriving at the conclusion, a richer and more acceptable evaluation process will result.

The second criticism is to be addressed at forcing the evaluation to converge on a single point position in the portfolio matrix, thus creating an appearance of accuracy which frequently does not exist. It may not exist because the available data are neither rich nor precise enough to place the SBA at a particular point in the matrix.

The third criticism is that when information is inadequate for a firm decision, managerial reactions need to be appropriately cautious, either delaying the decision or hedging against several different possibilities or making progressive commitments as better data become available. The point positioning fails to provide a basis for a choice among these responses.

The fourth criticism is that the preoccupation with arriving at a point position prejudices managerial thinking away from intuitive "soft" perceptions of reality, in favor of "hard" quantitative factual reality, and robs the decision process of the essential intuitive insights and "hunches."

The fifth and perhaps the most important criticism is that the point hypothesis encourages a spirit of conformity within the firm at a time when divergences and differences of perception and opinion must be encouraged.

Need for "Area Hypothesis"

The preceding remarks suggest that sophistication of strategic analysis must be matched with the level of external turbulence. When the level of turbulence is so low that the most probable estimate has a high probability of occurrence, it will do the job at least cost. But when the probability of its occurrence is low, a different, uncertainty preserving, method of SBA positioning becomes necessary. For this method, we suggest the "area hypothesis" approach described below.

Use of "area hypotheses" is also indicated when the firm's position on the main axes of the matrix are multidimensional (e.g., use of "competitive position" as opposed to market share and use of "future prospects" as opposed to "growth rate"). The judgment of the future competitive position of the firm must reflect the differences of opinions of qualified managers in the firm. There may be valid differences within a single function, such as marketing, as well as the typical interfunctional differences, such as between R&D, marketing, and finance. A forced reduction of these differences to a point estimate deprives management of the full appreciation of the future risks and uncertainties that must be taken into account in strategic decisions.

When managers whose views have historically been harmonious develop significant differences in their world outlooks, these differences may be an important symptom that extrapolation of the past experience is no longer a reliable predictor of the future. Or they may be a symptom that the future is becoming less predictable and that the firm will increasingly have to rely on "weak signals" if it is to deal with turbulence in a timely manner.[9]

We can summarize the preceding discussion by paraphrasing the requisite variety theorem, which was first enunciated by cyberneticist Roy Ashby. To succeed in the environment the firm must match the subtlety, complexity, and speed of its response to the urgency, complexity, and subtlety of the environmental challenges. Our argument is that today for many SBAs the point hypothesis no longer captures the requisite complexity and must therefore be replaced by the "area" or "dispersion hypothesis," which we will describe below. Our first step is to deal with the information intake by the firm.

ENLARGING THE INFORMATION BASE

Two Information Filters

Numerous writers, as well as managerial experience, have shown that in turbulent times there are usually significant differences between the information available in the environment and the information used in the decision mak-

---

[9]Ansoff, "Managing Strategic Surprise."

ing.[10,11] Ansoff has suggested that external information is processed through two filters. The first is the *scanning filter,* whose "filtering power" is determined by the match between the technique used in abstracting the information from the environment and the nature of the environmental turbulence. A dramatic typical example of a mismatch is offered by the current failure of the numerous input-output models, which are based on the assumption of a linear progress in the environment, to predict the behavior of the highly nonlinear and surpriseful international economy.

The second filter applied to the information is a *cultural filter,* whose "filtering power" is determined by views of the word (paradigms) that are held by the responsible decision makers. In practical managerial terms, the view of the world is described by the degree of reliance on past phenomena as indicators of future events, preparedness to accept novelty, perceptions of what kinds of behavior works best. For example, during the first thirty years of the century, it was believed that profits are maximized when the firm offers the customers the cheapest standardized product (recall Henry Ford's maxim: "Give it to them in any color so long as it is black").

The cultural filter becomes a block to progress when an organization needs to confront dimensions of reality that are significantly different from past history. Therefore "sensitizing" the participants to accept novel signals, and particularly "weak signals," is one of the key problems in enlarging the information perspective of the firm.[12,13]

Thus one step in closing the gap between the environmental information and the information that finds its way into decisions is to make sure that the methods of information gathering have the necessary richness and variety ("requisite variety") to capture the complexity of the environment. The second step is to adapt the culture of the firm to the new external realities.

The Problem of Cultural Transformation

Sociologists have repeatedly called attention to the tendency by managers to persist in using their prior model of reality, even when environmental turbulence demands novel responses. But practicing managers have been slow to give proper attention to this phenomenon. Major strategic reorientations have been

[10]Ibid.

[11]This refers to the concept of "intelligence failures." See W. Kirsch and W. Trux, "Strategische Frühaufklärung und Portfolio-Analyse," *Zeitschrift für Betriebswirtschaft,* Sonderheft 2, 1979, p. 53; W. Kirsch and H. K. Klein, Management-Informationssysteme II (Stuttgart, 1977), p. 152.

[12]H. Igor Ansoff, (with J. Eppink and H. Gomer), "Management of Strategic Surprise and Discontinuity: Improving Managerial Decisiveness," *Marknads-Vetande,* Utgiven au Sveriges Marknadsförbund, 4/79 argang 9.

[13]H. Igor Ansoff, *Strategic Management* (London: Macmillan, 1979).

introduced in firms without anticipation of serious organizational malfunctions that followed.[14] For example, during the post-World War period strategic planning has been repeatedly implanted in unready ground only to give rise to the phenomenon of resistance to planning that is due to a refusal by the dominant culture within the firm to accept the new mode of behavior.

In recent years the importance of cultural reorientation in the face of turbulence has received increasing recognition. The importance of the problem to the firm transcends the problem of SBA positioning and has been discussed in detail elsewhere.[15] However, as we will show below, when properly handled, the introduction and use of dispersed SBA positioning can make a major contribution to the cultural transformation of the firm.

"Hard" Facts and "Soft" Facts, and Weak Signals

Every management decision process is based on a combination of "hard" and "soft" facts. *Hard* facts are numerical and unambiguous, purported to describe in an impersonal manner "the way things are." They are obtained from observations and statistical data and are reduced and processed by logical processes (models, estimates, forecasts). *Soft* facts are typically qualitative, often ambiguous, expressing personal views and opinions of individuals who are frequently unable to provide a logical support for their positions.

Point positioning is based on both hard and soft facts, but the latter are used in a role that is secondary to hard analysis. Furthermore, soft facts are used to narrow estimates to the most probable position, rather than open the range of possibilities suggested by hard facts. As mentioned before, this approach is justified under conditions when the environment is perceived to have a small enough variance to permit use of most probable estimates.

In dispersion positioning soft facts must of necessity assume a different and a much more important role. In environments in which variance is high and relations among variables are poorly understood, attempts to generate hard facts on the basis of previous proven relationships and data become increasingly unreliable. In bridge terminology, a "finesse" becomes much more important when a "peek" is no longer available. Thus intuitions, feelings, "visions" of expert individuals begin to play a larger and larger role.

Second, in turbulent environments, efforts to converge on a hard estimate become counter productive because they violate the principle of requisite variety described earlier. As a result, the differences of views introduced by soft facts must be carried to the point of decisions.

As environmental turbulence increases, management is increasingly forced to rely on (soft or hard) weak signals. A *weak signal* is an early indication of a

[14]A. D. Chandler, Jr., *Strategy and Structures* (Cambridge, Mass.: M.I.T. Press, 1962).

[15]Ansoff, *Strategic Management.*

change whose impact is expected to be very significant, but the mechanism of impact cannot be described accurately enough to permit management to devise a specific "strong" response or to compute the size of an impact. For example, there is a generally shared conviction today that atomic fusion will be an enormously important source of energy in the future. But little can be said about the timing of its commercialization, the technology that will be needed, the costs of producing it, etc., etc.

Weak signals are a relatively new concept which was made necessary by the growing unpredictability of the environment. It introduces a new way of looking at information and opens a new range of responses to the firm. It has been described in detail elsewhere.[16] Its use for dispersed SBA positioning becomes necessary when unpredictability in an SBA reaches a point when it is no longer possible to respond in a timely manner by delaying response until signals become strong. Thus, depending on the level of turbulence within the SBA, dispersed positioning should be based either (1) on strong hard and soft facts or (2) on weak (as well as strong) hard and soft facts.

For the purposes of strategic decision making, use of soft facts and of weak signals offers two complementary advantages. The first is a realistic view of the state of uncertainty about the future prospects in an SBA and of the firm's competitive position within it. Skillful managers will of course choose to behave very differently in an SBA in which the future is clear and unambiguous, as compared with an SBA in which the future is murky and uncertain.

The second advantage is that through weak signals management is put in a position to react early to important but still poorly perceivable trends. We will discuss the use of both of these advantages later. For the moment, we turn to the problem of making dispersion estimates.

INTRODUCING DISPERSION ANALYSIS

Dispersion Analysis in Small and Medium-Sized Firms

Small and medium-sized firms will typically have limited staff resources. The managers who are responsible for strategic decisions are also the key experts on the future prospects and the firm's competitive capabilities. Some busy managers in such firms are prone to argue that concern with future uncertainties is a luxury that only the large firms can afford and that small firms must "keep things simple."

We suggest that the environment has no particular tolerance for small as opposed to large firms, and that when the environment is turbulent, the unfore-

[16]Ansoff, "Managing Strategic Surprise."

seen "slings and arrows" of change are much more damaging to small enterprises than they are to large ones. Thus well-managed small-medium enterprises have only two choices: either to stay out of turbulent environments or to face up squarely to the consequences of uncertainty and turbulence.

Fortunately, it is perfectly feasible for a small firm to develop a realistic view of its SBA portfolio within the resources that are usually available. One straightforward approach follows:

1. The key management group sets aside frequent periods (say one-half day twice a month) for strategic deliberation and analysis.

2. As a first step this strategic management group subdivides the environment of the firm into distinctive areas of opportunity called SBAs.[17]

3. The group, through discussion and argument draws up a list of key trends, threats, and opportunities that are likely to affect both the future prospects in the SBA and the firm's competitive position within it.

4. Using an appropriate version of the positioning matrix, the group next positions within it the future prospects of the SBA, and the future position of the firm. A simple procedure is to ask each manager (using the result of step 3) to make a judgment of a "low probable," "most probable," and "high probable" position.

5. The managers next "negotiate" to determine low probable and high positions, each citing his or her reasons and arguments for each of the positions. The result (for a two-SBA firm) may be that shown in Figure 1.

[17]Ansoff and Leontiades, "Strategic Portfolio Management."

Figure 1   Sample Dispersion Patterns Using Three-Point Evaluation

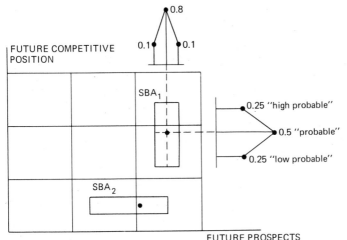

For SBA$_1$ the managers have decided that there is a substantial agreement that the future is excellent and that the uncertainty in this future is small. The future prospects might as well be represented by a point. On the other hand, there is a large uncertainty about the firm's ability to succeed in the SBA. The reason for this may be that the competitive future is murky. Or it may be that the firm's knowledge of the trends in competition is admittedly poor. The different action consequences in the respective cases would be obvious to an experienced manager.

SBA$_2$, which we show at the bottom of Figure 1, represents an opposite case in which the uncertainty about the future is large, but it is clear that in any of the futures the firm will be a weak competitor.

6.   It is important that a protocol be made of the views, arguments, and positions taken by the respective managers. A major aspect of such protocols should be diagnosis of the actual state of knowledge about SBAs. The dispersion region shown in Figure 1 may be due to uncertainty about well-understood outcomes in facts, or it may be due to a genuine unavailability of information about the future. For example, in some SBA everyone will agree that the potential emergence of a new technology will make the prospects "turbulent," but, for the moment, it is impossible to see what this "turbulence" will mean. It can easily be seen that management options for response to such early indications of turbulence are different from a situation in which the alternative outcomes can well be described but it is highly uncertain which one of them will occur.[18]

7.   Once the group has worked through the positioning of the individual SBAs, it will be ready to do two things: (1) balance the SBA portfolio and (2) take concrete action decisions in each SBA.[19]

8.   Once a cycle has been completed, the strategic management group continues to monitor the development of each SBA, review the list of key trends/threats/opportunities, and revise the matrix as new information develops.

As can be seen from the above, this approach is economical, requiring a minimum analysis of staff assistance. It is also highly informal, permitting and encouraging free expression of views and opinions. As a secondary, but extremely important, outcome, it is an excellent team-building device for the group responsible for the future of the enterprise.

In some situations it will be found that the power structure and/or presence of strong dominant personalities will tend to bias the discussion according to personalities and not to facts. In such situations, a relatively simple Delphi technique can be used which isolates judgments based on perceptions of facts from interpersonal influences.

[18]Ibid.

[19]Ibid.

As the preceding description shows, using this approach to SBA analysis requires a minimum of assistance from either outside or inside staff. However, when the system is first put in place, management would do well to seek expert advice, which usually cannot be found inside small and medium firms.

As a final remark, the dispersion analysis of SBA discussed above is an approach that is one step higher in complexity and sophistication than Strategic Issue Management (also highly adaptable to small firms). The choice between the two approaches depends on how the management perceived the future evolution of its SBAs. If the future trend is seen as satisfactory and the competitive position is both satisfactory and stable, strategic issue analysis will suffice to protect the firm from turbulence. Otherwise the dispersion SBA analysis is the more suitable technique.

Dispersion Analysis
in Large Firms

The large-firm situation differs in two aspects. Usually there is a staff charged with the task of environmental analysis and interpretation. One or more techniques—such as extrapolative forecasting, scenarios, impact and cross-impact analysis, environmental modeling, competitive analysis, and competition modeling—will be in use.

All of these techniques can provide a valuable "hard data" input into the dispersion analysis. The changes that must be made in order to modify the process from point positioning to dispersion positioning consist of two parts. The first is to make sure that the uncertainties and the variabilities inherent in both data gathering and processing are preserved (and not suppressed as is done in the point analysis), and that the SBA positioning results are presented to management in the form shown in Figure 1 (or a more refined smooth probability distribution). This presentation should be accompanied by an outline of the key assumptions and methodology employed and, particularly, explanations of the sources of variability.

The second extension of the staff contribution is to sensitize the data gathering and processing to the weak signals so that management can be alerted to vague but consequential developments as early as possible. We shall refer to this total process of staff inputs as *analytic dispersion positioning*.

The second distinctive characteristic of large firms is that in addition to the decision makers responsible for SBAs, there are many staff and line managers throughout the firm whose jobs bring them in contact with the actualities of the environment and who, as a result, have valid intuitions and judgments about both the impending changes in the environment and the firm's competitive future. Such managers usually work in the "interface" functions, such as R&D, marketing, sales, purchasing, and planning. This population offers a rich source of expertise that can be mobilized to augment and sometimes (in medium and large firms) replace the sophisticated analytic inputs by the staff. A procedure

Figure 2   SBA Positioning in Medium and Large Firms

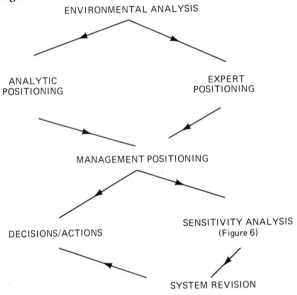

for incorporating these valuable inputs into the work of SBA positioning is illustrated in Figure 2.

1. The first step is identification of the SBAs in which the firm is doing and aspires to do business. This is followed by identification of the relevant "external" environments that are expected to have important impacts on both the SBA and the firm. Thus, in technologically intensive SBAs, the technology is a relevant external environment. In SBAs that are strongly affected by governmental action, the government policy and action with respect to the firm is a relevant environment, and so on.

2. The second step is to amend the analytic environmental surveillance and analysis that are already under way in the firm to make them yield dispersion results SBA per SBA.

3. The third step is to divide the totality of SBA into groups that require dispersion analysis and groups for which point position analysis will continue to be satisfactory. This is a key step because the total number of SBAs in medium and large firms is typically large (as many as twenty to forty or more) and even the point analysis involves a substantial amount of work. This work will be multiplied for SBA submitted to dispersion analysis. In the Appendix to this paper, we will suggest some criteria for sorting the SBA.

4. As Figure 2 shows, two parallel processes follow. First, all SBAs, are submitted to analytic positioning. Second, the SBAs selected for dispersion

analysis are analyzed by experts. The selection of the experts is an important step (see the Appendix).

The experts are given the relevant environmental surveillance data and are asked to give judgments that contribute to establishing the position dispersion. Depending on their expertise, some individuals will be asked to contribute to the future prospects, some to competitive position, some to both.

As stated above, the experts will seldom be in the position to render an overall judgment of, say, the competitive position. Technical people can contribute their views on the impact of technological change; commercial people, on the impact of the competition; external relations people, on the impact of government regulations, etc.

5. The substantial amount of disparate data thus obtained must now be consolidated to determine the positions. This involves two steps: consolidating the judgments of each homogenous group of experts, and consolidating the nonhomogenous judgments of the groups. The Delphi analysis is one of the most useful techniques for the first step. The second step lends itself to the Monte Carlo analysis. This statistical method of combining qualitatively different judgments has so far found little use in business firms. Therefore we describe it briefly in the Appendix.

6. The position dispersion, obtained from analytic positioning (accompanied by the relevant protocols of the data, reasoning, and methodology), is next superimposed on the expert positioning (also accompanied by protocols). The result, illustrated in Figure 3, is submitted for the group of responsible managers who must now *make a decision on the future shape of the SBA.*

In the illustration the experts and the staff are in substantial agreement on the future prospects, but the experts see the competitive position as being less predictable than does the staff. The decision group will ana-

Figure 3   Example of Managerial Positioning

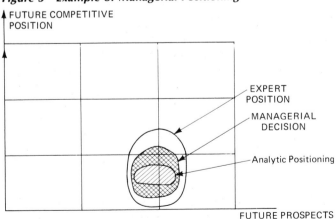

lyze the reasons for the differences, add its nonjudgments, and select the management position that, as illustrated, will frequently lie between the two extremes.

We are now in a position to discuss the action implications of positioning analysis. Before doing this, it is necessary to recognize that unlike the situation in a small firm, SBA positioning in a large firm is a complicated process involving many people.

It is essential therefore to make sure of two things: (1) that the system selected is cost-effective, that is, no more complex than necessary; and (2) that the "noise" and distortion in the system, rather than genuine future uncertainties, are not responsible for most of the resulting dispersion. To ensure these two conditions, the system must be submitted to periodic sensitivity analysis.

This may result in simplification, such as a conclusion that the use of experts does not add much to the analytic positioning. The role of experts will typically be important when the SBA under analysis is going through profound structural changes; it will be less important when extrapolation of past experience is valid for the future.

Sensitivity analysis may lead to a redesign of the process by which the dispersions are obtained. Typically introduction of dispersion positioning is a gradual "learning" process lasting several years. In this process, people become "calibrated," the expert population is identified, the cost-effectiveness of the Delphi technique (as opposed, for example, to consolidation by staff) becomes clearer, and so forth. We will have more to say about sensitivity analysis in the Appendix.

MANAGERIAL USE OF DISPERSION ANALYSIS

Enrichment of Managerial Decision Options

Dispersion positioning adds substantial costs and complexity to portfolio analysis. In recent years, faced with the growing internal complexity of management systems, some writers have reacted by a call to "keep it simple" and to eliminate complex analysis.[20]

Experienced managers will agree on the value of simplicity but will also warn against *simplistic* ways of attaining it. They will suggest that simplicity is not a "free good": While making the inside of the firm more manageable, it may cause the firm to lose touch with the complexities of the external realities. As we mentioned above, continued success (and even survival) in a turbulent environment requires a specific level of internal complexity, which must be maintained

[20]H. Igor Ansoff, "Strategic Issue Management," *Strategic Management Journal,* 1983

to enable the firm to capture the nuances and variabilities in external trends, threats, and opportunities.

When environmental turbulence increases to a point where decisions based on the most probable (point) positioning become too risky, the additional complexity of dispersion positioning pays for itself by enlarging the decision options available to the management.

This is illustrated in Figure 4. The first three steps, starting with environmental surveillance, are assumed to have been conducted in accordance with the

Figure 4   Strategic Decision under Weak Signal and Uncertainty

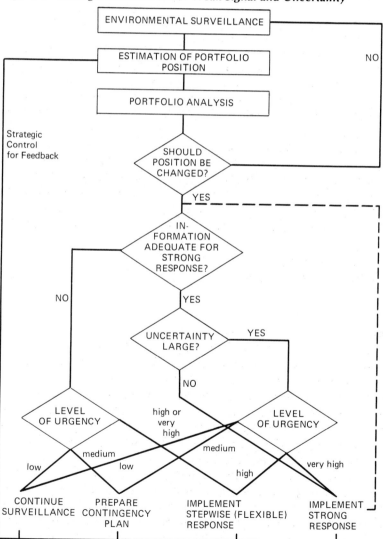

preceding discussion to produce a portfolio view of the firm's SBAs. Some SBAs will have been submitted to point analysis. For these, the decision options are twofold: (1) if the prospective position of the SBA is satisfactory, the environmental surveillance can be continued; and (2) if the position of the SBA should be changed, the dashed line indicates that the sole managerial option is to implement concrete strong response, which will change both the firm's investment in the SBA and its competitive strategy.

For SBAs that have been subjected to dispersion analysis, if the portfolio analysis suggests that the firm's position should be changed, the first step is to determine whether the dispersion is due to the weakness of the signals about the future (that is, lack of information about the nature of the trends or their impact) rather than by the uncertainty about which future will occur. To refer to an earlier example, all that may be known is that the SBA's environment will be highly turbulent, or that a particular technology is expected to have a major impact on the SBA. In such cases, the dispersion of probable impact will be large, potential impact on the firm will appear important, but there is not enough information to formulate a specific "strong response" or to change resource commitment to the SBA or to reformulate a new competitive strategy.

In this case, the answer to the question "INFORMATION ADEQUATE FOR STRONG RESPONSE?" in Figure 4 will be NO.

The next step is to determine the level of urgency of response. At one extreme, even if the information is poor, the potential impact may loom large and imminent. In this case, an initial flexible response must be made immediately based on the information available. In our two examples above, a high, but undifferentiated, turbulence can be met by increasing the intensity of environmental monitoring; if the technological source is known, the firm can enhance the monitoring and also begin to expand its know-how of the relevant technology. As the firm acts, and as the environment develops, increasing knowledge will make possible progressively more specific responses. This is the meaning of the option "IMPLEMENT STEPWISE RESPONSE" at the bottom of Figure 4.

At the other extreme, if the sense of urgency in the SBA is low (small and/ or distant impact), the preferred option is to "CONTINUE SURVEILLANCE."

Returning to an earlier step, if the information is adequate for defining and executing a strong response, but if the uncertainty is large, using the most probable future as a basis for response is not justifiable. The urgency must be examined and an appropriate response selected. If the most probable future is likely to occur, a strong response is both possible and justifiable in the manner illustrated at the bottom of Figure 4; otherwise one of the weak responses should be used.

Thus recognition of both weak signals and statistical variance puts management in a position to choose among four different response options ranging from direct response, to gradual and flexible commitment, to continued surveillance. By contrast, point positioning offers only one option ("IMPLEMENT STRONG RESPONSE"), shown by the dashed line in Figure 4.

Strategic Control

In point positioning a commitment is made to a strong response. Subsequent events may show that the environment has not developed as anticipated or the chosen strategy may not be as successful as planned. A number of research studies show that once a firm commits itself to a strong response strategy, it tends to stick to it even in the face of disappointing results. Thus strategic control is difficult under point positioning.

Dispersed positioning, through the options of partial and gradual commitment, offers an opportunity for revising the SBA startegy as new data become available. If a strategy turns out to be unpromising before major financial and psychological commitments have been made, it can be scaled down techniques of dispersion analysis, but they also need to transform the organizational outlook, the strategic culture of the organization. In fact, in many cases, the need for a cultural change may be more urgent than for the technical apparatus of the analysis.

The following features of dispersion analysis make it a potential instrument of cultural change:

1. It emphasizes, on being introduced into a firm, a faithful image of the environment with all of its uncertainties, ignorance about the future, and turbulence.

2. It stresses the use of managerial judgment and intuition in a role, coequal and sometimes superior, to quantitative analysis.

3. It encourages the dialectic constructive confrontation of differences among managers and the carry-over of these differences into decision making.

4. It involves all the managers who have relevant knowledge and/or responsibility for strategic action.

And yet, these advantages are easily lost if dispersion analysis is introduced and perceived as just another, even if superior, computational-analytic system for positioning SBAs within the matrix. A detailed discussion of how the advantages can be used to help a cultural transformation and how the typical "resistance to planning" that accompanies cultural change can be overcome is beyond the scope of this paper.[21,22] However, certain hints can be offered here:

1. As a first step, a strategic diagnosis must be made to determine what, if any, changes in organizational competence and culture and necessary.[23]

[21]Ansoff-Declerck-Hayes, *From Strategic Planning to Strategic Management* (London: John Wiley, 1976).

[22]Theodore Levitt, "A Heretical View of Management Science," *Fortune,* December 18, 1978.

[23]Kirsch-Esser-Gabele, *Das Management des geplanten Wandels von Organizationen* (Stuttgart: Poeschel, 1979).

2. As a second step, the ground must be prepared for organizational acceptance of the new approach. The relevance of the approach to current and important problems should be demonstrated; potential points of resistance must be identified and dealt with. This includes particularly the threat (real or apparent) that the new approach may present to influential managers.

3. The prerequisite organizational changes that must be in place in order to ensure effective conduct and use of the dispersion analysis should be identified and implemented. For example, all the participating managers usually need a period of training and familiarization with the relevant concepts and techniques. Also, a new decision implementation system is usually needed for carrying out the new types of decision made possible by the dispersion approach. This may lead to introducing *Strategic Issue Management.*[24]

4. The introduction and use of strategic dispersion analysis should be organized as a participative approach in which the contributions of all participants are encouraged, recognized, and used. For example, the contributing experts should not be made to feel like impersonal guinea pigs, isolated from one another and from the decision process by an impersonal Delphi process.

5. Rather than introduce dispersion analysis as a system, it is better to use it as a tool for resolving specific challenges that the involved managers consider important and pressing.

Summary

In this paper we have addressed what may be called the *requisite variety imperative.* This imperative states that if a firm is to succeed, the complexity, subtlety, and speed of its responses must match the complexity, subtley, and urgency of the environmental challenges.

We have suggested that strategic portfolio analysis, which is widely used today to select strategic responses, is not sufficiently complex, or subtle or fast for the environment of many firms.

To enhance complexity and subtlety, we have proposed dispersion positioning of the firm's SBA within the portfolio matrix, and we have shown how this enlarges the range of managerial response options. To enhance timeliness of response, we have suggested the use of weak signals in the positioning process.

Finally, we have suggested that dispersion positioning can serve two purposes within the firm: (1) technically, to make its decision processes more responsive to the environment, and (2) culturally, to realign the firm's view of the outside world with the realities of what is happening in the environment.

---

[24]H. Igor Ansoff, *Managing Discontinuous Strategic Change.*

APPENDIX
DESIGN AND "DEBUGGING"
OF DISPERSED POSITIONING PROCESS

Roles of Staff

The transition to dispersion position analysis has two major managerial consequences: increased involvement of experts throughout the firm who are specialists in various categories of both hard and soft facts, and direct involvment of key managers in determining the degree of dispersal of the positions within the matrix.

Both of these steps broaden, rather than narrow, the role of the strategic planning staff. On the one hand, the planning staff must now organize the soft data and weak signal collection from the experts; on the other hand, it must preprocess these data into forms useful for the work of positioning. The staff also retains responsibility for the generating of "hard" environmental data (for example, large societal trends). This last requirement has already led to the development of methodologies for identification of social, political, demographic, and technological trends and turbulence (e.g., scenarios, impact analysis, cross impact analysis, etc.), which are increasingly being used in enterprises. As mentioned earlier, all of these approaches remain useful for dispersed positioning.

So long as the emphasis rested on hard data and on the staff as its main source, strategic planners had little interest either in sociometric tools or in techniques of statistical analysis of the resulting data.[25] The shift to soft data adds another responsibility to the staff for introducing and using these techniques.

Selection of Experts

In involving a large number of managers in the positioning process, there is always the danger of bringing into the survey pseudoexperts who can provide statistical mirages that have little relation to environmental facts. This danger can be minimized by taking the following precautions:

1. One has to recognize that the expertise in any of the particular groups of specialists is typically limited. Experts in one field may have invalid prejudices, rather than knowledge, outside the field. For example, while members of the R&D department may produce valid judgments on the contribution of product quality to a firm's competitive stance, their judgments about the firm's marketing niche may not only be unreliable but negatively prejudiced.[26,27]

---

[25]Ansoff, "Strategic Issue Management."

[26]For strategies of planned change, see Kirsch-Esser-Gabele, *Das Management.*

[27]The tools have typically been developed for nonprofit organizations which typically lack a hard data base.

2. The identification of an individual as an expert on a specific class of questions is usually influenced by the personal perspective of whoever is responsible for the selection. If that person lacks expertise in the field, he or she should consult the peers of the intended experts.

3. Surveys can be designed to yield not only responses to questions but also information about the qualification of the respondents. Surveys can also be designed to have the respondent delimit his or her own area of expertise.

All efforts to use weak signals confront a dilemma: as the number of potential receivers is broadened to increase the probability of detecting weak signals, the danger of receiving a range of irrelevant background noises is also increased. This is particularly true when the signals are very weak and becomes less true as the signals become stronger. The solution to this problem lies in (1) designing appropriate filters, and (2) gearing the strength of the response to the strength of the signal.

But to repeat our discussion up to here, the solution of the problem to minimize the perceived range of irrelevant background noise cannot be to reduce the number of experts, but to make appropriate analyses of the received data, such as sensitivity analysis or further "deep analysis."[28,29]

Use of the Monte Carlo Method

In the application of the point hypothesis the effort is directed at converging on the point position of an SBA within the matrix through a combination of analysis and group consensus.

In the dispersion approach discussed, convergence to a single position is not forced, and divergence of expert opinions, as well as recognition of statistical variability, is encouraged.

One possibility is to estimate the variability of judgments directly along the principal dimensions of the SBA matrix: the probable future prospects in the SBA and the firm's relative future competitive position within. As we have seen, this approach becomes necessary when the firm is small and does not avail itself of expert opinions.

As discussed earlier, in large firms better results can be obtained if each expert makes a contribution in the area of his or her expertise and the judgments are then combined into an overall estimate of the position dispersion within the matrix.

But the penalty for encouraging each expert to confine judgments to his or

---

[28]For discussion of such functional myopia, see Ansoff, "Changing Shape."

[29]W. Trux and W. Kirsch, "Strategisches Management oder Die Möglichkeit einer "wissenschaftlichen" Unternehmensführung," *Die Betriebswirtschaft*, 1979, p. 228.

her own area of expertise is that these cannot be combined analytically into an overall range of judgments of the position within the matrix. An approach that is useful for arriving at such synthesis is the Monte Carlo method.

This technique, which was first applied to business problems by D. Hertz,[30] proceeds as follows. A random sample is taken from each of the component distributions contributed by experts, and these individual inputs and combined by applying agreed-upon weights of the importance of the contributing distributions. The result is one point on the final curve of the distribution of the position, as shown in Figure 5 where the process is illustrated. The complete procedure is then repeated to obtain a distribution of the future prospects, as shown at the bottom of Figure 5.

In Figure 5 the input likelihood distributions may be based on hard data (e.g., econometric analyses, market analysis, etc.), or on judgments of expert managers, or on both. The linear weighting, that is illustrated is used when it is not known how the individual inputs combine to produce the overall estimates of the market position. But the Monte Carlo approach is equally applicable when all the data are judgmental and the weighting is nonlinear, or when the data are hard and the relationship among variables is explicit. Thus Monte Carlo is a general method for combining several component probability distributions into an overall distribution.

Sensitivity Testing
of the Estimation Process

As noted earlier, large dispersion has important decision consequences. On the other hand, the positioning process is complex, based on human judgment, and subject to hidden distortions and errors. Unless the process is well designed, the dispersion introduced by system errors can easily exceed the dispersion contributed by environmental uncertainties.

Therefore a newly installed expert positioning procedure should be regularly examined critically and redesigned as necessary. After the procedure settles down, it should be checked periodically to guard against the excess complexity that all systems tend to acquire with time. This procedure is illustrated in Figure 6.

The process of management positioning involves a comparison of the analytic and expert positions with the judgments of the decision makers. If the differences are explicable by the nature of the three sources of results, and if no anomalies are observable in the results, the system should be examined for excess complexity and simplified if possible.

If anomalies exist, the first step is to trace them back to the analytic and/or to the expert positioning process. Then the key building blocks of each

[30]D. B. Hertz, "Risk Analysis in Capital Investment," *Harvard Business Review,* January–February 1964, p. 95.

Figure 5   Finding the Distribution of Market Attractiveness Through the Monte Carlo Method

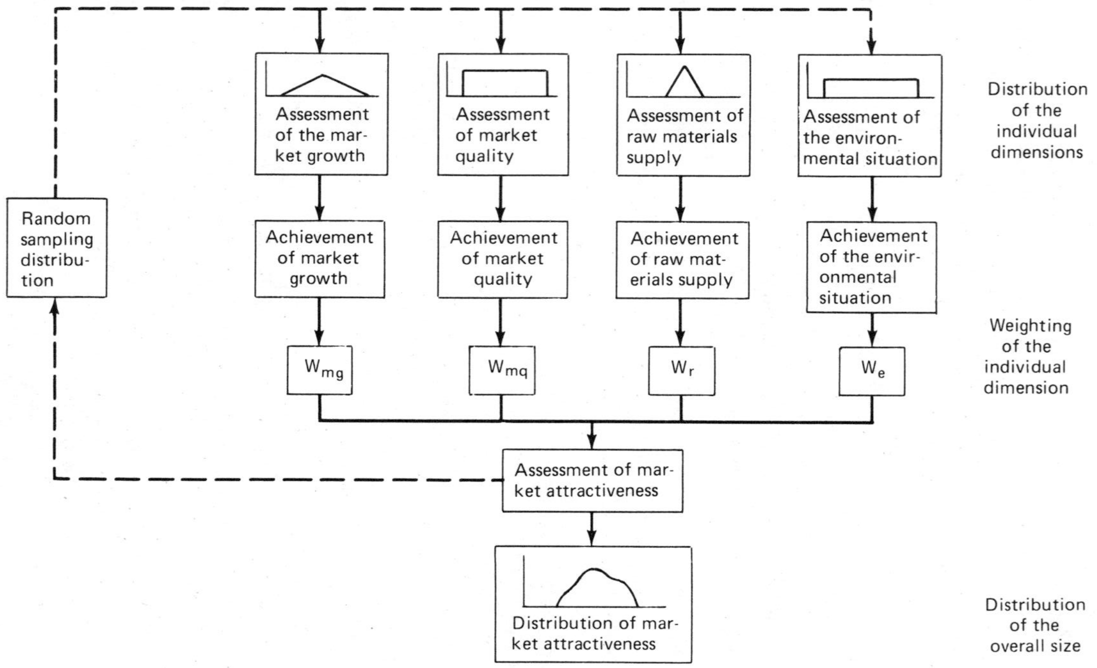

Figure 6   Sensitivity Analysis of Positioning

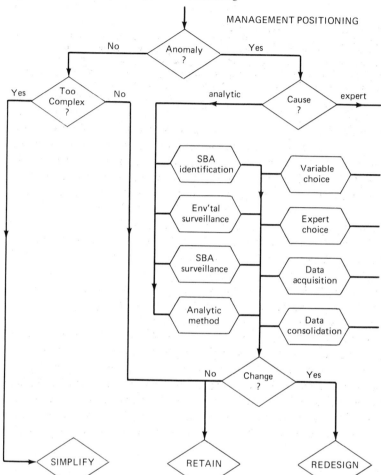

process shown in Figure 6 are checked to determine which changes should be made in the design of the positioning system.

The following sample questions will be asked of the positioning system:

1. Are the experts properly qualified?
2. Are they being used in their area of expertise?
3. Are all the key positioning variables included?
4. Are the data that are made available to the experts relevant to their judgment?
5. Is the data-gathering process free of personality factors, political influences, group effects?
6. Is the data-consolidation process appropriate to the available data?

The questions asked about the analytic positioning will include the following:

1. Are the SBAs clearly and unambiguously defined, without overlaps?
2. Are the external surveillance techniques complex enough to capture the nature of turbulence in the environment?
3. Are the SBA analysis and surveillance techniques complex enough to capture the nature of turbulence in the environment?
4. Do the models used for analysis match the complexity of the data?

As Figure 6 shows, sensitivity analysis leads to three possible results: system simplification, retention of the present form, and redesign of the system.

Choice Between Point and Dispersion Approaches

Experience shows that even under point hypothesis a firm with twenty or thirty SBAs (not an uncommon number in practice) must invest a very substantial amount in SBA analysis in order to produce point estimates. As the preceding discussion indicates, the question of how to determine an area dispersion multiplies this labor several fold.

An answer to this question is based on two criteria:

1. The importance of a particular SBA to the firm's profit stream. If an SBA is an important contributor to future profits, even a small dispersion can have important profit consequences. Therefore such an SBA should be submitted to a careful dispersion analysis. If the expected contribution is small, point determination will suffice for the portfolio analyses.
2. The *a priori* judgment of the future variability in the SBA. If the competitive environment in an SBA is expected to remain stable—that is, the future prospects are stable and predictable—there is no sense in "gilding the lily" through analysis that we expect will yield a small dispersion. On the other hand, if an SBA's future appears particularly turbulent, it may need a dispersion analysis even if its contribution to the firm is relatively modest.

To summarize, dispersion analysis must of necessity be used sparingly and in combination with point analysis. The commitment made in the first a priori judgments is not irrevocable. If, for example, in the course of point analysis variability and uncertainties appear large, a shift can be made to dispersion analysis. As an alternative procedure, the entire portfolio can first be submitted to point analysis and then selected SBAs can be analyzed in depth, according to the criteria presented above.

10

Strategic Control: Some Issues in Making It Operationally More Useful

PETER LORANGE

The Wharton School, University of Pennsylvania

I am indebted to Bala Chakravarthy, Edward Freeman, and Decklan Murphy for comments on an earlier version of the chapter.

This chapter discusses some issues relevant to the effective use of strategic control as a practical element of a corporation's overall strategic system. After a brief discussion of the need to reconsider the control process in the light of recent advances in strategic management, we will give a definition of what we mean by strategic control, and its function within the overall strategic system. The bulk of the discussion will then focus on how to measure various aspects of strategic performance, as well as on the issue of reconciling strategic and operating performance measures. Particular attention is paid to measurement of critical environmental assumptions. The roles of various executives in diverse aspects of the control tasks are also discussed. The practical implications of the various concepts introduced will be illustrated through an example. While most of the discussion refers to control at the business level, implications for the corporate (portfolio) level are also explored.

1. INTRODUCTION

The past decade has witnessed significant advances within the field of strategic management, in terms of both conceptual developments and new empirical research insights. Moreover, such approaches are winning increasing acceptance as good corporate practice. When it comes to one closely related management process, management control, there does not seem to have been the same degree of evolution. Management control practices still continue to play an important role as a vehicle for managing today's corporations, but they do not seem to have evolved significantly toward being more explicitly reconcilable with strategy-setting management processes. This chapter will suggest that it is useful to see strategic planning and control as separate aspects of an overall strategic process; hence the term *strategic control* is used.[1]

Exhibit One suggests an overall, simplified picture of the strategic direction-setting process. It also indicates the control process's relationship with this, emphasizing that control incorporates both an operative and a strategic dimension.

We must thus view the strategic process as consisting of a direction-setting subprocess, which takes place at discrete intervals in time, and a subprocess of modification, follow-up, and improvement of this direction, which takes place on a more continuous basis. The direction-setting subprocess might be broken down into a sequence of several discrete steps: (1) objectives setting—what direc-

---

[1]The term *strategic control* has been used with different intended meaning by several authors. The concept of strategic control developed in this chapter does not correspond to these. See J. H. Horovitz, "Strategic Control; A New Task for Management," *Long Range Planning,* June 1979; E. Gerald Hurst, *Controlling Strategic Plans,* in *Implementation of Strategic Planning,* ed. Peter Lorange (Englewood Cliffs, N.J.: Prentice-Hall, 1982); and Carter F. Bales, "Strategic Control: The President's Paradox," *Business Horizons,* August 1977.

Exhibit One: Control Process—Operative and Strategic

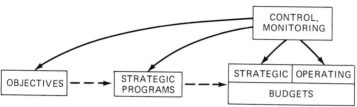

tion to go given that the attractiveness of the niche as well as one's own strength has been assessed; (2) strategic programming—how to achieve the intended strategic direction in terms of steps to be taken and resources required; and (3) the delineation of the near-term action aspects of the strategic programming that need to be carried out during the next year in parallel with the normal operating activities. These parallel activities converge into the "strategic budget" and the "operating budget," respectively. The direction-setting process has been well documented elsewhere[2] and will not be further discussed here.

The follow-up subprocess consists of assessing how we are actually doing relative to the stated plans. The common well-established form of this is budgetary control. However, in this chapter we will argue that the control function should also include explicit follow-up regarding strategic programs- and objectives-implementation. Further, the budgetary control should distinguish between follow-up vis-à-vis the strategic and the operating budgets. There are thus *four* dimensions of follow-up, as indicated by the four solid arrows in Exhibit One, and we will call this totality "strategic control." A key issue in strategic control, as it has now been more broadly defined, is to be able to reconcile the trade-off between near-term and longer-term emphasis and performance in a more explicit manner. Thus the control process should be able to monitor progress in terms of *both* an organization's ability to adapt (its effectiveness) and its integrative performance (efficiency).

As indicated, we might see the operationalization of strategic control as simultaneously monitoring four different aspects of performance: First, classical near-term operating performance measures, such as profits, costs, and/or ROI, must continue to play a role. Second, we must measure the organization's efforts at implementing strategic changes on a day-to-day basis in parallel with the operating activities, such as time and costs spent on new product and/or market development, research and development, and process improvements. Third, these near-term measures must be reconciled with measures of progress toward the implementation of specific strategic programming activities. Finally, all these measures in turn should be reconciled with measurements that capture changes in one's basic objectives. It thus seems necessary to consider all these

[2]See, for instance, Peter Lorange, *Corporate Planning: An Executive Viewpoint* (Englewood Cliffs, N.J.: Prentice-Hall, 1980).

four elements of performance as interrelated; they must be seen in context in order to give a significant picture of performance. If not, one can easily get a distorted view.

For instance, profit improvements alone can give an almost meaningless picture of performance unless one also examines the extent to which one's strategic programs have been maintained, such as promotional activities, research, and maintenance, all of which may diminish near-term profits. Analogously, a unilateral focus on a strategic measure such as market share improvement is not necessarily all that meaningful as a performance measurement signal when seen alone. However, when considered together with measures regarding the actual costs of market share improvements, then the market share signals easily become more meaningful.

In the rest of this chapter we will offer more specific suggestions regarding the measurement types that seem relevant and will show how these can be operationalized. We will in particular elaborate on those measurement types that typically seem relatively less familiar, most notably now to assess relevant environmental changes. We will also explore various implications of such a strategic control measurement approach, notably when it comes to assessing environmental exposure, task delineations ("Who does what?"), interpretation/reconciliation of multidimensional control measures (i.e., the four types of measurement outlined), and implementational issues when attempting to evolve an effective strategic control approach into a reality. However, it will be particularly useful at this stage to introduce an example to illustrate the context within which the strategic control approach should take place within a corporate setting that follows contemporary strategic management approaches. Throughout the discussion we will return to this example.

2. AN EXAMPLE: STRATEGIC AND OPERATING STRUCTURES WITHIN A CORPORATION; IMPLICATIONS FOR THE STRATEGIC CONTROL TASKS

Let us now address the task of actually implementing strategic control in real-life organizational settings. There are two related sets of issues that above all need to be addressed in this respect. First, who is responsible for monitoring, analyzing, and reporting on the various aspects of the control tasks? We recall from Exhibit One that the control task might be broken down into four interrelated elements. Particularly with the advent of so-called strategic structures, as reflected in the widespread use of SBUs, which do not (and often should not) coincide with the formal (operating) organizational structure, the issue of "who monitors what" needs careful delineation. A second and related issue concerns the reconciliation of the various submeasures into one managerial synthesis—

i.e., how to carry out a comparison of actual performance against all four dimensions (objectives, strategic programs, strategic budgets, and operating budgets).

In order to discuss these two issues—control task responsibilities and consolidation of several measures—we will make use of a brief example. Consider a corporation that started out as a small brewery making Pilsener beer, but which, as it grew, diversified horizontally into making other beers and had over time also expanded into related businesses, such as soft-drink bottling and manufacturing of packaging items: glass bottles, closures, and carton containers for outside customers. As can be seen in Exhibit Two, the formal organizational structure reflects that considerable vertical integration has taken place over the years, so that much of what is produced in one division tends to be for a "sister division" customer.

This organizational structure has evolved over time, enabling the cost-efficient operation of a large-volume, small-margin, essentially mature business. It reflects a high degree of specialization, avoidance of duplication, and utilization of scale economies, all essential requirements for success in these types of businesses. An elaborate, but conventional, responsibility center control system is in place.

With increased competition as well as more changes in customer tastes and purchasing behavior trends, the corporation embarked on delineating a strategic structure to reflect the specific businesses within which it was competing and to develop specific strategic plans, consisting of objectives and strategic programs for each of these businesses. The strategic structure that resulted from identifying the businesses within which the firm is active can be seen in Exhibit Three.

It should be noted that the company chose to see its own strategic position in terms of *two* business levels. The "business elements" can be seen as well-delineated product-market entities, for which a relatively unambiguous assessment of the business's future attractiveness can be made and for which one's competitive position can also be established relative to the specific competitors. The "business families" consist of related business elements, for which it would be difficult to carry out competitive strategies individually without assessing the impacts on the others.[3] There may be important synergies in the marketplace, so

[3]For a more detailed discussion of the business element and business family concepts, see ibid., pp. 76–81 and 100–105.

Exhibit Two: A Formal (Operating) Organizational Structure

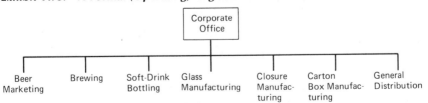

Exhibit Three: A Strategic Structure

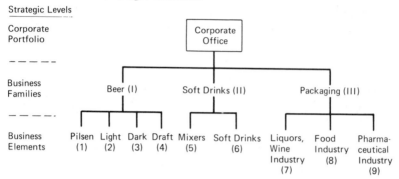

that the business elements can be seen as "colors on the (business family) pallet." There may also be internal organizational synergies such as in R&D, production, and distribution. The business families are similar to what General Electric originally denoted Strategic Business Units (SBUs)—i.e., freestanding businesses that, in principle, can be sold off.[4]

The major motivation behind the introduction of the strategic structure was thus to strengthen the firm's ability to adapt to environmental opportunities by formulating and implementing more realistic competitive strategies. At the same time it was still essential to maintain the efficiency-oriented focus reflected in the operating structure; for this reason a reorganization would be undesirable. Hence *both* the strategic and the operating structures would have to be in effect.[5] This was achieved by means of three interrelated vehicles. First there was the appointment of teams of executives to form business family and business element strategy groups. These executives continued to hold operating positions. (We will return to the appointment of these teams in Section 7 of this chapter). Second there was the delineation of strategic direction through the planning process, based on the analytical "building blocks" provided through the strategic structure. This strategic direction was then in turn "fed into" the operating structure in the form of strategically derived roles to be carried out, as reflected in strategic budgets (see Exhibit Four). Third, the control process was used as a major vehicle for integrating the strategic and the operating dimensions. It is this third aspect that will be elaborated in our present context.

Exhibit Four shows how the interrelationships can be established between a business element's objective(s), its strategic programs for implementing this di-

---

[4]For a discussion of General Electric's concept of strategic-operating structure, see Richard F. Vancil, *Decentralization: Managing Ambiguity by Design* (Homewood, Ill.: Dow Jones-Irwin, 1979). See also "General Electric Company" by Richard E. Vancil and Paul Browne, Intercollegiate Case Clearing House, 9-181-111, Boston, 1981.

[5]See Daniel Nathanson, Robert K. Kazanjian, and J. R. Galbraith, "Effective Strategic Planning and the Role of Organization Design," in Lorange, *Implementation of Strategic Planning*.

rection, and its strategic budgets for carrying out the near-term aspects of the strategic program's execution.[6] A particular objective (or set of objectives) has led to the delineation of a set of strategic programs (X, Y, Z, . . .) for implementing the objective. Each of these strategic programs tends to be crossfunctional. For instance, strategic program X of Exhibit Four is to be carried out jointly by Departments B and C. We see that each department thus is assigned a number of *derived* roles in carrying out its aspects of the strategic programs. Department A, for instance, has roles in connection with strategic programs Y and Z. From Exhibit Four we can therefore see that each department needs a strategic budget large enough to carry out all of these indirectly assigned strategic roles—i.e., the sums Σ_a, Σ_b, Σ_c of Exhibit Four. The fractions of each of these resources needed for next year might be denoted the strategic budgets for each department. As we can see, Exhibit Four highlights three of the strategic control dimensions, namely, whether each objective is still relevant (left-hand side of Exhibit Four), whether each strategic program is coming along as assumed (each horizontal line of the exhibit), as well as whether each operating organizational unit is car-

[6]Vancil initially suggested that the interrelationship between the strategic and the operating dimensions be formulated in this way. See Richard F. Vancil, "Better Management of Corporate Development, in *Stategic Planning Systems,* ed. Peter Lorange, and Richard F. Vancil (Englewood Cliffs, N.J.: Prentice-Hall, 1977).

Exhibit Four: The Delineation of Derived Strategic Roles for the Operating Structure, Based on the Patterns of Operating Department Involvements Needed to Carry Out Each Strategic Program

rying out its strategic roles (the vertical columns of Exhibit Four). Let us now discuss how the measurement types for controlling the four types of dimensions can be further operationalized.

3. MEASUREMENT TYPES

The measurement types vis-à-vis the operating budget, falling along the classical lines of responsibility center control, are of course well known and do not merit detailed discussion as such, given the context of this chapter.[7]

In order to delineate the measurement types appropriate for monitoring the strategic budget, we first need to establish a workable, practical distinction between what is an operating budget and what is a strategic budget. Lack of a clear definition of what constitutes strategic resources versus operating resources might have several dysfunctional effects. First, it might create unrealistic perceptions that strategic resources are "gifts" in addition to the ordinary budget. The way the dual strategic/operating resource pool concept is intended to be perceived, however, is to have each organizational unit develop a lean operating budget with no "fat" or "frills," for them to "add back" the resources necessary to carry out the strategic tasks. Second, without a clear definition the classification of what is "strategic" might tend to incorporate a fair number of activities that should actually be seen as operational. Organizational units may attempt to "get away with" less-stringent exercising of their judgments as to what is what and may feel tempted to throw marginal activities into the strategic pool.

A useful definition of what constitutes *strategic* resources might encompass the following:[8] First, strategic resources should be aimed at *changing* the course of direction of a particular business—i.e., be needed to carry out a *change in business strategy.* It follows that strategic resources are discretionary when seen in the context of current operations. Second, the strategic resources should be identifiable with specific strategic programs, as illustrated by Exhibit Four, and as such should be seen as "one-shot" or "zero-based" in nature. The justification for a particular allocation of strategic resources is that it should facilitate the improvement of long-term results for the business.

Let us also give a definition of what constitutes *operating* resources, since such a contrasting may shed further light on the distinction between strategic and operating. First, operating resources should be seen as necessary to *maintain*

---

[7]See, for instance, Robert A. Anthony, and John Dearden, *Management Control Systems* (Homewood, Ill.: Richard D. Irwin, 1980); Samuel Eilon, *Management Control* (New York: Wiley Interscience, 1972); Robert J. Mockler, *The Management Control Process,* (New York: Appleton-Century-Crofts, 1972); Allan A. Patz and A. J. Rowe, *Management Control and Decision Systems* (New York: John Wiley, 1977).

[8]This is consistent with the way Texas Instruments makes its distinction between strategic and operating funds. Patrick E. Haggerty, "The Corporation and Innovation," *Strategic Management Journal,* Vol. 2, No. 2, (April–June 1981).

the existing business,—i.e., for carrying out current operations at a successful level. Second, the operating resources should be consistent with the expected operating activity level for an organizational unit—i.e., what incremental changes from last year are necessary to meet this year's target, that is, operational goal. The fundamental purpose of the operational resources is thus to facilitate best possible year-ahead results.

In order to be useful in practice, it is necessary to realize that the available strategic resources will normally be scarce, and that hence careful choices should be made in order to prioritize selectively a small set of strategic program activities. This focus on a few significant strategic activities may also make it easier for the organization to come to grips with what constitutes a strategic budget versus an operating budget.

It is useful to classify strategic resources into several types.[9] First, the human resources needed to carry out strategic activities typically are most critical. These can be classified in terms of accounting for time-spending patterns, as well as in terms of salary expenditures. A second type of strategic resources are (non-personnel) expenditures associated with R&D, product testing and introduction, market research, process modification, and so on. Third, we have specific investment requirements for equipment, plant, and so on. Finally, working capital requirements stemming from inventory changes, credit volume, and/or term changes, and so on, should be considered a strategic resource when part of a specific effort to change strategic direction. It should be stressed that even though all strategic resources can be classified into one of the above four categories, it does *not* follow that all of these types of expenditures and/or investments are always strategic. For instance, research and development expenditures may have to be incurred to keep an ongoing business moving. Similarly, investments may have to be made in order to modernize and respond to ordinary demand increases, which is part of "business as usual."

In summary, the monitoring of strategic budget activities tends to encompass two measurement types—strategic expenditures measurements and accounting for executives' time-spending patterns. It is important to monitor the fractions of the use of the organization's resources that are being spent on strategic program implementation activities versus the operating activities, to ensure that the organization does not "borrow" resources intended for strategy implementation use to actually meet unexpected operating pressures. Also, the balance between the various strategic program-spending implementation activities should be monitored so that ad hoc overattention or underattention to particular implementation efforts might be avoided.

Let us now turn to the issues of measuring strategic program performance. There are four types of interrelated measures that we will recommend in this context, all to be applied to specific, individual strategic programs. First, one

[9]See Paul Stonich and Carlos Zaragossa, "Strategic Resource Programming," *Planning Executives Journal,* May 1980.

measure should capture the degree of physical completion of the intermediary stages in achieving a strategic program, what one might call "checkpoints" or "milestones." A second measure should address the time dimension—i.e., whether the achievement of a milestone takes place on target, or off schedule, or ahead of schedule. A third measure should deal with the actual resources spending levels in order to reach a strategic program target by a given date, the measurement units being expenditures and/or time spent on a particular strategic program phase. Are these resource expenditures as planned, or too high or too low? None of these measures is new as such; in fact, many companies have had considerable experience using these as part of their approach to project management.[10] What is lacking in many cases, however, is the reconciliation of these measures with operating measures as well as strategic position measures. Also, they should be reconciled with an additional often overlooked strategic program performance measure, which we will discuss.

A final set of strategic program performance measurement issues deals with assessing the degree to which the basic underlying environmental assumptions behind a strategic program are still valid. One example might be whether our key competitors react in the ways anticipated. If not, do we need to modify any of our competitive moves, such as pricing, advertising, and service efforts? Another example might be whether consumer and market reactions are turning out as planned. If not, do we need to modify, for instance, our promotion campaign, modifying a new product's features, and so on? Technological breakthroughs are examples of assumptions that might also be critical. Have we, for instance, reassessed pertinent new research and/or development findings that might have come about during the strategic program execution period? This might merit reconsideration of a project's feasibility and might potentially trigger a major reorientation of the strategic program. Assumptions relating to approvals and authorizations from various public-sector authorities may also frequently become critical for the continued viability of several types of strategic programs. These and other examples should illustrate the importance of the additional need to monitor whether the basic conception of a strategic program continues to be valid.

This reinforces our need to see the implementation of strategic programs in a dynamic context where our moves will typically lead to "responses" by outside forces, such as competitors and/or customers, which again might call for revised moves on our part, and so on. To monitor critical environmental factors in order to capture the dynamic, "multistage" nature of realistic strategy implementation is thus important. Changes in assumptions might often call for a subsequent redefinition or redirection of a strategic program. Environmental assumption analysis is thus in fact critical for reassessment of a strategic program's continued

[10]See, for instance David I. Cleland and William R. King, *Systems Analysis and Project Management,* (New York: McGraw-Hill, 1968); R. R. Miles and C. C. Snow, *Organizational Strategy, Structure and Process* (New York: McGraw-Hill, 1978).

"effectiveness." More traditional project management control measures might not adequately highlight this environmental exposure dimension.

Exhibit Five illustrates the interlinked tasks of controlling strategic programs and strategic budgets, based on our corporate example introduced in Section 2 of this chapter. Let us now more specifically focus on the beer business family and two of its business elements, "light" and "dark" (see Exhibit Three). "Light" is a new business element that is in the process of being introduced. The objective is to build a position for this beer in the higher-income, "younger"-consumer segment. Three strategic programs have been identified to attempt to achieve this: (1) the formulation of a new light beer, involving the brewing and beer-marketing operating divisions (consumer taste testing); (2) the development of an appropriate bottle and packaging, involving beer marketing, glass manufacturing, closures, and the carton plant as well as brewing (for usefully incorporating a new bottle dimension in the tapping plant); and (3) the actual launch, involving the beer marketing, brewing, glass-manufacturing and distribution divisions. "Dark" is an old, well-established beer, which traditionally has been perceived by the consumers as a nutritious drink, used for instance by mothers (in limited volume) during pregnancy. The objective is to relaunch and reposition the "dark" beer so as to appeal to the "mature" beer drinker who would appreciate a heavy-bodied beer. The strategic program that has been launched to achieve this involves beer marketing, to carry out a media campaign, and brewing, to develop a revised beer formulation and to prepare for production.

Regarding the control of the continued relevance of the objective, this might thus be done by following critical environmental assumptions. For "light," these might be to continue to assess the growth potential for this business in terms of the extent to which consumers' preferences might be changing toward this direction or not. Also it might involve monitoring factors that might possibly "dampen" this growth, such as governmental taxation and/or other regulatory moves. To monitor the development of one's own competitive strength, continued testing of consumer preference relative to other beers might be carried out. Relative market share might also give an indication of the strength position. Entry and/or exit of other brands must also be followed.

The control tasks go on along *both* the strategic and the operating dimensions of Exhibit Five. Each strategic program needs to be controlled in terms of making progress toward preestablished "milestones." For instance, the new beer formulation program (number 1 in Exhibit Five) will have to pass intermediary targets for completing initial formulation in the laboratory, limited-scale consumer taste testing, pilot-scale batch brewing, full-scale consumer taste and appearance testing, and full-scale trial brewing. The calendar must also be followed in terms of assessing whether stages are completed on time. Similarly, resource spending per stage broken down on each of the various departments must be checked. Finally, relevant environmental assumptions must be monitored: Do the customer target groups actually seem to "appreciate" this light-beer concept? If not, can our concept be modified? Are there indications that one or

Exhibit Five: *Two Objectives, to be Implemented by Means of Four Strategic Programs. This Leads to Derived Strategic Tasks for the Six Departments. Three Types of Control Tasks Arise; Vis-À-Vis Each Objective, Each Strategic Program, and Each Department's Strategic Budget.*

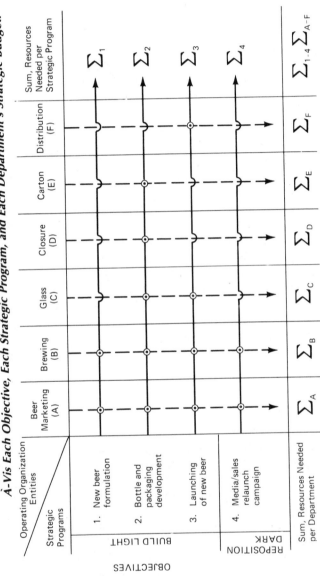

more of our competitors might also be preparing a light beer? If so, what actions might we take? Does the approval of the new beer run into problems with the Food Administration Agency, and, if so, what responses can we take? The second aspect of the control of each strategic program deals with the resource usage pattern. Has time been spent and have costs been incurred in such a way that each department is doing its part of the overall team task? While it is obvious that control for overspending must be made, it is equally important that one control for underspending. The latter may signal that one or more functional entities are not "tooled up" to carry out their strategic assignments—day-to-day pressures may be occupying all their capacity.

For each operating division the strategic budget also needs to be controlled. Let us take the glass division as an example. We see from Exhibit Five that this division is involved in two strategic programs, namely, to carry out the strategic task of developing a new beer bottle as part of program number 2, and of initiating new-bottle production as part of program number 3. The spending of the resources provided, the strategic budget Σ_c, should be monitored so as to establish that these are *not* made use of for operating purposes and "fire fighting" in the glass plant. Also, the monitoring should check to make sure that *both* strategic tasks are being pursued as was intended.

Let us now discuss the measures for monitoring the objectives dimension. One obvious approach would be to measure progress toward actual attainment of long-term goals. For instance, to what extent are planned growth levels in sales, market share, profits, and so on, actually being met? A major problem, however, in comparing actual performance with these kinds of prior sets of goals is that the prior-posterior time span usually becomes too long to make such measures meaningful as tools for intervening to modify and improve objectives. For instance, what is the practical relevance of knowing that one has actually not met one's growth goal five or ten years after this goal was set? The ability to use the control process as a self-corrective mechanism to respond to and ameliorate problems thus typically becomes quite limited in such cases. Useful control of objectives' fulfillment performance is thus difficult to achieve by following the classical control model mode.[11]

4. ENVIRONMENTAL MEASUREMENTS

There is, however, a useful indirect way of controlling objectives, which at least in part gets us around the long-control time-span problem. This deals with attempting to systematically assess changes in critical environmental assumptions

[11]See, for instance, William H. Newman, *Constructive Control* (Englewood Cliffs, N.J.: Prentice-Hall, 1975); Peter Lorange and Michael S. Scott-Morton, "A Framework for Management Control Systems," *Sloan Management Review,* 16, No. 1, pp. 41–51.

that underlie a particular objective. If substantial changes in critical assumptions turn up, then presumably we may feel compelled to reexamine whether the objective itself is still relevant or whether redirection might now be appropriate. Thus environmental assessment monitoring gives *indirect,* but usually early and relevant, indication that our objectives need to be reexamined.

How can we go about developing in practical terms an effective environmental assumption analysis as part of a strategic control process? We suggest a five-step approach.

The *first step* deals with developing an initial list of critical environmental factors that involved line management deems relevant vis-à-vis a particular objective. We recall that the objectives-setting stage attempts to establish what might be proper strategic direction, based on a reconciliation of assessments of a business's attractiveness as well as one's own competitive strength. Assumptions relating to business attractiveness fall into three categories. First, we have to address key factors underlying the future pattern of demand in the business. For instance, what, if any, might be impacts from changes in the economic climate at large, and so on? Second, we might assess the likelihood of the emergence of unexpected factors that might "derail" our basic business demand assumption. Prominent in this respect might be asumptions relating to technological developments, raw-material changes, legislative changes, and so on. Third, we might address assumptions regarding whether we might continue to enjoy reasonable general profitability levels in the business. This might be affected by entry and/or exit of competitors, overcapacity, and so on.[12]

When it comes to reassessing assumptions associated with our own competitive strength relative to competition, we might usefully divide this into two classes of questions. One question deals with whether we will continue to have anticipated quality-type competitive lead advantages, thus enabling us to take a higher price. The other question deals with whether we will continue to have assumed cost advantages relative to the competition. Regarding this, relative market share changes might indicate shifts in relative cost advantage. Capital investment patterns to enhance automation, productivity, and/or scale economies might also signify shifts in the relative cost assumption.

The *second step* deals with imposing some practical limits on the critical assumption list. Typically we find that for a specific business there tend to be only a few factors that are judged particularly critical. Positive as well as negative potential impacts from factors should be kept in mind when deciding on importance. Too often we might have a tendency to overemphasize potential negative impacts.

The *third step* is to attempt to build a more explicit understanding of how each of the critical factors might evolve. For this we might make use of a broad spectrum of available tools, from such classical approaches as statistical time-series analysis and lead indicators to more future-oriented scenario analysis ap-

[12]See, for instance, Michael Porter, *Competitive Strategy,* (New York: Macmillan, 1980).

proaches. The analysis may be based on internal and/or external sources, including econometric data bases (such as DRI, Wharton Econometrics, Chase Econometrics), financial performance data bases (such as Compustat, Value-Line), and business line competitive position/performance data bases (such as PIMS). There may be many relevant underlying disciplines for gaining insight into critical assumptions, including scenario analysis, market research, technological forecasting, and industrial economics. The overriding aim is to develop as good an understanding as possible of how a key factor might develop, based on whatever combination of information and know-how there is available. In the course of such probing, we should develop a "feel" for the degree of ability to predict the development of a particular environmental assumption.

The *fourth step* deals with examining how we might respond to anticipated development of certain factors by modifying our own objective(s). Again, we might typically have a large number of potential responses' ranging from major modifications of an objective to more specific decisions, such as pricing, new-product development, and advertising, or attempts to improve production or distribution processes. Providing a general catalog of response options is beyond the scope of this chapter; however, we can think about response options as falling into one of the following four categories, as indicated by Exhibit Six. First, we may have the task of responding to environmental factors that definitely indicate a long-term pattern, such as demographic shifts or changes in consumer taste. In such instances we may be able to carry out a planned, orderly, and often incremental response (Cell A). Second, we may have to face a sudden typically quite unpredictable development, such as a move by a competitor that involves pricing or advertising intensity. In this case it may be useful to have developed contingency plans (Cell B). Third, we may have to face a situation where we can in fact predict a critical environmental happening, such as observing whether competitors are adding plant capacity, but where there is little we can do in terms of responding except reconfirming our commitment to the business or withdrawal (Cell C). Finally, we may have the particularly difficult and

Exhibit Six: Pattern of Exposure from Critical Assumptions

PREDICTABILITY RESPONSE POTENTIAL	HIGHER	LOWER
MORE	A	B
LESS	C	D

often risky situation of a sudden, unpredictable environmental happening that leaves us with no response options, such as a major technological breakthrough by one of our competitors (Cell D). In all these situations, the critical challenge, however, is to develop a realistic organizational perception with respect to what response options we realistically might be able and willing to consider, taking our own resource availability into account (funds, people, critical know-how).

The *final step* consists of reconciling our view of all the key environmental assumptions in terms of their comprehensibility and predictability, as well as in terms of the extent to which it offers a response potential. This might be summarized through a plotting of the factors onto a chart such as Exhibit Six. The purpose of such a plotting is, of course, not to pretend that we are dealing with an exact exercise. Our "measures" are highly judgmental and are not based on cardinal or ordinal scales. Rather, this final step should be seen as an attempt to develop some overall visualization or mapping of the pattern of critical environmental factors that may confront a business. Thus Exhibit Six should be considered a summary of our initial environmental assumption analysis providing a picture of what is the emerging environmental exposure.

The procedure of identifying, classifying, and analyzing the key environmental assumptions just discussed might be seen as a necessary precondition for environment-based monitoring as part of our strategic control approach. The five-step approach for identifying and analyzing key environmental assumptions is an iterative one. The overriding purpose is to better understand the counterfocus that the organization is exposed to in its environment. A trial-and-error approach for developing such a feel for these dynamic forces is critical. In the next sections we will discuss how we might make further use of this analytical basis through strategic control.

5. RISK ASSESSMENT IMPLICATIONS OF ENVIRONMENTAL EXPOSURE ASSESSMENT APPROACH

In this section we focus on some implications from the environmental exposure analysis, in terms of how they might affect our assessment of risks involved. The positioning of the relevant critical environmental assumptions gives insight with respect to the riskiness of a particular objective as a function of how it is exposed to the environment. If one or more critical environmental factors, for instance, are "located" in the lower-right corner of Exhibit Six (cell D), then we might say that the particular objective in question could be quite risky, as a consequence of this environmental exposure. If, on the other hand, an assumption is "located" in the upper-left corner of Exhibit Six (cell A), then the risk might be seen as much less, given that we can both predict and respond reasonably well.

It should be emphasized that the expected frequency or likelihood of a factor's occurring, a major determinant of risk, is only indirectly accounted for in the risk exposure concept discussed here, in that this constitutes one of the important criteria for limiting the list of critical environmental assumptions, as discussed under step 2 as part of the five-step approach outlined in Section 4.

It is important that the strategic control process examine whether there seems to be a *change* in environmental risk exposure over time. This might manifest itself by changes of some sort or another affecting a particular environmental assumption in such a way that our ability to predict and/or respond might improve or diminish. For instance, it is commonly assumed that a new start-up business (a "question mark" business) would normally be more risky than a well-established business (a "cash cow" business). We should monitor whether such a lessening of what might seem to be the riskiness of environmental exposures in fact seems to take place as the business evolves toward a more mature stage. If we find that a business seems to become more and more risky as it evolves over time, this might be an important signal that its environment is changing in an undesirable direction, and that the business might in fact become quite unsuited to play its role as a "cash cow" element in the firm's portfolio of businesses. To understand this early is of course critical so that we can examine what ameliorating actions to take when it comes to modifying the business strategy in question and/or the corporate portfolio strategy.

We might search in at least three types of directions in order to explore the potential for reducing a given business risk exposure. First, time is of the essence. Early realization of changes in critical environmental factors might lead to corrective action at a time when the span of options might typically still be wide. Late awareness and acknowledgement of key environmental shifts, on the other hand, is in many instances a handicap because the degrees of freedom tend to be less. Second, we might attempt to increase our ability to understand and predict a critical factor, say, by stepping up internal analytical and know-how capabilities and/or carrying out research to increase our insight into this particular phenomenon. Also, we might be buying relevant outside expertise and services, such as employing consultants and making use of outside econometric forecasting resources. Third, we might attempt to increase our own response potential. One way to do this is by investing in more-flexible equipment. As an example of this, we might, for instance, build a power plant in such a way that it can alternatively burn gas, oil, or coal. We might also invest in a broader product line, which would allow us to respond with different brands to different competitive pressures. These are situations where added costs might legitimately be incurred so as to increase our flexibility to respond vis-à-vis a critical environmental factor.

The issue of reducing risk should, of course, also be addressed in connection with the overall corporate portfolio balancing. The levels and changes in each business's environmental risk exposure positions will be essential inputs for the corporate level in carrying out such a portfolio-balancing task. Attempts to achieve an acceptable overall risk exposure balance should be one of the criteria of the corporate-level resource allocation process. It is critical that the environmental risk exposure properties of each business lead to an overall fit that provides a satisfactory exposure balance. It is thus neither good nor bad whether a business is exposed to high or low environmental risk levels *per se* (assuming, however, that the risk is not higher than necessary because of management neglect). What matters is each business's fit within the overall portfolio. Systematic control of key environmental factors is thus critical for maintaining a portfolio strategy; changes in each portfolio element's risk exposure must be monitored.

6. CONTROL MODES

We now turn to a second set of implications of the environmental exposure/risk analysis, dealing with how this might affect the mode of control.[13] Let us first consider the tasks of controlling and responding to lower-risk-exposure situations (the upper-left corner, cell A, of Exhibit Six). We are here in a position to monitor the environment relatively closely and to interpret the implications of such changes. Also, we are able to make responses as necessary. We might in fact think about the process as being quite analogous to the steering of a rocket toward a target, with relatively frequent but typically small corrective actions, based on a more or less continuous scanning of the critical environmental factors in question.

If, on the other hand, our ability to predict is small, while the response potential still exists (the upper-right corner of Exhibit Six, cell B), there is a significant change in the implementation of the control tasks. The environment's evolution will typically no longer be as easily understood but will rather present us with "surprises" that demand a response. Thus we might develop what might be labeled "contingency control"—i.e., relatively elaborate steps of action to take if a particular positive or adverse environmental development occurs. The mode of scanning continues to be to follow the environmental phenomena relatively closely and more or less continuously. However, we would seldom expect changes and modifications in our objectives or strategic programs. When necessary to make a change or modification, however, these tend to be quite large. Under circumstances like these, it is important that we guard against a slackening off of our environmental-scanning efforts. This would inevitably raise the danger of scanning being seen as monotonous and nondecision oriented.

Let us now consider the situation where we are usually able to predict relatively well, but where the response potentials tend to be smaller. In this setting it seems essential to scan the environment so as to take advantage of our potential

[13]This section has been significantly influenced by Newman, *Constructive Control.* See also Ben C. Ball and Peter Lorange, "Managing Your Strategic Responsiveness to the Environment," *Planning Executives Journal,* Fall 1979.

to gain insight into and understanding of how a key factor might evolve. We might call this an anticipative go/no go control mode, in that the response options typically are few. These might be either to withdraw from the business, say, by selling or closing it, or to continue as before. Time is of course essential when making such decisions. It seems particularly critical to keep in mind that we are often dealing here with behavioral and/or political barriers that may create "wishful thinking" within an organization and hence may make it difficult to act. When, for instance, a key environmental assumption relates to fluctuations in a commodity market, we might easily decide to "stay on" in the hope of recuperating later when, in fact, this might be quite illusory, unrealistic, and thus dangerous. The strategic control approach might thus provide an opportunity to institutionalize the monitoring and reporting in such a way that the tendency to delay the signaling of "bad" news might be counteracted. Thus the process might provide a vehicle whereby lower-level management might find it more "politically" feasible to bring up unfavorable changes in circumstances earlier, as part of their regular reporting on critical environmental assumptions. Thus the strategic control process institutionalizes a set of rules that "protects" lower-level managers so that they might be more easily encouraged to bring adverse factors to the attention of higher-level management, forcing an earlier and more realistic decision-making focus on whether to withdraw from the business or allowing oneself to continue.

We need to consider one final type of control situation, namely the one associated with the lower-right (cell D) corner of Exhibit Six—i.e., a high-risk exposure setting. This final type of control may be labeled post-factum go/no go control. It is here typically not possible to do much in terms of changing objectives or strategic programs in time. Rather, we are faced with merely registering that our position has significantly improved or deteriorated. We might see the control process more as one of learning from these experiences so as to avoid the same "errors" in the future.

Of the four modes of control of key environmental settings that thus emerge, it may possibly be most difficult to grasp the intuitive difference between an anticipative and a post-factum go/no go control setting. Therefore let us give an example to illustrate the difference between these two types of control. Consider the situation of a shipowner who is involved in the supertanker segment of the industry. During the early 1970s there was a strong boom in the tanker market. A very large crude carrier (VLCC), which might be purchased for a price of U.S. $40–$50 million, could earn enough revenue to pay for itself within a few years. After the first OPEC oil crisis the rate of increase in the volume of oil to be shipped dropped dramatically. This coincided with an exceptionally high rate of delivery of new VLCCs, which had been ordered during the boom. There was thus a dramatic fall of the tanker charter rates, and the profitability of the business deteriorated rapidly. In fact, the spot market rates became so depressed at times that they did not even cover the price of bunker, with no contribution to other cost items, such as crew costs and financial costs. The only alternatives for VLCC owners who had lacked the foresight to secure longer-term time charters for their ships were to lay them up or to sell them in a very depressed secondhand market. Let us, however, examine the development of the pattern of prices for VLCCs during the period just after the collapse of the spot market. Maybe to our initial surprise, we find that it took approximately nine months before the secondhand market became significantly weakened. Thus, due to widespread expectations or beliefs that the "good old days" would come back, the secondhand market acted "irrationally," with a substantial lag. Examining the history of the falls in the spot market and the secondhand market at earlier periods in time, we find analogous lagged patterns for the drop in the secondhand market. Thus, in a mode of anticipative go/no go control, the spot market moves might be an indicator of when to sell the VLCC and get out with one's assets virtually intact. However, most tanker owners did not use an anticipative go/no go control approach. They did not see the signals to sell in time; by practicing post-factum control, they often incurred straggering losses.

7. TASK DELINEATION; CONTROL SIGNAL RECONCILIATION; DECENTRALIZATION

Let us now turn to the question of delineating managerial responsibilities for the various monitoring tasks, interpreting the various types of control signals, reconciling these types of signals, and taking managerial actions. Recall from our discussion of strategic and operating organizational structures that these normally are *not* congruent below certain levels in the organization. As also noted in our earlier example (see Exhibits Two and Three), this implies that the task of performance monitoring along all four control modes (i.e., objectives, strategic programs, strategic budgets, operating budgets—see Exhibit One) does *not* normally fall on one person or organizational unit. This is reflected by the fact that different groupings of people tend to be involved in the formulation of objectives and strategic programs on the one hand, and in the carrying out of strategic and operating budgets on the other hand. Several of the organization's members are "wearing two hats"; the executives involved are largely the same, but they have delineated the way they distribute their tasks differently when it comes to the strategic dimension versus the operating dimension. For this reason the question of who is responsible for the various monitoring tasks is not immediately evident and needs clarification.

Experience has shown that it might be useful to appoint specific teams of executives to carry out the strategy-formulation tasks. The delineation of a strategic structure is thus normally not sufficiently operationalized unless it is also clear that certain executives are to be responsible for the various strategy-formulation tasks. These executive teams might also be natural focal points for the continuous monitoring of key assumptions underlying objectives, as well as for following progress on strategic programs. The teams should be drawn from across the organization, with the primary criterion being to involve those executives who might best be able to contribute to relevant strategy articulation. Thus, while being relatively free from constraints set by formal organizational structure and hierachy lines, it is still important that key operating executives be included when it is clear that these will subsequently be directly involved in the carrying out of given strategies.

Let us illustrate how a hierarchy of strategic teams might be established by drawing on one example with the strategic structure illustrated by Exhibit Three. The first step is to appoint three levels of strategy teams: the corporate strategy team, three business family strategy teams, and nine business element strategy teams. The corporate strategy team might consist of the chief executive officer as chairman and the chairmen of each of the three business family strategy teams as members. Typical operating jobs for executives such as these three might be as follows: The chairman of the business family I team is also vice-president in charge of beer marketing; the chairman of the business family II team is vice-president in charge of soft-drink bottling; and the chairman of the business family III team is vice-president in charge of glass manufacturing. The members of each of the business family strategy teams should include the chairman of each of the business element teams that are associated with a business family. Thus, for the beer business family strategy team, members might include the chairman of the "pilsen" business element strategy team, whose operating assignment might also be manager of sales, beer marketing division; the chairman of the "light" business element strategy team, who might also be vice-president in charge of the general distribution division; and so on. The members of each business element strategy team should be selected in such a way so as to represent the most relevant organizational resources for formulating the business strategies in question. For instance, the "pilsen" business element team might have the following four members (in addition to the chairman): the member/brewmaster of brewery X (from the brewing division); the assistant manager of glass plant Y (from the glass manufacturing division); the manager of distribution (from the distribution division); and the director of corporate marketing (from the central corporate staff).

Membership on all strategy teams should be seen as a *temporary* assignment. All teams should be appointed anew each year so as to underscore that for the strategic structure *change is normal:* The very purpose of the strategic structure is to be able to adapt quickly to changing environmental circumstances with modified and realistic organizational focus, reflecting the new circumstances. Thus, too much institutionalization of the strategic committees might defeat the very purpose of a strategic structure. While an evolutionary perspective on strategic focus should be maintained when feasible and natural, it is also essential that membership changes be made when strengthening of a team thereby is perceived as possible.

The corporate strategy committee should appoint the business family strategy teams. Each of the business family teams might in turn propose its respective business element teams. The corporate strategy team may wish to approve these appointments. One should avoid making the teams too large for working efficiency reasons, say, ideally four to six members. One might also attempt to avoid having the same executives be members of too many teams. Each of the strategy teams' monitoring tasks is to be carried out along the guidelines discussed earlier in terms of which types of variables to focus on and how to measure these.

A critical question deals with the strategy teams' power and responsibility to intervene under various circumstances when their control efforts suggest deviations that point toward the need for ameliorating action. We need to establish how such a pattern of decentralized authority might be delineated. In this connection, let us distinguish between two types of potential interventions. When it comes to following up on the implementation efforts of strategic programs, carried out by various parts of the operating organization as their *derived* strategic roles, a strategy committee should have the authority to intervene in case of problems—i.e., interact with one or more operating elements as appropriate to keep the strategic program evolving. When, on the other hand, it comes to interpreting major unexpected impacts from environmental forces, implying that one might potentially have to modify a strategic program significantly or even have to change the basic direction for an objective, then a careful procedure for "upward signaling" should be established. Critical environmental factors that are relatively difficult to predict or understand as well as relatively difficult to respond to, as identified in our analysis summarized in Exhibit Six (i.e., being located in the lower-right part of the figure), should be reported upward to the next-level strategy team as soon as possible. The analysis of the impact(s) of such developments should be done jointly by the two team levels. The nature of the monitoring task, the need for a more corporate-wide focus in analysis, and the decision-making discretionary level call for a higher degree of centralization than when it comes to intervening to maintain progress in the execution of strategic programs if no major changes in environmental premises are involved.

Each entity within the *operating* organization is responsible for monitoring progress along its respective operating *as well as* strategic budgets. In these instances, too, an operating organizational entity should have the authority to make corrective decisions in response to operating budget deviations in accordance with established standard operating procedures. Minor strategic budget deviations should also be dealt with in this way. However, when it comes to more substantial strategic budget deviations, then contact should be made with the relevant strategy team to which this strategic program refers. Ameliorating actions should be taken as a result of interaction between the two organizational entities. A final type of strategic budget deviation might emerge as a result of shifting resources to or from the operating budget from or to the strategic budget, say, to respond to an unexpected operating crisis or to take advantage of an unexpected strategic opportunity. These budgetary deviations imply shifts in the agreed-upon resource allocation pattern and the strategic direction and should thus not be allowed to be initiated by an operating organizational entity. One should not allow the strategic budget to be treated as a "slush fund" to be used whenever it is convenient from an operating point of view.

From the preceding paragraphs it is becoming clear that conflicts might arise between strategic and operating considerations for which there is no "right" answer. Such strategic-operating trade-off considerations should be carried out at the lowest organizational level at which the strategic and the operating structures become congruent. Exhibits Two and Three indicate that this congruence takes place at the level of the chief executive officer and the corporate strategy team. In other organizations the strategic-operating reconciliation level might be at a lower level than in our example. It should be stressed that the following must be made explicit: at what level the strategic-operating reconciliation is supposed to take place and which executives are involved at this level.

An overall challenge is to establish a significant pattern of decentralization, given the management capacity constraints will be in effect, as usual. We have seen that the pattern of environmental risk exposure may have potential consequences in terms of decentralization of aspects of the control tasks. The task of scanning a certain environmental factor can probably be less easily delegated when this factor involves a major risk exposure. Factors associated with less environmental risk, on the other hand, can typically be more easily delegated in terms of who does the scanning. Similarly, reporting on deviations and initiation of corrective actions along previously developed contingency tracks can typically be more easily delegated in lower-risk settings than in situations with perceived higher-risk exposure. We thus have a more flexible way to decentralize than the traditional responsibility center approach. Senior management can institutionalize the follow-up and reporting on selected environmental assumptions that might complement the financially based responsibility center control. Thus some critical aspects of monitoring the continued relevance of a business's basic objective might remain quite centralized while allowing the business's operating performances to be monitored in a rather decentralized manner.

Although a full-fledged discussion of the issue is beyond the scope of this chapter, we can still point out that these arguments might also have implications for the way the boards of directors might be specifically involved in a corporation's control activities. While a major responsibility of a board of directors presumably is to execute control, it might be difficult to carry this out in a satisfactory sense when only engaging in budgetary-based control discussions at this level, easily getting lost in the details and often only being able to react too late. To put some of the key assumptions on the board's agenda, on the other hand, and emphasizing aspects of strategic control might be more useful for the board.

8. CONCLUDING ISSUES

In this chapter we have argued that strategic control should be seen as an integral part of the overall strategic processes of a corporation. Although considerable progress has generally been made on strategy formulation, there seems to be a broad group consensus that strategy implementation, control, and follow-up tend to be less well emphasized in many corporations.

Which potential implementational barriers could frustrate the development of a strategic control approach along the lines discussed in this chapter? First, it should be stressed that past tradition with and exposure to related management processes seems important. For instance, a well-established procedure of responsibility center accounting might provide the organization with the necessary discipline to benefit from a control approach. Exposure to strategy formulation models (such as the BCG approach)[14] might similarly improve the organization's ability to establish strategic targets against which to control. Thus it seems that strategic control might be seen as a follow-on stage in the evolution of a firm's management processes after the establishing of business strategy-planning procedures.

Second, there could be barriers to implementation from established staff groups that might see themselves as having vested interests in parts of the management process, such as the control department, the strategic-planning department, or the MIS department.[15] Top management should establish sufficient coordination among these existing departments to ensure that their subsystems evolve in ways that will be consistent with each other. Rather than putting one of the existing staff departments in charge of developing strategic control, a senior staff executive could be given the responsibility for this, together with coordinating the evolution of the other management subsystems.

Finally, it seems critical that there be a high degree of explicitness regarding various aspects of the approach: This includes the delineation of the strategic and the operating structures; the patterns of derived strategic tasks to be carried out by each operating entity, as exemplified in Exhibits Four and Five; and the distinction between what constitutes strategic and what constitutes operating resources. Above all, however, the strategic control conceptual logic should be clear and understood.

We have argued that strategic control is the key to better implementation, on at least three accounts. First, the emphasis on articulating strategic programs as well as on the strategic budgets that can thereby be derived provides an element of realism when it comes to ensuring that sufficient strategic resources are available. Second, separate monitoring of the uses of strategic operating resources helps ensure that day-to-day crises and "fire-fighting" do not always

---

[14]For an overview of models of behavior strategy formulation, see Yoram Wind and Vijay Mahajan, "Designing Product and Business Portfolios," *Harvard Business Review,* January–February 1981.

[15]Vijay Sathe *Controller Involvement in Management,* (Englewood Cliffs, N.J.: Prentice-Hall, 1982).

arise in efforts to implement strategy. Finally, the most important benefit, in our opinion, is the explicit focus on changes in assumptions underlying objectives and key strategic programs and thus the recognition that strategic plans should always be considered "temporary." The environment always changes. Hence most written plans tend to be more or less obsolete relatively soon after they have been written. Strategic control can thus help management by modifying and improving strategic plans as needed on a more or less continuous basis. The value of the written planning document becomes one of providing a basis, an initial position for further improvements. Thus strategic control seems essential for strengthening our ability to react, frequently allowing us to gain time and flexibility in terms of response options. We feel that we well see a strengthening of the strategic control emphasis among many corporations over the next decade.

11

Seizing Competitive Initiative

I. C. MacMILLAN

Columbia University

The author wishes to thank the Strategy Research Center, Columbia University Graduate School of Business, for support. Reprinted by permission from *The Journal of Business Strategy*, Vol. 2, No. 4, Spring 1982. Copyright © 1982, Warren, Gorham & Lamont, Inc., 210 South Street, Boston, Mass. All Rights Reserved.

The purpose of this paper is to explore the concept of strategic initiative—the ability of a company or strategic business unit to capture control of strategic behavior in the industries in which it competes. To the extent that strategists can capture and maintain the initiative, their competitors are obliged to respond thus being forced to take a reactive role rather than a proactive role.

The company with the initiative is better able to dominate the competitive game, and ultimately to maintain control of its own destiny. This much is self-evident—the fundamental strategic problem lies in *how* to actually capture the initiative, and once having secured it, how to retain it in the face of competitive countermoves.

To obtain and retain strategic initiative appears to require a number of critical conceptual skills. These are a thorough understanding and anticipation of the following: response barriers; intelligence systems; pre-emption potentials; infrastructure requirements; calculated sacrifices; general management challenges; and what can only be called "punch and counterpunch" planning. Each will be discussed in turn.

RESPONSE BARRIERS

Porter has perhaps done more than anyone else to draw the attention of strategists to the need to analyze mobility barriers, particularly entry barriers.[1] Harrigan[2] and MacMillan and McCafferty[3] have in more detail discussed the concepts of exit barriers and inertia barriers. Entry barriers (see examples in Box 1) are characteristics of the industry or business that prevent, or seriously inhibit the movement of competitors into a product/market position, perhaps already selected by the company with strategic initiative.

Exit barriers, on the other hand, inhibit or prevent the movement of competitors from a position they have already occupied, while inertia barriers are characteristics of the competitors themselves which seriously slow down their responses to moves made by others.

It is axiomatic that the strategist who elects to secure and maintain the strategic initiative needs to know and understand such barriers intimately. In particular, the conceptual challenge lies in the ability to anticipate the emergence of *future* barriers.

This is important for three reasons:

Anticipation of emerging *entry* barriers allows a strategic aggressor to take

---

[1]M. E. Porter, *Competitive Strategy* (New York: Free Press, 1980).

[2]K. R. Harrigan, *Strategies for Declining Businesses* (New York: Lexington Books, 1980).

[3]I. C. MacMillan, and M. L. McCafferty, "Strategy for Low Entry Barrier Markets such as Service Industries," *Journal of Business Strategy,* 1982.

Box 1   Some Common Response Barriers*

1. *ENTRY BARRIERS* (Identified by Porter [1980] and others)
   Economies of Scale: High investment is needed to be cost competitive.
   Differentiated Product: Customers identify and are loyal to a specific product or brand.
   Capital requirements: Large amounts of capital required to provide credit, leased equipment or build image by advertising.
   Switching costs: Customers would have to pay a lot to switch brands.
   Distribution Channels: Access to channels are blocked.
   Components and raw materials: Access to supplies are blocked.
   Prime locations occupied:
   Preferential treatment from Governments:
   Experience benefits: Know-how and experience benefits kept from competition.
   High expected retaliation: If competitor will retaliate violently.
   Price cutting:
   Lack of opportunities to share costs: Among many other products and markets.
   Specialized skills: Access to critical skills blocked.
   Interest group: Threat of, or actual, government, union etc. objections to move by competitors.
   Patents:
2. *EXIT BARRIERS* (Identified by Porter [1980], Harrigan [1980] and others)
   Effect of large investment write-offs
   Damage to prestige/image of company
   Damage to ego of management
   Government proscription: Government prevents exit.
   Large clean-up costs: To leave sites in original condition.
   Union agreements: Prevent exit.
   Shared costs: Which would have to be borne by other products/markets.
   Suppliers, customers, distributors: Prevent exit.
3. *INERTIA BARRIERS* (Identified by MacMillan and McCafferty [1982])
   Strategic choice: To control the move would be counterstrategic.
   Strategic challenge: Move regarded as nonthreatening.
   Distraction: Competitor distracted by major problems or opportunities.
   Visibility: To move is not visible to competitor.
   Portfolio position: Division affected has low priority in company.
   Structural: No specific division responsible, or motivated to respond.
   Procedures: Correct response calls for major policy revisions or costly revisions of procedures.
   Bureaucratic politics: Response creates jurisdictional disputes and bureaucratic disruptions.

*A specific industry could well have unique response barriers. In fact the greater part of the creative challenge lies in identification of the barriers unique to the industry.

the initiative by positioning itself to enter the segment ahead of the barriers and even use its "first occupancy" position to create/erect the barriers for competitors, who then have to surmount the entry barriers. Texas Instruments has consistently used experience curve effects to create cost barriers for other entrants.

Anticipation of emerging *exit* barriers allows the aggressor to time exit ahead of the actual formation of such barriers, thus increasing flexibility of movement from undesirable positions while the competitors are held back by the exit barriers. For instance, several "first exits" from increasingly regulated businesses received less public interference than subsequent exits. It is also possible that the aggressor can exit and then help shape exit barriers to prevent others from exiting. This has happened frequently in exits from foreign countries, where the departure of the first major competitor had precipitated government action to prevent/hinder others from leaving.

Another problem is to find oneself in a situation where a competitor which would very much like to leave a segment (and thus make life easier in the segment) cannot do so because of exit barriers which are generally of the competitor's own creating.

In many cases, actual entry barriers may be rather low, in which case, anticipation of emerging *inertia* barriers of the competitors allows the strategic aggressor to improve judgements as to what is the most appropriate *timing* of the contemplated strategic move, as well as to improve judgements as to the likely *duration* that the initiative will be retained before competitors start responding in sufficient numbers to erode the advantage of the initiative. This has been a characteristic of many of Citibank's new products introductions in the 1960's and 1970's.

A thorough analysis and understanding of such barriers lays the groundwork for determining future opportunities for capturing the initiative. In effect it is the equivalent of careful analysis of the competitive terrain. The next challenge lies in analysis and determination of how the terrain will be, and is being used. This requires the development of appropriate intelligence systems.

INTELLIGENCE SYSTEMS

Without appropriate intelligence it is impossible to retain strategic initiative. In the first place intelligence provides a basis for anticipating changes in product/market/competitor positions in the industry. In the second place it provides the *only* basis for anticipating the countermoves by competitors, suppliers and customers.

It is clear that there are three major areas to which resources must be deployed for intelligence to be effective.

First is *product intelligence*—the information relating to the nature of the product and its production, delivery, and substitutability by other products.

Second is *market* intelligence—information concerning the current and emerging needs, values and relative power of major distributor and customer groups.

Finally there is *competitive* intelligence—information concerning the current and emerging positions of existing and potential competitors. In particular it is important to be able to anticipate responses of competition to moves initiated by the strategists.

An important conceptual challenge for the strategist is the decision as to *which* of the major intelligence activities deserves most emphasis. This judgement can be considerably aided by considering product life cycle implications.

Product intelligence can have high importance in the early stages of the product life cycle, when the desired nature of the product, its desired characteristics, production methods, delivery methods and service requirements are still being articulated by the developing market. *Market intelligence* can be particularly important in the mature stage when the emergence of new needs or changes in old needs signal opportunities for segmentation. *Competitive intelligence* is always important, but emphasis switches from direct competition in the early stages of the life cycle to substitute competition as the product matures.

What appears to be vital to effective intelligence activities is that the emphasis be focussed on anticipating expected *behavior* by key competitors, suppliers, customers or distributors. Several firms have successfully institutionalized this emphasis on anticipating behavior or responses by key players by assigning to line managers the role of a "shadow" competitor, supplier etc., as part of their line responsibility. (Much in the same way as the British opposition party has a "shadow" cabinet minister whose role it is to keep fully up to date on the important issues in the real minister's area of responsibility.) In strategy meetings, it is expected of these "shadow" executives that they be able to present their best judgement as to how their particular "shadow" will respond to the strategic moves being considered.

This has had several salutory effects: First, people in the company soon become aware of the fact that there is such a shadow position and start to forward information that would otherwise lie around in "stagnant pools" in the organization. Thus the shadow competitor becomes an information sink.

Second, with some assistance the shadow executive soon develops a fairly sophisticated mental model of the opponent, which includes its philosophy, strategy, long run resources, commitments, bureaucracy and power position in relation to its own stakeholders. These insights are vital for anticipating the responses of opposing organizations.

Third, the inclusion of the shadow role as a formal responsibility helps ensure that specific *line* attention is given to the difficult intellectual problem of second guessing the opponent.

Fourth, the mental model of the opponent provides the basis for testing new data about the opponent for consistency. Formally, if the data does not "fit" the model it is required that such data be checked and accuracy confirmed.

This assures that incorrect data tend not to be accepted, but at the same time the checking of "maverick" data, rather than automatic rejection of it, ensures that if the opponent's organization is undergoing change, the shadow executive discovers this. This second phenomenon helps prevent self-delusive assumptions that the opponent will continue to act forever in the way that it has in the past.

Finally, the shadow executive system tends to be less costly and more effective than the enormously complex and highly bureaucratic formal information systems that appear to be the popular alternative.

The three types of intelligence described above, together with the analysis of response barriers, provide the backdrop for the formulation of the actual strategy. With this background, it is possible first to identify pre-emption potential.

PRE-EMPTION POTENTIAL

Key to capturing and retaining initiative is an intimate understanding of what potential pre-emption options are possible—moves where once one competitor has taken the initiative, others find it extremely difficult to follow. Porter discusses pre-emption explicitly in connection with capacity expansion. In a mature industry, the first competitor to expand capacity may discourage others from expanding, thus pre-empting market share. However the rich potential for pre-emptive moves is also apparent in many of Porter's entry barrier discussions.

It is critical to understand the importance, for pre-emption, of marginality. Take key accounts, for instance. It is a common phenomenon that a relatively small proportion of key accounts account for a disproportionately large proportion of total revenues and/or profits in an industry, or for a company. The phenomenon also applies to distribution channels, market segments, customer types, geographic locations and so on.

So by moving rapidly to occupy the highly concentrated, first few positions and consolidating its position in these, the strategic aggressor may be able to pre-empt the competition and thus gain the initiative. This has a double advantage. First the slower competitors must now compete for the remaining positions with successively decreasing marginal return on effort. Second, in competing for these smaller positions the strategic aggressor already has a large base of revenues over which to cover fixed costs, which base is denied to its competitors,—thus creating significant cost barriers for the late entrants.

Thus an important component of developing strategic initiative lies in being able to visualize which pre-emptive potentials exist, or are emerging, as the industry evolves. This can be a two-edged sword, in that the pre-empted positions of the past could create exit barriers for the future: For example many organizations who achieved dominance of a "traditional" distribution system found themselves unable to switch to a new, emergent distribution system for fear of retaliation by existing distributors who carried a very large proportion of their sales. This is why emphasis is placed on pre-emption *potential*—potential for *both* the company *and* its competitors to pre-empt emerging customers, markets, channels, supply sources, geographic locations or key accounts.

A second major class of pre-emption opportunities lies in the areas of technology application. At different stages of the life cycle technology can be applied to secure initiative by exploiting the advantages of: patents, new applications, new features, process improvements, new distribution systems, enhanced reliability, or better service. For instance, Sears with its huge consumer data base may use the emergent self diagnostic systems on appliances to pre-empt a substantial number of appliance purchases by offering "one-stop" appliance servicing for all Sears' appliances with each service call.

A thorough understanding of pre-emption potential requires thorough assessment of emerging infra-structure requirements. These will be discussed next.

INFRASTRUCTURE REQUIREMENTS

As with nations, each industry is constrained by its own infrastructure; and as with nations, the infrastructure requirements change as the industry develops and evolves.

By infrastructure is meant the set of organizations and institutions which provide the means for the products to be produced for, delivered to, and serviced in, the market. Without the correct configurations of suppliers, distributors and support service organizations, industry growth is severely constrained and without the correct configuration of *skills* in the industry or industry chain, the ability to compete is severely constrained.

Strategic initiative calls for an ability to assess and anticipate infrastructure requirements for two reasons. First, lack of awareness of the constraints caused by infrastructure shortcomings causes companies to undertake inappropriate moves (like attempting to sell technologically complex equipment in underdeveloped countries), and subsequent difficulties of coping with this inappropriate move push the company into a reactive mode so it loses the initiative. *Second,* early identification of emerging infrastructural requirements creates the opportunity for gaining initiative by securing (or even developing) the critical parts of the infrastructure themselves. Thus: IBM was able to secure substantial market position by a huge investment in programming education, long before such activity became part of school curricula; and Citibank has positioned electronic teller machines as part of its major investment in electronic distribution systems.

The pragmatic problem of the above arguments is that, despite all the analyses, there is likely to still be a great deal of uncertainty concerning the outcome. Moves to secure initiative generally demand some level of calculated risk taking, for there comes a stage when action must be taken, and taken knowing that major sacrifices are being made (or may have to be made, once the real world responses of the competitors become known).

CALCULATED SACRIFICES

The challenge lies in addressing sacrifices a priori: to identify what type of sacrifices must be contemplated, to recognize their implications and to ensure that they are appropriate to the circumstances. For instance when IBM invested five billion dollars in the development of their system 360 series, a number of sacrifices in terms of alternative new products (like super-large computers and/or micro-processors and mini-computers) had to be made. At the same time the company had to sacrifice the ability to expand more rapidly internationally. But these sacrifices were explicitly recognized and were highly appropriate for the stage of development of the industry and the status of the competition—what was called for in the face of a threat of an increasing domestic challenge was a product line which would maintain the *initiative* in the traditional customer base. This 360 series was that product line.

The recognition that the capturing or retention of strategic initiative may require substantial sacrifices gives rise to a problem of morale. This is but one of several general management challenges which are associated with pursuit of strategic initiative.

GENERAL MANAGEMENT CHALLENGES

General management must be keenly aware of several key challenges that they face as the leadership of the businesses which seek strategic initiative. The first is a clear definition of the "strategic role" the business will play. This is particularly important if the business happens to be part of a larger organization and the business has a definite strategic role to play in the larger portfolio.

In recent years it has become increasingly apparent that the prescriptions of the more simplistic portfolio approaches are not justified. However it is clear that some vehicle for allocating resources among different SBU's provides a useful start for planning a corporate strategy. What is more important is for management of individual businesses to be clear as to what their strategic role is in the company. The definition of an appropriate strategic role is a major general management challenge.

Regardless of what particular portfolio approach has been selected, it is possible to identify a number of major strategic roles which could be played by an SBU.[4] Such strategic roles also need to be defined for *independent* businesses. These are specified and discussed below:

1. *Build aggressively.* The business is in a strong position in a highly attractive fast growing industry and management wants to build share as rapidly as possible. This role is usually assigned to an SBU early in the life cycle.

2. *Build gradually.* The business is in a strong position in a very attractive, moderate growth industry and management wants to build share.

3. *Build selectively.* The business has *some* good positions in a highly attractive industry and wants to build share where it feels it has strength, or can develop strength, to do so.

4. *Maintain aggressively.* The business is in a strong position in a currently attractive industry and management is determined to aggressively maintain that position.

5. *Maintain selectively.* Either the business is in a strong position in an industry that is getting less attractive, or the business is in a moderate position in a highly attractive industry. Management wishes to exploit the situation by maximizing the profitability benefits of selectively serving where it best can do so, but with the minimum additional resource deployments.

6. *Prove viability.* The business is in a less than satisfactory position in a less attractive industry. If the business can provide resources for use elsewhere, management may decide to retain it, but without additional resource support. The onus is on the business to justify retention.

7. *Divest/liquidate.* Neither the business nor the industry have any redeeming features. Barring major exit barriers the business should be divested.

8. *Competitive harasser.* This is a business with a poor position in either an attractive or highly attractive industry and where competitors with a good position in the industry *also* compete with the company in other industries. The role of competitive harasser is to sporadically or continuously attack the competitor's position, not necessarily with the intention of long run success. The object is to distract the competition from other areas, deny them revenue for other businesses, or to use the business to cross-parry,[5] when the competition attacks an important sister business of the strategic aggressor. Such competitive harassers are popular in the chemical industry.

[4]W. E. Rothschild, *Strategic Alternatives* (New York: ANACOM, 1979); and R. E. Biggadyke, *Becton-Dickinson,* proprietary case prepared for Becton-Dickinson Corporation, 1980.

[5]Porter, *Competitive Strategy.*

Clearly each of these strategic roles poses specific leadership challenges to general management. As one progresses *down* the list of roles there is an increasing need to maintain *morale* in the business and the last three roles pose a serious challenge as far as maintenance of morale is concerned.

Conversely, as one goes *up* the list there is increased need for building "autonomous self discipline," namely a challenge to put in place systems which will not constrain the exercise of initiative by business managers, but at the same time will ensure that resources are not squandered as a result of excess enthusiasm.

Finally, if initiative is to be captured and retained, there is a key general management challenge required in anticipating what the *basis of industry leadership* will be for the next round of strategic plays. Management must be able to decide, out of an analysis of the emerging response barriers, pre-emption potentials, and infrastructure requirements, what will be the basis of industry leadership and what will be needed to deliver this, for a given strategic role.

More specific management challenges will be discussed for each strategic role below, but for every role the general management challenges are: definition of the appropriate role, maintenance of morale, development of self disciplining systems and determination of the basis of industry leadership.

PUNCH AND COUNTERPUNCH PLANNING

The final conceptual skill required for securing and retaining strategic initiative is an ability to clearly identify the prime targets of the strategic move and to generate countermoves to competitors' responses that will throw them off balance once they do respond.

Clear identification of prime targets.   A strategic move generally has a differential impact on different competitors. To the extent that the strategist clearly identifies this, and specifically identifies which competitors are to be attacked by the move, it is possible to better judge what the most likely counter-response will be, and where it will come from. Thus it is important to know whether the target of the attack is the leading competitor or one or more smaller ones, or whether the *apparent* target is the leader but the impact is really on the smaller ones (as happened with Avis' "We try harder" campaign). To the extent that the strategic move is visualized in a generalized way, with no detailed thinking going into the specific impacts on different competitors, the strategist will be unable to identify counterresponses and will end up reacting to unanticipated countermoves, thus losing the initiative. Thus it is important for the strategist to be clear who is on the "hit list" when the move is made.

Counterpunch planning.   Equally important for retention of the initiative is the planning of the series of moves which will be undertaken to recapture the initiative, if competitors attempt to gain the initiative: pre-planned actions aimed at throwing the competitors off-balance. This can consist of programs for attacking the competitors' major accounts, the development and maintenance of fighting brands,[6] programs for invading territories of competitors, or attempts at taking away key distributors. As mentioned above, the main purpose of such moves is not necessarily to succeed in capturing the positions attacked, but rather to seriously threaten and endanger the competitors' position if the competition does not respond to the attack. So the strategic aggressor is able to put the competitor back on the defensive and regain the initiative. In the discussion below, the set of programs held in reserve for counterpunching will be called the "counterpunch" list.

With the development of a "hit list" and a "counterpunch list" all the key concepts are in place for the development of a discussion of strategies for gaining initiative for specific strategic roles. Each will be discussed in turn. Some suggestions shall be made as to when each role may be strategically appropriate. *This is not to say that the role is totally inappropriate under other conditions, only that it may be more difficult to accomplish.*

STRATEGIC INITIATIVE FOR THE AGGRESSIVE BUILD ROLE

The aggressive build role is *strategically appropriate* to the rapid growth stage of a product or service.[7] Under conditions of rapid growth the competitive situation can be likened to the colonial landrush by the European powers in the fourteenth to seventeenth centuries. There is an immense pressure to occupy territory as quickly as possible, at the same time when the territory is poorly explored. If at any stage one stops to engage an enemy power, precious time and resources are lost, which could be deployed to occupying and consolidating in other territory. But if one does *not* engage the enemy where encountered but instead bypasses them, one may be creating a highly strategic sore spot into which the opponent can firmly entrench (as did the British in Gibraltar, for example).

Clearly the major conceptual challenge here is to be able to judge the conditions under which to engage the competition, and when to bypass or ignore competition, leaving the segment for "mopping up" later. This requires a good assessment of the major entry barriers for that segment. In order to make this assessment, strategic *intelligence* is needed. It would seem that the prime de-

[6]Ibid.

[7]Rothschild, *Strategic Alternatives.*

mand at this stage is for *product* intelligence, followed by market intelligence. Retention of the initiative involves being able to identify ahead of competition the largest and most rapidly developing uses and applications of the product and service. Thus the early identification of the "spare parts delivery" market was critical to the success of Federal Express. It is incumbent on the strategist to identify, as rapidly as becomes available the *real* needs that the product serves, and develop the production, delivery and service systems to support these needs.

The second challenge is that having identified the key product characteristics required, the strategist move as rapidly as possible to incorporate in the product those characteristics which are expected to be most in demand. The purpose is to take control of what Abernathy and Utterback call the "dominant design"—the configuration of product characteristics and specifications that become the reference base for the industry and around which the industry eventually competes.[8] To the extent that the company product is the dominant design product, the company has the initiative. This is the most important *pre-emptive move* that can be accomplished.

Clearly the third challenge is that once a particular segment has been occupied, that strategist start seeking to build *entry barriers* as rapidly as possible. Thus the strategist should focus on pre-emptive moves such as cornering the largest accounts, raising the capital requirements for entry, securing key distributors, occupying prime locations, building up switching costs and so on. The creative skill lies in identifying which entry barriers are relevant to the specific industry.

The fourth challenge lies in being able to develop the *infrastructure* to support rapid growth. A major problem faced by rapidly developing industries is a shortfall in the logistical capabilities of suppliers, distributors and service deliveries.[9] Critical skills are in short supply throughout the industry chain. In order to support the "land rush" conditions discussed above the strategist may find that resources need to be deployed to nurture, develop and support critical infrastructure organizations. This needs also to be done with minimum resources, since there is great pressure to use resources for growth. The identification and development of *key* infrastructure components also creates opportunities for pre-emption. By creating, and consolidating, positions with key suppliers, distributors or support services, the strategist can also create response barriers. Irrespective of whether infrastructure demands create entry barrier opportunities, the rapid building of a suitable infrastructure is critical to long run initiative, for it is where there are shortcomings in the infrastructure that competitors can wrest away the initiative.

A fifth challenge is the recognition that in the early stages, when the de-

---

[8]W.J. Abernathy and J. M. Utterback, "Patterns of Industrial Innovation," *Technology Review,* June–July 1978.

[9]Porter, *Competitive Strategy.*

sired product characteristics are still being articulated in the market place, it may be necessary to invest substantial sums in *"sacrificial products"*—namely products which are developed and tested in the market and become obsoleted precisely because the business then learns more about the real product need. In other words, often the only way to determine what the market really wants is to put the product on the market and learn, with the market, what the real product requirements are. This could take several generations of product but may be the only way to gather product intelligence, particularly if the product is complex. If management requires that each generation of product be profitable, instead of regarding the early models as sacrifices, the rate of intelligence gathering could be seriously impaired.

The final challenge is a *general management* challenge—how to conceptualize what the long run markets and competitors will really be at the early stages of the game. Often the whole shape of the industry changes once the dominant design emerges and enough volume of sales is being generated to warrant the serious attention of major competitors. (This could well be the case in the word-processing industry.) The entry barriers which the strategist erects should address the long run competition as well as the more immediate competition.

To summarize, it appears that the initiative in aggressive build situations where the market growth is rapid is attained by rapid occupation of the largest, fastest growing segments—filling key market spaces as quickly as possible, and throwing up entry barriers as quickly as possible. The basic dilemma is whether to engage the competition while doing this, or to bypass them and postpone engagement with them until the company moves over to a gradual build role, which is discussed next.

STRATEGIC INITIATIVE FOR THE GRADUAL BUILD ROLE

The gradual build role is *strategically appropriate* when the industry starts to emerge from the frenetic pace of the rapid growth stage, but is still growing well.[10] To justify pursuing this strategy, the firm should at this stage have a generally strong position and be determined to steadily improve this position.

By now the desired product characteristics are likely to be fairly clearly identified. The nature of competition will tend to move more to expanding applications, expanding territory (particularly overseas), enhancing services and reducing costs. So *market intelligence* and *competitive intelligence* start to take precedence over product intelligence at this stage. Product intelligence activities have to do with one of the major sources of *pre-emptive* potential—the dominant next generation product. The challenge lies in identifying, from market and competitive intelligence, what the "compelling" characteristics of each next gen-

---

[10]Rothschild, *Strategic Alternatives.*

eration product line will be, and to introduce the successive generations of such products in such a way as to continuously pre-empt the competition (recall the IBM System 360 example).

Critical to maintaining the initiative is a thorough understanding of the *response barriers*—both of the competition (in order to judge the best timing of each product introduction) and of the business itself (in order to minimize the response lag to initiative seeking moves by the competition). Competitive intelligence should also provide information for anticipation of the competition's major moves: For instance, once the product requirements have been articulated in the market place, there arises the opportunity to pre-empt foreign markets by rapid movement into the richest of these markets with marginally modified, current generation products. Competition may elect to do this, in the process creating substantial entry barriers by exploiting a "first occupancy" position. So the strategic aggressor needs to be alert to the first indications of such moves, so that they can be matched or defused.

In the gradual build role—particularly as the market growth eases off and the customers become aware of, and knowledgeable about, the full potentials of the product, the type of *infrastructure* demanded may start shifting to an increased need for application engineering, or equivalent support services. If dominance can be built in this area it creates some additional *potential for pre-emption*.

Another major pre-emption potential is the development or securing of distribution systems and service systems which provide *low cost* access to large numbers of smaller secondary markets, territories and accounts, thus profitably denying such accounts to the competition. Since these "second stage" segments can be very diverse, an important pre-emptive option is the ability to customize, via some modular approach, a relatively standardized product. (The use of *basic* hardware with *specific* software in data processing and word processing, or basic insurance policies with multiple options are examples.) In the event that this is not possible, the strategic aggressor could well face the dilemma of having to cope with competitors who decide to attack by building customized products for selected segments.

If this occurs, a well conceived *sacrifice* may become necessary. The dominant producer can ill afford to match every specialization or segmentation move adopted by each of its competitors, if it wishes to retain strategic initiative. Thus a conscious sacrificial decision may have to be made *not* to provide full coverage for all markets but to yield certain markets to these competitors. Ideally these should be markets in which the entry barries are low, and are expected to remain so; or markets in which entry barriers are expected to reduce substantially in the future (for instance via learning curve benefits to reduce entry costs). Then if the competitors get too powerful, they can be more easily attacked, either for "hit list" purposes (to completely defuse them) or for counterpunch purposes (to throw them off balance if they try to move out of their "reservations"—namely those markets which have been strategically yielded to the competition).

The fundamental *management challenges* at this stage are two-fold. First is the conceptual ability to recognize when the point of negative marginal returns on effort has been reached for each segment, territory or distribution system. Inability to make these hard nosed assessments causes management to squander valuable talent, ingenuity and resources trying to scrape the bottom of each market barrel. The second challenge is, once having recognized these turn points, to anticipate the appropriate basis of *industry leadership* for the coming slower growth phase: At different times, in different industries, the initiative goes to those few competitors who correctly anticipate, and prepare for, the leadership capabilities which drive the market—be it quality, cost, value, marketing skills, service coverage, distribution skills or combinations of these.[11] Since the time to develop dominance in these strategic capabilities is long, and the capacity to dominate in more than a few capabilities is limited, it is truly important for management to *anticipate* which capabilities will be needed in the next stage, rather than find itself without the time to develop the required dominance.

In summary, strategic initiative for a gradual build role calls for: control of next generation product introductions, anticipation of competitive moves, pre-emption of second-stage segments and key international segments, identification of emerging bases of industry leadership, sacrifice of full coverage and ability to clearly identify when points of negative marginal return on endeavor are reached in each position.

The major alternative to a gradual build role is a selective build role. This is discussed next.

STRATEGIC INITIATIVE
FOR THE SELECTIVE BUILD ROLE

The selective build role is *strategically appropriate* either when there are insufficient resources for a gradual build role, or the business has a *moderate* position in an industry where growth is still solid but had started to slow down. The role calls for focus on growth in selected segments, territories or market positions rather than across all fronts. Clearly the main thrust of this role comes from the careful assessment of the strengths and vulnerabilities of the key competitors as well as the business itself. Strategic initiative is retained by being able to focus on emerging rich market segments. Thus, the *strategic intelligence* requirements call for a focus on competition and markets. *Market* intelligence is necessary for the identification of general opportunities but this is not sufficient: *Competitive* intelligence provides the basis for identifying those *specific* opportunities that the business, but few of its competitors, can follow. Thus what is sought is the capacity to carve out niches in the market that the competitors either cannot follow (because of some entry barrier) or will not follow (because of some response

[11]Ibid.

barrier), and exploit the niche for the duration of the time that the competitors do not follow. Thus competitive intelligence is needed for identification of existing and emerging entry and response barriers so that defensible niches can be identified. (In the 60's and 70's Digital Equipment's focus on mini and micro processing markets was a conscious strategy to serve a segment that IBM *could* have attacked, but *would* not attack).

Critical to the success of such a role is the clear identification of which of the competitors are on the "hit list." The essence of the strategic role is to choose time, place and conditions of attack and to attack under conditions that suit the business rather than the competitors. MacMillan suggests several such conditions:[12] These include concentrating effort on limited segments at a time rather than on several; attacking areas where the competition have overextended themselves (usually manifest by customers complaining about quality, support service or delivery); avoiding prolonged wars of attrition by choosing segments where a strong position can be achieved quickly; developing and paying detailed attention to the logistics required to support the move; developing loyalty with specific key decision makers in carefully targeted accounts; and ensuring that the management and firing line employees (like sales people) have a high degree of autonomy as well as commitment to the strategic move.

Of additional importance is a realistic and pragmatic assessment of the business' *own* current and emerging *vulnerabilities,* because it is where the business is vulnerable that competitive counterpunches can do the most damage.

In many cases the defensibility of a niche depends on a clear understanding of what is valued by the customer. In the high, but decelerating, growth stages the market is in a better position to assess value (quality, reliability, support service versus life time cost of the product) than in the early very high growth stage. What constitutes value tends to differ from segment to segment and thus the prime areas for *pre-emptive potential* will tend to lie in the identification of emerging value—segments that fit the particular skills available in, or generatable by, the business. This was characteristic of the entry of the Japanese into the photo-copying business. There existed a feasible and unserved market for simple, inexpensive copiers whose copy quality was not excellent but whose value, in terms of life time cost to the customer, was high. The manufacturing skills were in place in Japanese industry to produce such a copier, and the Japanese were able to pre-empt this business segment with a low cost strategy, which was counterstrategic to the dominant U.S. competition.

A further valuable *pre-emptive potential* lies in positioning. If one does not intend to dominate, one can clearly pre-empt and exploit a lesser position, particularly if that position can be supported by a "cause"—a slogan which one can use to rally customers, distributors, suppliers and/or employees and which the competition finds hard to deny. A famous example is Avis Corporation's "We're

[12]I. C. MacMillan, "How Business Strategists Can Use Guerilla Warfare Tactics," *Journal of Business Strategy,* Vol. 1, No. 2 (Fall 1980).

number two, so we try harder." But was it clear, in the Avis case, that the major impact of the positioning strategy would be on the shares of the smaller competitors, rather than on Hertz? The need for accurate "hit-listing" is repeated: It is critical for the strategist to decide whether the real attack is aimed at gobbling up one or more smaller competitors, or taking a bite out of one of the larger competitors, for their responses mut be anticipated if the business is to retain initiative. There may even be a real need to develop signals to the market place[13] to obviate the panic responses from non-targeted competitors.

The major *sacrifice* called for in the selected growth role is the obvious one: the recognition that full coverage of large markets (with concomitant economies of scale) is foregone. In the long run this could lead to severe cost disadvantages, when the market slows down and becomes more competitive. Therefore a key general management challenge lies in somehow delivering high value to the customer while at the same time continuously reducing costs. It is too easy to get enticed into a high service, high margin segment, and end up being a high quality, but high cost and *unwanted* participant, as the industry moves into maturity.

In summary, the selective build role appears to call more than anything else for creativity in choosing the time and conditions of competing, and thus in pragmatic assessment of the key emerging vulnerabilities and strengths both of the competition and of the business itself, in an increasingly *value* driven market.

STRATEGIC INITIATIVE
FOR THE AGGRESSIVE
MAINTAIN ROLE

This role is *strategically appropriate* when the business has a strong position in a mature market. This type of business can deliver steady profits for long periods, and resource commitments must be committed to maintenance of the strong position achieved. However, if there is limited potential for strong growth, resource commitments should be *limited* only to such maintenance of position.

In these slower growth conditions, competitors are likely to be much more *directly* competitive, so the need for competitive intelligence is very high. Market intelligence becomes less important, as a need for product intelligence re-emerges, particularly in terms of maintaining and developing more efficient supply, delivery, production and service. Further there emerges a need to monitor for the less obvious threat of competition via substitutes. In fact a conceptual challenge for management is to avoid developing a "conventional wisdom" about the industry[14] which denies or decries the threat of substitutes. The point is that by this stage the market has fully articulated the needs to be satisfied by

---

[13]Porter, *Competitive Strategy.*

[14]Ibid.

the product or service, and now that the need *is* fully specified, it becomes easier to find other ways of satisfying the need. At this stage the desired characteristics of the product are well known by the customers, who should by now be buying on the basis of value to them; so cost, quality and reliability are likely to become prime considerations in the purchase decision. So strategic attention also needs to be given to how to build entry barriers for substitutes, and these barriers tend often to revolve around pricing, cost reductions and economies of scale.

Hence key *infrastructure requirements* will tend to revolve around *continuously* improving the efficiency in the entire infrastructure (production, distribution, supply and service systems)[15] and not allowing slack[16] to develop. In fact it is another serious challenge for management to avoid the erosion of the infrastructure, which happens if they tolerate a slow but inexorable reduction of efficiency, discipline and competitiveness. By so doing the business eventually creates massive response barriers to invasive moves by aggressive (often new) competitors.[17]

A second challenge for the management is the anticipation of what the basis of industry leadership will be for each successive round of strategic plays (discussed above in the gradual build role, in which anticipation of the *first round* basis of leadership was called for). Since there are not the resources to achieve dominance in cost, quality, distribution, marketing, sales, service and so on, the initiative tends to go to the businesses which have achieved dominance in the strategic capability critical for the *current* period. Then while competitors are matching this capability, the strategic aggressor can build dominance in the capabilities critical for the *next* round of competition.

It is in the light of a need to *be able* to move from one dominant capability to the next that some of the principles of aggressive defense become important. Maintenance of flexibility is essential to strategic initiative, and so the aggressive maintainer must start paying attention to anticipating exit barriers.[18] so that it does not find itself locked into situations that were appropriate for the past strategic round but not for future rounds. (For instance, the dilemma of finding oneself locked into a powerful group of independent distributors at a time when the consumers have moved their purchasing behavior to supermarket chains). Equally important is the need to reduce response barriers of the business itself, so that it can move rapidly to recover the initiative from aspiring usurpers. Since the business is likely to find itself the target of attacks by competitors aspiring to its strong position, it has the choice of waiting for, and responding *directly* to, each initiative by its competitors (in which case it will surely find itself on the

---

[15]Abernathy and Utterback, "Patterns of Industrial Innovation."

[16]R. M. Cyert and J. G. March: *A Behavioral Theory of the Firm* (Englewood Cliffs, N.J.: Prentice-Hall, 1964).

[17]A. Meshulach, personal communications to author.

[18]Harrigan, *Strategies for Declining Businesses.*

defensive and lose the initiative), or it can maintain an inventory of powerful, highly aggressive counterpunch moves targeted at strategically sensitive areas of the competitors, to be used to knock the competitors back in line if the competitors do attempt to gain the initiative. A well prepared counterpunch list is fundamentally important in maintaining the initiative.

At this stage of the game, a major source of *pre-emption potential* is in the area of pre-empting capacity: either of suppliers, production facilities, distribution systems or support service organizations. The anticipation, and first introduction, of major features/support services, for a basically standard product, is another area with pre-emptive potential. So ability to modularize becomes an even more important skill than in the gradual build role. Finally, in the international arena key skills may be required in the area of government relations, to pre-empt (or block pre-emption by competitors of) positions in the international chessboard.

For the aggressive maintainer, the *major sacrifice* involves the trade-off between maintenance of position and profitability. It is imperative that the strong position that has been built be maintained. This may require substantial investment in *replacement* of old facilities to remain competitive in costs. This investment may not appear as attractive as high growth alternatives, yet to maintain the strong stable position some of these more attractive, more exciting (but riskier) alternatives may have to be sacrificed. To do this, fully depreciated plant (capable of high *accounting* profits) may have to be scrapped in order to install modern, more efficient plant which will give low *accounting* profits. In recent decades, several industries slowly became uncompetitive because they could not make that sacrifice.

The major *general management* challenge appears to be in the capability of building and sustaining a degree of autonomy that allows lower management to aggressively respond to competitive moves, yet also ensures that such aggressive responses do not disrupt the business, which needs a high level of balance and co-ordination to capture the efficiencies needed to keep costs down. Critical to resolving this dilemma is the ability for senior management to explicate the simplest, shortest set of guidelines, which define the "ideology" of the business and by which lower level management can assess the suitability of their "parochial" responses to the business as a whole. Some chief executives have taken the trouble to do a lot of soul searching and then to develop a set of "10 commandments" for their businesses which are the absolute minimum set of rules by which to assess the suitability of alternative courses of action. The idea of this minimal set of broad rules was approached as follows: The chief executives were asked to generate a set of rules that would be issued under the assumption that they would be stranded on a desert island for two years. On their return, they should be able to review all the decisions made by subordinates and feel satisfied that even if it were *not* the exact decision they would have made, they would still feel that it was a feasible and acceptable decision. To test the rules as they evolved, the chief executives were then asked to review all the important decisions made in the past two years and decide whether the rules would have led to essentially similar decisions had they been absent. These rules were given to middle management, who were then given autonomy to select any alternative they desired as long as it kept within the confines of these rules. This has had salutory effects in increasing the morale, as well as the flexibility of middle management responses to competitive moves. If such autonomy is not developed, the aggressive maintainer runs a serious risk of becoming mired in its own bureaucracy.

In summary, the aggressive maintenance role calls for: sustained attention to cost reduction in the entire infrastructure; avoidance of the erosion of this infrastructure (and hence competitive position) a clear set of counterpunch plans to protect initiative; the development of a clear, simple ideology which will enhance flexibility of responses to competitive moves; and a strong sensitivity to the threat of substitutes.

STRATEGIC INITIATIVE FOR THE SELECTIVE MAINTAIN ROLE AND COMPETITIVE HARASSER ROLE

These roles are *strategically appropriate* when the business has a subordinate position or a poor position in a very high growth market. The first alternative is to carefully select and occupy only favorable positions which will assure profitability with *minimal* commitment of resources, while less favorable positions are conceded to the competition. The clear alternative to conceding the unfavorable positions is to use the weaker position to harass those competitors in the industry.

Selective Maintenance

In the event that a selective maintenance role is chosen for the business, there are major inertia barrier problems to be overcome. First is to select segments where some entry barriers or response barriers either exist, or can be built. This can usually be done by careful segmentation. Second, is the dismantling of exit barriers (or avoidance of emerging exit barriers) for those segments that will be conceded. A great deal of creativity may be needed to find inexpensive ways of bypassing or overcoming the objections of committed distributors, customers, labor unions, government agencies and other such interest groups that may object to the exit.[19] In addition, plant and equipment, or property may

---

[19]Ibid.

have to be creatively disposed of to avoid enormous write-offs, and/or costly programs for restoration of sites.

A concomitant set of general management challenges exists. First, the concession of segments to the competition needs to be done under conditions of strategic withdrawal, and not of complete abandonment, withdrawal encourages competition to attack, and this may precipitate a wide-scale competitive assault on the entire market.[20] So competitors need to be prevented from assuming that the entire market is being hastily abandoned and thus being encouraged to try to invade those segments that the business intends to hold. There is a particular need to maintain "counterpunch" lists for the segments being abandoned. Use of these counterpunches whenever competitors attempt to penetrate a selected-to-hold segment helps the strategist signal determination to maintain the selected positions.

On the positive side, there lies a challenge similar to that of the selective growth role: to identify those conditions of competing that suit the business, rather than the competition. Even more than in the selective growth role, creative attention must be focussed on the careful selection of niches, and the formulation of strategies for entering and developing entry barriers to these niches without having much resources to do so.

The successful development of such niches provides a key for resolving the most *crucial general management challenges* for the selective maintain role, which is in effect a *retreat*. Retreats are generally bad for morale. Building of morale is critical to the success of this role, and the way that morale is built and maintained is for management to focus subordinates' attention on the modest, *achievable,* successes in the niches selected. Warren has stressed the need, in building morale, to focus on achievable success rather than focus on potential failure *or* on grandiose targets.[21] If morale is to be built, this is precisely what can be done with the aggressive niche strategies called for in a selective maintenance role.

In the process of selection of such niches, the major *sacrifice* that has to be made is the fundamental trade off between value *of* the customer and value *to* the customer. Management cannot afford to continue to satisfy the demands of the customer unless the customer in turn has real value to the business, measured in terms of profits. Management may have to face up to the tough decision to refuse uneconomical demands of substantial high value customers, thus incurring the risk of losing these customers entirely. Unless such risks are taken, the business will find itself being drawn via creeping commitment into competing under terms that are dictated by customers, rather than the business itself. Ultimately initiative is lost to the customer.

The major *intelligence* requirements for this role call for identification of segments where specific strengths existing in, or inexpensively generatable by,

[20]Meshulach, personal communications to author.

[21]E. K. Warren, personal communication to author.

the business can be used. To the extent that these strengths also create entry barriers for other competitors, these segments may be pre-empted by concentrating on these segments, and entering rapidly in order to take full advantage of any response lags created by response barriers of the competitors.

Competitive Harassment

If the business is to be used primarily for harassment of competition, it is a foregone conclusion that the prime focus of intelligence activity is competitive. In particular the extent to which the business maps onto the competitor's product/market portfolio is important in determining the nature of the harassment role. For instance, if the business occupies the weaker position in a highly attractive growth industry, the harasser can be used as a distractor, diverting attention from the second industry. If the business occupies a weaker position in an attractive industry in which the competition enjoys strong profits from a stable moderately growing condition, the harasser can be used to drive down prices and thus deny revenues to the competition. If the competitor appears to be attempting to enter an industry in which the parent company enjoys a good position, the harasser can be used to cross parry by attacking the competitor's product and forcing it to turn its attention back to "home base." The feasibility of these alternatives clearly depends on a good assessment of the relative positions the various SBU's occupy in the competitor's portfolio, hence the need for good competitive intelligence.

As far as *infrastructure* is concerned, there is a real need for the competitive harasser to find ways of keeping costs to a minimum, particularly fixed costs. Thus the management should seek ways of subcontracting as much of the business as possible in order to maintain a very low, but permanent, presence in the market which does not detract resources from other businesses. But at the same time there is a need to be able to mobilize substantial increases in activity, if the need arises to carry out an harassment ploy very high flexibility is needed.

The business must be able to exit when the usefulness of the business as an harasser has expired. There is a danger that it may find itself locked into an unsatisfactory market once its usefulness is over.

Certain entry and response barriers preclude effective harassment—for instance high customer loyalty, strong distributor loyalty or high switching costs make it difficult for the market to respond to harassment moves. Thus a good assessment of *all* inertia barriers, of competitors and of the business itself, is important.

The great management challenge lies in morale. It is important for management to develop success criteria which focus on competitive impact rather than on the volume of business accomplished, since this will vary according to the need for harassment. It is likely that only a few people will derive motivational challenge from the strategic role, but these people will find the harassment role a particularly challenging one.

STRATEGIC INITIATIVE
IN THE PROVE VIABILITY
AND DIVEST ROLE

These roles are *strategically appropriate* when the business occupies an unsatisfactory position in an unsatisfactory industry. Unless the business can clearly demonstrate some future potential there is little value in devoting further time, management talent or scarce resources to maintaining its existence.

Prove Viability Role

Here, more than any other role, management must find ways of deriving profitability by strategic moves chosen so that, ideally, the probability of success is maximum, and the amount of resources used to pursue the move is a minimum. Here, more than any other role, it is essential for the business to choose the time, place and conditions for competing, so that it competes under conditions that suit the business, not its competitors. Here, more than any other role, it is necessary for the business to develop counterpunch plans that allow it to demonstrate intense commitment to those markets that it chooses to fight for, and that it will retaliate violently if its key markets are attacked.

This creates a challenge to management to very carefully consider several factors. First, management must get to grips with what the minimum justifiable scope of the business shall be—in other words what level of business there must be to justify the effort of sustaining the business in the long run. Next it must decide whether there is sufficient market *potential* to achieve this scope, without requiring resources. In so doing it has to take into account whether there are compelling economics for keeping the business, not only from the point of view of the business itself, but also its customers, its suppliers and its distributors, perhaps even unions and government agencies. Unless there is justifiable potential from the point of view of *all* these stakeholders, it is unlikely that the business will receive the environmental support it needs to prove long run viability.

The greatest challenge in developing a viable strategy will be to find ways of getting *other* stakeholders to commit resources to support of the business. Since it will receive few company resources, the business must identify which stakeholders have a vested interest in the survival of the organization, and pinpoint what the bases for such vested interests are. Having identified these, the strategist is in a position to decide how to enlist aid, support and resources from those parties that *do* have a vested interest. This conserves the limited resources of the strategist for those truly important moves which take advantage of every available inertia barrier to secure and establish market niches. With the prove viability role it is imperative that focus, concentration and precision be used in selecting conditions of competition. The role generally requires substantial retrenchment from the existing positions, particularly in capacity. Real creativity, discipline and sacrifice is called for to squeeze every form of slack from the business,[22] and to convert these slack resources to those resources which are deployable to the task of demonstrating viability.

In the event that viability cannot be proved, the final sacrifice of closing down or divesting the business needs to be considered.

Divest/Liquidate Role

Here the essence of the strategic initiative lies in the dismantling of exit barriers, for unless the exit barriers can be scaled, the company can be locked for years into a totally unrewarding situation.[23] To the extent that allies can be found to reduce the burden of removing these exit barriers, such help must be enlisted. (Several companies have been able to persuade their employees or the employee union to take over the ailing business, thus bypassing enormous exit barriers created by union and pension agreements).

A major consideration is the decision as to how to exit. Once again the position of the business in the competitor's portfolios of business is relevant. At the one extreme, by combining the business with a competitor's business, it may be possible for a high salvage value to be obtained[24] in which case the greatest co-operation is called for with competitors. At the other extreme, if there are competitors who are competing fiercely with the company in other industries, it may be possible to precipitate tactics that will cost the company little, but be highly disruptive to competitors, thus detracting from their capacity to compete in those other industries. In this case minimal co-operation with competitors is indicated.

An analysis of stakeholders' vested interest can also give some indication of which, if any, of the stakeholders may be interested in the purchase or support of the business—this may create some opportunity to leverage a better price for the business.

Finally, the key pre-emptive challenge may lie in being able to anticipate whether othe competitors will also exit. As Harrigan points out,[25] if enough competitors depart the industry may become "comfortable" again. If not enough exit, then the best price and conditions may go to the company that pre-empts the first exit. Thus competitive intelligence focussed on the competitors' exit intentions becomes vital to the timing and pricing of the exit.

In both the divest/liquidate and the prove viability role the challenge of morale maintenance must be addressed. Once again, what becomes important is how success is defined to the subordinates, how skillful management is in setting challenging but achievable targets for them and how adept they are at reinforc-

[22]Cyert and March, *Behavioral Theory of the Firm.*

[23]Harrigan, *Strategies for Declining Businesses.*

[24]Ibid.

[25]Ibid.

ing the success achieved. The skill of great military leaders at accomplishing this in adverse circumstances bears testimony to the need to focus on *success,* however modest, when building morale.

This concludes the discussion of strategic initiative for different strategic roles.

CONCLUSIONS

What was attempted was to show how general principles evolved in the first part of the paper could be applied more specifically to each strategic role in the second part of the paper. What has not been discussed is an alternative approach, which looks at the application of strategic initiative concepts to different industry structures (fragmented versus concentrated, regional versus national versus global), primarily because the focus has been on the strategy of the strategic business unit or its independent equivalent. What has been attempted is to use the idea of strategic initiative to bring together concepts of corporate strategy (which define a strategic role for the portfolio of SBU's) with the concepts of business strategy formulation (which addresses the problem of how to compete in a specific SBU).

The approach of looking at strategic initiative takes the policy field a step closer to the study of strategy as a dynamic problem, in which competitive countermoves are a fact of life in strategy formulation, rather than a static, unilateral process.

REFERENCES

1. HARRIGAN, K. R., *Strategies for Declining Businesses.* New York: Lexington Books, 1980.
2. MACMILLAN, I. C., and M. L. MCCAFFERTY, "Strategy for Low Entry Barrier Markets such as Service Industries," *Journal of Business Strategy,* 1982.
3. PORTER, M. E., *Competitive Strategy.* New York: Free Press, 1980.

12

Designing the Innovating Organization

JAY R. GALBRAITH
Management Consultants, Ltd.

Innovation is "in." These days, as never before, new ideas that can be implemented are being promoted in order to restore our worldwide technology leadership, our growth in productivity, and our business competitiveness. Other ideas are being sought to conserve energy and to adapt to new energy sources. The popular press uses words like *revitalization* to capture the essence of the issue. The primary culprit of our undoing, up until now, has been the short-run earnings focus of management. However, even some patient managers are finding that they cannot buy innovation. They cannot exhort their operating organizations to be more innovative and creative. Patience, money, and a supportive leadership are not enough. It takes more than that to get innovation.

The argument of this paper is that innovation requires an organization that is specifically designed to innovate. That is, organization structure, processes, rewards, and people must be combined so as to create an innovating organization. An innovating organization is one designed to do something for the first time. The point to be emphasized here is that the innovating organization is completely different from and often contrary to our existing organizations. Our existing organizations are operating organizations. They are designed to efficiently process the millionth loan, produce the millionth automobile, or serve the millionth client. An organization designed to do something well for the millionth time is not good at doing something for the first time. Therefore organizations desiring to innovate or revitalize themselves need two organizations—an operating organization and an innovating organization. In addition, if the ideas produced by the innovating organization are to be implemented by the operating organization, a transition process to transfer ideas from the innovating to the operating organization is also needed. This paper is intended to describe the innovating organization. That is, if one wanted to create an organization that would produce innovations, what would it look like?

In the next section the innovating process that is to be managed is described by means of an example. In this example are a number of lessons from which the innovating organization can be discerned. The following sections then describe the role structure, the key processes, the reward system, and the people practices of the innovating organization prior to summarizing the argument.

THE INNOVATING PROCESS

This section describes the typical process by which innovations occur in organizations. But first some definitions of innovation are needed. The usual distinction between invention and innovation is made. *Invention* is the creation of a new idea. *Innovation* is the application of a new idea to create a new process or product. Invention occurs more frequently than innovation. In addition, the kind of innovation that is of interest is that which arises when a new idea is not consistent with the current concept of the business. Many innovations are generated routinely in some companies. But these are inventions that are consistent with the current concept of the business. Here we are concerned with applying inventions that are good ideas but not quite consistent with the current business concept. Industry has a poor track record with this type of innovation. Most major technological changes come from outside an industry. The mechanical typewriter manufacturers did not innovate by introducing the electric typewriter, the electric typewriter people did not invent the electronic typewriter, vacuum tube companies did not introduce the transistor, and so on. Our objective is to describe an organization that will increase the odds that these nonroutine innovations can be made. The following example of a nonroutine innovation contains a number of lessons from which we can design an innovating organization.

This example organization is a new venture that was started in the early seventies. A group of engineers came up with a new electronics product while working for one of our more innovative electronics firms. However, they were in a division that did not have the charter for their product. A political battle ensued, and the result was that the engineers left to form their own company. They successfully found venture capital and introduced their new product. Initial acceptance was good, and within several years they were growing rapidly and had become the industry leader.

In the early 1970s, however, Intel invented the microprocessor. By the mid to late seventies this innovation began to spread through the electronics industries. Manufacturers of previously "dumb" products now had the capability to spread intelligence into their product lines. A competitor who understood computers and software introduced just such a product into our new venture firm's market. It met with initial high acceptance. The president of our firm responded by hiring someone who knew something about microcomputers and some software people and instructed the engineering department to respond.

The president spent most of his time raising capital to finance the venture's growth. It occurred to him one day that the engineers had not made much progress. He instructed them to get a product out. They did, but it was a half-hearted effort. The new product contained a microprocessor but was less than the second-generation product that was needed.

The president then pursued international opportunities. He started in Europe and Singapore. But he noticed that the competitor was growing faster than his company. Then the competitor started to steal market share. The competitor became the industry leader. The president decided that he had better take charge of the product development effort.

Upon his return he found that the hardware types and software types were locked in a political battle in engineering. Each felt that its "magic" was the more powerful. Unfortunately, the lead engineer and cofounder was a hardware type, and the hardware establishment prevailed. However, they then clashed head-on with the marketing department, which agreed with the software types. The result was studies and presentations, but no new product. So here we have a young, small (twelve hundred people) entrepreneurial firm that cannot innovate. The president wanted innovation and provided resources to produce it. The lesson is that more is needed.

The president became more involved. Then one day he received a call from his sales manager in the New England territory. The sales manager said, "I think you should come up here. A field service engineer has made some modifications to our product and programmed it in a way that my customers are asking us to do. We may have something here."

The president was impressed with what he saw. The engineer wanted to use the company's product to track his own inventory. He wrote to the company headquarters to get some programming instructions. The response from headquarters was that it was against company policy to send instructional materials to field engineers. Undaunted, the engineer bought a home computer and taught himself to program. He then modified the product in the field and programmed it to solve his problem. When the sales manager happened to see what was done, he recognized its significance and immediately called the president.

The field engineer accompanied the president back to headquarters. He presented his work to the engineers who had been working on the second-generation product for so long. Their response was that the application was nice but idiosyncratic. They said that their planned product would be superior. The hardware types prevailed again. The field engineer was thanked and returned to his position.

A couple weeks later the same sales manager called the president again. He said that the company would lose this talented guy if something wasn't done. Besides he thought that the field engineer was right, not engineering. The president recalled that he had been impressed and that the field engineer had produced something more than his entire engineering department had. So he brought him back to headquarters and tried to find something for the field engineer to do while he decided what should be done. Within a few days the president received a request from the European sales manager to assign the engineer to him.

The European sales manager was visiting headquarters for a period of training. During that time he heard of the field engineer, sought him out, and listened to his story. It turned out that the sales manager had a French bank that wanted the kind of application that the field engineer had created for himself. A successful application would be worth an order for several hundred machines. The president gave the go-ahead and sent the field engineer to work in Europe. The engineering department said it wouldn't work. Three months later the field engineer successfully developed the application and the bank signed for the order of several hundred machines.

When the field engineer returned, the president assigned him to a trusted marketing manager who was told to protect him and get a product out. The engineers were told to support the manager and reluctantly did so. Soon they created some applications software and a printed circuit board which could easily be installed in all existing machines in the field. The addition of this board and the software temporarily saved the company and made its current product slightly superior to that of the competitor.

The president was elated. He congratulated the young field engineer and gave him a good position on the staff working on special assignments to develop software. Then he began encountering problems. The president tried to get personnel to give the engineer a special cash award. Personnel was reluctant. "After all," they said, "other people worked on the effort, too. It will set a precedent." And so it went. Then the finance department wanted to withhold $500 from the engineer's pay. He had received an advance of $1,000 for his European trip but had only submitted vouchers for $500 upon his return.

The young engineer didn't help himself very much either. He was hard to get along with and refused to accept supervision from anyone except the European sales manager. The president therefore arranged to have him permanently transferred to Europe. The personnel department prepared the necessary paperwork three times, and three times the engineer waited until the last minute and then changed his mind about going. At the moment, the president is still wondering what to do with him. End of story.

In this not uncommon story, we have a number of lessons from which we can construct an innovating organization. The next section takes these lessons and elaborates on them in order to see the structure, processes, reward systems, and people practices that make up the innovating organization.

THE INNOVATING ORGANIZATION

The vignette above contains a number of lessons from which we can construct the innovating organization. In order to construct it, it is important to note that the innovating organization is no different from an operating organization in the makeup of its component parts. That is, it consists of a task, a structure, processes, reward systems, and people, as shown in Figure 1. The accompanying table contrasts the components of the operating organization with those of the innovating organization. Under each component are the design parameters that make up that particular component.

*Figure 1   **Organization Design Components***

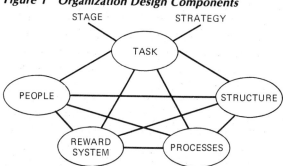

	Operating Organization	Innovating Organization
Structure	Division of Labor	Roles—Orchestrator
		Sponsor
		Idea Generator (Champion)
	Departmentalization	Differentiation
	Span of Control	Reservations
	Distribution of Power	
Processes	Information and Communication	Planning/Funding
	Planning and Budgeting	Idea Getting
	Performance Measurement	Idea Blending
	Departmental Linkages	Transitioning
		Program Management
Reward System	Compensation	Opportunity/Autonomy
	Promotion	Promotion/Recognition
	Leader Style	Special Compensation
	Job Design	
People	Selection/Recruiting	Selection/Self-Section
	Promotion/Transfer	Training/Development
	Training/Development	

The message to be communicated by Figure 1 is that each component must fit with each other component and with the task. A basic premise of this paper is that the task of the innovating organization is fundamentally different from that of the operating organization. The innovating task is more uncertain and risky, takes place over longer time horizons, assumes that failure is good in the early stages, and so on. Therefore the organization performing that task should be different as well. Therefore a firm wishing to innovate needs both an operating organization and an innovating organization. But what is the innovating organization? The next sections describe the structure, processes, rewards, and people practices of the innovating organization.

Structure

The innovating organization has a structure of its own. It consists of several roles. These roles as well as the degree of differentiation and reservations make up the structural dimensions of the innovating organization. Each dimension relates to some lessons that can be learned from the example.

1. Roles. Like any organized phenomena, innovation occurs from a combination of roles, whether the innovation occurs inside or outside an organization. Innovation is not an individual phenomenon. There are three main roles in the commercialization of any new idea. These three roles are well illustrated in the example.

Every innovation starts with an *idea generator,* or idea champion. In the above example the field engineer was the person who generated the new idea. This is the inventor, the entrepreneur or risk taker on whom much of our attention has been focused. The main conclusion of this attention is that an idea champion is needed at each stage of an idea's development into an innovation. That is, at each stage a dedicated, full-time individual whose success or failure depends on developing the idea is necessary for innovation. Very little more will be added here. It is the other roles that will receive our attention. The need for other roles begins because the idea generator is usually a low-level person who experiences a problem and develops a new response to it. The lesson here is that many ideas originate down where "the rubber meets the road." The low status and authority level of the idea generator creates a need for the next role.

Every idea needs at least one *sponsor* to promote it. In order to carry an idea into implementation, someone has to discover it and fund the increasingly disruptive and expensive development and testing efforts that shape it. Thus idea generators need to find sponsors for their ideas in order to perfect them. In our example the Hartford sales manager, the European sales manager, and finally the marketing manager sponsored the idea of the field engineer. Thus one of the functions of the sponsor is to lend his or her authority and resources to an idea to carry it further toward commercialization.

The other function of the sponsor is to recognize the business significance of an idea. In any organization there are hundreds of ideas being promoted at any one time. The sponsor must select among these ideas to find those that might become new business ideas. Thus it is best that sponsors be generalists. That is not always the case, as is illustrated by the above example.

Sponsors are usually middle managers who are distributed throughout the organization. They work for both the operating and the innovating organization. Some of the sponsors manage divisions or departments. It is also their task to balance the operating and innovating needs of their business or function. Other sponsors work full time for the innovating organization when the firm can afford the creation of venture groups, new-product development departments, and the like. In the example, the sales managers spontaneously played the sponsor role. The third sponsor, the marketing manager, was formally designated. The point here is that by formally designating the role or recognizing it, funding it with monies earmarked for innovation, creating innovating incentives, and developing and selecting sponsorship skills, the organization can improve its odds at innovating. Not much attention has been given to sponsors. They need equal attention for innovation, which will not occur until all three roles are present.

The third role illustrated in the example is that of the *orchestrator*. The president played this role. An orchestrator is needed because new ideas are never neutral. Innovative ideas are destructive. Innovation destroys investments in capital equipment and people's careers. The management of ideas is a political process. The problem is that the political struggle is biased toward members of the establishment who have authority and control of resources. The orchestrator is to be a power balancer to give the new idea a chance to be tested in the face of a negative establishment. The orchestrator is to protect idea people, promote the opportunity to try out new ideas, and back them when proved effective. This person is to legitimize the whole process. The president did exactly that with the field engineer. But before he became involved, the hardware establishment prevailed. Without an orchestrator, there can be no innovation.

Orchestrators play their role by using the processes and rewards that will be described in the following sections. That is, one orchestrates by funding innovating activities and creating incentives for middle managers to sponsor innovating ideas. Orchestrators are the top managers of the organization. It is their task to design the innovating organization.

The typical operating role structure of a divisionalized firm is shown in Figure 2. The hierarchy is one of operating functions reporting to division general managers, who are, in turn, grouped under group executives. The group executives report to the chief executive (CEO). Some of these people play roles in both the operating and the innovating organization.

The role structure of the innovating organization is shown in Figure 3. The chief executive and a group executive function as orchestrators. Division managers are the sponsors who work in both the operating and the innovating organization. In addition, several reservations are created whereby managers of R&D, Corporate Development, Product Development, Market Development, and

Figure 2   A Typical Operating Role Structure

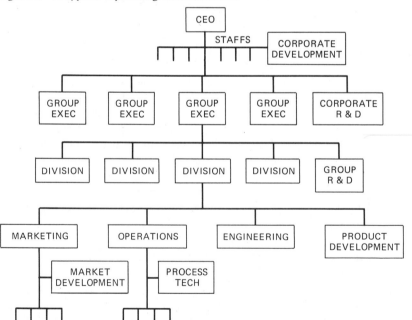

Figure 3   An Innovating Role Structure

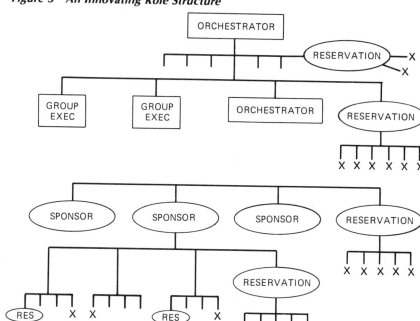

ORCHESTRATOR   SPONSOR/RESERVATION
X   IDEA GENERATOR/CHAMPION

New-Process Technology function as full-time sponsors. These reservations allow the separation of innovating activity from the operating. This separation is an organizing choice called *differentiation*.

2. Differentiation.   Another lesson from the story is that the idea was perfected at a remote site and was relatively advanced before it was ever discovered by management. Thus if we want to stimulate new ideas, the odds are better if the early effort is best differentiated from the operating organization in order to perfect and test new "crazy" ideas. An effort is differentiated when it is separated physically, financially, and/or organizationally from the day-to-day activities likely to disrupt it. If the field engineer had worked within the engineering department or at company headquarters, his idea would probably have been snuffed out prematurely.

Another kind of differentiation is to free initial idea tests from staff controls that are designed for the operating organization. At one company, managers used to make decisions on whether to buy a new oscilloscope in about fifteen to thirty minutes with a shout across the room. After being acquired, that same decision took twelve to eighteen months because the purchase required a capital appropriation request. Controls based on operating logic reduce the innovating organization's ability to test and modify new ideas rapidly, cheaply, and frequently. Thus the more differentiated the initial effort, the greater the likelihood of innovation.

The problem with differentiation, however, is that it decreases the likelihood of transferring a new proved idea back into the operating organization. Herein lies the differentiation/transfer dilemma. The more differentiated the effort, the greater the likelihood of producing a new business idea, but the less the likelihood of transferring the new idea into the operating organization for implementation. The dilemma occurs only when the organization needs both invention and diffusion for innovation. That is, some organizations may not need transfer to an operating organization. When Exxon started its information systems business, there was no intention to have the products implemented by the petroleum company. The executives had to establish their own operating organizations. Therefore they maximized differentiation in the early phases. Alternatively, when Intel started on the 64K RAM, the effort was consistent with its current business, and transfer into fabrication and sales was critical. Therefore the effort was only minimally separated from the implementing division producing the 16K RAM. The difficulty arises when a new product or process is different from the current ones but must be implemented through the current manufacturing and sales organizations. These organizations need both invention and diffusion. The greater the need for invention and the greater the difference between the new idea and the existing concept of the business, the greater the degree of differentiation that is needed to perfect the idea. The only way to accomplish both is to proceed stagewise. That is, differentiate in the early phases and then start transitioning so that little differentiation exists at implementation. The transition process is described in the "Key Processes" section.

In summary, invention occurs best when initial efforts are separated from the operating organization and its controls. Separation is needed because innovating and operating are fundamentally different and opposing logics. Separation allows both to be performed simultaneously. Separation also prevents the establishment from prematurely snuffing out a new idea. The less the dominant culture of the organization supports innovation, the greater the need for separation. Often this separation occurs naturally, as in the example, or it may occur clandestinely, such as in "bootlegging." If a firm wants to foster innovation, then it can create reservations where innovating activity can occur as a matter of course. Let us now turn to this last structural parameter.

3. Reservations.   Reservations are organizational units such as R&D that are totally devoted to creating new ideas for future business. The intention is to reproduce the garagelike atmosphere where people can rapidly and frequently test their ideas. Reservations are to be havens for "safe learning." When innovating, we want to maximize early failure to promote learning. On reservations separate from operations, this cheap, rapid screening can take place.

Reservations contain people who work solely for the innovating organization. The reservation manager works full time as a sponsor. Reservations permit differentiation to occur. They are also located in the divisions and at corporate headquarters to permit various degrees of differentiation.

Reservations can be *internal* or *external.* Internal reservations are like research groups, product and process development labs, market development, new ventures, corporate development, and some staff groups. They are organizational homes where idea generators can contribute without becoming managers. This was one of the intentions of staff groups. However, staffs often assume control responsibilities or are narrow specialists who contribute to the current business idea. Since these groups can be expensive, outside reservations like universities, consulting firms, and advertising agencies are often used to tap nonmanagerial idea generators.

Reservations can be *permanent* or *temporary.* The reservations described above, such as R&D units, are reasonably permanent entities. In temporary reservations, members of the operating organization can be relieved of operating duties to develop a new program, a new process, or a new product. When developed, they take the idea into the operating organization and resume their operating responsibilities. But for a period of time they are differentiated from operations to varying degrees in order to innovate, fail, learn, and ultimately perfect a new idea.

Collectively the roles of orchestrators, sponsors, and idea generators working with and on reservations constitute the structure of the innovating organization. Some sponsors and orchestrators play roles in both organizations, but reservation managers and idea generators work only for the innovating organization. Virtually everyone in the organization can be an idea generator, and all middle managers are potential sponsors. However, not everyone chooses to play these roles. People vary considerably in their innovating skills. By recognizing these roles, developing people for them, giving them opportunity to use their skills through key processes, and rewarding innovating accomplishments, the organization can do considerably better than just allowing the spontaneous process to work as described in the example. Across this structure of the innovating organization are several key processes. These are described in the next section.

Key Processes

In our example the idea generator and the first two sponsors found each other through happenstance. The odds of such match-ups can be significantly improved through the explicit design of processes to help sponsors and idea generators find each other. Processes of funding, idea getting, and idea blending are key ones for improving match-ups. In addition, transitioning and program management are processes for taking ideas from reservations into operations. Each of these processes will be described below.

1. Funding. One of the key processes involved in increasing our ability to innovate is an explicit funding process for the innovating organization. A leader in this field is Texas Instruments. It budgets and allocates funds for operating and funds for innovating. In essence, the orchestrators make the short-run/long-run trade-off at this point. They then orchestrate by choosing where to place the innovating funds—to division sponsors or corporate reservations. The funding process is a key tool for orchestration.

A lesson from the example is that it often takes multiple sponsors to launch a new idea. The field engineer's idea would never have been brought to management's attention without the New England sales manager. It would never have been tested in the market without the European sales manager. Multiple sponsors keep fragile ideas alive. If engineering were the only sponsor for technical ideas, there would have been no innovation.

Some organizations purposely create a multiple sponsoring system and make it legitimate for an idea generator to go to any sponsor that has funding for new ideas. Multiple sponsors duplicate the market system of multiple bankers for entrepreneurs. At 3M an idea generator can go to his or her division sponsor for funding. If refused, the idea generator can go to any other division sponsor or even to corporate R&D. If the idea is outside the current businesses, the idea generator can go to the New Ventures group for support. If the idea is rejected by all sponsors, it must not be a very good idea. However, the idea is kept alive and given several opportunities to be tested. Multiple sponsors keep fragile, young ideas alive.

2. Idea getting. The idea-getting process occurs by happenstance in all organizations, as it did in the example. The premise of this section is that the odds of match-ups can be improved by organization design. First, the natural process can be improved by network-building actions such as multidivision or multireservation careers, companywide seminars, and conferences. All these practices plus a common physical location facilitate matching at 3M.

The process is formalized at TI. It has an elaborate planning process called the OST System (objectives, strategies, and tactics), which is an annual harvest of new ideas. Innovating funds are distributed to managers of objectives (sponsors), who fund projects from idea generators which become tactical action programs. Ideas not funded go into a creative backlog to be tapped throughout the year. Formal, as at TI, or informal, as at 3M, there is a known system for matching ideas with sponsors.

Ideas are also obtained by aggressive sponsors. Sponsors sit at the crossroads of many ideas and often arrive at a better idea as a result. They then pursue an idea generator to champion it. Good sponsors know where the proved idea people are located and attract them to come and perfect an idea on their reservation. Sponsors can go inside or outside to pursue these idea people.

And finally, formal events can be scheduled for matching purposes. At 3M there is the annual fair at which idea generators can set up booths to be viewed by shopping sponsors. Exxon Enterprises held a "shake-the-tree event" at which idea people could throw out ideas to be pursued by attending sponsors. The kinds of events are endless. The point is that by devoting time to ideas and making innovation legitimate, the odds of having sponsors find new ideas are increased.

3. Idea blending.   An important lesson to be derived from our scenario is that it is no accident that a field engineer produced the new-product idea. Why? Because the field engineer spends all day working on customer problems and also has knowledge of the technology. Within the mind of a single person, there is a blending of knowledge of a need and a means for satisfying that need. In addition, our field engineer had a personal need for which the technology could be designed. The premise being espoused here is that innovation is more likely to occur when knowledge of technologies and user requirements are combined in the minds of as few people as possible, with one being optimal.

On other occasions a debate has taken place as to whether innovations are need stimulated or means stimulated. Do you start with the disease and look for a cure or start with a cure and find a disease for it? Research shows that two-thirds of the innovations are need stimulated. But this argument misses the point. As shown in Figure 4 (a), the debate is over whether use or means drives the downstream efforts. This thinking is linear and sequential. Instead, the model suggested here is shown in Figure 4 (b). That is, for innovation to occur, knowledge of all key components is simultaneously coupled. And the best way to maximize communication among the components is to have the communica-

Figure 4   Linear Sequential vs. Simultaneous Coupling of Knowledge

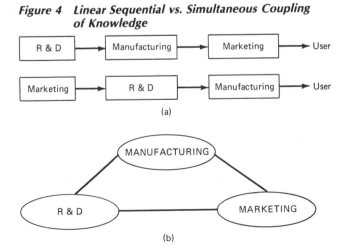

tion occur intrapersonally. If not intrapersonally, then as few people as possible will effectively communicate interpersonally. The point is that initial innovative ideas occur when knowledge of the essential specialties is coupled in as few heads as possible. This coupling can occur intrapersonally by growing or selecting people. These practices will be discussed in the "people" section. The other way is to couple knowledge through interpersonal processes.

A variety of processes are employed to match knowledge of need and knowledge of means. IBM has placed marketing people directly in the R&D labs where they interpret the market requirements documents. People are rotated through this unit and a network is created. Wang holds an annual users' conference at which customers and product designers interact over the use of Wang products. Lanier insists that all top managers, including R&D management, spend one day per month selling in the field. It is stated that British scientists made remarkable progress on developing radar after actually flying missions with the RAF. In all these cases there is an explicit matching of the use and the user with knowledge of a technology to meet the use. Again these processes are explicitly designed to get a user orientation among the idea generators and sponsors. They increase the likelihood that inventions will be innovations. The more complete a new idea or invention is at its inception, the greater the likelihood of transfer into the operating organization, thereby becoming an innovation.

4. Transitioning.   The most crucial process is the transitioning of an idea from a corporate reservation to an operating organization for implementation. This process occurs stagewise, as in the example. First the idea was formulated in the field before management ever knew about it. Then it was tested with a customer, the French bank. And finally development and full-scale implementation was the third stage. In other cases several stages of testing and scale-up may occur. Transitioning should be planned stagewise. At each stage the orchestrator has several choices that balance the need for further invention with the need for diffusion. The choices and stages of idea development are shown in Figure 5, with the choices as rows and the stages as columns.

The following choices face the orchestrator at each stage: Who will be the sponsor? Who will be the champion? Where will be the source of the staff for the effort? At what physical location will work be performed? Who will fund the effort? How much autonomy is involved or how differentiated should the effort

Figure 5   Stagewise Choice of Transitioning Ideas

Choice/Stage	I	II .... Nth	Implementation
SPONSOR	CORPORATE	CORPORATE	DIVISION
CHAMPION	CORPORATE	CORPORATE	DIVISION
STAFFING	CORPORATE	CORP.–DIV.	DIVISION
LOCATION	CORPORATE	CORPORATE	DIVISION
FUNDING	CORPORATE	CORPORATE	DIVISION
AUTONOMY	COMPLETE	COMPLETE	MINIMAL

be? An idea must be transitioned from a reservation to an operating division in this stagewise manner. For example, at the initial stage of new-idea formulation, the sponsor could be the corporate ventures group with the champion working on the corporate reservation. The effort would be staffed with other corporate reservation types and funded by corporate. The activity would be fully separate and autonomous. If the results were positive, the next stage would be entered. If the idea needed further development, some division people would be brought in to round out the needed specialties. If the data were still positive after the second stage, then the effort might be transferred physically to the division but the champion, sponsor, and funding would still be corporate. In this manner, by orchestrating through choice of sponsor, champion, staff, location, funding, and autonomy, the orchestrator balances the need for innovation and protection with the need for testing against reality and diffusion.

The above is an all too brief outline of the transition process. Entire books have been written on the subject of technology transfer. The goal here was to highlight the stagewise nature of the process and the decisions to be made by the orchestrator at each stage. The process is crucial because it is the link between the two organizations. That is, in order to innovate consistently, the firm needs an operating organization, an innovating organization, and a process for transitioning ideas from one to the other.

5. Program management process.   The last process necessary is the program management process of implementing new products and processes within a division. That is, the idea generator usually hands off to a product/project/program manager at the time of implementation. The product or process is implemented across the functional organization within the division. The systems and organizational processes for project management have been discussed elsewhere and will not be discussed here. The point is that a program management process and skill are needed.

In summary, across the innovating structure run several key processes. These are the funding, idea getting, idea blending, transitioning, and program management processes. Many of these occur naturally in all organizations. The implicit hypothesis of this section is that odds for successful innovation can be increased by the explicit design of these processes and the devotion of corporate resources to them. The same argument applies to the next section. The idea generator in the example voluntarily chose to innovate. So do hundreds of people in all organizations. But if a reward system exists for these people, more will choose to innovate and more will choose to stay in the organization to do their innovating. The reward system is the next component to be described.

Reward System

The innovating organization, like the operating organization, needs an incentive system to motivate the needed innovating behavior. Since the task of innovating is different from the task of operating, the innovating organization needs a different reward system. The innovating task is riskier, is more difficult, and takes place over longer time horizons. These factors usually require some adjustment to the reward system of the operating organization. The amount of adjustment depends on how innovative the operating organization is and on the attractiveness of outside alternatives.

The functions of the reward system are threefold. First, the rewards are to attract and hold idea people to the company and to the reservations. As firms have different attraction and retention problems, they will vary in their reward systems. Second, the rewards are to motivate the extra effort needed to innovate. After failing nineteen times, something has to motivate the idea generator to make the twentieth attempt. And finally rewards are given to reward successful performance. These rewards are to be given to idea generators primarily. However, the reward-measurement system for the sponsors is equally important. Each will be discussed in the next sections.

1. Rewards for idea generators.   The choice of reward system consists of mixtures of internal motivation provided through opportunity to pursue one's ideas, promotion, and recognition systems and special compensation. First, people can be attracted and motivated intrinsically by simply giving them the opportunity and the autonomy to pursue their own ideas. Autonomy is provided by a reservation. Many idea people are internally driven, as was the field engineer in our story. As such, the provision of opportunity to an idea generator to come to a reservation, pursue his or her own ideas, and be guided and evaluated by a reservation manager constitutes the minimal level of reward. If the minimal level attracts and motivates idea people, the innovating organization should go no further in creating a separate reward system.

Additional motivational leverage can be obtained if needed through promotion and recognition for innovating performance. The dual ladder is the best example where an individual contributor can be promoted and given increased salary without becoming a manager. At 3M a contributor can rise in the organization to an equivalent of a group executive and not be a manager. The dual ladder has always existed in R&D but is now being extended to other functions as well. Other firms use special recognition for career performance. At IBM there is the IBM Fellows Program in which a "fellow" is selected and can then work on projects of his or her own choosing for the next five years. At 3M there is the Carlton Award, which has been described as an internal Nobel Prize. The promotion and recognition systems reward innovation and aid in building an innovating culture.

When greater motivation is needed and/or the organization wants to signal the importance of innovation, special compensation is used in addition to providing opportunity and recognition. Different systems have been used. They will be discussed in order of increasing motivational impact and of increasing dysfunctional ripple effects—the implication being that the firm should use special compensation only to the degree that the needs for attraction and motivation dictate.

Some companies reward successful idea generators with one-time cash awards. For example, International Harvester's share of the combine market jumped from 12 to 17 percent due to the introduction of the axial flow combine. The scientist whose six patents contributed to the product development was given $10,000. If the product continues to succeed, he may be given another award. IBM uses the "Chairman's Outstanding Contribution Award." The current program manager on the 4300 series was given a $5,000 award for her breakthrough in coding on her last assignment. These awards are post hoc and serve to reward primarily as opposed to attract and motivate.

Stronger motivation is achieved through programs to give a "percentage of the take" to the idea generator and early team members. Toy and game companies give a royalty to inventors, internal and external, of toys and games that are introduced. Apple Computer claims that it gives employees a royalty for software programs they write and which will run on Apple equipment. A chemical company started a pool that was created by putting 4 percent of the first five years' earnings aside from a new business venture. The pool was to be distributed to the initial venture team. Other companies create pools from percentages (2–20 percent) of cost savings created by process innovations. In any case a predetermined contract is created to motivate the idea generator and early joiners of the risky effort.

The most controversial efforts to date are those attempts to duplicate free-market rewards inside the firm. Several years ago ITT bought a small company named Qume, which made high-speed printers. The founder became a millionaire. He had to quit his initial organization to found the venture capital effort. If ITT can make an outsider a millionaire, why not give the same chance to entrepreneurial insiders? Many people agree with that premise but have not found the formula to implement the idea. One firm created some five-year milestones for a venture, the accomplishment of which would result in a cash award of $6 million to the idea generator. However, the business climate changed after two years and the idea generator, not surprisingly, tried to implement the plan rather than adapt to the new, unforeseen reality. Another scheme is to give the idea generator and the initial team some phantom stock. That stock gets evaluated at sale time the same way any acquisition would be evaluated. This process duplicates the free-market process and gives internal people the same venture capital opportunities and risks that they have on the outside.

The special compensation programs produce motivation and dysfunctions. Other people often contribute at later stages and feel like second-class citizens. Also, any program that discriminates will produce equity perceptions and possible fallout in the operating organization. Care should be taken to manage the fallout if the benefits are judged to be worth the effort.

2. Rewards for sponsors. Another lesson from the example is that sponsors need incentives, too. In the example, the salespeople had an incentive to adopt a new product because they were being beaten in the market. The point is that sponsors will sponsor ideas, but they need not be innovating ideas. They will not sponsor innovating ideas unless the sponsor has innovating incentives. The orchestrator's task is to create and communicate those incentives.

Sponsor incentives take many forms. At 3M the division managers have a bonus goal that 25 percent of their revenue should come from products introduced in the last five years. When the percentage falls and the bonus is threatened, these sponsors become amazingly receptive to new-product ideas. The transfer process becomes much easier as a result. Sales growth, percentage of revenue increase, numbers of new products, and so on, are all bases for creating incentives for sponsors to adopt innovating ideas.

Another controversy occurs when the idea generators get phantom stock. Should the sponsors who supervise these idea people get some phantom stock too? Some banks have created separate subsidiaries so that sponsors can get stock in the new venture. To the degree that sponsors contribute to idea development, they will need to be given the stock options.

Thus the innovating organization needs its own reward system for idea generators and sponsors. The firm should start simple with the reward system and move to more motivating, more complex, and possibly more upsetting rewards as attraction and motivation problems require.

People

The last policy area of the innovating organization is that of people practices. The assumption is that some people are better at innovating than others and that these people are not necessarily those who are good at operating. Therefore the innovating organization's ability to generate new business ideas can be increased by systematically developing and selecting those people who are better than others. But first the attributes to be selected and developed must be identified. These characteristics are discussed for the idea generators and the sponsors.

1. Attributes of idea generators.   The field engineer in the example is the stereotype of the inventor. He is not mainstream. He is hard to get along with, and he broke company policy in order to perfect the idea. These people have strong egos which allow them to persist and swim upstream. They generally are not those types of people who get along well in an organization. However, if there are reservations, innovating funds, and dual ladders, these people can be attracted and retained.

The psychological attributes of successful entrepreneurs are those of high need for achievement and risk taking. But several other attributes are needed to translate that need into innovation. First, there is usually an irreverence for the status quo. These people often come from outcast groups or are immigrants. They are less satisfied with the way things are, and they have less to lose with a change to the current business idea.

Another attribute is "previous programming in the industry." Successful innovation requires in-depth knowledge in the industry gained through either experience or formal education. Hence the innovator needs to obtain a knowledge of the industry but not the religion. Previous start-up experience is also associated with successful business ventures. Attracting people from incubator firms (high technology) and areas (Boston, Silicon Valley) can increase the odds of finding innovators.

The amount of organizational effort to select these people varies with the ability to attract them to the organization in the first place. If idea people are attracted through reputation, then by funding reservations and employing idea-getting processes, idea people will select themselves and over time earn a reputation for idea generation. If the firm has no reputation for innovation, then idea people must be sought out or external reservations used for initial idea generation. One firm made extensive use of outside recruiting. A sponsor would develop an idea and then attend annual conferences of key specialties to determine who was best in the area, interview them, and then offer the ones with entrepreneurial interests the opportunity to develop the venture.

Another key attribute of successful business innovators is varied experience. This variety creates the coupling of knowledge of means and use in the mind of a single individual. It is the generalist, not the specialist, who creates an idea outside the current business idea. Specialists are inventors; generalists are innovators. These people can be selected or developed. One firm selects the best and the brightest from the ceramics engineering schools and places them in central engineering in order to learn the system. They are then assigned to field engineering where they spend three to five years with the customer and customer problems. They then return to central engineering product design. Only then do they design products for those same customers. The internal coupling can be created by role rotation. Some aerospace firms rotate engineers through manufacturing liaison.

Thus there are some known characteristics of idea generators. These people can be attracted or selected. By role rotation the needed varied experience can also be created. These people will be retained, however, only if there are reservations for them and sponsors to guide them.

2. Attributes of sponsors and reservation managers.
The people who manage the idea development process must also be attracted, developed, retained, and trained as well as those who generate and test ideas. Again some people and management skills are better suited to managing ideas than others, and therefore the innovating organization needs those who have learned the idea management skills. The attributes to be selected and developed are a management style for idea people, early experience in innovating, idea-generating capabilities, skills at putting together deals, and generalist business skills. Each of these attributes will be described below.

One of the key skills of the innovating organization is to manage and supervise the kind of person who is likely to be an idea generator and champion. In the preceding section these idea people were described as those who do not take to being supervised very well. That is true. Idea generators and champions have a great deal of ownership in their ideas. They gain their satisfaction by having "done it their way." The intrinsic satisfaction comes from the ownership and autonomy. However, idea people also need help, advice, and sounding boards. The successful sponsor learns how to manage these people the same way that producers or publishers learn to handle the egos of their stars or writers. The style was best described by a successful sponsor:

> It's a lot like teaching your kids to ride a bike. You're there. You walk along behind. If the kid takes off he or she never knows that they could have been helped. If they stagger a little, you lend a helping hand, undetected preferably. If they fall, you catch them. If they do something stupid, you take the bike away until they're ready.

This style is quite different from the hands-on, directive style of an operating organization. Of course the best way to learn this style is to have been managed by it and seen it practiced in an innovating organization. Therefore experience in an innovating organization is essential.

More than the idea generators, the sponsors need to understand the logic of innovation and to have experienced the management of innovation. Like any activity, the managers of it must have an intuitive feel for the task and its nuances. Managers who are only experienced in operations will not have developed the managerial style, understanding, and intuitive feel that is necessary to manage innovations. The reason is that the logic of operations is counterintuitive to the logic of innovations. This means that some of the idea generators and champions who have experienced innovation should become managers as well as individual contributors. The president in the example scenario was the inventor of the first-generation product and therefore understood the long, agonizing process of developing a business idea. It is also rare to find an R&D unit that is managed by someone who did not come up through the ranks of R&D.

The best idea sponsors and idea reservations managers are people who have experienced innovation early in their careers and are comfortable with it. They will have been exposed to risk, uncertainty, parallel experiments, repeated failures that lead to learning, coupling as opposed to assembly line thinking, long time frames, and personal control systems based on people and ideas, not numbers and budget variances. Other managers who have already developed their intuition and style in operations have difficulty in switching to the innovating organization late in their careers. These sponsor and reservation managers can be developed or recruited from the outside.

Sponsors and reservation managers need to be idea generators themselves. Ideas tend to come from two sources. The first is at low levels of the organization where the problem gap is experienced. The idea generator who offers a solution is the one who experienced the problem and goes to a sponsor for testing and development. One problem with these ideas is that they are partial, since they come from a specialist whose view can be parochial and local. But sponsors are at the crossroads of many partial ideas. They may get a larger vision of the emerging situation as a result. These idea sponsors can generate a business idea themselves or blend several partial ideas into a business idea. These sponsors and reservation managers at the crossroads of idea flow are an important second source of new ideas. Therefore they should be selected for and trained for idea generation.

Another skill the sponsors and especially reservation managers need is deal making and brokering. Once an idea has emerged, a reservation manager may have to argue for the release of key people, space, resources, and charters and for production time, or a customer contact. These deals all need to be made using persuasion. In that sense it is no different from project or product management roles. But people vary in their ability to cut a deal and bargain. Those who can should be selected. Those who have the other idea management skills can be trained in negotiating and bargaining.

And finally the sponsors and reservation managers need to be generalists with general business skills. Again the skill is needed to recognize a business idea and to shape partial ideas into business ideas. They need to coach idea generators in specialties in which the idea generator is not schooled. Most successful research managers are those with business skills who can see the business significance in the good ideas that come from scientists.

In summary, the sponsors and reservation managers who manage the idea development process must also be recruited, selected, and developed. The skills that these people need relate to their style, experience, idea-generating ability, deal-making ability, and generalist business acumen. These skills can be either selected or developed.

Thus some of the attributes of successful idea generators and idea sponsors can be identified. In creating the innovating organization these attributes can be recruited, selected, and/or developed. In so doing, the organization improves its odds at generating and developing new business ideas.

SUMMARY

The innovating organization is one that recognizes and formalizes the roles, processes, rewards, and people practices that naturally lead to innovations. The point emphasized throughout is that by purposely designing these roles and processes, the organization is more likely to generate the innovations that are now being sought. This purposely designed organization is needed to overcome the obstacles to innovation. Innovation is destructive to many established groups and will be resisted. Innovation is contrary to operations and will be ignored. These obstacles and others are more likely to be overcome with an organization designed to innovate.

Managers have tried to overcome these obstacles by creating venture

Figure 6   The Innovating Organization

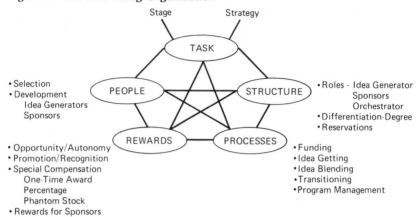

groups, hiring some entrepreneurs, creating "breakthrough funds," or offering special incentives. These are good policies but by themselves will not generate innovations. The message to be conveyed by Figure 1 was that a consistent set of policies concerning structure, process, rewards, and people is needed. The innovating organization is illustrated in Figure 6. It is the combination of idea people, reservations for them, sponsors to supervise them, funding for ideas, and rewards for success that increases the odds in favor of innovation. Simply implementing one or two of these practices will result in failure and will teach people that such practices do not work. A consistent combination of such practices will create an innovating organization that will work.

13

Strategic Planning and Human Resource Management: At Rainbow's End

CHARLES FOMBRUN
The Wharton School, University of Pennsylvania

NOEL TICHY
University of Michigan

INTRODUCTION

> Perhaps the single most important factor in our pursuit of productivity through people is helpful direction and support from experts on human resource management. . . . I did not come to this conclusion quickly but as I review our most and least successful ventures in recent years, the difference keeps coming down to people; how well we matched the right people to the critical jobs.

So spoke the chairman of a major corporation. He went on to note that for years his vice-president of personnel had been pushing to be included on the company's executive committee in order to have a more direct role in shaping key decisions:

> Well six months ago, I added him to the committee and, with other members, developed a list of "people issues" we need help with. So far, all personnel has sent us are requests for extensions while they try to get what we need. Frankly, I'm not optimistic.

Over and over in our study of the relationship between strategic-planning practices and human resource management we have heard the same concerns voiced by senior-level executives. For one reason or another, they are convinced that senior personnel officers should play a more proactive role in the formulation of strategic directions if those strategies are to be successfully implemented. Yet, when they turn to their personnel departments for help, all too often they find them ill equipped to deliver either information or expertise.

What a nightmare for some personnel vice-presidents! After years of explaining mediocre status by bewailing their lack of support and attention from the CEO, they are now getting both and find themselves unable to deliver the goods.

In working with senior executives on a variety of consulting and research projects over the last ten years, the authors found a familiar complaint of personnel officers to be their exclusion from active involvement in sessions where strategic decisions are made. Typically, top management would meet annd review a host of external trends (political, social, technological, as well as economic and competitive) and proceed to balance these against internal strengths and weaknesses. In the latter were usually included a relatively superficial assessment of human resource capacity. Decisions were made to enter new markets, develop new products, and pursue new technologies. Decisions were made to withdraw from markets, abandon products and technologies, or put them on hold. Millions, if not billions, in sales and profits were to be impacted. Cigars were passed, glasses lifted, and a call put through to personnel with instructions to find three of "these," four of "those," fifty of "these," and five hundred of "those" and then figure out what to with the fifteen hundred "thems" no longer needed in implementing the new strategies.

In a recent survey of a sample drawn from the Fortune 500 industrials, both senior-planning and senior personnel executives were asked to rate the degree to which human resource activities are being and should be used in formulation strategies. Only 20 percent responded that human resource considerations had a substantial impact on strategy formulation. However, 51 percent thought they should be instrumental in shaping strategic decisions.

Many have sought for some time to help shape the strategic direction of their organizations by requiring decision makers to see human resource issues as among those considered and given great weight *before,* not after, decisions are taken. Now it would appear that many personnel officers are gaining the CEO's attention before they have built the ability to deliver what is needed.

The purpose of this article is to examine

How personnel departments came to be in a position of potential influence

What strategic decision makers need from personnel

How personnel can more effectively meet strategic-planning needs while continuing to satisfy traditional expectations

MANAGEMENT: FROM EASY TIMES INTO THE 1980s

From 1946 to 1970, American industry experienced a period of unparalleled growth in sales and profits. All the latent demand that went unmet during the Depression and World War II exploded into the marketplace. By the time domestic growth slowed, firms were already turning their sights to the potential of the overseas market and called themselves multinationals. The "merger mania" of the 1960s produced multiples magic on American GNP, creating additional growth, albeit somewhat illusory. Even the reversals of the early 1970s were regarded as little more than "a rolling readjustment." Not until 1973–74 did more sanguine economists and business leaders acknowledge that the "party" was over, that we were in the midst of a decade of slow growth, that we needed to make some fundamental changes to remain competitive on the world scene.

To be sure, excessive regulation, discouraging tax laws, and perhaps an outdated intrepretation of antitrust laws have contributed to our current industrial situation. These factors, along with the perhaps unpredictable actions of OPEC, can be added to our reindustrialization of defeated nations as factors contributing to our current position. But they cannot be held as the collective cause of our current woes. Throughout the postwar "boom," all too many corporations relied on strategies that *exploited* existing technology and *neglected* longer-term investments. While this was clearly true in terms of plant and equipment, the point of this article is to stress that it was especially manifest in a neglect of the human resource base of the firm as well.

Looking back at this period, it seems clear that most executives continued to focus on short-term profit and activities designed to achieve it. First marketing and then finance became the "in" departments, with production, distribution, and data processing as important but clearly secondary support systems. Long-range planning groups grew in size but not stature during the 1960s, as corporations recognized the need for the activity, if not its implications.

In the past several years, however, attention has turned to where it should have been all along. The question senior executives are increasingly asking is provocative, deceptively simple, and full of implications. They ask, How do we implement these laudable strategies?

Unfortunately, a spate of articles, books, and consulting pitches has ensued on "strategy implementation" but fails to address the full complexity of strategizing. The implementation of strategic or long-range plans involves a vital set of activities having to do with structure, organizational processes, and people. The point we stress, however, is that sound strategy formulation must from the onset include implementation in the early iterations of the planning process.

Nowhere is this artificial separation of formulation and implementation more common and more dangerous than with regard to human resource issues. People are too often the implicit part of the plan, the unknown factor.

Exhibit 1 summarizes some of the current environmental pressures on organizations. The trends suggest that competing in the 1980s will require a sophisticated set of tools for dealing with the problems of a highly educated work force in a slack labor market, competing for fewer jobs in an increasingly service economy. Organizations will have to consider carefully the implications of alternative recruitment and training strategies to ensure effective implementation of

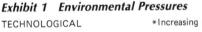

Exhibit 1   Environmental Pressures

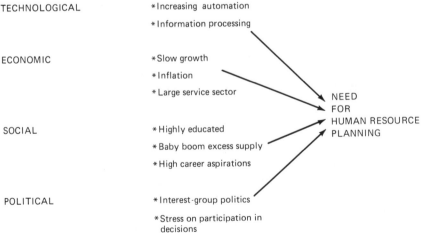

TECHNOLOGICAL
  * Increasing automation
  * Information processing

ECONOMIC
  * Slow growth
  * Inflation
  * Large service sector

SOCIAL
  * Highly educated
  * Baby boom excess supply
  * High career aspirations

POLITICAL
  * Interest-group politics
  * Stress on participation in decisions

NEED
FOR
HUMAN RESOURCE
PLANNING

their plans. Indeed, the viability of these plans may largely depend on how well human resource needs and implications are understood and built in to the planning process in the early stages of formulation.

In the rest of this article we discuss the informational needs of an effective human resource planning system and present some systematic steps for linking strategic planning to human resource management concerns.

STRATEGIC HUMAN RESOURCES MANAGEMENT

The personnel function, or human resource function as it is increasingly being labeled, has three sets of roles it can potentially play in helping organizations cope with an environmental context of slow economic growth, disillusioned workers, and fierce competition. Which of these roles it takes on is partly a matter of choice and competence, and partly a reflection of its current power in the organizational vis-à-vis top management and the planning group.

At the *operational level,* it can merely serve as a retriever of information. The human resource function of most organizations houses the data files, performance evaluations, and general records of the employee population. Setting up efficient and possibly computerized systems for retrieving data about the organization's human resources would give the human resource function some added measure of influence in the organization, given the need for quantifiable information on human resources in making decisions. In its operational role, the function serves as the organizational librarian.

On a more *managerial level,* the human resource function could, after monitoring the strategic plans of the company, develop its own projections of human resource needs and concerns and could communicate those to the planners, who would then decide on the basis of human resource's information and recommendations how and where to allocate scarce resources, given the human limitations of the company and labor market.

Human resources could be involved at a *strategic level* by direct participation in the formulation of the strategic directions of the company. Such a role would place human resource concerns on a par with financial, marketing, and technical concerns in the formulation of strategy.

Two strategic roles for the human resource function can be distinguished:

1. It could provide assistance in the formulation and implementation of corporate strategy by helping decide what set of businesses to be in and how the different businesses should relate to each other.

2. It could provide assistance in the formulation and implementation of specific business strategies by helping develop the distinctive competencies and competitive advantages needed for success in a particular business.

Exhibit 2 **The Role of the Human Resource Function**

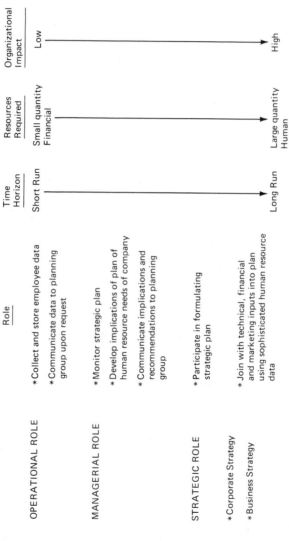

	Role	Time Horizon	Resources Required	Organizational Impact
OPERATIONAL ROLE	*Collect and store employee data *Communicate data to planning group upon request	Short Run	Small quantity Financial	Low
MANAGERIAL ROLE	*Monitor strategic plan *Develop implications of plan of human resource needs of company *Communicate implications and recommendations to planning group			
STRATEGIC ROLE *Corporate Strategy *Business Strategy	*Participate in formulating strategic plan *Join with technical, financial and marketing inputs into plan using sophisticated human resource data	Long Run	Large quantity Human	High

Exhibit 2 presents these three sets of possible roles for the human resource function. Clearly, strategic involvement would considerably empower the human resource function. That this power is becoming increasingly conferred upon the traditional personnel function is manifest in the small but significant number of highly paid senior human resource officers reporting directly to the CEO in such large organizations as IBM, Chase Manhattan Bank, Exxon Corporation, and General Electric.

For years the human resource staff has been content with an essentially operational role, worrying more about service delivery on a mundane level. The call for strategic involvement that issued from the cutting edge largely terrified most human resource functions in the 1970s. The threat of the 1980s is not that the human resource function will not be asked into the executive suite. Instead, it is a fear that the door will be opened only too quickly, with the human resource function unprepared and unable to deliver.

For a human resource management department to successfully play a strategic role in the company, it will have to carefully prepare, "tune up" as it were, for service delivery in a highly uncertain, long-run, and poorly structured decision-making context.

HUMAN RESOURCES INFORMATION

Two kinds of data are particularly relevant to corporate decisions. Regardless of the role personnel takes on, storing and retrieving the following data are critical to effective human resource management:

1. Internal human resource stock
2. External labor market data

Internal data must describe the company in terms of both past experience and future potential. As such it must be stored in a flexible format that is retrievable and interpretable in different ways. For instance, appraisal information, while useful to describe the current performance of an employee, should also capture the developmental needs of the employee. When aggregated across employees, it describes the human resource strengths and weaknesses of the company. Measures of entrepreneurship, ambition, and leadership, as well as attitudes toward transfers, expatriation, and promotion, could prove invaluable in formulating strategic investment decisions where successful implementation requires human resource skills and abilities.

Having these data about the internal population means building a systematic attitudinal survey mechanism in addition to storing quality appraisal data. To be maximally useful, these data must be tied to the demography and skills and profile of the internal population.

Strategic decisions, however, require information about the availability of external labor as well. The characteristics of the labor market in terms of wage structure, geographical location, supply in terms of job categories, and demand in terms of competitive pressure from other employers are necessary statistics for strategic decisions. Again, the human resource function must systematically store these in an easily retrievable fashion. The increasing sophistication of computerized decision support systems makes it possible to store vast data banks and reduce them to manageable proportions by using statistical models that can be developed on line by managers and decision makers themselves.

While both sets of data are vital, they are not sufficient, for they only describe the organization and its context in the present. The true task of strategic planning is projection and scenario forecasting. Thus a strategic role for the human resource function must involve the forecast of internal potential, as well as labor market trends. Exhibit 3 draws out the human resource dimension and its relationship to the business plan.

Two principal linkages describe the relationship between the human resource plans and the business plans:

1. Formulation linkages
2. Implementation linkages

Horizontal linkages in Exhibit 2 describe implementational concerns over time. A strategic business plan is designed to move the company to competitive

Exhibit 3   Strategic Transitions

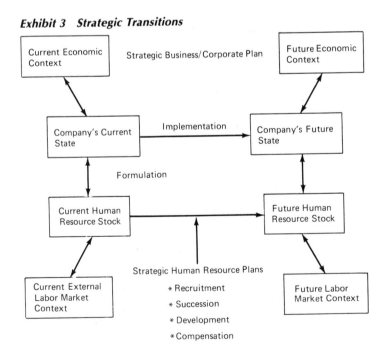

or profit position in some future product or market context. Paralleling it, a set of strategic human resource plans is formulated to guide the company's human resources in the desired direction. Through recruitment and training, the current human resource stock is transformed into an inventory of requisite skills and abilities for the company of the future. The critical task is to maintain consistency between both dimensions of the plan, and this means

1. Designing a strong link from the human resource function to the strategic-planning function at the formulation stage in order to ensure their consistency
2. Building a sufficient information base for human resource projection to support the business and corporate plans

Human Resource Management and Strategic Planning

All human resource functions have some responsibility for four generic activities that service the line organization:

1. Selection: recruiting qualified personnel
2. Evaluation: managing the performance appraisal process
3. Rewards: maintaining adequate compensation and fringe benefits packages
4. Development: creating systems to enhance skills, promotional opportunities, career paths

These four sets of activities are necessarily involved in the company's strategic plans. At a minimum, these activities on a day-to-day operational level must support the current operations. The right people must be hired to fit current vacancies. Compensation must be adequate for competitive recruitment. In a more strategic sense, however, the human resource activities must also reflect long-term considerations raised by the corporate/business plans. These involve projecting the internal and external labor market information into the future, and designing the collective thrust of the company's human resource plans. What will the organization look like in twenty years, and what kind of people will it need? What will they value as rewards for performance?

Exhibit 4 diagrams three levels of activity for the human resource function and the questions and jobs they imply. The point of the exhibit is to stress that a strategic involvement for the human resource function means not only building a link with the strategic corporate/business plan but increasing the long-range thinking of the function itself within each of its four sets of activities.

Most personnel functions are undoubtedly fun at the operational level. To determine why, it is useful to look to the past. Most personnel departments grew from reactive responses to environmental problems. For example, the shift in the labor force from blue collar to white collar called for recruitment strategies more closely tied to the collegiate educational system. More recently the push for equal employment opportunity and affirmative action has provoked a series of responses that include workshops for women and minorities, adjustments in pay, and more attention to the promotion of women and minorities. Few organizations have done significant work at the managerial level in any of the human resource functions.

The strategic issues noted in Exhibit 4 focus on longer-term, policy, and system issues. Only a handful of U.S. organizations approach human resource management in such a systematic way at the strategic level today. Nevertheless the challenge is to do so. Several examples of strategic human resource management follow.

Strategic selection is often a vital determinant of success in diversification strategies. This requires matching executive characteristics with the suitable strategic jobs to be done. For instance, General Electric parallels its portfolio analysis of business with a categorization of managers as "growers," "caretakers," and "undertakers" in terms of their suitability for performance in business at different stages of the product life cycle.

Strategic selection also means identifying the characteristics of managers needed for implementing strategic plans, and formulating staffing plans that will ensure an adequate supply of human resources for implementation.

Strategic appraisal requires doing more than gauging current performance; it requires appraisal in terms of both current performance and future potential. Moreover, strategic appraisal means understanding the need for a set of criteria to evaluate performance that may vary across strategic activities. For instance, in terms of the Boston Consulting Group Matrix, different performance criteria should apply across the business units of a portfolio. Profit does not adequately estimate a manager's success in minimizing the losses of a "dog" business. Nor is it adequate for gauging effective management of a "cash cow."

A *strategic reward* system must encourage performance in line with long-

Exhibit 4   Linking Corporate/Business Plans With Human Resource Activities

CORPORATE/ BUSINESS PLAN	Human Resource Activity			
	Selection	Appraisal	Rewards	Development
Strategic ←→	Kinds of people needed to recruit to manage long-run business	Criteria needed to measure performance in the long run	Values of the work force in the long run	Skills, experiences, and attitudes the current stock of HR needs in the long run
Managerial ←→	Recruitment/market plan Validate recruitment criteria	Identification of potential Assessment center for development	Five-year compensation program Cafeteria fringe benefits	Identify career paths Management development programs
Operational ←→	Staffing plans Day-to-day monitoring systems	Annual appraisal Training for performance appraisal	Wage and salary administration Benefits package	Fit individual to job Job training

run objectives. Compensation and benefits packages are often indomitably static and uniform, often incapable of recognizing individual performance. However, such companies as Texas Instruments, Crown Zellerbach, Santa Fe Industries, and Twentieth Century Fox have moved to institute large bonus plans for their senior executives that are tied to three- to five-year objectives of the units.

Strategic development programs are targeted to the future. Strategic development involves conducting programs and planning executive experiences that build the skills needed for effective performance in jobs five, ten, or twenty years hence. It means designing the future stock of human resources that will be needed to implement the company's strategic plans. Exxon's COED system is a formalized process of career pathing and job rotation that is specifically targeted to succession management at the executive level.

Overall, strategic activities must also be consistent, and that requires a philosophy of management that can only come from the top. The kinds of individuals that are recruited, the basic stance the organization takes to the retention, use, and development of its human resources, all stem from a basic philosophy that in most organizations remains implicit. Whether implicit or explicit, it is this management philosophy that provides the cohesion between the four generic human resource activities. For example, when Thomas Watson said that "IBM means service," he articulated a philosophy that came to permeate the selection, appraisal, reward, and development systems.

In summary, if the human resource function is to move from a strictly operational and reactive function to one involved in strategy formulation and implementation, three changes must take place:

1. Improve data collection and retrieval systems. Attitudinal appraisal and skills data must be readily available in flexible form.

2. Encourage strategic thinking within the different activity units of human resource management. Officers must be educated to the realities of corporate planning and constantly monitor trends in terms of their consequences for the company's human resources.

3. Link the activities of the human resource functions to the strategic plans of the company. Interact with executive line officers around strategy formulation.

DESIGNING THE CORPORATE HUMAN RESOURCE STRATEGY

Although we have discussed some elements of the strategically managed human resource function, what are needed are some guidelines for designing the overall corporate-level human resource strategy. Exhibit 5 illustrates how the human resource needs and tasks vary across the different businesses in a portfolio as a function of the product/market life cycle of each business. The critical corporate

Exhibit 5 *Corporate Human Resource Strategy*

BUSINESS LIFE CYCLE

HUMAN RESOURCE FUNCTIONS	Start-up Businesses	Growth Businesses	Mature Businesses	Declining Businesses	
Selection/Placement	Recruitment New activities Recruit Entrepreneurial style	Recruit for future business	Lateral moves and advancement for enhancing efficiency	Transfers to different businesses Outplacement Early retirement	Corporate human resource staff, policies designed to integrate human resource functions across businesses
Appraisal	Appraise milestones linked to plans for the business, flexible	Linked to growth criteria, e.g., market share, volume unit cost reduction	Evaluate efficiency and profit margin performance	Evaluate cost savings	
Rewards	Salary plus large equity position	Salary plus bonus for growth targets, plus equity for key people	Incentive plan linked to efficiency and high-profit margins	Incentive plan linked to cost savings	
Development	Minimum until a critical mass of people in business —then job related	Good orientation program for fast start-ups Job skills Middle-management development	Emphasis on job training Good supervisory and management development programs	Career planning and support services for transferring people	

Organization and design of the human resource functions within businesses task is to design a corporate human resource strategy that will line up with the corporate strategy for the range of businesses. Thus, in companies with a portfolio of businesses at different stages of growth and/or decline, there should be a clearly articulated human resource strategy, one that describes a differentiated view of what different businesses need in the way of human resource services which will result in different systems for the delivery of those services.

Managing the Marginals

Once the human resource needs are identified for different types of businesses, then the corporate job is twofold. First, an appropriate human resource function must be designed for each distinct set of needs. This is the task identified in the marginal at the base of the matrix. It entails ensuring that each business has an appropriately designed and staffed human resource function. For instance, the function in a start-up business will emphasize recruiting, whereas a mature business will emphasize development and training.

Second, the corporate human resource strategy must be responsible for integrating the human resource functions across lines of business. The more one differentiates the functions in order to match the distinct needs of businesses, the more difficult it is to achieve consistency across businesses. Thus selection policies may be diametrically opposed in two businesses. Or, more likely, the reward systems may not mesh. This can pose problems for the transfer of employees across businesses. The corporate stance should be to keep differentiation across businesses where necessary and carefully look for ways of integrating. A comprehensive corporate philosophy, as William Ouchi has stressed, is one way to cement the building blocks of a human resource strategy across businesses. Some key human resource policies should cut across businesses. No matter how it is done, the corporate human resource strategic role entails not only maintaining a suitable level of differentiation to human resource delivery as indicated by the lower marginal of the matrix but also developing integration through management of the right-hand marginal.

CONCLUSION: GETTING STARTED

If the human resource management function is to move out of the doldrums of operational servicing, and if it is to survive in the strategic arena and actually deliver when challenged to perform, it must begin to recognize and understand the managerial nature of its activities and their importance to organizational effectiveness. The following steps can help in getting started:

1. *Design a corporate philosophy*—Decide what the critical thrust of the strategic plan will be, and what kind of organization should follow. Whether the critical values the organization will adhere to involve product quality,

customer service, or employee satisfaction, they should be specific enough to represent an organizing principle for the company.

2. *Create formal systems that reflect corporate philosophy*—If the corporate philosophy involves treating its employees like members of a family, then job security should be a key reward for performance. Such a value should be reflected in all the human resource systems; it should be stressed as a recruitment criterion, tied to compensation, and built in as an assumption of development programs.

3. *Make management process the target*—The objective of injecting human resource management into the strategic arena is not to enhance the status of traditional personnel resource staff. Rather, it is to alter the way managers set priorities and make decisions. Thus the major change must be in the behavior of line management, getting them to consider human resource issues both as they think about future strategies and as they attempt to implement them. The first step in developing a strategic human resource function, therefore, calls for a careful analysis of the management process of the company to understand the interplay between marketing, financial, technical, and human resource inputs.

4. *Design targeted information systems*—A sure way to remain irrelevant is to develop sophisticated computerized systems without the involvement of the line. Management must begin by identifying in cooperation with human resource staff the type and format of the human resource data they need for strategic decision making. The human resource function should be prepared with some basic data and analysis that are not excessively complex, but simple and pragmatic.

5. *Grow systems over time*—The organization should start with only some rudimentary human resource systems. These should only be expanded and made more complex as pressure builds up externally from the marketplace, and internally from management. The systems should evolve as they clearly demonstrate utility in the strategic arena.

Following these five simple, but fundamental, steps should create the context for effective integration of human resource issues in the strategic management of the firm.

14

Paying for Strategic Performance: A New Executive Compensation Imperative

LOUIS J. BRINDISI, JR.
Booz·Allen & Hamilton Inc.

For the past 25 years, almost all executive compensation programs in American companies looked basically alike. They have consisted primarily of cash compensation (salary and annual bonus), long-term compensation (stock options and ownership plans) and employee benefits. The package provided to a particular executive or manager reflected the level of his or her function in the corporation or business unit, industry standards (often determined by simplistic salary surveys), and *financial* performance—that is, achievement of the corporate or business unit's *financial* goals.

As such, these schemes were "systems" unto themselves, developed with little, if any, thought of tying them to strategic management. In fact, in some cases, compensation systems proved counterproductive, actually inhibiting strategic performance. On the short-term side, business units whose primary mission was market share growth were often saddled with dysfunctional return-on-investment (ROI) bonus plans. On the long-term side, incentives for specific earnings-per-share (EPS) growth goals over a three-or four-year planning period inhibited real portfolio and asset management. While these goals were being achieved, businesses were being milked and price/earnings (P/E) ratios declined.

But today, in our highly competitive business environment, executive compensation must be much more clearly linked to *strategic* performance—to the management of the corporate portfolio, to the business unit's mission, to short-term financial performance as well as long-term strategic performance, and, finally, to the degree of risk involved in managing the portfolio effectively and productively. The new emphasis does not eliminate financial performance; indeed, the short-term financial goals of cash flow generation and returns are still vitally important. Nor does it eliminate the use of competitive market intelligence about pay in comparable corporations to determine compensation strategy. Rather, it reflects management's recognition of the fact that the management compensation system can now be used to gain competitive advantage and achieve long-term success.

But how can the management compensation program enhance strategic performance and how can it be designed to reflect and reward business unit mission?

In brief, management must first define and segment its portfolio of businesses. Then, for each business, it must assess the external competitive environment, market attractiveness, and growth opportunities, as well as internal financial performance (e.g., revenue and profit contributions, return on investment). Next, management must determine the mission and role of each business in achieving established corporate strategic and financial goals, and to what extent that business enjoys—or lacks—a competitive advantage.

Such an examination allows management to focus available resources—financial and human—on those businesses in which competitive advantages are held and which are imperative for overall strategic success. It highlights the strategic goals at both the corporate and the business unit level that will be used to measure short-and long-term performance. And it suggests the kinds of tasks corporate and operating management will need to carry out successfully in the strategic fight ahead—tasks that will shape overall executive compensation strategy and the magnitude and design of the programs.

EXECUTIVE COMPENSATION STRATEGY: THE CONCEPT

Clearly, then, corporate and business unit strategy shapes executive compensation strategy; in combination they are designed to achieve higher earnings growth and return on equity that will lead to the ultimate goal of high market to book ratio.

But corporate strategies obviously vary from company to company. And business units within a corporation differ from one another in terms of their basic economic structures, varying market positions, and cash use/generation. Consequently, each corporate and business unit strategy requires a specific executive compensation strategy—one fitted not only to the execution of strategy and the achievement of strategic and financial goals but also to the difficulty and risk of the management tasks involved and to the criticality of the function or business units to long-term success.

Each scheme will consist of some combination of cash compensation—that is, salary and annual bonus—and long-term incentives such as stock options, restricted stock, and long-term bonuses in the form of performance units or shares, which reward financial performance as measured by relative EPS growth, returns and other performance criteria.

The balance between base pay (salary) and incentive compensation (bonus), and between short-and long-term rewards depends on a number of factors.

THE MIX FOR THE CORPORATE EXECUTIVE

At the corporate level, the balance to be struck, the compensation elements to be used, and the total financial reward to be provided depend on corporate strategy and goals and the type of management task ahead. If growth through acquisition is a key corporate goal, for example, then long-range rewards should be a significant part of the total compensation for a corporate CEO, to reflect the long-term nature of acquisition planning, selection, and integration.

In the case of the management-task factor, restructuring a portfolio of businesses to attain cash balance, for example, or to divest businesses with poor earnings or low growth potential, is usually a more complicated and lengthy process than simply maintaining or upgrading a portfolio. In a state of portfolio flux, it is difficult to set specific earning growth goals because of the varying impacts of acquisitions and divestitures on earnings. Although relative performance measures—earnings growth and return on equity, measured against those of comparable companies—can be used to compare corporate performance, the determination of an appropriate sample of competitors is not always easy.

A corporate CEO responsible for restructuring a portfolio, therefore, should be awarded a compensation package in which the long-term incentives include stock options or restricted stock in special cases. In contrast, the corporate CEO responsible for portfolio maintenance and upgrading would be awarded a somewhat different package, with long-term incentives emphasizing performance units to reward maintenance of position rather than stock options because leverage may be limited. These differences are shown graphically in Figure 1.

Figure 1   Compensation Packages

Corporate CEO with responsibility for major restructuring of portfolio

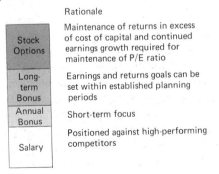

	Rationale
Stock Options	Low market-to-book ratio requires major acquisition and divestiture program
	Earnings growth and return goals cannot be planned easily
	Time period elastic
Annual Bonus	Market ultimate judge of long-term strategic performance
	Size of annual bonus reflects long-term focus
Salary	Based on extent and success of business portfolio changes
	Positioned against capital competitors at level at which current cash compensation is not a short-term issue

Corporate CEO with responsibility for maintaining/upgrading of portfolio

	Rationale
Stock Options	Maintenance of returns in excess of cost of capital and continued earnings growth required for maintenance of P/E ratio
Long-term Bonus	Earnings and returns goals can be set within established planning periods
Annual Bonus	Short-term focus
Salary	Positioned against high-performing competitors

Figure 2 Impact of Portfolio Restructuring (Stock Price)

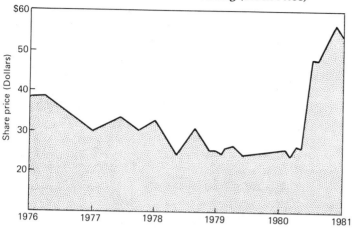

The proportion of these various components has shifted somewhat in the last few years to reflect changing attitudes about the appropriate make-up of compensation packages. Yet more dramatic shifts will probably occur as management seeks newer, more innovative ways to compensate its executives for managing in these more turbulent fast-moving times.

Until quite recently, American management has focused—some say fixated—on short-term profit results, cutting longer-payout research and development investment to the bone and harvesting business successes as early as possible. The reasons for that trend are pretty obvious: government tax and depreciation policy, investment-inhibiting legislation, and the ongoing pressure of the investment community to increase earning per share every quarter.

In recognition of and as reward for short-term performance, short-term incentives were implemented and that simply exacerbated the problem. Annual bonus plans created bigger annual bonus opportunities, which in turn intensified the short-term performance focus and in effect discouraged strategic management. In parallel, corporate financial controllers, with the help of technical compensation consultants, established short-term ROI formulas for all business investments—and that acted as a damper on growth investing.

The negative effects on growth and productivity have finally begun to trouble corporate America, and more and more companies are reexamining their short-term view of the future. So, once again, corporate executives are designing strategies that look for results a little farther down the road. In line with that longer lens, they are reshaping their compensation packages giving added weight to long-term compensation. In studies Booz·Allen has conducted over the past four years, we have found that long-term compensation can represent up to 50 percent of annual cash compensation. In some industries or industrial segments —e.g., petroleum exploration and production—it can reach 100 percent.

As one form of long-term compensation, stock options are making a strong comeback. Relegated to the closet in the '70s because of inflation, lack of real growth, and declining P/E ratios, stock options are once again respectable members of long-term incentive plans. We are convinced that the market will reflect corporate strategic performance in portfolio management. Figure 2 shows the stock price movement of one of our clients who successfully restructured a moribund portfolio. Indeed, in our view, the optimum long-range plan for the '80s, will be a combination of stock options and performance bonus to reward both improvement in stock price as a result of portfolio management and specific profit improvement gains.

THE MIX FOR THE BUSINESS
UNIT CEO

The executive compensation package for business unit managers depends on the portfolio roles and the profit-leverage opportunities of the business they direct. Is the business a cash user or a cash generator? That is, is it in the growth phase of its life-cycle, or is it a mature business with a stable, dominant market share?

The answers to these questions dictate the balance between short-and long-term compensation for achieveing strategic goals, as well as the basis of bonus payment for the achievement of financial goals.

For example, in business units with short-term cash-generation horizons, cash compensation is critical and should be leveraged in the form of an annual bonus—emphasizing short-term cash compensation over long-term reward.

The salary-to-bonus mix also depends on portfolio roles and profit opportunities. Executives managing business units in the growth stage—that is, cash users—should be paid for strategic performance. They should have a salary/bonus balance tipped toward bonus to reflect the entrepreneurial management skills needed to build volume and market share, strategic goals typical of the growth phase, and to emphasize management's willingness to pay for that strategic performance at a crucial point in the business's development.

However, the salary/bonus mix changes as the business unit moves along its life-cycle curve. As the business becomes a mature cash generator, financial performance—net cash flow, say, or return on capital—and maintenance of market share are critical to funding other businesses. Now the form of reward, as shown in Figure 3, which contrasts the executive compensation strategy for managers of cash users to that of cash generators, is primarily salary, supplemented by annual bonus and long-term performance bonus units. Stock options should be used only when the unit contributes significantly to earnings growth and market-to-book ratios.

At every turn, we see that executive compensation strategy is not only linked to corporate and business unit strategy, but driven by it. To demonstrate the point, I'd like to take you through the highlights of an executive compensation strategy study we recently conducted for a diversified corporation.

Figure 3   Compensation Packages

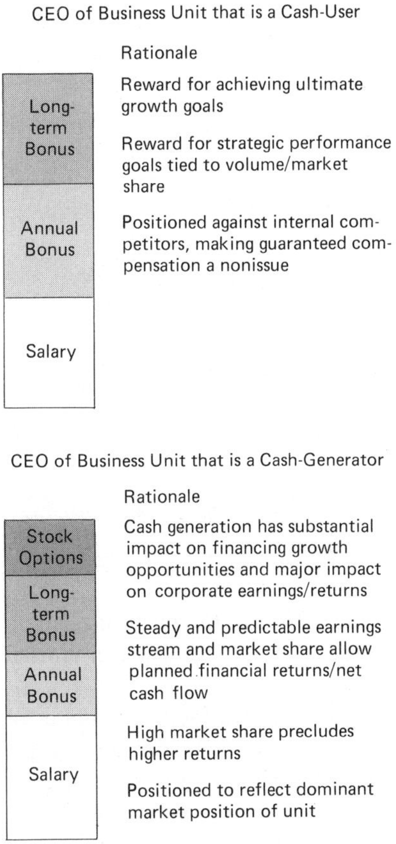

CEO of Business Unit that is a Cash-User

	Rationale
Long-term Bonus	Reward for achieving ultimate growth goals
	Reward for strategic performance goals tied to volume/market share
Annual Bonus	Positioned against internal competitors, making guaranteed compensation a nonissue
Salary	

CEO of Business Unit that is a Cash-Generator

	Rationale
Stock Options	Cash generation has substantial impact on financing growth opportunities and major impact on corporate earnings/returns
Long-term Bonus	Steady and predictable earnings stream and market share allow planned financial returns/net cash flow
Annual Bonus	
Salary	High market share precludes higher returns
	Positioned to reflect dominant market position of unit

EXECUTIVE COMPENSATION STRATEGY: REAL WORLD APPLICATION

After segmenting the corporation into its 10 businesses, we analyzed those units' revenue and net earnings growth; profitability, measured by ROI and earnings contribution; and competitive performance in terms of ROI and revenue growth. We discovered that the total corporate portfolio contained some growth businesses, several strong cash generators, and a number of marginal businesses that provided neither growth nor cash. In light of the corporation's profitability target of 15 percent after-tax ROI and 15 percent earnings growth target, the implication was clear (see Figure 4): *none* of the businesses met both the profitability and growth targets and only two exceeded the 15 percent growth target. Several met profitability targets only, and several were actually drains on overall operations.

Figure 4   *Portfolio of Businesses*

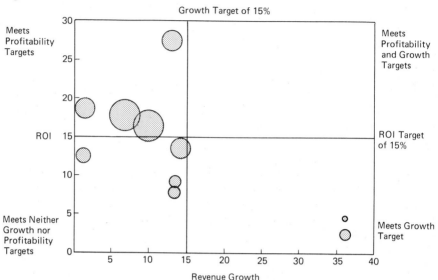

We discovered also a cash/growth imbalance. That is, the portfolio had an insufficient number of growth businesses in which to invest, resulting in unused debt capacity.

Turning to their executive compensation program, we found a number of dysfunctions in compensation practice stemming, primarily, from an archaic compensation philosophy. The program was traditional, with the bulk of cash compensation fixed on bonus leverage moderate. Long-term incentives were given in the form of performance units based on corporate EPS growth. Awards were small, unleveraged, and amounted to little value added.

The changes that were made in the executive compensation program were dictated by corporate strategy and goals, and by the portfolio of the various businesses.

The corporate goals over the next five years are to enhance the profitability of those businesses generating most of the earnings, invest in the fast-growth businesses, and turn around or divest several marginal businesses. In addition, major acquisitions will be sought to corrrect the cash/growth imbalance—i.e., the unused debt capacity will be employed to induce growth.

To realize these goals, *corporate* top management, which bears ultimate responsibility for overall risk, growth, and profitability, and for increasing value for shareholders, will need to identify and evaluate high-growth companies as acquisition candidates.

Top *operating* management will need to focus on the strategic management of their separate portfolios and on the performance of the businesses within those portfolios. They will need to address the internally focused goals—improving profit margins in the large, moderately profitable businesses by establishing highly cost-competitive positions in all businesses, exploring new distribution channels to build market share and spread overhead costs, and introducing new products to revive market demand; aggressively building market share for the high-growth businesses through new-product introduction and pricing strategies; and divesting those businesses with poor earnings or low-growth potential that drain corporate resources.

These roles dictated a market-driven compensation strategy that emphasized long-term incentives, namely, stock options and performance units, for both corporate and operating management. Stock options were reintroduced into the program.

The corporation mix recommended for *corporate* top management was salary and long-term incentive; annual bonus awards were to be modest, highly discretionary, and given only in recognition of incremental achievement of strategic portfolio goals. Long-term incentives would consist of both stock options and performance units, in roughly equal measure. The options will capture market appreciation and shareholder interest in tandem with performance units, which reward financial performance relative to earnings-per-share growth of selected competitors. A 4-year period of measurement was recommended. Total compensation will consist of salary (42 percent) and bonus (8 percent); the remaining 50 percent will consist of long-term growth bonus, and performance units (i.e., stock options with SARs).

The mix recommended for *operating* executives was salary plus annual bonus, to reward short-term performance, and long-term rewards in the form of long-term growth bonus and performance units, to recognize internal financial performance tied to market appreciation. Stock options are provided also to enable operating CEOs to take advantage of stock appreciation generated by their portfolio performance. A four-year measurement period was indicated (see Figure 5).

This complex executive compensation strategy, which is summarized here for reasons of confidentiality and space, is now being implemented. There is every indication that the components of this strategy are consistent with the corporation's long-term strategy.

Is this an exceptional case? Yes and no. Yes, in the sense of complexity, simultaneously adopting specific compensation strategy and then adjusting that strategy to reflect the new and more dynamic corporate and business strategies needed in the '80s. But no, in the sense of susceptibility to the theoretical approach I outlined earlier. Once we did the required internal and competitive financial analysis, the pieces of the compensation puzzle fell into place rather quickly, perhaps a bit more slowly than solving the *Sunday Times* crossword, but a light year ahead of realigning the colors of Rubik's Cube!

This is not to say that the approach outlined here uses set formulas to provide pat answers. Rather, it is a very sound technique for ensuring that compensation strategies reward those individuals who make the decisions and take the

Figure 5 *Profile of Strategy-Driven, Annual Executive Compensation Packages ($ Thousands)*

actions that will give the corporation a competitive edge in the '80s and carry it successfully into the new century.

The key requirement in developing a strategic executive compensation program is corporate and business unit strategy formulation. This provides the basis for resolving the "how much" issue; the size of total executive rewards is related to management task, and the "for what" issue: the tasks rewarded relate to corporate strategy.

The strategies identified here are critical to corporate and business unit success and, indeed, survival. They *must* form the basis for both short-and long-term incentive payment. Traditional compensation systems driven by "philosophy," "competitiveness," and "job evaluation" are archaic and unworkable in a strategically managed environment. Throughout the '80s success will belong to those companies which not only provide strategically driven levels of reward, but which also pay for strategic performance.

15

Strategy:
A Bureaucratic
and Political Process

RENATO MAZZOLINI
Columbia University

The aim of this paper is to develop a framework describing how corporate strategy is formed. The basic argument is that strategy is the product of set organizational processes plus key individuals' interventions.

We define *strategic decisions* as the commitments to action and the resource allocations that determine the field of activity of the firm—what endeavors to pursue, i.e., what goods or services it produces and what markets it serves. Strategic decisions also refer to how such endeavors are pursued in terms of the way key corporate resources are raised and allocated. These decisions are unstructured or nonrepetitive—as opposed to routine operating decisions.[1] This paper is an outgrowth of a study of strategic decision making conducted in Europe from 1975 to 1978.[2] In this study the first step was to formulate a model of how strategic decisions are made. This was derived from existing organizational politics and process literature. Then this model was tested empirically (304 interviews, in 123 organizations, primarily with CEOs). Our purpose here is not to report the findings of this study. Rather, it is to build on it to develop a theoretical construct of how strategic decisions are made.

The preeminent trait of organizational activity is its programmed character: It is the bureaucracy that governs most of the actions of the firm. This means that there is an inherent tendency to perpetuate the *status quo*. Organizations, however, do occasionally engage in novel kinds of actions. For this to occur, an intervening force must step in during the normal decision process. Such intervening forces are represented by individuals with influence on the firm's strategy.

We must be more specific about an enterprise's bureaucracy and the way strategy emerges from it. And about the role of key individuals and the way they interact with the bureaucracy to bring about strategic change.

I. THE BUREAUCRACY'S OUTPUTS

Notwithstanding intervening forces, the ongoing behavior of a firm is the product of organizational processes: Whereas the outcome of a strategic decision tends to be different each time (strategic decisions are decisions never "encountered in quite the same form and for which no predetermined and explicit set of ordered responses exists"),[3] the way a course of action is first elicited, then formulated and approved, and finally implemented, is determined by set procedures.

---

[1] J. L. Bower and Y. Doz, "Strategy Formulation: A Social and Political Process" (Working Paper, Division of Research, Harvard Business School, Boston, 1977), p. 10; and H. Mintzberg, D. Raisinghani, and A. Theoret, "The Structure of 'Unstructured' Decision Processes," *Administrative Science Quarterly*, 21 (June 1976), p. 246.

[2] R. Mazzolini, *Government-Controlled Enterprises* (Chichester: John Wiley, 1979).

[3] Mintzberg, Raisinghani, and Theoret, 'Structure of 'Unstructured' Decision Processes," p. 246.

A. Decisions—Need Identification

The information that causes a problem or an opportunity to be identified is collected and distilled according to certain agreed-upon procedures. Procedures are designed to gather, formalize, and transmit data according to standardized patterns, that is, collect and process the particular type of information that they are programmed for; the way the information is presented is equally determined by routines which thus influence the message conveyed by the information; and processes are responsible for appraising the information. Mintzberg found that "the need for a decision is identified as a difference between information on some actual situation and some expected standard."[4] This is comparable to Bower's concept of discrepancy. "The first step in a long process which ends with the expenditure of capital funds, begins when the routine demands of a facility-oriented job indicate the need for a new facility"[5]—when there is a "discrepancy" between performance expectations by the organization and actual results (or the results that are forecast given the type of activity in which the organization is currently involved). The identification of such differences or discrepancies rests upon routines and so does the determination of the standards: Standards evolve from a process—they are based on past trends, projected trends, standards in some comparable organization, the expectations of other people, and theoretical models.[6]

Certain opportunities and problem areas only are identified. A threat or an opportunity in an area on which SOPs do not gather information may long remain uncovered.

B. Search for Alternatives for Action

Processes are responsible for finding solutions. Set procedures trigger search and direct search toward particular areas. Not all theoretically possible avenues are considered. Rather, the actions contemplated are a limited set of alternatives selected according to a particular routine. This procedure seeks to follow known paths—the range of actions considered and the way these actions are investigated are outputs of set organizational processes. Precedents are accepted as binding.[7] The environment is scanned for familiar courses of action, and op-

[4]Ibid., p. 253.

[5]J. L. Bower, *Managing the Resource Allocation Process* (Boston: Division of Research, Harvard Business School, 1970), p. 50.

[6]W. F. Pounds, "The Process of Problem Finding," *Industrial Management Review,* Fall 1969, pp. 1–19.

[7]R. M. Cyert and J. G. March, "Organizational Factors in the Theory of Oligopoly," *Quarterly Journal of Economics,* 70 (1956), 52ff.

tions are appraised according to preestablished criteria.[8] The possibility of looking for an investment opportunity in an area in which the firm is not already involved does not usually come up. For this to occur, an initiating force must intervene.

Two questions must be asked.

First, *when* does search occur? Search can be triggered by a deterioration in the firm's performance or by an opportunity. Such an opportunity can be identified from within the firm (e.g., a division pushing for an extension of its field of activity) or by an outside unit (e.g., a bank).

Second, *how* does search occur? The way search is carried out and its stopping point are largely determined by organizational procedures. The way alternatives are looked for, the way the investigation process is conducted, and the way in which alternatives are evaluated are dependent on routines. Further, search is simple minded: It looks first at the neighborhood of problem symptoms, then at the neighborhood of the current alternative. This means that if a strategic problem arises, the search for alternatives to solve it will start by looking for a similar problem encountered in the past and go on by looking at what courses of action were used to solve that problem previously. Yet, given the nonrepetitive character of strategic problems, only rarely can familiar problems actually be found. So, familiar solutions are applied to new problems: Search looks for solutions within a rather limited range of alternatives for action known to the organization. Whatever the newness of the problem, the range of effective options tends to be limited to what the firm has done already or at least done partially in similar fashion.

The search process is fairly stable over the short run. It evolves however, over time, gradually improving as new situations are assimilated and experience is gained with particular types of problems.

Solutions are sought in a repertoire of known alternatives, and the routines for investigation and evaluation, while improved over time, normally do not change radically. Confronted with a performance deterioration, the organization will try to correct it with a course of action that was experienced elsewhere; confronted with an opportunity, it will tend to seek to exploit it via courses of action that have been used before.

As suggested earlier, for a radically new area of activity to be pursued, a force must intervene. This does not mean, however, that this force will necessarily have a bearing on what alternatives will be considered. Even when a new type of problem is raised by a force, that problem will be solved via conventional routes unless a force acts also on the search process *per se*. In other words, for a new route to be pursued, an initiating force not only has to cause the need for innovation to be felt but also has to actively promote a new route itself.

---

[8]Y. Aharoni, *The Foreign Investment Decision Process* (Boston: Division of Research, Harvard Business School, 1966), p. 42; and G. T. Allison, *Essence of Decision* (Boston: Little, Brown, 1971), p 79.

C. Investigation of Courses of Action

The data that are analyzed to appraise an alternative cannot be complete. It is practically impossible to look at all the factors that might have a bearing on the issue, since time and money as well as analytic capabilities are probably limited. Thus decisions have to be made on the basis of partial and selected information. And there has to be a procedure for gathering certain data rather than others. An investigation is carried out in successive phases with built-in check points, and data are collected, processed, and evaluated according to distinct patterns: Information is increasingly elaborate as one goes on in the process, and more and more precise rules are used to evaluate it.[9]

When a new type of alternative is considered, the investigation is by necessity often ill adopted. Misevaluations and errors tend to be inevitable. Forces cannot determine this phase of decision making. Still, they can occasionally step in and correct one aspect of the process or another.

D. Approval

It is difficult to determine at what point and by whom a decision is made.[10] A decision to follow a particular course of action evolves over time as resources are allocated to define and refine the particular course. Thus decisions themselves are outputs of organizational processes: The very conception and elaboration of an alternative involve a progressive decision to pursue that very alternative; as a course is investigated, there is a cumulative process of individual and organizational commitments to pursue it. The key issue is not who made a particular decision to allocate certain resources to a given action but what conditions created commitments resulting in the acceptance or rejection of that action.[11]

When a new type of strategy is considered, there are no procedures specially tailored to appraise it. It is existing procedures that must be employed. Thus a reviewing unit may simply not get involved and indeed may be skipped altogether. Alternatively, a reviewing unit gets involved no matter what. Approval is then cumbersome. A good illustration is that of a government-controlled enterprise.[12] Many such companies are accountable to state-owned holding companies. Their plans are thus first integrated in the overall plan of the holding. This plan is then submitted to the ministry for state holdings. The ministry in turn presents a report to parliament. In addition, certain special organizations be-

---

[9]Aharoni, *Foreign Investment Decision Process,* p. 37.

[10]Bower, *Managing the Resource Allocation Process.*

[11]Aharoni, *Foreign Investment Decision Process.*

[12]Mazzolini, *Government-Controlled Enterprises.*

come involved—e.g., regional development agencies, interministerial committees for price controls, industrial planning departments. For new types of actions, delays on decisions can run as high as thirty-four months.[13] Granted this is an extreme case, but large diversified firms can be expected to run into similar problems with novel kinds of decisions. It is only with experience that approval becomes swifter as routines are adapted to appraise new courses.

Furthermore, the pace and effectiveness of change is dependent on the degree to which the proposed change affects the expectations of many suborganizations. In particular, a shift in strategy entailing the discontinuance of a given course of action will be all the more difficult to accomplish when it entails upsetting several suborganizations' expectations that are satisfied up to that point.

E. Implementation

The accomplishment of an action plan rests on set procedures. Organizations have a limited range of things they know how to do—they know how to do what they have been doing already. Each suborganization has a finite set of routinized programs of action which it has learned "by doing." Over time, via a process of incremental learning whereby organizational units change adaptively as the result of experience, relative efficiency is reached—i.e., suborganizations adopt patterns of behavior that are relatively effective in performing the task expected of them.[14] This, however, is only true until the overall posture of the total organization remains stable. But when a new path is sought, organizational units will, at least initially, perform according to patterns of behavior with which they are familiar. Considerable distortion can therefore result between plan and action. "Projects that demand that existing organizational units depart from their established programs to perform unprogrammed tasks are rarely accomplished in their designed form. Projects that require coordination of the programs of several organizations are rarely accomplished as designed."[15] Indeed if a plan requires the concerted action of several units, it will be accomplished less effectively than if it can be handled in quasi-independence by one or a few units. The organization's structure is thus a key variable. Mazzolini found that a foreign expansion strategy is a case in point.[16] If a company is organized with an international division, the strategy is implemented relatively smoothly because it is handled for the most part autonomously by the division without need for much concertation with the rest of the organization. If the structure is, say, a functional

---

[13]Mazzolini, "The International Strategic Behavior of Government-Controlled Enterprises: Hypotheses and Some Evidence" (Paper presented at the "State-owned Enterprises" Conference, Harvard University, 1979).

[14]R. M. Cyert and J. G. March, *A Behavioral Theory of the Firm* (Englewood Cliffs, N.J.: Prentice-Hall, 1963).

[15]Allison, *Essence of Decision,* pp. 93–94.

[16]Mazzolini, *Government-Controlled Enterprises.*

one with no separate unit for foreign operations, the entire organization is likely to be affected by the strategy. Extensive coordination is required among suborganizations and considerable inefficiencies in implementation are typical—especially in the early stages of the strategy.

II. THE POLITICS OF LEADERSHIP

In this standardized context, top management has three major roles.

First, substantive interventions.[17] While strategic behavior does rely on set processes if the organization's scope and posture are to remain unchanged, a shift in strategy must be originated by active leadership. This is the case when a new type of opportunity is to be uncovered and when a new solution is to be pursued. There are three types of situations:[18]

A highly visible exogenous event (e.g., the oil crisis) calling a key executive's attention to a particular new type of activity

An outside force (e.g., a consultant) actively eliciting interest in a novel opportunity

A new kind of expertise being introduced in an organization (e.g., an individual with an international background pushing for foreign expansion)

Particularly when key individuals involve themselves in the development of a specific action plan, they heavily tint the output of the search process. Moreover, intervening forces can step in in one part of the process or another. They can correct inadequacies of the planning process, those of the investigation or implementation phases, and try to expedite approval by acting on one reviewing unit or another.

Second, shaping the process. A key function of leaders is to shape and reshape the structure in a manner that causes subunits to behave in a particular way rather than another.[19] Managing the structural context—the formal organization, the information, control, measure of performance, and reward and punishment systems—thus becomes a key to influencing strategy.[20] Aharoni found that suborganizations are often created to pay special attention to a neglected problem.[21] If top management feels that a given type of activity should receive

[17]Bower and Doz, "Strategy Formulation," p. 24.

[18]Mazzolini, "International Strategic Behavior."

[19]Bower, *Managing the Resource Allocation Process.*

[20]Bower and Doz, "Strategy Formulation."

[21]Aharoni, *Foreign Investment Decision Process,* p. 93.

special attention and be considered as part of the normal fields of endeavor of the firm, a special unit responsible for that activity may be created. This increases the range of options available to the organization, for the new unit will time and again propose an alternative for action in the field it is responsible for. This will also affect the probabilities of actual resource allocations in that area, for the unit will also generate data tailored to make the selection of its proposals more likely.

Third, in the decision itself to pursue a course of action. As argued above, commitments are built up around a particular strategy as its feasibility and attractiveness are investigated and analyzed. Top management has to give its approval for such investigation and analysis. The more it approves, the greater the commitments, and the higher the likelihood that the particular course will in fact be pursued.

Thus leadership's options for shifting organizational behavior include (1) "triggering program A rather than program B within a repertoire [i.e., the list of programs relevant to a type of activity], (2) triggering existing organizational routines in a new context, (3) triggering several different [organizational units'] programs simultaneously. Additional leeway can be won by feeding an issue to one component of an organization rather than another; for example, raising a strategic issue in a budgetary guise or vice versa. Over the long run, leaders can create new organizations. Occasionally, they may even effect deliberate change in organizations by manipulating the factors that support existing organizational tendencies."[22]

Still, leaders are not a unified group. "Rather, each individual in this group is, in his own right, a player in a central, competitive game. The name of the game is politics: bargaining along regularized circuits among players positioned hierarchically within the organization."[23] Leadership is not the product of a rational solution to a problem but rather the result of pulling and hauling, compromise and confusion between key individuals pursuing different ends and with different degrees of influence.

We ought to be more specific.

A. Who Are The Players?

The players are individuals whose interests and actions have a bearing on the organization's behavior. Within the firm, essentially top managers, staff people who can influence top management, and "executors"—people in the field in charge of executing plans. And outsiders: key government people with a say in business decisions, union leaders, members of the press or public opinion spokesmen, and suppliers—bankers as well as major customers.

[22]Allison, *Essence of Decision,* p. 87.

[23]Ibid., p. 144.

B. What Determines
a Player's Stand?

A player's stand consists of an individual's attitude or posture vis-à-vis the issue under consideration. This hinges upon two elements.

1. Perception of the situation. This depends first on the player's position. The task each player is responsible for encourages him or her to focus primarily on certain types of problems. Specialized attention to particular problems will cause a player to be sensitive only to those issues involving such problems. This responsibility-influenced perception will be enchanced by factors such as selective information available to the person who occupies a particular position, group pressures within the suborganization in which the individual finds himself or herself, or the rewards and punishments attached to that position.

Second, an individual's own intellectual abilities and knowledge (e.g., training) will cause him or her to see problems in one way rather than another. Cultural or social factors are also important. Moreover, their role in other games distorts players' perceptions. Individuals are influenced not only by other organizational games in which they are involved but also by their roles outside the organization.[24]

2. Stakes. These are the potential benefits or losses individuals can expect from the outcome of a situation. First, players' goals and interests directly related to the issue under consideration. While there is usually a consensus on broad issues—e.g., return on investment—there is generally disagreement about specifics—what actual steps to take or how to accomplish such steps. Second, goals and interests as they relate to other games. Players are normally engaged in many different though overlapping games simultaneously. A move in one game often affects the course of other games and players' posture in them. Not infrequently are such indirect consequences more important to a player than the outcome of the event itself. Third, goals and interests as they relate to motives that are not directly connected with the life of the organization in which they arise. Players' activities outside the organization involve the building up of commitments to other organizations as well as to other individuals. Such commitments influence the stands players take on company affairs.

C. What Determines
Each Player's Power?

A player's power is his or her ability to influence the outcome of the games in which that player is involved. Since the overall behavior of an organization emerges from the aggregation of the various simultaneous and overlapping

---

[24]Aharoni, *Foreign Investment Decision Process.*

games played in the organization, a player's power in the context of the total organization is his or her capacity to affect the doings of the total organization.

There are at least seven sources of power: (1) formal authority stemming from a given position, (2) the ability to review and veto others' decisions, (3) direct control of resources necessary to carry out action, (4) control over vital information, (5) vital expertise for planning and implementing action,[25] (6) direct access to other players with power plus the ability to modify their behavior, and (7) personal traits such as charm or credibility based, say, on professional reputation or academic titles.

D. What Are The Rules of The Game?

Organizational politics do not occur in a disorderly, random, and confused way. Rather, they take place in a regularized fashion. Orderliness stems from set codes and principles and methods for the conduct of political activities. First among these are action-channels—"regularized means of taking [organizational] action on a specific kind of issue."[26] An action channel is a course through which influence may be moved and directed to yield actual organizational behavior.

Furthermore, politics follow certain rules determining what should and should not be done. Certain rules are explicit, others implicit; some are stable, others changing; some are clear, others fuzzy. Written rules include not only legal codes, statutes, and bylaws but also the formal organizational structure and each position's authority as well as formal "orders" or operating guidelines or procedures (e.g., the requirements imposed by the budget). Tacit rules include economic and cultural norms both within the company and within general codes of good conduct.

E. What Is The Game?

How are players' actions combined to yield organizational behavior?

1. How is an issue raised?   Except in the case of a major event raising a glaring opportunity or threat, most problems are defined "actively": The matter of whether to pursue a new course stems from the conscious, deliberate positioning of the existing strategic posture.

An issue arises thanks to one or several individuals proposing a new idea for action. Individuals may have an idea for a variety of reasons—from personal to company or outside motives. For example, a division manager can make a proposal for his or her division, which has important implications for the overall

[25]Andrew Pettigrew and Enid Mumford, *Implementing Strategic Decisions* (London: Longmans, 1975), p. 109.

[26]Allison, *Essence of Decision,* p. 169.

strategy of the firm; or the manager can even directly formulate ideas that directly concern the total enterprise. Depending on their standing in the organization, such individuals will command more or less attention to issues they raise.

2. How is an issue forwarded once it is raised?   An action is proposed by one or several players who champion it. The proposed action then typically attracts others who give it their support. Widespread backing is normally necessary for a novel, complex, or controversial idea to make its way and be pursued. Thus coalitions are formed. These are temporary alliances among individuals from many origins, functions, responsibilities, and interests, for the purpose of fostering the adoption or pursuit of particular decisions or actions. While all members of the coalition back the same basic idea, their motives may be quite varied. Generally those who proposed the issue in the first place have interests closest to the issue *per se*. Supporters are more likely to be motivated by the side effects of the proposed decision and action—i.e., the byproducts in terms of the consequences for them in other games or their own personal endeavors. In particular, they can join a coalition merely to help other coalition members for the simple purpose of doing them a favor which they hope they will be paid back in one form or another.

3. What is the structure of the game?   Power, responsibilities, and judgments are shared among several players. This basic fact conditions the overall way decisions are taken. Decisions and actions are not taken as choices of a unified group, nor are they the product of a formal summary of leaders' preferences. Instead they result from bargaining among players, each fighting for his or her own point of view. And the adoption of a course of action is not a function of what might objectively appear the most efficient means of reaching an aim or the objectively optimal way to solve a problem. Rather, it is a function of political resultants: the result of power plays and settlements (or quasi-settlements) of differences among players. A particular decision can be the product of one player's (or one group of players') standpoint. Generally, however, a compromise has to be reached between various points of view, and what is finally done often does not correspond to anybody's original idea: Ultimate behavior is a collage of partial demands and ideas of players who see different faces of the issue and pursue different ends.

4. Implementation.   When a decision about an organization's behavior is reached formally, the larger game is by no means over. For relatively minor or operating issues, decisions by leaders can be ignored altogether. This is rarely the case for strategic issues. Yet there is considerable room for interpretation in terms of the accomplishment of a decision. The chances of slippage are considerable, since many players are involved and opportunities for close control of each more eleatory.

Three points are especially critical.

First, how specific is the formal decision? In particular, the most controversial issues require strong backing; promoters need to secure the most widespread support possible. To do this, it is often necessary to leave some ambiguity around the proposed action and its reasons. Clearly, however, the more vague the decision, the greater the opportunity for distortion of what was originally intended. This is particularly serious for decisions that are taken at the top of an organization and that involve the functions of the entire organization. Top managers or leaders then take the formal decisions but have to delegate not only most of the implementation but also most of the implementation's control. Deciders themselves, therefore, cannot even monitor how others put their decisions into practice and have to rely on intermediaries to do so. The task of controlling a decision's accomplishment for someone who has not taken it is particularly arduous when the decision's formulation is fuzzy. Even in the best of all cases, when intermediaries are genuinely committed to making sure the decision gets implemented as intended, they may fail in their mission simply because of the vagueness of the prescriptions they are to monitor.

Second, who is to accomplish the decision? Some decisions are quite specific in this respect. Others are vague. For example, a multidivision company's top management may decide that a particular diversification is desirable. If it is not made clear what division ought to pursue this line, considerable room for debate will be left. One can expect a new game to develop once the decision to diversify *per se* has been reached. There will first be the resurgence of the old opponents of diversification, who will try to delay action and to foster the wrong kind of action. In so doing, they both hope to delay what they see as an undesirable outcome and to generate enough ill will about the practical aspects of the decision so that it may be revoked or abandoned or at least revised. Further, there will be various players fighting to get the action assigned to those individuals or that organization which they consider most fit to achieve their expected results. Thus several leaders of divisions may have supported the general decision to diversify. Once it comes to settling which division should actually do so, there may be considerable divergence of opinion, various division heads arguing that their own division should be the main vehicle for diversification.

Third, what about normal foul-ups? To repeat, organizational action is a blend of formal decisions and agglomerations of quasi-independent actions of players. In the formulation stage of a given pattern of behavior, formal decisions obviously prevail. Usually, for strategic decisions, relatively few players are involved, and communication between them is relatively effective, thus avoiding too many misunderstandings and blunders. In the implementation stage, however, it is the actions of many individuals that are critical. Over and beyond any attempt by such individuals to manipulate the decision, some errors, miscommunications, and omissions are inevitable. This again is all the more likely for those decisions whose accomplishment calls for the mobilization of the entire organization. The difficulty of making sure that the actions of the many individuals concerned are consistent is exacerbated by the simultaneity and interdependence of the many games involved. The information that has relevance is so vast and comes from so many sides that it can be absorbed but scantily: Due to the many interlockings of the games, the flow of pertinent communication is so dense that it is by necessity elliptic and thus often ambiguous, and it takes place in such a noisy environment that parts of it are inevitably lost. Indeed, considerable misperception, miscommunication, and misinformation are a standard part of any organization's functioning.

III. CONCLUSION

Our framework is summarized in the following exhibit.

Unless leadership actively intervenes, it is a firm's bureaucracy that determines its strategy. This means the existing strategic posture tends to be perpetu-

Exhibit

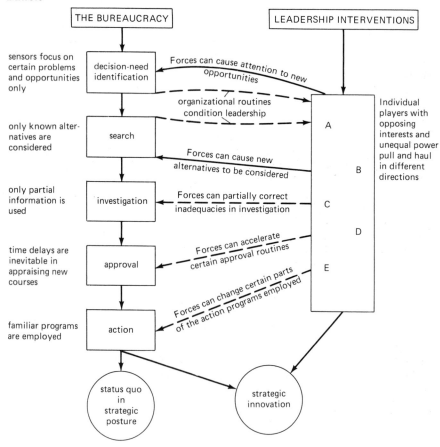

ated. To understand how decisions are made, one must explain the functioning of organizational processes. Thus, to understand what will trigger search, one has to look at what information routines are designed to collect and process; to understand what alternatives will be considered in given circumstances, one has to look at what past circumstances are closest to the present ones and what was done then, and so forth.

It is only when an influential force intervenes that a novel course of action may be pursued. Therefore one must analyze which such forces have influence to cause an organization to look at new types of strategies, and one must understand how these forces emerge. This means uncovering key players' identity—their position, their personality, and their preferences. And one must display the interfaces between players often pulling and hauling in different directions—the power plays, the give and take, the cabals, the collusions and intrigues. Furthermore, one must account for the confusion and foul-ups that also make up the political game from which forces result.

Yet, one must not lost sight of the fact that while forces can indeed provide the impetus for new problems or opportunities and courses of action to be considered, their influence beyond that is critically conditioned by existing processes. Leaders themselves are constrained by the bureaucratic setting. On the one hand, set procedures condition the type of information players get and the nature of the interfaces between them. On the other, leaders must rely on existing routines for the implementation of their decisions. Once a novel idea for action is introduced, standard procedures must take over, players having but limited influence on what happens in the accomplishment of a plan: Decisions are carried out via familiar programs and leaders can only intervene occasionally to amend but certain aspects of these programs.

REFERENCES

1. AHARONI, Y., *The Foreign Investment Decision Process.* Boston: Division of Research, Harvard Business School, 1966.
2. AIKEN, MICHAEL, and JERALD HAGE, "Organizational Interdependence and Intraorganizational Structure," *American Sociological Review,* 33 (December 1968), 912–30.
3. ALLEN, S., "Organizational Choices and General Management Influence Networks in Divisionalized Companies," *Academy of Management Journal,* Vol. 21, 341–65.
4. ALLISON, G. T., *Essence of Decision,* Boston: Little, Brown, 1971.
5. ANDERSON, C., and F. PAINE, "Managerial Perceptions and Strategic Behavior," *Academy of Management Journal,* 18 (December 1975), 811–23.
6. ANSOFF, H. I., *Corporate Strategy,* New York: McGraw-Hill, 1965.
7. BLAU, P. M., *Exchange and Power in Social Life,* New York: John Wiley, 1964.

8. BOURGEOIS, L. J., "Economic Performance and Dominant Coalition Agreement on Means versus Ends in Second Order Strategy Making," Academy of Management Proceedings, San Francisco, 1978, pp. 101–6.

9. BOWER, J. L., Managing the Resource Allocation Process. Boston: Division of Research, Harvard Business School, 1970.

10. BOWER, J. L., and Y. DOZ, "Strategy Formulation: A Social and Political Process." Working Paper, Division of Research, Harvard Business School, Boston, 1977.

11. CANNON, J. T., Business Strategy and Policy. New York: Harcourt Brace, 1968.

12. CARTER, E., "The Behavioral Theory of the Firm and Top-Level Corporate Decisions," Administrative Science Quarterly (1971), pp. 413–28.

13. CHANDLER, A. D., Strategy and Structure. Cambridge, Mass.: M.I.T. Press, 1962.

14. CHRISTENSEN, C. R., K. R. ANDREWS and J. L. BOWER, Business Policy Text and Cases. Homewood, Ill.: 1973.

15. CROZIER, MICHEL, The Bureaucratic Phenomenon. London: Tavistock, 1964.

16. CYERT, R. M., and J. G. MARCH, "Organizational Factors in the Theory of Oligopoly," Quarterly Journal of Economics, 70 (1956), 52ff.

17. CYERT, R. M., and J. G. MARCH, A Behavioral Theory of the Firm. Englewood Cliffs, N.J.: Prentice-Hall, 1963.

18. DAHL, R. H., "The Concept of Power," Behavioral Science, 2 (1957), 201–18.

19. DEWEY, J., How We Think, Boston: Heath, 1933.

20. GODWIWALLA, W. M., W. A. MAINHART, W. D. WARDE, "Strategic Configurations and Influence Mixes of Organizational Functions for Overall Corporate Strategy." Academy Management Proceedings, San Francisco, 1978, pp. 111–15.

21. GUTH, W. D., "Formulating Organizational Objectives and Strategy: A Systematic Approach," Journal of Business Policy, Fall 1971, pp. 24–31.

22. GUTH, W. D., "Toward A Social System Theory of Corporate Strategy," Journal of Business, 49 (July 1976), pp. 374–88.

23. HALL, R. H., "Intraorganizational Structural Variation: Application of the Bureaucratic Model," Administrative Science Quarterly, 7 (December 1962), 366–76.

24. HALL, R. H., "The Concept of Bureaucracy: An Empirical Assessment," American Journal of Sociology, 69 (July 1963), 32–40.

25. HARSANYI, J., "Some Social Science Implications of a New Approach to Game Theory," in Strategic Interaction and Conflict, ed. K. Archibald, p.i. Berkeley: University of California Press, 1966.

26. HILSMAN, ROGER, To Move a Nation, New York: Doubleday, 1967.

27. KATZ, R. L., Cases and Concepts in Corporate Strategy. Englewood Cliffs, N.J.: Prentice-Hall, 1970.

28. LINDBLOM, CHARLES, *The Policy-Making Process.* Englewood Cliffs, N.J.: Prentice-Hall, 1968.

29. LITSCHERT, ROBERT, and T. W. BONHAM, "A Conceptual Model of Strategy Formulation," *Academy of Management Review,* 3 (April 1978), 211–19.

30. MACMILLAN, IAN., *Strategy Formulation: Political Concepts.* St. Paul, Minn.: West, 1978.

31. MARCH, J. G., and H. A. SIMON, *Organizations.* New York: Graduate School of Industrial Administration, Carnegie Institute of Technology, 1959.

32. MAYES, B., and R. W. ALLEN, "Toward a Definition of Organizational Politics," *Academy of Management Review,* 2 (October 1977), 672–78.

33. MAZZOLINI, R., *Government-Controlled Enterprises.* Chichester: John Wiley 1979.

34. MAZZOLINI, R., "The International Strategic Behavior of Government-Controlled Enterprises: Hypotheses and Some Evidence." Paper presented at the "State-owned Enterprises" Conference, Harvard University 26–28, 1979.

35. MINTZBERG, H., *The Nature of Managerial Work.* New York: Harper and Row, 1973.

36. MINTZBERG, H., "Policy as a Field of Management Theory," *Academy of Management Review,* II (January 1977), 88–103.

37. MINTZBERG, H., D. RAISINGHANI, and A. THEORET, "The Structure of 'Unstructured' Decision Processes," *Administrative Science Quarterly,* 21 (June 1976), 246–75.

38. NEUSTADT, RICHARD, *Presidential Power.* New York: John Wiley, 1976.

39. NEWMAN, WILLIAM, "Intra-organizational Politics." Graduate School of Business, Columbia University, New York, 1975.

40. NEWMAN, W. H., and J. P. LOGAN, *Strategy, Policy, and Central Management,* Cincinnati: South-Western Publishing Company, 1976.

41. NEWMAN, WILLIAM, and KIRBY WARREN, *The Process of Management.* Englewood Cliffs, N.J.: Prentice-Hall, 1977.

42. OUCHI, W., "The Transmission of Control through Organizational Hierarchy," *Academy of Management Journal,* 21 (June 1978), 178–92.

43. PETTIGREW, ANDREW, *The Politics of Organizational Decision-Making.* London: Tavistock, 1973.

44. PETTIGREW, ANDREW, and ENID MUMFORD, *Implementing Strategic Decisions.* London: Longmans, 1975.

45. PFEFFER, T., and G. R. SALANCIK, *Organizational Decision-Making.* London: Tavistock, 1973.

46. PFEFFER, T., G. R. SALANICK, and H. LEBLEBICI, "The Effect of Uncertainty on the Use of Social Influence in Organizational Decision Making," *Administrative Science Quarterly,* 21 (1976), 227–45.

47. POUNDS, W. F., "The Process of Problem Finding," *Industrial Management Review,* Fall 1969, pp. 1–19.

48. QUINN, JAMES, "Strategic Goals: Process and Politics," *Sloan Management Review,* 19, No. 1 (Fall 1977).

49. SAYLES, L. R., *Managerial Behavior: Administration in Complex Organizations.* New York: McGraw-Hill, 1964.

50. SCHELLING, T., *The Strategy of Conflict.* New York: 1960.

51. SCHILLING, W., P. HAMMOND, and G. SNYDER, *Strategy, Politics and Defense Budgets.* New York: Columbia University Press, 1962.

52. SIMON, H. A., *The Shape of Automation.* New York: Harper & Row, 1963.

53. SIMON, H. A., *Administrative Behavior.* New York: Free Press, 1976.

54. SALANICK, G. R., and J. PFEFFER, "The Bases and Use of Power in Organizational Decision Making: The Case of the University," *Administrative Science Quarterly,* 19, No. 4 (1974), 453–73.

55. TUSHMAN, MICHAEL, "A Political Approach to Organizations: A Review and Rationale," *Academy of Management Review,* April 1977.

56. TWOMEY, D. F., "The Effects of Power Proportion on Conflict Resolution, *Academy of Management Review,* 3 (January 1978), 144–50.

57. UYTERHOEVEN, H. E. R., E. W. ACKERMAN, and J. W. ROSENBLUM, *Strategy and Organization.* Homewood, Ill.: Richard D. Irwin, 1973.

58. WILDAVSKY, A., "Budgeting as a Political Process," in *The International Encyclopedia of the Social Sciences,* ed. David L. Sills, pp. 192–99. New York: Crowell, Collier and Macmillan, 1968.

59. ZALEZNIK, A., "Power and Politics in Organizational Life," *Harvard Business Review,* 48, No. 3 (1970), 47–60.

16

Directors' Responsibility for Corporate Strategy

KENNETH R. ANDREWS
Harvard University

This article is adapted from a talk given by the author to a *Business Week* conference on corporate strategy and the board of directors in New York City, October 14, 1980.

The strengthening of the corporate board of directors has not yet produced a clear or widely accepted conclusion about the board's role in formulating, ratifying, changing, or evaluating corporate strategy. Discussion of this subject among chief executive officers (who are often also board chairmen) does not thrive.

Previous articles in *From the Boardroom*—for instance, Samuel M. Felton's "Case of the Board and the Strategic Process"[1] and William W. Wommack's "The Board's Most Important Function"[2]—produced little response. Not much has been said elsewhere. Audit committees, compensation committees, and social responsibility committees have all become commonplace, yet the pressures bringing them into being have only rarely produced strategy committees.

We do not have to look far to find out why. Many chief executive officers, rejecting the practicality of conscious strategy, preside over unstated, incremental, or intuitive strategies that have never been articulated or analyzed—and therefore could not be deliberated by the board. Others do not believe their outside directors know enough or have time enough to do more than assent to strategic recommendations. Still others may keep discussions of strategy within management to prevent board transgression onto management turf and consequent reduction of executives' power to shape by themselves the future of their companies.

Few chairmen whom I have encountered in my experience, research, or correspondence share the wish of Robert A. Charpie, president of Cabot Corporation, to "see a board 100% involved."[3] Able, amiable, and competent as they are, even fewer chairmen want to undertake the work and turmoil required to make such involvement useful.

But even if strategy were not such a sensitive topic, invoking latent tension between CEO and independent directors, it would require more time and sophistication than chairmen or outside directors, however willing, could easily summon to the task. At best, original contribution by outside directors is limited and infrequent. Nonetheless, the forces shaping corporate governance, including restlessness among independent directors, are pressing boards toward greater participation in determining the future direction and character of their companies.

I will make a careful statement now that, however harmless it looks, will certainly not win the commitment of most chief executives for some time:

A responsible and effective board should require of its management a unique and durable corporate strategy, review it periodically for its validity, use it as the reference point for all other board decisions, and share with management the risks associated with its adoption.

---

[1]HBR July–August 1979, p. 20.

[2]HBR September–October 1979, p. 48.

[3]Quoted in HBR July–August 1979, p. 26.

WHAT CORPORATE STRATEGY IS

Virtually every word of so summary a statement requires definition before the statement can be fully understood. By the fashionable phrase, "corporate strategy," for example, I mean the pattern of company purposes and goals—and the major policies for achieving those goals—that defines the business or businesses the company is to be involved with and the kind of company it is to be.

A statement articulating corporate purpose differentiates the company in some way from all its competitors and stems from a perception of present and future market opportunities, distinctive competence, competitive advantage, available resources, and management's personal aspirations and values.

Corporate strategy reconciles what a company might do in terms of opportunity, what it can do in terms of its strengths, what its management wants it to do, and what it thinks is ethical, legal, and moral.

This concept of strategy thus involves economic, social, and personal purposes—not financial objectives alone. Although it evolves with the development of markets, company strengths, and institutional values, corporate strategy marks out a deliberately chosen direction and governs directly the investment decisions, organization structure, incentive systems, and indeed the essential character of the company. It embodies a disciplined unity of purpose, a purpose which—to be powerful—must be clear and worthy of the commitment of energetic and intelligent people.[4]

Such a concept of strategy makes an important contribution to management. It forces continuous sensitivity to changes taking place in the company's environment and resources. It requires managers to lay conflicting personal agendas on the table and to look beyond immediate opportunities toward long-term growth and development. Such strategy summons up imagination, innovation, and a zest for risk; and it focuses the work of specialists as well.

The concept of corporate strategy has its shortcomings, as well, for it demands tough, high-risk commitment to a choice of direction. Because it means that a company must sometimes forgo immediate profits for long-term superiority, it can seem inconvenient. For instance, an acquisition that raises current earnings per share but has no future fit with either market development or distinctive competence will be ruled out. Corporate strategy demands that companies examine carefully the muted demands of the future and suppress the clamor of the present.

In both business and government, "muddling through" is the classic response to politically confused decisions about purpose. It has its proponents not only among practitioners but also among scholars. The coalition theory of R.M. Cyert and J.G. March substitutes internal bargaining among special interests for corporate strategy—on the assumption that organizations do not have purposes;

---

[4]For a fuller description, see my book, *The Concept of Corporate Strategy,* revised edition (Homewood, Ill.: Dow Jones–Irwin, 1980).

only people do.[5] David Baybrooke and Charles E. Lindblom, without so much as a smile, call their view of purposeless organization "disjointed incrementalism."[6] And in 1967 H. Edward Wrapp published his beguiling but no less anti-strategic "Good Managers Don't Make Policy Decisions."[7]

If a management group cannot decide on a loftier or more practical purpose than adapting to whatever comes, improvisation becomes its limited strategy and the planning horizon closes in. Should this occur, the board must look for an early breakout—even demanding new leadership if necessary—before its company flunks out of national and international competition.

WHY REQUIRE A CORPORATE STRATEGY?

My argument thus far has been that it is better for corporate management to have a strategy than not. But why should a board concern itself with the strategy's content? I submit four principal reasons:

First, the board needs specific evidence that its management has a process for developing, considering, and choosing among strategic alternatives operating within the company.

Second, especially if they have no personal experience in the industry, independent directors need to understand the characteristics of their company's business. Knowledge of strategy makes intelligent overview feasible.

Third, knowing the company's strategy can give the board a reference point for separate decisions that come before it and insight into what matters should be presented to it. If their approval is to be more than routine assent, board members must be allowed to assess the impact of proposals—whether for capital appropriation, a new R&D facility, or an acquisition in an exchange of stock—on their company's strategy.

If management can answer the directors' questions about the strategic impact of a single proposal, the directors will be reassured not only about the soundness of that proposal but also about the continuing objectivity of management. Through a series of specific questions related to management's stated intentions, the board can prevent the company from straying off its strategic course, without resorting to overcautious conservatism.

The *fourth* reason for directors to insist not only that a company have an explicit strategy but also that it present the strategy to them is that evaluation of

[5]R.M. Cyert and J.G. March, *A Behavioral Theory of the Firm* (Englewood Cliffs, N.J.: Prentice-Hall, 1963).

[6]David Baybrooke and Charles E. Lindblom, *A Strategy of Decision* (New York: The Free Press, 1963).

[7]H. Edward Wrapp, "Good Managers Don't Make Policy Decisions," HBR September–October 1967, p. 91.

corporate strategy and of management's adherence to it allows continuous evaluation of management.

Short-term measures are unsatisfactory for evaluation. The best criterion for appraising the quality of management performance, in the absence of personal failures or unexpected breakdowns, is management's success over time in executing a demanding and approved strategy that is continually tested against opportunity and need. The combination of short-term return and long-term investment can only be evaluated over several years.

How to interpret windfall advantages and undeserved misfortune—and to judge skill against results—becomes straightforward when a board can observe executive performance against a consciously considered and explicitly stated corporate strategy. Discussion of strategic issues in the context of the company reveals executives' quality of mind and depth of judgment and gives directors a foundation for later interpretation of results.

ROLE IN STRATEGY DEVELOPMENT

How should the board participate in the development of strategy? This is a tough question to answer. A board does not formulate strategy; its function is *review*—a word as slippery in meaning as it is soft in sound.

If the reviews process leads the board to approve corporate actions, the board must stand behind its assent. This support entails sharing with the CEO the risks of the decisions it approves, and the board should not approve decisions until it is fully willing to accept those risks.

The review process, by which a management recommendation wins rather than coerces board approval, begins only after full-scale presentation of strategy to the board. The process resumes, as indicated earlier, whenever a capital appropriation, unexpected shortfall, or other strategically important matter comes before the board.

Review is principally discussion sparked by questions and answers. The rejected alternatives are discussed until the directors are satisfied that the process which produced the recommendation was thorough. Discussion concludes in consensus, either to approve or to support withdrawal of the recommendation. The degree to which the directors are convinced that the recommendation meets the strategic tests applied to it in advance affects their subsequent loyalty to the CEO if and when the project fails.

However, review of strategic recommendations goes beyond establishing the board's satisfaction with the strategic process. For example, a publishing house decided that, because of the progress of information technology, it should expand beyond a solely book-producing orientation. At a board meeting, the president proposed the acquisition of two small supplier companies involved in electronically accessible data bases. The entrepreneurial founders of the data base companies were present at the publisher's board meeting to discuss the synergy that would be made possible by the acquisition. An urbane, high-speed summary of the proposed acquisition, allegedly backed by extensive management inquiry, produced the board's expected affirmative vote—which was apparently justified strategically.

After the meeting, two of the outside directors (who had asked questions and received "answers") met at the elevator. Without speaking, they both shook their heads. Each had formed a negative opinion about the education, breadth, competence, and integrity of the entrepreneurs and about the future of the publishing company if these people became part of management. Subsequent to the acquisition, the two subsidiaries were eventually disbanded for reasons that appeared to justify—at least in the view of these skeptical directors—the wholly unexplored and uncertain distrust they had felt when the board made its original "strategic" decision.

Of course, the outcome might still have been the same, even had the consideration of these small acquisitions been more extensive. Perhaps the judgment, skill, and practice required for such a major decision were lacking among both management and the board.

Nonetheless, hindsight makes clear that the board's discussion should have led to further consideration of the proposal and to more skeptical appraisal of the two data base proprietors. The directors' questions, which could not have been wholly clear in the presence of the visitors, should have led management to realize that it needed better answers and that it needed to withdraw the proposal until it understood the import of the questions and had gotten those answers.

Special full-scale strategy reviews.   A director cannot be incisive and influential unless he or she is familiar with the issues involved. Consideration of new strategies, complex annual reviews, and corporate updates are hard to fit into board meetings of ordinary length. A number of companies have undertaken a special two- or three-day strategy meeting at a location apart from the company, and sometimes with spouses invited for a partially separate program. Senior members of management and planning staff are included.

In such a setting, the systematic presentation of the past year's results compared to the year's plan (with analysis of discrepancies) is accompanied by the presentation of the following one- or two-year plan. The latter plan is then considered against the long-range plan.

More important, in informal sessions at the bar or at meals, the participants' concept of the company and its future is discussed without the usual constraints. Such discussion sometimes includes the board's role and how effectively it contributes to the strategy process.

Assigning more time to the formal consideration of the company's future does not of course guarantee useful contribution from the board, but it does contribute enormously to the board's education. Everyone is exposed to people they might not meet otherwise—directors, managers, staff members, and spouses—

and this wider acquaintance leads to (1) greater knowledge of the company and its people, (2) greater trust in individuals' competence and goodwill, (3) understanding of the unevenness of management strength and the opportunity for management development, (4) relaxation of the tension between outside directors and chief executive officers, and (5) keener interest in future opportunities.

To prepare for and schedule a special full-scale strategy review meeting is a formidable undertaking. In fact, the time-consuming nature of the task lends support to Courtney Brown's arguments that the chief executive officer should not be chairman of the board.[8]

Although such a meeting need not culminate in a two- or three-day retreat every year, any effort to prepare a board to understand and play some part in the strategic decisions of a complex company requires more time than a CEO may be able to give it. A separate chairman to look after this and other board functions, or (as William Wommack suggests) a chief strategic officer in management ranks, or a massive delegation of operating responsibilities by the CEO may be necessary to allow time for strategic leadership.

But no matter how strategy sessions are arranged, good chairmanship—to provoke productive discussions or identification of the more debatable issues—is indispensable. At a minimum, careful reading of well-prepared staff reports, with discussion focused on issues that cannot yet be finally resolved, clarifies insight and informs subsequent judgment.

CORPORATE STRATEGY COMMITTEE

Especially since the collapse of Penn Central led to the proliferation of audit committees, organization by committee has been the board's means of coping with its increased workload. The audit committee performs the watchdog function by monitoring compliance with SEC regulations and the Foreign Corrupt Practices Act and by investigating problems of ethical conduct. The compensation and nominating committees often not only establish executive compensation and recommend new candidates for election but examine the qualifications and performance of senior management and of the board itself.

Organization by committee economizes the time of directors, puts the most qualified people in charge of given issues, educates directors, and provides a relatively private context for discussion of sensitive subjects.

The arguments against a strategy committee are the same arguments used against any form of board involvement in strategy. These arguments ignore powerful trends in corporate governance, minimize directors' potential contributions, and reduce the possibility of building a strong and able board. They will

[8]See Courtney C. Brown, *Putting the Corporate Board to Work* and *Beyond the Bottom Line* (New York: Macmillan, 1976 and 1979, respectively).

almost certainly fall on deaf ears with the onset of a new generation of chief executive officers, the developing awareness of responsibility among independent directors, and the possibility that conventional management practice tends to undermine productivity.

Composition & function. For a strategy committee to work, it should be composed of carefully chosen outside directors who have shown interest and talent in considering strategic questions brought to the board. New directors can be recruited especially for this function.

In the few companies I know of in which a strategy committee has been established, the committee members started off slowly, hearing from one segment of a business at a time and acquainting themselves with the information as well as the managers presenting it. A second level of sophistication would be to have committee members prepare for meetings by reading staff studies that discuss future risks, possibilities, investments, and projects.

After it had become familiar with current strategy, the committee's function would be to assess the strategy's strengths and weaknesses and to consider what measures might improve the strategy. The committee would also discuss the issues being debated within management and consider key proposals before they reached the board. It would note whether other committees—like finance, investment, or pension management—had interest in a proposal.

One of the principal functions of the committee would be to encourage the strengthening of the strategic planning process within the company—to get to know the key participants and to appraise the context within which capital projects and new product ideas originate.

Character of discussions. Participation in the strategy formulation process made possible by an active committee could become so intimate as to make CEOs very nervous. Putting information about many possibilities in the hands of outside directors who have become opinionated in their own success and self-esteem can lead to snap-judgment preferences hard to dislodge later.

In some boards where the strategy committee approach has been tried, the unwritten rules constraining discussion have been relaxed to the point that partisanship or bias has been avoided. Individual directors and the CEO challenge each other, and—their relationships strengthened by associations developed in such situations as off-site discussions—they explore things informally as well as more seriously. Directors too quick to substitute their opinions for those of management can be called for interference. Assured that the strategy committee members are not going to take a position prematurely or fault them for indecision, some CEOs have brought to the committee vexing problems, serious threats, and impending choices well before management was ready to make a formal recommendation to the board.

Besides encouraging directors to produce ideas, this strategy committee process could still the restlessness of directors who are uneasy at the yes or no choice given them when a new proposal arrives with a firm recommendation.

The basis for saying yes is loyalty to management; the case for the proposal contains little basis for saying no. Prior discussion would let the directors be heard and might make them more understanding and less resentful if they were later overruled. The lines between management and board authority must remain clear, but the more communication across them the better.

The strategy committee would neither create nor dispose of problems of board-management relations. It would simply be a device to make practical the convergence of varied points of view and the dissipation of provincial, functional, or occupational bias. It would do what the board as a whole should but cannot do; it would segregate—like all effective committee structures—the appropriate problems, questions, and recommendations to those most interested and qualified. Like the other committees of the board, it would be shaped by its leadership, composition, and assigned function.

CONTRIBUTION TO CREATIVE STRATEGY

No discussion of board involvement in strategy formulation, full-board strategy sessions, and corporate strategy committees should conclude without attempting to dispel the solemnity that usually descends on the subject. For individual directors, strategic participation means more work, more time, more thought, and probably at times more uncertainty, frustration, and concern.

Nonetheless, the most common response to exposure to central management issues is stimulation, excitement, satisfaction, greater confidence in being able to contribute, and ideas and knowledge to take back to one's own company. The opportunity to consider someone else's problems is usually exhilarating. The convergence of new points of view on long-standing problems previously viewed between one set of blinders sometimes produces dramatic and satisfying results.

The normal routine of assent to management proposals, based on general confidence in management as justified by past performance, is essentially boring. When participants have reason to wonder whether their confidence in past performance is a sound basis for expecting adequate future performance, they feel frustrated. If in their relationship the CEO is overly forceful and the board overly acquiescent, an unproductive, even dangerous, situation results.

Freer participation by the board in contributing to strategy formation would be of no great importance unless such participation produced better decisions by management. The heart of the strategic process is the generation of alternatives—combining in new ways market opportunity, customer needs, and company capabilities. If a company is to stand apart from its competitors with superior returns on its equity (and why not?), then it must nurture the kind of creativity that finds new applications and new definitions of its distinctive competence.

The current erosion of assets under inflation, the decline in productivity, the temporary collapse of our automobile industry, and the lessening of U.S. competitive capabilities all call for more boldness and imagination in the management of innovation and the undertaking of risk. The leaping innovation that is occasionally produced by imagination and creativity cannot be decreed or simulated. It is throttled by the fear of failure, the cracked voice of experience, the tyranny of plans mechanically requiring an arbitrary percentage growth rate quarter by quarter.

Nonetheless, imagination exists in all questing organizations and people; it can be released and encouraged. The articulated goal to be first in a chosen technology or market, supported by money and people focused on bold objectives, can produce a Wang or Intel at the expense of many a pedestrian competitor. Boards of directors do not themselves create or invent, but they can take into their overview the innovative processes of the company and support their strengthening.

Through its concern with its company's strategy, a board could emphasize and contribute to the search for new opportunity. "What's new?" is a question that should have an unending series of answers in the execution as well as formulation of strategy. Every qualified director has some special skill or experience that could be brought to bear without short-circuiting the authority of management.

Creativity can be served, in short, by realizing the potential for board contribution to corporate strategy. The variety of experience, points of view, technical and general knowledge, and quality of judgment present in a well-put-together board can extend management's constrained view of the world and bring stimulation and new ideas to executives grooved by their company's experience to stereotyped policymaking and behavior.

This variety can be made fully effective only by involving boards in the most critical issues facing their chief executive officers—the identity and mission of their companies, the direction they are to maintain in a fast-changing world, and the innovative decisions that will make their strategies successful.

17

Replaying the Board's Role in Formulating Strategy

KENNETH R. ANDREWS
Harvard University

Three issues ago I wrote in this space on the board of directors' responsibility for corporate strategy.[1] I claimed then that "a responsible and effective board should require of its management a unique and durable corporate strategy, review it periodically for its validity, use it as a reference point for all other board decisions, and share with management the risks associated with its adoption." I predicted that this statement and the supporting argument would not overwhelm many board chairmen with its wisdom or result in a new rush of strategy committees and annual strategic reviews.

In the main, I was right. I sent reprints to many of my colleagues on four boards. They are responding, when I see them in passing, with friendly groans about having too much to read and with interest that derives from how directly our common boards review strategy. A handful of letters has appeared, mostly from friends.

For example, Ernest C. Arbuckle, former dean of the Stanford Business School and chairman of Wells Fargo and now chairman of the Saga Corporation, wrote to say that most CEOs aren't ready to set up formal committees of the board to review strategy. He believes, and I agree, that informal discussions of the CEO and outside directors reviewing alternative corporate strategies should come first.

Such sessions, he thinks, stimulate CEOs to move faster than they might otherwise to consider basic strategy questions and should assure them of their directors' support and willingness to take part in periodic discussions leading eventually to conclusions.

Arbuckle would find it more exciting, he added, to be a member of a strategy committee that might finally be set up by the CEO than to serve, say, as chairman or member of several audit committees. Most of us who experienced our first really important committee assignments on audit committees during the questionable payments days would say amen.

As time goes on, I hear in quick airport encounters or telephone calls of other interest. The board whose approval of two dubious acquisitions I used as an example of the extraction of consent, rather than the achievement of free board approval, recognized and discussed the incident despite the disguise in which I meant to conceal it from them and everybody else.

I will watch requests for reprints. This activity, or lack of it, will be a clue to whether my longtime hope that boards will become usefully involved in the most critical issues facing their chief executive officers is being seriously considered. In the crowded world of top management (in case you haven't noticed), the lead time to consider and discuss ideas that imply change and more hard work is long. Obtuseness is not the problem; it's time.

---

[1]"Directors' Responsibility for Corporate Strategy," HBR November–December 1980, p. 30.

THE ART OF IMPRECISION

During the course of the original article, I took a potshot or two at "muddling through" as the classic response to politically confused decisions about purpose. In criticizing improvisation as a very limited strategy, I cited a widely reprinted article by H. Edward Wrapp, "Good Managers Don't Make Policy Decisions,"[2] as "beguiling but antistrategic."

His response to this allegation has corrected my longtime misunderstanding of his title and clarified the main difference between us—the degree to which corporate strategy can or should be made explicit. The resolution of this question is crucial to board participation in a company's strategy-determining processes.

Ed Wrapp, once himself in business and a valued former student and colleague of mine, teaches business policy in the executive program (which he formerly directed) at the University of Chicago; his consulting experience and board service are extensive. The foreword of his article reads in part as follows:

"The successful general manager does not spell out detailed objectives for his organization . . . nor does he make master plans. He seldom makes forthright statements of policy. He is an opportunist, and he tends to muddle through problems—although he muddles with a purpose. He enmeshes himself in many operating matters and does not limit himself to 'the big picture.' "

As I read Ed's article again, I conclude that though still beguiling, it is not antistrategic. He defines a good manager, in fact, as one who is "able to move his organization significantly toward the goals he has set, whether measured by higher return on investment, product improvement, development of management talent, faster growth in sales and earnings, or some other standard."

Ed identifies five important management skills. His "good manager" keeps himself informed about a "wide range of operating decisions being made at different levels in the company." He saves his energy for those few "issues, decisions or problems to which he should give his personal attention." He (think *he* or *she* throughout) is sensitive to the power structure in his organization, works through people in different parts of the organization who have ideas he likes, and develops a hazy set of goals, a hazy timetable, and a "hazier notion of how he can reach these goals" and find "corridors of comparative indifference" that he can use to bypass opposition.

You can begin to see why I went astray; this is skill indeed. If we read on, paradox deepens. We find that the fourth skill of the successful manager is "knowing how to satisfy the organization that it has a sense of direction *without ever getting himself committed publicly to a specific set of objectives.*" Practicing the art of imprecision, he communicates objectives over time by promoting a consistency or pattern in operating decisions and avoids management by objectives and other policy straitjackets.

The most important skill assumes the futility of trying to push total packages of purposes and policies through an organization. Instead, the astute manager combines and restructures the separate proposals before him to move partway toward his objectives. He identifies "opportunities and relationships in the stream of operating problems and decisions."

Paradoxically enough to trick my own memory, Ed emphasizes, after all, that the good manager is "a planner and encourages planning by his subordinates" but recognizes that even if a plan is sound and imaginative, its implementation will be a long and painful process.

In his letter to me, Ed quotes his statement that good managers will "make strategic change a way of life in the organization and continually review the strategy even though current results are good." He writes:

"My complaint is with the highly formalized strategic planning which I observe in many companies, a process which is sterile, but one which is promoted by professional planners. The most imaginative strategy seems to me to emerge in organizations where senior managers are willing to help in the search for solutions to serious operating problems.

"The best managed conglomerate I know of (most of them are dismally managed) has no planning department and no required planning mechanisms for its divisions. But this same company has a powerful flow of new products. What better way to ensure the long-term success of an enterprise."

"I won't rest easy," Ed Wrapp concludes his letter, "until the antistrategic indictment is lifted."

The indictment, such as it was, should indeed be thrown out.

But an interesting question remains. How explicit and articulate should be the pattern of purposes and policies that defines the business of a company and the kind of a company it is and should become?

The uses of ambiguity are sensed by every politically wise administrator, who by definition is sensitive to the ways in which the purposes and perception of individuals divert or even disrupt cooperative action. But unless a board of directors knows what the purposes and policies of a company are, it can hardly review or take part in the subtle processes that produce them, approve the outcome, or have confidence in the wisdom of the risks being undertaken.

Let us look first at the case *against* making a clear statement of strategy and then at the case *for* it. The outcome will doubtless not be a vote for one and against the other. But if the differing circumstances become clear that make the strategist's clarity more or less important than the intuitive incrementalist's imprecision, then this excursion into an important difference of opinion, which extends far beyond Ed Wrapp and me, will be worthwhile.

THE CASE AGAINST
BEING EXPLICIT

Wrapp opens the argument with the statement that the good manager shies away from "precise statements of his objectives for the organization" mainly because he finds it impossible to set down "specific objectives which will be relevant for any reasonable period into the future." It would be difficult to persuade the organization to turn to different goals, in any case, when needs and conditions shift.

Although the public must perceive the organization as having a clear sense of direction, the good manager is seldom so certain. Furthermore, he knows that objectives cannot be so clearly stated that everyone in the organization knows what they mean. Subordinates who press for more precise objectives find that their freedom to operate and accommodate ideas flowing upward from their sectors of the organization is reduced.

A fuller development of this point of view can be found in James Brian Quinn's *Strategies for Change: Logical Incrementalism.*[3] After studying nine multibillion dollar companies and interviewing ten executives in each, Quinn finds that managements "arrive at their strategic goals through highly incremental processes, rather than through the kinds of structured analysis often prescribed or 'required' according to management dogma."

From his interviews with those 90 senior executives, he concludes that they avoid strategic pronouncements to prevent four bad results: (1) undesired centralization, (2) a focus for otherwise fragmented opposition, (3) the rigidity that closes down options and makes announced goals hard to change, and (4) breaches of security when executives move to other companies or when strategies for diversification, consolidation, or plant closures create anxiety.

Because the companies in Quinn's study were General Mills, Pillsbury, Exxon, Continental Group, Xerox, Pilkington, General Motors, Chrysler, and Volvo, we must take the inquiry seriously. I think we are supposed to approve what the interviewed executives say they actually do rather than evaluate it as less than strategic management.

This point of view has wide support, especially among students of organizational behavior. Henry Mintzberg, author of *The Nature of Managerial Work*[4] and the three HBR articles,[5] believes that strategy is a pattern in a stream of

---

[3]Homewood, Illinois: Richard D. Irwin, 1980.

[4]New York: Harper & Row, 1973.

[5]"The Manager's Job: Folklore and Fact," July–August 1975, p. 49; "Planning on the Left Side and Managing on the Right," July–August 1976, p. 49; "Organization Design: Fashion or Fit?" January–February 1981, p. 103. See also Henry Mintzberg and James A. Waters, "Tracking Strategy in an Entrepreneurial Firm," unpublished paper, McGill University, 1980.

decisions and can be quite divorced from intent. Strategy emerges from behavior and, if articulated, may so coerce and constrain creative members of the organization that the stream of innovation will dry up.[6]

Before turning to the case for articulating corporate strategy, we should note that Wrapp, Quinn, and Mintzberg are in part reacting against the artificialities of strategic planning systems, which seldom, if ever, produce fundamental strategic decisions. The precise, specific, and quantitative objectives they repudiate have little to do with what I think corporate strategy is or with what the board, in its responsibility for overseeing the nature and direction of its company, should be interested in. I will return to this point later.

THE CASE FOR BEING EXPLICIT

Much more than Wrapp, Quinn acknowledges that general goals may be promulgated openly for cohesion and élan and that specific goals can usefully be announced when action is necessary, a major transition is undertaken, and after a crisis has passed. Quinn comes near the camp where I pitch my tent in asserting that "the essence of strategy is to identify [a] small number of truly essential thrusts or concepts and to marshal the organization's resources and capabilities consciously toward them."

What in this context he calls "proper goal formulation" has the virtue of making the best use of an organization's information sources, securing the commitment of those who must achieve the goals, and maintaining the opportunism and flexibility essential to effective strategy. The open sharing of common purposes (now Quinn has entered camp and tent) permits individual freedom under the control of purpose, sustains morale (which is after all a goal-oriented phenomenon), and provides a way to sense emerging problems.

What is meant by corporate strategy, it now is clear, is crucially important in the decision whether to make it explicit. I certainly do not mean that management should devise and boards of directors ratify elaborate planning systems that, in caricature, (1) classify all the companies' businesses by market share and rate of market growth and (2) imply or recommend that cash cows be milked, dogs divested, and fishhook question marks turned into stars—to borrow the vulgar and destructive vocabulary of some approaches to strategic planning.

Certainly management should not confuse results with purpose and put growth goals first. Concentration on high-percentage increases in sales and profits, without attainable programs to match, wrenches resource allocation out of shape or ends in frustrating underachievement and such other byproducts as empty manufacturing space, excess staff, and ill-considered acquisitions.

[6]The idea in this sentence comes from a recent conversation with Mintzberg.

What corporate strategy is.   Boards of directors, when they discuss corporate strategy, must have some common idea of what is meant by the term. As I have proposed before, it can be considered the evolving pattern of decision that both determines and makes clear what a company's purposes, goals, and principal policies have been and now are. Without precluding response to (and indeed seeking out) new opportunity that is related to its resources and special competence, it defines generally the range of business the company intends to pursue and excel in.

But corporate strategy is more than a set of product-market decisions. It reflects qualitatively what kind of business organization the company intends to be for all its constituents—shareholders, employees, customers, and communities. Aspirations of quality, style, and social responsibility belong in this determination. This kind of summary statement of corporate purpose is clear enough to set the company apart from its competitors but general enough *not* to prevent the generation of innovative, detailed action programs and the participation of people who are motivated by their perception of purposes that have opportunity and attraction for them.

A strategy that meets these specifications is always the proper subject of discussion by the management and the board, for strategy in a changing world and company should always be evolving with experimental offshoots and informative forays. Plenty of room exists in the course of these determinations for incremental processes and intuitive judgment.

Within flexibly defined markets, strategically disciplined management deliberately (but not too soon) adapts purposes to problems encountered and successes achieved. Implementation feeds back to formulation in continuous interaction. Corporate strategy is a living concept, with certain fundamental character-determining purposes remaining essentially unchanged and more sensitive elements like product characteristics, technical capabilities, and marketing policies assuming new forms.

Corporate purpose thus has both enduring elements and short-term aspects that should change, not disjointedly or adventitiously but in innovative response to changing market opportunity and capability and to developing personal values within management and its maturing organization. Acceptance of the essential mixture of policy that enables a company to set and predict direction, but leaves unsettled commitments that cannot or do not have to be made, should end the dispute between those who think that corporate purpose should be kept close to the vest (to hide uncertainty and indecision, among other things) and those who believe that, within reasonable regard for security, it should be made available to all who are interested.

Why the board should know.   In any case, whatever can be said at any one time about corporate strategy and strategic issues still unresolved should be communicated to the appropriate key persons in the company for a number of good reasons. What has not become clear and what has not been decided should obviously not be broadcast to the public or to the whole company. Issues not resolved should be of intense interest, however, to a board able to provide support in the reduction of uncertainty or the risks to be taken in its face. I assume that the board or a small committee of its members is not a security risk.

The main reason for attempting to make strategy explicit is to identify areas of indecision and expose indecisiveness to reasonable discipline. Ed Wrapp's incrementalist, with his hazy and personal purposes, may be as politically astute as he is inscrutable, but he may also go private to preserve his power over the eventual outcome and to keep his uncertainty and indecision from becoming known.

The master who knows but won't tell is worthier than the pretender who doesn't know and therefore *can't* tell. But neither gets the benefit of counsel from his associates in management or on the board. Opposition is sometimes better faced in open argument than manipulated in accordance with a hidden and perhaps confused agenda. Candor is becoming recognized more and more widely as administratively useful and also informative.

Making strategy as deliberate as it is practicable enables good managers to know what they are really doing and to know what, more than momentum, is going for it. If the goals of the corporation and the principal means for getting there can be communicated, then people of like mind, attracted and held to a company because of what it seeks to be, can commit their energy and creativity to it—without forever being told or having to improvise what to do.

If the strategy is challenging, members of the organization can be stimulated to respond with more than routine performance, with new ways of reaching goals, and with solutions to problems encountered on the track. A band of people casually gathered to work for a livelihood can be made into an institution embodying values, creating loyalty, and providing non-material rewards, to say nothing of profiting from efficient or first-class performance.

Do we need more? If so, consider this. If the strategy is known, rather than obscured in incremental wandering where only the leader (and often not even he) knows what is really going on, then its evolution can be monitored from more than one point of view in a changing company uncertainly coming to terms with a changing environment. Its financial, technical, material, and human resources can be planned for and sought out in advance. The organizational structures and systems can be dominated by the company's general purpose rather than by the special purposes of specialists.

For a board the opportunity to consider an articulated strategy, whatever shape it is in or whatever uncertainty still attends it, can be a productive way to perform its twin functions of supporting and evaluating the performance of its chief executive officer and his immediate senior associates. The support is essentially that suggested earlier by Ernest Arbuckle: the encouragement and help of the board in identifying strategic issues and considering alternatives without exacting premature resolution from an unconvinced CEO or substituting its own preferences for management's unreadiness to recommend resolution.

Chief executives must be made comfortable in such discussions. Opening up previously private purposes to directors' scrutiny is a severe test of CEO's security and their grasp of strategic issues—the most administratively and intellectually demanding of all those awaiting their attention.

Exposing the process of deciding strategy to board review and participation, then, invites the best effort and support of directors in the process of encouraging continued management attention to the toughest questions. It also opens the CEO's management of the future of the company to evaluation prior to proof by profit.

EVALUATING PROCESS AND OUTCOME

A corporate strategy can be subject only to judgment, not to definitive evaluation in advance of its validity. How clear it is in words or practice, how fully it exploits domestic and international market opportunity, how consistent it is with corporate competence and resources (both present and projected), and how internally consistent it is can all be submitted to qualitative analysis. How much it reflects the values and aspirations of the key persons in the company, how much it constitutes a clear stimulus to effort and creativity, and whether in ethical and moral terms it inspires commitment and the required quality and class can also be estimated in the light of relevant, if unquantifiable, evidence.

The fitness of the match between resources and market opportunity and its profit potential can be quantified. The level of risk, likely to be adjustable, should be determined jointly by board and management. For if a board is going to sign off on a strategy, it is sharing its risks with the chief executive and must not turn on him as a scapegoat at a later time only for the reason that he was wrong.

It is true that, in the board, dissatisfaction may develop with the way in which management handles strategic issues. The silent strategist may postpone the eruption of such uneasiness indefinitely, until bad results make his removal inevitable. It is surely better to arrive at considered approval and agreement in the board in the first place than to have a highly emotional crisis at last.

Whether to make strategy explicit, then, turns on how one defines strategy, how much the participation of managers other than the CEO is required, and how much the board is to take part in the process. It is of course true that the determination of strategy and the consideration of strategic issues is a highly political process. It is true also that many times strategic issues are not identified because nobody knows what to do with them.

The nine multibillion dollar companies Quinn examined have had before them some of the most complicated decisions that exist in the world of corporate management because their size, their resources, the range of choices, and the strengths of special interest and convention are so great. It can be said almost for certain that most of them did not give earlier as much deliberate attention to what seem now to be their life-and-death issues as they in retrospect would like.

Myopia resulting from acceptance of industry wisdom and conditions, preoccupation with current political and economic problems and scapegoats, and confused national policy cloud all in-company identification of major strategic issues. It may be too much to expect the perspective of independent directors to illuminate early enough such problems as the success of Japanese competition,

---

The Central Art of Effective Strategic Management

In recent years there has been an increasing chorus of discontent concerning corporate strategic planning. Many managers are concerned that despite elaborate strategic planning systems, costly staffs for this purpose, and major commitments of their own time, their most elaborate strategies never get implemented. These executives and their companies have generally fallen into the classic trap of thinking of strategy formulation and implementation as separate sequential processes. They have relied on the awesome rationality of their formally derived strategies and the inherent power of their positions to cause their organizations to respond. When this does not occur, they become bewildered, if not frustrated and angry. Instead, successful managers who operate with logical incrementalism build the seeds of understanding, identity, and commitment into the very processes that create their strategies. By the time the strategy begins to crystallize in focus, pieces of it are already being implemented. Through their strategic formulation processes, they have built a momentum and psychological commitment to the strategy, which causes it to flow toward flexible implementation. Constantly integrating the simultaneous incremental processes of strategy formulation and implementation is the central art of effective strategic management.

Significant strategic shifts in large enterprises take years, if not decades, to accomplish. Consequently, it is rare for a single person to mastermind a complete change in a major organization's total strategy—although this can occur in a time of crisis or when an individual's tenure is exceptionally long. What one sees in the short run as an important strategic shift very often turns out under investigation to be part of a much longer continuity that has been building for some years and will later gently mutate and evolve into a quite different form than it now possesses. Those who wish to shape strategy in large organizations must learn to live with and manage this continuously evolving consensus-creating process.

From James Brian Quinn, *Strategies for Change: Logical Incrementalism* (Homewood, Illinois: Richard D. Irwin, 1980), p. 145.

the changing structure of the world automobile industry, and the world energy situation. That perspective may not have been applied to the problem at all.

Although the problems other companies face are less global, and often much more tractable, they are almost always difficult. It is true also that time and understanding of strategic choices are limited among outside directors, many of whom are immersed in their own unanswered questions.

The astute executive, however, senses what is ready for discussion and what is not. He (you are still thinking *he* or *she*) knows the value of a single idea not thought of before. He is aware that the more he knows about the way his managers and directors think about strategic problems, the more likely he is to arrive at a solution that is politically acceptable as well as economically sound.

Rather than inscrutably keeping his peace, he has the opportunity to open up the process, to raise questions, to encourage but not to force the facing of strategic reality, and to lead a process of decision that can enlist the total strength of management and the support and detached insight of the board.

The "continuous, evolving, incremental, and often highly political process that has no precise beginning or end," as Quinn characterizes the formulation of strategy, poses a subtle requirement for understanding and leadership on the part of chief executive officers and boards. Directors are compelled by this imperative to realize that reviewing an incremental process that shapes a company's future over time and approving its periodic outcomes is not merely a matter of poring over mechanical and highly quantified analyses of the results and prospects of separate businesses or of briskly requiring that management decisively submit its recommendations on fundamental, separate issues.

The level of attention, understanding, and knowledge of content made necessary by viewing strategy as at the same time a rational, intuitive, and political process makes a director's role even more sophisticated and demanding than it has conventionally been considered. Does this observation make it less likely that directors and CEOs will undertake discussions of strategy? I hope not.

18

Corporate Strategy as a Vital Function of the Board

KENNETH R. ANDREWS
Harvard University

A year ago in these pages I argued as strongly as I knew how for the fuller engagement of the board of directors in the design and execution of corporate strategy.[1] It was my intention to stir up the kind of discussion I thought was being resolutely avoided by corporate chief executives unwilling to have directors discuss strategic issues before, or even much after, management recommendations were presented to the board for acceptance.

I was aware of most of the reasons why director participation in strategic decisions had not flourished. And from earlier contributors to *From the Boardroom* and discussion with some executives, I knew that effective board participation in strategic processes could make an important long-term difference in a company's performance and contribute to the longevity and pride in achievement of chief executives.

Six months ago I reported on the opposing school of thought that believes in incremental and implicit strategy and documents its approval of intuitive, improvisatory, and undiscussed purpose with abundant evidence of its occurrence in practice.[2] Correspondence and conversation immediately picked up.

I'd now like to report some of the issues raised and views presented in amplification or rejection of the viewpoint I advocated. The topic is at least being talked about in some of the symposia and seminars on boards in the United States and abroad. In fact, some boards address issues of corporate strategy for as long as three or four days.

How much *effective* board contribution actually takes place is not easy to determine, but at least such sessions provide information applicable to strategic questions. Because directors do not seek credit for or retain ownership of ideas offered or questions raised that may influence management's decisions, it is difficult to accurately measure the value of board input to corporate strategy. The tributary can't find its contribution to the river.

Nonetheless, any sort of discussion of strategy presents individual directors the opportunity to find out whether management does indeed have a unique and durable corporate strategy (however sparsely stated), to get some idea of its validity, to relate to it individual project and capital appropriation decisions, and to raise strategically relevant rather than captious or random questions.

When the chairman opens the door to discussion, the interested outside director begins to participate; ultimately, the kind of information and talent required can together effect understanding, testing, reasoned ratification of the future direction of the company, and a commitment shared with the chief executive to the success of his or her strategy—or to its timely modification.

The unresolved problems delaying productive board participation are many. We can agree quickly that:

---

[1] "Directors' Responsibility for Corporate Strategy" (*From the Boardroom*), HBR November–December 1980, p. 30.

[2] "Replaying the Board's Role in Formulating Strategy" (*From the Boardroom*), HBR May–June 1981, p. 18.

It is not the board's function to formulate strategy but to review it and to monitor the process that produces it.

What is meant by corporate strategy and how clearly it should be set forth are not generally understood.

A chief executive used to thinking that the board's principal function is to select, support, and replace him (think *him or her* henceforth) will approach enlargement of the board's strategic role with much hesitation and little experience.

Outside directors are very busy and are not usually well informed about the strategic recommendations they may be asked to evaluate and approve.

Central decisions that will determine the company's nature and performance 10 and 20 years into the future are laden with risk, uncertainty, and contention.

Putting most of these undeniable realities to one side, let's turn to the letters and notes I have before me and to some subjects in the developing conversation in which you might like to join, specifically: (1) the degree to which strategy is the business of the board, (2) whether it should be made explicit at some levels of generality but not at others, (3) the advisability of establishing a strategy committee, and (4) the differences between useful director involvement in small and large companies.

Without intending violence to the writers' views, I will try a respectful synopsis of what seem to me opinions useful in sorting out the entanglements of logic, attitude, experience, and differences among situations that complicate any consideration of corporate boards. We will come at length to how well boards are chaired and what modest beginnings some chairmen have undertaken.

STRATEGY AS THE BOARD'S BUSINESS

I was naturally cheered, to begin with, by letters from a small group of supporters. Bryan Smith, general director of Texas Instruments, is an articulate expositor of TI's longstanding program to make its board a visible, important organ of corporate governance.

The TI board attends a four-day strategic planning conference in the first quarter of every year to discuss business opportunities of the next decade. In addition, several board members attend the following two days of management meetings with 500 managers from all the company's activities. By the time the board comes to approve the company's plans, via ten days' annual work of the corporate objectives committee, it is presumably informed enough to play an important role in the company's planning processes.

Smith is encouraged by the enhanced role of the board in many companies. "The conscription of active, independent boards," he concludes, "is important—even vital—to the cause of rejuvenating America's drive to technological and commercial leadership."

Texas Instruments' record is good; it would be fascinating to have an objective and documented analysis of its strategic review process. However, the proprietary nature of its discussions makes it unlikely that researchers interested in analyzing board effectiveness can be admitted to these elaborate proceedings.

In any case, separating the contributions of the board from those of management in such an interactive process would be difficult. But to make converts out of skeptics, we need more objective observation and analysis of board and committee activities over an extended period of time.

Happily, our file of cases based on direct observation is beginning to accumulate. Daniel T. Carroll, president and CEO of Hoover Universal, whose incisive article "Boards and Managements: Ten Challenges and Responses" appeared in HBR's September–October issue, refers in a recent letter to the usefulness of board cases in an interesting way:

"I think the whole matter of board involvement in corporate strategy will be better served by a series of persuasive cases than by logical arguments. . . . Cases will help to express the varied nature and form of corporate strategy and thus differentiate it from 'motherhood' statements on the one hand and rigid statements about market share and growth rates on the other. Cases could also demonstrate wide-ranging approaches to director involvement and thereby reduce director and management apprehensions."

This passage means to me that case discussions by chief executive officers and board chairmen would do more than exhortation can to persuade individuals, via prescriptions developed for another set of problems, of the possibilities in their own unique situations.

Dan Carroll acknowledges as unarguable my premise that boards should play a role in corporate strategy. He brings, however, the same realistic caution to director recruitment as to the effectiveness of logical arguments like mine in changing the minds of chief executive officers:

"I wonder whether we aren't expecting more of directors than most can provide in terms of time and talent. As an alternative, greater use of professional directors has its advantages and at least one serious disadvantage. The professional director would have the requisite experience, the time, and, in all probability, the manner needed to reduce a chief executive's anxiety.

"But I fear that an overreliance on professional directors can introduce into board deliberations an undue influence by 'noncombatants' whose familiarity with the verities of business is either remote, theoretical, or nonexistent. I don't have a satisfactory solution, only an uneasiness about the probable impracticability of an obvious one."

After reading Carroll's responses to the challenges posed by the liberated board seeking its proper place in governance, I am not dismayed by his caution. The author of that idealized prescription for enlightened board management has to be as prepared to see major constructive change as I am.

The General Electric Company, which has been into strategic planning to the top of its monogram for at least a decade, evidently attempted long ago a connection between strategic management and the activities of its board, which has been one of the most illustrious in membership in corporate history.

Robert M. Estes, long GE's general counsel and an important contributor to *From the Boardroom,* recalls the undertaking of GE's management to do an "honest, thorough strategic planning job in close cooperation with keenly interested board members—not only interested in the GE future but also motivated by the desire to go back to each of their boards and get the same type of job done."

Estes remembers also Ralph Cordiner's deadly serious effort to do a kind of strategic planning that would transform a tradition-ridden giant into a modern, fast-moving high-technology company.

It is interesting to note that one of the fastest ways to spread enlightened management practice at high altitude is to expose chief executives to a view of it in their outside boards. Independent directors are supposed to introduce ideas and perspectives from the outside, serving as a "window to the world." They may also find things they had never dreamed of in their philosophy as they lean on the sill looking in.

PROBLEMS IN MAKING STRATEGY EXPLICIT

To turn now to the degree to which strategy should be made explicit in discussions with the board, the management, or the outside world, Richard V. Dempster, chairman and CEO of McCulloch Corporation, speaks for many in finding that I want "to bring the board into strategy review a little more than boards wanted to be brought in and a little more than managers wanted the boards to be brought in." (To this I admit cheerfully; I am in the unenviable position of advocating duty and responsibility—over the easier course!)

Dempster finds in Ed Wrapp's defense of unstated incremental strategy a welcome avenue to flexibility, dynamism, and escape from public explanations of necessary changes of direction. The ground he takes is between Wrapp and me.

As implied earlier by Dan Carroll, Dempster thinks that "in encouraging the selection process by a board nominating committee, one must be sure to nominate directors who are (1) qualified to think about corporate strategy and (2) willing to spend the necessary time to do the necessary homework. In a truly multinational corporation, it is particularly important to obtain directors who are not nationalistic and who, above all, do not take a 'U. S. only' view."

Still on the subject of how explicit corporate strategy should be, we should look at Wrapp's reply to my call to directors to insist that management present them a clearly thought-out strategy and that it be understood, questioned, and evaluated before it is approved and used subsequently as the framework for investment, compensation, and executive selection decisions.

Because of the variety, length, and depth of his experience (to say nothing of my obligation this time to let him express his views in full), I give you, with his permission, vintage Wrapp, down-to-earth and undiluted:

"Your ideas on corporate strategy and the board of directors in *From the Boardroom* are opening up for discussion a subject that many a chief executive officer, given a choice, would keep in the closet.

"Over the past several years, I have talked in a personal vein with a number of chief executive officers in small to large companies. Some still held the position, others had moved to the sidelines via such bumpy routes as normal retirement, early retirement, takeovers, shareholder disputes, and outright discharge. The validity of the sample cannot be judged, for the sources must remain confidential. Fault it for pent-up frustrations, failing memories, or my inability to cross-check the opinion.

"Nevertheless, the conclusion must be that CEOs depend only obliquely on their boards of directors for guidance on corporate strategy. The reflections of the ex-chief executives were much harsher than those still in power.

"For a reason I will get to later, I want to describe four strata of corporate strategy that emerged from these informal off-the-record talks:

"*Stratum I—corporate strategy for the annual report.* Usually this version is sterilized by top management and edited by the public relations staff. For the shareholders, it conveys a sense of direction, an assurance that management knows where it is trying to take the company. The pressure for such a statement is growing, even though it may read like a treatise on planning written by George Gilder.

"*Stratum II—corporate strategy for the board of directors, financial analysts, and middle management.* Somewhat more comprehensive and revealing than Stratum I, most boards of directors must settle for this level of enlightenment, particularly in the larger, multibusiness companies.

"Here we get glimpses of the segments of the company and perhaps good hints as to where management sees the growth opportunities. As top management discusses Stratum II with the intended audiences, the game plan usually calls for keeping it simple and camouflaging the deeper potholes.

"*Stratum III—corporate strategy for top management.* In an organization of any size or complexity, several members of top management can be expected to participate in discussions approaching a full consideration of moves and countermoves, the strength of the competition, the competence of operating management, and perhaps a hot topic such as odds for survival of the current management. Needing the support of this group, the CEO will usually try to reach agreement in these discussions.

"*Stratum IV—the CEO's private corporate strategy.* If the CEO is a strategic thinker, he is seldom inhibited by anyone—not by his top managers, not by his directors, not by his professional planners, and not by his outside advisers. He may be mulling a range of moves that he discloses to almost no one. In trying to gain a deeper comprehension of who exerts the most influence with a CEO and why, I have discovered that even when he shares his innermost thoughts with one or two managers or directors or advisers, his strength of will and conviction dominate the discussions.

"The reasons for reticence are usually a complex tangle. Parts of the private strategy may be dictated by the CEO's self-interest; or he may be analyzing developments that those around him are not yet ready to recognize and diagnose; or he may not be willing to share knowledge of delicate maneuvers for fear of premature disclosure; or, as is often the case, he may believe he is the best qualified to sort out the pros and cons and decide how to proceed.

"Putting my finger on our apparent differences of opinion about the board and corporate strategy, I am persuaded that one of the problems is that we may be comparing notes on different strata of strategy. Many of your observations seem to relate to Stratum II, whereas I tend to be more preoccupied with Stratum IV, and there is no suggestion here of which level may be more perceptive.

"All four strategy levels can be found in many organizations, but direct questions about their existence will not elicit an open admission from anyone near the top. A skillful strategist can probably weave an internal consistency through all four levels, so that different discussants never suspect that they are participating in anything but the full picture.

"Let me share some occasionally earthy quotes:

'It was a tortuous task to build a consensus in the top management group. As we began to agree on a direction for the company, I kept a couple of my board members informed. Hearing no flat turndowns from them, we began to use the strategy as a checkpoint on the big issues. All the while, we had a planning department grinding out PR documents that were not inconsistent with our strategy but not very revealing either. The idea of exposing my strategy for a full discussion by the board never crossed my mind.' (*former CEO of a large conglomerate*)

'My board members spent too much time talking about how they did things in their own companies. We listened to their stories, but for the most part they had remote relevance to the matter I had brought up for discussion. The best argument for putting a professor on the board is that you don't have to listen to "how we do it in my company." ' (*former CEO who was merged out of his post*)

'Many of our board members may have been risk takers in their own companies, but when they came to my meetings it seemed they were more concerned with their legal liabilities than with encouraging management to be aggressive. We kept the board members splashing around in the shallow end of the pool, never letting them venture into deep water. One or two hand wringers on a board can pursuade the others to an ultraconservative position.' (*retired CEO*)

"One final conclusion. Everyone will agree that predicting whether a company will grow and adjust to change and prosper is a high-risk game. What is the best clue to future success: A written strategy, a large planning department, detailed planning mechanisms, a demanding board of directors, burgeoning markets, superior technology?

"My choice would be to determine whether the CEO and the other important general managers are strategic thinkers. Strategic thinkers, as contrasted with bureaucrats and administrators, seem to find ways to turn lackluster prospects into healthy businesses. And how, you ask, does one recognize a strategic thinker? There's the rub."

WHAT DO WE MEAN BY
CORPORATE STRATEGY?

All of us have a long way to go before we make clear to each other what we mean by corporate strategy. It is actually Stratum III (not Stratum II) that I would choose for deliberation by a board. I would want a board to know the agreements reached by top management about how the company should position itself to take advantage of future market opportunity and to outdo its competition.

The board must sense at least how well the chief strategic officer of the company (in almost all cases the CEO) has investigated market opportunity, appraised and invested in the distinctive competence and total resources of his company, and combined opportunity and resources, consistent with the economic goals, personal values, and ethical aspirations that define the character of the company.

Since no one has a monopoly on insight, not only should top management agree on what it will try to accomplish, but so should the board. I feel as obliged to make the utopian tendency of my argument as clear as is Ed Wrapp's appreciation of reality.

I see now that Stratum IV is what really interest Wrapp. I recognize the private world of the unfettered leader as the wellspring of what in time would be discussed openly as strategic alternatives. As a naive proponent of what might be in contrast to what is, I confess I would like to see this creativity come out of the political closet and become a candidly participative process.

That all four strata should be consistent and internally reinforcing seems to me not only highly desirable but quite feasible. But differences of opinion are what make not only horse races but good conversation as well; I am glad to have Ed Wrapp's important elaboration of his position.

To return to Wrapp's last question, how to recognize a strategic thinker is indeed a central problem that I hope contributors to these pages and those who preside over management development and appraisal systems will address. If I remember his comment on Samuel Felton's case,[3] Bob Charpie, CEO of Cabot Corporation, cited as the key indicator of management ability a potential executive's talent to reconcile current results with investment in long-term growth. Protection of the future against the overwhelming pressures of the present is easy to specify as essential; bringing it off and surviving requires magnanimity of judgment on the part of superiors.

That latitude may not be provided by an executive who is not a strategic thinker. Yet it is the long-term strategy that governs diversion of maximum present profit to produce future advantage over competitors. Nobody can describe the judgment applied to this trade-off, but strategic thinkers know it when they see it. At middle management levels, strategic thinkers are often killed off or taught better by seniors pressing for planned quarterly profits against what is always immediate adversity or unexpected shortfall.

STRATEGIC THINKING IN SMALLER COMPANIES

One of the most interesting letters that this discussion of strategy has produced is from Richard Chapin, who was recently president of Emerson College and is presently a director of the Norton Company and several smaller companies. His first reaction to both my HBR pieces is that they apply to big companies.

He recognizes life in a company without a fully developed appartus of corporate governance in Ed Wrapp's "playing things close to the chest, . . . the hazy set of goals and timetable, the hazier notion of how to reach these goals, and the continuing search for soft spots in the roadblocks." Chapin continues:

"Someone long ago observed that small organizations inevitably have one engine, one person who provides the power and direction and who probably controls much of the stock. I have been on three such boards, and I empathize with the natural tendency to accept less explicit definition of objectives and plans and less sharing with the board.

"The last few years have taught me that I had better resist that natural tendency. While the lack of an explicit set of strategies, plans for implementation, periodic review, and so on may be a beguiling aspect of small business, it can also mean the difference between being in a position to optimize opportunities and 'muddling along'; or worse, it can lead all too quickly to deep trouble. And no one can know how long the road back is until one has been there. Here are two examples of the former and one of the latter.

[3]"Case of the Board and the Strategic Process" (*From the Boardroom*), HBR July–August 1979, p. 20.

"A small bank where I am a director muddled along for years seeking and taking any kind of business it could get from automobile loans to student loans. Last year the directors and management decided to concentrate on providing full services to very small businesses. In effect, we put down the shotgun and picked up a rifle. Since that simple identification of a strategy, shared with the board, brings in a lot of customers, profits have consistently exceeded plans.

"Last year I did some consulting work for a small manufacturing company with annual sales in the range of $5 mllion to $6 million. For years the company had traded successfully on a high-quality, sort of mystical guru, reputation of its founder and his fine-tuned intuition about the marketplace. He died, and the current owners have tried to carry on with a strategy that seems to be best summed up as 'don't do anything Martin wouldn't have done.' Martin didn't need to find out about the market; he made it when he owned the business.

"For the current owners to state that they need to develop explicit market and financial planning strategies would be to admit a new weakness. Therefore, contrary to the infinite wisdom of this consultant, they continue to favor intuition over a product strategy based on a simple market segmentation study. This especially rankles because it appears that none of the competition is operating with any coherent set of strategies either.

"A somewhat larger, though still small ($26 million to $27 million), company where I am a director is just now beginning a process of defining quite specifically what businesses it wants to be in, where, with what people, and with what financial plan.

"This is all in response to a disastrous 18 months, which included an acquisition in an area completely unrelated and in which we have no expertise and excessively rapid expansion in areas more closely related to our business, which we should have tried one at a time. Getting in trouble took about six months; getting out will take at least three years—if sales projections hold up.

"Incidentally, up to this point the board had been satisfied with rather hazily implied definitions of mission. The board is now locking the barn door—participating with management in developing strategy guidelines and timetables for the recovery and future directions for the business. For us, at least, a big part of periodic review of the efficacy of the plan will be inputs of various environmental factors affecting the business.

"Having been badly burned, my concern is that we not go so far in making every capital expenditure, new product line, staff addition, development, and so forth pass a litmus test that we hog-tie the CEO or take the fun out of it.

"My hope is that the process will instead retain a reasonable level of management option and flexibility, provide for timely review, and—above all—provide baselines and key indicators, all of which will make it virtually impossible for directors not to ask the right questions.

"While I suppose it is by definition clear that larger companies need more of what you are urging, these experiences suggest to me that the need exists too in smaller enterprises to be just as explicit as possible, though obviously far less complex."

OPPOSITION TO STRATEGY COMMITTEES

This sample of reaction to the proposition that boards should be organized to evaluate a conscious, carefully developed, and articulated strategy has been instructive to me. My suggestion that a board almost totally preoccupied by its full-time responsibilities establish a strategy or corporate objectives committee has produced an unexpected small furor, despite the existence of such committees (effective or not I do not know) in a number of companies. The objection, most eloquently phrased by Karl Bays, CEO of American Hospital Supply, is that strategy is too important to relegate to a committee; it should be the function of the full board.

I find it hard to resist this argument, for corporate strategy is more important than the control system, the committee structure (external audit, executive compensation, public responsibility), the selection of new directors, and most of the other matters delegated to committees for disposition or detailed processing of recommendations prepared by management for eventual submission to the full board.

Assigning strategic decision making and preparation for participation in it to the full board requires ruthless elimination of routine matters and lengthy presentations of reports that could be studied in advance, longer and more frequent meetings, and disciplined, skillful chairmanship.

As I say amen to all of this, I have the unworthy suspicion that I have been defeated by the most sophisticated put-down of all. That is, the chief executive who does not really want his board to delve deeply into strategic questions—for whatever reason—will keep strategy *out* of the hands of a specially qualified and informed committee.

He will submit strategic decisions directly to the formal board meeting, where the open consultation of wristwatches by uninterested directors (those who prefer to substitute confidence in the management for inquiry into what it is up to) will speed the discussion past the rate of comprehension of the real issues and reestablish routine approval of management recommendations as the substitute for evaluation.

At any rate, I promised Karl Bays, as I will any other board chairman, that if he would assure me that he knew how to engage his whole board in an appropriately thorough consideration of the strategic issues confronting American Hospital Supply, I would stop hassling him and others about the desirability of a strategy committee. I hope sometime to find out how he does it, for I have no reason to suspect his good intentions or associate him with the doubts I confessed to a moment ago.

IMPORTANCE OF BOARD
CHAIRMANSHIP

However it is approached—through a committee structure or not—the work of a board these days requires superb chairmanship. The board as an institution of corporate governance is coming alive as a body with the needs of any sophisticated organization—that is, to be (a) effectively supplied with a succession of members with complementary experience and skills, (b) informed and educated for its responsibilities, (c) compensated and otherwise motivated to be conscientious, productive, and creative, and (d) committed to what it understands as its mission.

To lead the board into and out of the consideration of the strategic issues most central to the long-term survival of the company requires an even more fully developed talent than that required to develop a strategy with senior management. Within management, the chief executive's power can suppress disagreement, if necessary. Within the board, he has more subtle means to contain discussion, secure loyal assent, and avoid searching inquiry. To conduct discussions within management and in the board that do not provoke such measures with persons well enough informed and qualified to take part and to advance them to new high ground calls for rare gifts not specifically cultivated in the managerial careers of most chief executives.

Because so many problems attend the entry of a board into strategic considerations, the wisest course is to begin slowly, without commitment to grandiose procedures or fanfare of any sort—or the ambition to emulate Texas Instruments. A chairman can ask his directors, singly or collectively, what they believe the function of their board to be. For example, he can:

> Bring to each board meeting the head of an important division or function to describe the product/market strategy and the expected future development of the company's markets or the function's role in the company.

> Invite board members to attend management meetings in which operating and long-range plans are presented and discussed.

> Offer to individual directors access to any information they want in developing their own knowledge of the company or in pursuing any question or doubt they may harbor.

> Hold separate conversations with directors who appear to him especially knowledgeable about specific markets, technologies, or organization structures.

> Move slowly and tentatively in the face of the limitations he senses or the dangers he foresees.

Initial experiments with little risk of overinvolving the board may be informative; directors may respond with unexpected enthusiasm and indicate early how they would behave if presented with larger questions.

Now that almost everything obvious that is related to board matters has been said more than once, it is time to address, especially in this space, the advanced questions of board management. To get going the conversation from which I have drawn this sample has taken a while. I hope enough momentum has been achieved to move some more of you to record your views even as you act them out.

19

The Strategy
of Diversification

HAROLD S. GENEEN

ITT

Statement by Harold S. Geneen to the Antitrust Subcommittee of the Committee on the Judiciary
House of Representatives, November 20, 1969.

Mr. Chairman, members of the Subcommittee and Staff, I am Harold S. Geneen, Chairman and President of International Telephone and Telegraph Corporation.

Perhaps at the outset it might be desirable to outline my business experience briefly in order to provide some perspective to the background from which I make my statement. I have been President and Chief Executive Officer of ITT for slightly more than ten years.

In the course of my business career I have served as an officer with four of the companies of the so-called list of the 200 largest corporations. These include Raytheon Corporation, Jones & Laughlin Steel Corporation, American Can Company, as well as ITT.

These companies comprise a cross-section of traditional heavy industry, traditional light manufacture and the new and less traditional field of electronics. In addition, I have held positions in smaller companies such as Bell & Howell, The New York World Telegram, Mayflower Associates, and several small brokerage firms, and have been an accountant with a CPA title in the state of New York.

I started my business career in 1926 as a runner on the floor of the New York Stock Exchange, obtaining my education at night at New York University and working my way through a succession of business enterprises.

I say this only to give you a full understanding that when I speak of traditional companies or of modern competitive companies or of performance—or of meaningful competition, that I do so from a background of over 44 years in business that has afforded me an unusual span of exposure in these competitive fields.

At the outset I would like to make it clear that ITT and its management welcome the opportunity to appear before this distinguished Subcommittee.

We believe that the subject matter of these hearings is so important that it deserves the widest possible discussion and impartial analysis.

What is clearly at stake in these proceedings and in the information to be derived, in our opinion, is the question of whether the government will allow *"meaningful,"* new competition to flourish within our free enterprise system in the future. By "meaningful" I mean adequate and frequent enough new entry into established industries to provide, rapid, broad, and effective additions of competition on a scale which will provide economies to the consumer and strength to the economy.

There is an impression in the business community that a large-scale offensive war has been declared on American business growth, business change and business diversification. All of these trends are being attacked. If this offensive war has indeed been launched then it has been done without all of the facts, without meaningful and impartially interpreted data and without consideration of the serious consequences.

For example, the recently issued FTC report entitled "Economic Report on Corporate Mergers" dated October 1969, is a classic example of basically unsupported hypothesis and theory. Even critics of diversified or conglomerate companies concede many virtues to diversification and to diversification mergers.

However, this FTC Staff report, in 700 pages, does not even concede one valuable contribution of these diversified companies, whether old or new.

This is hardly the objective approach that is needed. And because this FTC Report is a Government-sponsored report, there can be little question of why business has this impression.

In fact, in presenting the FTC Report to the Senate Subcommittee on Antitrust and Monopoly, Professor Willard Mueller called for immediate action in curtailing diversification of American business. He said, and I quote, "As I balance the course of inaction, a policy of wait and see, against the course of action *that subsequent scientific inquiry might prove to be a too-zealous policy,* I choose the latter course without hesitation or reservation. For in the present circumstance, should a bold course of action prove later to have prevented some increases in economic efficiency, the matter can be righted by changing policy." (Italic added)

However, despite this recommendation, the 700 pages in the report give no reason nor is any evidence presented to show that diversified companies or diversified mergers actually have any unfavorable effect on competition or on the economy. Professor Mueller's statement is therefore a demand for sentence first, verdict afterward, and then of belated inquiry into the facts because, per chance, there may be some loss of economic efficiency. On this basis any policy, however damaging to the economy and to efficiency, could be justified, since it could later "be righted by changing policy."

What has happened, in my opinion, is that because of a lack of any real information the critics are creating a smokescreen of confusion.

Confusion arises in the first place by the *impression* that the issue for public debate is whether conglomerate companies should be allowed to make conglomerate mergers.

The *real* issue, however, is whether any company, young or old, should be allowed to diversify into fields unrelated to its traditional industry position and by so doing add competition the economy would not otherwise enjoy.

While there has been much said and written on the point that it is better to stimulate internal growth of competition in new fields, let me say clearly that as a matter of business judgment that for virtually all situations of real diversification into unrelated business this is impractical and uneconomic and just will not happen. It is far better that everyone concerned should know and understand this than to make incorrect decisions based on erroneous assumptions.

Companies can, perhaps, move through internal growth into an industry which is very similar in technology, production know-how and marketing to the company's existing operations. But in real product diversification situations new entry innovations, change and growth in production capacity can be accomplished in a meaningful way only by entering through an acquisition of a reasonably sized company already in that field.

There has been some acknowledgment of this fact even by the Justice Department which has recognized the need for "foothold acquisitions" as a necessary nucleus of this entry process. Unfortunately, there have been no official guidelines published on this point, and it is our general impression that the word "foothold" will in practice be thought of as a size so small that it will not provide a viable base for the kind of modern management systems and business techniques that a diversified company such as ours can apply in attempting to improve efficiencies and provide meaningful competition.

Therefore, while it is clear that the Department of Justice agrees in principle with the need for diversification mergers, it is unwilling to follow where its own logic would lead in order to encourage really meaningful competition.

Simply stated, a policy denying access to change, innovations and new industrial competition by the route of diversification acquisitions of meaningful size, will result in a stagnant status-quo of the existing large companies within an industry regardless of efficiency or competitiveness or the resulting values offered to the consumer. It prevents the functioning of a market in corporate assets thereby lowering the efficiency of the industry. In short, it prevents the natural transfer of assets to more efficient managements and also deprives stockholders of the real value of their investments.

It is precisely for these reasons that many informed people have come to the conclusion that the recent trends of our antitrust enforcement with respect to large diversification mergers are perhaps unintentionally really preventing new and increased innovation and new competition—and are operating to protect industry incumbents from new competition.

It is obviously timely that this whole aspect of enforcement in respect to diversified companies be reviewed.

An examination of the top 200 or top 500 companies or the top 1000 companies will disclose that an overwhelming proportion of the so-called old-line companies are already widely diversified into numerous industries. This is not really a new development or a new trend, or an unusual situation.

In fact, it is clear from general published information that most companies, large or small, are to varying degrees already diversified—and to use another word—at least partly conglomerate. This fact is readily apparent from the FTC report itself.

Diversification itself has many merits from the standpoint of the nation, the consumer, and the stockholder.

Diversification provides a form of security and insurance and a method of adapting to the real quickening tempo of change that we are all experiencing—change in technology, change in markets and consumers, and change in foreign competition. It therefore underlies *continuity* of employment and unity of corporate effort—it is a *constructive* influence on our economy. It is a vital necessity to management with concern for its trusteeship for the long-term future of its employees, stockholders, and the communities in which it operates. Diversification is, in short, an "insurance" policy for orderly future growth and thus has important positive values as a concept in itself.

This does not mean that a diversified company is not responsive to each of the markets in which it operates, or can be indifferent to its profit or loss there. But a diversified company is able to ride out the occasional and unforeseen vicissitudes of a particular market and depend on the long-term profit opportunities there. It is for this reason that communities welcome the new plants of a diversified company which are less likely to be shut down because of a short-term hardship or a fortuitous change in the market.

It is for sound reasons such as these—constructive reasons—that we see most of industry, large and small, either already diversified or becoming more diversified.

Factually then, what we really have are only "old" or "new" diversified companies—or conglomerates.

But just as we have always recognized "well managed"—or "less well-managed" companies—so too do we have "well-managed" or "less well-managed" conglomerate or diversified companies. And the investor and marketplace have always recognized this difference—and have usually rewarded it in kind by valuation and stockholder investment action. This corrective factor can be relied upon. Inefficient companies must either change and become efficient, or they will wither away.

But it is well-managed and well-run companies, whether old or newly diversified, that we are talking about here today. They are constructive and represent a sound economic organization with *positive* economic and social impact.

Therefore, the *form and structure* of diversification should not be confused with the problem of individual company management. American industry, in fact, provides far more examples of successfully well-run diversified companies—old and new—than it does of "unsuccessful" ones. This large group of successful diversified companies should not be lumped together with the few less well-managed ones. It is important, therefore, to recognize that what is necessary to consider here today, in our opinion, is the value of diversification itself, not the history of a few particular managements—each of which will differ in methods and performance—and in the magnitude of the problems they had to face in their particular industries.

One last general comment. Much has been said in the public debate about the effects of diversified companies on communities, yet the fact remains that diversified companies are constantly seeking good communities in which to build plants and companies—just as good communities are seeking diversified industry. Our operating units which are responsible for the location of their new plants are constantly seeking new area communities. And ITT's operating units receive scores of visits in the course of a year from representatives of villages, towns, cities and states over the country who are interested in having ITT operations in their communities where environment and labor are available. One of the greatest trends of constructive economy and social uplift that has been seen in this country, far more effective than any local government could achieve, has been the vast number of plants that have been built in small towns throughout the newer and less developed areas of the country. Far from detracting from community growth, they have added greatly to it. In this respect, large and diversified companies have been fluid and responsive, providing employment and continued community support.

So, generally, it is my belief that the issues here today are constructive ones, issues of permitted new industry competition *without* any increase in market concentration—issues of continuity of employment—of growing communities—of encouraged corporate effort through permitted diversification—all to the benefit of the nation's consumers and the economy.

In this respect, the statement that Congressman McCulloch of the Committee made last July 30 is worth repeating, and I quote:

". . . the intensive study by the House Antitrust Subcommittee should provide answers to many of the questions raised by the so-called conglomerate corporations. Proceeding with great care and fairness—I repeat, and fairness—to protect and accommodate the legitimate interest of the companies involved, the enforcement agencies and of the Congress, these hearings should provide a more clear assessment of the motivations and methods by which these companies have proceeded, a more accurate picture of their effect on our society and a more perceptive basis upon which to judge whether legislation is needed to insure a free and competitive society."

This statement stands forth as the basis on which we say that the work of this Committee is timely in the national interest. And it is in this same spirit that we welcome the opportunity to appear here today.

It is against this background that I would like now to deal with the position of ITT and its work, and its contribution to the economic and competitive stream of our economy.

First, let me explain the motive behind our diversification.

The origins of ITT go back to 1920 at which time it started as a small service company in the communications field in the Caribbean.

This company grew under the leadership of its founder, Mr. Sosthenes Behn, until at the outbreak of the 2nd World War it had grown to a company of about 75,000 employees and approximately $92 million of sales.

It is important to realize that while almost 100% of ITT's stockholders were American citizens at that point, almost all of its activities were abroad.

During World War II, practically all of ITT's companies in Europe were overrun and seized. Currency conversion problems which persisted for many years after the War, and the necessity for rehabilitating and rebuilding our companies, were ITT's primary concerns and difficulties. I might point out that these serious losses and difficulties occurred at a time when most U.S. companies were rapidly expanding from the U.S. plants which had been developed for war time purposes and were quickly converted to peace time capacity usages, thus providing an uninterrupted flow of growth and earnings for their stockholders.

ITT had no such advantages. In fact, many of our companies have not been recovered from the World War II expropriations. And even more recently, our Cuban telephone company was expropriated without compensation by Mr. Castro. A short time later, our Brazilian telephone company was also expropriated. And only two weeks ago, we sold our Peruvian telephone company to the Government of Peru in recognition of their national aspirations.

Experiences of this kind, therefore, regarding the business risks involved in foreign operations convinced the management and Board of Directors of ITT of the necessity and of our obligation to diversify into the relatively secure and growing U.S. and Canadian economies. Our first point of entry into the domestic market might logically have appeared to be the telephone equipment manufacturing business, as this was our major field abroad. However, ITT's traditional areas of telecommunications were essentially foreclosed in the U.S. because of the captive market position and vertical integration of AT&T and its manufacturing subsidiary Western Electric Co., and General Telephone and Electronics and its manufacturing subsidiary Automatic Electric Company.

The very small portion of the independent telephone market which remains open for competition leaves the prospects for future growth as minimal. Additionally, governmental decisions have given the Communications Satellite Corporation a monopoly position in the operation of communications satellites and a virtual monopoly in U.S. ground stations, thereby foreclosing significant growth in our other traditional field.

The basic purposes and goals of ITT's diversification efforts are therefore intended for the long-term protection and profit of its family of shareholders. We believe the purposes of such diversification are highly important to long-term stability, as well as growth. Business is facing an increasingly fast-paced technical obsolescence trend as well as increasing international competition based on world economies of low labor costs and constantly increasing technical capabilities within these low labor cost areas. Diversification and the consequent development of broad professional management skills are a necessity for protection and future development. Diversification is therefore a necessary type of corporate insurance which sound management must achieve on behalf of its stockholders, so that the risks of separate sectors are pooled and alternatives of internal fiscal investment are provided. The purposes of diversification in our case, therefore, can be summarized as follows:

1. To diversify into industries and markets which have good prospects for above average long-term growth and profitability;
2. To achieve a sound balance between foreign earnings and domestic earnings;

3. To achieve a sound balance between high risk capital-intensive manufacturing operations and less risky service operations;

4. To achieve a sound balance between high risk engineering-labor-intensive electronics manufacturing and less risky commercial and industrial manufacturing;

5. To achieve a sound ratio between commercial/industrial products and services, and consumer products and services;

6. To achieve a sound ratio between government/defense/space operations, and commerical/industrial/consumer/products and services in both foreign and domestic markets; and

7. To achieve a sound balance between cyclical products and services.

Those are our motives and our purposes. These motives are designed to provide growth, and security for our employees and stockholders.

Now—to our methods.

There are many kinds of diversified companies—or "conglomerates." There are old, respectable diversified companies. There are new diversified companies. There are different degrees of product and market diversification. Most significantly, there are differences in management forms and methods. Some of them differ in emphasis on operations versus, let's say, simple financial management. Others may be engaged primarily in securities promotion. In making acquisitions, some companies use straight equity securities, others use warrants, debentures, installment payments and deferred pricing. There are friendly mergers. There are hostile tenders and proxy fights; there are examples of retained managements; and there are replaced managements. There are resulting efficient companies and there are resulting relatively inefficient companies.

Unfortunately, all of these differences are being indistinguishably merged into a generic term "conglomerate" which is now being widely and confusedly used.

But the important *fact* is that *each* company is a different company and they cannot be thought of meaningfully as a "class" any more than the general term "corporation."

For example, diversified or conglomerate companies divide in one essential area.

This point of division is whether they operate as a financial holding company or as a coherent operating company. That is—whether they provide within the parent company a broad group of central management skills, applicable not only to the over-all corporate areas such as financing, legal, and stockholder relations, but also to the *operating* areas of the company. Such areas, for example, as production, marketing, planning, research and development, product development, and foreign operations.

ITT operates as a coherent *operating* company with a substantial central *operating* management. In fact, we have slightly over 1,000 industrial and operational specialists in our central management group. We have developed this expert group in order to improve our competitiveness and our efficiencies and to support our operating companies in improving operations in those fields, either new or old, that we have entered.

Again, acquisition policies are *not* the same for all diversified or conglomerate companies. The "pro" and "con" of the legal methods used and the economic justification of even "hostile tenders" have been well-aired in the press. Let me say—for the record—that we have never made a hostile tender.

Let me point out instead the management and business *value* of friendly acquisitions which, by far, represent most mergers. For example, with the central management capabilities that ITT has assembled, we can provide receptive and constructive bases for merger—bases that will pay off in increased efficiency for *both* parties. For example:

1. We offer an assurance of continued support and growth in an innovative climate leading to new products and fields through our informed management support of such a company.

2. We offer a concerned, helpful, and invigorating management atmosphere in which the new management members can grow. Opportunities for advancement are created within such an environment; and since these mergers are arrived at with the concurrence of management and stockholders, there is a "mutual accord" on improved objectives from the very start.

3. We can afford to price fairly and to exchange our own *equity* stocks with the shareholders of an incoming company. We can improve operating efficiencies and profits sufficiently to make this valuation worthwhile to both sets of shareholders. By exchanging equity stocks, the shareholders of the original company continue as equity participants in the family of ITT shareholders. We have used no unusual financial packages to support our growth.

It is significant, therefore, that many of the allegations leveled against a few conglomerates are simply not applicable to us or to the vast majority of diversified companies.

These methods and the economic results brought about by the diversified companies such as ITT are thoroughly pro-competitive, pro-growth, and in the national interest.

Other allegations which have been leveled against conglomerates include those of reciprocity, concentration of power, questionable economic performance of acquired companies, predatory pricing and finally the allegation that the decision-making process is removed from the acquired company to the corporate headquarters of the conglomerate.

In considering each of these allegations I think it well to define the starting place. ITT, like all companies, is in business to earn a fair profit commensurate with its competitive performance in full compliance with the law and the responsibilities of good corporate citizenship. We cannot afford to do anything which would conflict with this. I will explain therefore why we cannot engage in reciprocity or predatory pricing, etc.

RECIPROCITY

Efforts to purchase or sell goods or services on the basis of so-called "reciprocity" violate basic management principles of building a business soundly and permanently by being at all times capable of meeting open competition and having a trained business organization capable of meeting the challenges and problems created by competition. Only in this manner can a secure foundation and future be developed and built for a company. The theory of "reciprocity" is therefore repugnant as a basic business philosophy. And furthermore, it is my firm belief that efforts to purchase or sell goods or services on the basis of so-called "reciprocity" are completely uneconomical and are, in fact, a very unsound business practice. Such a practice dulls and distorts the efforts of both sales and purchasing staffs which should be directed toward selling and buying products on the basis of price, quality and service; it dilutes the management responsibility for profits; and, in the long run, it is certain to be costly and enervating to any company that practices it.

I am, of course, aware that there has been considerable talk during recent years about "reciprocity" and in some companies certain people have endeavored to create for themselves an executive-level career as a "Trade Relations" director. However, it is my opinion based upon my 44 years of business experience in a rather wide variety of companies, that reciprocal buying and selling "gains" are largely illusory—and are more often "talked about" or "claimed" by self-serving Trade Relations directors than ever realized or actually practiced on any significant scale. In addition, on the other side, I have observed that salesmen must often have some excuse for losing a sale, and may blame their failure to sell on what they think they see as reciprocity where none in fact exists.

Most importantly, within ITT the very structure of our organization and the very wide variety of our products and markets, create the necessity for our profit center organization. Under such a "profit center" organization, it is simply impractical to attempt to practice reciprocity; and in fact, we do not even assemble the data that would be necessary to do this. I think, therefore, it is quite clear that there is no "interest" in reciprocity under our philosophy of management, nor would reciprocity even be practical under our organization. Let me be more specific as to this structure and organization, and how it works. The structure and organization of each ITT operating unit, for the reasons already stated, is a separate "profit center" with its own *decentralized* purchasing department and its own *decentralized* sales department. This structure effectively eliminates both the motive as well as any practical opportunity for any attempt to utilize the volume of purchasing activities of one ITT profit center to try to benefit the sales activities of another ITT profit center. Since the professional reputation, compensation and, most importantly the business career progress of the manager and management of each ITT profit center, are dependent upon their record of performance as shown by their individual profit center, it is clear that these local managements have the strongest possible professional and career motivation to achieve maximum efficiencies in their own purchasing department. Consequently, they would not only strenuously resist any possible attempt to interfere with the efficiencies of their own purchasing departments for any claimed reciprocal benefit to any other profit center, but would consider this as a restraint on their own professional careers. In this day of shortage of executives and unlimited outside career opportunities, no company could afford to alienate its management by affecting their careers in this manner. Moreover, this would be alien to the entire philosophy of performance and efficiency, which is the very basis of ITT's whole management approach.

The practical situation, and the ITT management attitude, is best illustrated by the fact that ITT does not even waste the time or energy to accumulate the purchasing and sales data which would be necessary for "reciprocity" or "reciprocity effect." When the Department of Justice has on several recent occasions asked ITT to accumulate this data for the Department's current investigation, it has been necessary for us to send out special questionnaires to each of the local profit centers and then specifically to assemble and compile the data to answer the Department's questions. This task was accomplished only after considerable effort and, I might add, complaining by the local purchasing departments about the tremendous waste of their valuable time which was involved in assembly of what they considered useless data. And even this data which was assembled for the Department will rapidly become obsolete. The reluctance of our local managements and purchasing agents to spend their time in assembling this type of data further illustrates the complete lack of application of such information in our business operations and the lack of any significance to any allegation of "reciprocity" or "reciprocity effect." I might add that as a matter of our corporate policy, when we first assembled this type of purchasing information for the Department of Justice in 1966 we established procedures for the careful protection of the resulting list of large suppliers to make sure that it was limited to purchasing and legal channels and was not made available to any ITT personnel responsible for sales or marketing. At the same time in 1966, in order to make sure that ITT's corporate policy against the practice of reciprocity was fully and clearly understood throughout the System, we issued a formal ITT Company Policy stating as follows:

Reciprocity
The United States Supreme Court has held that reciprocal buying practices or "reciprocity," is "one of the congeries of anticompetitive practices" at which the antitrust laws of the United States are aimed. Reciprocity is also an unsound busi-

ness practice, since it distorts the market process and the normal development of economic efficiencies and product improvements. Consequently, for both legal and business reasons, it is the policy of ITT to purchase and sell products and services on the basis of the commercial criteria of superior quality, suitability, efficiency, service, and price.

No attempt shall be made to develop sales of any service or product through the use of, or threatened withdrawal of, any existing or potential reciprocal buying leverage of "reciprocity."

In this connection, information concerning ITT System purchases from particular suppliers shall not be made available to personnel who are concerned with developing sales and marketing.

This policy is still in effect, and we have recently taken extra steps to make sure that all ITT System purchasing and sales personnel are familiar with this Corporate Policy.

CONCENTRATION OF POWER

Concentration of power, perhaps, is the subject that is the most misunderstood of any concerning the so-called conglomerate or diversified company. The problem is one of inadequate statistics and of misinterpretation which seems to prove a point. In the FTC report which I referred to earlier, for example, it is stated that merger movements around the turn of the century and in the 1920's "left an indelible imprint on the structure of the American economy," and resulted in, and I quote, "an increase in market concentration."

This subject of "market concentration" is in fact, the only real economic issue. Market concentration does have a bearing on competition because competition or monopoly can only exist in some *particular market.* This voluminous FTC Report is a massive evasion of the real need for careful and real analysis of market concentration. The reason so much time is spent in the FTC Report on the irrelevancy of "aggregate" or "overall concentration" or "super concentration" is simply to distract the reader's attention from a very important fact. The figures on market concentration have been so "unobliging" as to have shown no increase since World War II (and since long before then). Indeed, there may possibly be some tendency the other way. That is why the FTC Report despite its 700 pages says very little on the key issue of "market concentration" and, in fact, provides us with only some very questionable statistics and conclusions— and some truncated comparisons. (See appendix 1)

I do not make this assertion as an idle statement. While the FTC Report is too recent and too bulky to permit full and detailed study and analysis of all its deficiencies, we think that the facts set forth in appendix 1 to this statement give forcible support to the very basic criticism of the Report. Consequently I urge you most strongly to read the appendix to this statement in full because of its conclusive importance to these proceedings.

Moreover there is further serious "blurring" of the statistics as used.

There is no distinction made in these statistics, for example, between a company such as ITT, which has about $4 billion in sales and revenues, about 50 percent outside the U.S. and spread thinly over some 35 industries, and on this basis is ranked as the 11th largest U.S. industrial firm, and, for example, the company which is ranked 12th—Western Electric—which also does $4 billion, but this time *entirely in the U.S. and all concentrated in one industry.* Nor, for that matter do the FTC statistics adequately distinguish between manufacturing activities as contrasted to service activities or the geographic source of income and the relation of these activities to the so-called "manufacturing assets." In the case of ITT, the FTC statistics commit an *error of almost one for one*—or 100%—by including ITT's worldwide manufacturing and service activities in this sort of exercise. Similar substantial errors result with respect to many other large companies, such as the mining and oil companies, automobile, business machine and others with high foreign growth.

One must question, therefore, the accuracy and meaningfulness of these FTC statistics when one considers the rapid growth of services and the rapid growth of overseas activities of all large American companies in recent years.

Perhaps even more important is the fact that the *implication of continually increasing aggregate concentration in a small group of companies does not follow from the statistics* since the list of 100 or 200 largest companies keeps changing. It is a mathematical certainty that there will always be 100 largest companies, but it is important to recognize that they are not the same companies from period to period. This only again indicates the conclusive effects of competition and change. In fact, less than one-third of the top 100 companies in 1909 are still in it. What happened to the golden names in the other two-thirds? What happened to the traction companies? What happened to the gas companies? And what happened to the railroads? The emergence of the aviation and electronics industries and other new industries would be part of the answer. But I think the basic answer is in the failure of the managements of these companies to grow, diversify and change along with the economy, in other words—the effect of competition. For example, of the 50 largest manufacturing corporations, in 1947 as tabulated by the Bureau of the Census, only 25 were among the 50 largest in 1966.

Also disregarded by the FTC statistics is the simple fact that with respect to the growth in assets of the 200 largest companies between 1948 to 1968, only about one-fifth of the apparent aggregate increase in such assets can be ascribed to *all large mergers* by the 200 largest companies—horizontal, vertical, or conglomerate. Consequently, at least four-fifths of the apparent increase in assets was simply the result of non-merger growth all by the traditional horizontal companies. It is obvious that practically nothing significant of that apparent increase in assets is attributable to diversification mergers by the "new conglomerate" companies.

The FTC statistics on aggregate concentration ignore the very important fact that about 85 percent of the assets of the top 100 companies in 1968 are accounted for by companies in the fields of chemicals, oil, primary metals, fabricated metals, machinery, electrical equipment, automobiles and aircraft. These are all highly capital-intensive manufacturing operations; and so perhaps all the FTC statistics on the assets of the top 100 companies really tell us is something of the increasing capital costs of heavy goods industries, of off-shore drilling, of foreign oil investment and of the growth of the automobile and airplane industries.

It is clear that ITT's diversification acquisitions do not pose any threat of aggregate concentration of U.S. manufacturing assets. Although *Fortune,* and presumably the FTC, rank us as the 11th largest U.S. industrial company, actually about half of our operations are located outside the U.S. And a very substantial portion of our U.S. activities are not in the manufacturing area at all, but are in the field of services and financial services. For example, in the U.S. ITT has a total of about 66,000 employees in its manufacturing operations; this represents about 0.3 percent of the total number of about 20,045,000 employees on manufacturing payrolls in the U.S., according to the Bureau of Labor Statistics.

Consequently, I submit that it is unsound for anyone to suggest that ITT represents any kind of a threat of "aggregate concentration" or other kind of threat to the competitive structure of U.S. industry.

I believe one could properly ask now what has this talk about increasing "aggregate concentration" to do with conglomerates—or ITT—or adverse effect on competition? And the answer is clear—almost nothing.

But what are the important stakes for the American citizen and the national interest? We have agreed that excessive concentration within markets is not desirable because it reduces competition, and competition is what spurs efficiency. We have also shown that diversified mergers do not increase market concentration but *do increase competition.* Efficiency is always desirable, but never more so than today. America's position as a world industrial leader is challenged today by the resurgent nations of Europe and Asia, most particularly Germany and Japan. It is quite conceivable that without increased competition the U.S. could start on the downhill economic road and our industrial economy could become second-rate. If we thwart our companies from growing, changing, and becoming more efficient, even when their growth has no effect on concentration within markets, we may be starting on that downhill road as the traction companies and the other "golden names" from the past I referred to.

At first glance, our current balance of payments deficit may seem only remotely connected to the subject of our meeting here today. But the fact remains that our increasing deficits in the Balance of Payments area are bluntly telling the cost of this mounting efficient foreign competition. This same story is being told by the increasing variety and abundance of imported goods within the country. It is not my purpose to object to the flow of foreign competition for the benefit of the American consumer. It is my purpose to point out the need for greater efficiency and performance on the part of our domestic companies, and to point out that a better understanding and support of the needs of American business by its government is of vital importance to the U.S. national interest—and one of those needs is the ability to diversify and enter new competitive fields.

THE ALLEGATION
OF QUESTIONABLE PERFORMANCE
OF ACQUIRED COMPANIES

We have furnished the Subcommittee staff with a great volume of financial and other business information concerning ITT and the companies which have joined the ITT System.

What does this information show with respect to the profit performance of these companies after they joined the ITT System? The recent FTC Economic Report on Corporate Mergers points out that "it is not possible to measure efficiency from merger by simple before and after comparisons" since prices and costs vary over time, there are changes in product development strategies, capital investment programs, research and development expenses. There are also important changes in markets, customers, general economic conditions, inflation, taxes and many other factors.

The FTC Report states that the recent performance of a few conglomerates "indicates that they are not immune from ordinary management problems."

I would like to make it very clear that we do not claim that our form of diversified corporate organization or our form of open management system makes ITT immune from ordinary management problems or any other kind of economic or business problems. We do not claim that our management system provides a cure-all for every problem that may arise within one of our subsidiaries or profit centers. However, I am convinced from my own 44 years of business experience, and from the experience of the large number of other experienced and capable corporate executives who constitute the ITT management team, that the ITT System can provide the maximum assistance to the operating units that intelligent and responsible professional management can produce.

Keeping in mind the practical problems I have just mentioned with respect to the lack of direct comparability of "before" and "after" profit performance figures, I believe that the companies which have joined the ITT System have successfully met the problems of drastically increasing labor and material costs, the problems of higher state, local and federal taxes of all kinds, and the problems of increasing competitive pressures in every market we serve and have generally increased their profits at average rates between 10 and 15 percent per year.

To give you a rough idea of the magnitude of these practical business problems, the U.S. Department of Commerce has reported an increase of 56.1 percent in average weekly earnings for U.S. manufacturing workers during the period from 1958 to 1969, including an increase of 6.1 percent in the last year alone! The increase for contract construction workers was 80.6 percent during the period from 1958 to 1969, including an increase of 9.8 percent in the last year!

Just this month, the Bureau of Labor Statistics has reported that the nation's unit costs have increased by 1.6 percent in the third quarter and that the national productivity has actually *decreased* in this same period by .4 percent. And, therefore, the best the U.S. economy can hope for during the year 1969 is the poorest productivity increase since 1956. This is the old cost-price squeeze and business has got to handle it.

These increased wage rates are reflected in both our own direct labor costs and in the costs of all the materials and supplies which we purchase.

For example, the U.S. Department of Labor reports the following substantial increases in the wholesale price index for common purchased metals and metal products.

	(in percent)	
	Percent increase 1958– August 1969	*Percent Increase August 1968– August 1969*
Semi-finished steel products	13.3	5.3
Gray iron castings	30.6	3.4
Copper, wirebar electrolytic	64.8	14.6
Copper water tubing (in coils)	51.9	28.0
Zinc, slab, prime western	30.0	7.2
Red brass ingot	76.8	18.5

Now how has ITT's U.S. operations and manufacturing units coped with this very serious problem of the cost-price squeeze?

If we take the year 1968, for example, we find that our profit margins have narrowed, yet we have been able to increase our profits through plain hard work, new plant investment and by achieving cost reduction efficiencies in our plants, increased productivity, increased capacity utilization and increased sales per employee. Vigorous and increasing competition from both U.S. and foreign competitors makes it impossible to try to meet this squeeze by trying to pass on the entire increase in our own pricing. You have seen the results of this in increasing foreign imports of steel, autos and electronic products.

But despite these continual problems of inflation, mounting unit costs, and increasing competition in all markets and lower margins, and despite the specific problems experienced by any particular ITT profit center along with the other members of their particular industry, and despite the occasional mistakes which will inevitably be made by any company, the performance record of the ITT System as a whole by any comparison would be outstanding over a ten-year period. That record is one of a stable annual compounded increase in earnings per share at the rate of 11 percent over each preceding year for 10 successive years. We believe this ten-year record speaks for itself with respect to the soundness of our form of diversified corporate organization, as well as our management systems and techniques. We have appended to this statement the 10-year summary of this growth from our 1968 annual report which shows our increase in earnings per share from 95 cents per share in 1959 to $2.58 per share in 1968. (Appendix II).

PREDATORY PRICING

I can assure you that, as businessmen, we at ITT don't like to lose money and we don't intentionally price below our cost. Indeed, the managers in charge of our individual profit centers work hard to reduce their costs when they see that their competitors are in a position to sell at lower prices over the long term. I believe that theories that big diversified companies can and will engage in "predatory" pricing, subsidizing one profit center with the earnings of another, in an attempt to monopolize a market, is folklore—not fact. Such allegations may be numerous but the evidence is practically non-existent. While the businessman who lost a sale on price would like to think his competition is indulging in sales below cost, I have found that in reality the rival's lower price means that he is more competitive, and that his costs are actually lower.

THE DECISION-MAKING PROCESS

Insofar as ITT is concerned, nothing could be further from the truth than the allegation that the decision-making process is removed from an acquired company to corporate headquarters. If the decision-making process were removed from the divisional level, we would be unable to retain the excellent management we have been able to assemble to run our various operations—and it would be impossible to run it from headquarters.

ITT Headquarters personnel act essentially as an expert management consultant staff. We do not manage any of the line operations from the Headquarters in New York City. Our policy is to have each operating unit do as much of its own work as possible.

The major contribution which ITT brings to the companies which join the ITT System is the approach and atmosphere of a sound and effective modern management system. The ITT management system emphasizes detailed and realistic short and long range planning and budgeting developed by individual profit centers, effective controls for the ascertainment and measurement of actual performance in comparison to budgeted performance, prompt ascertainment of problem areas and effective and prompt constructive and corrective action, and the utilization of an effective expert consulting staff to give advice and assistance in these matters and other matters, such as quality measurement and control, cost effectiveness, greater operating efficiencies through industrial engineering, installation engineering, manufacturing engineering, product and value engineering, production and inventory control, transportation and traffic cost control, purchasing techniques, real estate procurement and disposition, technical and R&D programs, effective control of accounts receivable, legal patent and tax advice, personnel recruitment and the many other aspects of business management where the advice of trained, qualified and proven professional experts can be of assistance. We encourage and assist our profit centers in establishing unusually high goals for growth and profit performance—ordinarily a goal of a 15% increase in net earnings each year—but we also assist and support our profit centers in planning realistic methods and techniques for actually achieving those goals.

ITT could be described as a management cooperative. A group of smaller companies, each competing in its own industry and each sharing in and supporting the cost of a skilled central management it could not afford alone. We have an "open management" system which (1) stresses flexibility-continuous fact gathering and analysis and continuous questioning with the flexibility to change decisions and change direction (2) which stresses communications—including face to face communications on the details of problems, on a continuing basis (3) which is action-oriented stressing prompt action to solve business problems and (4) which stresses the early recognition and rapid development of individual management skills at all levels of the company.

No form of organization can be effective unless it develops and encourages the necessary management skills in its executives at all levels and offers them corresponding rewards in career progress and compensation. In time such an atmosphere of help and high goals encourages the utmost in hard work and outstanding performance. The wide diversification of ITT provides great opportunity for individuals to move to positions of responsibility and to secure recognition for their own contributions and to rise in the organization on merit, irrespective of age or seniority, or family connections or other barriers to achievement that are often associated with traditional business. For example, the average age of the executives in ITT's central management group is about 44 years—as compared to a range of 47 to 52 years in most other companies.

Despite, and perhaps even because of our ability to motivate, train and move able young executives to wide responsibilities—and despite our policy to pay high for high performance, it has become well known in industry that ITT constitutes an effective training school for management executives—and we find that our trained executives are in great demand for the top management positions in other companies. At least seven corporate presidents of substantial companies have come from the ranks of ITT executives in the last few years. While we naturally hate to lose our executives to other companies, we feel that this substantiates the nature of the corporate executive we are training—and more importantly the vast majority of this same caliber, remaining, is what makes our performance.

ACCOUNTING TECHNIQUES

Other questions have been raised concerning accounting techniques used by diversified companies. Particularly, there is great interest and debate now on the use of pooling of interest and the amortization of goodwill. Briefly, this is our position on these subjects.

ITT has not utilized any form of unusual accounting techniques to enhance the reported earnings of ITT. Our acquisitions, involving exchanges of stock have customarily been accounted for as pooling of interests with no material effect on the current reported earnings per share of the combined company; and the principles of pooling permit stockholders and investors to compare the combined company's current performance with the comparable restated earnings of the companies for prior periods so that there can be no illusory increase in performance.

Extensive discussions have been carried on during recent months, within the accounting profession with respect to the most desirable techniques for accounting treatment of mergers and acquisitions. ITT has always followed sound and conservative accounting principles, and we shall continue to do so.

We believe that the business future of ITT is dependent upon the utilization of good management techniques, sound business principles and sound use of available capital resources in order to develop a strong and continuing stream of earnings in growth industries. We believe it is obvious that this type of sound business growth can not be constructed out of other than sound accounting techniques. We believe that merger accounting principles should be neither pro-merger nor anti-merger, but should simply endeavor to reflect as clearly as possible for stockholders and the investing community the effect of a combination of two earnings streams and two sets of economic values. We believe that the pooling of interests principle is a convenient and accurate method of accounting for business mergers. We believe that reasonable provisions can be established by the accounting profession and the SEC to eliminate any accounting abuses or deficiencies which may exist and the entire business community will support efforts in that direction. However, there have been no such problems in the diversification mergers made by ITT.

Earlier in my testimony, I said that I would make a specific recommendation to this Committee. I would like to do that now.

Certainly a highly diversified company—like ITT—produces a beneficial impact on the U.S. economy. Companies like ours contribute directly to economic strength by checking inflation by decreasing costs through more efficient production, by stabilizing employment, by adding to the financial strength of local communities and by insuring a fair return to the investors.

When we talk of the economy, we are also talking of an important consumer—the thirty million stockholders who make the American economy go. These people need protection against the kind of strange financial packages which have made it difficult for even experts to determine the true values. These people may need protection against packages of any kind when offered in a manner to bypass the counsel of their own elected boards of directors.

Therefore, I recommend that a new division be organized within the Securities and Exchange Commission ... to be consumer-oriented to protect those thirty million investors from these strange financial packages. I believe this would give needed protection to the investing consumer, and aid the nation's economy to continue to grow.

Finally, gentlemen, I would like to thank you for this opportunity to present our views. I hope these thoughts will be of value to you and I sincerely believe that the findings of this Committee should support diversification and continued resulting growth in competition in American industry.

Thank you.

20

Strategic Interaction: Some Lessons from Industry Histories for Theory and Antitrust Policy

MICHAEL E. PORTER
Harvard University

The author has benefited from comments by R. E. Caves.

Antitrust policy has been constructed from a foundation of models of competition that are largely static and cross-sectional, reflecting the bulk of research in mainstream industrial organization. The focus has been structural on the one hand, taking the industry as the unit of analysis, and behaviorial on the other, with a preoccupation with the motivations for and consequences of particular competitive practices.

While studying the same market outcomes as antitrust investigations, the tradition of research on corporate strategy has been quite different. Here research has emphasized the study of in-depth case histories of firms' strategic interaction over a substantial period of time. The industry history, as practiced at business schools,[1] has had a number of distinctive elements when compared to bread-and-butter research in industrial organization. First, its emphasis is longitudinal, built around a careful re-creation of competitive moves and other events in the sequence in which they occurred. Second, it is broad and quite detailed in coverage of firm behavior and industry events rather than focusing on one or a few elements of competitive behavior such as investment or pricing. Third, it emphasizes the uncertainties present in predicting the future that bear on the decisions facing firms. Fourth, it places great emphasis on a full and complete description of each major competitor, including its full range of activities in all markets in which it competes, and a great deal of emphasis on "internal" factors such as the identity and backgrounds of management, the evolving organizational arrangements in place, et cetera.

The industry-history approach to studying competitive outcomes, then, rests on some explicit or implicit premises about their determinants that differ from those of past emphasis in industrial organization research.[2] While making no claims to be an expert in antitrust or of covering the concerns of antitrust systematically, I will attempt to outline in this paper some of the important issues for antitrust policy that seem to arise from the study of strategic interaction through industry histories, as well as some tentative policy modifications that result. In raising these issues, I will make use of an extended discussion of the disposable-diaper industry. The diaper industry is a strategic example because it illustrates richly the general possibilities for strategic interaction as well as poses, in the extreme, the specific dilemma of strategic behavior designed to achieve scale or learning economies. It is hoped that the discussion here will also contribute to the building of increasingly rich models of strategic interaction in industrial organization research.

---

[1]And originally in a somewhat different form by Edward Mason and his followers.

[2]Recent industrial organization research is changing to some extent in this regard. More on this below.

I. THE CONCEPT OF STRATEGY

Industry histories show that strategic interaction among firms is often guided by a strategy, or a coordinated plan consisting of a set of economic (and sometimes noneconomic) objectives and time-dimensioned policies in each functional area of the firm (e.g., marketing, production, distribution, and so on) to achieve these objectives.[3] The objectives and policies are simultaneously determined and reflect the firm's assessment of its capabilities and limitations relative to competitors and its search for a distinctive competitive advantage. Since each firm is seen as a unique collection of tangible and intangible assets and skills built up through its past activities, the emphasis in strategy formulation is in staking out a position based on the firm's unique capabilities that can be defended (that is, which possesses mobility barriers—see below) against competitors. Strategic interaction among firms is the playing out of strategies over time through investment decisions and tactical moves and countermoves. Successful strategies are those that are internally consistent and accurately reflect the firm's strengths and weaknesses relative to its competitors and its competitors' expected behavior.

The concept of strategy implies that antitrust analysis cannot form normative judgments about one aspect of firm behavior, or design remedies to correct it, in isolation. For example, a firm might have a distribution policy of exclusive dealers. Looking at its other activities, this firm might also be emphasizing high-quality products, an active product-innovation policy, fast service, extensive dealer support, and advertising stressing product quality, placed primarily in specialized magazines and trade journals. All these policies form a consistent strategy. Another firm practicing exclusive dealing in the same industry, on the other hand, might offer little service, products of only acceptable quality, minimal efforts in sales promotion to the retailer, and heavy television advertising. The first firm's exclusive dealership network could be socially desirable on balance, depending on the market shares of other competitors. The second firm's strategy, on the other hand, implies that its policy of exclusive dealing is probably designed to create a strategic entry barrier with little offsetting social benefit.

That an overall strategy guides strategic interaction also implies that a remedy aimed at one aspect of a firm's behavior must be probed to see how it will affect the ability of the firm to carry out its previous strategy, and whether the firm is likely to adjust other elements of its strategy to compensate or redefine its strategy completely. The firm will strive to maintain an internally consistent approach to competing, and one to which it is uniquely suited. If an antitrust remedy eliminates a key part of the strategy, then the firm may be forced to adjust its entire strategy to one that may or may not lead to an outcome that is

---

[3]See K. R. Andrews, *The Concept of Corporate Strategy* (1971). The concept of strategy has been institutionalized in nearly all major corporations, through the widespread adoption of formal systems for strategic planning.

better from a social viewpoint than the original position. For example, if a firm is blocked from a particular vertical contractual arrangement with its customers, it may turn instead to heavy image advertising. Or if antitrust restraints on predatory pricing prevent a market leader from disciplining its rivals and signaling potential entrants using price, it may turn instead to the myriad other disciplining tactics available (see below) to preserve its strategic position, which may have the same effect but be extremely difficult to police effectively.

II. STRATEGIC HETEROGENEITY

Industry histories and my discussion of strategy highlight the fact that firms compete with quite heterogeneous strategies, despite the fact that they are in the same industry. Heterogeneous strategies reflect firms' efforts to achieve a sustainable competitive advantage, given their differing and evolving bundles of tangible and intangible assets and skills, as well as the presence in many industries of market segments consisting of clusters of buyers who place differing weights on the market attributes under a firm's control (product characteristics, price, marketing practices, distribution channel, et cetera). A necessary corollary to these sources of strategic heterogeneity is that the pattern of strategies being followed in an industry will often shift over time and vary from industry to industry.

As I have argued elsewhere, heterogeneous strategies imply diverse bases for market power of different firms in the same industry.[4] The notion of entry barriers protecting all incumbents in an industry must be supplanted by a broader concept of mobility barriers, or factors that deter other firms from replicating a particular strategic configuration. Strategic interaction, then, is the process by which firms seek to get behind or create sustainable mobility barriers. Within the same industry, firms with different strategies will possess differing types of mobility barriers as well as mobility barriers of varying overall height.

The mobility barrier concept calls into question intent as an operational indicium in antitrust. Firms, once in an industry, are no longer "equal" except in size. There are often a variety of different protected positions in an industry. Mobility theory implies that all firms strive to drive other firms out of their strategic territory and create a well-protected strategic group. This "intent to monopolize" is pervasive, where the monopoly is sought over a particular strategic configuration.

Similarly, Salop's[5] interesting formulation of entry deterrence as natural or

---

[4]R. E. Caves and M. E. Porter, "From Entry Barriers to Mobility Barriers: Conjectural Decisions and Contrived Deterrence to New Competition," 91 *O. J. Econ.* 241 (1977); M. E. Porter, "The Structure Within Industries and Companies," 61 *Rev. Econ. & Stat.* 214 (1979); M. E. Porter, *Competitive Strategy: Techniques for Analyzing Industries and Competitors* (1980); A. M. Spence, "Entry, Capacity, Investment, and Oligopolistic Pricing," 8 *Bell J. Econ.* 534 (1977).

[5]S. C. Salop, "Strategic Entry Deterrence," 69 *Am. Econ. Rev.* 335 (1979).

strategic may not represent a clear distinction. Scale economies, for example, do not exist but are created by a firm's investment decisions based on choices about strategic configuration. The firm invests in research to perfect larger scale facilities, and in the facilities themselves, to create a mobility barrier or defend itself against another firm that has attempted to create a mobility barrier. The mobility barrier is hardly unintentional nor a side effect of innocent profit maximization, as Salop's formulation of natural barriers (of which scale economies are cited as an example) implies.

The theory of mobility barriers also implies that antitrust analysis of market power and remedies aimed at reducing market power cannot always be industrywide but rather must be directed at the groups of firms following similar strategies (strategic groups). There is generally no single test for the presence of market power that can be applied to any industry. An industry need not be concentrated overall for a particular strategic group to have enormous market power. Remedies aimed at the sources of market power of one strategic group may have little impact on that of another group; worse yet, they can allow another strategic group to reinforce its market power.

III. DYNAMIC COST REDUCTION

The recent attention in corporate planning on strategies based on the "experience curve" has emphasized the importance of dynamic cost reduction in strategic interaction. Much of the recent discussion has centered around the so-called "experience curve." The term "experience curve," popularized by the Boston Consulting Group (BCG), mixes together two familiar but quite disparate phenomena—(static) economies of scale and (dyanamic) product and process technological changes (learning) that lower cost. These together, holds BCG, propel real costs down in proportion to the firm's cumulative production volume.[6]

For purposes of understanding strategic interaction, the BCG formulation is unsatisfying because it mixes static economies of scale, learning that depends on time, and learning that depends on cumulative production volume. Because the operation of static economies of scale is well known, I will concentrate here on the learning aspects.

Learning reduces costs over time as the firm discovers how to do things better in product design, process layout, job design for workers, machine operating rates, organizational coordination, and the like. Thus, firm learning can be very broadly based and involves managerial as well as technological dimensions. Some learning and the associated product and process changes can increase possibilities for static economies of scale, while other learning leads to absolute cost improvements.

---

[6]The overall decline of cost in proportion to cumulative volume is offered by BCG as an empirical regularity. For a fuller description of the BCG formulation, see O. Abell and S. Hammond, *Strategic Market Planning* (1979), and Porter (1980), note 4 *supra*.

There are three plausible ways to formulate the rate of learning, with very different implications for strategic interaction:

a. as a function of cumulative volume;
b. as a function of time in the industry;
c. as a function of exogenous technological change.

The one most often stressed in the corporate strategy field is that learning is a function of cumulative volume.[7] In this formulation, the firm growing the fastest will be gaining cumulative volume (and lowering cost) the fastest. Thus the optimizing firm should price even below cost in the growth stages of an industry's development to gain market share and hence reduce cost relative to rivals. As the industry matures, this strategy can lead to a dominant firm with a large cost advantage over its competitors. All firms, including entrants, are compelled to seek market share—the firm with the greatest risk-taking ability and staying power will ultimately win out.[8]

The formulation that learning is strictly a function of cumulative volume forces us to confront some familiar tradeoffs in economics, those between market power or monopoly (allocative efficiency) and cost (technical efficiency) on the one hand, and between market power and innovation on the other. A learning curve based on cumulative volume implies that the large-market-share firm, since it generally has the greatest "experience," will often be more efficient at any given time, even though it may have a great deal of market power. The learning curve also implies that the largest-market-share firm (that is accumulating volume the fastest) will likewise be the most innovative in improving product or process to lower cost. Thus, any policy that limits a firm's ability to strive for and later occupy a dominant market position will have negative consequences for long-run costs.[9] This affects not only the appropriate policy towards what is an acceptable market share, but also complicates policy towards so-called "predatory" behavior. Pricing below variable costs in pursuit of market share may be justified by dynamic efficiency considerations, even though such behavior would violate even the lenient Areeda-Turner test recently proposed in the literature on predatory behavior.

While the strict cumulative volume formulation of the learning curve

---

[7]Note that this is not precisely equivalent to the Boston Consulting Group formulation, which is that *overall* cost declines are based on cumulative volume, made up of a learning and scale economies component. Because they are usually so collinear, the empirical evidence presented by BCG does not allow a discrimination among the significance of the various sources of cost decline, nor the alternative formulations of the rate of learning.

[8]The nature and duration of the battle for dominance will clearly depend on the extent to which one firm can get out in front in cumulative volume due to early entry or because rivals fail to recognize or act on the learning curve in their behavior.

[9]In the short run, holding back a leader from gaining share many lead to faster cost declines by followers and thus, perhaps, lower average industry costs.

raises these problems, it is critical to recognize the conditions that underlie this strict formulation, because they often do not hold in practice. The strict formulation assumes that the process of learning based on accumulated volume goes on indefinitely, which is probably not true in all situations where much of the learning occurs early in the industry's development. The strict formulation also assumes that the leader's learning can be kept proprietary. If it can be copied, the leader may indeed be learning the fastest; but this does not imply greater efficiency for the leader, nor that the leader will pull away from the pack. Moreover, if we added the assumption that learning is costly and requires R. & D. spending, then the opportunity for low-cost copying can put the leader at a disadvantage, which will reduce incentives for learning.

Another qualification to the strict cumulative volume formulation of the learning curve is the possibility that innovations may change product or process technology enough to create a new learning curve that the leader is ill prepared to jump onto because of his past investments.[10] Or, competitors may be able to chip away at a leader's market share by focusing on particular parts of the product line or customer segments, taking advantage of the leader's inflexibility due to high volume. The risks of these sorts of outcomes will rationally deter firms in many industries from even attempting learning-curve-driven strategies.[11]

A second formulation of learning is that it is a function of time in the industry. Here costs decline for many of the same reasons, but the innovative process that discovers opportunities to lower costs is a function of how long the firm has been looking. If learning is a function of time, rather than cumulative volume, the implications for strategic interaction are much different. Here firms will strive for early entry or acquisitions of early entrants as a base of subsequent strategies. New entry and growth by followers do not threaten the learning advantages of leaders. Conversely, there is no mechanism for leaders to get further ahead. Rather, the cost differences are stable but shrinking as a proportion of total cost as the industry and firms grow older. The only way a firm can improve its relative position in such a world is to acquire an older firm (or its personnel). Unlike the cumulative volume formulation, however, the learning *rate* cannot be accelerated, and hence the ability of a firm to alter its position (and hence the incentive to do so) is much less pronounced.

Learning as a function of time raises few special problems for antitrust except in the premium it places on early entry. Since technical efficiency is maximized if there are many early entrants, policy that prevents one early entrant from erecting entry barriers towards others is indicated. While prevention of artificial entry barriers is a bread-and-butter concern of antitrust, however, what is novel here is the need to do so very early in an industry's development. Antitrust

---

[10]Cumulative volume learning is most likely to lead to dominant outcomes in markets where innovation is incremental and correlated to the level of R. & D. spending. Here the market share leader can readily preserve its low-cost position.

[11]For a more detailed discussion of these risks, see Porter (1980), note 4 *supra,* chs. 1 and 12.

has, by and large, ignored this period of an industry's development, focusing rather on more mature industries, when remedies can have little or no impact on time-related learning.

A third formulation of learning is that it depends on exogenous technological changes, such as improvements in machinery purchased from equipment suppliers, improvements in raw materials, exogenous inventions such as computer controls, and so on. Here there is no link between learning and market position, except insofar as market position cuts against the ability of firms to assimilate exogenous developments. For example, exogenous learning may involve new scale-sensitive machinery, in which case small-scale firms then fall behind in cost position.[12]

Exogenous learning also offers few novel concerns for antitrust. Where its employment in the industry is scale-related, exogenous learning can raise or exacerbate the static-efficiency/market-power dilemma. Where diffusion of exogenous learning is not scale-related, the primary antitrust concern is to insure that all firms in an industry get access to the learning and no firm is able to prevent diffusion to others through contractual arrangements or other practices. Policies to reach these ends should raise few dilemmas, because the fact that learning is exogenous to the industry should mean that there is little chance of blunting the incentives for innovation in the process controlling practices that impede wide diffusion.

This discussion suggests that the nature of the antitrust policy problem raised by dynamic cost reduction depends centrally on the precise nature of dynamic cost reduction present in the industry. Thus, policy towards monopolization can no longer aim for sweeping rules (like maximum market shares) or get lost in debates over intent, but must proceed on a market-by-market basis governed by the economic structure involved. Where conditions lead to learning curve strictly related to cumulative volume, then the policy dilemma is perhaps most acute. Here a firm's desire to drive competitors out of a market to increase its market share can, in some industries, have a legitimate positive justification in efficiency. Antitrust policy must get over its preoccupation with sorting "good" monopolists from "bad" monopolists and confront directly the tradeoff between efficiency and market share that exists in such industries. Since appropriable learning curves based on cumulative volume clearly occur empirically, enhanced attention to dynamic cost reduction should add new respectability to the cost justification for firm behavior, which has had a tendency to be viewed as a smokescreen used by business to further its own ends. Some more specific policy options will be discussed below.

In practice, static scale economies and dynamic cost reductions of all three kinds often interact to cause a competitive process resulting in a dominant market leader with significant and stable cost advantages over existing and potential competitors. For example, Procter & Gamble (P&G) has dominated the huge

---

[12]Though it may well be sensible for small firms to wait and let others make the first mistakes in introducing exogenous innovations.

disposable-diaper industry largely through the operation of scale economies and the learning curve. Appendix A shows an estimated income statement for P&G in disposable diapers, compared to that of an entrant into the market aiming at a nationally branded position who begins an entry in 1974 and reaches equilibrium market share in 1980.[13] The assumptions which yield the entrant's income statement are relatively optimistic, and P&G is assumed *not* to retaliate. P&G's estimated cost advantage of 15 percent once the entrant reaches equilibrium (with an even greater cost advantage while the entrant is reaching its target share) is due to a sharp proprietary learning curve in manufacturing and product development, significant static economies of scale in research, advertising, sales force, transportation, and (to a lesser extent) in manufacturing, product differentiation, and absolute cost advantages due to raw material access and favorable access to hospital sampling kits for new mothers. The bulk of these cost advantages are due to true economies due to scale and learning curve phenomena and not to bargaining power.

Appendix A clearly illustrates the degree to which static and dynamic considerations cumulate and interact to produce a low-cost dominant leader, and the enormous risk an entrant would have to bear to enter the disposable-diaper market.[14] It is also easy to see, using such a calculation, where P&G's costs of entry were lower than the hypothetical entrant's, largely because P&G avoided some of the fixed costs the entrant must bear once P&G is in the market. Remedies that would induce entry into disposable diapers or allow followers to gain significant market share from P&G must be extreme. Eliminating all P&G advertising, for example, would only lower P&G's cost advantage by perhaps 3 percentage points out of 15. Any effective remedy, further, would force a significant loss in efficiency. Breaking P&G into two equal pieces and forcing it to divest one might come close to restoring competitive balance, but would lead to higher costs as a percentage of sales in R. & D., manufacturing, sales, and transportation.[15]

IV. THE FIRM AS AN INTERRELATED PORTFOLIO OF BUSINESSES

Industry histories reveal that in strategic interaction, firms must often be viewed as portfolios of activities rather than as entities competing independently in each industry in which they have operations. Widespread diversification in the U.S.

---

[13]Essentially, the same situation will face a follower in the market who aspires to national-brand status.

[14]This risk of entry is made even greater by P&G's likely retaliation to entry. Another calculation that illustrates this point is found in R. G. M. Sultan, *Pricing in the Electrical Oligopoly*, volumes I and II, Division of Research, Harvard Graduate School of Business Administration (1974).

[15]And raise difficult problems with the brand name.

since the 1960's has led to business units of multibusiness firms being the rule rather than the exception as competitors in most industries. Not only does logic argue that firms will simultaneously optimize over their entire range of business units, but modern strategic planning practice emphasizes that firms should view their businesses as a portfolio and should manage them accordingly.[16] Modern portfolio management approaches place great stress on taking cash from less favorable or slow-growing business units and plowing it into gaining market share in promising business units, making the firm an internal capital market with a deep pocket. There is widespread belief among managers that the diversified firm gains resulting advantages in access to capital compared to single-business firms, implying imperfections in the external capital market.[17]

Going hand in hand with the fact that many of today's large firms are managed as portfolios of businessess is the existence of pervasive interrelationships among the activities of many diversified firms. These interrelationships range from relatively intangible forms—like the fact that P&G has a high degree of accumulated knowledge in market research and consumer testing that can be applied to any of its consumer products—to actual sharing of brand names, distribution channels, purchases, logistical networks, service organization, sales forces, component fabrication, assembly plants, and so on, among often disparate products.

Such interrelationships can have a major impact on costs, and mean that traditional product or industry boundaries are no longer sufficient to define relative cost positions among firms. For example, P&G employs the same retail channels, sales force, and logistical system in disposable diapers as it does in its other paper products (bathroom tissue, paper towels). It saves perhaps 2 to 4 percent of sales by using its Charmin Division sales force to sell both diapers and paper products during the same sales call, spreading the fixed costs of the call over more units. Before its diaper volume became large, P&G saved transportation costs (about 10 percent of sales) relative to a firm that only sold diapers, by shipping full carloads combining diapers and other paper products. P&G has probably taken advantage in diapers of expertise in paper products gained in its other paper products businesses and Buckeye Cellulose Division (and vice versa). Finally, P&G reportedly eliminates additional costs by not having to offer as many promotions to the retailers to secure favorable shelf positioning as other diaper brands, because of its presence in other grocery-store product lines as well as its diaper-market share. The competitor that is not optimally diversified, then, faces a significant cost disadvantage relative to P&G in disposable diapers, even before considering industry-specific economies of scale or other mobility barriers. Savings of this order of magnitude due to appropriate

[16]See, for example, a summary of the popular Boston Consulting Group's, McKinsey & Company's, and PIMS' approaches to portfolio planning in Abell and Hammond (1979), note 6 supra.

[17]The social efficiency of this internal allocation of capital advantage must still be regarded as dubious and depends critically on still-undeveloped understanding of the capital market's imperfections and distortions introduced through the tax system.

diversification are not atypical in my study of a wide range of industries, and they often involved cost savings in groups of products more disparate than those in the P&G example.[18]

Where firms have interrelated portfolios of businesses that are managed as such, some important behavioral and normative implications are raised for examining strategic interaction in a particular industry. First, the objectives (and behavior) of a particular business unit can only be understood by studying the firm's entire portfolio. The firm will invest scarce capital, managerial time, and attention in pursuing learning curves or otherwise gaining market share in some businesses, while allowing market share in others to erode ("harvesting"). Further, a diversified firm's behavior in one business will be affected by how that behavior will impact interrelated businesses. The firm may rationally price below variable cost in one business in order to build market share and volume that will lead to cost reductions in shared distribution or logistics facilities that lower cost for the whole group of related businesses using these facilities. Conversely, a firm may defend a particular business against competitive attack to a degree that appears irrational (or "predatory") until one recognizes that if market share is lost in that business, the market position of other related businesses will be damaged. Thus, the complications raised by the learning curve for determining predation will be exacerbated by cost-related diversification. Any industry-specific test for market power or for the social appropriateness of a particular competitive practice becomes similarly suspect. Preventing an industry leader from defending its share in an industry may allow a related diversified firm to build even greater barriers through improving its position in that industry on top of superior volume in related industries.

Another consequence of the existence of interrelated businesses managed as portfolios is that there will be strong pressures in many industries for offensive or defensive related diversification or vertical integration. Firms will be motivated to search for related diversification in order to create strategic cost advantages that carry over to their other businesses. A firm making sophisticated castings which it assembles into one end product, for example, may look for other (otherwise unrelated) industries using similar castings, so that it can reap economies of scale that lower overall costs. Conversely, P&G's presence in disposable diapers in combination with facial tissue, bathroom tissue, and paper towels placed strong pressure on Scott Paper and Kimberly-Clark (Kleenex) to enter the disposable diaper field defensively. If they did not, both firms might face serious disadvantages in transportation costs, selling costs, relationships with retailers, and even raw material purchasing costs.[19] Offensive and defensive motivations for related diversification can both be present in a given situation.

---

[18]Note, also, that many of the cost savings enjoyed by P&G are real economies and not the fruits of bargaining power.

[19]This is the same basic motivation as that identified by Knickerbocker, *Olgopolistic Reaction and Multinational Enterprise* (1973), in his study showing the marked tendency of multinationals to defensively enter a country market if one of their competitors did.

Johnson & Johnson (J&J), for example, is the preeminent firm in many baby-care product lines. Disposable diapers represented the only rapidly growing new product area in the baby care field and offered obvious possibilities for transference of the J&J brand name and distribution system. Hand in hand with these as motivations for J&J's entry into disposable diapers was the threat that P&G and other diaper firms posed for entry into J&J's traditional baby care products, as these firms developed brand names associated with baby care and sales volumes that offered possibilities for economies of joint operation in several baby-care product lines.

The result of such offensive and defensive motivations for related diversification is that we should (and do) observe many situations in which firms are diversified in parallel or nearly parallel ways and compete with each other in multiple industries. For example, John Deere, Caterpillar Tractor, International Harvester, Ford, and J. I. Case, among other firms, all have come over time to operate in multiple and overlapping product areas in the farm equipment, construction equipment, and light- and heavy-truck sectors. Related diversification driven by the search for strategic interrelationships has become the dominant motivation for diversification in the 1970's and now the 1980's, supplanting the conglomerate diversification of the 1960's.

Such related diversification with important cost consequences raises some vexing questions for antitrust policy above and beyond confusing what is predatory behavior. On the one hand, cost-motivated offensive- and defensive-related diversification increases efficiency, and can and does have the procompetitive effect of encouraging entry when diversification involves greenfield expansion or acquisition of a base that is subsequently developed. Often the synergies of related diversification allow entry into industries that might in their absence seem to offer insurmountable barriers. On the other hand, the process of offensive and defensive entry into related clusters of businesses may ultimately lead to a significant increase in overall entry barriers by forcing a newcomer to enter the whole cluster of businesses (be optimally diversified) or face a serious disadvantage.[20] Further, related diversification can exacerbate the efficiency/market-power tradeoff posed by the learning curve when they occur together.

Another consequence of the existence of interrelated businesses managed as portfolios is that strategic interaction can and does involve multiple industries. Where businesses are interelated, firms rationally formulate strategic plans in related groups of businesses simultaneously. A move by a competitor in one industry can be met by a response in that industry or in another related industry in which that competitor also operates. To preserve overall balance, for example, Scott Paper could counter a P&G move in facial tissue either through a response in facial tissue or one in bathroom tissue designed to preserve the total volume of product moving through the same sales force and distribution system (and thereby its relative cost position).

Where strategic interaction among firms occurs simultaneously in several

---

[20]The basic problem bears some resemblance to the familiar vertical integration problem.

industries, this in some ways complicates the achievement of tacit collusion by greatly increasing the number of variables in the implicit bargain. It also means that a firm's improvement in market share in one industry can have benefits elsewhere in the portfolio, raising the incentive for attempting to gain share. However, there are also some reasons which suggest that competition in multiple industries can facilitate tacit collusion. Competition in multiple industries offers possibilities for various forms of side payments. For example, one firm could yield share in an industry, allowing the leader to raise entry barriers to new firms, while the firm was allowed to gain share in another industry without retaliation. Furthermore, firms can maintain equal profits and market power despite unequal shares, as long as they divide up markets in such a way as to preserve balance in the volume of shared components, the volume of products moving under shared brand names, and volume through shared channels, sales force, or logistics facilities.

Competition in several industries may also allow otherwise unavailable forms of market signaling and competitor disciplining that enhance tacit collusion by lowering the risk of competitive outbreaks. For example, what I have called a cross-parry is a situation in which a firm responds to a competitive threat in one industry with a response in another industry in which it and the threatener compete. Compared to having to meet the threat directly, such a response can credibly signal displeasure, while being relatively easy to disengage from without triggering a series of moves and countermoves. This is because of the risk that a direct response might be interpreted mistakenly as an attack rather than as a signal of displeasure. Further, where firms compete in several industries, a punishing retaliation to a move in one industry can be much more severe, because it can involve simultaneous attacks in a number of businesses. Finally, a firm can punish another's transgressions in one market in another jointly contested market where the defender's share is small, or where the aggressor is the most vulnerable, thus forcing the aggressor to bear a high relative cost. Thus, simultaneous competition in multiple industries raises new issues for antitrust scrutiny of competitve practices.

V. GLOBAL COMPETITION

Some important issues for antitrust are raised by the increasing incidence of industries in which strategic interaction is global, an observation that becomes apparent when one examines industries such as automobiles, television sets, broadcast equipment, and many others. Global industries emerge when there are sources of strategic advantage to competing in a coordinated manner in a number of national markets, such as large scale economies in manufacturing or research or internationally cumulative learning.[21] In some global industries the ad-

---

[21]See Porter (1980), note 4 *supra*, ch. 13, for a more extended discussion of the economics of global industries.

vantages stem from current scale economies or learning, while in others the global firm may be utilizing past investments in intangible assets.[22]

In global industries, while some mobility barriers are market-specific (e.g., distribution channels), other potentially larger barriers stem from the firm's *global* position (e.g., manufacturing scale economies). In such industries, the firm's behavior and market power in any one national market are determined by its situation globally. It may price below cost in the U.S. market, for example, so that it can gain enough volume to lower production cost to successfully compete against global competitors in Europe or Latin America. If such economies are in fact attainable, such behavior is not predatory but motivated by real efficiencies, though it surely leads to barriers to entry. Barriers to entry/mobility in global industries clearly often exceed those that can exist in national industries.[23]

Obviously, in global industries, antitrust analysis must be global. In an industry that is global, the tradeoff between domestic market and efficiency is eased because even the dominant domestic firm will face ample potential competition.[24] Structural remedies that increase competitiveness from the sole point of view of the U.S. market can seriously backfire in a global industry. Limiting a firm's market share in the United States can threaten its efficiency and hence competitive position elsewhere in the world, for example, and invite the entry of foreign firms into the U.S. market that might ultimately be able to erect even higher barriers.[25]

Global competition and related diversification interact in many industries to produce situations in which a firm must be both global in scope and optimally diversified in order to be competitive. For example, a television-set manufacturer that is not global and not diversified into videotape recorders will have little chance of success in the next decade. This exacerbates the policy considerations that have been raised.

VI. SIGNALING AND TACIT COLLUSION

Industry histories can reveal much about the sources of the current competitive equilibrium by uncovering patterns of market signaling among existing competi-

---

[22]For the classic treatment of the utilization of intangibles by multinationals, see R. E. Caves, "International Corporations: The Industrial Economies of Foreign Investment," 38 *Economica* 1 (1971).

[23]The increase in the number of industries in which competition is global has led to an increase in what I call coalitions, or transnational horizontal agreements among firms with different home markets. These raise some intriguing issues for antitrust.

[24]Unless all firms are global in parallel.

[25]Note, however, that if global firms have merely capitalized on past investments in intangibles, then the existence of worldwide competitors does *not* imply any efficiency gain to allow a dominant U.S. leader.

tors and potential entrants. These are myriad forms of market signals that communicate to competitors with varying degrees of credibility without the need for actual large-scale investments or moves in the marketplace, some of which I have attempted to catalog elsewhere.[26] Some of the most common are shown in Figure 1. Careful examination of competitive behavior and public and quasi-public statements by managements, with extreme attention placed on the sequencing of statements and events, can expose signaling behavior.

Since market signlaing can clearly facilitate tacit collusion, eliminating market signaling practices enhances competition. However, while I am generally skeptical of market signals, they raise some vexing issues for antitrust. While signals surely can have socially undesirable effects in deterring entry or facilitating tacit collusion among existing firms, the problem is that nearly all market signals have some socially beneficial component. Announcements of capacity expansion can promote efficiency through reducing excess capacity due to bunching of capacity additions. Publication of actual prices or pricing policies can allow buyers to bargain more effectively. Public comment by executives on industry events, or company announcements which state the logic of firms' moves, can increase the degree to which the capital markets are well informed. The problem is that market signals contain information, and information is beneficial to market functioning.

Another problem with policy toward market signals is that there are so many forms of market signals that limits on particularly obvious ones for which the positive social benefits seem negligible may do little to control undesirable signaling behavior. Since so many aspects of company behavior can be signals, banning signals is a bit like trying to keep firms in a tight oligopoly from recognizing each other's existence.

[26]Porter (1980), note 4 *supra*, ch. 4.

Figure 1   Forms of Marketing Signaling

Prior announcements

Public discussion of moves or industry events

Disclosure of data about costs, market position, or other company strengths

Publication of policies for pricing and determination of other competitive variables

Fighting brands

Form and timing of moves relative to industry convention

History of response to entry or competitor moves, in any of the industries in which the firm competes

Maintenance of retaliatory resources, such as excess cash

Actions against new competitors' products in test markets

Cross-parry in another jointly contested industry

Behavior divergent from apparent profit maximization

Binding (and communicated) commitments that raise exit barriers, such as long-term contracts, capital investments, and others

VII. ENTRY/MOBILITY
DETERRENCE

Study of strategic interaction in industry histories reveals a wide array of behavior available to firms to deter entry, much of which has been little studied by industrial organization researchers. Since the same entry-deterring tactics can also be employed to deter or defend against attempts at increasing share by incumbents, the analysis of that case (mobility deterrence) is parallel.

Some behavioral and normative issues in entry-deterring tactics can be illustrated through pursuing my example of the disposable-diaper industry. Figure 2 shows some of the feasible behavior available to P&G to deter entry (or discourage market share gains by incumbents) in the disposable-diaper industry. The tactics in Figure 2 are generalizable to many industries. Further, they reflect the fact that entry (and mobility) is not an instantaneous move but rather takes time and often occurs in a sequential fashion, involving the occupation of a series of strategic groups over time.[27] Thus, if the entrant or competitor seeking to gain share can be punished early in the process, he may give up altogether. Much of the recent literature on entry deterrence makes a sharp distinction between the pre- and postentry game which is inappropriate.[28] It may be rational for the incumbent to carry out a threat long after the entrant has first appeared in the market, for this reason and because the incumbent's reaction to this entrant (or uppity incumbent) can signal other entrants and incumbents.

The alternative entry-deterring behavior in Figure 2 varies along a number of significant dimensions for the competitive outcome. The tactics vary in the certainty with which they inflict a penalty on the potential entrant (or competitor) and in the certainty with which the potential entrant (or competitor) will notice them. This means that they have differing entry-deterring values.

More importantly, though, the tactics also vary greatly in their *relative* cost to the dominant firm (P&G) compared to the potential entrants (or competitors). Some tactics, like public comment, or forms of signaling such as speculative patent suits, or introducing a blocking brand into test market, cost the leader relatively little but can significantly raise the expected costs (or risks) of the entrant. Other tactics, like increasing advertising in an entrant's rollout markets or introducing a new generation of the product, have a considerable cost to the leader but inflict a proportionally even higher cost on the entrant or smaller-share competitor, because advertising and product development are subject to economies of scale. Furthermore, such entry-deterring tactics may raise product differentiation or overall demand, which benefits the leader and offsets some of

---

[27]See Caves and Porter (1977), note 4 *supra*. There are often one or more particularly desirable sequential entry paths.

[28]For example, Salop (1979), note 5 *supra*, at 335; R. Schmalensee, "Entry Deterrence in the Ready-to-Eat Cereal Market," 9 *Bell J. Econ.* (1978), pp. 313–14.

Figure 2   Possible Entry/Mobility Deterring Tactics in Disposable Diapers

	Cost to Procter & Gamble (P&G)	Cost to an Entrant (Competitor)
Signaling		
1. Signaling a commitment to defend position in diapers through public statements, comments to retailers, etc.	none	raises expected cost of entry by increasing probability and extent of retaliation
2. File a patent suit	legal fees	legal fees plus probability that P&G wins the suit with subsequent cost to the competitor
3. Announce planned capacity expansion	none	raises expected risk of price cutting and the probability of P&G's retaliation to entry
4. Announce a new generation of diapers to be introduced in the future	none	raises the expected cost of entry by forcing entrant to bear possible product development and changeover costs contingent on the ultimate configuration of the new generation
Capacity		
5. Build capacity[1] ahead of demand	present value of investment in excess capacity	raises the risk of price cutting and the probability of P&G's retaliation to entry
6. Cut price	across-the-board reduction in sales revenue	equal proportional reduction in sales revenue but smaller total lost revenue; demand for entrant more likely to be price elastic if have lower product differentiation
7. Cut price in "newborn" diaper sizes	focuses price cut on first diaper a mother will buy	greatly raises the cost of inducing trial by the new mother, who is most susceptible to switching brands
8. Increase cents-off couponing in test or rollout markets	focuses effective price cut on contested markets; most coupons will reduce revenues on sales P&G would have made anyway	most coupons redeemed will lead to incremental revenue from *new* buyers

Figure 2 (Continued)

	Cost to Procter & Gamble (P&G)	Cost to an Entrant (Competitor)
9. Load buyer with inventory by discounting large economy size package in roll-out markets	reduction in sales revenue part of sales; probably to price-sensitive customers most susceptible to competitor incursion	greatly raises the cost of inducing trial for the entrant

Advertising

	Cost to Procter & Gamble (P&G)	Cost to an Entrant (Competitor)
10. Raise advertising nationally	the cost of a given dollar increase in advertising will be spread over a large sales volume	must match P&G in absolute message volume to maintain relative position, but the cost of advertising is spread over much smaller base; may also suffer diseconomies by not having national media available

Price

	Cost to Procter & Gamble (P&G)	Cost to an Entrant (Competitor)
11. Spot advertising overlays in test or rollout markets	same, but focuses resources on contested markets	same, but no disadvantage due to national media access

Product

	Cost to Procter & Gamble (P&G)	Cost to an Entrant (Competitor)
12. Put a "blocking" brand[2] into test market	cost of product development and market testing	credible threat that second brand will be aggressively rolled out nationally if entry occurs; raise probability of closing off lowest-cost entry into the industry
13. Introduce a "blocking" brand[3]	cost of brand introduction	raise cost of entry by exposing entrant to more direct retaliation by the leader
14. Introduce a new generation of the product[4]	fixed cost of new product development expenditures and manufacturing changeover spread over large volume	fixed cost of product development and manufacturing changeover must be spread over smaller volume; also elevates the risk of potential entrants that future product generations will make existing investment obsolete

Figure 2   (Continued)

	Cost to Procter & Gamble (P&G)	Cost to an Entrant (Competitor)
Exit Barriers[5]		
15. Raise exit barriers through investment in specialized assets, long-term supply contracts with raw material sources, high labor severance or layoff benefits, etc.	increase cost of failure	credible threat that leader will defend his position

[1] This case was analyzed by A. M. Spence, "Entry Capacity Investment and Oligopolistic Pricing," 8 *Bell. J. Econ.* 534 (1978).

[2] A brand which occupies a natural market segment for entry. In the diaper industry, this is a premium brand. The second most natural segment would be a lower-cost, lower-quality brand positioned between the regular Pampers product and private labels. Given the product performance sensitivity of the customer, however, this is much less likely to succeed.

[3] This situation has been analyzed by Schmalensee (1978), note 36 *supra*.

[4] Under some circumstances, it can be more effective to introduce the new generation after the entrant has begun a rollout, because this makes the entrant's investment in rollout of the old generation obsolete and damages its brand reputation, as well as forcing it to match the new generation. The entrant can be more likely to withdraw under these circumstances.

[5] For a discussion of exit barriers, see Caves and Porter (1976); Porter (1980), note 4 *supra*.

the cost to him. On the other extreme, competitive price-cutting inflicts a huge cost on the leader because of the leader's large overall volume and the fact that price cutting by the leader will induce few customers to switch to him because of his already large share. Offering cents-off coupons in the market where an entrant is introducing his product ("rolling out") can target the entry-deterring investment better than an across-the-board price cut, but still it is relatively more costly to the leader because of his larger share and the fact that unlike the entrant, most coupons will be redeemed by the leader's already existing customers.

Entry/mobility-deterring behavior also varies in its ability to be localized to a *particular* potential entrant or competitor. Advertising in test markets can localize the defense to the particular product features stressed by a particular entrant. Couponing, on the other hand, will affect (and thereby cause response from) all competitors in the market. The potential entrant or competitor is clearly placed in the best possible situation where the leader must make investments in entry/mobility deterrence across the board rather than being able to target its moves to the particular geographic market or part of the product line under siege.

This analysis of alternative entry-deterring behavior suggests that the form of competitive behavior often attacked in antitrust investigations of predatory aggressive price cutting may be the most benign in terms of the exercise of market power. Entry/mobility deterrence through predatory pricing is across the board and offers the dominant firm none of the scale economy benefits that some other forms of behavior do. The preoccupation of the predation literature (and antitrust scrutiny) with price is unfortunate, in this light, and might be better spent on finding ways of preventing tactics that deter entry or mobility which are effective and yet low-cost to a dominant firm.

A final case in entry/mobility deterrence is the apparent paradox that it may well be rational for the firm to *encourage* entry of appropriately positioned and weak firms in order to block other more threatening firms, or to preserve such weak firms when they get into difficulty.[29] The presence of other weak incumbents, for example, may lower the prospective entrant's initial share or force the entrant to bear retaliation from these incumbents as well as the leader. The leader may well encourage entry of weak firms into segments that offer natural possiblities for sequenced entry, in an analogy to the brand-proliferation argument.

VIII. DIFFERENCES AMONG FIRMS' OBJECTIVES AND ABILITIES

Study of industry histories suggests that firms' objective functions in a given industry can differ a great deal. The first reason has already been discussed; firms in a particular industry will have differing patterns of related diversification. Further reasons stem from uncertainty and from lack of owner control.

Where there is uncertainty about the future, managers use various mechanisms for predicting the aspects of the future relevant to their decisions. Industry histories illustrate that managements often place great reliance on their past backgrounds and experiences as analogies to the current situation.[30] Particularistic company norms or rules of thumb are followed. Crude signals are employed, such as the widespread use of the rate of market growth as an indication of future industry attractiveness. All this implies that firms may react differently to a given market situation, and the particular forms of predictive mechanisms employed by individual firms can affect the manner in which investment decisions are made and how the industry evolves. These considerations must be factored into analyses of firms' responses to antitrust remedies, mergers involving their competitors, and so on.

Interacting with these considerations is the separation between ownership and control. The essence of the separation is that managers do not perceive their personal interests to be coincident with maximizing the long-run value of the firm. This can be because of bankruptcy fears, monetary incentives based on

[29]Entry can be encouraged through licensing, selling of component parts, and the like.

[30]See Porter (1980), note 4 *supra*, ch. 3.

short-run profitability, criteria for promotion that often stress short-run performance, and other failures of reward systems that stem from imperfect information.[31] Separation between ownership and control also allows other forms of managerial utility maximization, such as pursuit of status, exit barriers due to emotional attachments, and the like. Finally, separation of ownership and control, coupled with various transactions and information costs, also gives room for differences among companies in the decisionmaking power and authority of different functional departments or individual executives. The degree of separation between ownership and control and its internal consequences can and does vary among firms in a given industry, with the result that competitors can differ sharply in their motivations.

Varying separation between ownership and control, differing internal reward systems, and varying approaches to dealing with uncertainty imply that firms may differ greatly in their time horizons, willingness to bear risk, and what they derive utility from. Such factors can strongly influence the pattern of strategic interaction in an industry as well as structural outcomes, by leading to some firms investing earlier and more aggressively than others or defending their positions more stubbornly.[32]

As firms' objectives vary, so do their abilities, a straightforward corollary of much of my earlier discussion in this paper. Thus, some firms may have more capital to invest to grow more rapidly than others, or more skill in marketing or in cost minimization. All this can also influence strategic interaction and structural outcomes.

IX. THE DETERMINANTS OF MARKET STRUCTURE

One of the most striking points that emerges from the study of strategic interaction through industry histories is the extent to which history and chance play an important role in interacting with economic variables to determine the structural outcome in an industry. Buyer characteristics, technology, and cost functions are surely important determinants of industry structure that have been empha-

---

[31]For example, a manager may be better off if he makes an incorrect move in an expected value sense that all other competitors also make than if he does not follow competitors' behavior. The fact that other competitors made the move may well insure a favorable evaluation of the manager under imperfect information, or at least allow him to keep his job. If the manager diverged from the industry and proved to be wrong, on the other hand, he would almost certainly lose his job. See M. E. Porter and A. M. Spence, "The Capacity Expansion Process in a Growing Oligopoly: The Case of Corn Wet Milling," Harvard Graduate School of Business Administration Working Paper (October 1978).

[32]This analysis may explain some of the differences in "animal spirits" of different competitors, observed by F. M. Scherer, A. Beckenstein, E. Kaufer, and R. D. Murphy, *The Economics of Multi-Plant Operation: An International Comparisons Study* (1975), in explaining different proclivities of aggressive addition of large-scale capacity.

sized in previous research. The discussion here suggests that a dynamic view of cost functions should be added to this list of structural determinants. Yet economic structure does not map fully to the industry outcome. There are at least four other important determinants of structure: various kinds of first-mover advantages, chance discoveries or decisions, the identity of industry participants, and the level of uncertainty during industry development.

The disposable-diaper industry discussed above provides a good example of the first two—chance decisions and first-mover advantages. As the data in Figure 3 illustrate, P&G held a dominant position in the disposable diaper industry as of 1974. Its 70 percent market share is well protected by significant mobility barriers, and P&G has maintained its position through 1980, despite serious challenges by the likes of J&J, Kimberly-Clark, Union Carbide, and a number of other Fortune 500 firms. Industry structure in the disposable-diaper industry in 1980, now an over-$1-billion market, is highly concentrated, and informed estimates give P&G well-above-normal returns on investment.

Why did this structural outcome occur in disposable diapers? Part of the answer surely lies in the potential economies of scale and learning that we presented to be reaped by the firm that reached high production volume and national distribution, had the appropriate kind of diversification to allow cost sharing, and won the largest market share. P&G pursued these aggressively and is by far the most efficient firm in the industry. Yet almost a dozen firms (including Scott Paper, Kimberly-Clark, J&J, Borden, Colgate-Palmolive, and others) in 1965 had the potential to be in P&G's position in 1980—each with substantial resources, appropriate diversification in related products, and probably the corporate capabilities to master the required technology. The history of disposable diapers reveals an intriguing sequence of events that has had a major impact on the current structure. Several firms were producing disposable diapers before 1966, when P&G introduced its Pampers brand nationally—among them a unit of J&J, Kendall Corporation, and Parke-Davis. These firms sold crude disposable diapers as a costly speciality product, largely through drugstores. P&G correctly perceived the possibility to make disposable diapers a mass-market product, and developed a way to manufacture diapers at high speed and correspondingly low cost.

While P&G got the jump on the preexisting disposable-diaper competitors, however, a number of other firms also perceived the opportunity posed by disposables. Companies of the stature of Borden, Scott Paper, and International Paper were in the market about the same time, or soon after P&G, with their own disposable diapers. Unfortunately, however, all three of these companies bet on the wrong product technology. Each produced a two-piece diaper, consisting of reusable plastic pants and a disposable liner—the product configuration that had become standard in Europe some years previously.[33] By the time that it became

---

[33]The two-piece variety was much cheaper and more nearly cost-competitive with the prevailing substitutes for disposable diapers—diaper delivery services and home laundering.

Figure 3   A. Estimated Diaper Unit Cost for Procter & Gamble*

	1974 Dollars per Unit	Percent of Total
Raw materials—		
Fluff pulp	$.006	15.0%
Cover sheet	.005	12.5
Backing sheet	.001	2.5
Packaging	.003	7.5
Manufacturing labor	.003	7.5
Depreciation and maintenance	.001	2.5
Utilities	.001	2.5
Total manufacturing costs	$.020	50.0%
Freight	.004	10.0
Selling, general, and administrative costs	.006	15.0
Pretax profit	$.010	25.0%
Manufacturer Sales Price	$.040	100.0%

*Based on Bruce Kirk, *Disposable Diaper Investment Potential,* R. W. Press-pich and Co., Inc.

clear that P&G's one-piece diaper was the preferred alternative in the U.S. market, P&G was already national and enjoyed most of the mobility barriers outlined above. While all this was occurring, several other companies, including J&J and Kimberly-Clark, saw the possibility for a superior one-piece diaper using a better liner material and a more absorbent pulp pad. Though their improved diaper indeed proved to be superior by most accounts, by the time these firms got their product on the market, P&G already had a dominant market share and significant cost advantage.[34] P&G was able to modify its diaper to incorporate the new features pioneered by competitors in time to counter the entries of these new firms as they rolled out their products nationally.[35]

   Thus, the disposable-diaper market was dominated by P&G through a combination of the extent of latent scale and learning economies combined with P&G's ability to be the first mover. The structure of the industry was largely determined for the next 20 years in the first 4 years after P&G's introduction of Pampers, in 1966. In the high uncertainty that prevailed during this period, P&G bet correctly on basic product technology, was able to achieve some manufacturing process breakthroughs, and built its share and volume quickly. Once

[34]It takes approximately 6 years to roll out a diaper brand nationally because of natural lead times, the requirement to have regional plants because of high transport costs, and the risks of investing in several highly specialized plants all at once before customer acceptance has been tested.

[35]This raises another important structural feature of the diaper market, which contributed to the dominated outcome—the fact that technological change after the initial one-piece breakthrough was incremental and more a function of R. & D. spending than chance or creativity. Hence, R. & D. became largely a fixed cost necessary to remain viable in the industry, thereby subject to scale economies and giving the leader (P&G) an advantage.

Figure 3 B. Sample Investment Decision Facing Entrant into the Disposable-Diaper Industry in 1974 (1974 dollars in millions)

	Pre-1975	1975	1976	1977	1978	1979	1980	%
Total Estimated U.S. Market	—	—	—	—	—	—	$700	100
Potential Entrant Operating Statement								
Sales		$ 5	$20	$60	$100	$150	$200	100
Implicit market share							29%	
Contribution		1.38	5.5	16.5	27.5	41.3	55.0	27.5
R. & D.		10.0	10.0	10.0	10.0	10.0	10.0	5.0
Sales force		.25	1.0	3.0	5.0	6.0	8.0	4.0
Advertising		2.8	5.6	8.4	11.2	15.0	11.0	5.5
Coupons		.5	2.0	6.0	5.0	1.5	2.0	1.0
Samples		1.3	1.9	2.5	3.1	3.6	3.0	1.5
Pretax cash flow*		(13.5)	(15.0)	(13.4)	(6.8)	6.2	21.0	10.5
Capital Investment (before operating losses)								
R. & D. prior to startup	$20.0	—	20.0					
Plants	20.0	20.0	20.0					
Cumulative capital investment	40	60.0	80.0	100.0				

*Depreciation is included in manufacturing costs.

Assumptions in Figure 3B

1. Total market in 1980
   3.8 million births
   75 percent penetration of disposable diapers
   55 changes per week
   baby in diapers an average of 25.5 months
   manufacturer's selling price $.04 (same as 1973)

2. Six-year rollout, reaching national distribution in 1980.

3. Five regions in the United States of equal baby population. Enter one new region per year.

4. Assume pattern of sales growth similar to that of Kimberly-Clark.

5. Assume 27.5 percent contribution to advertising, sampling, couponing, sales force, and profit. Baseline for this figure is figure 3A above, which gives the estimated income statement for Procter & Gamble (P&G):

   —assume no purchasing disadvantage (materials 37.5 percent)

   —assume entrant's manufacturing cost = 20 percent (instead of 12.5 percent) due to learning curve and scale economies

   —assume entrant's freight cost = 13 percent (instead of 10 percent) due to lack of full carload shipments

   —assume administrative costs = 3 percent (best guess for P&G)

Revenues		100%
Materials	37.5	
Manufacturing	20.0	
Freight	13.0	
Administrative	3.0	
Total	73.5	
Contribution		27.5%

6. Assume product and process R. & D. a fixed cost of $10 million per year (estimate of expenditures of major competitors).

7. Assume use of food brokers until 1979 (at cost of 5 percent of sales) and own sales force thereafter (4 percent of sales).

8. Assume advertise on a regional basis untl 1980. In each region, spend at a level to match P&G's 1973 spending plus a catch up of 15 percent plus a penalty for not being national of 10 percent (P&G's network advertising is approximately 1/3 of total advertising; network discount estimated at 30 percent).

9. Assume cents-off couponing at rate of 10 percent of sales price in 1975, 1976 and 1977, 5 percent in 1979, and 1 percent of sales thereafter.

10. Assume 600K babies born per region per year. Babies in diapers 25.5 months. Sample costs $1.00. Send a sample to each baby initially. Once in region, sample only new babies.

11. Assume up-front R. & D. investment of $20 million (2 years at assumed required rate).

12. Assume construction of five plants with enough lines to produce a total of $200 million in diapers. Investment $10 million for initial four-machine facility plus $1.0 million for each additional line added to the facility. Sales rate per line $5.0 million. Will require 40 lines.

its volume, and other first-mover advantage like product differentiation and favorable access to hospital sampling kits, had allowed it to rapidly build mobility barriers, P&G was able to neutralize subsequent attempts by entrants to gain market share at its expense, despite the fact that the entrants had the necessary financial resources and were diversified in such a way as to allow them to enjoy shared costs with other of their businesses.

Imagine, however, that Scott Paper and Borden had not introduced a two-piece diaper but rather had correctly perceived the one-piece diaper to be the preferred alternative of U.S. consumers. With three capable competitors starting at the same time, it is quite likely that the structure of the disposable diaper industry in 1980 would be a great deal different. Unless other chance events occurred, no one firm would have likely gotten far enough ahead to gain a significant competitive advantage. With incumbents each holding much lower market shares than P&G has had, other entrants would have faced lower barriers to entering the market than those implied by appendix A. The industry in 1980 would likely be one with much lower concentration, but perhaps higher average cost levels.

Would society have been better off with the latter structure? Perhaps, if the equally balanced market shares of three or four competitors promoted vigorous rivalry and nearly normal returns. Yet the socially desirable outcome would depend on whether the differences between these lower returns and P&G's current returns offset the low costs P&G currently enjoys because of its dominant market share.

This example illustrates that in markets with scale economies and/or learning curves, a significant first-mover advantage is simply getting ahead in the race down the cost curve. Another common first-mover advantage is favorable access to raw material supplies or other inputs. In a world of imperfect contracting, early entrants can often develop loyalties to raw-material or component suppliers that allow them to get first claim on inputs in the periods of shortage that often accompany the rapid-growth phase of an industry's development. Or they can tie up raw materials before market forces bid up their prices.

Another form of first-mover advantage, operative in the diaper industry, is potentially lower-cost brand development into a market. An interesting case of this, recently analyzed by Schmalensee,[36] shows that this effect does not depend solely on advertising, but can occur in a world where firms do not advertise at all.

The impact of the second important historical determinant of industry structure—chance decisions—goes beyond the interaction with first-mover advantages discussed in the diaper example. Early strategic choices made by incumbents in an industry are usually made under great uncertainty. The uncertainty present in the disposable diaper industry early in its development is

---

[36]R. Schmalensee, "Product Differentiation Advantages of Pioneering Brands," Working Paper, Alfred P. Sloan School of Management (August 1980).

typical of many industries in this state. During this period, firms must decide among alternative product configurations, marketing approaches, and manufacturing technologies, among other things. Which of these product configurations, marketing approaches, and/or manufacturing technologies becomes the industry standard is partly a function of which is "best" in an underyling structural sense but also can be a function of which alternative happens to be chosen and developed by the largest number of most capable firms. Once a given alternative is developed and refined, adopting another one that could ultimately be better may face substantial catch-up costs or other barriers. Since differing product configurations, manufacturing technologies, marketing approaches, et cetera, may have very different consequences for industry structure, history can influence structure through this mechanism as well.

A third determinant of industry structure revealed by industry histories is the identity of the particular firms that happen to be participants in the industry during its infancy.[37] The strategic choices firms make are usually influenced by their objectives as well as their stock of resources and skills. I have argued above that these will differ among firms. In the U.S. wine industry, for example, early entrants were generally independent, family-controlled companies that had been started de novo. Their resources and skills limited their strategies to ones based on regional distribution, little advertising, and emphasis on quality. The structure of the wine industry that emerged was one characterized by low concentration. In the mid-1960's, however, Gallo had grown to significant size, and a number of large consumer marketing companies entered the industry through acquisition. These firms applied tried and true consumer-packaged-goods marketing techniques to wine. They increased the rate of product introductions (many of them lower quality wines or mixtures of wine and other juices), raised advertising rates, took advantage of established distribution systems to achieve national market coverage, and automated production.

The latter two historical determinants of structure reveal an important cause of structural change in mature industries. Mature industries often undergo structural change because of the entry of new firms with significantly different resources and skills than incumbents, even though underlying economic structure is unchanged. Such an entry can allow the pursuit of new approaches to competing that had latent potential but were unreachable or passed over by previous incumbents. Mature industries also often undergo major structural change when a competitor discovers a way of competing that was overlooked in the early choices among alternative strategies, even though the underlying economic structure is constant.

A final historical determinant of industry structure in maturity, exposed in joint work with Michael Spence, is the level of uncertainty about future demand

---

[37]The identity of early incumbents is partly endogenous as a result of industry structure but has a high random component in a world of uncertainty, transactions costs, and diversification of established firms. To cite just one example, not all established firms who would be favorable entrants into an industry will be seeking diversification during any given time period.

and technology during the developmental period.[38] High uncertainty in the developmental period tends to limit the optimal size of moves, temper investments to reap first-mover advantages, and thereby promote the development of a more competitive industry structure in equilibrium. Certainty, conversely, encourages attempts at preemptive behavior during the industry's developmental period to reap first-mover advantages and deter subsequent entry.[39] While preemptive forays can lead to intense competition in the short run, preemptive strategies tend to result in higher concentration in maturity.

This analysis of the determinants of structural change besides underlying economics illustrates the potentially high leverage that antitrust policy can potentially have early in the development of an industry compared to its ability to change structure in the mature period. Yet, during this early period, most industries are usually ignored from an antitrust point of view. While exactly which firms reap a first-mover advantage or an advantage from a chance innovation is not in itself usually normatively significant, the process by which the structural outcome is determined (which does have normative significance) may be influential in ways that have little cost in social terms.

X. SOME ADDITIONAL IMPLICATIONS FOR ANTITRUST POLICY

I have identified a number of implications of strategic interaction for antitrust policy above. However, a number of more general points emerge as well as some more particular policy implications in several important types of industry settings. A general point that seems hard to overemphasize is that there seem to be few standards for unreasonable market power that apply to all industries. The normative significance of market power can differ a lot, depending on its bases and the manner in which it was achieved. Second, the traditional focus of antitrust on the narrowly defined (based on product substitutability) industries with geographic market boundaries stopping at the U.S. border has been made obsolete in many situations by recent developments in strategic planning practice and shifts in the fundamental ways in which major corporations compete in the 1980's.[40]

In pursuing more specific policy recommendations, we must treat separately those industries where a significant efficiency-competition tradeoff exists because of large scale economies, related diversifications, or long-lived propri-

---

[38]Porter and Spence (1978), *supra* note 31.

[39]With certain future demand, the firm that can credibly commit to build capacity to meet this demand may be able to keep others from trying.

[40]This is not to say that some antitrust analysis and proceedings do not take such things into account, but rather that many still do not.

etary learning based on cumulative volume.[41] In all three of these situations, a dominated outcome is likely. Except in the case of pure static scale economies, conventional standards of predation should not apply, because the usual definition of variable cost is not appropriate. In such industries, we are in a second-best world where the focus of policy ought to be on encouraging competitive pressure on the leader without sacrificing efficiency through tempering incentives for growth and market share. Direct intervention in the competitive process is generally bad policy. Some policy alternatives will be described below.

In industries where efficiencies due to scale, diversification, or learning are only moderate, strategic interaction can still lead to a dominated outcome if a leader can move aggressively to get out ahead and bolster his position with other barriers or first-mover advantages. Once the industry becomes so dominated, practical remedies are limited. Hence, the best hope for improving the outcome is to act during the developmental process in the industry, before the leader gets too far ahead. Unfortunately, the decision to take an antitrust action early in the life of the industry requires a forecast of what the structural outcome in the industry will be—an uncertain prospect at best—and we must still be concerned about tampering with incentives for static and dynamic cost reduction.

These reasons lead me to believe that the most desirable goal for policy in developing industries is to work to insure indirectly that one firm does not unnecessarily get too far ahead, to facilitate the right kinds of firms entering, and to stimulate competitive pressure from sources other than direct U.S. competitors. This might consist of the following kinds of policy, many of which could also improve performance in industries with large economies of scale, cost sharing, or learning:

1. Selective relaxation of the standards for horizontal mergers among non-leaders. While mergers do not necessarily lead to efficiencies, in some circumstances they can be pooling learning or providing the volume to construct efficient scale facilities, logistics systems, et cetera.

2. Selective relaxation of standards for related acquisitions of nonleaders, and even, in some cases, leaders. Some related acquisitions can, through opportunities for cost sharing, give rise to real economies and allow followers to seriously challenge leaders. Such acquisitions may well lower the cost of entry for outside firms bent on challenging a leader and thus yield an effective entrant whose entry would not occur de novo. The usual concern that such an acquisition will not be used as a base for aggressive growth is minimized where industry structure promises to yield a dominated outcome, because a follower acquired and not invigorated will likely be driven out of the market. Further, where related diversification produces significant real economies, even acquiring a leader may be justified, though our tolerance for such acquisitions should be much lower.

---

[41]If the industry is global, of course, there is no problem.

3. Elimination of artificial barriers that allow a leader to get ahead of followers, and entry-deterring tactics that do not involve any countervailing social benefits. In many industries, artificial barriers such as unresolved patent suits filed by the leader, licensing delays, delays in product certification, and the like, give a leader what turns out to be an unsurmountable jump. Antitrust authorities should work actively to reduce such barriers to a minimum by working with sister agencies and the courts to get expeditious resolution of decisions, consistent with protecting the rights of those involved. Furthermore, entry-deterring tactics which merely delay or punish competitors, rather than propelling the incumbent down the cost curve or improving its product offering, should be eliminated. Eliminating these offers no risk of compromising social goals.

4. Preserve customer bargaining power. Customers with bargaining power can ensure that even a strong leader passes on many of the benefits of his efficiency. Policy towards vertical contractual relationships needs to be particularly sensitive to agreements which co-opt customers in industries prone to a dominated outcome.

5. Open trade policy and elimination of any artificial barriers to entry by foreign multinationals. Elimination of governmental as well as any other trade barriers or restraints on foreign multinational entry can yield effective competition despite a tendency towards concentration in the U.S. market.

6. Approval and encouragement of cost-saving contractual arrangements among competitors. A second-best approach to preserving competition, while at the same time not sacrificing too much efficiency, is to allow competitors to form joint ventures to perform scale- or learning-sensitive production or distribution operations, or to sell scale- or learning-sensitive component parts, services, or even portions of the product line among themselves. As long as such arrangements are sanctioned only with due warnings about the consequences of abuses, they seem to offer a possibility of both low costs and a reasonable number of competitors.[42] Such arrangements are common among foreign firms such as Japanese producers. Despite very favorable cost positions, for example, there are five major Japanese television set producers who sell scale-sensitive color picture tubes among each other.

XI. MATURE INDUSTRIES

Once an industry has become mature, tough standards for predation begin to make more sense, with the caveat that cost sharing or global competition should lead to viable defenses. Given the often entrenched positions of leaders in mature

---

[42]Some parallel suggestions are made by Scherer et al. (1975), ch. 9, note 32 *supra,* though largely in response to static single and multiplant scale economies and not to learning effects.

businesses, however, the best hope for increasing competitiveness in concentrated, mature industries seems to rest in encouraging the entry of optimally diversified (or global) firms that can thereby offset the advantages of incumbants, have the resources to support major investments to overcome barriers outright, and/ or can perceive new ways of competing that allow them to vault mobility barriers cheaply or nullify past learning or scale advantages of incumbents. Since internal entry is perceived to be very risky against entrenched incumbents, this implies that related acquisitions by established firms of industry followers or near-leaders be actually encouraged. Existing merger policy is most appropriate in mature, unconcentrated industries, to keep them that way, rather than in mature oligopolies.

21

Competition, Entry, and Antitrust Policy

A. MICHAEL SPENCE
Harvard University

I am grateful to the Federal Trade Commission for providing the opportunity to reflect on these problems and to the participants in the FTC Conference for their comments. I am particularly indebted to Bruce Owen and to Steven Salop for many insights and observations on an earlier draft. Finally, I want to thank the lawyers at the FTC for their interest and their patience with an economist's attempt to understand the relevant features of the antitrust laws.

I. INTRODUCTION

My purpose in writing this paper and in speaking today is to explore the relevance and applicability of the American antitrust laws to various aspects of the competitive processes. As economists, lawyers, and business people, we have come to understand these processes in different ways. It therefore seems to me useful from time to time to try to discuss the nature of competitive interaction in terms that help to reduce the dissimilarity of perspectives.

The antitrust laws (as written and interpreted through cases) are, broadly speaking, the principal regulatory instrument with respect to competitive interaction at the industry level in the United States.[1] One can ask several basic questions with respect to the regulation of competitive interaction and industry structure. They concern the range of circumstances to which the law is applicable and the welfare consequences (and by that I mean the performance of industries and markets) of the application of the law in those areas where it has jurisdiction. I should like to make clear at the outset what aspects of antitrust law and policy are the focus of attention here.

To this observer, the antitrust laws have their clearest and least ambiguous application to explicitly cooperative behavior and to merger on a scale that is functionally equivalent to complete cooperation. Generally they prohibit it. They make explicit agreements, or conspiracies with respect to price and other variables, illegal. They prevent horizontal mergers that create unnecessary reductions in numbers of competitors, and they prevent trusts. Although the imaginative observer can always locate exceptions, by and large this seems to me to be the least controversial aspect of antitrust regulation.[2] By that I mean that the welfare consequences of these prohibitions (assuming that their enforcement has had a deterrent effect—and it seems to me that it clearly has) are generally desirable.

There are at least two broad areas in which the applicability of our antitrust law has a considerably more ambiguous applicability. One concerns formally noncooperative behavior that gives rise to cooperative-like results, usually in concentrated industries. While it is tempting to digress into a discussion of this type of competitive interaction and to the regulatory alternatives for dealing with it, I will not so digress (at least not for long), for it is not the subject in which I am primarily interested today. Suffice it to say that there has been a

---

[1]There are other regulatory bodies and activities. But they focus either on particular industries or sectors, or on problems like the environment. There is also foreign trade policy, which has a significant influence on competition and industry structure in the United States. Because of its importance, I shall comment more extensively on its relation to antitrust policy later in the paper.

[2]There are examples of U.S. industries that have been adversely affected by foreign competition, where the problem can be traced, in part, to an inefficiently fragmented structure in the U.S. industry. Such cases are not common; in those cases, antitrust policy is not reasonably regarded as the source of the structural problem.

great deal written about the subject.[3] At the level of policy, there are at least two schools of thought. One school takes the view that regulating conduct is doomed either to failure or to inconsistency and that the only effective relief is structural. Structural relief, of course, runs squarely into the problem of efficiency and the related question of what initially created the level of concentration actually observed. These questions are not always addressed properly in the policy debate. Another school of thought takes the view that certain practices (open competitive policies by trade associations, "most-favored-nation" clauses in contracts being examples) make avoidance of profit-reducing competition easier, and that these facilitating practices should be banned or circumscribed.[4]

This brings me to the second ambiguous area and the third broad area of antitrust policy—the "monopoly" problem. The monopoly problem is the central focus of most of what I have to say today. In referring to the "monopoly" problem, I mean to include not only monopoly in the sense of a single seller, but also high concentration, large amounts of market power, and rates of return above risk-adjusted costs of capital. I do not want to tackle the monopoly problem directly; that is, I do not want to begin with what the law either is or ought to be. Rather, I should like to discuss what we know and (perhaps equally important) what we do not know about competitive activities and processes, especially the dynamic aspects of competitive interaction, because I believe that an understanding of these processes will and should influence our thinking about public policy in this broad area.

I have in mind, under the heading of "competitive activities and processes," a number of specific topics. They include entry and entry deterrence, investments and other activities that constrain the opportunities of one's actual or potential rivals, the intertemporal aspects of competition, and the structural features of industries that are influential in determining competitive strategies and industry evolution. I will try to summarize and interpret some of the writing on these subjects and to identify areas in which relatively little is known. My reasons for subjecting you (and many of you are primarily interested in antitrust policy and not the evolution of microeconomic analysis) to such an enquiry are

---

[3]Much of the relevant part of economic theory has focused on oligopolistic interaction in mature industries.

[4]I do have one observation concerning this broad area. There is a subset of industries that have real problems with price competition (in the sense economists mean it). They are industries where, because of demand fluctuations, lumpy additions to capacity, and capital intensiveness, marginal costs are below average costs. Under these conditions, competition would bid prices down to the level of marginal costs—not all the time, but often enough to create problems. Such industries find ways of preventing prices from being bid down below average costs to marginal costs. I have seen a number of cases in which devices that facilitate the avoidance of the bidding process have been attacked as collusive. Such cases are sometimes brought without consideration being given to industry's rate-of-return figures. Such cases strike me as expensive; and in some cases, futile. But the main point I want to make about them is that they should not be brought without some analysis of what the Government would like the firms in the relevant industry to do in lieu of what is being proscribed in the bringing of the case.

twofold. First, it seems to me essential to the development of a consistent and effective policy with respect to monopoly concentration and market power to have some insight into the ways in which individual firms and groups of firms acquire and maintain positions of market power. The problem with examining these questions in the context of particular antitrusts suits at the time they are brought is that one is often looking for items on a list of "bad" or "unacceptable" competitive practices. At the very least, this tends to divert attention from the structural and strategic origins of the market power.

The second reason for delving into the processes whereby market power is acquired is that the performance of an industry or market is in part determined by the evolution of its products and structure, and not just by the competitive structure of the mature industry. Indeed, in some industries the technology and its evolution produce persistent changes in structure, so that their structure and performance when they eventually mature and stabilize is not the central issue from a welfare standpoint.

The remainder of the paper is divided into four sections. In section II, I discuss entry and entry deterrence and then try to assess how antitrust policy is likely to affect entry-deterring behavior and market performance. The underlying models are essentially static in a sense that will be clear (I hope) in the discussion. The longest section is the third. It focuses on the dynamic aspects of strategic investment and competitive interaction. Much of it consists of a discussion of the ways in which a number of structural features of markets influence intertemporal competition. The fourth section deals with foreign competition, in a somewhat abbreviated fashion. Logically it might have been included in section III, but because of its importance and some special considerations that are relevant, it rates a separate section. In the fifth and last section, I have tried to reflect on the implications of the foregoing for antitrust policy. Those who are looking for or expecting a comprehensive policy proposal will be disappointed. But I think there remain some useful propositions to help guide prosecutors in selecting cases, if not courts in deciding them.

One further comment is in order. I refer repeatedly to welfare and market performance in what follows. Whenever these terms occur, they stand for the sum of the benefits to consumers and to producers in a market. Producer benefits are profits. Sometimes it is necessary to add up benefits over time, and that is done by taking a present value using some suitable discount rate. Thus, for my purposes, market performance is measured by the discounted present value of the benefits to consumers and/or producers.[5]

---

[5] As a number of observers have pointed out, performance in this sense is arguably not the only objective of antitrust policy. And I agree. Some would argue that no firm can be deprived of its market by inappropriate means without due process of law, regardless of whether or not the market is more efficient without that firm. Therefore, let me simply acknowledge at the outset that improving market performance in the sense defined above is not the sole objective of policy, and that there are other purposes that may override in particular cases.

II. ENTRY DETERRENCE

Any firm or group of firms that is able to maintain a position of market power and high profitability over an extended period of time must have some form of protection from the expansion of potential or actual competitors. That protection (if it exists at all) consists of a combination of structural features of an industry (economies of scale, for example), and activities (of the firm[s] seeking protection), that deter the expansion of rivals. The activities and the structure interact to create the barriers and to produce profitable operations.

When economists use the term "structure," they mean two different things. Sometimes the term refers to exogenous characteristics of an industry such as the technology, the production function, or the demand. At other times it refers to concentration, which is the result of a combination of the decisions of firms and of exogenous structure. Naturally, this produces considerable confusion. To avoid some of it, I shall refer to technology and the like as "exogenous structure," meaning that it is not the result of the behavior of firms or their customers. The antitrust laws cannot do much about underlying exogenous structure. They must, therefore, operate either on conduct (so as to alter the incentives for erecting entry barriers), or on the endogenous aspects of structure (like high concentration). The question naturally arises then as to what kinds of conduct are to be deemed acceptable or unacceptable, and in what circumstances.

To answer this sort of question, one probably wants to acquire some familiarity with how entry deterrence is managed in a variety of contexts. It would be foolhardy of me to attempt to offer generalizations that are intended to be without exception. Industries and markets are far too complex and varied to permit that. But there are some tendencies and some propositions that I believe withstand both theoretical probing and exposure to evidence from case histories reasonably well. My intention is to discuss some of these propositions which I believe characterize the competitive structure of many industries, and then to reflect on the kinds of policies that would make sense in light of the underlying economics.

The first proposition is that the deterrence of entry or expansion has at least two logically quite distinct parts. One consists of the actions that will be taken (or potential entrants anticipate will be taken) if entry occurs. (Henceforth I shall refer to established firms and entrants. The reader should interpret "entrants" broadly to include firms that are expanding or changing their strategies as well as those that are actually newcomers to an industry). The second class of actions are those that are taken prior to entry. These actions of established firms are designed to influence their own incentives with respect to their reactions to entrants. Therefore they also influence the perceptions of potential entrants about the likelihood of those actions. The moves made prior to entry can be thought of as *positioning*. The actions in response to entry might be referred to as *reactions.*

Positioning and reacting are distinct types of activity. But they are strategically related. Positioning affects the incentives of the established firms with respect to reactions. To the extent that these effects are accurately perceived, positioning will influence the profit calculations of potential entrants. The trick in entry deterrence is to find a positioning strategy that is (a) not too costly and (b) creates the incentive for the established firm to react to the entrant in a way that is destructive to the latter. The established firm(s) want to position themselves in such a way that their self-interested reaction to a potential entrant is damaging to the entrant's profitability without being self-destructive. Or, to put the matter another way, if the established firm does not create a situation in which self-interest makes the entrant unprofitable, then entry will be deterred only if the potential entrant can be otherwise convinced, notwithstanding the economic incentives, that the established firm will act so as to make the return to the entrant's investment unacceptably low. Credibly conveying the intent to destroy—when after the fact of entry it is demonstrably not in the established firm's interest—is not only difficult, it is legally hazardous, because it exposes the established firm to the charge of predatory behavior.

A simple example of positioning would be the construction of production capacity by the established firm sufficient that upon entry, ordinary competitive prices and output would ensure that the entrant was unprofitable.[6] The capacity can be thought of as an investment by the established firms. Part of the return to that investment consists of profits that would have been lost in the event of entry. This sort of investment occurs commonly in manufacturing sectors. It need not be undertaken only to deter a potential entrant. The capacity may be intended to reduce the return to capacity expansion by other firms already in the industry. And the phenomenon is not confined to manufacturing. One can observe expansion-deterring investment in retailing, for example, where a firm may "overstore" a geographic area to limit the expansion of rivals.

The rate of return to this kind of investment depends upon a number of factors. Usually an important one is economies of scale, or a structural feature that is functionally similar. Scale economies can be found in marketing as well as production. In many situations the costs of advertising per dollar or revenues generated decline with share of market. Thus the entry- or expansion-deterring investment may be in advertising rather than production capacity or retail outlets. Or the investment may consist of a combination of these variables. There are many variants of the same theme.

---

[6]This issue and other related issues are discussed more fully in A. M. Spence, "Entry, Capacity, Investment and Oligopolistic Pricing," 8 *Bell J. Econ.* 534 (Autumn 1977); A. M. Spence, "Investment Strategy and Growth in a New Market." 10 *Bell J. Econ.* 1 (Spring 1979); A. Dixit, "A Model of Duopoly Suggesting a Theory of Entry Barriers," 10 *Bell J. Econ.* 20 (Spring 1979); E. C. Prescott and M. Ursscher, "Sequential Location Among Firms with Foresight," 8 *Bell J. Econ.* 378 (Autumn 1977); S. C. Salop, "Monopolistic Competition with Outside Goods," 10 *Bell J. Econ.* 141 (Spring 1979); R. Schmalensee, "Entry Deterrence in the Ready-to-Eat Breakfast Cereal Industry," 9 *Bell J. Econ.* 305 (Autumn 1978).

A second factor that affects the entry-deterring investment decision at the positioning stage is the aggressiveness with which the established firm competes with the entrant or the expanding firm. For the firm there is a tradeoff between prior investment and aggressive competition after entry, in deterring entry or expansion. The extent of the prior investment affects the need for being aggressive ex post. It also affects the credibility of the threat to the entrant. This is especially true in markets where the investment is largely irreversible so that the established firm does not have the option of changing its mind. Conversely, aggressive reactions postentry reduce the need for investment at the positioning stage.

Much of the policy embodied in the corpus of the antitrust laws deals with the entry problem by defining what will (from a legal standpoint) be regarded as excessively aggressive or "predatory" competitive behavior, or what I am calling reactions to entrants or expanding firms. Such policies should not be evaluated in a vacuum but rather in terms of the incentive effects they are likely to have. Increasing the stringency of the standards for predatory or unfair competition can have different impacts in different market situations. In some cases it will tip the balance against the strategy of entry deterrence. But in others, it will cause firms to increase the magnitude of their prior investments. It does this by altering the tradeoff referred to above between the positioning investment and the reaction to entry or expansion, after the event. To the extent that prohibitions against predatory behavior constrain firms' reactions to entrants, the prohibitions will increase the incentive for firms to make prior investments that reduce the need for aggressive reactions to deter entry.

As a result of these two possibilities, the welfare effects of increasing the stringency of the definition of predatory behavior are far from unambiguous. I suspect the majority view used to be (and probably still is) that more entry is better than less, and that the hoped-for effect of stringent standards would be exactly that—more entry. It is not my intention to deny that there are instances in which this view is correct. But it is far from being well established empirically that this is the normal case. It is probably true that a majority of economists would assent to the proposition that most concentrated U.S. industries are more concentrated than necessary to be efficient. Although I have considerable doubts and uncertainties about this proposition, let us accept it for the moment. Even if it is true, there remains the possibility that the primary effect of changes in policy directed toward predatory conduct would be to alter prior investment behavior rather than to produce more entry. Then one needs to ask whether those effects are ones that on balance improve or diminish market performance.

Even in the simplest cases, the answer is—it depends. I used the example of capacity as an entry-deterring prior investment earlier. The effect of constraining an established firm with respect to pricing or expansion of output in that case is to cause the established firm to increase its capacity. If it uses the capacity fully, the welfare effect is positive. But it may not. And in real market situations where demand is growing, uncertain, or fluctuating, and investments are lumpy, it is not easy to impose the desired outcome or to devise standards of conduct that induce it. When the prior investment is in advertising or retail capacity, the effects on market performance are even less clear.

My instinct as an economist is to study industries on a case-by-case basis, applying and adapting models as appropriate. For those of us who do this kind of work, the differences among industries sometimes seem more important or interesting than the similarities. And thus we are uncomfortable with general rules. That, of course, is not very useful to courts or litigators, who require some general principles or rules on which to hear and argue cases.

There has been a considerable debate about appropriate standards for identifying predatory behavior recently.[7] I am not sure that any consensus has emerged from that debate. Probably the most widely accepted standard is the one that prevents pricing below average cost. I shall express some reservations about this rule in the next section on the dynamic aspects of competitive interaction. Its virtues are that it is simple and that there is a reasonable possibility of detecting violations through examination of figures on rates of return. The principal alternative is a marginal-cost rule. A marginal-cost rule is not only based on a quantity that is difficult to measure; it is also a *less* stringent standard in a declining-cost technology. If average costs fall with output, marginal costs are *below* average costs.

But the point I wish to emphasize is that whatever standard you find most reasonable, a great deal of effective entry deterrence would pass the test rather easily. There are exceptions. The WEO campaign of price cutting in food retailing in the early 1970's by A&P probably violated an average-cost standard. Certainly the stock market reacted strongly and quickly to the low rates of return of A&P and its competitors.

But in many industries, the barriers to entry and the barriers to expansion are the result of the competitive strategies adopted by the major firms, including high rates of investment in advertising and new product introductions. An example might be the ready-to-eat cereal market, which is involved in an ongoing FTC antitrust case. It is not clear that prohibitions against predatory responses to potential entrants would have any material effect on the performance of this type of industry.

Since there are problems with operating on the incentives to deter entry entirely by regulating conduct undertaken in response to entry, one might reasonably ask about regulating the prior investment behavior. There is some precedent for this approach. In the Alcoa case, it was argued that it may not be acceptable for a monopoly to build capacity sufficient to meet a growing demand, thereby effectively preempting potential competition. In the FTC's titanium dioxide case, the Commission's lawyers argued that Du Pont's capacity expansion

---

[7]See, for example, P. Areeda and D. Turner, "Predatory Pricing and Related Practices Under Section 2 of the Sherman Act," 88 *Harv. L. Rev.* 679 (1975); M. Scherer, "Predatory Pricing and the Sherman Act," 89 *Harv. L. Rev.* 869 (1976); O. E. Williamson, "Predatory Pricing: A Strategic and Welfare Analysis," 87 *Yale L. J.* 284 (1977); P. L. Joskow and A. K. Klevorick, "A Framework for Analyzing Predatory Pricing Policy," 89 *Yale L. J.* 213 (1979).

program had the effect of preempting the competition and of creating a dominant-firm industry structure and that that was unacceptable in that market context.

While these approaches seem to me to have some merit, I shall argue shortly that there are no known, unambiguously beneficial, simple rules that can be applied to investments prior to entry or expansion. Once again, that negative conclusion is of little use to courts. But at least, focusing on the entry-deterring investment process in particular cases does seem to me to be an investigatory strategy that is more likely to capture the economically important aspects of competitive interaction and market performance. Since investment behavior is best discussed in an explicitly intertemporal setting, I am going to interrupt the discussion of policy to turn to the dynamic aspects of competitive interaction.

III. INDUSTRY DYNAMICS AND STRATEGIC BEHAVIOR

The preceding discussion of entry deterrence was couched in static terms. It is implicitly assumed that entry deterrence has two phases; one of them—the positioning phase—logically precedes the other. It assumes the established firms are already there in the market. Such an approach is conceptually useful for analyzing mature industries. But it leaves unanswered several important questions. For example, there is no explanation of who the established firms are and how they acquired positions of market power. An important question in an antitrust case is whether market power was acquired by legitimate means or not. The problem of regulating or influencing the evolution of industry structure before it becomes a problem is not therefore easily discussed with a static model. Moreover, the underdeveloped area of evaluating and measuring the intertemporal efficiency of a market gets set aside altogether.

My aim in this section is to describe some of what is known about the evolution of industries and about strategic interaction in the dynamic sense. And then, with that as background, we can reflect on policy options and the desirability or undesirability of regulating investment behavior. I should say in advance that the state of economic theory is not particularly advanced in the area of intertemporal competition.

For the purposes of the ensuing discussions, it will be useful to imagine an industry that is new and growing, or one that is in disequilibrium because of a major technical advance. An industry is in disequilibrium if firms are making investments that cause the structure of the industry to change. If one were trying to predict how such an industry were going to evolve, and whether it would evolve into a dominant-firm structure as in computers, a concentrated oligopoly as in autos, or a relatively competitive and unconcentrated industry like semiconductors, what would be the structural features of the industry that one would study? Or, to put the matter differently, what are the structural features that influence the strategic choices that firms make and the consequent evolution of an industry's structure?

A. The Magnitude of the Required Investment

The magnitude of the investment required to participate in the market efficiently is a factor that tends to create concentration in several ways. It limits the market to firms whose financial and managerial resources are sufficient to achieve the requisite scale. To the extent that there is uncertainty about the potential size or the rate of growth of the market, the need to make substantial investments to be efficient or cost-competitive increases the riskiness. While investors in securities can diversify the risks away to a large extent, firms and managers can diversify only to a limited extent. Uncertainty, however, is a two-edged sword. While it interacts with scale effects to increase the risk and hence deter the entry of the small or the risk-averse, it may also blunt the incentive for firms to attempt to move quickly and first into dominant positions. Calculations in the context of specific examples suggest that concentration may be a U-shaped function of demand uncertainty. That is, the least and most risky markets tend to produce investment behavior that gives rise to the highest levels of concentration. These calculations are far from definitive, and more work is required to understand the interaction of demand uncertainty and scale economies in influencing the dynamic equilibrium. But they are suggestive of the importance of uncertainty in conditioning the evolution of industry structure.

B. Differential Costs of Expansion in a Market

Firms can differ in the investment required to expand in a market, depending on their starting points. Let me illustrate with an example. General Foods and General Mills probably have lower distribution costs than Kellogg in the cereal market, because they distribute other products through the same retail outlets. Kellogg has a compensating advantage in the form of large market shares on a brand-by-brand basis and overall. Share in this context creates lower advertising costs per dollar of revenues. A logical potential entrant to the market is Procter & Gamble, which has a marginal distribution cost advantage similar to that enjoyed by GF and GM.

In extreme cases, the initial asymmetries can create rather pronounced concentration. IBM's customer base in the business sector in the tabulating machine market, and the expertise that went with it, gave it a significant cost-investment advantage in the early 1950's in computing equipment. That advantage rapidly (within 3 years) turned into a dominant market share in the business segment of the computer market.

One could go on with examples, but the point would be the same. Diversification and history create asymmetries among firms with respect to their strategic opportunities, which, when exploited, can give rise to high concentration and to initial or early positions of market power. There remains of course the question of whether and under what circumstances these initial positions can be maintained.

C. Reversibility of Investment

One significant factor in deciding the latter question concerns the extent to which the investments are reversible or not. Generally, irreversibility creates more permanence and higher concentration. Not only by increasing the exit costs but also by credibly committing the firm to defend its investment, it reduces the anticipated returns to potential rivals. As with uncertainty, irreversibility is a two-edged sword. It protects the firm with the market power position, but in the context of uncertainty, it increases the risk of the initial investment and hence may blunt the incentive to try to acquire a large relative share or to monopolize a segment of the market.

D. Uncertainty

I have adverted to uncertainty at several points without formally announcing it. It is clearly an important influence on industry evolution. As we have seen, the influence of uncertainty is somewhat complex. It is further complicated by the fact that it tends to be resolved over time. This gives rise to a number of interesting possibilities in the evolution of an industry. It is not uncommon (for example) that a market is initially developed by small and medium-sized firms; and then when it begins to accelerate in growth, the market is entered by larger firms, which then grow very rapidly. At the end of that phase, there is often a period of near-excess capacity and pressure on margins.

Why might this pattern be observed? One explanation is that large and small firms differ in the rates at which they can grow, because of differences in organization and in managerial and financial resources. Large firms exploit that advantage by waiting until some of the uncertainty about the market's potential is resolved. Thus the fact of uncertainty and the speed with which it is resolved as the industry develops can affect the timing and magnitude of the investments by entrants. An industry that evolves in the way I just described may become an oligopoly in its mature phase. But is not likely to evolve into a dominant-firm structure or a near-monopoly.

E. The Learning Curve

Closely akin to scale economies is the learning curve or experience curve. On the cost side, the learning curve depicts the relationship between unit costs and accumulated production to date. Generally it is a declining function. The rate of decline varies from industry to industry. In some industries the rates of decline are quite dramatic, on the order of 15 percent every time accumulated volume doubles. While the data required to estimate learning curves accurately have not generally been available to researchers, the emphasis on them by firms in some industries and by certain consulting firms is sufficiently widespread that it seems to me safe to include them on a list of potentially important structural features of an industry.

The competitive implications of the learning effect are interesting. As with scale economies, there is a premium (in the strategic sense) to early entry, rapid growth, and large relative share of market—all of these for the obvious reason that these things, in conjunction with the learning effect, confer cost advantages. The cost advantages in percentage (as opposed to absolute) terms may or may not diminish over time. But even if they do, the relevant time horizon may be so long as to be largely irrelevant.

The observations concerning the importance of share and of the head start do not tell us much, by themselves, about the competitive process, the evolution of the industry, or its performance in the absence of regulation or constraint. So let me turn to these issues.

When there is a learning curve, the marginal cost of additional output is not the current unit cost. Rather it is the current unit cost minus the present value of the reduction in all future costs which results from the fact that additional output at a particular time will lower unit costs at all future dates. This means that any firm, even a monopoly, will price more aggressively than it would in the absence of the learning effect. Indeed, the prices can be below unit costs, at least initially. It is easy to see that such behavior would be difficult to distinguish from, and could be confused with, predatory pricing. It is this fact, among others, that causes me to be concerned about average cost standards for predatory pricing—at least in relatively new and growing markets.

I have done some calculations of dynamic equilibria in models with learning effects in order to determine, in a rough way, what the impact on competition of this aspect of industry structure might be.[8] Some of the conclusions, which should be regarded as tentative at this stage, are the following. Learning curves are powerful sources of entry barriers. With substantial learning effects, it is not uncommon for the equilibrium number of firms to be three or four. Entry barriers are greatest when the learning curve is neither very steep (rapid learning) nor very flat (slow learning), but rather somewhere in the middle. It is the moderately rapid learning that creates the largest cost differentials among firms—and hence the greatest entry barriers.

From the standpoint of market performance, there is clearly a tradeoff between competitiveness (as measured by the number of firms) and price/cost margins on the one hand, and technical efficiency on the other. A single firm

[8]A. M. Spence, "The Learning Curve and Competition," Harvard Institute of Economic Research, Discussion Paper No. 766 (June 1980).

would be most efficient—that is, could produce at the least cost but would price monopolistically. If there are many firms, the price/cost margins are more nearly optimal, given the cost, but the costs are higher than need be, because the learning is dissipated across competitors. My calculations to date suggest that entry ceases in the neighborhood of the point where competition and cost efficiency are optimally traded off. That is to say, at the point where further entry is unprofitable, the benefits of an additional firm from more price competition about equal the cost increases resulting from dividing the cumulated industry output among more firms. I emphasize that this observation is not a logical deduction from a model but rather a generalization from calculated equilibria for numerous cases. The cases are distinguished by having widely different values for the important parameters, like the elasticity of the learning curve with respect to volume, the elasticity and growth of demand, and so forth.

A monopoly performs very poorly relative to two or more firms. The greatest improvement in market performances comes from the move from one to two firms. Of course, the two firms have to compete (i.e., behave noncooperatively) for the benefits to be realized.

A second observation concerns the case where the learning effects spill over to some extent from one firm to the next. One can think of this as a case where the unit costs of an individual firm depend on both its own accumulated output and the accumulated output of the industry. The relative importance of these two variables in driving unit costs down is a reflection of the extent to which the individual firm's production experience is or is not transmitted to other firms. My tentative observations concerning the impact of this kind of structural externality are based on the kind of calculations referred to above. Industry learning effects appear to reduce the aggressiveness of the output decision, to reduce the entry barriers, and to improve market performance. On the face of it, these effects are not surprising. Economists, however, will develop the sneaking suspicion that there is a potential market failure here, because some of the benefits of a firm's output decision are not appropriated by that firm. This might lead one to suspect that output would be too small. That line of reasoning, however, ignores the social benefit of increased competition. In fact, it is true that profits are lower with industry learning effects. But the impact of the transfer of the learning effects is to permit more competition for any level of industry cost reduction. That benefit tends to accrue to consumers. And the net effect is an improvement in market performance. There is more that could be said about the learning effect, but dwelling further on it in a survey such as this is probably not the best use of the available space.

F. Demand-Side Structure

Let me turn to the demand side of markets. Thus far I have concentrated primarily on investments and costs. But the demand side deserves (although it has not yet received) equal prominence. Indeed, a survey of U.S. industries in

1980 would, I think, tend to confirm one of Professor Barn's conclusions in his remarkable work on entry barriers; namely, that entry barriers based on product differentiation are generally the most potent sources of above-average rates of return.

There are many aspects of demand structure that can influence concentration and market power. There are, for example, a variety of kinds of effects that are analogous to the learning curve. In fact, in markets where the products are complex and/or new, there is exactly a buyer learning effect. Thus the demand for the product of an individual firm can depend upon the accumulated purchasing experience of consumers with that firm's products. The experience reduces the uncertainty associated with the characteristics and uses of the products, relative to those of rivals. The competitive implications of this sort of buyer learning are very similar to those found in the context of cost-reducing experience. Indeed, one can, in certain circumstances, formulate the problem in such a way that the models are formally equivalent. Since the effects are so similar, it is not necessary to repeat the conclusions we drew earlier.

The buyer learning effect is magnified if consumers invest in the product or its use. A well-known example is the computer industry, where there is not only consumer learning but also consumer investment in software that is largely equipment specific. The fact that it is equipment specific is, of course, a matter of strategy and not an act of God. When the buyer invests in the use of the product, the effect is to reduce the relative attractiveness of the products of rivals. Formally, this aspect of structure can be captured by allowing demand to depend on accumulated sales, and it magnifies the accumulated volume effect.

As in the case of cost-side learning, some of the demand-side learning may be an industry effect. Or, to put it another way, experience with one firm's product can have a positive influence not only on that firm's product, but also on those of rivals. And as in the cost case, this aspect of structure tends to reduce entry barriers and concentration for exactly the same reasons.

There are other reasons why demand may depend on accumulated volume other than learning. If the product is durable, there can be a negative effect of accumulated volume associated with saturation of the market. The durability effect causes a damping of the rate of growth of demand as the industry matures. Once again there is a premium on rapid growth and early entry, particularly if the effect is combined with either scale economies or learning on the production side.

G. Advertising

The subject that is most discussed in the context of demand-side structure and market power is advertising. The technology of advertising is such that the expenditures required to reach consumers with messages tend to be relatively fixed with respect to sales in units or market share. This had led analysts to conclude that there is a rather strong element of economies of scale in advertising that may explain the empirically well-established positive correlation between advertising intensity and profitability. It is also recognized, however, that "scale economies" is not exactly the right concept. Advertising, after all, operates on the demand and hence influences unit sales. It seems somewhat peculiar, therefore, to take the latter as fixed in explaining why advertising results in share of market cost advantages.

There is relatively straightforward way of avoiding this theoretical box. One can think of a firm as using resources to produce a product and then using more resources to sell it. Or, more usefully, one can think of it as using resources to generate revenues: some of those resources are used in creating a production to sell; other resources go into selling it. If you take the latter view, then advertising and selling activities are inputs to a process that generates revenues. That production function often exhibits economies of scale; hence, there are potential entry barriers associated with it.

H. Interdependencies Between Supply and Demand

There are some additional elements of structure that researchers have observed in case studies of particular industries, which I should like to comment on briefly. One of them concerns a relation between supply-side concentration and demand growth. It is not hard to find examples of industries in which buyers are reluctant to become dependent upon one or a small number of firms because of the loss of bargaining power. Where possible, buyers will avoid buying from concentrated industries, and that acts as a *negative* entry barrier in the industry. The buyers may actually favor (and, to some extent, protect) the new entrant. This feature is easy to observe in the high fructose market that developed in the 1970's as a substitute for sugar.

A second phenomenon concerns the investment by factors of production in the technology of a particular firm's products. It has been argued that part of IBM's market power stems from the fact that with a large share, most people who are trained in programming and software development are trained on IBM equipment and systems. A buyer who wants to hire programmers will, therefore, find a larger and better developed market if he purchases the equipment of the dominant firm. Formally, this phenomenon would have the features of the demand-side learning effect. The demand would increase with accumulated volume.

I. Product Development Costs and Economies of Scale

Let me finally describe what I believe to be an increasingly important aspect of industry structure. In some industries, product development costs represent a substantial fraction of total cost, as a result of the opportunities for developing new products or reducing costs. Sometimes high development costs result from rapidly changing demand. The latter can be induced by changes in prices elsewhere in the economy or by other factors. The computer industry is one in which product development costs have historically figured prominently. And it appears to be increasingly characteristic of the automobile industry, where petroleum prices and some regulatory activity have pushed up the product development costs and the rate of product change.

Product develoment costs are largely fixed costs. Their impact on average costs is therefore smaller, the larger the sales volume over which those costs can be amortized. Industries with these characteristics will exhibit a strong tendency to become highly concentrated, and the dominant-firm structure is common. While more work needs to be done on the question of what kinds of equilibrium market structures are likely to emerge under these conditions, my conjecture (if you will permit me one) is that symmetric equilibria in terms of market share are unstable. That does not mean that the end result is a monopoly (in the literal as distinct from the legal sense). While the cost functions may appear to have the characteristics of a natural monopoly, it is by now well known that driving smaller competitors out of business in a dynamic setting is not always, or even usually, a good investment for the large firm.

I mention this aspect of industry structure in part because I believe that there is an important subset of American industries that will find that the fixed costs of staying in business are a rising fraction of total costs. The forces causing the changes are diverse; they include rapid change in technology (especially in the semiconductor and integrated circuit industries), rapid changes in relative prices in sectors like energy, and the advent of significant foreign competition in many sectors. In the not-too-distant future, many of the affected markets will become antitrust concerns. It is probably useful to begin now to think about what the best policy responses might be.

In the course of the evolution of an industry, firms make investment decisions based on calculations of the returns to the investments. The decisions are interactive in the game-theory sense. Part of the process of developing a coherent investment strategy is the calculation of the moves that are likely to be made by rivals, because those moves will affect one's rate of return. The most likely investment decisions of one's rivals are not independent of one's own investment decisions. And therefore part of the return to most investments consists of the deterrent effect it will or may have on one's rivals' investment behavior. The point I want to make is simply that most strategic investments are entry- or expansion-deterring. That is not their only objective, but it is almost always part of the calculation of the return. It is difficult at best—and, quite conceivably, logically impossible—to distinguish between entry-deterring investment and other kinds of investment.

A combination of structure, timing, and past history will create strategic opportunities which firms will exploit by committing resources to the point where the marginal returns equal the perceived costs of capital. Part of the marginal return will consist of the damping effect of the investment on the extent of rivals' expansion. Many investments have this preemptive component. Its importance varies from industry to industry with the structural characteristics I adverted to earlier. In a dynamic context, entry or expansion deterrence is an integral and ordinary part of the competitive process; it is not something that can be isolated as unusual or abnormal and then eliminated by regulation. Nor does taking into account the deterrent effects of one's own investment behavior involve peculiar business planning or practice. On the contrary, ignoring these effects would seem to businesspeople to be unusual in the extreme.

IV. INTERNATIONAL COMPETITION

I adverted to foreign competition in a previous section without dwelling on it. For several reasons, it deserves a prominent place in a general discussion of competition policy. I will not expose you to a long discussion of the subject, but I do want to make some observations that might influence the way in which foreign competition is viewed in an antitrust context.

Foreign competition is not ignored in antitrust proceedings. For example, it is a legitimate counterclaim to a charge of monopolization that there is competition from non-U.S. firms and from imports. But there is still a strong tendency to treat the U.S. market as the relevant market and to regard foreign competition as a minor qualification. In fact, there is a growing number of markets in which the relevant market is the worldwide market.

Foreign competitors are potentially a powerful competitive force, because they can and do sell into the large U.S. market at something approximating marginal cost. This is particularly true of competition emanating from relatively protected, and large, domestic markets like that in Japan. The costs associated with product development, learning, and the like, are recovered in the domestic market, while the costs of exports are treated as incremental. The domestic market may be protected to ensure that cost reductions achieved through serving the domestic market are not diluted by imports. Historically, such a strategy at the national level was necessary to be competitive by U.S. standards. Even without the aid of a protected domestic market, a firm that can achieve a large share of market worldwide can afford higher product development costs, which result eventually in competitive advantages.

This paper is not the place to attempt a lengthy explanation of the internationalization of many domestic markets. But certainly the trend has been created by a combination of forces. Tariff and other trade barriers have been negotiated downward. The relative size of non-U.S. markets has been growing and providing arenas where foreign competitors can expand to become cost-competitive. And the economies that were severely damaged by the Second World War are building back to more normal levels of activity, investment, and consumption. All this is creating a situation in which U.S. firms and industries face increasingly powerful competitors who have large bases in non-U.S. markets and who often operate in cooperation with their respective governments.

From an antitrust standpoint, increasingly effective foreign competition presents some interesting problems and possibilities. From a strategic standpoint, U.S. policy should be devoted in part to ensuring that non-U.S. markets are not effectively blocked to U.S. corporations at the same time as U.S. markets are relatively open. A failure to pursue such policies will ultimately result in an erosion of the competitive positions of U.S. industries. For competition policy, foreign competition represents an interesting alternative to operating directly or indirectly on domestic industry structure. Exposing a domestic industry to foreign competition and reducing the domestic industry's concentration are alternative ways of achieving competitive outcomes. In fact, we ought to use a combination of foreign competition and domestic structure to achieve the desired competitive outcomes. Foreign competition, I should say, is regulated by tariff and nontariff barriers.

I am currently involved in some research that focuses on the tradeoffs involved in optimally exploiting antitrust and trade policy. Let me briefly try to provide the flavor of the problem. If, for structural reasons of the type discussed earlier, there are efficiencies associated with high concentration, some of the benefits of concentration can be obtained without having the kinds of pricing problems that would normally occur in a closed economy, by matching increases in concentration with tariff reductions. Such a policy has two effects: it will increase the competitiveness of U.S. firms in non-U.S. markets, and it may reduce tariff revenues. Both these factors need to be taken into account.

To implement coordinated policies in the trade and antitrust areas, we need to become more knowledgeable than we currently are about the answers to a number of questions. For example, how does the optimal combination of trade and concentration vary with the size of the domestic market relative to the worldwide market? How is it affected by the comparative advantage or disadvantage of domestic and foreign firms in terms of costs (and by costs I mean cost functions: actual costs are endogenous and responsive to policy), the concentration of the nondomestic part of the supply side of the market, the policies and strategies pursued by other countries, the magnitude of economies of scale, learning effects, and product development opportunities and costs?

These are hard questions to answer, but certainly not impossible. And I believe they are important enough to invite the attention of academics and policymakers in the relevant areas of microeconomic regulation, including especially antitrust.

V. ANTITRUST POLICY

The time has come to try to say something about what all this means for antitrust policy in the monopoly area, broadly defined. Let me preface these remarks by saying that I do not regard myself as an antitrust expert. These thoughts are at best a basis for discussion, and certainly not well-worked-out policy proposals.

My first observation is this. To the extent that one's objective is the improvement of market performance as conventionally measured by the present value of the net surplus, then it is not at all clear that preventing market power from developing (even if one could) would be desirable. In industries where the structural basis for market power is a scale economy or a learning effect, relatively efficient market structures may entail having powerful firms or groups of firms.

A second observation is that the structural environment of industries that evolve toward monopolies, near-monopolies, or concentrated oligopolies, is often such that behavior that is normally considered to be predatory is *not* required for the concentrated outcome to occur. It seems to me unreasonable to expect firms to calculate the returns to their strategic investments in abstraction from what their rivals are expected to do. And what rivals will do depends on precisely those investments. These mutually recognized interdependencies are factors in the investment decisions of firms. The result is an equilibrium in the dynamic sense. Dynamic equlibria often result in market power positions and the dominance of market segments by individual firms, for structural reasons discussed in the previous two sections.

On the other hand, while market power is the natural result of strategy and structure, I can think of a few industries that require a monopoly structure to be efficient markets as large as those in the United States. (I would not say the same thing about smaller countries, whose problems in this area seem to me rather different from ours.) Hence, there is some merit in looking for ways of preventing unnecessarily high levels of concentration, ways that do not place arbitrary restrictions on the private sector and that run minimal risks of impairing market performance and the competitive position of the U.S. industry in world markets. The extent to which this is possible will almost surely depend upon the structural characteristics of industries and hence will vary from one industry to the next.

A third observation would be the following. Attempting to prevent monopoly power by looking for predatory or unfair conduct whenever and wherever monopoly power develops, strikes me as a costly and ineffective policy strategy. Standards for predation sufficiently stringent to prevent monopoly power in all cases would be considerably more stringent than those we have now. And they would run the risk of constraining firms in ways that are counterproductive and arbitrary. I want to make it clear that I am not arguing against the existence or enforcement of laws prohibiting predatory behavior. The point is rather that this will not and should not serve effectively as the *main* weapon in the arsenal for dealing with the market power and related performance problems.

There is a related point that deserves comment. Neoclassical price theory notwithstanding, there is a partial conflict of objectives between business and the public sector. There are instances in which the formulation and implementation of strategies by businesses that are in every sense effective and normal business practice, result in market outcomes that are not ideal from the broader perspective of overall market performance. There is a widely accepted myth that the pursuit of profit by "legitimate" means will always result in the right results. Not only is it not true, unless one defines "legitimate" in such a way as to make a tautology; acceptance of it biases the process of changing the market outcome toward a search for what must be there according to the theory, namely, some kind of unacceptable conduct.

In saying there is partial conflict of objectives, I do not mean to imply that all instances in which the conflict surfaces should be regulated. Sometimes the cure is worse than the disease. Indeed, the policy problem is to know or to learn what if any market processes are regulatable at reasonable cost and low risk, and by what means. It is hard to start thinking about this problem if one believes that except in a few unusual regulated sectors, the problem does not exist.

One way to deal with these problems is to define activities which result in the acquisition of a monopoly position in a market as unacceptable. That is a logically coherent position, but it amounts to prohibiting monopoly. In particular, the distinction between legitimate and illegitimate means of acquiring monopoly power would essentially disappear. There is, however, a difference between operating directly on structure and operating on conduct at the level of remedies. Preventing monopoly by conduct restrictions may involve the plaintiff in guessing what combinations of activities would, if excluded, have prevented the evolution toward monopoly. When the basis for the monopoly power is largely structural, that game can be frustrating and ineffective.

I do not want to convey the impression that I believe there are no instances in which monopoly power is acquired by economically illegitimate means. On the contrary, examples of predatory conduct do exist, and the law as I understand it is adequate to deal with them.

But the study of strategic investment behavior, intertemporal industry evolution, and the underlying structural determinants of both of these—theoretically, and in the context of case studies—suggest to me, and I hope to others, that there is and will continue to be a significant subset of industries that do not lend themselves to this approach to regulating market power. And I would therefore conclude that we ought either to find alternative ways to regulate, or not regulate at all.

Because structurally based monopoly problems usually stem from some scale economies (broadly defined to include demand-side phenomena and dynamic effects like learning) that are large in relation to the size of some market or market segment, I find the idea of actively using foreign competition as a regulatory device attractive. Considerable expertise is required to do this, because the tradeoffs between efficiency, competitiveness, and the benefits of foreign profits and domestic tariff revenues are complicated, to say the least. And there are other complicating factors. At the moment, trade and competition policy are implemented by different organizations operating relatively independently. That would have to change. In addition, the problem of negotiating general reductions in trade barriers, while at the same time employing potential foreign competition as a regulatory instrument at the industry level, should prove challenging to the best minds we have. But in spite of these problems, I believe that there is a subset of U.S. industries where controlled import competition is a more sensible and effective regulatory device than deconcentration, constraints on investment behavior, or other remedies that would fall within the scope of domestic competition policy.

Obviously, foreign competition is not a short- or medium-run solution to market-power problems in all afflicted industries. There is, for example, a collection of oligopolistic consumer goods industries in the United States that have persistently achieved high rates of return with no obvious concomitant risks that might justify the observed returns. These industries have been a source of concern to antitrust agencies for some time. Many such industries have little or no foreign competition, essentially because the market expertise required to compete tends to be country-specific. Some of the attempts to deal with market-power problems in these industries within the framework of existing law seem (to this outside observer) to have involved excessively creative applications of the law, to the point where the whole process looks like a costly and somewhat indirect form of rate-of-return regulation. Once again, it appears to me that our regulatory approach through antitrust has been ineffective because of the apparent need to claim that the market power stems from abnormal business behavior, when it may in fact be the result of normal dynamic competitive interaction and underlying structure.

It is perhaps useful to note that other countries deal with the monopoly problem in somewhat different ways. The British Monopolies Commission, for example, appears to be able to intervene rather more directly in industries that are identified as having some sort of performance problem. I hasten to add that I am not an expert on the Monopolies Commission, but my impression is that the legal context in which its decisions are made and reviewed is somewhat more flexible than our antitrust law.

In certain industries, the entry barriers may result from practices that one would not want to argue are per se illegitimate, but which are in the context of a particular industry rather powerful entry-excluding devices. Some of the examples I have in mind involve exclusive dealerships, with possible examples being the automobile industry (historically) and hearing aids. I am sure there are others. It seems to me that it ought to be possible to devise a regulatory mechanism that permits the Government to disallow such practices in particular cases, after a suitable investigation into the costs and risks of taking that action, without having to argue either that the practices are the result of collusions or that they are unacceptable in all cases.[9] To an economist, the problem with the antitrust

---

[9]Exclusive dealerships, in fact, may be an area in which the law has been applied flexibly and with some sensitivity to the structural differences among markets.

law in the monopoly area is not so much what it contains as what it does not contain. It correctly identifies and prohibits classes of actions that are both outside the range of normal competitive business behavior and likely to result in poor market performance. Where it is less effective is in dealing with the existence of market power whose origins do not fit the above description. One might argue that the law was never intended to apply to the latter cases. But if that is true, then I think it would be hard to defend some of the monopolization cases brought in the past 10 to 15 years. The arguments in a number of cases with which I am familiar have an air of economic unreality that is associated with the need to make the arguments fit the facts of the case to a model that does not apply. The cases I have in mind are ones in which there is little or no dispute about the presence of market power, notwithstanding endless debates about the definition of the relevant markets.

In reviewing some of the forces and strategic considerations that influence the evolution of industries' structures, I hope to have created the impression of a rich variety of possibilities and outcomes. This is entertaining for academics who enjoy trying to untangle the web of interacting influences. And it is of course all too easy to apply that knowledge critically to the activities of those who try to modify and enforce the rules within which the economy will operate. There will always be some tension between the general rule and its application to the particular case.

Nevertheless, I believe that recent research provides some help, and future research will provide considerably more help in understanding the process of industry's structural evolution. More to the point from a policy point of view, it provides some categories and some structural phenomena with which to classify industries into groups. Groups of industries will differ by the sources of the market power of the firms that have it. And they will therefore also differ in the ways in which they will respond to policy intervention. It is the last fact that is most relevant from a policy standpoint.

The ability to group industries on the basis of their structural similarities and hence the sources of the market power ought to provide a useful input to the process of selecting and screening cases, and to the formulation of policy at that level. It does not provide simple answers concerning what rules or standards to apply in judicial proceedings. My own view is that the state of our understanding of both dynamic strategy and intertemporal market performance is currently insufficient to justify confident conclusions with respect to rules and standards. But I do think that it is better to admit ignorance than to defend rules based on incomplete static models of industries.

The only conclusion about which I am sure is that the effectiveness of the antitrust process in the United States, insofar as it regulates monopolies and market power, will be substantially affected for the foreseeable future by the sophistication that can be brought to bear in the analysis and selection of cases and by the imagination that is exercised in finding alternative ways of achieving the objective of improving market performance.

22

The Strategic Exit Decision: Additional Evidence

KATHRYN RUDIE HARRIGAN

Columbia University

The author wishes to acknowledge the computing assistance of Muhd Daud and Brenda K. Kocian in completing this project. Also, the criticisms of Donald C. Hambrick and an anonymous reviewer helped in the paper's revision.

INTRODUCTION

When its markets sour disastrously, when profitability plummets hopelessly, or when (for other reasons) an SBU no longer "fits" with the rest of a corporate entity, the firm contemplates exit. Yet sometimes the timeliness of its divestiture (or liquidation) can be blunted as the firm responds to the deterrent effect of exit barriers. Some exit barriers are elements of an industry's structure. As such, they will affect the competitive requirements of doing business, particularly the firm's ability to withstand intensified price competition, because they can disrupt the smooth retirement of redundant facilities and increase the volatility of an industry.[1] A substantial exit barrier can develop when the firm becomes reluctant to sell or abandon its investments in a particular business because it cannot retrieve their value, due perhaps to depressed market conditions such as are commonplace within industries where it is becoming increasingly evident that demand is declining, for example, and few alternative uses for the business's assets will exist.

This paper compares findings concerning exit behavior within *non-declining* industries with findings from a study of exit within declining industries.[2] It argues that the firm's ability to implement its strategic decisions successfully (in this case, to exit) depends not only on the presence of relatively low industry *structure* exit barriers which should permit marginal (i.e., nondominant) firms to exit with ease but also on the height of firms' *strategic* exit barriers which will differ according to how particular firms have competed in the past. In addition to articulating how the effects of exit barriers might be expected to vary within nondeclining businesses, the paper suggests that firms should carefully consider how to build or avoid creating forms of these barriers in order to maintain control of how their industry evolves.

The sections that follow relate this study of exit to other studies of industry structure and of decline. The theory of exit barriers is reviewed and additional variables affecting exit behavior are suggested. These are subsequently tested in a model of exit within mature industries. Its findings are contrasted with those of decline and some distinctions are noted.

The model of exit builds on Harrigan's endgame theories by adding variables suggested by corporate planners who divested unsuitable business units. The basic form is an econometric analysis tested on a sample of sixty firms from five nondeclining industries. Like the PIMS database, several years of data for each firm were utilized to study the effect of various structural factors on this strategic decision, each year of data comprising an observation.

[1]Michael E. Porter, *Competitive Strategy: Techniques for Analyzing Industries and Competitors* (New York: Free Press, 1980).

[2]Kathryn Rudie Harrigan, "Deterrents to Divestiture," *Academy of Management Journal,* 24 No. 2 (June 1981), 306–23.

THE USE OF STRUCTURAL
STUDIES IN STRATEGY RESEARCH

Studies mapping the competitive environment using the structure-conduct-performance paradigm of industrial organization economics can offer managers an improved understanding of the environmental factors that may influence a particular strategic decision. The entry barriers that firms overcome in undertaking competition become, in many cases, the very forces that will deter their departure later. A model that describes the forces affecting exit—which estimates the magnitude and direction of their effects—becomes particularly germane within planning systems that must cope with rapid product obsolescence brought about, in some cases, by frequent technological innovation.

Although mature industries can be guided in their development by the introduction of timely technological improvements, conditions of excess capacity are an inevitable and fundamental difficulty that firms must confront in this environment. Because increases in productive capacity must be brought into line with slowing increases in demand, early identification of the forces that could discourage marginal competitors from making timely exits and that may suggest tactics for ameliorating their effects are of particular interest to managers charged with strategy formulation.

Strategists could use these findings as warnings concerning undesirable industry conditions which could develop if the informed manager did not undertake efforts to staunch their growth. Students of strategy formulation could gain from these types of studies improvements to existing contingency theories of business strategy and the beginnings of what may become an optimality theory of strategies for environments of slowing demand.

THE MATURE INDUSTRY
ENVIRONMENT CONTRASTED
WITH DECLINE

Competition within some declining industries has been marred by panic-stricken behavior (resulting in substantial write-offs of assets) and destructive rounds of price cutting as firms burdened with excessive productive capacity tried to fill these plants to breakeven levels. During such periods of volatility, average industry profits remained depressed until a sufficient number of redundant factories were removed to equilibrate industry capacity with reduced levels of demand. But if demand were indeed declining without reasonable expectations that the factors affecting the industry's demise would be reversed, firms seeking to exit from endgame would undoubtedly encounter some difficulty in disposing of the physical assets they had once employed because the value of their assets would probably soften over time as the recognition of industrywide decline became increasingly widespread.

Within mature industries where the rate of growth in demand is slowing, by contrast, competitive behavior should be less panic stricken due to a more resilient resale market for firms' assets. Price-cutting behavior may be similar to that expected within declining industries plagued by excess capacity, however, because the mismatch of demand with capacity coming onstream may require a period equivalent to technological lead times to be resolved. In this study we assume that multiplant competitors facing conditions of excess demand could close a plant to ease these conditions, but smaller, single-plant competitors would face only the choices of remaining doggedly in the industry or of exiting. We introduce this subgroup as the focus of this study in the following section.

A comment concerning "fringe" competitors.   Firms that possess large market shares are generally believed to possess substantial power to influence prices and other conditions of competition. Although Markham[3] has suggested that the firms acting as pricing leaders need not be those possessing the largest share of the market (an observation of pricing behavior substantiates his assertions), firms continue to seek market share because it is believed to confer cost economies due to the larger scale of production, advertising, R&D, or other competitive activities that is needed to serve a larger sales volume.[4] These market leaders are core competitors because their strategic postures (and market shares) place them at the center of industry influence.

Fringe competitors, by contrast, are firms whose strategic postures (and market positions) place them at the periphery of industry influence.[5] If smaller, they are less likely to enjoy the economies of scale in their operations; if publicly traded, they are less likely to engage in kamikaze pricing maneuvers to fill their idle plants. Because they suffer both cost disadvantages and tactical inflexibility, these firms are among those we would expect to be driven from the industry when competition became more volatile.

A comment concerning the behavior of "core" firms.   Within established industries where growth is slowing, firms that possess substantial market shares, the competitive core firms, would press their smaller, less-successful rivals in order to maintain their previous growth rates and profitability goals. This group, which would be less likely to exit from their mature industry environment, would set the standards for competitive behaviors, however.

A comment concerning the measurement of exit.   The population densities studied were obtained from industry counts in Dun & Bradstreet indi-

[3]Jesse W. Markham, "An Alternative Approach to the Concept of Workable Competition," *American Economic Review,* June 1950, pp. 349–61.

[4]Robert D. Buzzell, Bradley T. Gale, and Ralph Sultan, "Market Share—Key to Profitability," *Harvard Business Review,* January–February 1975, pp. 97–106.

[5]Michael E. Porter, "The Structure within Industries and Companies' Performance," *Review of Economics and Statistics,* 60 (May 1979), 214–27.

ces and from *Census of Manufactures* reports of firms in operation. This count included privately held as well as publicly traded firms. Exit was indicated as a binary code (where "1" indicated exit occurred); acquisitions (even by direct competitors) would alter this tabulation only if the operations of the two firms were subsequently integrated and operated thereafter as one entity. Yet because antitrust laws prohibit most horizontal mergers, few such integrations were expected to occur.

As we will explain below, this tabulation of the occurrence of exit can be related to information concerning exit barriers and other structural traits for the industry in which the business units operate, the economy, and the traits of "core" competitors. These data are used to construct independent variables. Although the occurrence of exit may arguably indicate the *absence* of exit barriers and other structural conditions, the data file does inform us about the traits of firms that did not exit. The "core" firms' traits are assumed to exemplify the industry. There is a chance that these characteristics systematically misrepresent those of the industry, of course. Therefore we proceed as follows. Measurements of the reporting businesses are taken on the assumption that their characteristics typify the industry, but we will discuss individual attributes where this is a less-sensible suggestion as they occur. A measure of the relative magnitude of certain attributes was constructed by dividing the measure of the reporting firm by the industry average, where available, or by the harmonic mean of the reporting firms' attributes if an industrywide measure was not available. We infer that industry structure data gleaned from published data describing leading, publicly traded competitors would also describe the environment faced by follower firms.

INDICATORS OF AN INDUSTRY'S ATTRACTIVENESS

All businesses do not offer the same potential for profitability. The average return on invested capital for some businesses, such as steelmaking, is lower than for others, such as pharmaceuticals. The variation in potential average industry profit levels is, in part, attributable to differences in industry structures. These structural conditions can influence whether informed organizations enjoy the potential to earn profits in excess of average returns across all industries. As such, they are a major influence on the perceived attractiveness of an industry environment with respect to future resource allocation decisions.

Industry attractiveness is used as a major criterion for classifying business units by planners using various portfolio schemes. An important, and sometimes overlooked, feature of this group of attributes is their mutability. Industry structure changes as demand slows, as competitors invest in new forms of vertical integration and technologies, or as structural changes occur in the markets of firms' customers (or in the technologies of their suppliers). The firm must understand the effects of structural changes that can accompany these slowdowns in order to create contingency plans for such environments.

Harrigan's study of decline,[6] which investigated those environmental and corporate factors that encouraged firms to either divest (or liquidate) declining business units or take actions to fortify their competitive positions therein, has identified several groups of factors that influenced the perceived attractiveness of an industry. Some of these were traits of industry structure. Others included variables influencing the outlook for continuing demand and the pattern of tactics firms had pursued with success within their industries. The expected effect of each of these variables upon exit behavior within mature industries is discussed below.

THE OUTLOOK FOR GROWTH IN DEMAND

Mature industries are characterized by a high degree of market saturation. Fewer significant product innovations coupled with high purchase prices and widespread customer acceptance in earlier years have led in many cases to a market where buyers are experienced (i.e., they understand the products' attributes and can compare them among rival vendors), where dealers are exerting increasingly stronger pressures for price breaks upon vendors, and where annual consumption is becoming primarily for replacement needs once the initial purchase has been made.

This stabilized repurchase rate could offer ample sales volume for a reduced number of competitors to serve. Under such a scenario, a relatively steady stream of production could be planned for and capacity expansions could be eased onstream. Profit levels could be steady, albeit at lower levels than within some growing markets. But cost-saving adjustments could be made in competitive tactics such as advertising campaigns or in standardization of manufacturing or distribution operations in order to bolster the flagging profitability that is frequently associated with slowing sales growth. This hopeful scenario could be realized as long as competitive equilibriums can be maintained and price wars avoided.

In decline, favorable expectations concerning demand for the products of an individual firm could keep competitors that served lucrative subsets of the market invested even in the face of adverse demand conditions. Empirical studies of this phenomenon have indicated that expectations can be highly significant influences on exit decisions. In a mature industry environment, where conditions of low or stagnant sales growth could persist for decades, the individual outlooks of successful competitors regarding demand could keep them invested while less

[6]Kathryn Rudie Harrigan, *Strategies for Declining Businesses* (Lexington, Mass.: D. C. Heath, 1980).

successful firms (or those firms whose products have become commoditylike but do not possess the absolute costs advantages needed to support this posture) may be squeezed out.

In estimating this effect, it was assumed that the growth in sales volumes would be slowing more profoundly for follower firms if the sales volumes of core competitors were increasing more rapidly than average industry sales growth rates. Our measures of less than proportionate sales growth (which have been deflated by GNP growth rates) amplify the advantages enjoyed by firms whose growth rates exceed the average. These firms would be less likely to exit than those firms from whom sales volume was taken. Therefore the probability of fringe competitors exiting would be greater and the sign on this factor would be positive.

If, however, the mature industry environment seems to reward additions to capital investments, an incentive to remain invested may exist. This effect, which relies on perceptions, is difficult to measure. Our proxy for these encouraging conditions, an estimate of the apparent attractiveness of capital formation for fringe competitors, π^*, was the percentage of capital expenditures accounted for by each industry's four largest competitors multiplied by the average capital turnover ratio. The sign of π^* was expected to be negative because high capital turnover enjoyed by leading firms could be expected to signal high potential returns for other competitors as well.

PROFITABILITY POTENTIAL
OF INDUSTRY STRUCTURE

Many of the independent variables we posit as influences of exit behavior are suggested by the literature of industrial economics. In theory building, industry structure variables, such as the presence of high levels of seller concentration, high entry barriers, and substantial product differentiability, suggest whether the opportunity for higher industry profits exists. Other traits, such as the presence of high levels of buyer concentration and high exit barriers suggest that industrywide average profits may be depressed. This section discusses the effects of industry structure upon industry performance.

Exit barriers.   If the firm is to attain its strategic objectives for a particular SBU, it must possess the flexibility to exit with relative ease from investments it no longer values. Firms face economic exit barriers, which are structural factors common to the particular market niches they serve, as well as barriers unique to their postures within those niches. They need to understand how to cope with each of these.

The economic barriers that are part of the industry context shared by competitors will be difficult to alter single-handedly unless the firm makes the types of strategic expenditures that force the industry's structure to evolve. Examples of such expenditures that force the industry's structure to evolve. Examples of such expenditures include (but are not necessarily limited to) changes in capital and technological scale requirements, changes in the degree of vertical integration, or changes in other factors that may have constituted entry barriers for the firm previously. One of the reasons for slow changes in many industry contexts may involve the substantial degree of risk associated with undertaking these types of expenditures.[7] If unprepared for exit, these expenditures can make divestiture difficult to implement.

Firms that should have abandoned the fight due to poor performance (but did not) would be expected to act similarly to firms in declining industries. They would avoid exit to avoid recognizing reporting losses which would be incurred on disposal or to avoid cash requirements to meet unfunded pension obligations which would be incurred by shutting down operations. Unlike firms in declining industries, firms within mature industries may postpone the recognition of these factors that act as barriers for longer periods of time, provided their losses do not become too large. Also, there is a remote chance within a mature industry that a buyer for the firm's assets may appear. For these reasons, the heights of exit barriers may be relatively higher in mature industries where less pressure to exit exists than in decline, and the industry may seem to be more attractive.

Although economic theory argues that the original costs incurred to acquire productive assets ("sunk costs") should not function as a deterrent to exit, some managers of declining businesses (in the acetylene business for example) acted as if they believed the substantial losses they would have recognized on disposal *did* matter to both the stock market and to their customers in other businesses of the corporation.[8] In these cases it was feared that their actions would communicate poor judgment. Some managers permitted this concern for managing reported performance to act as an exit barrier even in decline.

Similar forces could be operative in mature industries where excess capacity would depress profitability for many competitors until some adjustments to industrywide capacity were made. The disposal of productive assets should be less difficult to accomplish within mature businesses, however, unless the assets to be recycled were used specifically for the manufacture of those products for which excess manufacturing capacity exists.

Construction of exit barriers.   Accordingly, a set of variables was constructed to measure the height of exit barriers and the incentive forces of these other important economic factors. The magnitude of write-off losses were gauged by the age of industrywide physical asset accounts. High net to gross physical plant balances could indicate highly undepreciated assets. If such bal-

---

[7]Consequently, the structure will evolve, in most cases, at reduced speeds. In some cases the trend of structural evolutions may even reverse as demand and technological conditions change or as firms reposition themselves and change their emphasis on an SUB's mission.

[8]Harrigan, *Strategies for Declining Businesses.*

ances were prevalent among leader firms, they were assumed to indicate a trend of industrywide high balances.

Changes in these balances were also of interest. Although high absolute physical plant balances signaled the presence of high exit barriers, changes in these balances could indicate a trend toward liquidatioin or capital formation. If leader firms were liquidating, exit barriers related to the durability and specificity of physical plant would be relatively low. But if the physical plant accounts were increasing, this trend might indicate a revitalized commitment to remaining in this industry. If fringe competitors did not match these revisions, they might be left at a disadvantage which could be substantial enough to force their eventual exits. In that case the negative effect of the exit barrier would become positive.

Another exit barrier variable, height of barriers related to severance cost obligations, will be constructed in a section treating strategic exit barriers below because, although the extent to which an industry's manufacturing technology tends to be capital intensive (or labor intensive) is a structural characteristic of the industry, the trade-off between the relative amounts of automated versus hand placements, and the unique labor covenants negotiated (both degrees of technological advantage), are matters of individual corporate strategic choice. A different form of technological factor that can also affect exit behavior is formulated and discussed in the following section, which treats other elements of industry structure that are also germane to the exit decision within mature industries.

The construction of additional structural variables.   A mature industry with respect to increases in the rate of demand is not necessarily a stagnant one with respect to structure. Cost-reducing innovations and improved work methods are assumed to be occurring throughout this phase of competition. Indeed, these improvements which could place laggards at a disadvantage may exert substantial pressures on fringe competitors to retreat because if a firm does not possess one of the least costly technologies (or if its factories and other productive capacities are underutilized), the firm will suffer higher operating costs at a time when price competition is increasingly being emphasized. Accordingly, measures of the industry's structural context—physical plant size, efficiency, and utilization, as well as product differentiation activities—should be included in an analysis of exit behavior to capture the effects of competitive factors that may be important in forcing fringe firms to exit.

In a mature environment, the profitability of small competitors that do not serve specialized (protected) niches of the market will be squeezed by the price-cutting pressures of firms that operate the most-efficient-sized plants. Increasing capital requirements (needed to attain this scale of production) could squeeze out firms operating less-efficient-sized plants, assuming these competitors do not update their plants (due perhaps to a corporate decision to harvest the business in question), particularly if severe excess capacity is plaguing the industry. In that case, firms operating the smaller plants would be more likely to exit.

Capital requirements were measured by estimating the minimum efficient scale plant size.[9] The dollar value of MES was calculated from the *United States Census of Manufactures* measures of *M*, the number of establishments responsible for 50 percent of the industry's value of shipments. The value $1/M$ was multiplied by the dollar values (gross) of industry physical plants. Estimates of capital requirements could also be obtained using the "survivor theory," which holds that only the most-efficient-sized plants will survive under adverse industry conditions.[10] As capital requirements increase, as the number of dollars invested per plant rises, marginal competitors are expected to be more likely to exit. Accordingly, the sign of this variable would be positive.

Marginal firms may also suffer disadvantages if they have not kept abreast of changes in technology or work methods that improve the operating efficiency of their plants. The technological scale effect was estimated as (gross plant/number of employees), although other estimates of scale yield equivalent results.[11] Increases in scale effectively "raise the ante" in competition. If marginal firms cannot match these improvements and suffer cost disadvantages, they would be expected to exit. Therefore this factor's sign should also be positive.

Although economic and strategic exit barriers may discourage firms from executing timely exits, conditions of excess capacity should encourage marginally successful firms to exit because, during periods when aggregate productive capacity far outstrips the market's ability to absorb its output, price cutting becomes endemic. In such cases, smaller and inefficient competitors would be particularly hard pressed to maintain profitability due to the aggressive efforts of core competitors to fill their own underutilized plants to breakeven volumes. Some of them would be squeezed out.

The presence of excess industry capacity was estimated by subtracting practical (dollar) capacity utilized in a particular year from "optimal" or engineered capacity. The *U.S. Census of Manufactures* estimates of engineered capacity, which were employed, represent the percentage of total designed plant capacity at which the facilities are most likely to be operated when "fully utilized," an amount that is lower than designed output in many cases. The sign of this factor should be positive, indicating that when excess capacity is high, the likelihood of exit is greater.

---

[9]G. Rosenbluth, *Concentration in Canadian Manufacturing Industries* (Princeton: Princeton University Press, 1957); S. I. Ornstein, J. F. Weston and M. D. Intriligator, "Determinants of Market Structure," *Southern Economic Journal* (1973) pp. 612–25.

[10]Leonard W. Weiss "The Survival Technique and the Extent of Suboptimal Capacity," *Journal of Political Economy*, June 1964, pp. 246–61.

[11]See, for example, William S. Camanor and Thomas A. Wilson, "Advertising Market Structure, and Performance," *Review of Ecnomics and Statistics,* November 1967, pp. 423–40.

THE CREATION OF STRATEGIC
EXIT BARRIERS

Successful performance can pose an intriguing paradox. The successful tactics firms employed to achieve their performance goals can generate intangibles that act as strategic exit barriers. These are tactics, attitudes, and other impediments that can intensify the firm's reluctance to abandon a particular line of business. Although strategic portfolio approaches (such as the BCG grid) assume that managers can delete SBUs with relative impunity, the findings of Caves and Porter,[12] Porter,[13] and Harrigan[14] suggest that firms may have difficulty in getting out of businesses due to these barriers. Briefly, if the firm has attained successful ROI by being a superb marketing or R&D firm, its managers will encounter particular difficulty in divesting businesses that are close to the heart of their corporate image.[15]

The intangibles generated by firms' past strategic outlays do not affect all competitors equally because not all firms were serving the same niches of the market; not all firms pursued identical strategic postures. Strategic exit barriers will constitute particularly significant deterrents for firms operating within one strategic group, for example, but may not influence other competitors substantially. Also, firms may face differing barriers with respect to their relationships with customers that purchase other products from the firm.

Construction of strategic barrier variables. The intangible exit barriers generated by firms' past strategic outlays were estimated using measures of lagged advertising expenditures and labor severance costs. In environments of declining demand, expenditures for building trade relations, distribution networks, and brand images acted as exit barriers for firms that considered the declining business in question to be of relatively high strategic importance. This finding was consistent with those of Caves and Porter,[16] which indicated that expenditures for advertising and R&D seemed to be highly statistically significant influences on failures to exit.

The advertising variable compared individual firms' advertising-to-sales ratios with a measure of the dispersion of firms' advertising-to-sales ratios. This measure was constructed from the average advertising-to-sales ratio of each firm divided by the harmonic mean of the industry's advertising-to-sales ratio. Firms

[12]Richard E. Caves and Michael E. Porter, "Barriers to Exit," in *Essays in Industrial Organization in Honor of Joe S. Bain,* ed. David P. Qualls and Robert T. Masson (Cambridge: Ballinger, 1976), Chap. 3.

[13]Michael E. Porter, "Please Note Location of Nearest Exit: Exit Barriers and Strategic and Organizational Planning," *California Management Review,* 19, No. 2 (Winter 1976) 21–33.

[14]Harrigan, *Strategies for Declining Businesses.*

[15]Porter, "Please Note Location of Nearest Exit."

[16]Caves and Porter, "Barriers to Exit."

whose successful strategic postures were predicated upon the attainment of effective product differentiation (which we assumed would be indicated by this ratio) would be expected to face higher exit barriers. Resistance to exit would be particularly strong among those firms whose outlays were substantially higher than the mean. If competitors that were not in the core had advertised or promoted their products heavily in the past, they would also have created a strategic asset which they may have been loathe to abandon. Accordingly the sign of this variable should be negative.

Severance cost barriers were calculated as the ratio of pension expenses to earnings before taxes, multiplied by the average annualized employee wage and expressed as a percentage. The expected effect of this barrier would be negative, as in declining industries where firms would have faced sizable worker compensation lawsuits or been obliged to face substantial cash requirements for the funding of pension or other worker plans, had they exited. Some firms, which faced severance costs of this nature in declining industries, lowered their prices and struggled to capture enough sales volume to cover at least their operating expenses, rather than exit.[17] If the effect of labor costs were the same in mature industries, the sign on this factor would be negative.[18]

Caution must be exerted in representing the behaviors of fringe competitors in this factor, given differences in labor force characteristics among leader firms and followers. We assume some provision would be made for laborers employed in mature industries when they were idled by shutdowns. The approximate cost of this variable will represent those technologies that are more labor intensive as being those that would also face larger labor severance costs.

Construction of performance variables.   In addition to the improvements in market share that our sales growth variable assumes leading firms might enjoy, we estimated the effects of their ROI performance. Like assumed increases in respective sales volumes, our measure of corporate performance was expected to exert a positive influence on the likelihood of smaller firms to exit because positive feedback to leader firms in the form of high profits should intensify their determination to stay. The revitalized determination of these successful competitors would probably intensify rivalry, resulting in a greater likelihood that less capable firms would exit.

SUMMARY OF HYPOTHESES

Exit behavior (of firms listed in Dun and Bradstreet directories) was hypothesized to be influenced by (a) structural conditions within the industry during maturity (minimum efficient scale of plants, changes in technological scale, ex-

[17]Harrigan, *Strategies for Declining Businesses.*

[18]Many of the observations in the declining industry study (and in this one) covered years before federal legislation protecting pension systems was enacted.

Exhibit 1 Construction and Discussion of Independent Variables' Expected Effects Upon Exhibit Behaviors of Fringe Competitors

Variable Name [denomination]	Mean	Standard Deviation	Expected Effect	Explanation
1. *Capital Requirements:* $(1/M*$ total value of industry physical plants), where M equals the number of establishments responsible for 50% of the industry's value of shipments [Dollars per plant].	73.753	99.364	Positive	If the capital requirements for effective competition are relatively high and if leading firms possess this requisite critical mass, small firms (which may not) would be more likely to be squeezed out.
2. *Changes in Technological Scale:* (Gross plant/ number of employees)$_t$ less (Gross plant/ number of employees)$_{t-1}$ [Dollars per employee].	0.0134	17.663	Positive	An increase in scale investments effectively "raises the ante" in the game. Marginal competitors could be forced to exit if they can not match these investments.
3. *Change in Relative Age of Physical Plant:* [(Net plant/gross plant)$_t$ less (Net plant/gross plant)$_{t-1}$] divided by the industry average change in age of physical plant [relative percentage (decimal)].	−0.0006	.196	Negative	Relatively new assets may act as exit barriers (undepreciated write-off losses). They could also signal a renewed interest in the industry (or required pollution control investments). However, if many fringe competitors are liquidating, exit barriers are likely to be lower and exit is more probable. Exits are less likely if fringe firms increase their capital bases by updating their plant and equipment as core competitors may have done.
4. *Advertising Variability (Relative)* (Advertising/ sales) divided by average industry advertising intensity [Relative perentage].	4.855	45.979	Negative	If firms have engaged in product differentiating activities which entailed a relatively higher advertising or promotional intensity than competitors, these expenditures comprise an important element of their strategic posture and generate an intangible asset which they would be unwilling to sacrifice if no buyer for their business (and the product differentiation the firm had developed) was available.

Variable				
5. *Excess Capacity* (MOS plant utilization less level of capacity that was employed) [Average percentage (decimal)].	.0765	.1782	Positive	Significant excess capacity would likely squeeze out marginal competitors as leading firms filled the reduced capacity.
6. *Labor Obligations*: [(Annual pension expenses as a percentage of operating income) multiplied by (labor expenses per employee)]$_t$ less this quantity, the pension costs per earnings times the average employee wage, divided by industry average pension costs [relative percentage].	.0023	11.690	Negative	This exit barrier is both economic and strategic in nature. Recognition of these costs could act as a substantial (economic) exit barrier. If unionized, the unskilled labor force could act as a more substantial exit barrier to marginal firms than physical plant and equipment may be. Even if the firm were not unionized, it would be necessary to provide for the laborers who have been idled, lest the firm's subsequent bad reputation impede its future efforts to recruit manpower.
7. *Industry Attractiveness (π*)*: Percentage of industry capital expenditures made by four largest competitors multiplied by the capital turnover ratio [relative percentage].	1.1767	1.568	Negative	Exit should appear a less desirable action if the industry appears to offer attractive returns on additions to capital. Few firms would be likely to leave a promising industry.
8. *Relative Sales Growth*: Change in competitor sales deflated by CNP growth) divided by deflated industry sales growth [percentage].	−0.0001	.001	Positive	Leader firms whose sales growth exceeds the average industry growth rate would be less likely to exit. In a mature industry, the fringe firms whose sales growth was less encouraging would be more likely to exit.
9. *ROI (Past Performance of Leader Firms)*: Return on invested capital lagged one period [percentage (decimal)].	.0962	.249	Positive	Firms enjoying a high ROI would be less likely to exit, thus smaller, less successful firms would be squeezed out, hence more likely to exit.

Exhibit 2 Correlation Coefficients of Predictive Variables

	Capital Requirements t−1	Changes in Technological Scale t−1	Changes in the Relative Age of Assets t−1	Dispersion of Relative Advertising Outlays t−1	Excess Capacity t−1	Labor Cost Obligations t−1	Age of Physical Plant t−1	ROI (Past Performance) t−1	Industry Attractiveness Potential (π*) t−1	Sales Growth t−1
Capital requirements	1.00000									
Changes in technological scale t−1	−0.00264	1.00000								
Changes in the relative age of assets t−1	−0.02683	−0.03336	1.00000							
Dispersion of relative advertising outlays t−1	−0.07095	0.00034	0.14913	1.00000						
Excess capacity t−1	−0.21487	−0.00012	0.00585	−0.00002	1.00000					
Labor cost obligations t−1	−0.00131	0.00712	0.02738	−0.00002	−0.00008	1.00000				
Age of physical plant t−1	−0.01163	0.00207	0.20500	0.30746	−0.00992	−0.01365	1.00000			
ROI (past performance) t−1	0.07513	−0.00705	−0.16188	−0.02846	−0.05333	0.00164	0.30881	1.00000		
Industry attractiveness potential (π*) t−1	0.11745	0.00013	−0.02537	−0.06304	−0.23626	−0.00320	−0.06291	−0.04462	1.00000	
Sales growth t−1	0.04286	0.12931	−0.12904	−0.02490	−0.02312	0.04559	−0.02706	0.01213	0.00132	1.00000

540 observations of pooled time series data covering nine years.

cess capacity, and eocnomic exit barriers); (b) expectations concerning continued demand and profitability; (c) strategic exit barriers (these will not affect competitors homogeneously; and (d) past performance within the industry. Exhibit 1 summarizes the construction of these variables and hypotheses concerning their effects. Overall sample means and standard deviations are also presented therein.

Exhibit 2 summarizes the correlation coefficients of these variables. The "Technical Appendix" describes corrections that were made to reduce the heteroscedasticity introduced in cross-sectional analysis. Additional corrections could have been undertaken, but at the risk of introducing excessive collinearity among predictor variables. The results of these estimates are presented below.

THE DATA

The datafile constructed for this study examined five industry environments using information concerning the strategic outlays of sixty firms. As we explained above, data were available from surviving firms only. Supplementary data described the entire population, whether publicly traded, closely held, or privately owned. Information concerning exits was available, but inferences concerning the expected exit behavior of follower firms in the face of particular characteristics of mature industry environments were made, in part, using the COMPUSTAT I® file of leader firm behaviors.

Information concerning strategic expenditures, assets, and performance of firms from four-digit Standard Industrial Classification code industries characterized by relatively high specialization ratios was screened to obtain a set of relatively undiversified firms whose financial data would represent activities that were primarily within the principal SIC code category. (Firms that were substantially diversified, that is, greater than 30 percent of their sales were obtained from other activities, were removed from the datafile.) Information from firms' *Annual Reports* and from other financial statements, from the *United States Census of Manufactures,*[19] and from other published materials concerning competition within each industry supplemented these data for the meat-packing, distilled liquors, tobacco products, hydraulic cement, and aircraft industries. Exhibit 3 summarizes these data.

Exhibit 3 indicates high levels of excess capacity in the hydraulic cement and aircraft industries, reflecting a long-term problem in balancing demand with capacity which has taken the form of price cutting (and occasionally price fixing) in the hydraulic cement industry. On average, only firms in the aircraft industry were growing faster than the industry sales growth rate and faster than the growth rate of the entire economy.

---

[19]U.S. Bureau of the Census, *Census of Manufactures, 1973, 1977* (Washington, D.C.: Government Printing Office, 1977).

Exhibit 3 *Means (and Standard Deviations) of Leader Firms' Independent Variables by Industry*

Industry	Capital Requirements	Changes in Technological Scale	Changes in Relative Age of Physical Plant	Relative Advertising Intensity	Excess Capacity	Labor Obligations	Industry Attractiveness (π^*)	Relative Sales Growth of Leader Firms	ROI (Past Performance of Leader Firms)	Age of Physical Plant	Industry Growth Rate (ten-year average)
Meat packing	7.048 (1.418)	0.024 (12.208)	−0.002 (0.214)	1.299 (7.463)	0.110 (0.001)	0.001 (17.902)	1.481 (1.188)	−0.412 (6.198)	0.117 (.275)	.6139 (.1637)	.0555 (.2633)
Distilled liquors	65.374 (11.858)	0.029 (21.265)	−0.004 (.091)	.159 (.533)	.241 (.007)	.105 (3.772)	0.568 (.241)	−0.421 (7.644)	0.055 (.059)	.5474 (.0870)	.0253 (.2270)
Tobacco products	244.930 (114.284)	−0.033 (.372)	−0.003 (.134)	.393 (1.144)	.197 (.002)	−0.084 (.794)	1.333 (.455)	−1.723 (13.400)	0.166 (.246)	.6200 (.1459)	.0915 (.2974)
Hydraulic cement	22.534 (2.710)	0.026 (30.304)	.005 (.116)	.142 (.305)	.347 (.231)	.00001 (9.094)	.270 (.115)	−1.049 (10.843)	.067 (.045)	.5669 (.1141)	.0463 (.2580)
Aircraft	143.554 (13.279)	0.004 (.052)	−0.0006 (.358)	.575 (1.649)	.320 (.001)	0.019 (.782)	2.356 (3.579)	0.243 (10.780)	0.032 (.433)	.4987 (.1292)	.0528 (.3132)

Figures in parentheses indicate standard deviations.

Capital requirements were highest in the aircraft and tobacco industries, which also had the highest concentration ratios. Aircraft firms' ROIs were the lowest while tobacco firms' ROIs were the highest, on average. Aircraft and tobacco showed the highest R&D-to-sales ratios; meat packing and tobacco firms showed the highest advertising-to-sales ratios. The substantial variability among firms' R&D and advertising outlays within some industries indicated the presence of substantially different strategic groupings of competitors, one indication of a potentially volatile industry environment. These variations were captured in the advertising variable. Insufficient data prohibited use of the R&D-to-sales variable. Also, the variable was moderately correlated with the uncorrected advertising-to-sales variable, another factor that argued for its deletion.

All of these industries were growing at less than 10 percent per year and experienced their own set of problems in maturity. Many obsolete meat-packing plants were being replaced with newer ones, including some revolutionary technological changes in the packing process. Liquor distillers were adjusting to the change in consumers' preferences from brown to white liquors (from scotch to mixers like vodka). Tobacco companies were adjusting to tighter regulatory control during the seventies. The aircraft firms were finally recovering from the financial precipice by 1977. The means and standard deviations of Exhibit 3 represent the condition of the largest competitors, in many cases. The *Census of Manufactures* indicates that during the years 1968–77, the mean number of firms in each industry were as follows: meat packing, 144 firms; distilled liquors, 58 firms; tobacco products, 40 firms; hydraulic cement, 75 firms; and aircraft, 46 firms.

Although the COMPUSTAT® data used in this study are biased by accounting treatments and aggregation effects, they are ratio, not interval, scale in nature. Because nine years of data were available for most firms in the sample, a lagged structure could be imposed where the effects of a particular activity, such as the construction of additional plants, required more than one year to diffuse through the industry. The penalty for constructing a lagged structure was the loss of degrees of freedom and usable observations.

Data transformations were made to correct for errors introduced by heteroscedasticity from cross-section and time-series pooling according to standard corrections described by Pindyck and Rubinfeld.[20] Briefly, time-series data that have been transposed to cross-sections and pooled with data from other industries also required transformations to correct for autocorrelation and special interpretation of the error term that contains a time-series effect, a cross-section effect, and some interactions effects. The financial data were converted to ratios (e.g., advertising-to-sales) to reduce the difficulties that would have been encountered in interpreting the slope of the model that was generated using data from differing industries. A "Technical Appendix" summarizes the other corrections made to obtain unbiased and consistent estimators.

[20]Robert S. Pindyck and Daniel L. Rubinfeld, *Econometric Models and Economic Forests* (New York: McGraw-Hill, 1976).

Exhibit 4 Regression on Exit Behaviors

	Age of Physical Plant $t-1$	Changes in Technological Scale $t-1$	Changes in the Relative Age of Physical Plant $t-1$	Relative Advertising Intensity $t-1$	Excess Capacity Within Industry $t-1$	Labor Cost Obligations Incurred Upon Exit $t-1$	Capital Requirements $t-1$	ROI (Past Performance) $t-1$	Industry Attractiveness (Potential π^*) $t-1$	Relative Sales Growth $t-1$	Intercept	R^2 Coefficient of Multiple Determination	F-test Significance of Multiple Determination Coefficient
1.	-0.09038 (.0298)	0.00003 (.0016)	-0.02582 (-.0116)	-0.00037 (-.0395)	0.00679*** (.2798)	0.00008 (.0022)	0.00034* (.0790)	-0.09656 (-.0555)	-0.03101*** (-.1124)	0.32940* (.0725)	0.27984 (.0000)	.1142 (n = 517)	6.67***
2.	-0.09975 (-.0328)	0.00004 (.0018)		-0.00038 (-.0402)	0.00679*** (.2799)	0.00006 (.0018)	0.00034* (.0790)	-0.09162 (-.0527)	-0.03095*** (-.1122)	0.33560* (.0738)	0.28481 (.0000)	.1141 (n = 518)	7.41***
3.	-0.14072 (-.0463)			-0.00026 (-.0269)	0.0074*** (.3075)		0.00029* (.0686)			0.33822* (.0744)	0.26098 (.0000)	.1005 (n = 522)	11.66***

(Figures in parentheses indicate standardized parameter estimates, assuming unequal standard deviations.)

*Significant at the 10% confidence interval testing the null hypothesis that the parameter equals zero.

**Significant at the 5% confidence interval testing the null hypothesis that the parameter equals zero.

***Significant at the 1% confidence interval testing the null hypothesis that the parameter equals zero.

Average likelihood of exit = 25%

n = number of degrees of freedom

THE MODELS TESTED

The exit model, after corrections, was specified in the form of a generalized least-squares model:

$$P_i = {}_{ai} + b_i x_i + e_i$$

where p_i = probability of exit; where 1 = exit occurred, 0 otherwise; and x_i (where $i = 1, 2, \ldots, 10$) represents the variables developed above and reported in Exhibit 1. These were lagged one period relative to exit because illiquid assets would slow the speed with which firms could respond to the negative stimuli that might encourage exit.

The binary dependent variable (see page 472) indicates the probability of exit by fringe competitors. The coefficients of the independent variables indicate relative contributions to the probability of exit occurring. Standardized parameter estimates (sometimes known as standard partial regression coefficients) are presented in conjunction with the results of the models in Exhibit 4.

THE MODEL'S RESULTS

Three specifications of the regression model are presented to indicate the effects of deleting independent variables upon the explanatory power of the equations (indicated by the R^2 and F-statistic) and upon the standardized coefficients of the variables. Each independent variable's effects are discussed below. The low R^2 is not unusual for cross-sectional studies where many variables influencing corporate behaviors (in this case, exit decisions) are unobserved or not measurable.

The full specification of the model (Equation 1) indicates that the labor cost barrier variable and performance variable (return on investment) do not have the expected signs (but they are also not statistically significant). Other variables do have the expected signs, but relatively few of them are statistically significant. In the interests of parsimony, the lesser variables were deleted in Equations 2 and 3.

The excess capacity variable was statistically significant in all of the specifications presented and was positively signed. Its standardized coefficient indicates that this variable contributed most substantially to the explanatory power of the model. This result is consistent with findings from previous studies of excess capacity and industry performance.[21] The presence of significant excess capacity would be expected to create unpleasant competitive conditions which would make breakeven difficult for weaker firms to attain. Exits would be expected as excess capacity grew large.

---

[21]See, for example, L. Esposito and F. F. Esposito, "Excess Capacity and Market Structure," *Review of Economics and Statistics,* 56 (May 1974), 188–94.

The relative sales growth variable was positive and slightly statistically significant. It contributed substantially to the likelihood that a follower firm would exit if core competitors' sales were growing faster than average industry growth rates. The growth variable also contributed substantially to the explanatory power of the model.

The industry attractiveness variable was negative as expected and statistically significant. It indicated, as expected, a deterrent to exit. This finding suggests that where leader firms are enjoying success in obtaining acceptable returns to capital investments in a mature industry, smaller firms would be encouraged to remain invested too, assuming other conditions of competition are not too adverse. Deleting it increased the standardized coefficient of the age and excess capacity variables.

The capital requirements variable was positively signed and statistically significant. This result suggests that capital requirements, which have frequently acted as an entry barrier in earlier studies (preventing firms that did not operate minimum efficient scale plants from earning acceptable returns), may be a formidable obstacle *for core competitors* in mature industries. If the MES plant size of an industry were large, few firms would be needed (each operating one or more minimum efficient scale-sized plants) to satisfy industry demand. The presence of redundant plants would exacerbate conditions of excess capacity, a factor that also encouraged follower firms to exit in this model.

The change in technological scale variable was positive as expected but was not statistically significant. Its effect was similar to the capital requirements variable; it indicated that smaller or disadavantaged competitors operating less-efficient plants (of smaller scale) would be relatively weak if competition on a low-operating-cost basis became necessary. Such inefficient competitors would be likely to be forced to exit as technological scale requirements increased unless they were insulated by loyalties created from product differentiation activities (discussed below). The inclusion of this relative change variable contributed little to the coefficient of multiple determination (R^2) and it was deleted in Equations 2 and 3.

The return-on-investment variable was negatively signed and not statistically significant. The variable's effect appeared to be similar to the industry attractiveness variable; high ROI appeared to encourage the fringe competitors to remain invested. Since few new insights would be gained by retaining this variable, it was deleted in Equations 2 and 3.

The age of physical plant variable was negative but not statistically significant. Its coefficient as not as large as had been expected, indicating perhaps that economic exit barriers based on durable and specific assets were present but did not weigh as strongly in the exit behaviors of follower firms as did other factors. Deleting it in Equation 2 increased the negative effect of the standardized coefficient of the advertising variable.

The change in age of physical plant variable did not add much explanatory power to the model and was deleted in Equations 2 and 3. The change variable indicated an exit barrier, as expected; by contrast, the labor costs change variable did not indicate the deterrent effect that was expected. The labor variable was deleted in Equations 2 and 3.

The advertising variability variable was negatively signed, indicating an exit barrier, but it was not statistically significant. This variable represented the product-differentiating activities some firms would have undertaken as a strategic posture in lieu of other strategies, such as geographic specialization strategy based on price competition. The product differentiation strategy would be adopted by a subset of competitors, and a variable that proxied advertising-based exit barriers would not be significant for all firms in a mature industry. The variable's coefficients are not statistically significant in Exhibit 4.

In summary, the exit barriers that appear to deter firms within mature industries are those related to durable productive assets, intangibles related to product differentiation, and expectations. The following section summarizes the findings concerning exit within declining industries and compares them with findings concerning mature industries in this study.

COMPARISON OF RESULTS

Exhibit 5 compares the results of the two studies. The comparability of findings is limited by differences in datafiles and differences in the variables for which information was available. The data gathered for the declining industry study were scores scaled from low (.00) to high (.99) for each of the factors. They were gathered from interviews and cross-checked by subsequent questioning of industry participants and observers regarding their perceptions of the relative height of exit barriers and other factors influencing competitors' decisions.[22] This study used COMPUSTAT® data to test the effects of variables suggested by the declining industry study, economic theory, and interviews with executives who managed divestment decisions in mature industries.

The high-product-quality image variable indicated a strong deterrent to exit in the declining industry study. High-quality image could not be measured directly in this study. The advertising variability variable, a measure that would capture only one aspect of the differentiated product strategy, was a weak exit barrier in the results of this study. This finding differs from those concerning the effect of advertising and promotion-related exit barriers in declining industries where the factor was statistically significant, particularly where the business unit under study was of high strategic importance.

The mature industry study did not possess data concerning the effect of shared facilities or strong customer industries upon the decision to exit. We would expect these factors to act as exit barriers that would not be easily overcome unless operating losses were substantial. Of these two, many firms are ade-

---

[22]Harrigan, "Deterrents to Divestiture."

Exhibit 5 A Comparison of Results Concerning Exit Behavior Within Declining and Mature Industries

	Declining Demand Conditions		Mature Demand Conditions	
	Variable	*Effect on Exit Behaviors*	*Variable*	*Effect on Exit Behaviors*
	High quality	Significant exit barrier; may be the factor that makes a business strategically important to a firm.	—	—
	Promotion/advertising barriers	Significant exit barrier, notably where the business was judged not to be of particularly high strategic importance.	Relative advertising-to-sales dispersion	Not statistically significant, but negatively signed. A weak exit barrier, likely to be significant among firms offering differentiated products.
	Presence of strong customer industry	Significant exit barrier, particularly where the business was of high strategic importance.	—	—
	Shared Facilities	Significant exit barrier, particularly where the declining products possessed commodity like traits.	—	—
	—		Labor severance costs	Uncertain findings.
	Manufacturing/technology barriers	Very high statistical significance as an exit barrier, particularly where the product was highly differentiated.	Capital requirements	Significant factors encouraging exits (if plant are not MES).

		Changes in technological scale	Not statistically significant, but positive force upon likelihood of exit.
		Age of physical plant	Not statistically significant, but relatively strong exit barrier.
		Changes in age of physical plant	Not statistically significant, but negatively signed. A weak exit barrier.
Favorable industry environment	High statistical significance as an exit barrier. Expectations figured substantially in decisions to delay exit.	Industry attractiveness (potential π^*)	Strong exit barrier of high statistical significance.
	—	Excess capacity	Strong encouragement to exit of high statistical significance.
Losses	Strong encouragement to exit of high statistical significance.	ROI (past performance)	Not statistically significant but negatively signed. A weak exit barrier. The effect is essentially the same as the losses variable in the declining industry study.
	—	Relative sales growth	Encourages exit of smaller firms if larger firms' sales volumes are increasing faster than average industry growth. As a proxy for rivalry, it seems to suggest that smaller firms that possess no unique advantages in competing would be squeezed out of low-growth industries if leader firms maintain their increases in sales volume (and market share) goals.

quately aware of the dangers of commingling assets if an exit becomes necessary. Less attention has been given to the dangers of alienating important customers. The firm may jeopardize relations in other businesses where it hopes to thrive by cutting off dependent customers too abruptly. In decline, some exits were delayed until a reliable source of supply had been arranged for customers who continued to use the obsolescing product.

The expected exit barrier effect of idling workers did not yield definitive results in this test of exit behaviors. Although the variable was not measured in the declining industry study, the industry vignettes indicate that some firms did encounter substantive barriers related to labor unions. The factor did not appear to be statistically significant in this datafile, perhaps because of vast differences across publicly traded firms in severance costs and pension obligations.

Manufacturing and technological factors represented substantial exit barriers for firms in the declining industry study. The measures examined in the mature industry study also indicate that technological factors weigh heavily in exit behavior. Firms not operating MES plants or not keeping abreast of technological improvements appear to be more likely to exit. The age of physical plant variable was an exit barrier. The means and standard deviations of Exhibit 3 suggest that this factor may have been more significant for those firms that had recently invested in new plants and equipment and were loathe to exit so soon after recommitting to their industry. In summary, the variables treating the technological exit barriers in mature industries yielded findings similar to those of the declining industry study. Yet, because the mature industry environment is characterized by slowing growth (rather than negative growth), we would not expect the markets for physical asset disposal to be as eroded as in declining industry environments. Therefore the age of the physical assets variable should not be as significant an exit barrier as in decline.

Expectations appeared to generate substantive exit barriers both in decline and in mature industries. Where there has been evidence or experience of attractive returns on investment or additions to capital, firms are more reluctant to exit. Thus the potential industry attractiveness variable (based upon the relationship of concentration and capital turnover ratios) exerts a substantial force to keep firms invested, as did the favorable industry environment variable in the declining industry study.

Excess capacity emerged as a strong incentive to exit in the mature industry study. This finding is consistent with the conditions described in the declining industry vignettes where some firms purchased the assets of competitors and retired them to ensure that productive capacity did not overhang demand severely, and thereby prevented a vortex of price cutting.

Losses strongly encouraged exit in the declining industry study. Similarly, ROI performance was negatively correlated with the likelihood that follower firms would exit in the mature industry study. Specifically, this result suggests that if leader firms' sales volumes (and market shares) were growing faster than the average industry growth in mature industry settings, as the results of this study indicate, then the likelihood that follower firms would be pressured to exit increases, particularly if their strategic postures and served market niches are quite similar to those of the leader firms that enjoyed relatively high increases in sales growth.

In summary, although the variables in the studies are not directly comparable and the methodologies differ, many of the findings regarding the forces that encourage firms to exit from environments of adverse competition (or deter their exits) are of the same nature. Where comparisons with findings from the declining industry study could be made, the signs of the variables measuring exit barriers were generally in agreement. This study contributed new measures of exit barriers (which were not available previously) which could increase understanding of an industry's effects upon exit behavior. It highlighted the effects of excess capacity on competition, but it suffers from shortcomings inherent in any study where publicly reported performance data and accounts of strategic changes could not be collaborated with testimony and insights gleaned from the industry participants that exited.

The findings from this study are biased because they could not incorporate the internal trade-offs incorporated in firms' strategies, a limitation of much research that lacks verification through field studies. In general, it would appear that the competitors that are least likely to exit are those that (a) have carved out a defensible niche bolstered by loyalties from product differentiation activities, (b) have attained the lowest-cost position through frequent updates of plant and work methods, or (c) have specialized their offerings in some other unique fashion. It is the uniqueness of each competitive situation that forces reseachers to qualify the generalizability of structural studies and temper their predictions regarding behavior to the specific idiosyncracies of particular firms in particular industries. These shortcomings limit the generalizability of the predictive model.

The findings from this study (and those of the declining business study) suggest that smaller firms that try to insulate themselves from rivals who compete on the basis of price will be stymied by factors acting as strategic exit barriers. Firms pursuing "focus" strategies or narrow specializations appear to be less affected by the types of exit barriers associated with low-manufacturing-cost strategies, such as durable and specific physical assets, and more strongly influenced in their competitive behaviors by illusions concerning demand and the nature of competition. Microeconomic studies have long considered the effect of expectations upon economic behavior. These studies of exit suggest that a variable that captures competitors' expectations would be a useful enrichment of strategy studies that use paradigms based in industrial economics.

This study is among the first to test these and the traditional exit barrier variables empirically. Its findings suggest that exit barriers do not affect competitors pursuing different strategic postures in the same manner. Some evidence is also found suggesting that of Bain's classes of entry barriers—capital requirements, absolute cost advantages, and product differentiation—those follower firms pursuing product differentiation strategies may be shackled by the very barriers they overcame to enter that particular business. (The effects of these barriers upon entry are explored in a companion paper.) Further study of factors that heighten asset inflexibility (as do exit barriers) might suggest also how to mitigate the effects of some of these barriers through timely resource reallocations.

Additional study of the capital requirements barrier is also warranted. The findings in this study concerning the effect of this variable suggest a refinement of Weiss's survival theory (of the fittest). Although minimum efficient scale plants provide advantages for entering firms (and for competitors protecting their niches from intruders), they also prevent these firms from exiting easily. As growth slows, these attributes become a liability that was previously not recognized.

LIMITATIONS OF THIS STUDY

The theory extrapolated above rests on assumptions reviewed in this section. We assume that price competition is generally undesirable when it becomes destructive to capital formation activities. Thus, structural conditions that would exacerbate normal competitive activities to attain breakeven sales volumes are generally regarded as undesirable in this study.

We assume that closely held firms may be less likely to exit than smaller, publicly traded firms. Market judgments are expected to force unsuccessful firms out of industries where privately held firms that do not require a predetermined rate of return can afford to remain in competition. Also, we assume that firms protected by mobility barriers will be less likely to be forced out than firms that have not captured dominance of small, but viable, market niches.

We assume that the presence of strategic exit barriers connotes an absence of some degrees of autonomy in competitive maneuvering. Firms that have achieved success through marketing tactics will continue to rely on marketing maneuvers to rescue problem businesses in mature industry settings until exit is executed.

Finally, sale of one's assets to another competitor would not be measured as exit in this study unless productive capacity were eliminated. A mere change of legal ownership would not ameliorate the pricing pressures endemic in industries where competitors built too much capacity in anticipation of demand that never materialized.

USING EXIT BARRIERS

Firms may be able to arrange their depreciation schedules to coincide with the actual useful lives of assets employed in mature industries. (Accelerated depreciation schedules that do not incur recapture on disposal would be a helpful public policy change that could lower economic forms of exit barriers.) Informed strategists should recognize how to use these exit barriers as well as the other factors this paper has suggested could influence exit behaviors.

For example, Harrigan's field studies of exit barriers indicated that certain barriers are emotional in nature; that is, the factors have significance for the individuals charged with evaluating the exit decision which defy economic rationalization.[23] Managerial reticence to shut down plants may be based on concerns for face saving or sorrow for the welfare of the bulk of an isolated community that will be left jobless. (These emotionally charged issues should be segregated from the economic barrier of terminating a unionized labor force of long seniority.)

Many firms do not operate as investment portfolios that can sell off unwanted units without incurring substantial transactions costs. Their flexibility is different. A planned liquidation is difficult at any time because labor unions' contracts must be satisfied in dismissal, customers must be persuaded to substitute other products, the trade must accept the firm's explanation concerning why the company is unable to cover particular needs of the customer, and the value of untold millions of dollars invested in competitive positioning can never be recovered if no buyer for the business unit can be found. That is why when the firm decides to exit, it is important to begin by eliminating products that will create the least disturbance of customer relations, particularly where these relationships could affect other operations of the firm. Most multibusiness firms recognize the need to inform important customers of their exit, to make provisions for customers' future inventory needs by offering a special last-run buy-out sale, to delete the offering at the end of their buying season, and to offer parts and replacement stocks or an alternative source to these customers. Even after making these provisions, some firms fear liquidation because their disgruntled customers may still retaliate in other markets.

Many firms resist liquidations because they involve shattered dreams, loss of jobs, confusion among suppliers and customers, and endless hassles over details. Frequently a firm's position in a particular industry has been the result of the driving force of the chief executive officer. After several generations of pride and loyalty have been bound up in a company's name and operations, the very idea of walking away from such heritage would seem heretical, as in the steel industry for example.

Short of relieving the manager charged with evaluating the shutdown, the firm could relieve some of the pressures that might prevent its managers from facing these problems by using objective, multidimensional performance measures, horizon budgeting, or a product manager organizational design that does not penalize managers for unearthing poorly performing SBUs and bringing them to the firm's attention.

It should be possible for the thoughtful manager who intends to lead an

[23]Harrigan, *Strategies for a Declining Business.*

industry to preempt the smaller, less-efficient competitors on the fringes of competition by staking claim to particular types of customers and market niches early. This means the firm must identify how the industry will evolve and where it wants to be in that industry. The fringe competitors will satisfy the less-desirable customer groups if leading firms pursue their targets aggressively with operating advantages and concentrated marketing efforts. Such maneuvers assume, however, that the corporation will permit its business unit to suffer some years of thin cash flows until the business repositioning has been achieved. That is why it is so important to make the effects of reinvestments in new plant, advertising, or managerial capital explicit. The forms exit barriers could assume can be estimated at the inception of an investment, and similarly the exit barriers of competitors can be discerned. That means the thoughtful firm can begin to manipulate the industry context early to facilitate the exits of redundant competitors later.

SUMMARY

Field studies of exit suggest that firms have achieved reductions in industry capacity using several clever methods of preempting competitors. This paper has focused on identifying the barriers that would impede exit in mature environments, not on the methods that might be employed to implement this decision.

The statistical findings from this sample are generally consistent with those of the declining industries study. Strategic and economic exit barriers frequently deter firms from making the types of timely and frictionless exits that are assumed to be possible in economic theories of competition. Firms that can anticipate these effects are more likely to relieve the friction that asset disposal may entail.

Further research is needed to assess the implications of these barriers for competition and for the wealth-maximizing mandate of professional managers. The well-informed strategist will surely consider the influences of these barriers on competitors' behaviors during those periods of "competitive shakeouts" that have been described in the product life-cycle literature. The presence of structural imperfections, such as exit barriers, call into reexamination economic assumptions concerning Darwinian equilibriums in competition; the strongest firms may not possess the longest staying power nor the commitment to fight it out in a mature industry if their exit barriers are relatively low. Relatively inefficient single-business firms may bloody an entire industry before conceding the need to retire if their exit barriers are high.

TECHNICAL APPENDIX

As we indicated on page 485, it was necessary to use generalized least-square estimators to correct for errors introduced by the pooled (cross-sectional), time-series design of our datafile. Corrections for pooling were made using a weighted least-squares procedure. Preliminary estimates of the error terms were obtained using ordinary least-squares models. Generalized differencing corrections were made by multiplying the variables of the first stage by this residual and using least-squares estimates following this procedure.[24]

After corrections, little serial correlation was indicated by the Dubin-Watson D-statistic, and the correlation coefficients of the absolute values of the observed residuals to the predicted values of the dependent variable were low, suggesting that the variance of the residuals generated by this process does not depend on the values of the independent variables.[25]

Heteroscedasticity from the cross section effect was minimized by the generalized differencing corrections. The financial ratio format of the model minimized the range of values under analysis. The testing of dummy variables to estimate the differing industry slopes was inappropriate in this file because it yielded a nonsingular matrix.[26]

[24]K. H. Johnson and H. L. Lyon, "Experimental Evidence on Combining Cross-Section and Time Series Information," *Review of Economics and Statistics,* 55 (November 1973), 465–74; Roger D. Blair and John Kraft, "Estimation of Elasticity of Substitution in American Manufacturing Industry from Pooled Cross-Section and Time-Series Observations," *Review of Economics and Statistics,* 56 (August 1974), 343–47; Cheng Hsaio, "Statistical Inference for a Model with Both Random Cross-Sectional and Time Effects," *International Economic Review,* 15, No. 1 (February 1974), 12–30; Hui-Shyong Chang and Cheng F. Lee, "Using Pooled Time Series and Cross-Section Data to Test the Firm and Time Effects in Financial Analyses," *Journal of Financial and Quantitative Analysis,* 12 (September 1977), 457–71; and Yair Mundlak, "On the Pooling of Time Series and Cross Section Data," *Econometrica,* 46, No. 1 (January 1978), 69–85.

[25]Pietro Balestra, and Marc Nerlove, "Pooling Cross Section and Time Series Data in the Estimation of a Dynamic Model: The Demand for Natural Gas," *Econometrica,* 34 (July 1966), 585–612.

[26]Marc Nerlove, "Further Evidence on the Estimation of Dynamic Economic Relations from a Time Series of Cross Sections," *Econometrica,* 39 (March 1971), 359–82.

23

Making Technology Work for Business

JOHN M. KETTERINGHAM AND JOHN R. WHITE
Arthur D. Little, Inc.

John M. Ketteringham is Corporate Vice President, Technology, at Arthur D. Little, Inc.; John R. White is Senior Vice President, Strategic Planning.

INTRODUCTION

Investment in technology has reemerged as an essential component of many corporations' plans for growth, competitive improvement, and diversification. The increased emphasis on technological investments by corporations are a result of the following:

Declining growth in base businesses

Dramatic developments in new technologies

Development of international competition

Vitality of the venture markets

During the past decade of introspection over the environment, energy consumption, and the implications of the Vietnam War, companies had relegated technology, a central factor in their original growth, to the back burner. With the growth rates and margins of large industries falling in many countries, companies are again turning to technology.

Coincident with this renewed interest by major corporations in technology is the increase in new venture activity. Both seem strongly linked to the remarkable advances in biotechnology and microelectronics, which will significantly affect most industries. Thus, at the same time that corporations are searching for new opportunities to enhance growth and profitability, they can see that dramatic technological developments are being highly valued by investors.

Another important technology-related development is the emergence of international competition. The traditional technological leader in the postwar period, the United States, is being challenged, not by Russia as postulated fifteen years ago, but by Europe and Japan. These newer entries into the development of business through research have yet to demonstrate that they can manage the innovative process as well as U.S. companies did in the growth eras of the 1950s and 1960s. Indeed, as we examine historically the competitive role of technology in various industries, we can detect other mature characteristics in the way in which companies in different countries use technology. These may influence the future exploitation of contemporary developments and are discussed latter.

In the current volatile and uncertain environment, companies articulate four main technological issues:

Identification of the corporation's technological assets that may provide opportunities in new businesses

Expansion of internal research and development efforts into new areas

Obtaining of technology (developed or being developed by others) by license, acquisition, merger, or joint venture

International deployment of investments in new research and development efforts

Announced in a variety of ways in annual reports and in commentary by corporate officers, these strategies are the most popular themes designed to encourage optimism in the corporate future.

Many recent announcements reveal a more aggressive and versatile approach by major companies to participation in new technological developments. Companies with a strong culture of internal dependence on research are now making investments in situations where they participate in the technology of others; for example, Merck's license agreement with Astra Pharmaceutical, Honeywell's joint venture with N. V. Philips, and Du Pont's acquisition of New England Nuclear. Other firms have shown a willingness to make highly speculative, long-range investments, such as Hoechst, Dow, and Mallinckrodt in biotechnology.

These activities illustrate the range of actions available to a corporation in the pursuit of business strategies based on technology. They also imply that judgments are made as to the potential yield of different technological endeavors, and the importance of these new developments to industries within the scope of their interest; they include targeted actions as well as investments in basic research.

While many corporations have stated their objectives, have assigned the responsibility for implementation of their programs to meet these objectives, and have, in some cases, made some significant investments, there is still considerable lack of confidence in the "what," "where," and "how" (see Figure 1)—What technologies will provide opportunities? Where will these opportunities be? and How do we go about pursuing them? Thus, strategic planning methodology embraced enthusiastically by many managers in the 1970s is now being accused of failing to deal adequately with the implementation issues in general and the question of technology in particular. Indeed, the need for a new plan-

Figure 1.   Forces Leading to Increasing Technological Investment

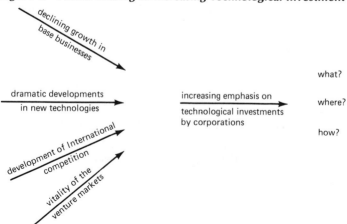

ning method is widely recognized. "The major unfinished business of the research literature is to provide managers with needed guidance in their formulation of a technological strategy for their companies."[1]

As managers struggle with their corporations' new expectations for technology, in this environment they are asking understandable questions:

A primary metal company—"In the future, how can we avoid repeating the failures we have experienced with new ventures?"

A telecommunications company—"We spend $10 million on research each year; how much should we be spending?"

From two chemical companies—"What are our technological strengths, and what new opportunities could they create?"

A European electronics company—"How can corporate management be more knowledgeable about the division's technological investments without invading its autonomy?"

An aerospace conglomerate—"How can we reinstill a technological culture into our nontechnical management?"

A medical products company—"How can the research and development groups communicate with the business planners?"

A chemical company—"We want to double research and development investment. What are our technological strengths and which programs should we choose?"

An electronics company—"How can we measure research and development productivity?"

A chemical company—"When will our new ventures become profitable? How can we improve them?"

A European manufacturing company—"What new technology will have the greatest impact on our business? What should we do about it?"

A medical products supplier—"Why won't our management let us pursue research we know is vital to our business?"

A diversified health company—"How do I recognize research developments of importance to my company?"

In addressing these and other equally profound questions concerning technology, we have found that developing a framework for dealing with technological issues is necessary.[2] Our incentive for doing this was largely derived from our

[1]Alan M. Kantrow, "Keeping Informed," *Harvard Business Review,* July–August 1980, p. 5.

[2]John M. Ketteringham, "Application of Strategic Planning to Investments in Health Care Technology" (Arthur D. Little publication presented at the Fourth Executive Forum in Health Care, Williamsburg, Va., March 1980), and Jean-Philippe P. Deschamps, W. Tom Sommerlatte, Kamal N. Saad, and John M. Ketteringham, "The Strategic Management of Technology" (Arthur D. Little publication presented at the European Management Forum, Davos, Switzerland, February 1981).

successful use of the framework method to rigorously analyze business issues over the past decade—an attempt to replace advocacy with analysis. The use of a disciplined methodology ensures that important issues are not overlooked, that a record is established for future reference, and that the judgments and their bases are communicated to all concerned, including nontechnical participants.

Important elements of this technological analytical framework include

A precise and useful definition of technology
The strategic role of technology
The linkage of technological strategies to business strategy
The changing nature of technologies
The international factors in the deployment of technology
The process of technological planning

These six concepts are explained in more depth in the remainder of this chapter.

A DEFINITION OF TECHNOLOGY

In our recent experience, companies asked to name the technologies in which they are the strongest have often answered by naming their strongest products or a scientific discipline in which they are particularly active. While useful to articulate the company's products and processes and to know the strength of its resources, such responses do not describe the technologies of the company. Confusion of the term *technology* with *science, products,* and *resources* is, in part, exacerbated by the terms *basic research* and *product development.*

Technology usually implies a "practical application of scientific or engineering knowledge." Thus, conceptually, technologies lie between the scientific and engineering disciplines (which may be pursued for altruistic purposes) and the products that the companies sell or use. To be a useful concept for analysis, a technology should fit the form:

We know how to _____ (verb)_____ (noun).
Example: We know how to formulate PVC resins.

By defining technologies in this way, we can relate them to products and processes, assess our relative technical strength in them against that of our competition, and evaluate them in many ways. For example, we can "unbundle" a product or process into its discrete technologies, as illustrated in Figure 2, and can identify the resources to practice these technologies. The application of technologies as a system to develop successful products or processes we regard as being in itself a technology. This is unique to the products or processes, and we call it a "systems technology."

Figure 2.   The Technologies Constituting a Technological Program

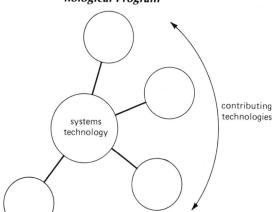

Figure 3 is a simple example of the relationship between the PVC products manufactured by a company with the technologies the company applies in their development and manufacture, and the scientific and engineering disciplines and knowledge it draws upon to practice these technologies.

This scheme can be generalized as presented in Figure 4. The flow of activity from bottom to top of the figure is representative of the familiar concept of "innovation." We find that breaking "innovation" into its actionable component steps this way allows an analytical approach to be taken in planning technology.

Figure 3.   Relationship of Technologies to Scientific and Engineering Knowledge and to Products and Processes

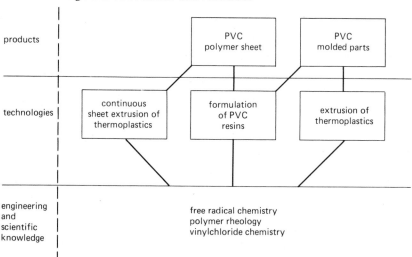

Figure 4   Generalized Relationship Positioning Technologies Relative to Products and Science and Engineering Know-How

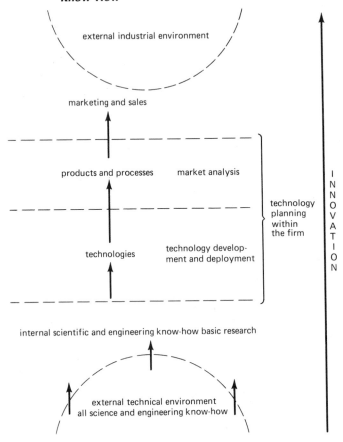

This goes further than the conventional way of looking at the innovative process as a combination of technical creativity and market awareness in that the firm's situation in the competitive technology and market environment can be described and assessed as a relative whole.

THE RELATIONSHIP OF TECHNOLOGICAL STRATEGIES TO BUSINESS STRATEGY

From the questions put to us by our clients and as illustrated earlier in this chapter, we conclude that the most challenging contemporary question facing managers is, How can we integrate business planning with technology planning? An example leads to a framework to address this problem.

The newly appointed director of research and development for a company producing high-technology consumable products, in preparing for a forthcoming planning seminar with his management, faced a dilemma. He was concerned that in the previous ten years his company had twice been beaten to the marketplace with innovative products, and he believed that to prevent this from happening again, he needed to embark upon aggressive research programs. Management, however, disagreed. The company recognized it was competing in a mature-to-aging industry and enjoyed a strong competitive position. The strategies chosen by management were therefore "maintenance" (to preserve their competitive position without seeking further market share) and "product rationalization" (seeking efficiency in product manufacture to maximize gross margin). To management, aggressive research did not seem to play a role in the implementation of these strategies. Indeed, the company had managed to achieve a very high market share even for those product areas where it had been beaten to market.

However, the research department knew they had been able to react quickly to these competitive threats by virtue of their strong technological position, even though they had not brought out the product first. Thus we articulated a technological strategy in support of the business strategy that had been highly sucessful in the past:

1. to maintain technological strength and flexibility in order to respond rapidly to competitive challenge in a business of technical volatility despite its otherwise advanced maturity

2. To adopt a conservative second-to-market approach and avoid risks incompatible with the company's competitive approach

Thus the apparent "failures" of the past were seen to be the result of a sensible, intuitive strategy; aggressive research was justified to retain technological second-strike capability.

Research and development programs may be linked to business unit or corporate strategies. This linkage implies that these programs should support the implementation plans of the company and its business units but also permits opportunities discovered by research and development activities to be fed into the business-planning process. Moreover, to maintain a scientific resource that can practice the required technologies, fundamental research may be addressed to maintain the vitality of the scientific personnel and provide access to technological developments. In practice, only the largest firms such as Bell Laboratories, IBM, and General Electric can afford investments in fundamental research.

A logical framework for this scheme is illustrated in Figure 5. The critical link between business planning and technological activities is provided by the setting of objectives gleaned from programs initiated to implement the strategies of the business units and the corporation. The setting of these objectives is discussed in the elaboration of the process presented later in this chapter.

Figure 5.   *Relationship of Technological Activities to Corporate and Business Unit Plans*

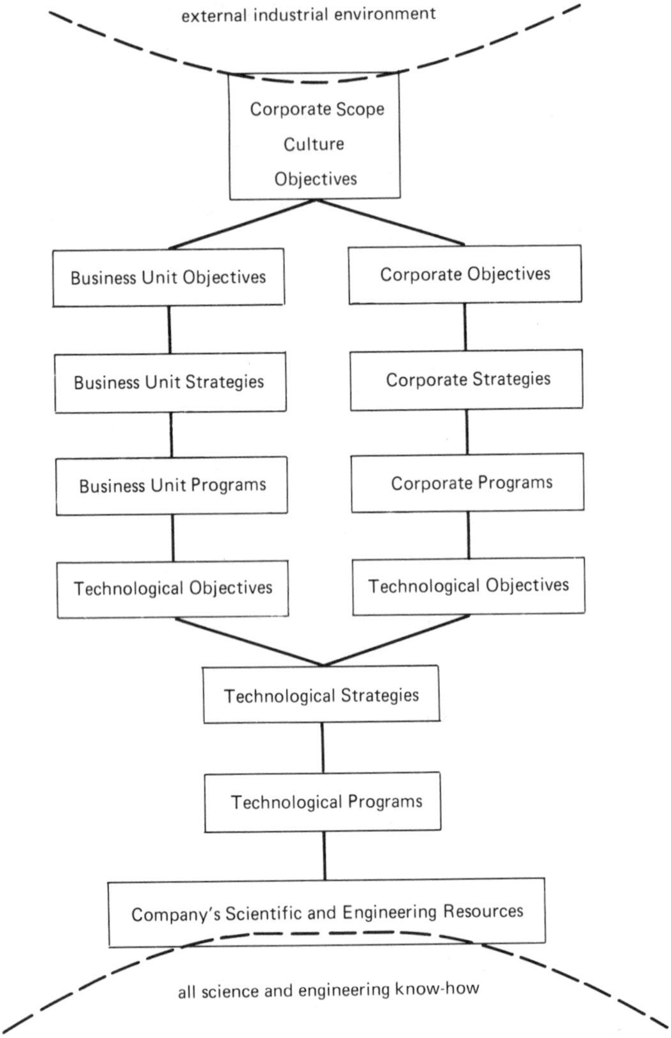

external industrial environment

```
                    ┌──────────────────┐
                    │  Corporate Scope │
                    │     Culture      │
                    │   Objectives     │
                    └──────────────────┘
```

Business Unit Objectives		Corporate Objectives
Business Unit Strategies		Corporate Strategies
Business Unit Programs		Corporate Programs
Technological Objectives		Technological Objectives

Technological Strategies

Technological Programs

Company's Scientific and Engineering Resources

all science and engineering know-how

THE NATURE OF TECHNOLOGIES

In the early 1970s the cardiac pacemaker industry was faced with a major strategic technological question. An obvious market need was the development of pacers that could be implanted for several years rather than the average twenty months typical of contemporary products. Several potential technological solutions to this objective were identified:

Mercury-Zinc Batteries—These power supplies were at that time used in the product. They could perhaps be improved further, although extensive effort in this direction in other industries had resulted in only incremental improvements in performance.

Nickel-Cadmium Rechargeable Batteries—This technology, worked on for years by the military and NASA, could represent a departure in clinical practice: The patient would need to recharge his or her pacemaker on a weekly or monthly schedule. It was questionable whether this product truly met the market need.

New High-Energy-Density Batteries—Several new systems in this area were under development, progress was impressive, and many groups within and outside the industry were active. While these batteries were promising, the potential for the technology was not certain.

Nuclear-Powered Batteries—This exotic technology had obvious drawbacks but was developing rapidly.

Biochemical Fuel Cells—This technology was far from a reality and was highly uncertain.

Management clearly faced a difficult decision—to choose among a wide range of technologies. Should they invest in the traditional technologies which offered little in dramatic potential but were relatively predictable, in fast-moving technology in alien fields, or in fundamental research in new emerging technology?

The technology that eventually succeeded was a high-energy-density battery system based on lithium and iodine. To date, all the other technologies have failed to play a significant role in the marketplace and, in our judgment, no longer are competitive threats.

The changing character of the technologies in this and other cases can be represented by a maturity curve constructed in a similar way to the concept used to describe the nature of industries. Technologies move through life cycles (just as industries do), emerging in basic research with a high degree of uncertainty and with few practitioners, through a stage of growth and high productivity, and eventually reaching maturity where advances are small and hard won. Figure 6 illustrates this for the battery example described above and for some other contemporary technologies.

The impact of technological changes on industry structure, in turn, is manifested in the embodiment of innovation in either products or processes. Products and processes also demonstrate changing characters analogous to industry life cycles. Product and process life cycles, in fact, tend to track industry evolution in characteristic patterns. They allow us to aid our clients in determining the technical character of industry maturity and the impact and utility of investments in technological programs.

Typically, as the work of Professor William Abernathy has shown, in in-

Figure 6.   The Maturity of Technologies

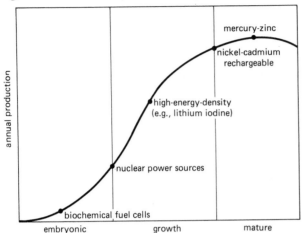

The maturity of power source technologies in the cardiac pacer
industry (1975)

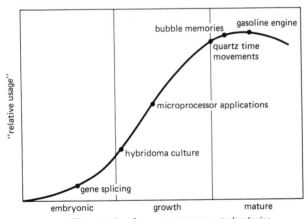

The maturity of some contemporary technologies

dustries in the embryonic or growth stages, the bulk of significant innovations
tends to involve enhancements in products that maximize performance.[3] When
the technologies supporting performance improvements trend toward maturity,
fundamental product design tends to solidify around a dominant configuration.
The bulk of significant innovations, in turn, trends toward manufacturing process enhancements that minimize cost. Industry structure where innovation is
manufacturing process focused tends to be that of the late growth or mature
stages of the industry life cycles.

[3]William J. Abernathy, *Productivity Dilemma: Roadblock to Innovation in the Automobile Industry*
(Baltimore: Johns Hopkins University Press, 1978).

   Characterization of technologies in this manner provides a powerful method for analyzing the risk and potential yield of a given technological program. Visualizing each technological endeavor addressing a market need as a group of discrete technologies (as in Figure 2), we need only to assess in our minds the maturities of the component technologies and their embodiment in product or process innovation to gain a measure of the risk of the program in terms of the certainty of the outcome and the potential yield of the endeavor. The concept provides a way of communicating to management the nature of its technological investment.

   This behavioral characteristic has been alluded to in the past,[4] but until now it has not been developed into a useful analytical approach effectively linked to operating strategy. For example, in a study of technical innovation in 1963, the relationship between the evolution of a technology and the eventual development of the industry was measured by the number of papers published and sales of product, respectively. In Figure 7, plots of these parameters show crudely the separate life cycles for the given technology and the industry (semiconductor). In our work today, we draw analogous curves of the rate of significant product and process innovation. Some revival of the technological maturity concept was evident in a recent *Harvard Business Review* article on the issue of

---

[4]"Patterns and Problems of Technical Innovation in American Industry" (Report to National Science Foundation by Arthur D. Little, Inc., 1963).

Figure 7.   The Correlation of Technological Maturity with Resulting Industry Maturity in the Semiconductor Industry

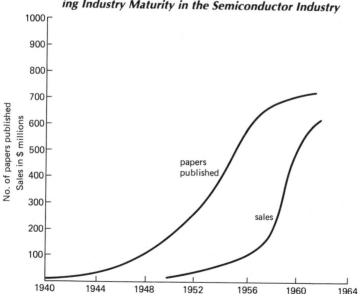

Source: "Patterns and Problems of Technical Innovation in American Industry," 1963.

selling corporate technology: "The technology life cycle can help companies decide when, how and whether to sell their know-how."[5]

We find that the concept of maturity is particularly useful in arranging the technological portfolio of a corporation when addressing some of the client questions enumerated earlier. These questions, generally concerned with the business opportunities and threats presented by the technological resources of the corporation, can be addressed by the following steps:

Identify the technologies relevant to the industry.

Assess their maturity and the impact on products and processes.

Estimate the competitive strength of the corporation in each technology.

In most cases the most powerful position is to be dominant or at least strong in a growth technology, as Polaroid was in the 1970s. Here the yield in terms of progress is likely to be high compared to a mature technology, and the uncertainty that progress will be made will be low compared to an embryonic technology.

In the past few years we have repeatedly encountered a typical scenario.

A large corporation (typically now in mature industries, such as chemicals, consumer goods, or primary metals) grew rapidly in the 1950s, 1960s, and early 1970s in its primary businesses based on the aggressive exploitation of its then growth technologies. Growth has now subsided in the industry, and the corporation is seeking new opportunities to rejuvenate its business portfolio. It again looks to its technology to provide these opportunities. What becomes apparent, however, is that its technologies have also matured and offer little promise of further advances. The corporation is seeking new applications for mature technologies—a frustrating task except perhaps in developing countries. (For example, Arthur D. Little participated in the introduction of nitrogen-fixing bacteria technology to legume growing in Africa.)

Conversely, the major investments in new technologies witnessed recently are not a symptom of the "awakening of the innovative spirit" or an overt dramatic shift in corporate philosophy, but one stimulated by the nature of the technology itself.

Certain technologies are in, or are moving into, the growth stage, as was illustrated in Figure 6. These technologies are principally in the areas of microelectronics and biotechnology. Not only do these technologies promise high yield, but they are significantly strategic to many industries.

Since technology offers one of the few means for shifting competitive position in more mature industries, and since most U.S. industries are mature, we have been especially interested in researching, both for and with our clients, the role of technology in the industries in which they compete and the way in which technology is managed within the businesses.

---

[5]David Ford and Chris Ryan, "Taking Technology to Market," *Harvard Business Review*, March–April 1981, p. 117.

THE STRATEGIC ROLE
OF TECHNOLOGY

In the cardiac pacemaker example discussed previously, the technologies mentioned were critically important at the time. As soon as the successful battery system was developed and established in the marketplace, this technology no longer differentiated the competition; the basis of competition became marketing intensive. The technology that evolved on the basis of competition was the electronic programming of the pacer function outside the body. Such changes in the identity of the technology critical to the competition as time progresses are common in many industries. Companies must be able to identify the technology of the moment—which we call the "key" technology—but must also recognize the threat of other technologies that may replace the "key" technology. We call these "pacing" technologies.

For example, the "key" technology in the computerized tomography arena in the early 1970s was the software algorithm that printed the picture to be computed from X-ray signals. EMI Ltd. pioneered this product. The key technology was followed in rapid succession by a series of other "key" technologies, such as the engineering of multiple arrays of sensors, the development of stable solid-state sensors, the development of efficient microprocessor-based, special-purpose computational systems. It will soon face the pacing technology of sophisticated high-resolution video displays.

We can relate the strategic role of a given technology (whether "base," "key," or "pacing") to its competitive importance, as illustrated in Figure 8. Along the shaded 45-degree axis, we identify three zones:

1. The "pacing" technology has the potential to overturn the existing competitive structure.

Figure 8. Strategic Role of Technologies

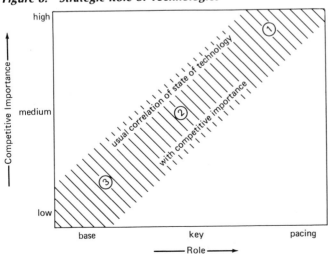

2. The better-positioned competitors are generally those strongest in this "key" technology as long as they are positioned well in the other factors making up the basis of competition.

3. While it is necessary, simply being proficient in the "base" technology is not enough—they do not provide competitive differentiation.

While often necessary, technology, even though "key," is seldom sufficient to establish the relative position of competitors in an industry because it is usually only one among several factors making up the basis of competition. Furthermore, because competitive dynamics depend so heavily on industry maturity, it is critical to recognize the difference between technology and industry maturities and their influence on the nature of competition.

For example, a company was formed to exploit a new technology for automatically performing biological assays in hospital laboratories. The company thought that this embryonic business was entering an embryonic industry; thus its strategies for investment in primary market development and its experience of losses and sustained negative cash flow were deemed acceptable—normal for the company's industry condition. As it turned out, the new products were substituting for (and competing against) existing manual laboratory techniques but were not, by virtue of their features and economies, increasing the number of such tests being called for by doctors.

It became apparent that the embryonic business was being launched into a mature industry. Overall demand for biological tests was growing little, if at all, because of underlying demographics and the maturity of hospital services in general. To get sales volume, the fledgling company had to take market share away from entrenched suppliers of competing materials and entrenched technicians manually performing the processes carried out by the new product. That the product had to displace its customers was an added, complicated irony.

Had the embryonic company been able to foresee that it was in the situation of elbowing its way into a mature industry rather than creating a new one, its strategies for investment in plant, equipment, and market development would have been very different, as would its financial performance. This example emphasizes our belief that strategy is as much condition-driven as ambition-driven and that industry maturity is a powerful determinant of the conditions in which a business competes, even though the business may have differentiating new technology.

Another side is evidenced by a better-known story. When Chester Carlson tried to market his new technology for making copies of printed and written materials using photoelectric properties of semiconductor material, a variety of equipment that utilized different technologies were already being supplied to the market: photostat (silver halide); various wet contact on coated paper-developing schemes; and thermofax, a dry, convenient though coated paper process. In addition, there were convenience printing systems like Ditto (dye-gel-solvent) and Multigraph (stencil). One major corporation after another declined the opportunity to take a license and introduce yet another competing product in an already crowded field. It was not then perceived that the market was already changing with, perhaps, Thermofax as the harbinger.

Carlson's story is, of course, now famous, and with twenty-twenty hindsight, we can all see clearly that what the Haloid Corporation succeeded in doing, as Xerox, was to accelerate the shift in the office copy industry through the creation of new primary demand. The capability and features of xerographic copiers were such that copies began to be used in situations where none had previously been used. It was not just that a Xerox copy substituted for other copy systems; it was that the convenience, speed, ease, and availability of the clean, dry, sharp plain-paper copy made it an increasingly common tool for intraoffice and interoffice communication. Demographics also helped as the economy shifted more toward white-collar employment during a period of great economic expansion. The key point, however, is the dynamic that engineers call "positive feedback," in which the availability of the capability provided by the new-product technology itself creates new demand for itself. Being able to predict, or even just to recognize, this bootstrapping feedback is the key to identifying the potential for industry rejuvenation, sorting mere substitution from self-generating demand creation.

Fast-growth segments with overall mature markets often look like embryonic industries. Blue jeans are such an example. The U.S. apparel industry is very mature, not only in its slow-to-no growth but in the stable positions occupied by principal suppliers of fabric. Although the apparel cut-and-sew industry is highly fragmented and fashion-driven in many segments, the industry demonstrated its mature structural characteristics by the extreme difficulty encountered by those who opted to enter against Levi and Bluebell, despite explosive growth in the conventional jeans segment.

One of the most remarkable phenomena in the history of industrial competition is the repeated failure of industry leaders to change their own technology when new technology is transforming the industry. Examples are legion: Curtiss Wright missed the shift to aircraft jet engines. In the shift from steam to diesel-electric locomotives, the major suppliers of steam, American Locomotive and Baldwin, were unable to respond, despite clear signals over a period of more than a decade. After the revolution, an entirely new set of competitors (General Motors and General Electric) led the industry.

Figure 9 shows one way to sort industries and technologies. The xerography story is illustrated in the upper-left quadrant. The bulk of basic industry is upper right.

In developed countries the truly embryonic industries are found in the lower-left quadrant. They exhibit all the embryonic traits; for example, many competing technologies, uncertainty as to which technology will prevail, many small competing ventures, and unknown market potential. The industries in the less-developed countries usually fit the description of the lower right. As a corollary, we find that technology-related rules for strategy formation are different in

Figure 9.   Categories of Industries and Technologies

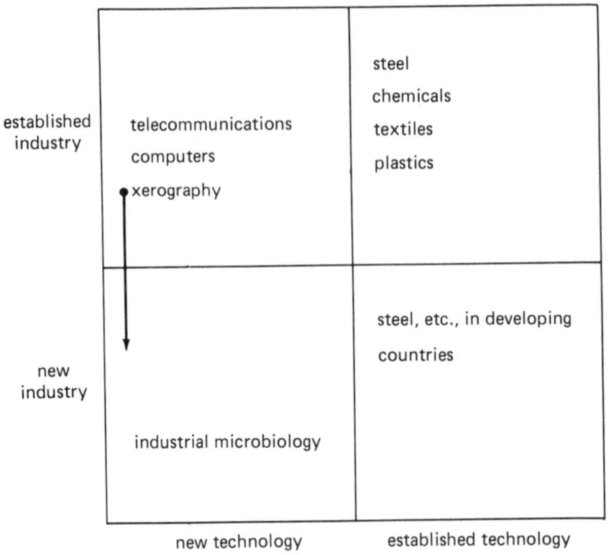

developing and developed countries; steel, aluminum, and chemicals may be embryonic industries, but politics, demographics, and resources are the prime movers, not new technology. Even the acquisition of required technology is political and resource dependent.

Thus the maturity of a technology is independent of the industry maturity, and technologies (base, key, or pacing) are of different strategic importance to industry and change with time.

These concepts about definition, nature, and role are exceedingly useful for:

> *Balancing the technological investment portfolio.* We urge that companies critically examine their investments in research into "base" technologies unless the technologies are in a growth stage or likely to become growth once again; they should seriously consider investing aggressively in their key technologies when technology is important to the basis of competition and, particularly, when it is in a growth stage. Also, a company may consider investing in one or more pacing technologies to prepare for, or accelerate, the replacement of the key technology.
>
> *Assessing the likely impact of technological developments upon industry maturity.* If promising pacing technologies are less mature than the industry (i.e., they promise dramatically greater yield than the industry has historically been used to), there is a strong possibility that the industry may become less mature, with attendant increases in market share volatility. Recent examples of this phenomenon can be identified: digital displays and

then crystal movements in the watch industry, microprocessors in the toy industry, and hybridoma technology in clinical diagnostics.

Assessing the business opportunities arising from a corporation's technological resources. This exercise is now particularly popular. (In many cases we suspect that the stimulation to undertake this analysis comes from being disappointed with the contribution of R&D to current businesses while being mindful that R&D was once very productive and, indeed, was the foundation of the company's businesses.) We conduct an analysis to

Identify the technologies of the company

Estimate the company's relative strength in these technologies (dominant, strong, favorable, tenable, or weak)

Assess its strategic role in the *current* industry segments (whether base, key, or pacing) and relative importance among the bases of competition

Identify any strategically important technologies not represented (usually new pacing technologies)

Identify new businesses where these technologies are strategically important (i.e., are key or pacing)

Thus we search for technologies in which the company is strong (or could be strong), technologies that are preferably in the growth stage of maturity and are key or pacing to the identified (thereby) business opportunities.

INTERNATIONAL FACTORS
IN TECHNOLOGY DEPLOYMENT

Using the concepts of technological maturity and strategic significance, we can also discern differences in the way companies of different nationalities exploit technology in international competition. Depending on the maturity of the industry and the maturity of the "key" technology, companies of different, but predictable, nationality appear to gain the competitive edge.

The volatile medical diagnostic imaging industry of the 1960s and 1970s provides a model for the following observations.

Figure 10 correlates the changing maturity of the diagnostic imaging industry segment over the past decade with changes in the maturity of the technology used by the industry. By the 1960s, the industry and its technology, represented primarily by X-ray equipment, were both mature. World-wide competition was dominated by a few large companies: General Electric and Picker with regional strength in the United States, CGR in France, and Philips and Siemens sharing much of the rest of the world market. Market shares were relatively stable and technological evolution was slow.

During the 1970s, emerging technologies—especially computed tomogra-

**Figure 10.   International Competitive Interaction
in Diagnostic Imaging Products**

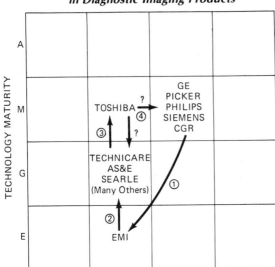

phy (CT), ultrasound, and computerized reconstruction of nuclear medicine images—were commercialized. The new technologies were of sufficient competitive impact to cause the industry to return to a growth phase, as represented by the arrow (1). EMI initiated this process with the then-embryonic CT technology but was closely followed by other manufacturers as the technologies concerned moved into the productive growth stage of maturity (2). Market shares became highly volatile as many new entrants appeared (over twenty-five in CT scanners alone). Most notable were Technicare (now part of Johnson & Johnson), American Science & Engineering, and G. D. Searle in the United States, as well as several foreign companies.

As the technology matured and became more widely accessible, other competitive factors—e.g., presence, service network, price—regained importance. The original leaders in diagnostic imaging regained strong positions, and many of the new entries abandoned the business or were acquired. Also, at this stage—i.e., a maturing technology in a still growing market (3)—the Japanese companies entered with a very strong marketing thrust, Toshiba being the most notable new entrant. Thus the competitors now strongest in the business are those that participated in the earlier mature industry, with the important addition of Toshiba, but with few other surviving new entrants.

For the future, we see two reasonable scenarios (4). As the technology matures and growth rates decline, the segment might return to its original mature state and stabilize. However, it is more likely that further new technological developments represent opportunities that will sustain the current growth of the industry. Increasingly sophisticated data management continues to affect all diagnostic imaging product lines, but the most significant development is the introduction of digital radiology. In this technology, conventional X-ray images are recorded electronically instead of on silver-based photographic film, which is becoming increasingly expensive. The images may then be improved by conventional image enhancement techniques and stored in high-density permanent memory devices such as video discs. The equipment being developed may be added to existing X-ray machines and thus represents a strong new opportunity to the majors in the industry as well as to potential new entrants. For example, American Science & Engineering, unsuccessful participant in the CT segment, is among a few companies that have already announced digital radiology products. The demonstrated clinical utility and cost-effectiveness of these new imaging products appear to promise continued customer acceptance of new diagnostic imaging products.

Indeed, based on similar studies in a number of other industries, it seems fair to summarize (see Figure 11).

The American economy is replete with examples of growth industries fueled by growth technologies. Xerox, IBM, and other computer companies, fast-food franchises, consumer goods of a variety of kinds and so on, all grew with their respective technologies in recent years; long ago, the growth of the automobile industry, of General Electric, of the plastics industry, and others occurred in periods of high technological growth.

The British experience is rather different. British industry—much in a ma-

Figure 11.   Nationality in the Competitive Use of Technology

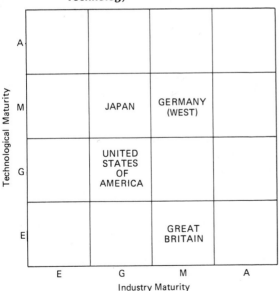

ture stage of its life cycle—appears bent on a strategy of using dramatic break-throughs in embryonic technology to regain competitive advantage. The CT scanner invention described above is but one example. Others include the super-sonic transport, the transverse engine automobile (which was eventually success-ful for the Germans, the Americans, and the Japanese), Pilkington float glass, and Dolby Sound (which were successful in different ways). We still see efforts in the same direction—the Bruce anchor is a notable example. Meanwhile Brit-ish industry lags in the growth markets fueled by growth technology based pri-marily in electronics.

The Japanese have historically exploited relatively mature technology but have nevertheless created high-growth industries by aggressive marketing and by concentrating on manufacturing efficiency even at the growth stage of maturity. Consumer goods such as cameras, radios, and calculators are typical. Recently the Japanese have made aggressive moves to invest in technology of earlier ma-turity, particularly in electronics and biotechnology—traditionally the province of the U.S. companies.

German companies, on the other hand, seem to excel in the use of mature technology (as used in precision machinery) in relatively mature industry seg-ments. Examples include the luxury automobile industry, manufacturing ma-chinery, and the earlier mature camera industry.

THE PROCESS
OF TECHNOLOGICAL PLANNING

These concepts and the experience we have gained in understanding technologi-cal change and its impact on industry have led us to develop a process for tech-nological planning that takes into account the methods of strategic planning de-veloped in the past decade.

Figure 12 shows an iterative planning process: The upper half of the figure illustrates a traditional business-planning activity. Information concerning con-ditions in the industry—the "situation analysis," the maturity of the industry, and the relative competitive strength of the company—is used to design appro-priate strategies for the business units and the corporation. Programs to imple-ment these strategies are then devised. Resources are appropriated to carry out these programs—where necessary, the strategies and programs may require modification to take account of the realities of resource availability.

The lower half of Figure 12 shows a similar technology-planning process which acts on the objectives handed it as part of the programs selected. To reach *these* objectives, technological strategies and programs are selected based on sim-ilar information inputs—the nature of the technologies involved, their respective maturity, and the relative technical strength of the corporation. Again, resources must be interrogated and iterations carried on with the business plans and the technology plans until a compatible and agreeable set of actions is reached. The

*Figure 12. Strategic Planning—Integration of Techno-
        logical and Business Plans*

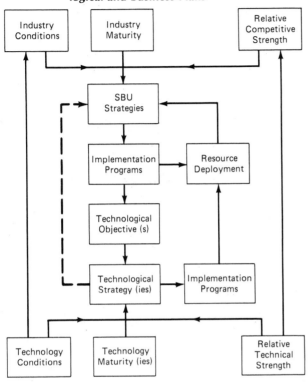

dashed path recognizes the possibility for the business strategy to be stimulated by the technology.

We find that this process can be conducted in structured workshops similar to those we use for business and corporate strategy formulation or off-line in a series of study activities, or perhaps preferably in a combination of the two approaches.

The strategic role of technology can be deduced from the "situation analysis," particularly the analysis of the basis of competition. For example, in a mature industry, a low total cost position is frequently a critical competitive factor, and technology may be employed to develop manufacturing efficiency. In a growth industry, technology's role is frequently to create new generations of product. As strategies are formulated and programs selected, certain of the actions planned will have implications for technology which can be stated in the form of an objective.

Taking these objectives, it is the responsibility of the technology function (research and development department perhaps) to choose the technology strategies and programs to best fulfill these needs.

24

Reinventing the Factory: A Manufacturing Strategy Response to Industrial Malaise

WICKHAM SKINNER
Harvard University

The key issue in manufacturing corporations in the Western world is how to respond to the problem of loss of competitive strength and industrial vitality. Western industry has lost market shares, millions of factory jobs, and its head start in equipment and process technology (EPT). Equally serious has been industry's failure to attract the best of our younger people and adequate reinvestment in new capital equipment as well. Without new people and new EPTs we have a state of industrial malaise that continues to erode.

What is being done? I have spent the past year asking this question in twelve large manufacturing firms in the United States and Europe. The focus has been on that very question with two subquestions: (1) What has your firm been doing to reap the benefits of apparently rapid recent advances in manufacturing technology (CAD/CAM, robots, lasers, new investments, etc.)? and (2) What are the career origins and characteristics of the next wave of manufacturing top managers (men and women who will be running manufacturing in five or ten years)?

With the present mass of difficulties surrounding manufacturing, one would expect a strong sense of urgency to adopt modern technology as we see our competitive positions eroding and productivity gains slowing. We have all kinds of obvious motives for trying to adopt new technology.

But, in the face of what appear to be exciting new technologies and opportunities all the way from flexible machining centers to computer-aided manufacturing and computer-aided design, the availability of these new equipment process technologies far outruns their adaptation and the realization of their potentials. On balance I conclude that the progress we are making is slow, hesitant, and, indeed, very spotty.

This leads to a strange paradox. While the factory is different from what it was twenty years ago, with working environments generally improved, computer terminals all around, and a few islands of automation, for the most part one sees much old equipment, a very slow rate of change, a modest evolution, and the same old problems: cost, quality, delivery, and problems with the work force.

History suggests that economics will create change and technology will create change, but where is it? The factory of the future is still out there in the future. Is technology to be the white knight that stops our industrial decline? Is there a possibility of a real "shoestring catch," a turnaround that solves the problems of our sick industries? So far the answer is no—it is not happening.

If a technological revolution is not what is happening, what is? Surely American managers with their tradition of activity and energetic response to problems are not going to sit and watch their manufacturing enterprises die on the vine. The answer to that is a firm *no.* that is not what is going on.

What is happening instead is extraordinary and patently impressive. In my experience, I have never seen anything like it in terms of its energy, its scope, its intensity, and its hopes. I see U.S. industry right now at its traditional best. We have the tradition of getting ourselves three touchdowns behind, but winning in the fourth quarter.

Examine what is happening: Top management is rediscovering the factory. Corporate management is newly interested in the factory, as it has not been in the last twenty-five years. It is perfectly obvious to them now—they have got to be. Company after company is going back to basics. Industrial engineering standards are being brought out and dusted off. Operations are being tightened. Managers are scrutinizing every operation for signs of inefficiency and low productivity. They are refocusing on the basics of quality, redefining what quality involves and requires. Production managers are being given courses, lectures, and all kinds of training on those kinds of subjects. Companies are setting up productivity czars, productivity committees, corporate productivity groups, corporate technology laboratories, corporate technology directors. Top managers are touring the country and speaking about the urgency of productivity, going before Congress, speaking to anyone and everyone who will listen. Business magazines are full of these issues and concerns.

The energetic, frenetic projects are taking many companies into addressing problems they have put off for years, such as their problems in all-purpose white-elephant plants. Now they are trying to straighten them out, trying to create turnarounds. Management is attempting to involve more workers. Companies are approving some capital appropriations that they would not have even thought about four or five years ago. There are closings of plants considered hopeless and moves South. We see some new greenfield plants. Managers of manufacturing are being admitted to meetings of their peers. At many companies now is the first time that manufacturing people have been invited to participate in a management development program.

What does all this really amount to? How do we interpret all this churning, this energetic and purposeful kind of activity? Is it going to save the day? Is it revitalization?

There is certainly a vitality that we have not seen in years. Is it "reindustrialization"? I don't know what that means, but what is going on is certainly a reaffirmation of an old faith and a longstanding ideology. For it clearly is reemphasizing the importance of productive facilities and the development of effective management. But is it going to save the day? I don't think so.

In the automobile industry today, for example, we see U.S. production management at its zealous best. We abhor waste, inefficiency, and laziness, and many a foreign country has learned that point of view from us. But what it amounts to is nothing more than dusting off the old game plan. They are back to basics and good industrial engineering. Its productivity, efficiency, and cutting corners. Is the modest productivity gain that renewed focus on productivity going to save a thousand or fifteen hundred dollars per automobile?

The old game plan, the paradigm of industrial management, is productivity, working on the numbers, and industrial-engineering basics: straight-line flows, controls, setting standards, standardizing, mass production. But one thing we have learned recently is that the Japanese borrowed that game plan from us a long time ego and they are now better at it than we are. So we must ask this question: Is the old game plan going to work as well as it used to? I don't think it is. So far there is no significant gain in productivity; we are still losing ground in industry after industry.

So what is to be done? First, we need to learn from the past five years that the single-minded pursuit of productivity is not working. It has not been working for twenty years and it is not working now. We have a productivity paradox.

Criticizing productivity is like saying that apple pie and meat and potatoes are no good or efficiency is no good. How could productivity be no good? Can we stop worrying about being cost effective? I'm not saying that. Improving productivity, of course, is absolutely necessary. But productivity is turning out to be something like happiness or fun—the more we pursue it directly, the more elusive it becomes. We need to begin to wonder whether it may be the wrong goal. It is a means to an end. It is a great byproduct; it is great to have it happen, but as a principal objective, it has caused and continues to cause increasing trouble.

Why is productivity proving to be so elusive? A minor but continuing problem is that its definition is unclear. Many tend to think about it first in terms of direct labor. But when indirect labor is added and analysts include overhead to other costs in the equation and finally end up with sales per employee, the data are too gross to help much. Statistics show that some companies with the largest sales per employee do not have the best bottom lines. What about capital when you are thinking about productivity? And how do you equate your investment in capital with your major focus on productivity?

Probably more important than problems with definitions and accounting is that productivity says "squeeze, cut, scrimp, work at the margin, don't spend any more than you have to, don't invest—work harder and smarter." Further focus on productivity is a focus on cost and efficiency instead of on competitive position or building the manufacturing resource to be a competitive weapon.

The biggest and most important reason that productivity has been a wrong goal and has led firms into trouble is simply that it is working at a marginal, modest, and nonstrategic objective. Studies of major competitive improvements in manufacturing over five-to-eight-year periods in a variety of companies demonstrate that the major improvements in performance have not come from "productivity" programs. I call it the 20-40-40 formula. Twenty percent of the gain comes from changes in productivity, while 40 percent results from changes in technology and 40 percent from major changes in manufacturing strategy—i.e., structural changes in how manufacturing is set up, organized, and managed.

Instead of focusing management efforts on strategy and structure, the obsession with productivity has diverted and is now diverting many top managements and manufacturing managements from the enormous potentials of improved, competitive performance in analyzing manufacturing structure and effecting structural change. The multiplier decisions are those having to do with capacity, with make or buy, with major choices of equipment and processes, with the number of plants, the size of plants, the location of plants, major production control systems, human resources and work resource management systems, quality-control systems and organization. I have seen too many tragic situations where fine, intelligent hard-working managers are putting in fifty to seventy hours a week and getting nowhere because the problems are structural in nature and beyond short-term solution. For if the problems are structural, no amount of work at the margin, or productivity and efficiency programs, will return the firm to competitive superiority.

We have a productivity mind set. We have a numbers mentality, which may be one of the biggest single barriers to the introduction of new technology. It has been a significant cause of the present deterioration and malaise in Western industry. It accounts in large part for the rationale by which top management cut off manufacturing from issues of finance and marketing and competitive strategy, and manufacturing managers allowed it to happen. For if manufacturing is merely a productivity game, it can be delegated to a low organizational level and handled by technologists and efficiency experts.

So much of our problem has been related to our way of thinking about it. Our concepts and understandings have led us down a useless path. And continuing productivity-focused efforts repeat the same noncompetitive results. But what about the "40" in technology and the "40" in manufacturing strategy and structure? Why are we moving so slowly on these fronts?

Many high barriers stand in the way of introduction of new technology. They divide into six groups: (a) problems with the new technologies themselves, (b) inappropriate/inadequate systems for capital allocations, (c) limitations of the vendors of the new technology, (d) personnel and labor problems in perceiving the new technology, (e) internal resistance and risk aversion on the part of manufacturing managers, and (f) lack of a manufacturing strategy.

First to the technology itself. Many of these new technologies are quite revolutionary. Few managers can really predict accurately what factories are going to be like ten or fifteen years after adopting these new highly computerized and mechanized technologies. And the payoffs are not only subtle—they are delayed. The delays are caused by years of problems, debugging, training, evolving new systems. Anyone who anticipates fully successful payoffs within five or six years is probably overoptimistic. And the payoffs are not always going to be in cost savings. They are more apt to be in strategic advantage, such as faster new-product introductions, ability to produce a broader product line, and superior product reliability. The bugs, the break-ins, and the problems signal a struggle of nightmarish years to get any of these things working. But if we think we can wait till the technology is frozen and let someone else go first, we face the dilemma of losing competitive positioning. Meanwhile the capital costs of new EPTs are skyrocketing. With such substantial risks and capital costs, the few companies moving ahead are acting either in desperation or the sheer faith of the CEO.

Second, the capital-budgeting systems in most of our companies have a one-year horizon and high hurdle rates, which have made new investment difficult. The capital-budgeting systems are fine for handling new capacity and new products. They require a high/short payback on cost-saving investments. But managers have a hard time selling a new competitive weapon that ought to be really great in five to seven years but must be started now.

The financial skills in our large corporations produce apparently precise pro formas, but that same mind set demands good returns. So we keep on turning down new technology based on financial considerations. Some firms have turned down new EPTs one by one, year by year, and have then awakened to find themselves nearly out of business. We need new ways of conceptualizing and evaluating these new technology investments which deal with more than the cost and productivity dimensions. Few capital budgeting systems handle the strategic dimension.

Third, vendors. Most of these new technologies consist of hardware and software, of many pieces and ingredients. The systems are disaggregated and no one vendor offers a whole system. There is no turnkey operation as there is in the chemical and utility industries. Most vendors supply components and lack any total, coordinated systems that they can install and guarantee. The vendors are cautious in what they offer. Our machine tool industry, for example, has acted on the assumption that in a cyclical industry companies should seek to have a one-year to two-year backlog and not lose money in the down years. With that philosophy it has lost market share year after year. Few vendors aggressively try to offer more complete factory systems with the service and assurance that it is going to work.

Fourth, the human resource dimension of new EPT introduction has been that of a cautious reserve toward new technology, not only because of the productivity backlash but because of a century of thinking that technology is the enemy. Workers fear not only the loss of jobs but the impact of new technology on their working environments. Furthermore we have shortages everywhere of excellent technicians, maintenance people, service people, supervisors, and trained knowledge workers. Looking ahead, the new technology will require a better selection, a new kind of supervision, more training, and more responsibility for more capital. These factors are causing managements to go slow and workers and unions to be cautious.

The fifth factor impeding new technology is internal resistance and risk aversion by manufacturing managers. They are realistic in predicting the problems, pressures, and difficulties that they will meet in trying to get new EPT appropriations through management. They need to ask for large amounts of capital, often in a sick industry or when depreciation cash flows fail to provide funds needed for the new EPT. They must make some big promises about this nice new computerized technology that is going to make a great contribution, when they well know that it is going to be a struggle for five years. And even if it works superbly it is difficult now to predict and promise the specific favorable consequences five years hence.

So few manufacturing managers are taking the personal career risks to ask for dollars for new technology in new facilities. The problem is made worse by the fact that many manufacturing managers get "chewed up" by sophisticated financial people who know the market, the business, and the strategic situation.

Most manufacturing managers have been, until recently, cut off from the top corporate councils for twenty-five years. There are career risks, and the rewards are very modest while the risks are very large. So what can we expect? Manufacturing managers act like good soldiers. They have the infantry mentality and that is the way, unfortunately, that they often get treated.

These five roadblocks are all set up by the lack of a manufacturing strategy. Without a long-term manufacturing strategy, it is impossible to make plans for a new, expensive, yet risky EPT that will not pay off financially for years and offers only a strategic long-term advantage. A manufacturing strategy would not only protect production managers, but in the process of developing it and getting it approved, manufacturing executives would think through and make plans for a long-term sequence of building the production function to be a competitive weapon.

A manufacturing strategy is derived from corporate competitive strategy. It describes in explicit terms just what it is that manufacturing must do exceptionally well in the face of precisely defined obstacles and difficulties to play a proactive part in the corporate strategy. From such a statement of task, each element of manufacturing policy and structure can be designed.

The new EPTs offer a new era to the manufacturing executives as they move from an operating posture to develop a strategic weapon. For not only is failure to move into and take advantage of the new technologies more competitively serious than ever before but the new microprocessor-based technologies offer new opportunities for companies to compete totally. This is because the new microprocessor technology's main advantage is an ability to be faster and more flexible on new-product development, offering marketing new possibilities in successful product variations.

So far it must be said that a single-minded obsession with productivity continues to keep many manufacturing managers down in the plant and failing to perceive new technology as a formidable potential competitive weapon. But without a process of manufacturing strategy development, they have lacked the essential tool that could help them break out of their confined and thereby conservative and cautious roles.

Is a new breed of manufacturing managers who will save the day coming along? We need some new set of skills, concepts, competences, and attitudes in manufacturing. Are such men and women working up the organization via normal processes? In most of the dozen companies studied in 1982 such a new breed is developing. They are "new" simply in that they think about manufacturing in long-term, competitive terms and are taking high risks and providing broad conceptual and specific personal leadership for rebuilding their manufacturing structures.

The differences between the "old" and the "new" are relevant to the problem of barriers to new technology. In terms of carreer paths, the old breed has moved up slowly and in a relatively straight line, staying within production, with relatively narrow rather than broad variety of experiences. They have a rather slower path up the ladder of promotion.

The new ones are coming from an astounding mixture and variety of assignments and responsibilities; they are coming from engineering, from sales, from manufacturing, some from finance; many have been project managers or program managers or have led human resource or computer-based information system innovations. They are coming from a much richer variety of experience than in the past.

In terms of breadth, the old ones have a depth of competence in the old tools of productivity. They are strong in industrial engineering, processes, methods, and labor relations. The new ones are apt to be a little weak in those areas, but they are stronger in terms of finance, accounting, and creative budgeting. And they are much stronger in terms of marketing, program, and project management, and they quickly grasp the concepts of manufacturing strategy. One surprising fact is that it has nothing to do with age. At some firms, the new breed consists of people in their fifties and sixties.

In attitudes, the old ones are the infantry—they are patient, dutiful, responsible. They keep appointments on time, they do everything on time. They have a strong sense of corporate loyalty; they have great respect for their bosses. The new ones, as you would expect, are impatient and frequently overconfident. They often believe they are better than they really are. They are in a hurry, but they are good at delegating and team building. They are somewhat loose and laid back; they delegate in ways that would scare many old managers, for they do not follow up with the same type of rigor. But they are outstanding at inducing people to cooperate and in coordinating new projects. They border on being disrespectful to the company and the industry and their colleagues while they are loyal to their functions and their own careers and self-esteem.

In skills, the old type can expedite and follow up, and they tend to focus on cost and delivery. The new ones can handle more ambiguity, change, discontinuity, and uncertainty. Nothing bugs them very much. They do not expect things to be the same tomorrow. And they seem to be good at new-technology development.

In executive styles, the old ones have much shorter fuses; they are more autocratic. At the same time, they are loyal team players; they support their peers and sustain their colleagues. The new ones have longer fuses with subordinates; they seem to be much more patient. They are more collegial and they excel at team problem solving.

There is a great variety among companies as to how they handle the developing and strengthening of this new breed. By and large, most personnel and human resource programs worry a great deal about employees at lower levels while neglecting where managers are coming from and how to develop managers with a broader diversity of competences.

In spite of the seriousness of the situation here in the early 1980s and the still negative trend in competitive strength in many industries, there is reason for optimism. While there are substantial problems ahead, industrial history is full of examples that demonstrate the fundamental lesson that technology totally affects economics. History shows managers as prisoners of technology, and for two hundred years we have seen a society and technology in collision.

Exactly the opposite is now beginning to occur. By some good fortune, technology and society are now lined up right, in a way we have seldom seen before. There are many indications that the new technology is good for society. The old technology was machines substituting for people, starting with the steam engine. It resulted in standardization and in long runs, and it was good for process industries and mass production. We surrounded workers with staff, indirect labor, and controls. We ended up with monotony, boredom, and specialization.

The new technology is entirely different. It requires a whole new role for workers and a whole new set of managment skills. In the handful of plants that have boldly moved into the new EPTs, we see workers doing much of their own scheduling, their own inspection, their own production planning and inventory control. They make decisions with information at their fingertips. High-school graduates with some training and with great pride are using on-site process computers. This is producing autonomy and involvement. And for the organization's competitive struggle, it is producing an opportunity for flexibility, shorter runs, and much more product variety.

The new technology will frequently provide a devastating competitive advantage for companies that learn it first. As one company in an industry finds new ways of producing and can supply new products quickly, it can be much more flexible and adaptable and can move faster in markets; the effect will domino right through that industry. And those who do not go first must then play catch-up ball. But to get in on the ground floor requires a long-term manufacturing plan.

Since the Industrial Revolution, the whole name of the game in the factory has been productivity. For what was a factory other than a set of facilities for mass production? The corporation objectives were productivity, efficiency, and return on investment. The technologies were power and steam, electricity, and mechanical advantage. How did we manage it? We managed it with industrial engineering, efficiency experts, standards, controls, schedules, discipline, and short-range operations. The attempt to get low-cost, standardized merchandise dehumanized factories. As a result, employees had to give up many rights and subject themselves to an organization. This created the backlash, the dullsville, the preoccupation with the numbers, the road we have been going down in the last twenty years.

What is a more productive way of thinking about the factory? Can we think of it as a competitive resource? Can we see a factory as a place where innovative people can produce outstanding products and meet market needs? And can we do this as the factory grows much more capital intensive? This requires concepts that are contradictory to the old nations. It requires much more strategy and genuine long-range planning. The factory as an institution has let us down. It has let us down because we let it down. We kept on seeing it as an efficiency machine, which it was in 1800. We managed it by and for productivity and profit. The irony is that we lost our productivity and our profit; now our golden prosperous dream is almost gone.

Now we have the technology and the ideas for reinventing the factory as an institution.

If we can see it and manage it as a place for innovative and independent people to produce great products and have full lives, and if we use technology as a primary resource rather than the last decision we make, we will reinvent the factory. If we do it we will do it from the inside out with a competitive manufacturing strategy. By reinventing the factory we may see it emerge as a successful institution in our society.

25

The Strategic Management of Technology

JOHN M. HARRIS, ROBERT W. SHAW, JR., AND WILLIAM P. SOMMERS

Booz·Allen & Hamilton Inc.

Copyright Booz·Allen & Hamilton Inc. This article and the methods it describes are the outgrowth of numerous client assignments performed by Booz·Allen's Technology Management Group and the firm's strategic and general management specialists. Among the key contributors to the methodology and its application are: Dr. Joseph Nemec, Jr., Dr. Eugene T. Yon, Bruce A. Pasternack, John W. Allen, Eric R. Zausner and Charles R. Engles.

It is clear that throughout the 1980s, competitive advantage, new product development, new markets, productivity and profitability will all be tied directly to technology. Advances on the technology front are revolutionizing both mature and high-technology industries, radically altering traditional business strategy and triggering dramatic shifts in global market share.

Traditional industry leaders are already reeling from the impact of unprecedented global competition, as once-clearcut industry lines are blurred, government-business alliances proliferate and newly emerged, world-class competitors outperform them.

The industrial winners in this era of economic imbalance and escalating competition will be those firms that *seize and exploit technology as a corporate strategic weapon*—an asset that can be effectively managed in support of business and corporate strategy. Less fortunate competitors, as the 1970s have demonstrated, will persist in treating technology as hard to manage, resistant to analytical planning techniques and as a secondary, noncritical factor in corporate planning.

The challenge for management—in *every* industry, not just high-technology ones—will be to recognize opportunities and marshal resources to provide sustainable competitive advantage in world markets. Integrating technology planning and management with business and corporate strategy is critical to this process.

What precisely *is* technology management? To borrow a definition from Peter Drucker's book, *Technology Management and Society,* technology is, quite simply, *know-how.* In most cases, it is scientific know-how embodied in people, plants, patents, laboratories and equipment. This know-how results in a manufacturing process or product, or a service (or all of these) that—if recognized as a resource—can be *managed.* When properly managed, technology complements business strategy in mature companies, drives business strategy in high-technology companies and, in most industries, can be leveraged to achieve a sustainable, competitive advantage in the marketplace. The key lies in formulating the right technology strategy and, ultimately, integrating it into the corporate planning process—not an easy undertaking by any means.

EMERGING TECHNOLOGY TRENDS

In the 1970s, as headline after headline announced, technology-driven events caused major shifts or "dislocations" in world markets. First, the rules of the global economic game changed in midstream, rewritten by OPEC, inflation and new players, such as Japan and the LDCs.

Second, the United States lost its competitive edge on the technology front in a host of industries. Spending on technology declined in the United States, and U.S. technology spending *as part of world share* declined as well. During the period from 1970 to 1978, for example, U.S. spending on R&D dropped from 2.5 percent of GNP to 2.1 percent. During that same time, R&D spending as a share of GNP in Germany rose from 2.0 percent to 2.1 percent, and in Japan, from 1.5 percent to 2.0 percent.

Despite this economic upheaval, selected technologies such as electronics, data processing, and telecommunications were funded and developed. New markets were created by industries that hadn't even existed just 10 years before. Those who opted to play the technology game—and played it well—were richly rewarded.

In the 1980s, technology will continue to trigger major market shifts as a new set of trends emerges.

First, technology is already transforming mature industries generally thought to be static and overdeveloped. In the automotive industry, for instance, we are seeing the widespread use of computer-assisted design and manufacturing, or CAD-CAM (including robotics), the penetration of microprocessor-based controls and feature sets, and the replacement of traditional materials by synthetic ones. The same types of developments are reshaping banking, manufacturing, publishing, retailing and other industries—all considered mature and low-growth by most of the business community.

At the other end of the spectrum, in a second key trend, high-technology industries are being revolutionized.

The semiconductor industry offers a compelling example. Between 1975 and 1980, the number of circuit functions per chip on semiconductor memories grew by a factor of ten, while the price per bit of memory decreased by a factor of three. The latest technology, very-large-scale integration or VLSI, will increase the number of circuit functions per chip by yet another factor of 10. And in the late 1980s or 1990s, new technology will make another quantum leap in microelectronics capability. Virtually every high-technology industry will feel the effect of this technology development—and the shortened product life cycle it produces.

The third trend emerging in the 1980s is perhaps the most far-reaching: Technology is totally changing business definitions and market segmentation, leading to radical shifts in world market share. When combined with broad economic forces, these shifts will dislocate *entire* markets. As a result, even technology leaders face increasingly fierce technological and market competition.

On a world scale, between 1960 and 1978, the United States lost world leadership in twelve key industries and gained position in none. Japan, by contrast, increased its competitive position in eight industries while losing ground in none.

The volume produced by world-scale manufacturing can provide significant learning-curve advantages and other benefits, resulting in lower production-and-distribution costs. It can also erect strong barriers to competition by concentrating technology in selected product lines and processes—a situation already evident in major industries ranging from chemicals, aerospace and automobiles to electrical equipment, steel and pharmaceutics.

On the positive side of the trends picture, technology will create huge new markets in the 1980s that will serve as springboards for still others in the 1990s. Robotics, CAD-CAM, bioengineering, energy management and telecommunications, to name a few, will all offer unprecedented market potential.

Capitalizing on this potential will demand that management firmly grasp technology as a competitive lever and strategic tool. It will also demand a new level of sophisticaiton in technology management, a discipline that encompasses the development of a technology strategy, the integration of technology decisions into long-term corporate strategy and a comprehensive technology investment program.

TECHNOLOGY: A TOP
MANAGEMENT PRIORITY?

The highly successful managers of technology included in a Booz·Allen survey in the late 1970s all shared a number of common traits: They generally adopted a long-term planning perspective and viewed technology innovation as the single most important factor in their success. Top management involvement in technology planning was strong and technology decisions were well integrated into overall business strategy.

By contrast, in our work with clients on a wide range of technology-based problems, we have found a pervasive, short-term, bottom-line mentality that often works against effective technology planning. Even more serious, perhaps, we have found that many CEOs—particularly in U.S. firms—have delegated their decision-making role on technology issues to middle management, thereby surrendering their control over a critical aspect of their business. We have also discovered that while management tends to publicly espouse the importance of technology, few CEOs approach it as a strategic issue.

Despite this lack of top-management involvement, in both 1979 and 1981 Booz·Allen surveys of officers and senior managers in *Fortune* 1000 firms, changing technology was ranked as one of the top four critical issues business faces in the 1980s (see article p. 548). Technology was also viewed as complex and difficult to manage. In the 1981 survey, some 86 percent of the respondents indicated that their lack of an analytical approach to integrating technology and business planning was a significant barrier to managing technology and 79 percent saw the limited involvement of technology managers in the planning process as another major drawback.

Citing these two problems as the principal causes, only 37 percent of the managers sampled thought that technology and strategy were being effectively integrated into their company in U.S. markets and only 13 percent, in world markets.

There is, then, a vast and growing strategic gap between the perceived importance of technology to business success and the attention and resources that it receives from top management. With the exception of a handful of leaders, management views technology as complex and difficult to manage. This view has evolved in an environment in which senior managers are not involved in the design of a technology strategy and technology managers are not involved in business planning.

INTEGRATING TECHNOLOGY AND STRATEGIC PLANNING

We believe that the key to closing this gap lies in repositioning technology as a strategic resource by elevating its importance in the business planning process. As a first step, based on our client experience and independent research, we've identified several emerging principles of technology management that appear to run counter to traditional management views. Chief among these:

Principle 1: To a large degree, the direction and timing of the technology evolution can be anticipated. Traditionally, technology has been viewed as unpredictable, extremely risky and unquantifiable. In a recent study, however, we found that once invention occurs, the steps in new product development leading to eventual market commercialization followed the same general pattern, and essentially the same timing, for literally dozens of inventions—from xerography to integrated circuits. As a result, we believe that a systematic approach to tracking innovations can be applied—and that it is a key ingredient in the effective management of new technology markets and products (see Figure 1).

Principle 2: Technology should be viewed as a capital asset. Traditionally, technology has been treated as an isolated, project-based phenomenon, rather than as a strategic resource. In contrast, we believe that technology position is critical to competitiveness, that technology changes and external competitive position can be analyzed and that technology can—and should—be treated as an allocable corporate asset.

Figure 1   Path and Timing of Technology Development

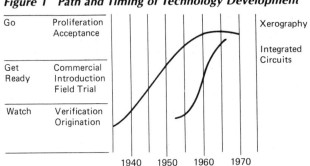

Principle 3: Assuring the congruence of technology investment and business strategy is essential to successful technology management. We believe that technology priorities should dictate investment thrust. In our work on technology-based problems, however, we have consistently found mismatches between our clients' strategic objectives and their technology investments. Inadequate investment, excessive investment and improper investment allocation are all common.

For example, we see companies making *inadequate* investment to maintain technological leadership once they have established it. Sometimes they stop investment just short of developing a proprietary technology Often they won't spend the time and money to monitor the competition—particularly on a worldwide basis. Or, they fail to invest heavily enough to improve their competitive position even when they have a market opportunity or a time window to do so.

On the other hand, we have seen clients spend *excessive* amounts to develop new products for maturing businesses—businesses that their competitors are harvesting, or with low opportunity for high yield. This happens most often when technology investments are based on, or influenced by, precent of sale measurements. Typically, the largest product group receives the largest R&D budget.

Finally, we frequently see *improper* allocation of investment: patent protection for mature products; cost reduction programs for embryonic products when the company should be investing to secure a market position; investment in technologies when gaining a competitive position is impossible; spending for defensive programs, or spending, which upon scrutiny, conflicts with the overall corporate portfolio strategy. In each case, the net result is the same: eroding competitive position.

The three principles outlined above, which we believe must drive corporate technology planning in the 1980s, are the basis of the analytical framework underlying Booz·Allen's approach to the management of technology.

TECHNOLOGY MANAGEMENT: A THREE-PRONGED APPROACH

To assist clients in planning their technology strategy, Booz·Allen has developed a three-part program for the effective management of technology. It encompasses *technology strategy development, technology commercialization (see page 545) and technology resource management (see page 542).*

In developing an approach to technology strategy, we have assumed that (1) the use of standard corporate planning terminology will speed understanding of our techniques and improve communication between technologist and planners in client organizations, and (2) most large companies have a corporate strategic plan pinpointing overall objectives and outling programs for important strategic business units (SBUs).

Generally, plans for describing the goals, programs and resources of major technology thrusts also exist and are used as the basis for technology planning. In many cases, a business situation assessment pinpointing markets, competition, and corporate priorities is also available as part of the overall corporate plan. This assessment is generally based on a traditional review of internal strengths and weaknesses and on the relative importance, attractiveness and financial profile of each business segment. The competitive position of each SBU is also addressed from a marketplace standpoint, as are the external forces that could affect its position. Based on this information, an evaluation of the attractiveness of each business is made. This traditional approach to strategic planning has proven successful—as far as it goes. Booz•Allen has found, however, that *integrating technology* into this process adds a powerful—and often overlooked—dimension to the traditional business segmentation assessment. It is this integration of technology and business into a comprehensive technology strategy that allows companies to leverage their technology and sustain competitive advantage in world markets.

Technology strategy—the management of technology for sustainable strategic advantage—is the keystone of this technology-management program. Planning a technology strategy is a complex and challenging, four-step process involving:

1. *Technology situation assessment:* an internal and external scan of the technology environment beyond the limits of the traditional business portfolio.

2. *Technology portfolio development:* a tool that can be used to identify and systematically analyze key corporate technology alternatives or "plays" and to set technology priorities.

3. *Technology and corporate strategy integration:* integrating the technology portfolio into overall corporate strategy assures consistent objectives and effective implementation.

4. *Technology investment priorities:* at this stage a specific technology strategy, critical to the survival and success of each business, is developed.

TECHNOLOGY SITUATION ASSESSMENT

As a first step, we take a product or business area and define it very broadly. Then we break down or "explode" each broad category into its components, until we arrive at a detailed, technology-by-technology analysis for each business.

As a next step, we analyze the specific technologies employed in each of the firm's businesses, products and processes. We also assess the importance of each technology to specific products and/or business, determine which technologies are shared among them and which are derived from purchased parts and materials. Next, we review—and rethink—the priorities dictating past and current technology investments.

Finally, we scan the external competitive environment to pinpoint the investment patterns of competitors on both the product and process side for each of the firm's vital technologies. We also evaluate the importance of evolving technologies: Which companies developed them? What is the likely path of future innovation?

TECHNOLOGY PORTFOLIO DEVELOPMENT

At this point we have thoroughly analyzed competitive position in each of our technologies and assessed each one's relative marketplace importance. With this information, we can develop a "technology portfolio" by creating a quadrant grid similar to that used in business strategy analysis (see Figure 2). "Technology importance" is based on criteria that include value added; rate of change; and potential markets and their attractiveness. "Relative technology position" is determined by assessing current and future position in a given technology and its expected future development. Some quantitative criteria used to determine these are previous results, as demonstrated by patents, product history and cost; human resource strengths; and technology expenditures, current and projected.

Looking at the grid, if you find yourself in the "Bet" quadrant, then you're in an excellent position technologically in a business segment where that technology is important—and your objectives should be high to sustain and increase competitive advantage. This is the business where you must commit to the newest equipment, the risky R&D project and new product experimentation.

If you're in the "Draw" quadrant, you're in a borderline position—or worse—competitively, but the technology you're involved in is important. You need to make one of two decisions: Either bet against the competition and invest to attain a leadership position, or develop a plan to disengage from, or even abandon, that technology and then invest in more lucrative areas.

Figure 2   **Developing the Technology Portfolio**

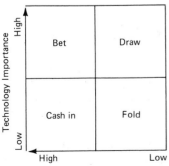

In the "Cash-in" quadrant, you're in a strong position technologically, but the technology you excel in is not really important in marketplace terms. This situation occurs most often in a rapidly changing industry such as electronics or engineered plastics, where existing technology is continually being supplanted by new techniques. We also find that technologies underlying aging product families—frequently a company's original product lines—tend to lie in this quadrant.

If you are in the "Fold" quadrant, you are weak technologically in an unimportant field. If you have invested heavily, you may have to view those dollars as a sunk cost. If not, then a financial redeployment strategy is essential—and the sooner the better.

TECHNOLOGY AND CORPORATE STRATEGY INTEGRATION

Generally, a business portfolio is *product oriented:* It measures a firm's product lines in terms of market position and importance. By contrast the technology portfolio is *technology based* and defines the firm's relative product and process technologies in terms of marketplace position and their importance to the basic business of the corporation (see Figure 3).

Though the business and technology portfolios provide fundamentally different perspectives, they must be compatible if you expect to gain advantage in a technology-related business. In other words, a technology portfolio will be effective only if it is consistent with the strategy implied by a company's business portfolio. Such consistency, we have found, is frequently the exception rather than the rule; far from complementing each other, the two portfolios often conflict.

The reasons for linking the business and technology portfolios and for ensuring their consistency are compelling. On the one hand, if they are incompatible, a company runs the risk of developing a potentially attractive strategy based

Figure 3   Matching Business and Technology Portfolios

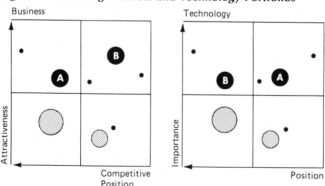

on financial data and other business portfolio information only to discover that it lacks the technology strengths needed to achieve its objectives. On the other hand, when analyzed in isolation, a technology portfolio can provide an unrealistic or distorted picture of market attractiveness and competitive position.

A technology portfolio, when viewed correctly, that is, in conjunction with the business portfolio, serves a number of purposes:

> It establishes a common planning base for all priority technologies.
>
> It provides an overview of a corporation's technological position, and a method for timing corporate technological investments in sync with its business plan.
>
> It identifies positions of strength to be leveraged and technology requirements to be strengthened or acquired to achieve corporate objectives.
>
> It provides a basis for focusing on high-potential, new business opportunities that could be built on current technological strengths.

DEVELOPING TECHNOLOGY INVESTMENT PRIORITIES

As a final step, a technology investment matrix of strategic plays versus relative technology expenditures can be developed from the technology portfolio analysis (see Figure 4). The matrix is a convenient tool for summarizing a company's technology strategy options and initiatives from an investment standpoint. It can be used to display individual technologies or the technological content of individual businesses with units or products that make up the overall corporate portfolio. Analyzing the matrix, it is clear that for a technology in the "Bet" quadrant, spending should be high relative to the leader—in fact, a company should concentrate on *becoming* the leader. In the "Draw" category, with a weak position in a technology of high importance, we need to increase expenditures (move to "Bet"), pull back if we can't make that increase, or perhaps continue to play

Figure 4   Technology Investment Priorities

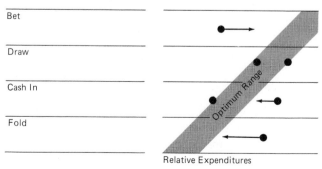

Relative Expenditures

another round (draw) with out current hand until a future date. With technologies in the "Cash-in" and "Fold" positions, we generally need to reduce or terminate investment and concentrate our recaptured resources on technologies with higher leverage.

Using the grid approach, we discover a number of key questions: What resources are required to achieve corporate strategic objectives? What should the level and rate of technology investment be? What additional investments are needed to achieve corporate goals?

As the following example demonstrates, the four-step approach outlined above can be a powerful analytical and decision-making process.

TECHNOLOGY STRATEGY IN ACTION: ENGINEERED MATERIALS

The client profiled here was a major multinational firm in a seemingly ideal situation: It had a strong competitive position with proprietary products in the engineered materials field.

The market was growing rapidly in response to 15 years of applications development work by leading manufacturers, including our client. Its synthetic materials were increasingly replacing glass and metals in transportation applications and a variety of consumer products, such as appliances, where their high strength-to-weight ratio was important. The business was both technology dependent and capital intensive, and becoming more so. Growth and profitability of their engineered materials business had been strong.

Our client, however, was concerned about maintaining a leadership position in light of some disconcerting trends. First, some of its original patents were expiring. Second, new competition appeared to be coming from world-class chemical and petro-chemical companies based in the United States, Japan and Europe. These firms were developing materials that competed well with our client's major products. Third, adding capacity and developing a really strong manufacturing-cost position would require a massive capital investment in world-scale plant—over a billion dollars. Finally, because of rapid growth, our client had been forced to allocate production, giving emerging competition an opportunity to "qualify" inferior products as second sources for some customer applications.

The business portfolio (see Figure 5) showed that the company was in a strong overall position with high market share in commodity products A and B, and with leadership positions in the downstream fabricated products businesses (C, D and E). Only product F, the past generation product that had largely been replaced by A and B, appeared in a bad position.

The technology portfolio (see Figure 5), developed after considerable competitive analysis, highlighted areas where the company's technology programs were out of balance with its business strategy: Recent emphasis had centered on

Figure 5   Engineered Materials: Matching Business and Technology Portfolios

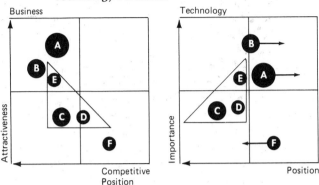

the downstream products—C, D and E—and, as a result, the company's position in the basic business—products A and B—had been allowed to erode. Management was surprised to learn that, relative to competitive activity, its position in the cornerstone technologies was being liquidated as it poured resources into developing markets for the fabricated products. Mangement felt their spending levels had been adequate on products A and B. The C, D and E teams did not appreciate their ultimate dependence on maintaining technology leadership in A and B. Secondly, Product F was suffering from the "young tiger syndrome." The product had been properly identified by the planning staff as being in the last stage of a distinguished career—clearly a "harvest" strategy was appropriate. However, several senior managers had favorable memories of the product and a succession of young tigers had been given a year or two opportunity to "reposition" F for growth. Consequently, a number of development projects had been initiated, directed toward improving our client's competitive position in this first-generation material.

The technology investment matrix (see Figure 6) was used to highlight these issues. As a result of the study, our client took the following actions:

Figure 6   Investment Strategy

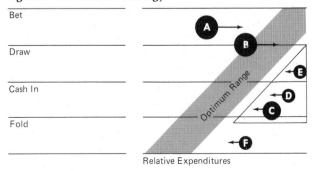

Technology budgets for A and B were increased by 40 percent and plant expansions were accelerated.

Programs for C, D, and E were modestly scaled back and some of their best people transferred to support the A and B programs.

Product F was handed over to a hard-nosed department veteran and managed for cash flow—not growth.

MANAGEMENT'S MANDATE

Mark Shepherd, the CEO of Texas Instruments, has called technology "the lifeblood of competitive leadership." We share this view; in the business environment of the 1980s, we believe that technology-based issues will underlie nearly every important decision that top management makes. Crucial to those decisions will be the ability to approach technology planning analytically and strategically.

As this article suggests, we also believe that technology *can* be planned and managed using formal techniques similar to those used in business and capital investment planning. An effective technology strategy is built on a penetrating analysis of technology strengths and weaknesses, and an assessment of the relative importance of these technologies to overall corporate strategy. Together with business strategy, the technology strategy defines how resources can be used most effectively to achieve sustainable competitive advantage.

The process is complex, but not mysterious; it can be planned, implemented and exploited. The alternative to managing technology is to be mastered, and finally, overwhelmed by it. Surely too high a price to pay in today's global marketplace.

TECHNOLOGY RESOURCE MANAGEMENT

John W. Allen
Booz·Allen

The management of technological resources is a complex task and one in which only a handful of U.S., European and Japanese companies have demonstrated preeminence over time. Yet throughout the 1980s, the ability to manage technology resources effectively will be a pivotal factor in gaining and sustaining technological leadership.

The first steps in confronting this problem—linking technology planning and business strategy, treating technology investments as capital assets and forging a link between senior technologist and strategic planners—are discussed elsewhere in the main body of this article.

However, after these steps are completed, several significant issues of *execution* remain. Once the technology investment decisions are made, how should those decisions be implemented? How should R&D be organized for the most effective use of human resources? How should new product/process programs be managed across business and product lines? How should the development and/or acquisition of technologies missing from a corporate portfolio be managed? How should technology transfer be undertaken? R&D interface with commercial organizations? How do we manage new technology-based ventures? The issue list can and does go on.

From our work with clients in a range of technology based businesses, we believe that there are three facets to successfully managing technological resources:

> strategically focused technology investment (as discussed in the main body of this article);
> management culture and policies;
> organization structure and dynamics.

All three facets are directly linked to and driven by corporate objectives and strategies.

MANAGEMENT CULTURE
AND POLICIES

Successful technology developments are the result of investments made over time—several years to several decades. Technology investments are primarily investments in people, particularly in senior technologists and technology managers. As a result, return on technology investment is directly related to the quality of a company's staff and its motivation. Prime requirements for success are the ability to attract and retain top technologists, to motivate them with sound compensation and career development programs and to create an entrepreneurial environment. Companies that treat technologists as second-class citizens or initiate frequent abrupt changes in corporate direction and personnel policies will experience high turnover (a direct loss of assets) and have a difficult time managing technology resources. In short, the effective management of human resources is vital to success.

Of equal importance are accurate business definition and the communication of goals, objectives and strategies: who you are, what you do, what you stand for, and how your firm relates to its customers, employees, suppliers, the financial community, society and government. We continually observe that the technologists in companies that manage these relationships well have "good" ideas, and those that don't, have poor or "dumb" ideas. New product/process ideas flow not only from market and competitive analyses, but also from a common understanding of the tenets and objectives that drive a company. This strong sense of purpose also creates an entrepreneurial environment.

Of overriding importance is the direct involvement of business managers at all levels of the technology management process, from CEO/COO to business unit general managers and middle management.

ORGANIZATION STRUCTURE AND DYNAMICS

How should technology resources be organized? Within strategic business units close to the market and manufacturing operations? In corporate R&D centers? Group level "centers"? Venture groups?

There are, of coure, no simple answers to these questions. However, we believe the structure of an organization is vitally important to the effective management of technology resources.

From a management perspective, there are four distinct stages in the technology life cycle: new ideas, emerging technology, venture management and commercialization. These are all highly complex activities: The time frame, the type of people needed and the mode of business leadership required are different for each stage.

Only a handful of firms—AT&T/Bell Labs and IBM, for example—have successfully managed R&D through the first two stages, idea and emerging technology. These stages require long-term staying power; the payoff usually comes only after ten years or more. This extended time frame needs a highly stable management that remains unchanged in direction and resource commitment, even through changes in administration. Technology in its earliest stages requires a clear mandate from top management and often should be conducted in a corporate lab directly responsible to that level. Since the emphasis at this stage is on exploratory research, the scientists, engineers and technology managers involved all need highly specific technical expertise. And they must be motivated by an incentive and reward system that is based on clearly defined and carefully negotiated goals and milestones.

By contrast, new venture management, the third stage in the technology life cycle, has quite a different focus and has been handled successfully by a somewhat larger number of companies, including Texas Instruments, Hewlett-Packard, DEC, Dow and General Electric. Although the time frame is shorter, five to ten years, perhaps, this stage still requires a long-term commitment, usually at higher cost and risk. Typically, the technology focus of venture management is on advanced product-process development, with the goal of creating a new business. Companies sucessful in venture management select manaagers with technology *and* commercial experience to lead their new business teams. Each team must blend technology, marketing and manufacturing skills, and should include future operations managers. New venture managers should report to the CEO/COO or another very senior executive, who must actively direct the program and measure progress against objectives. Due to the high costs and to the demands on top management, even very large companies can afford to launch only one to three major ventures at a time. In successful companies, the players receive significant incentive compensation for commercial success, and are not severely penalized for failure, if the venture was well managed.

Over three-fourths of all technology expenditures are invested in the commercial, or final, state of the technology life cycle. Here, the focus is on both strategic and tactical programs: advanced development and product/process development in support of ongoing businesses. These technology investments must be carefully aligned with the strategies driving each specific business; resource allocation should be the direct responsibility of a senior technology manager reporting directly to the strategic business unit general manager. It is critical that technology planning at this stage:

> focus on the key technology investment centers, balancing product and process technologies;
>
> foster communication and ensure coincidence of the interests and talents of technology and marketing groups on one hand, and manufacturing on the other;
>
> emphasize external communication—gathering key customer market intelligence, competitive intelligence, university and technical society participation and analysis;
>
> manage the technology investment portfolio, adjusting it to fit business strategy.

In a future issue of *Outlook,* we plan to give resource management in-depth treatment.

TECHNOLOGY COMMERCIALIZATION:
AN OVERVIEW

Joseph Nemec, Jr.
Booz·Allen

Technology commercialization provides the mechanism for introducing products into the marketplace, the ultimate determinant of profitability. Successful technology commercialization, therefore, is crucial to leveraging technological advantages in the marketplace.

In recent years, the margin of profit realized from new products appears to be shrinking rapidly, while the financial burden imposed by commercialization steadily grows. Chief contributors to that burden are a familiar litany of management problems: short-term planning horizons, the rapid dissemination of technology which quickly erodes competitive advantage, worldwide competition, and unpredictable regulatory changes. Compounding these already formidable obstacles to commercialization are the traditional problems created by technology transfer. All these factors have led to higher costs and higher failure rates for products and to a question asked incessantly by management: "Why aren't we successful in the commercialization of new products?"

The answer to that elusive question lies in the effective management of commercialization, which, in turn, is a key element in the effective management of technology.

NEW PRODUCT DEVELOPMENT: RECENT FINDINGS

A recent Booz·Allen study of new product development sheds an interesting light on the commercialization process and suggests some of the critical success factors that drive it. According to the study:

> Since 1976, fewer than 10 percent of all product introductions have involved products new to the world; the majority were adaptions of, or additions to, existing products.
>
> Compared to an earlier Booz·Allen study in 1968, management has improved the efficiency of new product expenditures, but the percentage of successful commercialized new products has remained unchanged.
>
> Despite the unchanging success rate, expectations for new products for the next five years are even higher.
>
> Major new product developments are driven mainly by technology and R&D.
>
> Key factors contributing to the ultimate success of new products include: the product's "fit" with market needs; its fit with the internal functional strengths of the company; technological superiority; and top management support.

As the findings suggest a successful commercialization strategy—like a successful technology stategy—is shaped by the relative assets that a company brings to a specific technology-dependent product.

A WINNING TECHNOLOGY COMMERCIALIZATION STRATEGY

Regardless of one's product, industry, market or competition, the goal of a commercialization strategy is the same: to achieve a successful position for a product in attractive markets. With that goal paramount, a winning commercialization strategy is built on two key elements: superior product performance and the shrewd assessment of market needs.

Attempts to commercialize products for low-potential markets or to develop technologies that are not important are irrational and costly. Yet many companies fall repeatedly into one or both of these technology traps. How does one identify and exploit the most attractive and potentially profitable options for product development? Briefly described there are two fundamental commercialization strategies (see Figure):

Figure   Commercialization Strategies

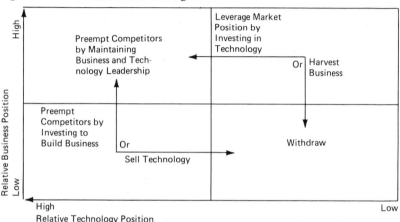

THE PREEMPTIVE LEADERSHIP STRATEGY

A preemptive leadership position can be achieved through technology advances or by aggressive market thrust. That leadership can be seized by being the first in the marketplace, by erecting market and technology barriers, and/or by investing heavily in technology to achieve superior position—and then continuing a high level of investment to maintain that position.

FAST-FOLLOWER STRATEGY

To leverage market strength, a fast follower can either acquire and develop the technology necessary for superiority or invest in expanded market presence through strengthened distribution channels, low-cost manufacturing, brand name visibility and related methods.

Each of the strategies outlined here has a different risk-return profile—and each is shaped by the combination of business and technology assets available to support specific product and process developments. The alternative to these two technology commercialization strategies—to be a slow follower—is clearly a losing approach and a costly one both in time invested and lost returns.

THE ROLE OF TECHNOLOGY
IN THE 1980s: WILL IT DEPEND
ON DOLLARS OR SENSE?

THE RESULTS OF A 1981
BOOZ·ALLEN SURVEY

Early in 1981, Booz·Allen & Hamilton conducted a survey of 800 executives in *Fortune* 1000 companies on the role of technology in corporate operations. We surveyed chief operating officers, research and development (R&D) directors, and corporate and divisional planners in seven major sectors of the U.S. business economy: energy, chemicals, basic manufacturing, electronics, aerospace, consumer packaged goods, and health and medical.

In summary, the survey findings show that, with respect to the future business environment, the most important influences on U.S. business in the 1980s will be economic, regulatory, and technological, with changing technology especially critical in high-technology industries. In the economic area, the cost of capital is expected to have the major impact, especially in industries heavily dependent on the purchase of basic materials and machinery. In highly regulated industries such as energy and chemicals, government policies are of greatest concern.

Particular technologies also are expected to affect business, with those related to advanced computer capabilities believed to have the greatest potential impact. Especially prominent in this category are microelectronics, computer-aided manufacturing, computer-aided design, and software engineering.

In the future business environment, some companies—both in the United States and abroad—believe they will be vulnerable to foreign competition, especially from Japan and West Germany. The electronics and basic manufacturing industries see Japan as an important competitor; the health and medical, chemical, and electronics industries view West Germany in the same light; and the aerospace industry perceives France as a market threat.

In competition with foreign industry, U.S. business feels it is at a disadvantage because of certain government regulatory requirements and tax policies (Figure 1). Government subsidies, labor costs and productivity, costs of capital and trade policies are other major disadvantages cited.

On the upside, American business executives believe they enjoy distinct competitive advantages around the world because of superior technological know-how. An abundant domestic supply of many natural resources is also an important plus in the minds of many of the survey's respondents.

Figure 1 *Competitive Advantages/Disadvantages (Percent of Responses)*

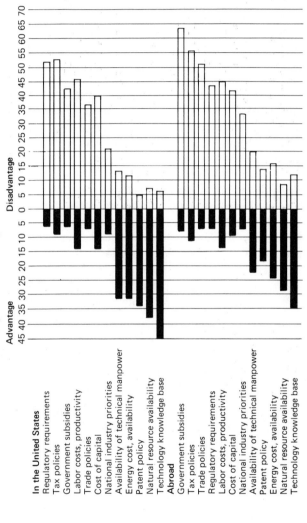

Despite this optimism, survey respondents believe that American management overemphasizes short-term profits *and* that the lack of involvement of top management in the technology process have resulted in the consistent underfunding of technology-related activities—such as R&D—in a wide range of industries and in emphasizing those functional areas that have a more immediate impact on profits.

TOP MANAGEMENT'S R&D ROLE

More specifically, the survey results show that relatively few top-level managers review all R&D programs early and often or actively participate in the firm's evaluation and management of its R&D program. Overall, only one in three conducts R&D program reviews regularly, and only two in five become actively involved in R&D program evaluation and management (Figure 2).

Top management appears to prefer "focused" reviews of their R&D operations. Almost three in five respondents indicate that top management's role in the technology process is limited to either reviewing major development programs above some dollar threshold, or singling out and following programs of key importance (Figure 2).

This limited involvement of top management in the technology process may be a major reason why technology functions are—or at least are perceived to be—significantly and chronically underfunded. One of every two respondents said R&D and new product development are underfunded, while two of every five perceive manufacturing and engineering as being insufficiently financed.

The combined effect of, at times, indifferent management attitudes and chronic underfunding of R&D probably has resulted in the weak roles that technology and technology-related functions are perceived to play in the overall performance of a company. Rather, marketing/sales and production/manufacturing are perceived to be most important or second most important to performance. Operations that contribute to a company's long-term growth are de-emphasized. For example, only two in ten participants ranked new product development or R&D in the first or second positions of importance to the overall performance of the company. Even fewer—one in ten—indicated that manufacturing engineering is important.

TECHNOLOGY UNDERVALUED

A second major finding about the role of technology in American business is that although most companies carry out technology monitoring and forecasting to identify threats and/or opportunities, technology appears to be given less weight in the short-term corporate planning process than factors that contribute to short-term profitability. Of twelve factors identified (Figure 3), the three most

Figure 2 Top Management's Role in the Technology Process

● indicates industry's emphasis significantly
  above sample average

Industry: Consumer Packaged Goods, Basic Manufacturing, Chemicals, Energy, Health and Medical, Aerospace, Electronics

Percentage of Responses: 58, 58, 46, 44, 39, 34

Top Management's Role

Singles out and follows programs of key importance

Reviews major development programs above some dollar threshold

Focuses on projects in trouble

Actively participates in firm's evaluation and management of R & D program

Monitors near-term profits, not technology

Reviews all R & D programs early and often

Figure 3 Factors Considered in Corporate Planning Process

● indicates industry emphasis significantly above sample average

* Basic manufacturing and consumer packaged goods significantly emphasized none of the 12 factors.

Factor	Percentage of Responses	**Industry***	Electronics	Aerospace	Health and Medical	Energy	Chemicals	Percentage of Responses	**Industry***	Electronics	Aerospace	Health and Medical	Energy	Chemicals	Percentage of Change
Product performance	51			●				55			●				8
Manufacturing economics	50							56							12
Capital requirements	42					●		42							0
Competitive position in U.S.	42							52							24
Availability of qualified technical personnel	36		●	●				47		●	●				31
New product development	31		●		●			55		●		●			80
Market growth expectations	27							41							52
Manufacturing capacity and demand	23							31							35
Competitive positions world	13				●			21							62
Expected technology changes	13						●	31		●	●				138
Management compensation and rewards	9							15							67
New technologies in other industries	4							10		●				●	150

important considerations cited for both short- and long-term planning are product performance, manufacturing economics, and competitive position in the United States.

A very different picture emerged when we examined the percentage of change in a factor's *importance* in short- versus long-term planning. The *extent* of the increase was significant for several factors. New technologies jumped 150 percent, expected technology changes increased 138 percent and new product development increased 80 percent.

What this suggests is that, although management considers, in the short term, factors that contribute to near-term performance and profitability, they do recognize, to some extent, the importance of factors that will allow U.S. business and industry to compete in world markets in the future. The problem, it would seem, is translating the long-term technological considerations into short-term planning commitments, when corporate goals argue for short-term, positive bottom-line results.

BARRIERS TO INTEGRATING TECHNOLOGY

This is very much in line with the third major finding about the role of technology in U.S. business—that the major barriers to integrating technology into the corporate planning process are management's short-term, profit-oriented perspective; the lack of formal analytical approaches; and failure to involve technical personnel in the planning process.

Survey participants believe that remedying this situation requires greater top-management commitment to *longer* term results, improved long-range planning of technology, higher R&D expenditures, greater emphasis on integrating technology and a tighter coupling of technology and strategic planning (Figure 4).

In 1978 we surveyed the top management of 12 companies considered to be technological leaders in the United States, Europe and Japan. The crucial differences between these leaders and those of other first-line organizations surveyed in 1981 are threefold.

First, the technology leaders have a long-term perspective and commitment to technology innovation and development, and closely monitor technological changes that might affect their markets. In contrast, our 1981 survey shows that many organizations have a short-term perspective, and that current costs and short-term profits weigh heavily in their technology development and funding decisions.

Second, the technology leaders have learned to manage their technology resources—human and material—*and* to integrate them into their overall business strategy, thus ensuring that technological investment is in line with corporate objectives. Most respondents in our latest survey believe their companies are

Figure 4   Means of Integrating Technology in Planning Process

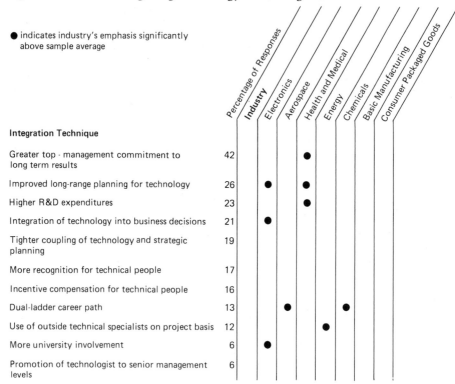

● indicates industry's emphasis significantly
   above sample average

Integration Technique	Percentage of Responses	Industry	Electronics	Aerospace	Health and Medical	Energy	Chemicals	Basic Manufacturing	Consumer Packaged Goods
Greater top - management commitment to long term results	42				●				
Improved long-range planning for technology	26		●		●				
Higher R&D expenditures	23				●				
Integration of technology into business decisions	21		●						
Tighter coupling of technology and strategic planning	19								
More recognition for technical people	17								
Incentive compensation for technical people	16								
Dual-ladder career path	13			●				●	
Use of outside technical specialists on project basis	12					●			
More university involvement	6		●						
Promotion of technologist to senior management levels	6								

not integrating technology with business strategy in any consistent or exemplary way.

Third, in the leading technology companies, management grasps the complexities of the technological environment and is able to help translate technological considerations into strategic business decisions. In contrast, the results of our 1981 survey show that most top-level managers do not review R&D programs early or often, and do not actively participate in evaluating and managing them.

What are the implications of our survey findings and comparisons?

Although the role of technology is critically important in American business, our survey results indicate there are significant barriers to integrating technology in the all-important corporate strategic planning process. Although the monitoring of emerging technologies is fairly widespread, many *believe* existing forecasting capabilities are not adequate to the task of predicting the precise timing and form of their development. Further, an appropriate analytical approach to integrating technology into the planning process does not exist in most corporate environments, nor is there sufficient top-management commitment to long-term results.

The survey results suggest that substantially greater emphasis needs to be placed on the importance of technology in long-range corporate success, identifying the specific means of integrating technology in the planning process and developing a sound analytical approach to carrying out technology planning. Without this readjustment in emphasis, U.S. business may well find itself not in first place, not an "also ran," not even in the race.

26

Towards a Strategic Theory of the Firm

RICHARD P. RUMELT

University of California at Los Angeles

Paper prepared for a conference on "Non-Traditional Approaches to Policy Research," Graduate
School of Business, University of Southern California, November 12–13, 1981. This version revised
November 16, 1981.

I consider myself a mainstream researcher in the field of business policy, and the ideas I want to describe in this paper concern the foundations of a theory of business strategy that is rooted in economics. But is such a paper, whatever its merits, really appropriate at a conference entitled "Non-traditional Approaches to Policy Research"? Surprisingly, it is. The use of economic theory to model and explicate business strategy, as it is understood within the field of business policy, is distinctly non-traditional.

To the uninitiated, it appears obvious that the study of business strategy must rest on the bedrock foundations of the economist's model of the firm and the theory of industrial organization. Nevertheless, until very recently, there has been a virtually complete absence of any intersection between business policy and economic theory. Few attempted a cross-fertilization between these fields; most who did reported results barren of much interest. This state of affairs did not reflect the unwillingness of policy researchers to learn economics. Rather, it came about because the neoclassical theory of the firm was created by assuming away the very existence of those phenomena that most concern students of business policy. it was sustained by the mainstream microeconomist's commitment to the position that the theory of the firm not be required to describe the actual behavior of firms.

This situation is beginning to change. The pioneering insights of Coase, Simon, and Stigler set in motion forces that are undermining the neoclassical theory.[1] Recent work by Williamson, Porter, Spence, and others demonstrates that economic concepts can model and describe strategic phenomena.[2] In this paper I want to look closely at this new confluence and suggest the outlines of a "strategic" theory of the firm.

BUSINESS POLICY AND NEOCLASSICAL THEORY

Business policy is concerned with those aspects of general management that have material effects on the survival and success of business enterprises. For about twenty years the central organizing concept in this field has been *strategy*. The concept is empirical rather than theoretical, having its roots in numerous field studies of business firms and the historical analysis of the evolution of business enterprises. In essence, the concept is that a firm's competitive position is defined by a bundle of unique resources and relationships and that the task of

[1]Ronald Coase, "The Nature of the Firm," *Economics,* 4 (November 1937), 386–405; H. A. Simon, *Administrative Behavior,* 2nd ed. (New York: Macmillan, 1961); and George J. Stigler, "The Economics of Information," *Journal of Political Economy,* 69 (June 1961), p. 213–25.

[2]Oliver E. Williamson, *Markets and Hierarchies: Analysis and Antitrust implications* (New York: Free Press, 1975); Michael E. Porter, *Competitive Strategy* (New York: Free Press, 1980), and A. M. Spence, "Investment, Strategy, and Growth in a New Market," *Bell Journal of Economics,* 10 (Spring 1979).

general management is to adjust and renew these resources and relationships as time, competition, and change erode their value. This way of looking at the firm is *not* a theory; it is a set of constructs that have proved useful in describing and summarizing the empirical studies of firm behavior that form the core of the business policy literature. Simply put, these broad empirical observations are:

1. The general managers of firms make choices, and some of these choices are considerably more important (having more impact on performance) than others.

2. Strategic choices are not necessarily explicit but may be characterized by infrequency, uncertainty, the irreversibility of commitments, and multi-functional scope, and they are usually nonrecurring.

3. The most critical strategic choices exhibited by a firm are those concerned with the selection of the product-market areas or segments in which the firm will compete and the basic approach to those businesses.

4. Similar firms facing similar strategic problems may respond differently.

5. Firms in the same industry compete with substantially different bundles of resources using disparate approaches. These firms differ because of differing histories of strategic choice and performance and because managements appear to seek asymmetric competitive positions.

What makes these apparently innocuous observations worth repeating is that they either contradict or stand completely outside the neoclassical theory of the firm and the standard models used in industrial organization.[3] For example, Cohen and Cyert's treatment of the theory of the firm begins this way:

> This book concentrates on the most significant institution in our economic system—the business firm—and the most important function of our economic system—resource allocation. It is impossible to have a clear understanding of the functioning of the modern American society without knowing a great deal about the firm and the role it plays in the economy's resource allocation process.[4]

Nevertheless, in the following four hundred pages of this well-written text, few real firms are mentioned and no model is discussed in which the firm's choice problem is anything other than the selection of a price or level of output for a homogeneous product with known production and demand functions. Monopolistic competition is discussed but rejected on theoretical and empirical grounds.

[3]They also contradict the environmental determinism viewpoint in organizational sociology. It is an intriguing example of disciplinary chauvinsim that organization sociologists tend to attribute the straightforward notion that senior management's choices influence the selection of an organization's tasks and internal structure to Child's strong reminder on this point. See John Child, "Organization Structure, Environment and Performance—The Role of Strategic Choice," *Sociology*, 6 (January 1972), pp. 1–22.

[4]Kalman J. Cohen and Richard M. Cyert, *Theory of the Firm: Resource Allocation in a Market Economy* (Englewood Cliffs, N.J.: Prentice-Hall, 1965), p. 3.

The problem with the neoclassical theory is that it is not really a theory of the firm. The existence of the firm is actually problematic within the axiomatic framework of the theory and must be justified by reference to entrepreneurship as a fixed factor. What the theory actually deals with is the workings of the price system in a setting in which nothing but prices need be known. It is a powerful intellectual achievement, but that power was obtained by assuming away such phenomena as (1) transaction costs, (2) limits on rationality, (3) technological uncertainty, (4) constraints on factor mobility, (5) limits on information availability, (6) markets in which price conveys quality informaiton, (7) consumer or producer learning, and (8) dishonest and/or foolish behavior.

In fact, many of the assumptions embodied in the neoclassical theory are only now coming to light as specialized models of markets are being investigated. One interesting example is Spence's discussion of signaling equilibria,[5] in which it is sensible to invest in otherwise useless activities in order to signal quality differentials. Another is Diamond's observation that the introduction of a small consumer search cost into a retail market model drastically alters the nature of the equilibrium.[6]

The situation with regard to industrial organization has been only marginally better. Within industrial organization there is a subschool which, like business policy, has recorded and commented on a wide variety of real-world business behavior. However, the theoretical structure of the field has never encompassed that richness. The traditional model of industry in industrial organization is taken from oligopoly theory[7] and remains that of identical firms or firms that are homogeneous but for scale. The effect of this modeling assumption has been to reduce the study of industrial competition to the study of relative scale, all other differences being ignored.

Industries differ, in the standard view, according to the degree of concentration, the presence of scale economies, and the degree of product differentiation or nonprice competition. Scale economies and product differentiation are viewed, in this framework, as properties of an industry rather than as the results achieved by firms and both are identified as barriers to entry, creating economic rents (profits that do not attract new production).

By taking the industry as the unit of analysis, industrial organization has largely ignored the theory and evidence of intra-industry differences among firms. Thus, while great efforts have gone toward explaining interindustry differences in the rate of return, it can be easily shown that the dispersion in the char-

[5]A. M. Spence, *Market Signaling: Informational Transfer in Hiring and Related Processes* (Cambridge, Mass.: Harvard University Press, 1974).

[6]Peter A. Diamond, "A Model of Price Adjustment," *Journal of Economic Theory*, 3 (1971), 156–68.

[7]In this regard it is important to note that oligopoly theory, far from providing a predictive model of firm behavior, represents the "edge" of economics in that a profit-maximizing assumption fails to define behavior. Oligopoly models are constructed by first assuming a pattern of behavior and then deducing the form of the resultant equilibrium, if one exists.

acteristic long-term rates of return of firms within industries is five to eight times as large as the variance in returns across industries.[8]

What has caused this mismatch between the concept of strategy and neo-classical theory? To say that the economic models are not "realistic" would be true, but unfair and beside the point. All models in the social sciences are unrealistic; good models are specialized and simple, generating descriptions of the phenomena of interest with the fewest necessary constructs and assumptions. This mismatch arises because policy researchers and economists have been interested in substantially different phenomena. The central concerns of business policy are the observed heterogeneity of firms and the firm's choice of product-market commitments. By contrast, the basic phenomena of interest in neoclassical theory is the functioning of the price system under norms of decentralized decision making.

In the language of economics, the chief concern of business policy researchers has not been static profit maximization[9] but profit seeking through corporate entrepreneurship and with the empirical observation that corporate entrepreneurship is intimately connected with the appearance and adjustment of unique and idiosyncratic resources. This view of corporate behavior is most closely associated with Schumpeter's vision of competition as the process of "creative destruction" rather than as a static equilibrium condition.[10] As Nelson and Winter have noted:

> The core ideas of Schumpeterian theory are of course quite different from those of neoclassical theory. For Schumpeter the most important firms are those that serve as the vehicles for action of the real drivers of the system—the innovating entrepreneurs . . . The competitive environment within which firms operate is one of struggle and motion. It is a dynamic selection environment, not an equilibrium one. The essential forces of growth are innovation and selection, with augmentation of capital stocks more or less tied to these processes.[11]

Thus the concepts of entrepreneurship and resource heterogeneity, so central to business strategy, have been either omitted or taken as preexisting givens

[8]See R. P. Rumelt, "How Important Is Industry in Explaining Firm Profitability?" U.C.L.A., 1981.

[9]The standard attack on the neoclassical theory has centered on the assumption of profit maximization. According to the behavioral theory of the firm explicated by Cyert and March, managers are only intendedly rational. Bounds on their information-processing capacities prevent firms from acting as true profit maximizers. Baumol's somewhat different argument is that the quantity corporations act to maximize is not really profits but sales (or growth, or some measure of manager's welfare). Current fashion terms these adjustments to the neoclassical model as highlighting information costs, computation costs, and agency problems. See Richard M. Cyert and James G. March, *A Behavioral Theory of the Firm* (Englewood Cliffs, N.J.: Prentice-Hall, 1963); and William J. Baumel, *Business Behavior, Value and Growth* (New York: Macmillan, 1959).

[10]J. A. Schumpeter, *The Theory of Economic Development* (Cambridge, Mass.: Harvard University Press, 1934; original publication 1911).

[11]R. R. Nelson, and S. G. Winter, "Neoclassical vs. Evolutionary Theories of Economic Growth: Critique and Prospectus," *Economic Journal,* 84 (December 1974), 890.

in neoclassical theory. Entrepreneurship is normally omitted because it has become by definition the repository of nonneoclassical phenomena. Entrepreneurs are seen to posses special information, to be unique, to create pure profit, and to act as the essential indivisibilities governing the size distribution of firms. Similarly, resource heterogeneity is taken to be an exogenous property of the physical world rather than an endogenous creation of economic actors. *Their omission has obscured the close logical connections between these constructs.* Without resource heterogeneity (and the equivalent of property rights to unique resources), there is little incentive for investing in the risky exploration of new methods and the search for new value. Given uncertainty, the *ex post* results of entrepreneurial activity will necessarily be resource heterogeneity. At the most primitive level, firms may simply differ in the relative efficiency with which they extract or process homogeneous goods. However, in the absence of perfect intermediate markets for these goods, firms will have incentives to integrate. Thus is born the *strategic* firm, characterized by a bundle of linked and idiosyncratic resources and resource conversion activities.

What accounts for the neglect of these important phenomena? Nordhaus and Tobin have argued that the problem is one of modeling:[12]

> Many economists agree with the broad outlines of Schumpeter's vision of capitalist development, which is a far cry from growth models made nowadays in either Cambridge, Mass. or Cambridge, England. But visions of that kind have yet to be transformed into theory that can be applied to everyday analytic and empirical work.[13]

I agree that there are substantial difficulties in creating formal models of Schumpeterian rivalry, but I do not see them as insurmountable. There may be, however, another factor deterring economists from such efforts—determining the welfare implications of Schumpeterian rivalry is markedly more difficult than modeling it. This implies that policy researchers, who are only secondarily concerned with the technical welfare implications of competitive activity, may well have a comparative advantage at producing descriptive theory in this area.

UNCERTAIN IMITABILITY AND AMBIGUITY

This section describes a simple theory of rivalry under conditions of causal ambiguity. I and my colleague Steven Lippman have named the theory and modeling concept it embodies "uncertain imitability." We model entrepreneurship as

---

[12]W. Nordhaus, and J. Tobin, "Is Growth Obsolete?" in *Economic Research: Retrospect and Prospect, Economic Growth,* Ed. R. Gordon (New York: National Bureau of Economic Resarch, 1972), p. 2.

[13]Also quoted in Nelson and Winter, "Neoclassical vs. Evolutionary Theories," p. 889.

the production of new production functions and generate firm heterogeneity as an outcome rather than as a given. The treatment here is only a rough sketch of the more complete theory, and interested readers are directed to the source.[14]

In neoclassical theory firms entering industries or undertaking substantial expansion efforts select their production functions from a known bundle of technological possibilities. Thus imitative attempts tend to equilibrate firm efficiencies, and long-term differences in profitability signal failures in either product or factor markets. But suppose that there exists an irreducible uncertainty connected with the creation (or production) of a new production function. Then the efficiencies achieved by entrants or major expansion programs will vary. Furthermore, if there is a nonrecoverable cost associated with such entrepreneurial activities, rational actors will stop short of seeking to imitate the best extant firm. Thus the ambiguity that generates the initial heterogeneity will also act to block its homogenization through imitation.

Uncertainty in the creation of new production functions is most likely to come about because there is ambiguity as to what the factors of production actually are and as to how they interact. The standard neoclassical assumption is that there is a finite set of known factors of production and that their marginal productivities can be discerned. However, if the precise reasons for success or failure cannot be determined, even after the event has occurred, there is causal ambiguity and it is impossible to produce an unambiguous list of the factors of production, much less measure their marginal contributions.

In order to model this situation, assume that a market exists for a homogeneous product. There is a known demand function and any entrant into the industry obtains a cost function $C(q,b)$ which is U shaped in q, the rate of output. The parameter b is a measure of relative efficiency and larger values of b imply lower unit costs. Each firm, once it is in the industry, acts as a profit-maximizing price taker. By adjusting output so that marginal cost equals the market price p, a firm with efficiency b obtains a level of profits $y(b,p)$.

If $C(q,b)$ exhibits fixed costs, firms may display negative profits when the market price falls below some level. Define $h(p)$ as the value of b that just allows the firm to break even at a market price p. Thus $y(h(p),p) = 0$, and if $b < h(p)$, the firm cannot make positive profits and is forced to withdraw from the industry.

Now assume that each entrant into the industry must pay a nonrecoverable "entry fee" K and then receives a cost function $C(q,b)$ in which b is a realization of a random variable X with cumulative distribution F and density f. Intuitively, it should be clear that firms will enter the industry and display a variety of efficiencies. As entry continues, the price will fall, forcing some firms that have received "poor" cost functions (low b's) out of the industry. Finally, the industry will reach a state that deters further rational entry attempts. In a sense, the final free-entry

[14]S. A. Lippman and R. P Rumelt, "Uncertain Imitability: An Analysis of Interfirm Differences in Efficiency under Competition," *Bell Journal of Economics,* 13 (1982), 418–38.

equilibrium is achieved through processes of variation and selection rather than neoclassical resource flows. In it, firms display a range of efficiencies and the most efficient display stable persistent rents.

In general it is quite difficult to characterize the final equilibrium in that the optimal entry strategy depends in detail up the mix of extant firms at each point. For simplicity, I will assume that each entrant has a negligible independent impact on the market price.[15] Now define $V(p)$ as the expected value of entry when the prospective entrant faces an *unchanging* price p. Taking the discount rate to be r, we have

$$V(p) = -K + (1/r) \underset{h(p)}{y(x,p)} \, dF(x). \tag{1}$$

For p sufficiently small, $V(p) < 0$ and entry is blocked—even the guarantee of a fixed price being insufficient to make entry attractive. Because V increases in p, there is a unique price p^* that solves $V(p) = 0$, and atomism ensures that the final entry-blocking equilibrium price will only be infinitesimally less than p^*. Each prospective entrant can therefore expect to receive at least $V(p^*)$ and entry will proceed as long as $p > p^*$.

When the price is p^*, the minimum b necessary for survival is $b^* = h(p^*)$. Firms in the final equilibrium will be those that received values of b greater than b^*. Thus the probability P_s that an entrant will survive the selection process and be a member of the final equilibrium is

$$P_s = 1 - F(b^*). \tag{2}$$

The distribution F_s of survivor's b's is $F(x)/P_s$ for $x > b^*$ and zero otherwise. Survivors of the selection process earn profits $y_s(b,p^*)$ in perpetuity and the expected level of survivor's profit is

$$Ey_s = \frac{1}{P_s} \int_{b^*}^{\infty} y(x,p^*) \, dF(x). \tag{3}$$

Combining (1) with (3) and the condition $V(p^*) = 0$ gives

$$Ey_s = rK/P_s \tag{4}$$

and defining survivors' rents as $R_s = Ey_s - rK$ reveals that

$$R_s = rK(1 - P_s)/P_s \tag{5}$$

---

[15]The nonatomistic free-entry equilibrium can be characterized if firms do not drop out of the industry. This result is obtained if fixed costs are zero, sunk, or scaled with the rest of the firm. With this specification, entry produces a renewal process in total industry capacity. For details, see Lippman and Rumelt, "Uncertain Imitability."

From (5) it is clear that the average survivor (and the industry as a whole) displays positive economic profits in equilibrium despite price-taking behavior and free entry. These rents are created by the failure of other firms to survive: if $P_s = 1$, then $R_s = 0$. More precisely, for each survivor there are $(1 - P_s)/P_s$ firms that fail to survive, each suffering a loss K. Consequently the net expected profit from an entry attempt is zero, and the survivor's rents exactly balance the failure's losses.

Another way of looking at (5) is that selection pressure ensures that the "average" entrepreneur will earn below-average profits. Indeed, if P_s is low enough, the mean of X will fall below b^* and the average entry attempt will not only earn poor profits but fail to survive.

In this equilibrium the extant firms have been selected for their unusual efficiency at production, and no outsider can expect to beat them at their own game. This result does not depend upon scale economies or sunk costs. Rather, it is the natural consequence of a nonneoclassical selection-based equilibrium. In the language of business policy, the more-efficient firms have "created" or discovered

Figure 1   Rescaling y_s

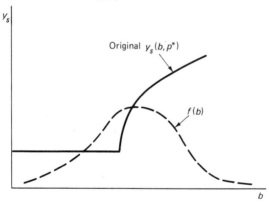

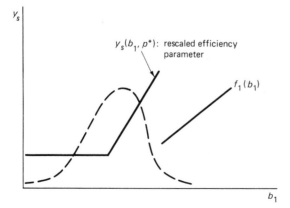

unique skills and strengths and will maximize their values by seeking other areas of activity wherein these special skills may also be of value.

What are the implications of increased riskiness? Figure 1 shows the shape of $y_s(b,p^*)$. Note that if y_s is not convex in b for $b > b^*$, it is always possible to find a monotone function $b \longrightarrow b_1$ together with its associated distribution and density functions, such that $y_s(b_1,p)$ is convex. This means that it is the riskiness of y rather than b that carries economic meaning. For simplicity, assume that the parameterization of $C(q,b)$ is chosen so that $y_s(b,p^*)$ is linear in b for $b > b^*$.

Given y_s convex in b, it can be seen from (1) that mean-preserving increases in the spread of F (or increases in variance) will tend to *decrease* the equilibrium price p^*. Equivalently, were such a pure increase in riskiness available privately to a prospective entrant, it would *increase* the expected value of that entry attempt. This "risk-loving" behavior also occurs in the case of call options; *ceteris paribus,* the owner of a call option prefers mean-preserving increases in risk to decreases. The principle also applies to the levered firm, a mean-preserving increase in risk shifting wealth from bondholders to stockholders.

A THEORY OF FIRM SIZE

The relationship between riskiness and private value has interesting implications for the optimal scope of entrepreneurial firms or risky projects. To begin, notice that irreversibly combining two separate entry attempts (paying $2K$ and receiving costs $C(b_1,q_1) + C(b_2,q_2)$) is never attractive. Intuitively, the relative draws from F are independent so that the relative riskiness has decreased, making the expected value of entry negative. Irreversibly combining two entry attempts would only be efficient if the draws from F could be guaranteed to be completely correlated. These considerations suggest that the entrepreneur's problem is not only to decide whether or not to enter but also to assemble the appropriate mix of assets for the attempt.

Which activities should the entrepreneur combine? The general answer is, *Those that will exhibit strongly dependent postentry efficiencies.* Given a bundle of activities with total postentry efficiency determined by the random variable X, adding new activities that involve sunk costs can never be profitable if their efficiencies are uncorrelated with X. Thus new activities are added until the point where further additions would not add sufficiently large expected profits or profit variance to justify the added sunk capital.

Note that this logic is opposite to that underlying diversification. Here the entrepreneur's objective is not to reduce risk, as the expected level of efficiency provides an inadequate return. Rather, the entrepreneur is attempting to concentrate only on those activities that are closely connected with success or failure in the market. Adding extraneous activities not only produces an unnecessary increase in the costs of failure but also may obscure important information regarding the success of the main endeavor.

Interestingly, *this perspective provides a theory of firm size that does not depend upon diseconomies of scale or control loss and is only tangentially related to the notion of a fixed entrepreneurial factor.* In addition, it explains why diversification, which reduces the risk of bankruptcy, is rarely undertaken by those facing the greatest risk—entrepreneurs entering or creating new markets.

SELECTION, ADAPTATION, AND ISOLATING MECHANISMS

Given uncertain imitability, in equilibrium the average firm earns positive economic profit and is more efficient at what it is doing than a new entrant should expect to be. Were this not true, entry would proceed until it was true. If the equilibrium is permeated by heterogeneous firms with evolved local advantages, there are a number of immediate implications. Among the most straightforward are these:

1. New entry activity will essentially be a function of market growth rather than industry profitability. High levels of profitability in stable markets may well signal incumbents possessing difficult-to-imitate skills and deter entry.

2. Firms that are successful in one endeavor will tend to seek out related activities in which their revealed special competences are useful.[16] Hence profitability and growth will be correlated even when the effects of demand pull are controlled.

3. If the basis for success in a market shifts to a new function, firms that have been successful in the past may now be at a disadvantage relative to outside firms possessing demonstrated skills related to the new required competence.

In industrial organization theory a barrier to entry exists when a prospective entrant is at a disadvantage relative to an incumbent.[17] In an important paper, Caves and Porter extend the entry barrier concept by defining *mobility bar-*

---

[16]Strictly speaking, a resource or competence will be fully utilized in one sphere of activity if it is a factor of production for a perfect commodity. However, if firm size is limited by differentiation, segmentation, and other exogenous sources of declining marginal revenue, unique factors may not be fully utilized in a single activity.

[17]Defining an entry barrier precisely is no simple task. Perhaps the most straightforward approach is to define it by its results—persistent surplus profits that do not induce entry. Stigler suggests that entry barriers exist when entrants would bear costs not borne by incumbents. This definition neatly separates the impact of scale economies, which are available to any producer, from sunk costs (idiosyncratic investment), which must enter into the entrant's cost prospective cost calculations but not those of the incumbent. See George J. Stigler, *The Organization of Industry* (Homewood, Ill.: Richard D. Irwin, 1968).

riers as asymmetries among firms within industries that act to limit differential expansion and the equalization of profit rates.[18] Their emphasis on heterogeneity deserves special attention:

> Limits on entry and limits on mobility remain stubbornly immiscible as long as we stick to conventional thinking about cost functions and intra-industry differences among firms. The conventional approach takes firms within an industry as identical in all economically important respects except for their size. Then cost conditions either define an optimal scale for the firm, leaving no explanation why size should change, or render scale indeterminate, providing no clue as to what could deter infinitesimal changes in a firm's scale. . . . The key to conjoining barriers to entry to a more general theory of interscale mobility of firms is the hypothesis that sellers within an industry are likely to differs systematically in traits other than size.[19]

In Caves and Porter's view, industries can be broken into *groups* of firms that exhibit distinct characteristics (e.g., broad-line vs. specialist). Mobility barriers both define these groups and are reinforced by the strategic activities of group members. The group concept is frequently all that is needed, but there is no theoretical reason to limit mobility barriers to groups of firms. I shall therefore use the term *isolating mechanism* to refer to phenomena that limit the *ex post* equilibration of rents among individual firms.

In the pure theory of uncertain imitability, the isolating mechanism is causal ambiguity. The inability of economic agents to fully understand the causes of efficiency differences limits competition by entry or imitation. However, many other isolating mechanisms exist. For example, mineral rights laws convert the results of risky exploration investments into *ex ante* uncertain but *ex post* persistent streams of rent. Similarly, patents, trademarks, reputation, and brand image serve to limit second-mover imitation of first-mover success. These and other important isolating mechanisms are listed in Table 1.

The importance of isolating mechanisms in business strategy is that they are the phenomena that make competitive positions stable and defensible. Many of them appear as first-mover advantages. For example, the first firm to commit idiosyncratic capital to serving a small market segment may gain a stable position serving that segment. From an equilibrium perspective, such events are inherently uncertain. That is, the existence of the market may have been problematic, the technology may have been uncertain, the information necessary to make the early move may have been unpredictably distributed, or by first-mover we may simply mean the first successful mover.

Although isolating mechanisms provide (*ex post*) stable streams of rent,

[18]R. E. Caves, and M. E. Porter, "From Entry Barriers to Mobility Barriers: Conjectural Decisions and Contribed Deterrence to New Competition," *Quarterly Journal of Economics,* May 1977, pp. 241–61.

[19]Ibid., p. 250.

Table 1   Elements of Strategic Position

Sources of Potential Rents	Isolating Mechanisms
Changes in technology	Causal ambiguity
Changes in relative prices	Specialized assets
Changes in consumer tastes	Switching and search costs
Changes in law, tax, and regulation	Consumer and producer learning
Discoveries and inventions	Team-embodied skills
	Unique resources
	Special information
	Patents and trademarks
	Reputation and image
	Legal restrictions on entry

the opportunities to create, "jump behind," or otherwise exploit them must arise from unexpected changes. Without uncertainty there is no wedge between the *ex ante* price of an asset or market position and its *ex post* value. It is the juxtaposition of isolating mechanisms with uncertainty that permits the modeling of heterogeneity in an equilibrium framework.

Table 1 emphasizes this point by also showing the important sources of potential rents. They are essentially unexpected changes in the environment. Thus Table 1 presents a simple theory of strategy: *a firm's strategy may be explained in terms of the unexpected events that created (or will create) potential rents together with the isolating mechanisms that (will) act to preserve them.* If either element of the explanation is missing, the analysis is inadequate.

IMPLICATIONS FOR NORMATIVE THEORY

Are there normative implications of this view of strategy or does it place the fortunes of the firm in the hands of exogenous events and impersonal isolating mechanisms? My view is that there are very real normative implications and they can be based on much sounder theory than much of the currently popular prescription.

First, it should be clear that a firm's stability and profitability fundamentally depend upon entrepreneurial activity. There cannot be a simple algorithm for creating wealth. Still, it is true that some ways of approaching the problem of strategy will be more fruitful than others. In particular, these points deserve emphasis:

1. The opportunities for strategic change occur infrequently, and their timing is largely beyond the control of management. The chance to substantially

improve one's competitive position does not arise out of pricing or advertising tactics, but the recognition of change in some underlying factor.

2. Unexpected events may change the distribution of sales and profits within an industry, acting as windfall gains and losses to incumbents. It is vital that management recognize and take full advantage of these events. The routine component of strategy formulation is the constant search for ways in which the firm's unique resources can be redeployed in changing circumstances.

3. More fundamental shocks act to change the very structure of the industry, altering the nature and magnitudes of the isolating mechanisms at work. Examples of such events are airline deregulation, the advent of small computers, and the impact of oil prices on the world automobile market. In such situations it is usually unclear what the eventual structure of the industry will be. Firms that are lucky or insightful enough to make early commitments to what turn out to be defensible positions can be stunningly successful. The implication is that a developmental theory of industry structure would be of significant value.

4. A critical strategic question in a growth industry is the shape of the final equilibrium. When industry growth is rapid, profits rates are normally quite high, but reinvestment rates that are even higher work to produce net negative cash flows. If firms misjudged the strength of isolating mechanisms in the final equilibrium, the slowing of growth will bring profit rates to below-normal rates; the industry will have functioned as a cash trap. Theory and empirical work on this issue would have obvious normative value.

5. If opportunities for significant shifts in strategic position are infrequent, and if isolating mechanisms create defensible positions, it follows that many firms can ignore strategy for long periods of time and still appeear profitable. As a corollary, high levels of profitability are not necessarily an indicator of good management. If a strategic position is strong enough, even fools can churn out good results (for a while).

6. Because strategic opportunities are by definition uncertain and connected to the possession of unique information or resources, strategy analysis must be situational. Just as there is no algorithm for creating wealth, strategic prescriptions that apply to broad classes of firms can only aid in avoiding mistakes, not in attaining advantage.

7. Because isolating mechanisms act to protect the first successful mover, speed is critical despite (and, in fact, because of) high levels of ambiguity. Good strategy is not necessarily enacted with a high level of initial confidence, although general management may appear confident in order to spur action. If firms wait until the proper method entering a market or producing a product is fully understood it will normally be too late to take advantage of the information.

CONCLUSIONS

The thesis presented in this paper is that it is both possible and fruitful to attempt formal modeling of Schumpeterian, or strategic, competition. One way this can be done is to model entrepreneurs as rational maximizers with bounded knowledge, making explicit the fact that our causal models of the physical and social worlds are incomplete and frequently in error. The model of uncertain imitability is an example of this approach.

By viewing strategy as entrepreneurship that both depends upon and creates interfirm heterogeneity, I have generated a number of propositions concerning the behavior of populations of firms. I have also drawn implications for normative theory. In particular, the area in which progress would be most valuable appears to be the creation of a developmental model of industry structure.

27

Strategy and Shareholder Value: The Value Curve

STRATEGIC PLANNING ASSOCIATES, INC.

INTRODUCTION

Managing for Shareholder Value

Esmark sells off a profitable business, and its stock price rises more than 100 percent. GAF divests about half of its assets supporting its unprofitable businesses, and its stock price jumps by 40 percent. In a similar move, Borden rids itself of its unprofitable businesses, but its stock price, which had risen in expectation of the announcement, falls back to its previous level.

Contradictions? Isolated pheneomena? Or nothing more than evidence of the stock market's reputed capriciousness?

Despite appearances to the contrary, logical explanations do exist.

However erratic the stock market may appear on a daily basis, our assessment of the evidence indicates that, in the long term, the stock market is an efficient and objective appraiser of company value. Within this system, the market's response to the actions of Esmark, Borden, and GAF is neither contradictory, atypical, nor meaningless. Instead, the response suggests a complex set of factors that underlie the determination of shareholder value.

If a company is to direct its strategy without ignoring its obligation to create shareholder value, it must understand the capital market's valuation process. What, then, *are* the critical requirements of the market? And what are their implications for strategic management?

SPA's Value Curve

To address these questions and to provide companies with guidelines for preserving and enhancing shareholder value, Strategic Planning Associates has empirically tested an approach to stock market valuation that synthesizes the work of many financial theorists into the Value Curve concept. The Value Curve addresses the two critical concerns of investors: (1) a company's cash flow, and (2) a minimum return on their investment that compensates them for risk and inflation. This minimum return, which we call the investors' required return, is the linchpin of SPA's Value Curve.

Implications for Profitability and Growth

The Value Curve has strong implications for setting profitability and growth objectives. It clearly suggests that *a company must set its long-term profitability goals to assure the investors' required return*. It furthermore suggests that much of the conventional wisdom about growth is misleading: the fact is that *growth by itself does not add to shareholder value*. Only when a company's long-term return on equity exceeds the investors' required return will the market reward growth in investment. *Otherwise, growth can have a neutral, or even negative, impact on a company's value.*

In sum, growth that does not provide the required long-term profitability can be a misdirected strategy.

Implications for Strategic Management

SPA's concept of the Value Curve provides clear guidelines for identifying and quantifying the cost of "cash traps"—that is, businesses with permanent, negative cash flows that act as a drag on a company's market value. In addition to making it possible to target cash traps for turnaround, harvesting, or divestiture, these guidelines enable a company to identify the businesses that warrant investment and to effectively screen acquisition candidates.

Implications for Financial Policy

The Value Curve has equally powerful implications for financial policy. Thus, the setting of debt and dividend payout levels should be evaluated in the context of the company's strategy and consequently its impact on shareholder value.

There is general agreement among corporate executives that the ultimate objective of all strategies is to create value for a company's shareholders. A critical first step in formulating strategies is to have a better understanding of the rules by which the capital market appears to assign value to corporations. By clarifying these rules, the Value Curve enables a company to establish goals, policies, and strategies that are in the shareholders' best interest. Thus, while the challenge to the creative strategist is still to develop effective strategies, it is crucial to take a shareholder perspective so that those strategies will be *rewarded* by the market.

How the Value Curve can help the corporation accomplish this goal is the focus of this [chapter].

I. TRADITIONAL APPROACHES TO VALUATION

Price-To-Earnings Approach

Traditional approaches to valuation have almost exclusively focused on earnings per share (EPS) as the key variable that drives share prices. And for seemingly good reason: companies reporting high growth in EPS tended to have high price-to-earnings (P/E) ratios. This P/E model of valuation has led many

Exhibit 1.   P/E Is Not a Direct Function of EPS Growth

COMPANY	EPS GROWTH RATE		P/E
	1975–1979	1980–1984*	
TRANSWAY INT'L	13.5%	12.0%	4.8
BORG-WARNER	14.5%	12.0%	7.3
TRW	14.5%	12.0%	8.0
GEORGIA-PACIFIC	11.5%	12.0%	10.3
POLAROID	15.0%	12.5%	12.9

*Source: Value Line

corporate executives to direct their strategies in order to maximize the growth of EPS, believing that this approach would also maximize the company's stock price.

This widespread view of the valuation mechanism fails to account, however, for observed inconsistencies. First of all, the causal connection frequently perceived between earnings growth and the P/E ratio is somewhat tenuous: high rates of earnings growth do not necessarily correspond to high P/E ratios; furthermore, companies with similar growth rates frequently do not sell at the same P/E ratio. The latter point is illustrated in Exhibit 1, where five companies with expected earnings growth of about 12 percent between 1980 and 1984 have P/E

Exhibit 2.   For Cyclical Companies, EPS and P/E Often Do Not Move in Conjunction

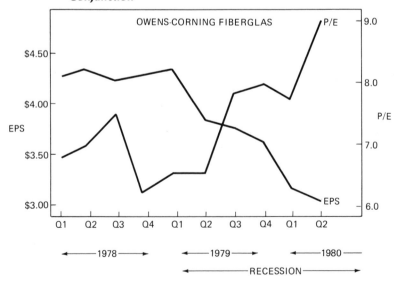

ratios ranging from 5 to 13, hardly a clear correlation. Secondly, contrary to expectation, cyclical companies often experience an increase in their P/E ratios along with a decline in their earnings per share, as seen in the case of Owens-Corning Fiberglas (OCF), a cyclical building materials company (see Exhibit 2). In this instance, OCF's price remained constant while its earnings fell, resulting in a higher P/E ratio. This pattern suggests that a high P/E ratio may merely reflect a temporary decline in earnings. In addition, the fact that OCF's price remained constant during this period of declining EPS implies that valuation is based on *long-term expectations* rather than on short-term earnings performance. Thus, the traditional interpretation of the P/E model does not adequately explain how stocks are priced, and therefore should not serve as the basis for long-term strategy.

Discounted Cash Flow Approach

Newer approaches to valuation, based on the discounted cash flow (DCF) method, are in SPA's view far more representative of the stock market's pricing mechanism. In general, the DCF model derives the price of securities by *discounting the cash flow stream* expected from the investment at the *investors' required rate of return*. The bond market offers a simple illustration of how the discounting mechanism works. Exhibit 3 depicts the pricing of three bonds having identical quality, face value, and maturity date. Each of these has been issued at a different time, and therefore has a different coupon rate. The investors' required return for bonds in this risk class is 13.8 percent for the year 1981. If the coupon rate, or return on face value, corresponds to the investors' required return, then the bond will sell at face value, as in the case of the Indiana and Michigan Electric bond. If the coupon rate is higher than the investors' required return, as in the case of the Ohio Edison bond, investors will price the bond up until the actual return equals the required return. If the coupon rate is lower, as in the case of the Georgia Power bond, the bond will sell at a discount, so that

Exhibit 3.   The Bond Market Illustrates the Discounting Mechanism

BOND		FACE VALUE	COUPON	REQUIRED RETURN	PRICE (JAN. 1981)
INDIANA & MICHIGAN ELECTRIC	1ST 13-7/8S 1987	$100	13-7/8%	13.8%	$100
OHIO EDISON CO.	1ST 15-1/4S 1987	$100	15-1/4%	13.8%	$105-7/8
GEORGIA POWER CO.	1ST 5-1/4S 1987	$100	5-1/4%	13.8%	$64-3/8

the actual return equals the required return. Thus, in the bond market, price is the lever which enables investors to obtain their required return.

The principle in the stock market is the same: the cash flow from equities is discounted at the investors' required return to yield the stock price. But there is one important difference: with bonds, the amount and timing of cash flows (namely, interest and principal payments) are known with certainty, so that given the price, the investors' required return can also be determined. With stocks, however, the investors' required return is more difficult to establish, since future cash flow streams cannot be estimated with absolute certainty, and stock price is the only known quantity.

The Investors' Required Return

Over the past two decades, several firms and academic institutions have been actively seeking workable methodologies for estimating the investors' required return for stocks. Security analysts, on the one hand, and academics, on the other, advocate two of the most frequently used approaches to establish the investors' required return.

The **security analysts' approach** estimates future cash flows for any company based primarily on fundamental research, and determines the implicit investors' required return that would yield the company's stock price. Depending on the cash flow estimate that is used, this approach yields required return estimates for the Standard and Poor's 400 ranging from 14 to 20 percent for the year 1979.

The **academics' approach,** pursued at schools such as Chicago, Sloan, and Stanford, estimates the investors' required return as a function of four variables:

- the real return on risk-free securities such as Treasury bills,
- the risk premium for all equities,
- an adjustment factor to account for an individual company's risk relative to all equities, and
- the expected rate of inflation.

This model has considerable intuitive appeal since it reflects the investors' requirement to be compensated *not only for the risks assumed in equity investment but also for inflation.* For the S&P 400, given historical risk premiums[1] and an inflation rate of about 9 percent, this method yields an investors' required return of about 18 percent for the year 1979, in contrast to the 14 to 20 percent range obtained using the security analysts' approach. Understandably, these widely

---

[1] For an estimate of historical risk premiums, see R. G. Ibbotson and R. A. Sinquefield, "Stocks, Bonds, Bills, and Inflation: Historical Returns (1926–1978)," *Financial Analysts Research Foundation.*

varying estimates have caused considerable confusion and skepticism in the business community.

Resolving the Issue

A practical way of resolving this issue would be to estimate the investors' required return for the S&P 400 by comparing its implicit value, calculated on the basis of a range of discount rates, with the actual price index. Using the S&P 400 enables us to make a reasonable estimate for the cash flow stream: since the S&P 400 is a broad-based aggregate of major companies, its growth potential is unlikely to deviate significantly from the growth forecast for the gross national product (GNP). The GNP growth rate can therefore serve as a proxy for the long-term growth potential of the S&P 400.

To derive an estimate for the required return, we extrapolated the average dividend index at the GNP growth rate. We then discounted the resulting dividend stream at various rates that represent the range of estimates for the investors' required return (see Exhibit 4). The evidence clearly indicates that a discount rate of approximately 18 percent yields an implicit value that coincides with the actual price index. On the other hand, a 14 percent discount rate yields a value that suggests that the S&P 400 is vastly undervalued; a 10 percent discount rate, that it is overvalued. It appears, then, that the investors' required return for the S&P 400, based on the DCF model, was about 18 percent in late 1979.

Clearly, despite general difficulties with estimating future cash flows and debates about the investors' required return, the DCF model has considerable

Exhibit 4.   The S&P 400 Index Can Help Determine the Investors' Required Return

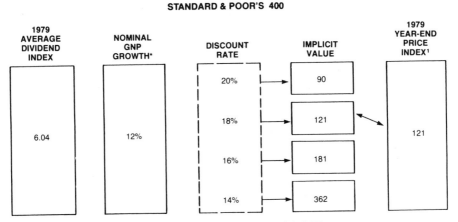

STANDARD & POOR'S 400

*Assumes 8.8% expected long-term inflation at the end of 1979. Current expected long-term inflation is higher

[1] Base year 1970

appeal: it not only focuses on a company's cash flow, which is the investors' primary concern, but also provides a mechanism for factoring in the need to compensate investors for their risks. Its usefulness for managing a company's value is limited, however, because it does not readily identify the key operating and financial variables that drive stock price.

To overcome this problem, SPA has formulated the concept of the *Value Curve.*

II. THE ALTERNATIVE: SPA'S VALUE CURVE

The Model

The Value Curve represents a model explaining the *market-to-book ratio* of a company in terms of three variables:

- the investors' *expectations* of the company's return on equity,
- the investors' *expectations* of the company's growth or reinvestment rate, and
- the investors' required return.

A company's return on equity is itself a function of its return on investment and its debt-to-equity ratio, while its reinvestment rate is clearly affected by its dividend policy. Thus, by linking stock price to critical operating and financial variables, the Value Curve enables companies to manage their strategies from the shareholders' perspective.

A basic assumption underlying this approach is that the company's rate of growth has reached a point of stability. Importantly, even if a company has not achieved this point, the strategic implications of the Value Curve concept are still absolutely valid: thus, regardless of a company's current growth profile, executives can always use the Value Curve concept to extract strategic insights essential for increasing shareholder value.

The Value Curve concept has profound implications for setting profitability and growth objectives.

According to the model implicit in the Value Curve, if investors *expect* that a company will continue to invest at rates below the investors' required return, then its shares will trade at less than book value; by the same token, companies expected to provide returns exceeding the investors' required return will trade at a price greater than book value. For example, if a company is expected to deliver a return on equity (ROE) of 12 percent in the face of an investors' required return of 18 percent, then the model suggests that the shares will trade at a market-to-book (M/B) ratio of 0.5; if, however, the company is expected to deliver an ROE of 24 percent, then its shares will trade at a M/B ratio of 2.0 (see

Exhibit 5.   An Explanation of the Market-to-Book Ratio

STOCK MARKET'S REQUIRED RETURN	COMPANY'S EXPECTED ROE	RATIO OF EXPECTED RETURN / REQUIRED RETURN	MARKET/BOOK RATIO
18%	12%	.67	.50
18%	16%	.87	.75
18%	18%	1.00	1.00
18%	21%	1.17	1.50
18%	24%	1.33	2.00

12% growth is assumed

Exhibit 5).[2] Thus, according to the model, the higher the expected ratio of the return on equity to the investors' required return, the higher the market-to-book ratio.

The Value Leverage Index

We refer to the ratio between a company's return on equity (ROE) and the investors' required return as the *value leverage index* or VLI.

The graphical representation of the relationship between a company's market-to-book ratio and the expected value leverage index for a given growth rate and investors' required return is what we call the Value Curve (see Exhibit 6).[3]

[2]These calculations assume an expected growth rate of 12 percent.

[3]It should also be noted that while the Value Curve model implies a linear relationship between the variables, the curve flattens out below a value leverage index (VLI) of 1.0. The reason for this is discussed on pp. 588–90.

Exhibit 6.   The Value Curve

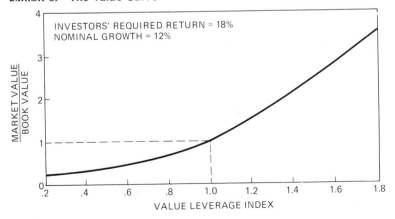

Empirical Evidence

The validity of the Value Curve model is supported, on the whole, by the market histories of hundreds of companies. In general, the correlation between a company's market-to-book ratio and its value leverage index (VLI) holds both across and within industries. For purposes of illustration, we have selected a number of companies across industries with the *same* growth in investment opportunities, and have plotted their observed M/B ratios (vertical axis) against their actual VLIs (horizontal axis), as seen in Exhibit 7. The Value Curve is plotted on the basis of the average investors' required return for the sample. To the extent that companies plot on or close to the Value Curve, the concept is validated.

Since all the companies in the sample have the same growth opportunities, what differentiates them in terms of their market-to-book ratio is their value leverage index. Clearly, as depicted in Exhibit 7, companies at the higher end of the VLI range tend to enjoy higher market-to-book ratios than companies at the lower end, thus confirming the correlation suggested by the Value Curve. For example, Wallace Business Forms, with a VLI of 1.4 enjoys a M/B ratio of 2.3. This implies that, on average, every dollar invested in the past has resulted in $2.30 of value. Scott Paper, on the other hand, with a VLI of 0.8 has a considerably lower M/B ratio of 0.7. The fact that companies in this sample plot on the Value Curve indicates that their current VLIs mirror the investors' expectations for the companies' future. The Value Curve implies, further, that companies create value for their shareholders, as 3M and Philip Morris have demonstrated, by achieving a profitability that exceeds the required return.

The Value Curve phenomenon that was observed across industries is also seen among companies *within* industries. We can see at a glance from the industry sample that most companies in each industry spread out along the Value

Exhibit 7. *Across Industries, the Higher the Value Leverage Index, the Higher the Market-to-Book*

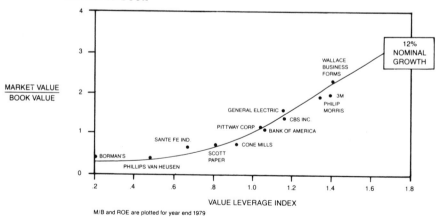

M/B and ROE are plotted for year end 1979

Exhibit 8.   The Forest Products Industry

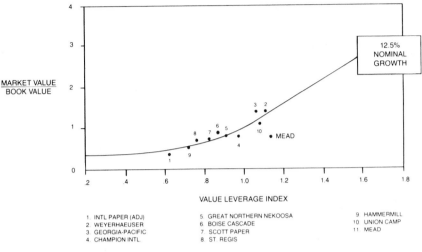

1. INTL PAPER (ADJ)	5. GREAT NORTHERN NEKOOSA	9. HAMMERMILL
2. WEYERHAEUSER	6. BOISE CASCADE	10. UNION CAMP
3. GEORGIA-PACIFIC	7. SCOTT PAPER	11. MEAD
4. CHAMPION INTL.	8. ST. REGIS	

M B and ROE are plotted for year end 1979

Curve, as predicted by the model (see Exhibits 8, 9, and 10). In the Forest Products industry, for example, Weyerhaeuser and Georgia-Pacific command much higher M/B ratios than International Paper and Hammermill (see Exhibit 8). The reason: substantial differences in their value leverage indexes. Similarly, in the Specialty Chemicals industry, the market accords Loctite, Nalco, and Lawter high premiums over their book value; by contrast, Reichhold and Sherwin-Williams tade at a considerable discount from book value (see Exhibit 9).

Exhibit 9.   The Speciality Chemicals Industry

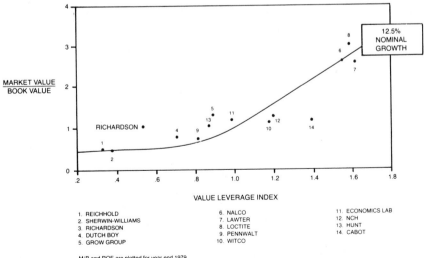

1. REICHHOLD	6. NALCO	11. ECONOMICS LAB
2. SHERWIN-WILLIAMS	7. LAWTER	12. NCH
3. RICHARDSON	8. LOCTITE	13. HUNT
4. DUTCH BOY	9. PENNWALT	14. CABOT
5. GROW GROUP	10. WITCO	

M/B and ROE are plotted for year end 1979

Exhibit 10.   The Food Processing Industry

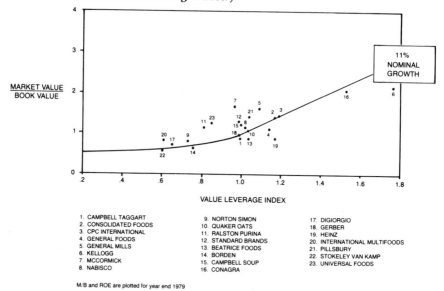

VALUE LEVERAGE INDEX

1. CAMPBELL TAGGART	9. NORTON SIMON	17. DIGIORGIO
2. CONSOLIDATED FOODS	10. QUAKER OATS	18. GERBER
3. CPC INTERNATIONAL	11. RALSTON PURINA	19. HEINZ
4. GENERAL FOODS	12. STANDARD BRANDS	20. INTERNATIONAL MULTIFOODS
5. GENERAL MILLS	13. BEATRICE FOODS	21. PILLSBURY
6. KELLOGG	14. BORDEN	22. STOKELEY VAN KAMP
7. MCCORMICK	15. CAMPBELL SOUP	23. UNIVERSAL FOODS
8. NABISCO	16. CONAGRA	

M/B and ROE are plotted for year end 1979

Again, in the Food Processing industry, companies like Kellogg and Conagra enjoy hefty market-to-book multiples relative to companies with lower VLIs, like International Multifoods and Stokely Van Kamp (see Exhibit 10). These examples from three different industries illustrate and reaffirm the Value Curve concept.

While most companies in these industries plot on or near the Value Curve, some companies, as we can see, do not adhere to this pattern. These include Mead in the Forest Products and Richardson in the Specialty Chemicals industries. The reasons for these apparent distortions are discussed in the following section.

III. APPARENT DISTORTIONS: CURRENT VS. EXPECTED PERFORMANCE

Where a company plots in relation to the Value Curve is a function of *when* you take the picture. A company's valuation reflects the shareholder's *expectations* for its long-term performance. But what the plotted value leverage index captures, for any given year, is the company's *current* performance. If, on occasion, current performance does not match long-term expectations, then a company will not plot on the curve.

This discrepancy may occur in three kinds of situations: when extraordinary events create abnormally high or abnormally low VLIs for a particular year; when the company in question is in a cyclical industry; and when the company is in the high-growth phase of its life-cycle.

(1) Extraordinary events.   When Bankers Trust divested its retail operations in 1979, it experienced a temporary surge in net income which was reflected in an inflated ROE and a correspondingly high value leverage index for that year. The company's market-to-book ratio, however, was lower than expected for the level of VLI, since the market recognized and discounted the extraordinary aspect of the 1979 net income; hence Bankers Trust plotted below the Value Curve in 1979 (see Exhibit 11).

Similarly, International Harvester achieved a 19 percent ROE in 1979—an exceptional performance in light of the company's history. One of the primary reasons for this high return was that the company built up its inventory in anticipation of a strike the next year, resulting in a fuller utilization of capacity. The market, however, remained skeptical about the company's ability to sustain such a high return in the future, and accorded International Harvester a M/B ratio more in keeping with its historical performance (see Exhibit 12). When the strike did materialize in 1980, the company incurred heavy losses that more than offset the 1979 performance, thus vindicating the market's assessment.

(2) Cyclicality.   In the case of a cyclical company like Allegheny Ludlum, the value leverage index has ranged from below zero to a high of about 1.0 over the past decade. However, the market-to-book ratio has remained fairly steady, at a level appropriate for the average VLI over the period (see Exhibit 13). This indicates that investors recognize the cyclical nature of the business and value Allegheny Ludlum on the basis of its long-term performance. Thus cyclical companies like Allegheny Ludlum can plot above or below the Value Curve in any given year.

Exhibit 11.   *Exceptions: Extraordinary Events*

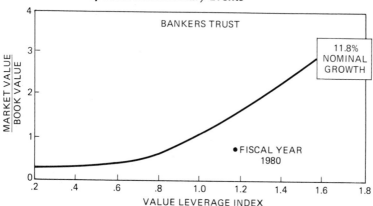

Exhibit 12.   *Exceptions: Extraordinary Events*

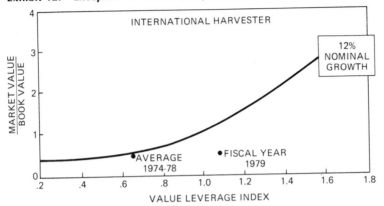

(3) High growth phase in the life cycle.   Companies in high-growth industries, such as Metpath and American Hospital Supply in the Health Care industry, frequently plot above the Value Curve—that is, they trade at market-to-book ratios well in excess of what might be expected given their current value leverage indexes (see Exhibit 14).

These companies currently enjoy high growth opportunities and are investing aggressively to build substantial market share. While such a strategy is very expensive in terms of the near-term ROE, investors clearly perceive that it will lead to very high returns in the future. The market thus accords such companies market-to-book ratios more in keeping with substantially higher returns on equity and, hence, higher value leverage indexes in the future.

Despite these apparent distortions, the valuation of companies tends to ad-

Exhibit 13.   *Exceptions: Cyclical Companies*

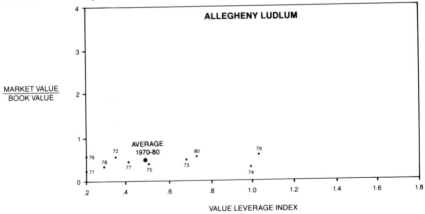

Exhibit 14.   Exceptions: High Growth Companies

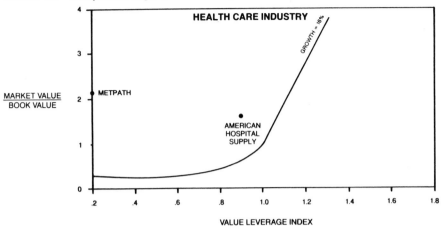

M/B and ROE are plotted for year end 1979

here to the main thrust of the Value Curve: namely, that valuation is based on the stock market's *long-term expectations* for a company as opposed to the company's *current* performance. Therefore, if a company occasionally plots above or below the Value Curve, this does not necessarily imply that it is over- or undervalued. *The Value Curve should not be used, then, as a tool to identify mispriced securities.*

IV. IMPLICATIONS FOR PROFITABILITY AND GROWTH

The Value Curve has tremendous significance for the strategist in setting profitability and growth goals. The key to setting these objectives is a value leverage index of 1.0.

Profitability Goals

A company must set its long-term profitability goals to assure the investors' required return. If it does not, it will trade at a discount from book value. Furthermore, as we saw earlier, a company with a higher VLI generally trades at a correspondingly higher market-to-book value. What this means for strategy is that any gains on an ROE base *near to or above the required return* can create tremendous leverage for increasing shareholder value.

This potential is best illustrated by McGraw-Hill's performance over the

Exhibit 15.   Impact of ROE Improvements: McGraw-Hill

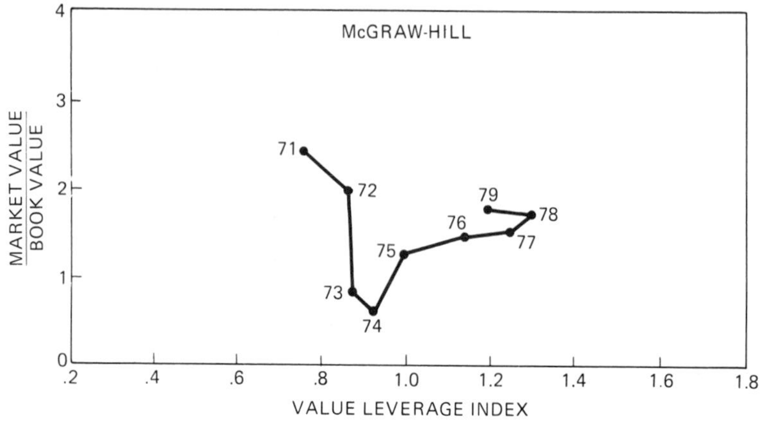

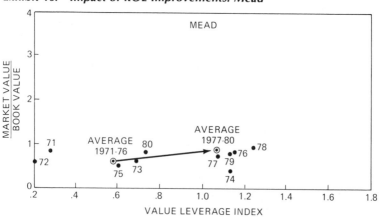

past decade (see Exhibit 15). Although McGraw-Hill's market-to-book ratio suffered a steep decline in the early seventies, in keeping with a general fall-off in market expectations for the entire publishing industry, it was able to effect an increase in its value leverage index from about 0.9 in 1974 to about 1.2 in 1979. This increase led to distinct market-to-book gains—moving from 0.64 in 1974 to 1.79 in 1979. As this case illustrates, even if the market has downgraded its expectations for an entire industry, a company, through strategic management, can counteract this reappraisal by achieving sustainable improvements in its value leverage index.

If, however, a company's value leverage index is considerably below 1.0, then substantial increases in VLI are essential to warrant any significant impact on the market-to-book ratio. Mead's performance over the past decade clearly illustrates this problem (see Exhibit 16). In the early seventies, Mead's portfolio

Exhibit 16.   Impact of ROE Improvements: Mead

contained a large number of low return businesses that severely depressed the corporate return on equity. By systematically repositioning its high potential businesses and divesting its low potential businesses. Mead was able to triple its ROE and, more importantly, double its VLI. In spite of this performance, Mead's market-to-book ratio improved by a mere 43 percent, while McGraw-Hill's 33 percent improvement in VLI was rewarded with almost a 200 percent increase in its M/B ratio. The reason for this difference is that Mead's improvement was effected over the flat portion of the Value Curve, in marked contrast to McGraw-Hill's improvement along the steep portion of the curve.

Growth Objectives

As discussed earlier, the Value Curve concept explains the market-to-book ratio in terms of the investors' expectations for the company's ROE, the company's growth rate, and its investors' required return. Through the value leverage index, we have thus far focused on the return on equity and the investors' required return; as such, we have restricted our analysis to companies that have similar growth opportunities. When we examine companies having *different* growth opportunities, however, we find that growth has tremendous implications for value. SPA's study of hundreds of New York Stock Exchange companies indicates that growth can increase a company's value, can have no effect on it, or can even decrease it, depending on where a company falls on the VLI spectrum. *Thus, contrary to popular belief, the rate of investment growth, by itself, does not drive stock prices.*

When Value Leverage
Index > 1.0

For companies whose profitability is greater than the required return (that is, those having a value leverage index greater than 1.0), a higher rate of growth resulting in a higher market-to-book ratio. This is evident in Exhibit 17, where we can see companies with similar VLIs trading at substantially different M/B ratios that reflect different rates of growth. Eli Lilly, with a M/B ratio of 2.7, and Philip Morris, with a M/B ratio of 1.9, are clear examples of the amount of leverage growth can have on value, when the VLI is greater than 1.0. Although both companies are providing the same return relative to the required return, in the case of Eli Lilly, the excess profitability is being compounded, through higher growth, at a faster rate. Hence the market is willing to pay more for Eli Lilly than for Philip Morris.

If, however, a company's return on equity equals its required return, a higher rate of growth, interestingly enough, has no impact on the market-to-book ratio. As we can see in Exhibit 18, both Clorox and Bell Industries trade at a M/B ratio of about 1.0, despite the vast difference in the expected rate of growth. We can attribute this to the fact that both companies have a value lever-

Exhibit 17.   For Companies with Value Leverage Indexes Greater than 1.0, Growth Has Positive Leverage

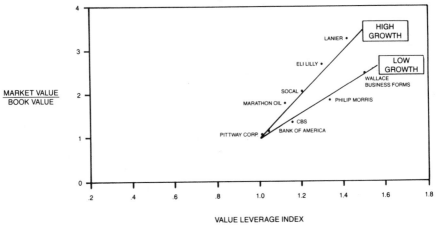

M/B and ROE are plotted for year end 1979

age index of 1.0, signifying that there is no excess return that can be compounded at the higher growth rate to warrant a higher market-to-book ratio. Thus, a growth rate double that of Clorox does not result in a premium market-to-book ratio for Bell, contrary to conventional wisdom about the value of growth. It appears, then, that investors are indifferent towards companies of varying growth when the return on equity equals the required return.

When Value Leverage Index < 1.0

Significantly, for those companies with a return on equity less than the required return, growth can have negative value—a fact that again defies the traditional belief about the effect of growth on value. As we can see in Exhibit 19, Carson Pirie Scott trades at a substantially lower market-to-book ratio than Arizona Public Service, despite having the same value leverage index. This observation can only be explained through the enormous difference in growth rates: since the VLI is below 1.0, the company with the higher growth rate com-

Exhibit 18.   For Companies with Value Leverage Indexes of 1.0 Growth Does Not Affect Market-to-Book Value

COMPANY	EXPECTED GROWTH RATE*	VALUE LEVERAGE INDEX	MARKET VALUE BOOK VALUE
CLOROX	10%	1.0	.99
BELL INDUSTRIES	20%	1.0	1.01

*Source: Value Line (July 1980)

Exhibit 19. *For Companies with Value Leverage Indexes Below 1.0, Growth Can Have Negative Value*

COMPANY	EXPECTED GROWTH RATE*	VALUE LEVERAGE INDEX	MARKET VALUE BOOK VALUE
ARIZONA PUBLIC SERVICE	5.0%	.80	.78
CARSON PIRIE SCOTT	9.5%	.80	.51

*Source: Value Line (September 1980)

pounds, at a higher rate, the "deficit" relative to the required return—hence its lower value.[4]

Floor for Trading

Extending this argument to its logical conclusion, we would expect a company's market-to-book ratio to drop to below zero for a sufficiently low value leverage index. However, as our study of hundreds of manufacturing companies with low VLIs suggests, this does not occur: a floor for trading exists, corresponding, in general, to the company's liquidation value. This is evident in the case of the Tire and Rubber industry, where many companies trade at liquidation values that are substantially higher than the value warranted purely on the

[4]Throughout this section, the implicit assumption has been that the ROE on incremental investment (i.e., the incremental profitability) is the same as the average ROE on existing investments. If this is not the case, it is the *incremental* ROE that should be compared to the investors' required return in order to assess the valuation implications of growth.

Exhibit 20. *A Floor for Trading Exists Corresponding to Liquidation Value*

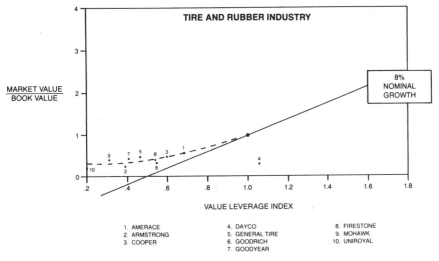

1. AMERACE	4. DAYCO	8. FIRESTONE
2. ARMSTRONG	5. GENERAL TIRE	9. MOHAWK
3. COOPER	6. GOODRICH	10. UNIROYAL
	7. GOODYEAR	

M/B and ROE are plotted for year end 1979

Exhibit 21.   Summary: Growth Is Not Always Valuable

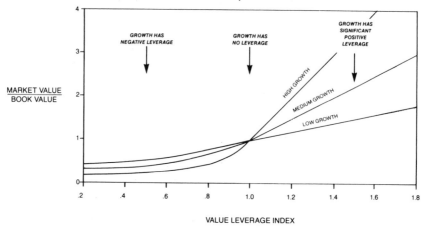

basis of their VLIs (see Exhibit 20). Thus, while the Value Curve implies a linear relationship between the M/B ratio and the VLI, the curve flattens out below a value leverage index of 1.0 in order to accommodate empirical observations about the floor for trading.

Summary

As summarized, then, in Exhibit 21, the market rewards a company's growth only when its return on equity exceeds the required return: otherwise growth has a neutral or negative impact on value. These findings have powerful implications for corporate goal setting. At the very least, they suggest that (a) corporate profitability targets must be set relative to the investors' required return, in order to preserve and create shareholder value, and that (b) growth that does *not* provide the required long-term profitability is a misdirected strategy.

V. NEGATIVE VALUE: THE NEED FOR ASSET REDEPLOYMENT

Positive Corporate Value

When a company is free-standing, it always has a positive market value, no matter how low its return on equity (ROE). Even when its ROE is clearly insufficient to fund its own inflationary growth requirements, a company continues to have positive market value because the market assumes first, that this condition is not sustainable, and second, that some value will be generated eventually either through new management, major restructuring, acquisition by another company, or even liquidation. This view is credible, if only because free-standing companies have no choice but to deal at some point with their cash flow imbalance.

Negative Business Value

Individual businesses within a company are valued similarly, but with one critical difference: unlike free-standing companies, *a business can have negative value* if its profitability is less than that required to sustain its long-term growth (see Exhibit 22). This critical insight makes intuitive sense: whereas a free-standing company must eventually face up to its negative cash flow, a "cash trap"—that is, a business with permanent negative cash flow—can be sustained forever with the proceeds from other businesses having positive cash flows. While, in general, the market may not be privy to the state of affairs of every business in a company's portfolio, cash traps effectively drag down the company's overall cash flow and ROE, and consequently its market value. Thus, by detracting from the value provided by other businesses, cash traps implicitly contribute negative value to the corporation. What this implies for individual businesses, then, is that the Value Curve remains linear over the entire VLI spectrum, and *does not flatten out,* as in the case of free-standing companies.

A simple example of the impact of a negative cash flow business can be seen in the case of Huffy, the nation's largest bicycle manufacturer. In 1975, Huffy was composed of a bicycle business and a lawn mower manufacturing business. A weak performer for years, the lawn mower business had such low profitability that its cash flow was negative even in a low growth market. When Huffy's management announced in 1975 that they would close down the lawn

Exhibit 22.   Businesses Within a Company Can Have Negative Value if Profitability Cannot Sustain Growth

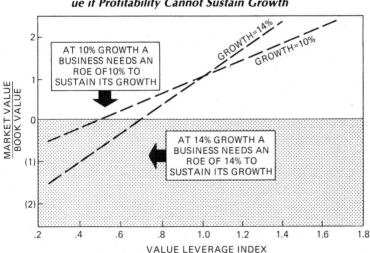

Exhibit 23.   The Market Reacted Favorably When Huffy Closed Down Its Lawnmower Division

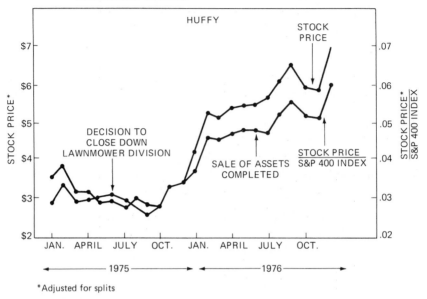

*Adjusted for splits

mower business, the market reacted by doubling Huffy's stock price, a response consistent with the removal of a high negative value contributor and the attendant improvement in corporate ROE (see Exhibit 23).

Exhibit 24.   GAF's Stock Price Rose When the Company Announced Its Intention to Divest Low Profitability Business

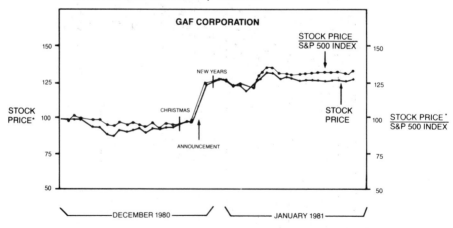

*Indexed at 100 on December 1, 1980

Exhibit 25.   Borden's Redeployment Strategy Disappointed the Stock Market

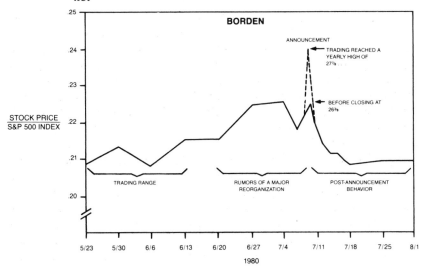

Towards the end of 1980, GAF similarly announced plans to divest almost half of its assets, which had inadequate profitability that acted as a drain on the firm's financial resources and value. Subsequent to the announcement, GAF's stock price jumped 40 percent in two weeks, reflecting the decision to remove negative value businesses from its portfolio (see Exhibit 24).

The Huffy and GAF examples notwithstanding, the mere elimination of cash traps is not sufficient to have a favorable impact on the company's stock price. Of crucial importance is the need to reassure investors on the soundness of management's plan for redeploying the proceeds from divestiture. Borden failed to provide this reassurance in 1980 when it announced a major divestiture of its problem businesses, and simultaneously publicized plans to reinvest those proceeds into businesses, such as PVC resins and ammonia, that are perceived to have low profit potential. Although the company's stock price rose while rumors of a major reorganization circulated, it plummeted again as shareholders perceived Borden's redeployment strategy as the trading of one set of inadequate investments for another (see Exhibit 25). In this case, Borden's decision to exit from businesses with high cost and weak competitive positions was consistent with strategic theory. But the company appears to have fully diluted the value of this move by reinvesting the proceeds in equally unattractive businesses.

Borden's experience illustrates a crucial point for companies that have negative value businesses in their portfolios: that it is not sufficient just to determine the best plan for mitigating the drag of negative value businesses on corporate resources and value, but that *it is equally important to develop a redeployment strategy that will enhance shareholder value.*

VI. IMPLICATIONS FOR STRATEGY

Investment Strategies

SPA's findings about profitability, growth, and negative value have critical implications for a company's investment strategies at the corporate and business levels, as well as for its financial policies.

The linchpin of SPA's Value Curve is the investors' required return. With respect to existing businesses, there are only three broad investment strategy options: invest, harvest, and divest. Traditionally, corporate executives have made their choice on the basis of a business's cash generation potential. According to SPA's Value Curve, however, this is only one of the considerations: how the current and future profitability of each business stacks up against the investors' required return is critical in determining the appropriate investment strategy for any business in the company's portfolio.[5]

Accordingly, a company can classify its existing businesses into three broad categories:

1. businesses that contribute positive value and have value leverage indexes exceeding 1.0,
2. businesses that contribute positive value, but have value leverage indexes less than or equal to 1.0, and
3. businesses that contribute negative value, and whose value leverage indexes are evidently less than 1.0.

Clearly, different strategies are called for in each instance, the appropriate strategy being dictated by an assessment of the strategic potential of the individual business. This assessment would have to focus, in particular, on the attractiveness of the industry and the business's own competitive strength.

Businesses in the first category clearly warrant further investment, unless an analysis of their strategic potential suggests an inability to maintain the value leverage index (VLI) above 1.0. Businesses in the second category warrant additional investment, if an assessment of their strategic potential reveals possible improvement to a VLI in excess of 1.0. Unless a business is already close to a VLI of 1.0, however, realizing such improvements frequently requires the development of a new strategy; clearly, the implementation of that strategy always carries the risk of falling short. If such improvement is unlikely, the business

---

[5]The investors' required return for any business within a corporation can be different from the investors' required return for the corporation as a whole; a business therefore needs to estimate its investors' required return on the basis of its own business and financial risk.

should either be harvested without allocating additional resources, or should be divested, depending on which option provides the greater value. Finally, since businesses in the third category rarely have the strategic potential to effect the dramatic turnaround required to warrant further investment, they become probable candidates for divestiture or write-off.

This investment framework is relevant not only for existing businesses, but also for analysis of new ventures and acquisitions. In the latter instance, however, a more explicit discounted cash flow analysis may be warranted to overcome the limitations of accounting measures.

Financial Policies

As mentioned earlier, a company should establish its debt and dividend policies within the Value Curve framework, keeping in mind the profitability and risk profile of the company's investment opportunities. Here, too, the investors' required return should guide the setting of these policies.

(a) **Debt policy.**   The debt decision for corporations has strategic significance, since debt can be employed as a powerful competitive weapon that could eventually result in greater value for the shareholder. This observatioin stems from the fact that, at any level of return on investment (ROI), the greater the proportion of debt in a company's capital structure, the higher its return on equity (ROE). What this implies is that, in order to achieve a particular investors' required return, a company could lower its minimum acceptable ROI by increasing its use of debt. With a lower ROI requirement, a company could have the flexibility to price below its competitors: lower prices in turn could lead to gains in market share, which in the long run could result in greater profitability, and hence higher value for the shareholder. Thus, from both a strategic as well as a shareholder perspective, a company should recognize that the use of debt can be advantageous.

The advantages of increasing debt levels, however, have to be weighed against the greater financial risk to both the corporation and the shareholder. The higher risk to the shareholder manifests itself through an increase in the investors' required return. Since a company's market-to-book ratio is dependent upon its value leverage index, or the ratio of its ROE to the investors' required return, its debt policy should address the tradeoffs between increasing the return on equity and increasing the investors' required return.

There are, of course, traditional considerations, such as the risk preferences of management and the constraints imposed by lenders, that should also be taken into account in a company's final decision on debt levels.

(b) **Dividend policy.**   Two situations warrant the payout of dividends to shareholders: first, when existing businesses do not have any investment opportunities that meet the ROE hurdle; and second, when new ventures and acquisition prospects also fail to yield the investors' required return. These criteria are in keeping with the principle enunciated earlier, namely, that the pursuit of growth which is not in the service of profitability is a misdirected strategy. According to SPA's Value Curve framework, a company's long-term dividend policy is, therefore, a "residual": it falls out of the company's growth opportunities, profit potential, and debt policy. Deciding whether the distribution should take the form of dividends or stock repurchase clearly depends on the tax situation of the company's shareholders, that is, whether the shareholders prefer dividend income to capital gains.

From the investors' perspective, a company's dividend policy has high information content—for example, investors could perceive a reduction in dividends as an indication of less favorable prospects for the future. It is therefore critical for a company to educate the investment community as to its intentions and goals in setting dividend policy, and, in particular, to communicate its decision in the context of the company's investment opportunities and overall strategy.

The past two decades have seen the impressive development of strategic planning concepts designed to improve business and corporate level strategy. SPA's Value Curve framework does not negate these concepts, but rather enriches, clarifies, and underscores them. The Value Curve helps link business strategy to such areas as asset redeployment, acquisitions, debt capacity, and dividend policy; it permits a company to assess its current portfolio of businesses more effectively; and most important, it provides tangible guidelines for making changes in that portfolio that will result in increased shareholder value.

For the strategist, the game has not changed. The rules of business strategy continue to drive profitability. However, the rules of the capital market *value* that profitability. Linking the two represents a major step toward integrated strategic management.

28

Risk Analysis: Important New Tool for Business Planning

DAVID B. HERTZ AND HOWARD THOMAS

University of Illinois at Urbana-Champaign

Reprinted by permission from the Journal of Business Strategy, Vol. 3, No. 3, Winter 1981. Copyright © 1983, Warren, Gorham and Lamont, Inc., 210 South Street, Boston, Mass. All Rights Reserved.

INTRODUCTION

It is argued here that risk analysis has an important role as an analytic aid in relation to strategic management. That is, firstly to serve as a "lens" for strategic thinking and, secondly, to provide analytic input into the process of dialogue about the organization's strategy options and, ultimately, strategy choice.

Recent contributions to the management literature mention the importance of risk in relation to strategic management in the environment of 1980's and 1990's, at the same time stressing the need for more adaptive and entrepreneurial forms of planning processes. As an article in *Business Week* (June 1, 1981) put it, some of the questions currently being asked by companies are:

1. How many businesses can we afford to be in without spreading ourselves too thin?
2. What particular strengths do we as a company have that will enable us to survive in those businesses?

The strategic focus in business organizations over the last 20–30 years seems to have moved from operations to strategy, and partially back to a focus on basic operations, i.e., understanding and developing individual businesses and searching for those relatively well-defined and less risky segments within which they should operate. Increasingly, managers are being charged with a mission of consolidating and improving their organization's strengths and capabilities, whilst simultaneously taking on as little risk as possible. Clearly, there is often more concern about risk aversion, such as limiting downside risk, than there is about gaining significant rewards. In other words more emphasis is now being directed towards understanding the impact of risk on business strategies.

This paper tries to examine how risk analysis should be used as an aid for the processes of corporate development and long-term portfolio planning.

THE PROCESS OF CORPORATE DEVELOPMENT

There seem to be two fundamental issues in this area. First, the determination of the set of activities to be undertaken. These might include such areas as new businesses, new products, new territories, new subsidiaries, divestment or consolidation of existing businesses and different segments in existing businesses. The second issue is the definition of the organization's need for resources and capabilities which will enable it to carry out the chosen set of activities in an effective manner.

In addressing these two issues, one of the main problems for the organization is that it does not know precisely what will happen in the future. This uncertainty about the future means that the organization must develop planning and allied approaches to handle and cope with the effects of uncertainty. Thus, it must build in flexibility and adaptability in order to cope with contingencies, and also be prepared to anticipate changes both in competitive behavior and in the underlying economic environment.

Another major problem is that the set of activities facing the organization is often quite small, i.e., the "menu" of available options is often restricted. Rather than having the problem of choice amongst a large number of possible options, managers are faced more often with a search process for scarce new opportunities and creative shifts in existing industries. Therefore, managerial thinking increasingly needs to be directed towards more insightful and creative decision-making as a prelude to choice.

Ultimately the organization requires to find that strategic combination of activities which makes sense in both aggregate terms and also at the level of individual business viability. In other words, top managers must develop an understanding of single business strategy and the synergy between it and overall corporate strategy. In order to determine such a strategic combination, the organization's corporate development function must, therefore, generate policy dialogue about the strategic options under active consideration. This can be achieved by viewing the options in terms of a number of alternative analytic "lenses" and thinking processes, about not only the ultimate *corporate development strategy* but, equally importantly, about the building blocks of *evaluation of existing and new activities* and of *examination of possible organizational activity portfolios.*

In the next section, we examine the role of one of the possible set of analytical "lenses" and approaches, *namely* risk analysis. This is discussed in the context of the strategic management of the corporate development process.

RISK ANALYSIS
AND THE CORPORATE
DEVELOPMENT PROCESS

In order to structure the discussion here we will categorize the following main activities in corporate development and, in turn, examine the contribution which *risk analysis* can make in relation to these activities. The set of activities we shall define are: *existing businesses and activities; new activities; portfolios of new activities; a combined portfolio* of new and existing activities, and a *development strategy.*

EXISTING BUSINESSES

In essence, the examination of existing activities requires the definitions of options, the resources they will consume, and the financial resources they will produce. (That is, we assume that the search and problem finding process has already been undertaken.)[1] In this area, therefore, the main contributions of strategic risk and decision analysis are in the areas of *financial planning and forecasting.*

Basic financial planning is a logical extension of the budgeting, cash flow, and funds flow projections normally developed within organizations. The initial stage is usually for the organization to specify its growth targets and acceptable financial policies. For example, a target of, say, 12% annual compounded growth in earnings per share may be suggested, and policies of avoiding overly high leverage may be implemented in terms of guidelines such as the statement of a maximum value for the debt to equity ratio.

Typically, in order to forecast cash flows, we need to develop uncertainty profiles for the underlying key system variables (which might include sales, costs, prices, inflation rates, environmental factors, etc.), during the planning horizon specified for the firm. Such profiles can be obtained using procedures for probability assessment discussed by authors such as Moore and Thomas, Raiffa, Schlaifer, and Winkler.[2]

The next step in the procedure is to gather the assessed probabilistic information into a structural risk-simulation model[3] of the firm's operations in order to determine the cash flow and probability effects of both the individual variables and their combination. Such a procedure will not only develop probabilistic cash flow and budget profiles over the planning period but also, more importantly, assess the sensitivity of the profiles to individual components and combinations of those components. Examples of forecasting approaches, including those which seek to widen the forecasting process to a consideration of more "fuzzy" futures, are given by Mao and Wagner.[4]

Perhaps one of the main problems associated with forecasting "fuzzy" futures is to be able to assess adequately all possible scenarios or future sequences of events which bear upon the forecast, and the assumptions which should underlie the construction of such scenarios. We have found that the probability

---

[1] For a literature review on this topic, see C. Schwenk and H. Thomas, "The Role of Decision Aids in Problem Formulation" (Working Paper, College of Commerce and Business Administration, University of Illinois, 1981).

[2] P. G. Moore and H. Thomas, "Measuring Uncertainty," *Omega,* 3, No. 6 (1975), 657–72; H. Raiffa, *Decision Analysis* (Reading, Mass.: Addison-Wesley, 1968); R. O. Schlaifer, *Computer Programs for Elementary Decision Analysis* (Cambridge, Mass.: Harvard University Press, 1971); and R. L. Winkler, *Introduction to Bayesian Inference and Decision* (New York: Holt, Rinehart and Winston, 1972).

[3] See, for example, D. B. Hertz, "Risk Analysis in Capital Investment," *Harvard Business Review,* September–October 1979, pp. 169–81; and D. B. Hertz and H. Thomas, *Risk Analysis and Its Applications* (Chichester: John Wiley, 1982).

[4] J. C. T. Mao, *Quantitative Analysis of Financial Decisions* (New York: Macmillan, 1969); and G. R. Wagner, "Strategic Thinking Supported by Risk Analysis," *Long Range Planning,* 13 (June 1980), 61–68.

tree, or "fault" tree as it is commonly referred to by engineers,[5] is a very useful aid for structuring the thinking process provided that the assessor is encouraged to think about extremes of the range of possible outcomes. This means that the 1% and 99% fractiles should be carefully considered and the assessor discouraged from "anchoring" his thinking[6] solely around the central values of the distribution. A number of corporate planning groups which encourage *scenario* construction for "futures" have identified this "anchoring" bias around "central" or "status quo"-type values, and have modified assessment to avoid asking directly for the "most likely" scenario. Further, they have consistently reported that decision-makers find difficulty confronting future events, despite the many suggestions, including brainstorming, which have been offered in various literature on futures research and technological forecasting. For an extensive study of real-life futures forecasting problems in a telecommunications situation see Burville and Thomas.[7]

NEW ACTIVITIES
AND PORTFOLIOS
OF NEW ACTIVITIES

The corporate development task in this area is to search for, and identify, potential new prospects and activities for the organization. It should then be possible to discover if there are groups of new activities which it might be sensible to launch and develop simultaneously as one entity.

In developing new prospects, there is a need to adopt sensitivity analysis and sensible screening approaches in order to identify and focus upon the number of options to be considered formally by the organization. A thorough risk analysis of even a relatively small set of options is extremely complex and time-consuming. It is evidently important in practice, therefore, to undertake the maximum amount of preliminary screening in order to reduce the initially envisaged set of options to a minimum set worthy of more detailed evaluation.

Two screening approaches merit practical attention. First, the multi-attributed screening model, the Churchman-Ackoff model,[8] expresses preferences for

[5]See B. Fischoff, P. Slovic, and S. Lichtenstein, "Fault Trees: Sensitivity of Estimated Failure Probabilities to Problem Representation," *Journal of Experimental Psychology Human Perception and Performance,* 4, No. 2 (1978), 330–44.

[6]See A. Tversky and D. Kahneman, "Judgment under Uncertainty: Heuristics and Biases," *Science,* 185 (1974), 1124–31.

[7]P. J. Burville and H. Thomas, *Strategy Planning; A Public Section Application* (London: Croom Helm, 1982).

[8]See C. W. Churchman and R. L. Ackoff, *Introduction to Operations Research* (New York: John Wiley, 1951).

options in terms of linear scoring measures. It has been widely accepted as a use-ful screening device, and in addition has intuitive appeal for managers, largely because it is a simple and easily understood formulation of the decision problem. Second, the mean/variance approach[9] offers a means of screening in an uncer-tain environment. It equates risk with variance of the outcome, and the issue is seen as one of balancing mean against variance. Thus, this approach consists of identifying the "efficient set" of options.

An equally important screen is the sensitivity analysis approach applied to a structural model of the new activity in order to more clearly understand the nature of uncertainty, and its impact on that activity. For a recent example of strategic sensitivity analysis see Dubourdieu and Thomas.[10]

In a recent article Hertz[11] examined the role of risk analysis in strategic decisions about new activities in the R & D area of a high technology corpora-tion. It should be noted that R & D was viewed by the corporate management as the principal base and the strategic competitive edge upon which the long-term growth of the company should be developed. This research example should fur-ther illustrate potential uses of risk simulation.

No area of risk-taking contains more uncertainty than research and devel-opment. In this area, simulation can help the senior executive to see the nature and consequences of possible choices more clearly, to weigh the uncertainties they entail, and to widen margins of safety in R & D investment through project "portfolios" designed to balance risks. For example, a technologically-oriented firm might develop a basic strategy to capitalize on the substitution opportuni-ties arising out of obsolescence. With the aid of an effective simulation model, the nature and probable impact of this obsolescence can be determined, and the ranking of alternative ventures can take into account the longer-term probabili-ties of profitable substitution.

United Aircraft Corporation, for example, employs a variety of manage-ment science methods, including technological forecasting, risk analysis, and systems dynamics models to help it shape R & D strategy. The company starts by identifying potential market needs. It develops a future-oriented scenario de-scribing in considerable detail—technological, economic, ecological, sociologi-cal, and political—the likely long-term environment for its present and potential products. The specific effects of various alternatives on possible market needs is simulated, and from these simulations new product concepts are developed. Thus, a scenario might be developed covering world energy requirements. By modelling the growth of energy demands and the constraints imposed by re-

[9]H. Markowitz, *Portfolio Selection* (New York: John Wiley, 1959).

[10]J. R. Dubourdieu and H. Thomas, "Strategic Sensitivity Analysis: The Case of an Electricity Gen-eration Project" (Working Paper, University of Illinois, 1981).

[11]D. B. Hertz, "Management Science and the Chief Executive," *Management Decision,* 10 (Winter 1972), 253–61.

sources availability and environmental considerations, a series of product needs could then be identified and a structure of product concepts proposed.

The next step is to develop and evaluate alternative R & D programs that could exploit these product concepts. The concepts are assessed from technical, technological, social, and environmental points of view, to produce recommendations for specific new products, along with useful data about their potential uses and market acceptance. These data are then used to estimate the risks of alternative R & D programs in terms of their probabilities of success.

If the success probability of a particular R & D program is high enough to warrant the commitment of the necessary resources, the company then develops quantitative models of the ventures necessary to exploit the new product results. Varying the inputs to these venture models permits management to determine which variables are most likely to influence their ultimate profitability.

Thus, the model building process at United Aircraft comprises a chain of analyses, starting with concept formation based on a broad view of the company's environment, through a series of stages culminating in the hypothetical marketing of a potential product. The next step is to determine, by means of a competitive model, what pricing policy would maximize the net present value of each venture. This model includes such variables as the initial market-share position, the market growth rate, the number of possible competitors, the slope of the manufacturing-cost learning curve, and the product life cycles of present and potential products. A computer simulation is utilized to determine the best policy; uncertainties are then introduced, their effects computed, and the estimated chances of achieving various levels of return charted in the form of risk analysis curves. This enables management to simulate the risks and returns associated with the various proposed product ventures as well as the cash-flow exposure involved at various levels of risk.

The final result is a portfolio of R & D investment possibilities, rank-ordered in terms of the trade-offs between respective rates of return and their risk exposure characteristics. To a company whose future depends upon orderly risk-taking and continuing investment in new product possibilities, such analytical information as an aid for decision-making could spell the difference between indifferent performance and brilliant success.

COMBINED PORTFOLIOS

In a combined portfolio not all strategic decisions, of course, are subject to the overriding uncertainties that characterize the previously described R & D environment. Many decisions, though less uncertain than R & D, are complicated by the necessity of satisfying several organizational objectives.

Any organizational portfolio must, therefore, simultaneously satisfy corporate objectives and also those of the divisions or strategic business units. What is needed, therefore, is a planning structure that enables the organization to organize "top down" and "bottom up" objectives and develop the plans and action programs for achieving the objectives.

Let us consider an example from an international chemical company which shows how a creative family of models can deal both with complexity and uncertainty. The family of models is shown in Figure 1.

The three types of models shown in Figure 1 are:

1. *Risk analyses.* These are used to test the attractiveness of diversification opportunities, as well as the potential range of future profitability for the company as a whole. They provide the basis for setting corporate and divisional profitability objectives, which are basic to the corporate decision-making process and are incorporated in the financial models.

2. *A corporate financial model.* This linear programming model provides "top-down" simulation of the financial consequences of alternative corporate objectives, policy guidelines and resource allocations. It checks their consistency and assesses the potential effects of incorrect or untrue assumptions on overall corporate performance.

3. *Divisional financial models.* These simulate alternative divisional objectives from the bottom up, and test their consistency with top-down corporate objectives. Proposed resource allocations to the division, and division profitability objectives, can be varied in the simulation until an alternative consistent with corporate objectives is identified. (If this cannot be done by varying resource allocations and divisional objectives and/or realistically reappraising their underlying asumptions, then corporate objectives may need re-examination.)

These models have given senior management a clear picture of the interdependencies between corporate objectives and financial policies, and enabled them to test the sensitivity of the results to changes in the assumptions. If corporate objectives turn out to be inconsistent with desired financial policies, the models provide a means of achieving the best possible compromise. In one instance, when a proposed increase in dividend payout threatened an unacceptable increase in external financing requirements, these models enabled the company to develop optimum combinations of equity and debt financing for each of several alternative dividend payout ratios.

Thus, the corporate model (essentially a set of logical statements about relationships with the business) utilizes the computer to balance asset, liability, and capital requirements within a framework of specified constraints and objectives. Meanwhile, the divisional model determines the financial consequences of various patterns of resource allocation, and their respective efficacy for the achievement of divisional profitability objectives. Alternatives within the divisional model are analyzed in terms of risks and probabilities. With the aid of two

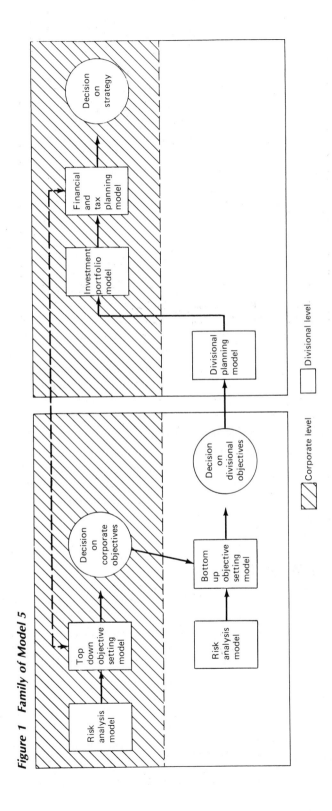

Figure 1 Family of Model 5

Divisional level

Corporate level

605

additional management science models, a set of high payoff projects is then chosen at the corporate level, aggregated in terms of planned investment expenditures, sales levels and cash flows, and finally checked for consistency with corporate objectives. In short, by displaying the entire corporate planning mechanism as a set of interrelated decision models, management science has measurably strengthened the effectiveness of decision makers at the top management level. For the complex, diversified enterprise especially, this last example suggests the possibility of attaining, through creative application of already available management science techniques, a really important improvement in the quality of their strategic decision making. Consider:

> Corporate objectives can be dovetailed with the projected financial results of existing and planned new investment projects.
>
> Investment decisions can be taken according to clearly defined strategic concepts. Projects with real potential for building up products and markets will not automatically be rejected just because high start-up costs make them initially unable to compete with investments in traditional product lines.
>
> Projects can be evaluated for their "fit" within a total portfolio, and overall portfolio performance can be significantly improved by balancing projects combining low return and low risk with projects combining high risk and high return.
>
> Strategic planning can be effectively linked to financial planning. Given pertinent information on the risks, returns, and timing of cash flows for each investment project, the financial planner will have a clear picture of the present and planned structure of assets and will, therefore, be able to make recommendations that better fit the requirements of the company as a whole.

DEVELOPMENT STRATEGY

At this stage, given a preferred portfolio, the organization must find an effective method of implementation which might involve training and skills development, acquiring management, businesses, other firms or finance, and changing existing organizational structures.

Successful decision and risk analyses, however, tend to have common ingredients for success which can usefully be categorized as *organizational, personal* and *technical.*

From the organizational perspective, there must be commitment and enthusiasm from senior managers for the analysis to be both carried out and implemented as a useful aid for problem sensitization and formulation. Many management techniques have failed to gain implementation because they have been pursued by rather isolated specialist groups; the typical operational research department is an example. It is essential for the success of strategic risk and decision analysis that there should be none of this "arms-length" consultancy. Insofar as the approach is mainly one of elucidating managerial expertise, it requires a close personal relationship between analyst and manager (or managerial group). Therefore, there must be sufficient time (and freedom from undue pressure) in which to carry out the analysis, and this factor alone suggests the decision and risk analyses will tend to be most effective in the resolution of those more complex tactical and strategic decision problems in which the typology of the problem structure is "fuzzy," the organizational mechanism for decision-making unclear, and both the level of risk and the scale of the decision significant.

At the *personal* level, managers must understand the broad-brush, strategic thinking flavor of the decision and risk analysis approach and effectively communicate their information needs in decision-making to analysis.

At the *technical level,* the major need in application is to get the manager to fully understand the nature of the problem and thus provide the analyst with an effective "model" of the problem. In particular, the analyst must be clearly informed about the nature of the decision-making process as well as the existence of decision support and information systems so that he can tailor the decision analysis to organizational needs. We have found that the decision tree framework provides a very effective discussion and communication vehicle, analogous perhaps to a "thinking algorithm," for formulating and structuring the essential elements and difficulties inherent in any reasonably complex analysis of strategy.

However, some articles have argued that there are risks in the application of risk analysis.[12] Some of their reasons are noted below:

i. The wrong problem may be solved due to inadequate *problem structuring.*

ii. There are many problems in assessing uncertainty and in getting managers to *confront events in the long-term future,* e.g., the future business environment.

iii. There are organizational problems associated with the implementation of risk analysis. For example, there needs to be a conducive *organizational structure* for strategic risk and decision analysis to be proven effective. In some cases, more decentralized structures (e.g., of divisionalized form with risk analyses carried at the division level) have proven to be effective but the common thread for success seems to be the need for *organizational commitment,* i.e., the approach is not forced by the CEO but through com-

[12]See, for example, E. E. Carter, "What Are the Risks in Risk Analysis," *Harvard Business Review,* July–August 1975; and W. K. Hall, "Why Risk Analysis Isn't Working," *Long Range Planning,* December 1975, pp. 25–29.

munication and discussion its value is perceived. Otherwise, sabotage by managers is likely to occur.

iv. Risk analysis cannot work because it smacks of "overkill," and the technique is generally too sophisticated for the present generation of managers.

v. Risk analysis encourages "tunnel vision," is not adaptive to change and does not eliminate the need for the manager to "take a gamble" once the results of the risk analysis are known (*because* it does not specify a clear-cut decision criterion).

Each of these criticisms can be addressed in turn.

PROBLEM STRUCTURING

We have stressed that problem finding and the search for options are the most creative parts of the decision process. This has also been recognized by writers and consultants in the field[13] and is an increasingly important research area.

We believe, however, that with the simultaneous improvements in decision aids[14] and in the increasing number of real-life case study applications, problem solvers can learn more about, and avoid problems in, problem structuring. However, structuring is an "art," not a science and in a sense practice makes perfect, through a process of "learning by doing."

UNCERTAINTY ASSESSMENT

We believe that the measurement problems in probability assessment can be overcome. Increasingly, the use of interactive programs[15] and fault trees[16] is helping managers to both understand the assessment process and structure complex assessments in a more effective manner.

We believe that most of the problems of probability assessment are not technical but behavioral,[17] and feel that behavioral implications such as task difficulty, analyst-manager interaction, etc. should be carefully considered when

[13]See, for example, C. H. Kepner and B. B. Tregoe, *The Rational Manager* (New York: McGraw-Hill, 1965); and G. M. Prince, *The Practice of Creativity* (New York: Collier, 1970).

[14]See, for example, R. O. Mason and I. I. Mitroff, *Challenging Strategic Planning Assumptions* (New York: John Wiley, 1981).

[15]See, for example, Schlaifer, *Computer Programs for Elementary Decision Analysis.*

[16]See, for example, Fischoff, Slovic, and Lichtenstein, "Fault Trees."

[17]See Moore and Thomas, "Measuring Uncertainty"; and R. M. Hogarth, "Cognitive Processes and the Assessment of Subjective Probability Distributions," *Journal of American Statistical Association,* 70 (1975), 271–94.

designing the assessment procedure for use by a particular individual or group. It should be noted that research is continuing to provide insights into the behavioral aspects of probability assessment.

STRATEGY AND STRUCTURE

Risk analysis clearly needs both organizational commitment and a sound organizational structure for effective implementation. In our experience, if strategic thinking is an acceptable norm within an organization, then strategic risk analysis can help formulate strategies which will typically be understood and subsequently debated for possible adoption and implementation. In our view, structure inhibits strategy whenever the strategy concept and strategic thinking are at variance with the organization's premises and belief systems (which we believe most often provides the driving force underlying the organization's decision processes). Some form of organizational design and restructuring is often necessary in order to implement risk analysis and other strategic "lenses" because this restructuring is often a *signal* for employees about the organization's commitment and belief in strategic thinking.

RISK ANALYSIS TOO SOPHISTICATED—LEADS TO OVERKILL

We feel that this criticism is largely unfounded. Where necessary, training is important both for the managers and the CEO of the organization for them to understand and appreciate the value of the risk analysis process. Such a training can also indicate the types of behavioral biases that commonly occur in judgement[18] and the heuristics (or rules of "thumb") frequently used in judgemental tasks. Thus, training should alert the manager to the nature of risk analysis as a thinking approach for his decision problem, which does not necessarily solve it or even prescribe what should be done. Rather, it encourages communication about the problem and its underlying assumptions, and ultimately leads to a more measured and balanced decision process.

POSTSCRIPT

Strategic risk and decision analysis is not an argument in methodology (in finance or any other area) but rather an approach which can be used to encourage problem solving and strategic thinking about the organization's future decisions,

---

[18]See Teversky and Kahneman, "Judgement under Uncertainty."

strategies and growth paths. It provides a means of structuring complex problems (which cannot be neatly categorized as, say, finance or marketing problems), and uses an extensive set of inputs from all relevant managers, disciplines, and external sources in its attempt to solve problems. It is, therefore, a multidisciplinary approach which enables people to understand strategic options more fully, and to make judgements in an atmosphere of greater awareness and understanding of future scenarios.

Such analyses provide managers with one of several possible "lenses" with which they can view the strategy formulation process. As inputs to this process of policy dialogue, they provide specific and valuable information about the impacts of uncertainty on policy options, and allow managers to judge and examine options in the light of changes in the wider social, economic and political environment and the organization's goal structures.

29

Linking Corporate Stock Price Performance to Strategy Formulation

BEN BRANCH
University of Massachusetts

BRADLEY T. GALE
Strategic Planning Institute

Reprinted by permission from the Journal of Business Strategy, Volume 4, Number 1, Summer 1983, Copyright © 1983, Warren, Gorham and Lamont Inc., 210 South Street, Boston, Mass. All rights reserved.

INTRODUCTION

Every chief executive officer worries about his or her company's stock price. He knows that the investment community uses both the analytical and emotional sides of its collective brain to assess a company. The stock market then assigns high multiples to some companies and lower multiples to others. A favorable stock-market evaluation of senior management justifies attractive compensation packages and keeps shareholders happy.

Stock prices also affect the availability of both equity and debit capital. The diluting effect of equity financing depends on a stock's multiple. High stock prices afford easier access to equity capital and, thereby, tend to reduce the cost of debt capital as well.[1]

A favorable stock-market evaluation also facilitates relatively inexpensive acquisitions and plays a crucial role in defending against takeovers. A stock that is too low relative to perceived value may make the company a tempting target for acquisition specialists. Since the pre-takeover managerial team is unlikely to survive intact, most executives do not want their company's stock price to fall low enough to encourage a takeover.

Everybody talks about the stock market but what can executives do about it? An investor relations campaign may help, but our findings indicate that high multiples are generally based on superior financial performance over a significant period of time.

In this article we will focus on how corporate strategy decisions can improve a company's financial fundamentals, and thereby, its stock price.

First, we develop a model that calibrates the relationship between stock price multiples and corporate financial performance. Then we describe how better business-unit strategy and better corporate-portfolio strategy can allocate resources to improve stock price performance.

I. PICKING THE RIGHT MULTIPLE FOR ANALYSIS

When is a stock price "high"? Viewed in isolation the per-share price reveals almost nothing. One stock at $300 may be very cheap while another at $1.50 could be overpriced. Obviously, stock prices need to be assessed relative to some reference base, such as earnings, past price levels, replacement values or book values.

A good reference base should reflect the resources available to management and provide a basis for comparing a rich variety of successful and unsuccessful companies. In addition, reliable data on the reference base should be available for publicly traded companies.

The P/E (stock price to earnings per share) ratio is a popular measure of

[1]*Business Week*, "The Perilous Hunt for Financing," March 1, 1982, pp. 44–50.

the market's opinion of a particular company.[2] A high (low) P/E indicates a positive (negative) market view of the company's future potential. The P/E ratio becomes virtually meaningless, however, when earnings are negative, very low, or highly volatile. Moreover, rather than poor potential, an individual low P/E may reflect very effective or very lucky management producing atypically high profits in a particular year.

While a rising stock price is generally favorable, the ratio of current to past prices is far from an ideal index of managerial effectiveness. Year-to-year stock price changes depend a great deal on specific stock market conditions. Moreover, an executive taking charge of a depressed company may be able to produce a substantial stock price rise with only mediocre financial performance. An already well-managed company's stock price is, in contrast, much more difficult to enhance.

Per-share replacement value of assets would be an ideal measure of the company's physical resources, but reliable data are rarely available. In contrast, per-share book values (a less accurate index of resources) are available for publicly traded companies. Let us consider the advantages and disadvantages of using book value of equity as a measure of a company's resources.

Relating stock price to book value introduces a number of potential problems.[3] Book values normally reflect historical costs less accumulated depreciation. Most cost-based estimates accurately reflect the market value of recently acquired assets. But the absence of inflation-correction and the mechanical nature of depreciation distort older book values.[4] Similarly, inventory book values are strongly influenced by whether LIFO or FIFO is used. Book values of companies with appreciable assets acquired through mergers will depend on how the acquired company's books were consolidated into the parent. Moreover, some companies' high R&D or marketing expenditures create values (product differentiation) that are not shown on the balance sheet. Finally, many companies have substantial foreign operations whose assets, liabilities and incomes must be converted to U.S. funds. Arbitrary decisions in areas such as these can distort book values appreciably.[5]

For cross-company comparisons, the frequent understatement of book values is less relevant than the degree to which the understatement differs across companies. Comparably understated book values can be appropriately used to measure relative resource availability. For companies having plant and equipment of similar average ages, the inflation impact and thus the degree of understatement should be similar. While the book value of start-up companies may

[2]S. Basu, "The Information Content of Price-Earnings Ratios," *Financial Mangement,* Vol. 4, No. 2, Summer 1975, pp. 53–64.

[3]A. Briloff, *Unaccountable Accounting,* New York, Harper and Row, 1972.

[4]A. Briloff, *The Truth About Corporate Accounting,* New York, Harper and Row, 1981.

[5]A. Getschow, "Slick Account, Ploys Help Many Companies Improve Their Income," *Wall Street Journal,* June 20, 1980, p. 1.

reflect very different degrees of understatement from those of mature companies, asset values of established going concerns should be understated to a similar degree.

Thus, book values should usually provide an acceptable measure of corporate resources. Moreover, book values are available and relatively stable over time. We have therefore selected the ratio of stock price to per-share book value (P/B) as the most effective stock price multiple for cross-company research. The P/B ratio is somewhat easier to work with than the P/E ratio, since, unlike E, B seldom goes near zero or becomes negative.

Many executives like to track their company's P/E multiple. For companies whose earnings are positive and stable, we can easily translate our P/B analysis into a P/E framework (by dividing P/B by earnings to book).

The extent to which price exceeds book reflects the "going concern" value that effective management adds to the resources under its control. A price that is less than book value per share suggests that management is imparting negative value to the company's resources. Because different industries have different opportunities, one would want to view P/B not only relative to the overall market but also relative to an average of the P/B's of companies in similar industries. For example, a P/B of 1.5 might be high for a railroad and low for a high-technology company.

II. CALIBRATING THE DRIVERS OF STOCK PRICE MULTIPLES

Many people can list the principal financial ratios that probably drive stock prices. But we need to calibrate *how much impact* each factor has on a company's multiple. Using public information, we constructed a data set of approximately 600 industrial companies covering the 1968–1981 period. The sample consisted of companies that had a complete set of relevant data and per-share book values appreciably above zero. About half of the PIMS member companies are in this sample. Other companies in the sample are similar to the PIMS companies in size, life cycle stage, and overall degree of profitability. We used this sample to test and quantify hypothesized relations between financial characteristics and stock price multiples.

Over the past decade stock price multiples have fallen dramatically (Exhibit 1). Beginning at a level of 2.3 in 1968, the average P/B had fallen to .9 in the depressed market of 1974. The average P/B recovered to 1.25 in 1976 but has been unable to go higher.

Low current P/B values clearly illustrate the investment community's increasingly critical view of corporate financial prospects. This changed outlook is due in large part to high interest and inflation rates. The nominal cost of capital has risen but nominal profit rates have not kept pace. Since fewer investments are beating the cost of capital, multiples are substantially lower now than they

Exhibit 1 Stock Price Multiples Have Declined Dramatically

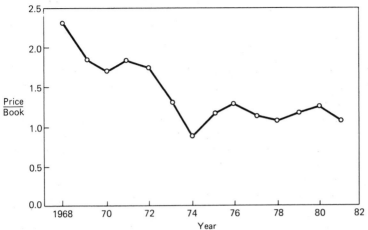

were a decade ago, and managers must now work much harder to achieve favorable stock prices for their companies.

P/B Ratios Differ Dramatically

The distributions of companies by P/B categories for 1968–73 and 1974–81 are shown in Exhibit 2. The percentage of companies achieving a P/B ratio greater than 1.0 has fallen from 75% (1968–73) to 44% (1974–81). In both time periods, the stock market valuations relative to book differ greatly from company to company. Some companies have market values several times their

Exhibit 2 At Any Specific Time, Companies Have Widely Differing Price-to-Book Ratios

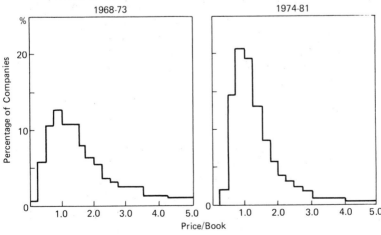

book values, while the market values of others are considerably below book. Why does the investment community assign high multiples to some companies and low multiples to others?

How Are Stock Price Multiples Set?

Investors are sensitive to the fact that stock prices approximate the present value of their expected future returns. Indeed, the appropriate discount rate is selected to make the expected returns stream equal to the current price. Stockholders receive dividends directly, while retained earnings are available to generate future profits and dividends. Thus, both components of profits are important determinants of stock prices.[6] Investors also try to assess growth prospects. The expected future income stream is related to both current profitability (a source of funds and predictor of future profitability) and growth potential.

In addition to a company's stream of expected returns, the rate at which the returns are dicounted also has a major impact on its market value. The relationship between a stock's P/B and the discounted value of its expected income stream is illustrated in Exhibit 3. The expected income stream depends on profitability and growth. The discount rate depends on the overall investment outlook and the company's risk position.

We have identified proxies for each of these P/B determinants. Specifically, ROE is a useful indicator of profitability; investment growth and R&D intensity reflect growth expectations and the average annual P/B is a proxy for the investment environment. While the firm's stock market beta serves as an ideal

[6]M. Nerlove, "Factors, Affecting Differences Among Rates of Return on Investments in Individual Common Shares," *Review of Economics and Statistics,* August 1968, pp. 312–31.

Exhibit 3 Key Determinants of Stock Prices

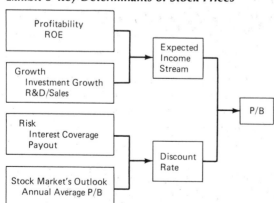

theoretical measure of risk, in practice we find interest coverage and dividend payout to work better.

Profitability Drives Stock Prices

The impact of profitability on stock prices is calibrated in Exhibit 4. Investors are particularly interested in *future* profitability. Current profit rates do, however, provide an indication of profit potential.[7] Companies with low current returns on equity (ROE) generally have very low P/Bs while those with higher ROEs have higher P/Bs. For example, the average P/B for companies with ROEs between 5 and 10 percent is .67, while for companies with ROEs of 20–25 percent the average P/B is 1.79.

The price/book multiple can be expressed as the price/earnings multiple times the ratio of earnings/book:

$$\frac{Price}{Book} = \frac{Price}{Earnings} \times \frac{Earnings}{Book}$$

OR

$$\frac{Price}{Book} = \frac{Price}{Earnings} \times \frac{Earnings}{Book}$$

[7] *Ibid.*

Exhibit 4 Profitability Drives Stock Prices

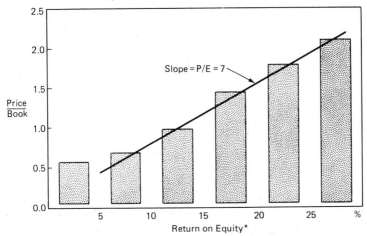

*Net Income/Common Shareholder Equity

In the context of Exhibit 4, the *slope* of the relationship between P/B and ROE is the price/earnings multiple. The slope shown in Exhibit 4 suggests a P/E of about 7 during 1974–81.

Growth Boosts Stock Prices Multiples

Exhibit 5 quantifies the effect of growth on stock prices.[8] Companies are better able to utilize their resources and sell their output for attractive prices when demand is pressing against their existing capacity. Usually increased spending on plant and equipment either forecasts further demand growth or reflects unsatisfied current demand. Accordingly, the stock market infers increases in future sales and profits from past investment growth.

Acting together the effect of growth and profitability is dramatic (Exhibit 6). Companies that are both very profitable and growing rapidly command P/B multiples which are on average about three times as large as those of low-profit slow-growth companies. Moreover, the positive effect of growth is greatest when ROE is high (.7 vs .3). Future growth is likely to yield a higher return where current profitability is high.

The price/earnings multiple (the slope of P/B vs ROE) for rapid-growth companies is much greater than the P/E for slow-growth companies.

[8]C. Ella, "After a Long Hiatus Some Analysts Again Stress Growth Stocks," *Wall Street Journal,* June 3, 1977, p. 29; C. Ella, "Large Growth Stocks Are Returning to Favor with Many Investors," *Wall Street Journal,* January 25, 1979, p. 1.

Exhibit 5 Growth Boosts Stock Prices

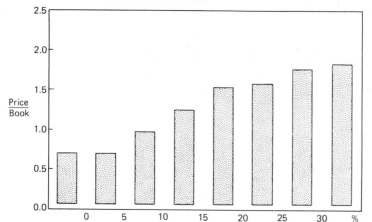

*Average annual percentage change in investment over 5 years. Investment is total assets minus current liabilities other than short-term debt.

Exhibit 6 Growth Boosts Stock Prices, Especially When Profitability Is High

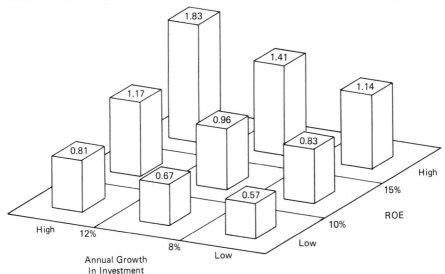

R&D Boosts Stock Prices Especially When Profits Are High

Taken by itself R&D intensity appears to have little or no effect on stock prices. A bar chart of P/B versus R&D sales (not shown) is essentially flat. When profitability effects are considered, however, R&D's stock price impact is clearly revealed (Exhibit 7). The stock price effect of R&D on P/B is particularly pronounced for profitable companies. As R&D intensity increases average P/Bs increase from 1.35 to 2.00 in high-ROE companies compared with an increase from .59 to only .73 for low-ROE companies.

The market views high R&D activity as an indicator of future growth-potential.[9] As the slopes of P/B versus ROE in Exhibit 7 indicate, the price earnings multiple is much greater for high-tech companies.

[9]*Business Week,* "Using R&D as a Guide to Corporate Profits," May 29, 1978, p. 75; C. Ella, "Ratio of Stock Price to Firm's R&D Spending on Per-Share Basis Found to Be a Useful Gauge," *Wall Street Journal,* June 19, 1980, p. 47; B. Branch, "Research and Development Activity: A Distributed Lag Analysis," *Journal of Political Economy,* September–October 1974; and B. Branch "Research and Development and Its Relation to Sales Growth," *Journal of Economics and Business,* Winter 1973, pp. 107–11; F. Scherer, "Corporate Investment Output, Profit and Growth," *Journal of Political Economy,* June 1965, pp. 190–97; W. Leonard, "Research and Development in Industrial Growth," *Journal of Political Economy,* March–April 1971, pp. 232–56; A. Severn and M. Laurence, "Direct Investment Research Intensity and Profitability," *Journal of Financial and Quantitative Analysis,* March 1974, pp. 181–93; J. Doyle and F. Navratil, "The Effects of Expectations on Industrial R&D Activity: Evidence Based on the Efficient Market Hypothesis," *Nebraska Journal of Economics and Business,* Autumn 1981, pp. 17–32.

Exhibit 7 R&D Boosts Stock Prices, Especially When Profitability Is High

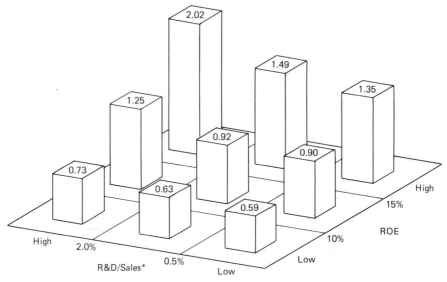

*R&D Expense/Net Sales

When Profitability is High, Payout Boosts Stock Prices

The payout story is similar to that for R&D intensity. Viewed in isolation, payout has little apparent stock price impact, but when profit effects are considered, its impact becomes clear (Exhibit 8). Average P/B rises from 1.5 to 1.9 with increased payout for high-profit companies and only from .60 to .66 for the low-ROE group.

Investors often view a high payout as reflecting management confidence in future profitability. Since managers are reluctant to set an unsustainable dividend rate, the market generally interprets a high payout as a signal that the current profit level is unlikely to decline.[10] When, however, the overall profit rate is low, a high payout may signal a possible decline in the dividend rate.

[10]C. Kwan, "Efficient Market Tests of the International Content of Dividend Arrangements: Critique and Extension," *Journal of Financial and Quantitative Analysis,* June 1981, pp. 193–206; J. Aharony and I. Swary, "Quarterly Dividend and Earnings Announcements and Stockholders' Returns: An Emperial Analysis," *Journal of Finance,* March 1980, pp. 1–12; "Dividend Announcement Security: Perforamnce and the Capital Market Efficiency," *Journal of Finance,* December 1972, p. 1006; R. Watts, "The Information Content of Dividends," *Journal of Business,* April 1973, pp. 191–211.

Exhibit 8 When Profitability Is High, Payout Boosts Stock Prices

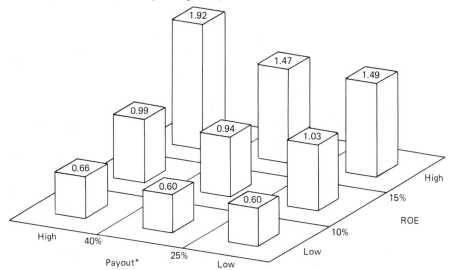

*Dividends per Share/Earnings per Share

A Low Interest Coverage
Reduces Stock Prices

A high level of interest coverage (earnings before interest and taxes relative to the interest obligation) implies a low default-risk.[11] The stock market tends to pay a higher price for this protection. Low interest coverage tends to reduce P/B (Exhibit 9). The interest coverage may be low because ROE is low or because debt is high relative to equity.

Debt's role is complex. On the one hand, leverage may raise ROE and therefore tend to increase P/B. On the other hand, debt imposes a legal obligation to pay interest whether or not the company earns a profit. This risk increases with the firm's debt-load as measured by interest coverage.

[11]James O. Horrigan, "The Determination of Long-Term Credit Standing with Financial Ratios," *Empirical Research in Accounting: Selected Studies,* 1966, Supplement to *Journal of Accounting Research,* Vol. 4, pp. 44–62; Thomas F. Pogue and Robert W. Soldofsky, "What's in a Bond Rating?" *Journal of Financial and Quantitative Analysis,* Vol. 4, No. 2, June 1969, pp. 201–208; Richard R. West, "An Alternative Approach to Predicting Corporate Bond Ratings," *Journal of Accounting Research,* Vol. 8, No. 1, Spring 1970, pp. 118–25; and George E. Pinches and Kent A. Mingo, "A Multivariate Analysis of Industrial Bond Ratings," *Journal of Finance,* Vol. 28, No. 1, March 1973, pp. 1–18; A. Bulkaou, "Industrial Bond Ratings: A New Look," *Financial Management,* Autumn 1980, pp. 44–51; M. Backer and M. Gosman, "The Use of Financial Ratios in Credit Downgrade Decisions," *Financial Management,* Spring 1980, pp. 53–56.

Exhibit 9 A Low Interest Coverage Reduces Stock Prices

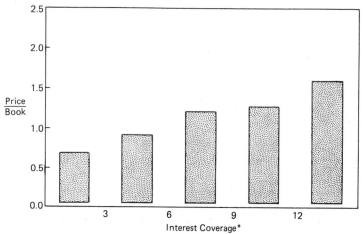

*Profits before interest and taxes divided by interest obligations

Interpreting the Drivers of P/B

The findings described above should be interpreted cautiously. While the stock market does tend to reward companies for high ROE, growth, R&D intensity, payout and interest coverage, the policy implications of these relations are less clear. For example, a company that sought to increase its growth at the expense of its ROE might adversely affect its stock price. Moreover, the tradeoffs between R&D intensity and ROE; payout and growth, etc., should not be ignored.

Investors do not reward companies for high ROE, interest coverage, R&D intensity, or payout per se. Rather, such characteristics are preferred only when they are viewed as forecasters of a favorable future.

III. WHAT P/B IS NORMAL (OR PAR) FOR MY COMPANY

When asked about the stock price performance of their company, most executives will focus on performance relative to competitors (industry peers). Industry peers have much in common. They buy similar raw materials, use similar technologies and sell the same kinds of products to the same group of customers. But there can be important financial differences among competitors. And these financial differences should lead us to expect different P/B ratios within a group of industry peers.

To obtain a benchmark based on industry peers, we just calculate the aver-

Exhibit 10   What P/B is Normal (or Par) for Your Company? (simplified illustration)

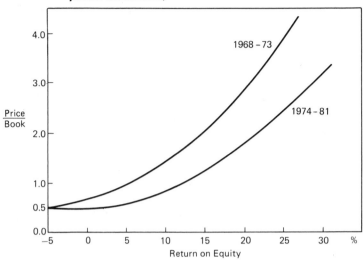

age P/B of companies that have similar raw materials, operations, products and customers. What are *financial peers?* How can we obtain a P/B benchmark based on financial peers?

Financial peers are companies that have a similar profile or financial fundamentals such as ROE, growth, R&D intensity, payout, and interest coverage.

We could develop a simplified P/B benchmark using only the P/B vs ROE relation. One merely identifies the P/B profile or financial fundamentals such as ROE, growth, R&D value which on average is associated with a particular company's ROE (Exhibit 10). This approximation works best if ROE has been stable over time and therefore is likely to remain stable in the future. Note, however that the relationship between P/B and ROE has shifted over time with the investment environment. Thus, in the 1968–73 period a much higher P/B tended to be associated with a given ROE than in the more recent 1974–81 period.

Moreover, a simplified P/B benchmark based solely on ROE does not reflect differences in growth rates among competitors. To obtain a P/B benchmark based on both profitability and growth one could look back at Exhibit 6, and plug in one's ROE and growth rate. Ideally, however, a P/B benchmark for financial peers should be based on the joint effects of *all* the key drivers of stock price multiples.

The P/B Model

To establish a performance standard that takes account of all the key drivers of P/B, we must step up from a *one* (bar chart) or *two* (cross table) dimensional relationship. Stock prices relative to book values can be explained by a model that includes variables related to a company's expected earnings stream and risk. More specifically the market focuses on profitability (measured by ROE), growth (measured by investment growth and R&D intensity), risk (measured by interest coverage and payout) and the investment community's outlook (measured by the average price/book). The resulting par P/B model explains about 70% of the P/B dispersion across companies.

Some people might wonder why beta is excluded from the P/B model. Betas are indeed a useful theoretical concept. The relation between beta and the rate of return from holding a stock is hypothesized to be positive because investors are risk averse and need to be compensated for the higher risk that a high beta indicates. In theory, the P/B mutliple should be low when beta is high because a higher beta implies higher risk and therefore a greater discount rate. When added to the equation however the estimated beta variable not only added little explanatory power but also had a positive sign which is counter to the theoretical relationship.

Several reasons may explain why beta did not have the expected impact on the P/B multiple. First, beta estimates are notoriously unreliable.[12] Second, the risk variables that are included in the model do have the correct relationship and are statistically significant. Apparently the investment community focuses on payout and especially on interest coverage when assessing the riskiness of companies.

Relative Importance of Stock-Price Determinants

Our focus is not on the overall level of P/B for the market as a whole, but rather on the differences in P/B across companies. We therefore estimated the P/B model on data from the 1974–81 time period, when the average P/B was fairly close to 1.0 in each year. Consequently, if only the market cycle variable is used as a model, only 5 percent of the dispersion in P/B multiples across companies is explained. The percentage explained rises to 48 (an increase of 43) when ROE alone is added. Adding the growth variables raises the percent of dispersion explained to 66 (a further increase of 18). The full P/B model has an explanatory power of 70 percent. Clearly the full model reveals much more about stock prices than ROE taken alone.

Establishing P/B Benchmarks

Our P/B model can be used to establish a "par" or normal stock price value. That is, we can compute "par P/B" for a particular company, which reflects its fundamentals and the investment community's overall outlook. This par value is designed to indicate how the stock market would generally value a company with similar fundamentals and in the current investment environment.

[12] T. Copeland and J. Weston, *Financial Theory and Corporate Policy,* Reading, Mass., Addison-Wesley Publishing Co., 1979, pp 272–326.

Exhibit 11 Stock Price Multiples of Food Manufacturing Companies

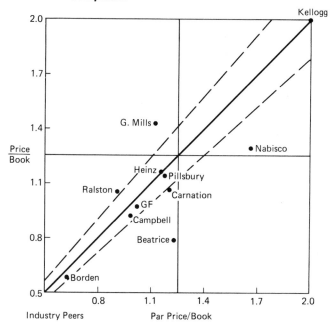

While some insights can be derived from a comparison against financial peers, others come from a comparison against industry peers. We can, however, take the best of both approaches, developing par P/Bs for all the industry peers and plotting them versus their actual P/Bs.

The 1981 year-end stock price multiples of eleven major food manufacturing companies are shown in Exhibit 11. Most of the companies fall along the 45 degree line where actual P/B equals par. They range from Borden, the least profitable company in 1981, to Kellogg, which was the most profitable by a considerable margin. Apparently the food companies taken as a group were neither in favor nor out of favor with the market.

General Mills was priced above its par. Beatrice Foods and Nabisco Brands were priced below their pars. Possibly the market prefers General Mills' largely internal growth over Beatrice and Nabisco's acquisition oriented growth.

Tracking a Company's Stock Price Performance

The par P/B model can also be used to diagnose your company's historical stock price performance or to simulate future stock price trends (based on projected financial fundamentals). Over the last ten years (72–81) the Dexter Corporation's stock price clearly outperformed the market (Exhibit 12). To under-

Exhibit 12 Dexter's Stock Price Outperformed the Market

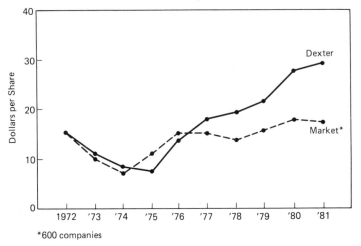

*600 companies

stand why, we can track Dexter's P/B multiple (Exhibit 13) and its rate of growth in book value.

Dexter's P/B moved well above the market during the mid 1970s. The major reason behind Dexter's improved multiple was its increased ROE (from 11% to 16%). This improved profitability drove up Dexter's *par* P/B relative to the market P/B.

Historically Dexter's *actual* P/B has tracked (about .3 to .4) below its par. Two possible reasons for this are Dexter's small size relative to other NYSE companies and its great diversity which makes Dexter difficult to compare

Exhibit 13 Dexter's P/B Has Tracked Below Par

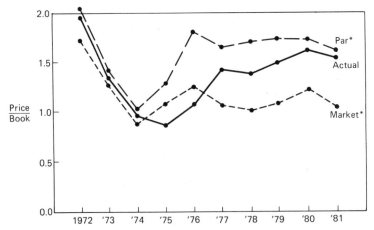

*5-year growth rate of investment, adjusted in 1977 to reflect acquisition of Mogul

against a set of industry peers. Different financial analysts (*Value Line, Media General,* F. Eberstadt) assess Dexter against *different* sets of "industry" peers!

Dexter's favorable stock price performance was due not only to its improved P/B multiple, but also to its above average growth in equity (about 15% per year compared to the market average of 10%). Dexter's strong performance stems from management's dual emphasis on careful strategic planning and rigorous financial control.[13]

How to Interpret Par P/B

Par P/B is the P/B value that a company with a particular set of fundamentals operating in the current investment environment would normally achieve. That is, with a specific current profitability, growth potential, risk and investment environment, one should expect a P/B approximately equal to the corresponding par P/B derived from the model.

The investment environment reflects the consensus view of the aggregate profit outlook and how those expected profits should be discounted. The investment community's outlook is related to current and expected future interest rates, inflation rates, energy prices, domestic and international competitive pressures, tax rates, environmental policy, rates of technological change, raw material prices, wage rates, productivity growth, regulatory policy and a host of other factors.

Average P/B multiples tend to approximate par (Exhibit 14). Companies with low pars tend to have low P/Bs and high-par companies tend to have high

[13]Worth Loomis, "Strategic Planning in Uncertain Times," *Chief Executive,* Winter 80–81.

Exhibit 14 On Average, Companies Cluster Near Their Par P/B

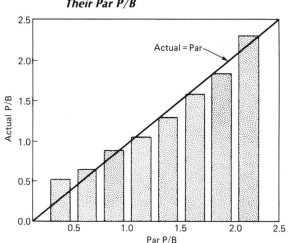

P/Bs. Note, however, that where par P/Bs are very low, average actual P/B is above par. Most companies are valued on a going-concern or income producing basis which par seeks to reflect. When, however, such values are quite low relative to their assets, investors may place more weight on liquidation values.[14] Investors apparently believe that, on average, even the assets of low-performance companies are worth at least half of their book values.

Why Do Some P/Bs Differ Appreciably from Par?

If all stock prices behaved exactly as our model predicted, each company's actual P/B would always equal its par P/B. While the average ratio of actual to par P/B is unity, the dispersion about this average is considerable (Exhibit 15).

Forty-six percent of the actual P/B values differ from their par values by more than 25%. Indeed, ten percent are more than 50% above their pars and four percent are more than 50% below. Clearly we would like to know more about those cases where the actual and par P/B values differ appreciably.

Actual and par P/B may differ for any of four reasons. First, the *par* P/B may fail to reflect some future development which the stock market anticipates. A par estimate based on past data can only reflect expectations that are embedded in the company's historical record. The investment community, in contrast, is free to take account of any relevant information.[15]

Second, the *actual* stock price may be too high or too low because of ran-

[14]*Business Week,* "When a Company Is Better Dead," *op. cit.*

[15]B. Malkiel and J. Cragg, "Expectation and the Structure of Share Prices," *American Economic Review,* September 1970, pp. 601–617.

Exhibit 15 Some P/Bs Differ Appreciably from Par

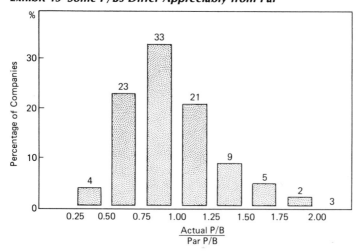

dom or transitory events or, more interestingly, because the market is simply misjudging the company's fundamentals. Thus a very large buyer or seller's trading may move a company's price away from par.[16] Similarly a brokerage recommendation or story in the financial press may cause the stock to be temporarily displaced from par.[17] Sometimes the investment community may seem to get carried away and then later become disgusted with an entire industry (genetic engineering, gambling, high tech, etc.)[18] Eventually such temporary influences fade away.

Third, as mentioned above, investors may value a stock on its liquidation value if that value substantially exceeds the company's going-concern (i.e., par) value. Fourth, errors in the par estimate may be due to shortcomings in the model's structure or in relevant input data. That is, the par estimate (based on relatively few variables) may neglect some factors which are important to some company's P/Bs or it may rely on misleading accounting numbers.

Large differences between actual and par P/B often result from a temporary disequilibrium or from the market anticipating changes in fundamentals. If this is the case, the difference should tend to narrow over time. If, in contrast, a difference results from liquidation value exceeding going-concern value or an inaccurate par estimate, the deviation should persist.

What Happens When Actual and Par P/B Differ Appreciably?

Large differences between actual and par P/B *do* tend to narrow over time (Exhibit 16). Those companies whose P/B values were furthest *below* par in the preceding year had, on average, the largest positive *increases* in their actual to par ratio. Similarly, those companies whose actual values *exceeded* their pars by the greatest amount, tended to have the largest *decrease* in their actual to par ratios.[19]

The tendency for the actual and par (P/Bs) to move closer together over time can be caused by changes in either the actual or the par values. Both tendencies have been observed. The movement of pars toward the actual levels im-

[16]L. Dann, D. Mayers, and R. Rabb, "Trading Rules, Large Blocks and the Speed of Adjustment," *Journal of Financial Economics,* January 1977, pp. 3–22.

[17]C. Bidwell and R. Kolb, "The Impact and Value of Broker Sell Recommendations," *Financial Review,* Fall 1980, pp. 58–68; D. Morse, "*Wall Street Journal* Announcements and the Securities Markets," *Financial Analyst Journal,* March/April 1981, pp. 69–76.

[18]J. Kessler, "The Wilted Beauties of High Tech," *Financial World,* June 1, 1982, pp. 16–20.

[19]Companies in intermediate ranges experienced intermediate changes. Note, however, that the *average* changes in the intermediate ranges include large individual positive and negative changes. That is, some companies with near-Par P/Bs moved substantially above or below par to repopulate the extreme ranges of performance relative to par (as the prior-period extremes tended to move in toward par).

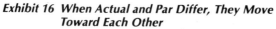

Exhibit 16 *When Actual and Par Differ, They Move Toward Each Other*

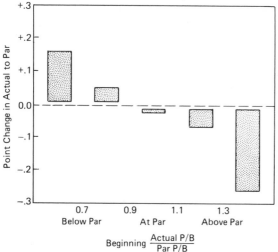

plies that the market was anticipating changes in company-fundamentals while the move of the actual toward par suggests that the market was mispricing.

The model explains why P/B is high or low for most companies. And for companies where the difference between actual and par is large, the difference tends to narrow in subsequent years. Thus, both the static and the dynamic relations between the actual and par values of P/B illustrate the model's accuracy.

IV. WHAT CAN MANAGEMENT DO TO IMPROVE ITS COMPANY'S STOCK PRICE?

Management can take three basic kinds of action to change its company's financial fundamentals and thereby improve its stock price. First, at the business-unit level, managers can use knowledge of the links between strategic position and performance to improve the profitability and growth prospects of individual business. Second, corporate-level portfolio strategy can channel incremental investment to businesses that have a high probability of beating the cost of capital. Third, corporate financial policy can affect the investment community's perception of a company's risk profile.

Business-Unit Strategy

Current profitability (which is taken as a forecast of future profit rates) as measured by ROE is a particularly important stock price determinant. A company's ROE depends, of course, on the profitability of its component business units. ROE itself is the product of the company's Return on total investment (ROI) and the ratio of investment to equity (capital structure). And corporate-level ROI equals the average of business-unit ROIs weighted by their proportion of the company's investment.

To improve business-unit profitability and thereby enhance the corporate stock price a company can take at least three steps. First, the company can educate line management on the links between a business unit's strategic position (its relative product quality, market share, investment intensity, productivity, etc.) and its profit performance.[20] The PIMS data base has shown that some two-dozen factors descriptive of a business and of its competitive environment account for 70% to 80% of the observed differences in profit performance across diverse business units. Second, enlightened managers can reposition weak business units to improve the odds of their beating the cost of capital. The odds of beating the cost of captial when investing in well-positioned business units are 2 or 3 times greater than for investments made in poorly positioned business units. Third, business units can improve productivity and operating effectiveness to realize their full potential.

A company's growth rate depends on the performance of its component businesses and on its acquisitions and dispositions. A business unit's growth rate depends largely on the growth of its served market and its market-share growth (Exhibit 17). To enhance growth a business unit needs to develop a high quality product for rapid-growth segments of the market.

Better strategic positioning by business units can help the corporate stock price in two ways. First, as we have just discussed, improved strategic position tends to improve the corporate profitability and growth rate. Second, as demonstrated in a pioneering research study by Sidney Schoeffler:

> The market pays a premium price for corporate profits that are secure, in the sense of being grounded in the "fundamentals" of a company's businesses. For example, wide profit margins coming from large-share businesses earn a higher P/B than equivalent margins coming from small-share businesses. The market appears to know that wide margins occurring in small-share businesses are more likely to decline than equivalent margins in large-share businesses.[21]

Investors pay a premium for quality earnings that are based on a substantial competitive advantage.

[20]Robert D. Buzzell, Bradley T. Gale, and Ralph G. M. Sultan, "Market Share—A Key to Profitability," *Harvard Business Review,* January/February 1975, pp. 97–106; Bradley T. Gale, "Can More Capital Buy Higher Productivity," *Harvard Business Review,* July/August 1980, pp. 78–86; Bradley T. Gale and Richard Klavans, "Formulating a Product Quality Strategy," The Strategic Planning Institute, Cambridge, Mass., 1982.

[21]Sidney Schoeffler, "Impact of Business Strategy on Stock Prices," PIMSLETTER No. 20, The Strategic Planning Institute, Cambridge, Mass., 1980.

Exhibit 17 Linking Corporate Stock Price to Business-Unit Profitability and Growth

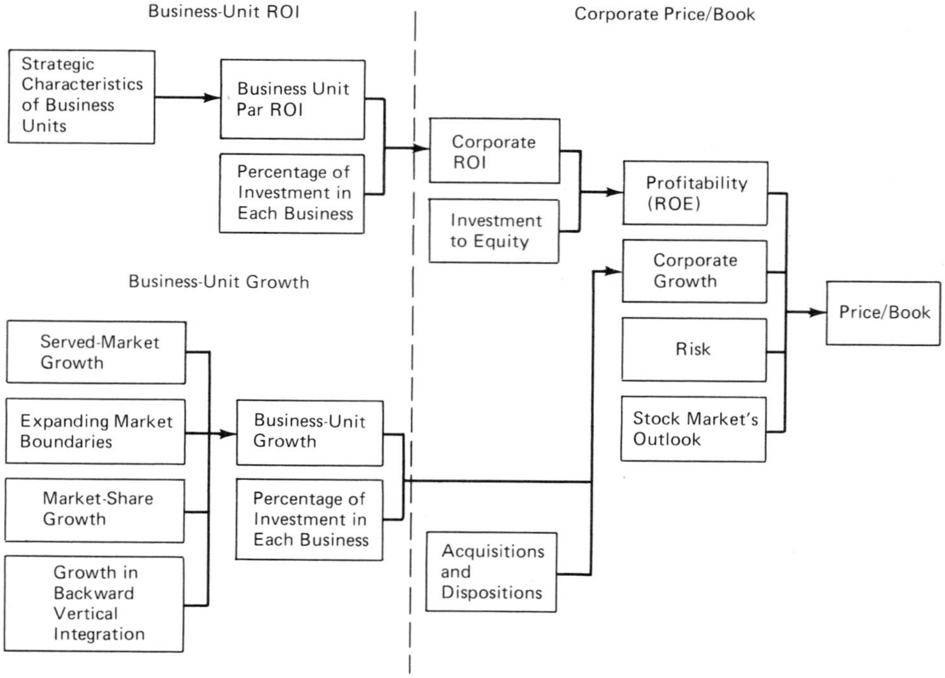

Corporate Price/Book

Business-Unit ROI

Business-Unit Growth

632

Corporate-Level Portfolio Strategy

A company's rates of profitability and growth depend not only on the profitability and growth rates of its component business units, but also on how the mix of investment in each business changes over time. A company can improve its financial fundamentals and stock price by (1) allocating capital to business with strategies that have a high probability of beating the cost of capital, (2) managing for cash (harvest, divest, liquidate) business units that are unlikely to be repositioned to beat the cost of capital, and (3) acquiring businesses that will improve the company's stock price.

Corporate Financial Policy

Capital-structure decisions are relatively complex requiring not only a determination of the optimal levels of debt and equity, but also a detailed assessment of the term structure of the company's outstanding debt. Our findings indicate that the investment community focuses not on how much debt a company has relative to its equity, but rather, on how much net income is available to cover interest payments.

The investment community seems to value a high payout rate for companies that are very profitable. Perhaps investors think very profitable companies with low payout rates will be unable to manage the very rapid growth implied. Capital structure and dividend payout policy should be tailored to reflect a company's profitability trends and growth prospects.

SUMMARY AND CONCLUSION

The increasingly critical investor evaluation of company potential (driven by high interest and inflation rates) has heightened the need for effective shareholder-oriented management. We have focused on the principal determinants of share prices and what executives can do to affect them.

With a greater understanding of how financial fundamentals drive stock price multiples and a better grasp of how a business unit's strategic position affects its profitability and growth prospects, management can formulate better business-unit strategy, more effective corporate-level portfolio strategy, and can deliver more value to shareholders.

30

Issues
and Strategic
Management

RENE ZENTNER*
University of Houston

*Formerly of Shell Oil.

ISSUES AND DECISION MAKING

In addressing the questions of issues, it is appropriate to begin by asking why managers should be concerned about their management. To answer this question, it is necessary to reflect on the historical development of corporate decision making in American business. For simplicity's sake, that history can be divided into three phases: the entrepreneurial phase, the managerial phase, and the societal phase.[1] In the first two, issues were less important than managers; in the third phase, issues have become at least as important as managers.

In the entrepreneurial phase, corporate decision making was principally the province of the founder of the enterprise. His ideas dominated the corporation, and his decisions directed it. This phase was succeeded by the managerial phase and was characterized by the emergence of the trained manager, the graduate business school, and the increasing perception of management as a profession. The corporation had become too large and complex for the entrepreneur to control, and he was replaced by a growing staff of specialized accountants, lawyers, marketers, and business school graduates. In both of these phases, it was the ability, skill, and perception of these leaders of the corporation that determined whether the enterprise was to prosper.

The third and most recent phase is that in which corporate decision making is as much affected by activities outside the corporation as by men and women managers within it. Although corporate decision making in this country has always been conducted within a framework of laws, it has only been in the last decade that such laws have had major impacts on all aspects of corporate decision making. Since about 1970, society has begun to share in such heretofore internal decisions as what products to manufacture, what manufacturing processes to employ, and under what conditions manufacturing should take place. Societal influence in the form of laws and regulations has affected how corporations make decisions as well as what decisions they make. For this reason, corporations have begun to involve themselves in the issues under debate in the societal forum, issues that when resolved become those laws and regulations.

Historically, the handling of issues was the responsibility of the public relations department. Managers generally believed that societal concerns could be dealt with through such conventional communications means as governmental relations press releases, speeches, and paid advertising. But as sophistication in understanding social forces and their impact on corporate decision making grew, it became increasingly clear that while some issues could be dealt with through communications methods, others had longer-range implications. Such issues affected not only present decision making but decisions about the long range as well. As such, these issues and their probable resolutions affected corporate goals and strategies in the long term in addition to corporate communications

[1] See in this regard the foreword by Elliot L. Richardson to John Paluszek, *Will the Corporation Survive?* (Reston, Va.: Reston Publishing Co., 1977), p. xi.

and behavior in the short term. It was out of this recognition that contemporary issues management methods arose.

As a consequence, a growing trend in American corporations has been organization for the management of issues. This trend has been evidenced by the emergence of an "issues management" literature, by the creation of new professional roles and titles, and by the proliferation of meetings and conferences on the subject.

This discussion will therefore deal with the nature of *issues management.* It will do so by endeavoring to define what the issues so managed are; why business believes they should be managed; and what organizational forms have emerged to provide the management required.

In doing so, however, the writer wishes to emphasize that issues management as a discipline is in the process of formation. There is little experience to rely upon, little theory to afford guidance, and few experts to provide leadership. Accordingly, this discussion should be regarded as a progress report on a new and possibly significant business trend, rather than an attempt to abstract general principles and lay down immutable rules. It will no doubt be another decade before those principles and rules can be deduced, and the reader should not seek them here.

THE NATURE OF ISSUES

Before turning to the question of managing issues, it is worthwhile to inquire what an *issue* is. To do so will help us understand what issues managers believe themselves to be managing. More importantly, such an inquiry will afford a yardstick against which various concepts can be compared, to determine whether or not they should be included in the issues management process.

We frequently find that when attempting to understand the special language of business, the conventional dictionary provides little guidance. For example, the *American Heritage Dictionary*[2] gives several inches of definition of the word *issue,* of which the most relevant are

  a. A point of discussion, debate or dispute
  b. A matter of wide public concern
  c. The essential point; crux: *the real issue*
  d. A culminating point leading to a decision: Bring a case to *an issue*

While these definitions are a place to begin, it is evident that they are too broad to provide the yardstick we are seeking.

---

[2]William Morris, ed., *The American Heritage Dictionary of the English Language* (Boston: Houghton Mifflin, 1976), p. 695.

As is so often the case, illumination of the field of issues and their management has been afforded by the Conference Board. In its 1979 publication *This Business of Issues: Coping with the Company's Environments,*[3] it set forth a definition of *issue* that covers the interests of business managers:

> An issue is a condition or pressure, either internal or external to an organization that, if it continues, will have a significant effect on the functioning of the organization or its future interests.

As the Conference Board publication points out, this definition implies that sooner or later an organization has to make a decision about each issue that confronts it.

The Conference Board definition gives more insight into the nature of issues business managers regard as necessary to manage. Its definition of *issue* provides the following two characteristics not included in the dictionary definitions:

> Relevance to the organization, either internal, or external
>
> Likely to have an effect on the organization that is more than trivial

Where the issue is to be found, however, is left comfortably vague.

It is less important to provide an exact definition than it is to understand the characteristics of relevant definitions. To this end, a final definition will be proposed in order to illustrate those characteristics. Thus it appears both from the writings on the subject and from what issues managers are managing that

> an issue is a social, regulatory, or legislative debate whose resolution may have the effect of preventing the organization from achieving its goals.

This definition provides the following characteristics that seem to be involved in current issues management:

> *Locus:* Issues are found in the social or public policy arenas, arising through some sort of debate.
>
> *Resolution:* More important than the issue is the consequence of its resolution.
>
> *Impact:* Organizations appear to be concerned only with issue resolutions that will set obstacles to achieving corporate goals.

These characteristics are helpful in determining whether an issue should be managed and, indeed, whether a topic is an issue at all.

---

[3]James K. Brown, *This Business of Issues: Coping with the Company's Environments* (Research Report from the Conference Board, New York, 1979), p. 1.

Issues have a number of dimensions; the 1979 Conference Board report presents several taxonomies to be considered:[4]

Environment: Internal or external to the organization
Content: Economic, Social, Political, Ecological, Technological
Timing: Current, Emerging, or Strategic

The duration of the issue is also considered, and its degree of impact on the organization.

Having identified what issues are in the language of today's business organization, it is now appropriate to turn to the emergence of need for their management.

WHY MANAGE ISSUES?

Historically, business and society met principally in the market. Accordingly, the attention of business managers was focused on markets and on consumer preferences and behavior. To the extent that social concerns and public policy affected business behavior, those concerns and that policy dealt mostly with the market behavior of business.

That business behavior outside the market became the focus of social concern and national policy after the 1950s is extensively documented elsewhere.[5] The ranks of activist social groups seeking political solutions to the growing problems of American society had originally been occupied by organized labor, organized business, and organized agricultural groups; they were increased during the 1960s and the 1970s by consumer organizations, environmentalist organizations, and a variety of groups advocating solutions to particular social or economic problems. The growth and effectiveness of these new organizations took business by surprise. After years of advocating national policies to the Congress and successive administrations, business leaders found themselves left behind in the advocacy of social, economic, and political solutions to the problems of American society. After years of developing effectiveness in replying to attacks from labor organizations—their traditional antagonist in the public forum—business leaders found that they had to defend themselves against attacks on new flanks from new antagonists raising new arguments.

The emergence of these new constituencies arose from changes in the nature of American society. Signs of those changes began to appear in the mid-1960s, fostered by changes in the demographic composition of American society,

---

[4]Ibid., pp. 9–18.

[5]See, for example, Paluszek, *Will the Corporation Survive?*

Table 1   High Confidence in Institutions

As far as the people in charge of running [each institution] are concerned, how much confidence have you in them?

	1966	1974	1976	1978	1980
	%	%	%	%	%
Higher educational institutions	61	40	31	41	36
Medicine	73	49	42	42	34
Television news	X	32	28	35	29
The military	61	29	23	29	28
U.S. Supreme Court	50	34	22	29	27
Organized religion	41	32	24	34	22
The press	29	25	20	23	19
Congress	42	16	9	10	18
The White House	X	18	11	14	18
The executive branch of the federal government	41	18	11	14	17
Major companies	55	15	16	22	16
Organized labor	22	18	10	15	14
Law firms	X	17	12	18	13

Source: Lewis Harris and Associates, Inc., *Harris Survey* (New York).

X = not asked.

the rising level of educational achievement, and increasing prosperity for all Americans. General public dissatisfaction with what was perceived as an unjust war in Indo-China and, later, government misbehavior at the highest levels, no doubt accelerated the change. As public opinion surveys revealed, public confidence in the leadership of all institutions declined precipitously from the 1960s through the beginning of the 1980s. Table 1 indicates that social confidence in business leadership has decreased, along with the decrease in confidence in other institutions.

The changes in the national environment found business unprepared. For the two decades between the end of World War II and the mid-1960s, American society had enjoyed comparatively smooth and steady economic growth, social stability, and political tranquility. Change had come smoothly and incrementally. Business thinking, business behavior, and business organization had accommodated to those conditions. The shocks presented by the new environmental situation took most businesspeople by surprise. In particular, the social and political forces that business decision makers were to encounter were those for which they had no training, no experience, and no way of responding. Accordingly, attention in business organizations became directed in the 1970s to methods for dealing with the new environment.

Needs for dealing with environmental change arose in a variety of business operations. The following organizations within the enterprise were particularly affected by changing social conditions:

Governmental Affairs
Public Relations and Communications
Corporate Planning
Marketing and Product Development
Employee Relations
Engineering and Manufacturing

The needs of these organizations to perceive, understand, and respond to environmental change provoked alteration in ways companies thought about managing their enterprise, beginning in the early 1970s. Out of these new perspectives came the concept of issues management.

As has been pointed out above, the term *issue* is one with many definitions. Similarly, a variety of definitions for the developing process of issues management exists. In his perceptive work *Will the Corporation Survive?*, John Paluszek suggests that issues management is the marshaling and organizing of resources to deal with social issues that have serious public opinion and regulatory implications.[6] Similarly, the Public Affairs Council defines *issues management* as having the elements of

Monitoring the social and political environment;
Analyzing and evaluating the impact of emerging issues;
Establishing priority among these issues;
Effecting responses to new developments in the environment.[7]

While other definitions abound, they all tend to contain these elements.

That issues management is still a developing process is recognized by the recently published report of the Task Force on Social Corporate Performance, *Business and Society: Strategies for the 1980s.*[8] That report points out that

it is only in the past few years that most companies have realized how important public policy and social issues are to their own survival and profitability. The effective integration of social performance issues into strategic planning has yet to occur in most major corporations. Most firms still conduct strategic planning exclusively as an economic exercise. In some cases, planning still deals only with investment allocation and projected returns on investment. In even the most sophisticated

[6]Paluszek, *Will the Corporation Survive?*, p. 245; also see Raymond P. Ewing, "Issues," *Public Relations Journal,* June 1980.

[7]Brown, *This Business of Issues,* p. 5.

[8]U.S. Department of Commerce, *Business and Society: Strategies for the 1980s,* December 1980.

companies, there are few effective socio-political inputs or outputs in the strategic planning process.

One sign of change is the increasing sophistication of issue analysis and issue management in many firms. This approach is, however, handicapped by its separation in most cases from the organized strategic planning process, its focus on public policy issues to the exclusion of many demographic or technological developments, its concentration on legislative and judicial developments, and the lack of a coherent method for selecting the most critical issues.[9]

Thus a growing number of U.S. corporations, responding to the need for organizing their resources to bring a sense of changing social environment into their decision making, have embarked on the creation of issues management processes. It is these efforts that we will now consider.

HOW COMPANIES MANAGE ISSUES

The literature of issues management is still small. Few companies are to date so sure of how to manage issues that they are prepared to discuss their efforts in public. Nevertheless, from a survey of what has been published, a general taxonomy of issues management methods can be proposed. Three categories of approach to issues management appear to be emerging in U.S. companies:

1. *Senior Management Responsibility*

    In some companies, responsibility for identifying, analyzing and dealing with issues is that of senior management, supported by individual staff. Characteristic of such cases is the existence at the board-of-directors or officer level of an appropriate committee.

2. *Staff Responsibility*

    In some companies, a staff organization holds issues management responsibility, reporting on its activities to corporate officers or organizations as appropriate. Typically, such staff organizations are positioned in the Planning or Public Affairs departments.

3. *Joint Management/Staff Responsibility*

    In the balance of companies having issues management functions, responsibility for managing issues is divided between staff and senior management. In these companies, each level plays an appropriate role in the several stages of the issues management process.

A fourth category, of course, embraces firms that have no organized or consistent system of issues management.

[9]Ibid., p. 159.

One important point that should be made at the outset of this discussion is that the term *issues management* is a misleading one. The term incorrectly suggests that issues can be managed; there is no indication that they can.[10] Examination of company activities suggests that the role of issues management in most companies is to manage the company's awareness of and response to issues. That distinction should be kept in mind when considering the various examples of the issues management process.

The first category of issues management organization shown in the classification system above is that in which issues management is the responsibility of senior management. Illustrative of companies that practice this method is E. I. du Pont de Nemours and Company, the largest U.S. chemical company. A four-man senior management committee is the focus of issues management activities; staff work for that committee is provided by a manager in the Public Affairs department. At Koppers Company the chief executive himself has taken the issues management responsibility. According to a recent Conference Board report,[11] every month three different groups of about twenty-five middle and junior executives in the twenty-five to forty age cohort gather with him to discuss a provocative book they have been assigned to read. Examples of authors read include John Kenneth Galbraith. In each of these cases, the effect of senior management interest on issues addressed is likely to ensure general corporate attention to those issues.

The nation's largest bank, the Bank of America, carries out its issues management program through the use of two committees made up of senior managers: the Public Policy Committee and the Social Policy Committee. The Public Policy Committee is composed of six members of the bank's board of directors; the senior vice-president—School Policy serves as the committee's secretary. The committee identifies and monitors broad environmental, political, and social trends that would directly or indirectly affect the bank's activities and performance, and it advises bank management on long-range plans and programs reflecting the new social requirements. It also reports to the full board on the status and adequacy of the bank's overall public policy activities and makes appropriate recommendations for improvements as necessary.

The Social Policy Committee, composed of senior managers from many of the bank's operating and administrative departments, is chaired by the senior vice-president—Social Policy, who thus provides a link to the Public Policy Committee. The Social Policy Committee identifies emerging social policy issues and considers as well the changing needs of groups to which the bank must be

---

[10]Robert H. Moore, "Research by the Conference Board Sheds Light on Problems of Semantics, Issue Identification and Classification—and Some Likely Issues for the '80s," *Public Relations Journal,* November 1979.

[11]James K. Brown, *Guidelines for Managing Corporate Issues Program,* Report No. 795 (The Conference Board, New York, 1981), p. 31.

responsive. The committee sets priorities and standards for responsible action and initiates changes in bank policies, positions, and practices. It also plans specific programs to help the bank meet its social responsibilities and monitors the implementation and effectiveness of these undertakings.[12]

Another prominent American organization taking advantage of senior management commitment to the management of issues is the Allstate group of companies. To render that group able to deal with the changing social environment, a Strategic Planning Committee was created in 1977, and an Issues Management Committee in 1978. Both of these committees utilize the matrix form of organization and have interlocking members drawn from the Executive Committee, which reports to the chief executive officer. This use of the horizontal project management method to bridge the vertical organizations within the Allstate group facilitates access to senior interdepartmental thinking as well as commitment to Allstate corporate objectives.

The Issues Management Committee is chaired by Allstate's vice-chairman, who is also a member of the Strategic Planning Committee. It has as members the president and chief operating officer; the executive vice-president, who is also chairman of the Strategic Planning Committee; two senior vice-presidents; and departmental vice-presidents in charge of corporate relations, public law, and strategic planning. Secretary of the committee is the Allstate director of issues management. Charge of the Issues Management Committee is to define the issues, to formulate Allstate policy and action plans for the Executive Committee's approval, and to determine the communications to be made to such Allstate constituencies as employers, consumer groups, policyholders, public-interest groups, and legislators.

Issues of different time scales are divided between the two committees. The Allstate Issues Management Committee concentrates on emerging issues whose definition and contending positions are evolving and on which legislation or regulation is likely within a prospective time frame of eighteen to thirty-six months. In contrast, the Strategic Planning Committee concerns itself with those strategic issues that are important in long-range planning, with probable impact at least three years in the future. Both issues management and strategic planning are directed to the best way to serve Allstate's primary stakeholders: the public, Allstate's customers, its employees, and its shareholders.[13]

In the second category of issues management systems, responsibility for dealing with issues lies with a corporate staff organization. For example, in Sperry Corporation, the communications section of Sperry's corporate staff has responsibility for collecting and coordinating intelligence about issues. It is the

[12]Ibid., p. 27.

[13]Archie R. Boe, "Fitting the Corporation to the Future," *Public Relations Quarterly,* Winter 1979, pp. 4–5.

communications section that meets with senior management division managers and other internal and outside groups for this purpose.[14]

No discussion of issues management would be complete without reference to the pioneer work thereon carried out by the General Electric Company. Integrated as part of its formal strategic planning process has been the development of a long-term environmental forecast of social, economic, political, technological, and competitive trends and developments. In 1970, responsibility for strategic planning was given to a newly created corporate executive staff; the Business Environment Studies Group, which had prepared the long-term forecasts, became a part of that group.[15]

The Business Environment Studies Group developed a number of sophisticated methods for the analysis of social and environmental issues. Over the succeeding decade, however, the General Electric business operations, divided into strategic business units, gradually assumed responsibility for their own environmental assessments. In 1975 a Public Issues Planning Staff was created in the Public Relations Operations group. The Public Issues Planning Staff has gradually absorbed most of the functions of the Business Environment Studies Group.

Currently the Public Issues Planning Staff's major responsibility is to link analysis of the sociopolitical environment to both the development of public policy issues and to the activities of General Electric's government affairs program. The staff also affords advice about the preparation of corporate-level environmental assumptions to the Corporate Planning and Development Staff. The Public Issues Planning Staff is thus linked both to General Electric's public affairs and to planning activities.

Other major corporations with effective issues management staffs include the American Telephone and Telegraph Company and the New York Telephone Company. The oil companies, which have been among the organizations most affected by environmental change, have also been active in the field of issues management. Gulf Oil Company has a manager for Planning and Policy Analysis in its head office organization in Pittsburgh. At Exxon Company U.S.A., the U.S. operating company of Exxon Corporation, issues management is the responsibility of the Planning Staff in Public Affairs. Planning works with senior Exxon management, the Exxon headquarters operating and staff departments in Houston, and the field offices to

Identify the issues that the company should address

Determine which department has lead responsibility for the issue and assign it a priority

Establish with the function the objectives the parties hope to achieve

[14]Brown, *Guidelines for Managing Corporate Issues Programs*, p. 6.

[15]*Business Society: Strategies for the 1980s,* pp. 162–65.

Determine the strategy to be followed

Develop an action plan to implement that strategy

Thus the Exxon Public Affairs Planning group takes the lead in issue identification and development of issue management programs. Actual implementation of such programs is up to two other Public Affairs groups: Government Relations and Public Relations. These groups in turn coordinate implementation strategies with line management in the operating functions so that the efforts of the entire Exxon Company U.S.A. organization are effectively brought into play.[16]

In the third category of issues management organizations, both senior management and staff interact in the management of corporate issues, according to their special skills. Thus senior management representatives are effective decision makers but lack time for research and development of information on issues. On the other hand, public affairs staff are effective at research and development of such information but lack the perspective of senior management. At Shell Oil Company those special skills have been combined to take advantage of the strengths provided by each.

In the first stage of the Shell issues management process, public affairs staff develops an initial list of issues. They do so in consultation with government relations staff and representatives of the operating functions. The result of these studies is the provision of a list of candidate issues considered important to the corporation, ranging from disposal of hazardous chemical wastes to the ability to conduct exploration for oil and gas on government-owned onshore and offshore areas.

In support of each issue, the public affairs staff prepares an Issue Scope Paper, which outlines the issue and its potential impact on Shell. The issues are then reviewed with senior Shell management. Management assigns priorities and categories to each issue. In this way the issues are divided between those in which action is to be taken and those that are merely to be followed. Issues of most importance are those that senior management decides require action in governmental or public arenas.

Once management has assigned priorities to the issues, the public affairs staff works with the operating and other staff organizations to develop policy options papers on the key issues. These papers set forth discussions of feasible alternative company positions, and the strengths and weaknesses of each position. The options on each of the key issues are then presented to senior management, which decides which option to adopt.

Once that option is adopted, the public affairs staff drafts a full position paper on the particular issue for senior management approval. Only after the position is approved can the strategy planning and execution for that issue go for-

---

[16]Remarks by J. J. Graham, Manager, Public Affairs Department, Exxon Company U.S.A., at the U.S. Army War College, March 20, 1979.

ward. Action then includes setting objectives for public affairs activities on the issue, developing strategies for governmental and communication activities, and deciding upon company actions, including special studies, employee communications programs and potential changes in operations.[17]

A similar approach is that employed by the Union Carbide Corporation in its Key Issues Program. That program was begun in 1976 and authorized by the corporate Management Committee in the conviction that the program was needed to focus the corporation's communications resources on a limited number of vital public issues. Objectives of the program are

> To effectively present Carbide as a responsible corporate citizen
>
> To enable Carbide to play a significant role in the development of reasonable policies affecting key issues
>
> To provide an articulate voice on major public issues that affect Carbide at the national, state, and local levels

The program is implemented through Carbide's matrix system of management. Once a slate of issues is selected, an appropriate team for each issue is created. Each team is headed by a Carbide executive having primary functional responsibility for the issue. That executive is in turn supported by a Communication Issue Manager, and by those Carbide employees who have expertise or accountability on that particular issue. It is this team that has the responsibility for developing a Carbide position on the particular issue assigned and for designing and implementing an appropriate communications strategy for internal and external audiences.

As a result of major emphasis from the top management of the Connecticut General Insurance Corporatioin on the importance of external affairs, an external affairs unit was created in 1977. Its functions include administering government and industry relations, developing corporate and divisional issue management systems, and organizing resources for tracking and analyzing key social, political, and business issues.

In the Connecticut General issues process, a list of corporate issues is developed by the corporate staff, on the basis of suggestions from each operating division head. Each issue is then assigned to a division head. Aided by the corporate external affairs staff, these lead officers and their staffs develop formal work plans for research and analysis on the assigned issues. Through this process, explicit company positions on the key issues are developed and communicated. The Connecticut General plan also contemplates that there will be quarterly discussions of the corporate issue process by senior officers.[18]

---

[17]Remarks by John Quinn, Manager Communications, Public Affairs, Shell Oil Co., to SIPC Marketing Communications Managers, Wiesbaden, November 5, 1980.

[18]Brown, *Guidelines for Managing Corporation Issues Programs,* p. 27.

IMPLICATIONS FOR STRATEGIC MANAGEMENT

It is evident that in the United States at least—and probably in the world in general—social, political, and economic changes are occurring at an unprecedented rate. It is also evident that these changes are having important impacts on the organization and behavior of business organizations of all kinds and sizes. Not only are the changes occurring outside the business organizations, but they are occurring within the organizations as well.

To respond both to the changes in the business environment and to the changes within the organization, the discipline of issues management has been created. As this summary has endeavored to show, organization for issues management has differed widely among corporations. In view of that diversity of organization, it is worthwhile to consider what similarities characterize the process. Examination reveals that such similarities exist.

First, a growing number of companies in all fields are creating issues management activities. In most instances the companies that have established such activities are the leading companies in their field—the best managed, the most efficiently organized, the most innovative. The increasing creation of issues management activities suggests that there is a growing awareness of the need for new organizational mechanisms for relating internal decision making to external change.

Second, the nature of each issues management process appears to depend greatly on individual corporate style—the personality of the chief executive officer, the internal decision-making dynamics of the company, and the field or fields in which it operates. Such diversities seem to account for the range of organizational forms in which issues management is currently being practiced.

Finally, there appears to be growing recognition that issues management has several important time dimensions: short term, medium term, and long term. Each of these dimensions involves a different kind of corporate activity. These dimensions are outlined in Table 2.

In the short term, issues management addresses the relationship between the corporation and its present internal and external environments. It is therefore dealing with the actions of marketing, public relations, and marketing functions. Typically, the short term generally embraces the current congressional session.

The medium term embraces a period ranging from three to five years; it includes either immature issues or issues not yet visible, but whose impact will be felt within a comparatively short time. These matters tend to be dealt with by the emerging issues staff and to be important to personnel and public affairs planning functions. Organizations responsible for health, safety, and environmental affairs would also be concerned.

The long term generally embraces a period consisting of about twenty years from the present and includes future threats and opportunities the corpo-

Table 2

Dimension	Duration	Organization Affected
Short term	Present–1 year	Marketing Public Relations Personnel Governmental Relations
Medium term	1 year–5 years	Emerging Issues Engineering Personnel Public Affairs Planning Environmental
Long term	5 years–20 years	Planning Financial Research and Development

ration will encounter in the dimly perceived future. At this writing it extends to the year 2004. As such, the long term is principally of interest to strategic planners, and perhaps to financial staff. Research and development groups are also concerned with the issues of the long term, since they are involved in initiation of activities whose impact on the corporation will come in the long term.

Thus, wherever the issues management process may be located organizationally, it must have links to both current corporate decision making and medium- and long-range planning. Moreover, because of its extensive impact on all facets of organizational activities, the issues management process must have the attention and involvement of all levels of corporate management. It must affect not only what corporate spokespeople say but also how corporate decisions are made and how corporate activities are conducted.

Issues management is rapidly being institutionalized in American business. That it is doing so reflects the ability of business executives to sense change, to organize for change, and to incorporate change in their decision making. As American society transforms itself during the remaining decades of the twentieth century, issues management will be the catalyst of corresponding change in the American corporation.

31

Planning for the 1980's: Corporate Planning with Government and Unions

BERNARD TAYLOR

Henley-on-Thames, England

Publication of the European Cooperation Fund 51, rue de la Concorde, 1050 Brussels. Tel: (02) 512.89.38—Telex: 21504 FEC BxB.

INTRODUCTION

The aim of this paper is to analyse what form of Strategic Planning is likely to be most effective in the emerging conditions of the 1980's. We can already see the broad outlines of what is required. We have a new highly-politicised business environment with increasing pressures from society, growing government involvement, strong trade unions and groups of shop-floor workers who can cause damaging dislocations in society. In fact there has been a major shift of power in European society—away from employers and management, towards other groups—employees, social pressure groups, politicians and public officials.

The evidence is all around us in the restrictions and vetoes which are imposed on the plans of management. Corporate plans produced unilaterally by management and presented to the work force as a "fait accompli" are just not implemented. Production targets are not achieved. Productivity is curtailed and restrictive practices are perpetuated. New equipment is not operated. Industrial stoppages multiply. Plants scheduled for closure stay open and workers who were to be laid off remain in work—even when they have no work to do.

Plans to open or close major facilities such as oilfields, mines, chemical plants and refineries, are a matter for public debate and sanction. Established products have to be withdrawn, re-designed or re-labelled. New products like drugs and pesticides are subjected to even more lengthy and expensive testing processes.

Many strategic decisions now require government approval. In companies which produce consumer goods such as food, drink, tobacco and petrol, profits and cash-flow depend on negotiations with government over prices and sales taxes. In large companies which are vulnerable to government sanctions, labour costs are largely determined by incomes policies. In several countries the rate of dividend paid to shareholders has to be within specified limits. The cost of debt capital is fixed according to government interest rates.

Large acquisitions require the consent of public bodies concerned with monopolies and mergers. The closure of large production units in effect requires government agreement and the minimum level of compensation to redundant employees is fixed by law.

The independence of private business is being threatened. Privately-owned businesses are coming into the public sector, through expropriation and bankruptcy. Domestically, many European businesses e.g. in textiles, only continue to exist because of government grants and protection against imports. In some fields, e.g. in steel, ships, aircraft and power plant, international competition is between government-business alliances. In other markets firms require powerful government support in the form of loans and export credit guarantees. In developing countries, multinational companies are being compelled to turn their subsidiary companies into joint ventures with a substantial local shareholding.

A cursory examination of this business environment makes one question the traditional view of business planning as an activity which:

1. is internal to the company
2. is the prerogative of managers
3. produces managerial decisions which are then received by the community and implemented by the work force.

The traditional managerial system is based on the premise that management has the power and authority to carry out its decisions.

This assumption may be true as regards administrative and operational decisions, but it is no longer valid for major strategic issues. In Europe, society has clearly decided that the planning of industry is now too important to be left in the hands of businessmen.

It is generally expected that businessmen will in future negotiate their plans: with the work force and their representatives; with public officials and politicians—and with community groups where their interests are involved.

It is also abundantly clear that businessmen must become involved in finding solutions for the important social and economic problems which are facing Europe today:

high and persistent unemployment,

shortages of energy and raw materials,

inflation at historically high levels,

the need to re-structure major industries,

control of pollution and dangerous chemicals,

conservation of natural resources such as fish and forests,

moderation of the fluctuations in financial markets and exchange rates,

the undermining of the motivation to work and to take risks, because of high levels of taxation,

the development of a more satisfying work environment, etc.

It seems unlikely that we will find satisfactory answers to these problems without the participation of businessmen as well as the representatives of government, labour and other interested parties. Industrial planning is coming more into the political arena. It means negotiating plans with governments and unions and communicating much more effectively with shop-floor workers. But we are only just beginning to develop the people in business, in government and in the trade unions, who can make strategic decisions in this way. It means:

1. a thorough re-orientation in the thinking and practice of Corporate Planning,
2. the development of new relationships and new understandings between businessmen, government officials and trade union leaders and possibly the establishment of new institutions and new procedures,

3. the appointment of new kinds of top managers, administrators and trade unionists and an ambitious progamme of training and development to give them the necessary skills to cope with the new planning environment,

4. the use of new approaches and new techniques for forecasting, analysis and planning—what we might call legislative planning or political planning, both for the short term and the long term.

THE NEW POLITICAL ENVIRONMENT

During the last decade, the social, political and legal framework of business has been transformed. The businessman's traditional "right to manage" his own enterprise has been repeatedly and successfully challenged by one pressure group after another, in the cause of equal rights for women, racial equality, consumer protection, pollution control and "the quaity of working life." *Social responsibility which was once an option has become a legal requirement.*[1]

The new-found power of blue-collar workers has resulted in an extension of the legal rights of employees and their unions. And in Western Europe, the limited liability company and the Board of Directors are now in the process of being reformed to provide for the improved representation of employees.[2]

A natural response of businessmen to this avalanche of legislation is to look for a moratorium on new laws, a breathing space in which to allow their organisations to absorb the changes which have occurred. But there seems to be little chance of this. Instead, the 1980's offer the prospect that government involvement in business will continue and will probably increase.[3]

In retrospect, the Energy Crisis of 1973/74 appears as a watershed in the history of the Western World—the end of an era of affluence, continuous growth and relative stability. Since then, the business environment has changed fundamentally and, I would argue, it is essential for us to arrange new forms of collaboration between government and industry, employee groups and the public in order to deal with the problems which have emerged. I believe that these problems are outside the scope of an individual company's management. They require action on the level of a community, a region, or on a national or international basis. It could be that they will prove to be temporary difficulties which will disappear over the next few years. I think that they will probably remain with us throughout the 1980's and businessmen will have to get involved with

[1]For a discussion of social and political pressures on business see: William D. Purdie & Bernard Taylor (Eds.) *Business Strategies for Survival—Planning for Social and Political Change,* Heinemann, London 1976.

[2]Renato Mazzolini, "The Influence of European Workers over Corporate Strategy," *Sloan Management Review,* Spring 1978, pp. 59–81.

[3]For a review of the growth of government intervention in the U.S.A. see "Government Intervention" Special Issue, *Business Week,* April 4, 1977.

government bodies, trade unions and other social groups in the search for solutions. Among the most important challenges facing Western governments and businesses are the following:

1. **Lower growth in world markets and intensive international competition**
    Much of the competition—from Japan, Russia and the Third World countries—is seen by our competitors as part of a national economic strategy which includes the availability of cheap finance and protected domestic markets.[4]

    This trade war has resulted in demands from western industrialists for similar support and protection from government.

2. The stagnation or decline of major industries—which have been traditionally regarded as the main supports of our economies: railways, docks, steel, shipbuilding, aircraft, textiles, shoes, motor cars, power plant, machine tools, etc.[5] This has led some companies like British Leyland and Volkswagen to become dependent on government support and has resulted in the nationalisation of industries like aircraft manufacture and shipbuilding.

3. **High unemployment and the shortage of key skills**
    The present high levels of unemployment will probably persist throughout the 1980's owing to the combined effect of the reduced demand for labour from manufacturing industry and an increase in the working population, and the large numbers of unemployed in development areas and among particular groups e.g. teenagers and especially black youths, will present our societies with major social problems.[6] At the same time business growth is held back by shortages of skilled workers. Despite high unemployment, instrument maintenance personnel, computer staff, electronics engineers and tool-makers are all in short supply.[7]

    The planning of manpower is complicated because of the long lead times involved, in educating and training new staff, in re-training existing employees for new jobs, in laying off people in declining industries and creating jobs for them elsewhere, and in persuading employees to accept new technologies.

[4]On the importance of the Bank of Japan in financing Japanese companies see: James C. Abegglen (Ed.) *Business Strategies for Japan,* Boston Consulting Group, Sophia University, Tokyo, 1970 (p. 61).

[5]For details of the decline in Steel, Textiles and Shipbuilding, see: "Europe's Ailing Industries," *Time,* October 16, 1978.

[6]For forecasts of unemployment and the underlying trends see: Colin Leicester, *Unemployment 2001 A.D.* (1977) and *Manpower Policies for the 1980's* (1978) Institute of Manpower Studies, Sussex University.

[7]For an attempt at forecasting the future demand for skills on an industry basis see: Chemical and Allied Products Industry Training Board, *Working at the Future: Strategy for 1977/1982,* Staines, Middlesex, 1976.

4. **Producer Cartels and Shortages in Supply Markets**

Since 1973 businessmen in the industrialized world should have learned not to take the supply of energy, food and essential raw materials for granted. To achieve secure sources of supply for important commodities in the future will probably require international agreements by national governments and free trade areas like the EEC. The price of oil is negotiated annually with OPEC countries. And there is now a continuing North-South dialogue aimed at stabilising commodity markets. I believe that long term contracts for raw materials will probably form an essential element of planning in the 1980's.[8]

Already we have international supply agreements on energy, food crops and fishing. The Japanese also have long term contracts for the supply of metals, rubber and other key commodities. And access to the major commodity suppliers in Africa and the Middle East has become a key political issue between the West and the Communist bloc.

5. **Hyper Inflation and Fluctuating Exchange Rates**

The years since 1973 have sent the highest rates of inflation since the Second World War and popular demands for governments to control wages, prices and dividends. Also, exchange rates have fluctuated violently and governments have tried to defend their currencies by increasing interest rates and by imposing stringent controls on the export of capital.

This turbulence in financial markets has added a new dimension of uncertainty to business management and governments have made regulations affecting the most important decisions in management—the levels of prices, wages and dividends, the cost of money and the prices of raw materials.

I believe that these problems are with us to stay and represent *a changed political environment for corporate planning.*

PLANNING AS A POLITICAL PROCESS

Corporate Planning was originally conceived in the 1960's as a mechanism for internal coordination and control within a company hierarchy with a single decision-making system focused on the chief executive and the Board.[9]

---

[8]See: David Novick, *A World of Scarcities: Critical Issues in Public Policy,* Associated Business Programmes, London, 1976, and: G. F. Ray "Raw Materials, Shortages and Producer Power," *Long Range Planning,* August 1975, also David H. Farmer and Bernard Taylor (Eds.) *Corporate Planning and Procurement,* Heinemann, London, 1975.

[9]For a review of recent research into Corporate Planning see: Bernard Taylor "Strategies for Planning" in Bernard Taylor and John Sparkes (Eds.) *Corporate Strategy and Planning,* Heinemann, London, 1977. Also Reports on current practice by the Conference Board, New York: *Planning and the Chief Executive* (1972), *Corporate Planning and the Corporate Planning Director* (1974), *Corporate Guides to Long Range Planning* (1976) and *Planning Under Uncertainty: Multiple Scenarios and Contingency Planning* (1976).

But, to work effectively today, Corporate Planning needs to be developed as an inter-organisational process so as to include relationships with other organisations and interest groups (inside and outside the business) whose decisions and actions are likely to have an important impact on the firm.[10]

We can all think of important projects—new factories, mines, reservoirs, airports and new products—motorcars, aeroplanes, drugs, pesticides—whose progress was delayed or stopped because of opposition from some social or political group.

And we know of industries where production targets and delivery dates are never met, where restrictive practices continue to hamper production and factories are grossly over-manned but workers are not made redundant because the production system is in fact controlled not by the management but by the trade unions and the work force.

We are also aware of the growing involvement of government in business over the last decade—controls on prices and incomes, legislation for the protection of employees, consumers and the environment, and to provide equal opportunity to women and ethnic minorities; direct intervention in specific industries through the use of incentives, sanctions, outright expropriation and nationalisation.

In the 1970's there has been a dramatic decline in managerial power and authority and many planning failures have been caused because management are overestimating their power to carry through their decisions. A manager can only plan with confidence *managerially* to take decisions which are under his own control. For decisions which are made by other groups or individuals outside his control he must plan *politically* to influence their decisions.[11]–(See Table 1)

Managerial Planning applies where management's authority is accepted. It does not work in a "political" situation i.e. where other organisations and interest groups are involved. Many important business decisions now come into this category. The location of a new plant involves negotiation with national and local authorities, with representatives of local communities and with trade unions and employee groups. The design of new products, particularly in sensitive areas like pharmaceuticals, construction, aircraft or automobiles, means protracted negotiations with regulatory authorities, professional bodies and consumer associations. The introduction of new labour-saving equipment such as computers is usually the occasion for extensive bargaining with representatives of the work force, as newspaper proprietors have discovered.

Wage negotiations and productivity deals which are aimed at reducing manning and eliminating resrictive labour practices may involve management in

[10]On Corporate Planning as an inter-organisational process, see John K. Friend, John M. Power and Christopher J. L. Yewlett, *Public Planning: The Inter-Corporate Dimension,* Tavistock, London, 1974.

[11]For an interesting analysis of the political aspects of Corporate Strategy, see Ian C. MacMillan, *Strategy Formulation: Political Concepts,* West, St. Paul, Minnesota, 1978.

Table 1   Two Styles of Planning

	Managerial Planning	**Political Planning**
POWER	Management's authority is unquestioned	Management's authority is limited in practice by the actions of other groups
FOCUS	Co-ordination and control of management decisions within the firm	Influencing decisions and policies of other groups inside and outside the firm
THEORY OF PLANNING	A "scientific" process of problem-solving and decision-making	Planning to be effective requires the agreement of the major power groups
PLANNING METHODS	Management formulates objectives, strategies and plans; other groups receive and implement them. Management makes the final decision	Management maintains information networks, forms alliances, uses persuasion and coercion, negotiates and bargains with other groups

elaborate bargaining rituals, with Departments of Employment and Industrial Tribunals, as well as Trade Unions and groups of blue-collar and white-collar employees.

Political Planning therefore involves the *negotiation* of management's policies with a whole range of organisations and groups:

major "stakeholders" e.g. key customers, large suppliers, financial institutions and banks;

local authorities, public utilities and government agencies;

trade unions and employee groups;

professional and industrial associations;

international agencies such as the European Community and the World Bank;

community action groups representing various interests.

In these political areas management must expect not just the usual internal discussion about budgets, targets and ways and means of achieving them. They must anticipate a real conflict of interests. Other groups and organisations will have their own objectives, policies and plans. The remedy for this conflict does not lie as is often suggested merely in the improvement of management's communications with its employees and with the public, though this is part of the solution. Other parties may understand management's position very well. They may simply disagree. If a real conflict exists it must be resolved through different processes—not via better communication and control systems, but by the use of power and influence, and often through formal negotiation and arbitration.

Much of the uncertainty which managers complain about is the result of unilateral planning. If businessmen prepare detailed plans without adequate consultation, expecting government and unions and other interest groups to comply with their requirements, then they are likely to see their organisations "blown off course."

Where other power groups are involved, management must be prepared to negotiate within broad guidelines, considering various alternatives. To quote the researchers of the Tavistock Institute:[12]

"The goal of imposing a comprehensive solution to the organisation of planning activities is bound to be illusory . . . the innovator should recognise the limitations of what he can achieve through the medium of central control systems of a kind that rest on explicit ground rules for dealing with clearly defined classes of situations."

"Corporate Planning is not enough—the making of strategic decisions must be considered not merely as a corporate but also as an inter-organisational process. The more comprehensively those in large organisations seek to plan the more they find themselves dependent on the outcome of other agencies, both public and private."

In many companies, Corporate Planning is largely concerned with internal coordination. In such firms, the planning activity should be expanded to include a "foreign policy" towards other organisations and interest groups. In a "politicised" industrial environment, inter-organisational contacts are vitally important. In practice, an organisation's scope and influence tend to be defined through bargaining with governments, unions and other organisations, and a firm may increase its effectiveness in negotiation by building and maintaining "information and support networks" with other organisations. Also, if a business is to operate effectively in the political arena, the management should not rely on random contacts and *ad hoc* arrangements—the personal flair of the Chairman and the negotiating skills of the Personnel Director.

In a political situation, businessmen are frequently at a disadavantage. Business executives are (rightly) promoted for their effectiveness in achieving management targets, not for their political skills. So the top management of a business may be brilliant technologists, accountants or salesmen and completely at sea when faced by politicians, civil servants, militant employees, leaders of social pressure groups or a television interviewer.

For a firm to become effective in the political arena therefore usually requires an investment: in staff and advisers with inside knowledge and practical experience—ex-civil servants, former trade union officials and politicians:—in the education and training of managers in politics, industrial relations and social responsibility to help them to understand the groups which they are dealing with and to acquire new skills they will need for negotiation, public speaking and dealing with the media—and in management time: spent in playing a leading

---

[12]John Friend et al. op. cit. p. 375 & p. xxiii.

role in trade and professional associations, representing the industry on sector working parties and Commissions of Enquiry, talking regularly to groups of employees, to teachers and students, and to residents in local communities, etc.

To avoid planning failures in the 1980's it is important that senior managers should take a realistic view of their power position. In most cases they should abandon any illusion that they are "the captain on the bridge" guiding the corporate destiny, and recognise that they must often operate like a politician, maintaining formal and informal contacts with other organisations, negotiating and bargaining with them, forming alliances with friendly groups and trying to influence potential opponents.

Some industries, e.g. armaments, energy and transportation, are traditionally close to government, and political activity there has always been an important part of management. Others, e.g. some consumer industries have been less subject to government intervention and for their management politics is a new world.

Regardless of the management's political experience, "Corporate Affairs" or "External Relations" is an important area of business which requires increasing top management attention and should be the subject of plans, forecasts and analyses, like other corporate functions such as finance, marketing or manufacturing. And some companies will need to employ specialists who know the relevant politicals systems. In many cases, the Corporate Affairs activity fits conveniently in the Chairman's Office alongside Corporate Planning.[13]

MODERN CAPITALIST PLANNING

Political debates about national economic planning usually propose two alternatives—Centralised Planning, or communism on the one hand, and Free Enterprise with a minimum of government interference on the other.

Industrial planning in Britain has been bedevilled by this kind of ideological battle ever since the Second World War. The example of the British Steel industry is a classic case—first nationalised then de-nationalised, then nationalised again. As a consequence vital investments in the industry were put back for a decade and we are now trying to re-structure the industry in the middle of an international economic recession.

It is generally assumed that businessmen are in favour of free enterprise. In my experience, businessmen are not so much concerned with the colour of the government as with achieving some kind of stability in government policy. However ridiculous the government policy, businessmen will adapt to it in time. What management find difficult to cope with is a policy towards industry which

[13]For an analysis of the activities of Public Affairs departments see The Conference Board, New York, Reports: The Role of Business in Public Affairs (1968), Organising for Effective Public Affairs (1969) and Public Affairs in the U.S. and Europe (1972).

changes every four or five years—not on the basis of rational analysis but because the new politicians have a different dogma from the ones they replace.[14]

In any case, the politicians are offering a false choice. Central Planning and public ownership of the means of production would be unacceptable to the majority of the population in Western Europe. And it would take strong action on the part of West European governments to break the monopoly power of large companies and large unions if we wished to develop free market economies. In Britain, for example, the Trade Union Closed Shop has legal support and in 20 out of 22 major industrial sectors, three firms control over 50% of the market.[15] The only feasible alternative for us is a form of industrial planning on the pattern which is already well developed in France, Japan and Sweden and exists in most other European countries. This is *not* centralised government planning of all areas of economic activity on the East European model. Nor is it Corporatism such as was common under the National Socialist governments of the thirties—where the government often achieved a consensus by force and free and open debate was prohibited.

In broad terms, Capitalist Planning means a process similar to that described below:[16]

1. Government puts forward certain broad economic policies and strategies or priorities for industrial and regional development.

2. These guidelines then become the basis for widespread debate among industrialists who are represented on a number of councils or committees. In these meetings businessmen discuss with government officials and trade unionists the prospects for their particular sector of business activity. And the government representatives offer incentives in the form of cheap credit, loans and grants or sanctions such as restrictions on building and limits on the import of technology.

3. In addition to these private negotiations, there is often—as in Sweden—a public debate in the course of which businessmen, government officials, political parties and other interest groups put forward their own "long term forecasts" for particular industries or regions.[17]

4. This could be described as "convergent planning." In most cases, by a process of negotiation, government officials and the leaders of business reach an understanding and the open debate where this occurs serves to test pub-

[14]See, for examaple, Arthur Knight, *Private Enterprise and Public Intervention,* Allen and Unwin, London, 1974.

[15]S. J. Prais, *The Evolution of Giant Firms in Britain,* National Institute of Economic and Social Research, Cambridge University Press, 1976.

[16]Stephen S. Cohen, *Modern Capitalist Planning: The French Model,* University of California, London, 1977.

[17]David Lundberg, "Pluralist Organisation and Consensus in Swedish Planning," *Long Range Planning,* December, 1976.

lic reactions to the proposed economic and industrial policy. Occasionally, as with the proposed rationalisation of the Japanese automobile industry, businessmen and government officials agree to differ.[18]

If this is the likely future, how should we prepare for it? In countries like Britain which have little experience of this kind of dialogue between government and industry, we have a great deal to do:[19]

1. We need to develop the relationships and the mutual confidence which is necessary before government officials and industrialists can work effectively together. Often it seems that they live in separate worlds and speak a different language.

2. New procedures and possibly new institutions are required to enable civil servants and businessmen to discuss industrial planning—both formally and informally, on a continuing basis.

3. A great deal of research and data collection will be required before industrial regarding market trends, trends in technology, availability of skilled manpower, etc.

This is broadly the approach which is being adopted in the British National Economic Development Office through the activities of the Sector Working Parties. We could regard the activities of NEDO as sector planning in the embryo stage.

NETWORK ORGANISATIONS

Research in Sweden and Britain emphasises the need for new kinds of institutions which can accept responsibility for regulating whole industries.

Metcalfe and McQuillan in their study of NEDO quote the case of an emerging industry concerned with large industrial construction sites, which had problems of "poor performance, escalating costs, long delays in completion and a strike record comparable to the worst in British industry. There was nowhere that clients, contractors and unions could meet and resolve their differences before a new series of problems sparked off more inter-organisational conflicts."[20]

Gunnar Hedlund and Lars Otterbeck in an investigation entitled "Futures of Sweden in a Global Industrial System" also identified the need for new kinds of "network organisations" to arrange collaboration *between* organisations. In

[18]P. Trezise and Y. Suzuki, "Politics, Government and Economic Growth in Japan," Hugh Patrick and Henry Rosovsky (Eds.) *Asia's New Giant,* Brookings Institution, 1976 (pp. 753–812).

[19]D. Berry, L. Metcalfe and W. McQuillan, "Neddy: An Organisational Metamorphosis," *Journal of Management Studies,* February, 1974.

[20]Les Metcalfe & Will McQuillan, "Managing Turbulence" in P. C. Nystrom & W. H. Starbuck (Eds.), *Prescriptive Models of Organisation,* North Holland, Amsterdam, 1977.

particular they recommend the formation of "coalitions" between organisations in different countries "to collaborate in the regulation of multi-national business."[21] Both of these pieces of research appear to support Emery and Trist's theory that "network organisations" might be an effective way of achieving stability in "turbulent environments."[22]

What then are the implications for businessmen? They must:

1. make effective contact within the various government departments which they deal with;

2. work directly within Trade Associations and in other forums like NEDO and the Industrial Training Boards: to recommend *positive policies* which will encourage the development of the industry and to minimise the impact of regulations which may be damaging:

3. work with government where possible in planning jointly for the future development of their industry—helping government officials to understand the industry's problems and opportunities for the future.

There are other tasks for government officials:

1. to develop continuing contacts with businessmen and a real understanding of industry's problems;

2. to advocate to politicians a stable industrial policy which can be maintained over a period of time;

3. to try to coordinate the policies of different departments so that industrialists do not continually receive conflicting messages, e.g. from an industrial policy which encourages the rationalisation of industry and a competition policy which tends to discourage the concentration of market power;

4. to attempt to develop jointly with industry broad strategies to guide the future development of key sectors.[23]

Trade Unions will also need to adapt and reorganise in order to play a fuller part in industrial planning

1. The Trade Union movement will no doubt continue to fight for a right to participate in industrial planning at national and international level. Trade Union interests are already well represented in socialist governments e.g. in Scandinavia and Britain. However, in some other parts of Europe e.g. in France, trade unionists claim that employee-interests are under represent-

---

[21]Gunnar Hedlund & Lars Otterbeck, *Futures of Sweden in a Global Industrial System,* Norstedt, Stockholm, 1974, pp. 204–209.

[22]F. E. Emery & E. L. Trist, *Towards a Social Ecology,* London, Plenum Press, 1973, p. 76.

[23]Arthur Knight, op. cit.

ed and trade unioin leaders have at times disassociated themselves from
the industrial planning process.

2. With the spread of sector planning, increasing numbers of trade unionists
    will be required to represent the views of the work force about the future
    development in their industries e.g. in Sector Working Parties.

3. Trade unionists will play a bigger role in *manpower planning* e.g. in fore-
    casting changes in employment patterns and in planning the education and
    training for various grades and skills, on a national and regional level.

PLANNING WITH EMPLOYEES AND UNIONS

The question for management in Europe is not *whether* we should try to involve
employee representatives in Corporate Planning but *how* we should involve
them. The last decade has seen an increase in the power of employees and unions
to the point where in general they can, and in many cases do, prevent the
achievement of corporate objectives and the implementation of company plans.
In part, their power arises from the vulnerability of large technological systems
to industrial action by a few workers, e.g. computer staff, power workers and air
traffic controllers. The power of the trade unions also arises from their effectiveness as political organisations, in particular the alliances which they have forged
with left-wing political parties.[24] One might contrast the comparative weakness
of businessmen in putting their case in the media, in parliament and on public
platforms.

In most European countries employees have now been granted certain legal rights to participation in management—on the shop-floor, in works councils,
and through direct representation at Board level. Also, the employers' rights
have been tightly circumscribed in relation to health and safety at work, sickness
benefits and pensions and the compensation of workers in cases of redundancy.
If management continue to present their plans to their work forces as a fait accompli they must not be surprised to find their employees delivering a veto to
the plans in the only way available to them—by taking industrial action.

In many industries, employees and trade unions are now involved in Corporate Planning *destructively* i.e. they usually play no role in setting objectives
and formulating strategies, but they can prevent plans being implemented by
maintaining restrictive practices and taking industrial action. An important task
for the present generation of managers is to find ways of involving employees
and their representatives in the planning process *constructively*, in order to use
their ideas and harness their energies in the development of the enterprise. Bob

[24]John F. B. Goodman, "Trade Unions and Collective Bargaining Systems" in Derek Torrington
(ed.) *Comparative Industrial Relations in Europe*, Associated Business Programmes, London, 1978
(pp. 30–48).

Wright, a senior official in the British Engineering Union, was recently quoted in *The Times* as saying:

"We don't plan strategies, we react to situations and this means we don't involve ourselves in production the way German unions do."

The contrast with the situation of unions in Japan is startling. For example, when Saint-Gobain decided to build a new fiberglass factory in Japan the management were surprised to receive from the General Secretary of the Japanese trade union involved, a statement which said:

"In view of the benefits which you are bringing and the risks which you take in opening this factory, the workers pledge that they will never go on strike."[25]

Attitude surveys indicate that there is a large untapped potential of energy and ideas among employees in Britain. In a study conducted on behalf of the Confederation of British Industry in May 1976, a majority of workers in nationalised industry (57%), a large proportion of employees in private industry (42%) and around one in three managers (29%) agreed with the statement:

"I could do more work in my present job without much effort."

The same survey revealed that employees were poorly informed about their own firm's financial results. 60% of employees had *no idea* what profits their companies had made. Also, they estimated the average company's pre-tax profits at £ 30 on every £ 100 of sales—which is about three times the actual figure and, as one might expect, 60% of them felt that a greater share of these huge profits should be shared among the work force and less should go to shareholders and directors. In these circumstances it is not surprising to find that employees would dearly like to have "more information from the top about what is happening and why." They would also like to be consulted about operational matters—particularly decisions affecting the way their work is planned and organised.[26]

Recent experiments in employee participation, organisation development and autonomous work groups, have led some trade unionists to conclude that any form of participation which includes no say in formulating objectives and plans but concentrates on discussing how the plans might be achieved is likely to be something of a charade.[27]

Four approaches are being advocated (see Table 2):

[25]Georges Valance, "Le Formidable Défi Japonais," *L'Express,* 4–10 April, 1977.

[26]*Study of Employee Attitudes and Understanding,* C.B.I., London, May 1976 and Opinion Research Centre, *Survey of British Workers,* November, 1974.

[27] Ake Sandberg, *The Limits to Democratic Planning,* Liber Forlag, Stockholm, 1976.

Table 2 Participation in Planning—Four Views

	Conflict	Consensus	Tripartite Planning	Alternative Planning
VIEW OF SOCIETY	Class conflict	Managers have power legitimately	Management must collaborate with unions and government	Struggle for the future
VIEW OF PLANNING	Management plan & employees oppose	Management plan & consult; Employees implement	Management plan & negotiate plans with unions & government	Management plan & employees plan too
ROLE OF UNION	To contest management plans in the interests of employees	To act responsibly; to keep conflict to a minimum	To implement plans which have been jointly agreed	To produce alternative corporate plans and negotiate them with management
IMPLICATIONS	Danger of industrial chaos & loss of international markets	Requires a participative management & a committed work force	Involves interminable delays. Difficulties in committing employees to plans	Requires industrial—union Organisation with research support. Can lead to confrontation

1. Consensus

This is the traditional managerial approach adapted to take account of the legitimate demands of employees and unions. It is assumed that management has the right to manage and the duty to take decisions in the interests of the company as a whole, i.e. not only the shareholders but employees, society, customers, suppliers and other interested parties. However, it is recognised that employees, like shareholders, have a special interest in the firm because they have invested not money, but time and effort, and because they depend on the company for their livelihood. It is therefore right and sensible that employees and their representatives should be kept informed about the company's plans and that they should where possible be consulted in advance about any important changes (e.g. investments in new facilities or new machinery) which are likely to affect employment. However, it is assumed that managers will make the final decisions and that, even where particular groups of employees disagree with these decisions, they will accept the plans and implement them for the good of the organisation as a whole.

The consensus view may also be broadened to encompass

a.   Work Groups for shop-floor employees which will enable them to have a say in how their work is planned and organised;

b.   Works Councils and Company Councils which will ensure that employees are kept informed and are consulted about important developments;

c.   Employee Representation on Boards—again, to ensure that there is adequate communication of information to employees, and to indicate that their interests are represented at the highest level.

2. Tripartite Planning

This suggests that employee representatives at different levels in the business should be consulted and involved at various stages in the preparation of the Corporate Plan. The work force should be made aware of the broad objectives and plans for their part of the organisation and performance should be reviewed against these plans on a regular basis.

The public interest should also be considered through regular consultations between management and government officials.

This is the form of Corporate Planning which is being adopted by the British nationalised industries under pressure from the government. A similar tripartite pattern of corporate planning is envisaged in the government's proposals for Planning Agreements which have so far appeared in private industry only in Chrysler U.K., and in a modified form in British Leyland.[28]

---

[28] *The Industry Bill,* H.M.S.O., 1975.

3. Conflict

Another view adopted by many trade unionists suggests that the interests of the work force and management will always be different. Agreement can therefore only be achieved on a temporary basis through negotiation.

Any attempt by management at achieving a consensus through employee participation is therefore doomed to failure and moreover entails the risk that trade union representatives will be implicated in decisions for which management should take the responsibility.

4. Alternative Plans

A fourth view envisages that trade unions may seek to become involved in Corporate Planning through an extension of the collective bargaining process. Unions may merely ask for the disclosure of more information about the company's future plans in order to consider the implications for their members before management takes any action.

Or, in critical situations, trade union representatives may come together, e.g. in shop stewards' committees at various levels in the enterprise to develop their own *Alternative Corporate Plans*. This has already happened in the U.K. in Lucas Aerospace[29] and in parts of the British Steel Corporation,[30] and in Norway in the Union of Computer Staff.[31]

It is apparent that the involvement of employees in Corporate Planning is going to place stresses on both Trade Unions and on management.

1. In the individual enterprise and at divisional and factory level, trade union leaders will be expected to respond to management plans and to produce their own proposals for: improving productivity, reducing industrial stoppages, introducing new technologies, closing obsolete plant and making new investments of various kinds.

2. Clearly, as industrial planning develops, the role of the trade union will be expanded. Trade union officials who have been trained in the procedures of pay bargaining will require further training in business management if they are to cooperate in planning the business in which their members work. Just as businessmen may be expert financiers and marketing men but are often novices in politics and mass communication, so trade unionists may be effective public speakers and skilled negotiators but have usual-

---

[29]Lucas Aerospace Combine Shop Stewards Committee, *The Corporate Plan: A Positive Alternative to Recession and Redundancies,* Hayes, Middlesex, 1978.

[30]Peter Bowen, *Social Control in Industrial Organisations,* Routledge and Kegan Paul, London, 1976 (pp. 136–164).

[31]Kristen Nygaard, *Trade Union Participation,* Working Paper, Norwegian Computing Centre, Oslo, 1977.

ly had little experience in actually running a business. If trade unionists are to become partners in management—on the Board, in the Works Council and on the shop-floor, there is a massive training job to be done.

Swedish experience with co-determination indicates the size of the training task. In Sweden, which has a population of 8 million, the state provides a subsidy of around £ 1 million (9.1 million Kroner) per annum for trade union education. In 1973 when Board representation was permitted by law, 1600 Board representatives were put through a four-week residential course. When the Act on Co-determination in Decision-Making was passed in January 1977, Parliament voted £ 8.5 million (60 million Kroner) for education and information material on this subject.[32]

3. Some Socialist writers insist that the workers' point of view must be put forward in the form of Alternative Plans for the future of the enterprise. This is a noble idea and a number of experiments are already under way. In a few cases public money has been made available so that researchers can help groups of workers to develop plans within their union branch. Figure 1 illustrates a pattern of planning which is being used by a number of union branches in Scandinavia.

4. There are also indications that employee participation will encourage

[32]Tom Gore, "Training Patterns of Swedish Trade Unions," *Industrial and Commercial Training,* May 1977.

Figure 1   Planning in a Union Branch

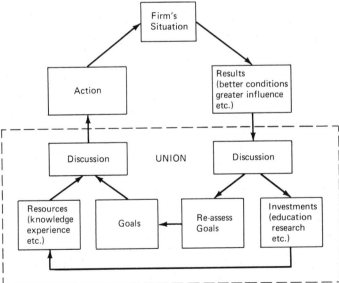

Source: K. Nygaard & O. T. Bergo, "The Trade Unions: New User of Research," University of Gothenburg, 1974.

changes in union organisation and may force mergers between unions. Where one union is able to represent all the employees in an industry or a firm, consultation is fairly straightforward. But if a number of unions are involved, complex processes of joint consultation are necessary to work out a consensus. Also, smaller unions may not be able to afford the research staff and the training facilities which will be necessary for them to fully represent their members in forward planning.[33]

Experience to date has also revealed a number of tasks for management:

1. to develop an atmosphere of trust in which two-way communication is possible;
2. to re-train supervisors and middle management so that they can adopt a participative style;
3. to keep employees and unions informed about company performance against objectives whilst maintaining normal commercial security;
4. to discover ways of minimising the delays in communication through several levels;
5. to maintain a sense of enterprise and risk-taking and avoid the tendency to make decisions on the basis of compromises and playing safe;
6. to assist trade union officers in sorting out inter-union conflicts and in gaining commitment from their members.

TECHNIQUES FOR POLITICAL PLANNING

The management tradition, in the U.K. at least, is one of political neutrality. Politicians are elected by the democratic process and it is expected that the government will act in the best interests of the nation as a whole. On the other hand, it is widely assumed that business is best left in the hands of businessmen with a minimum of government involvement.

For a variety of reasons, the energy crisis, unprecedented levels of inflation, persistent unemployment, the need to rejuvenate declining industries, etc., *the rules have changed.*

In recent years there has been:

1. a rapid growth in government spending and purchasing power,
2. an expansion of public ownership of industry,
3. the use of new government agencies to regulate and restructure industry,

[33]Lief Mills, "The Role of Trade Unions in Strategic Planning," *Long Range Planning,* April 1979.

4. an attempt to intervene in specific industries and in individual companies to influence management decisions on investment and employment, and

5. a flood of legislation expanding the range of government controls over prices and incomes, industrial democracy, "the quality of working life," environmental protection, race relations, equal opportunity for women and consumer protection.

In the face of continuous pressure from government agencies, left wing politicians, trade union officials and members of various social pressure groups, management have belatedly begun to realise that whether they like it or not their

Figure 2   *Management Decision-Making in a Mixed Economy*

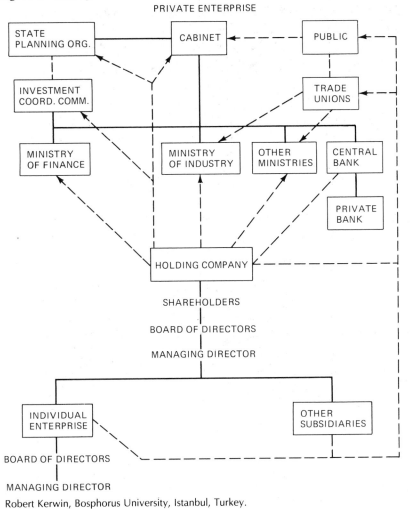

Robert Kerwin, Bosphorus University, Istanbul, Turkey.

businesses are involved in a political process. There is a debate going on continuously about the future of industry and its place in society. Proposals are being made by various pressure groups which are likely to have a critical impact on business and to contribute effectively to the discussion and management's interventions must be planned well in advance.[34]

It is not at all clear what form political planning or legislative planning will take. It will naturally vary with the size of the business, the degree of government influence and the issues at stake. However, the broad outlines of political planning are evident.

1. Political Mapping

The first stage is to gather information about the nature of the political environment. This means producing a "political map" of the main organisations and pressure groups which are active in an industry or region and in relation to

[34]Bernard Taylor, "Conflict of Values: The Central Strategy Problem," *Long Range Planning,* December, 1975.

Figure 3　Political Systems in the Food Industry—Introducing Margarine into South Africa (1966)

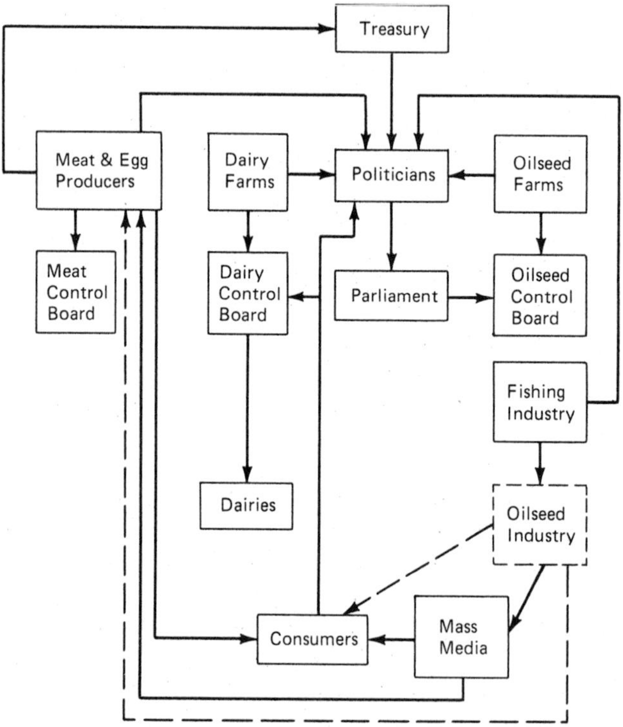

I. C. MacMillan, "Business Strategies for Political Action," *Journal of General Management,* Autumn 1974.

Figure 4   The British Hotel & Tourist Industry

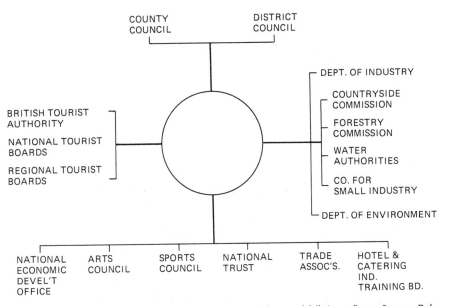

ASSOCIATIONS & OFFICIAL BODIES

COUNTY COUNCIL

DISTRICT COUNCIL

DEPT. OF INDUSTRY

COUNTRYSIDE COMMISSION

BRITISH TOURIST AUTHORITY

FORESTRY COMMISSION

NATIONAL TOURIST BOARDS

WATER AUTHORITIES

REGIONAL TOURIST BOARDS

CO. FOR SMALL INDUSTRY

DEPT. OF ENVIRONMENT

NATIONAL ECONOMIC DEVEL'T OFFICE

ARTS COUNCIL

SPORTS COUNCIL

NATIONAL TRUST

TRADE ASSOC'S.

HOTEL & CATERING IND. TRAINING BD.

Note: Most of these organisations have both elected members and full-time oficers. Source: Robert Perrin, Stanford Research Institute.

important issues e.g. legislation, planning permission, purchasing policy, government grants, import duties, etc. A number of political studies of this kind have been made.[35]

Figure 2, produced by Professor Robert Kerwin, former Director of Public Affairs with Mobil Oil Company, maps the external relationships of a private enterprise in Turkey. This makes the point dramatically. To quote Uwe Kitzinger, Dean of the European Business Institute at Fontainebleau: "To be in business is to be in politics because public policy is the dominant factor in the business environment." Figure 3 is an analysis by Professor Ian MacMillan of Columbia University, New York, showing the political relationships in the South African Food Industry produced in 1966 when a new margarine was introduced. Figure 4 by Robert Perrin of Stanford Research Institute displays the main associations and official bodies involved in the British Tourist Industry. Figure 5 from the British Gas Corporation, indicates the environmental interest groups which ought to be consulted in planning the construction of a new facility such as a gas holder.

[35]For example, I. C. MacMillan, "Business Strategies for Political Action," *Journal of General Management,* Autumn, 1974.

Figure 5 Consultation of Interest Groups—British Gas Corporation Project Planning

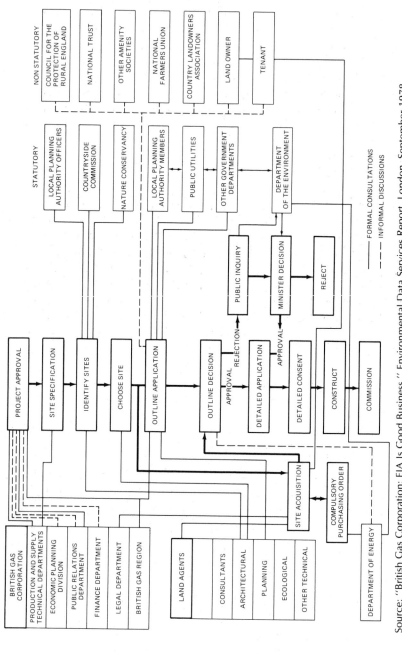

Source: "British Gas Corporation: EIA Is Good Business," Environmental Data Services Report, London, September 1978.

2. Analysis of Political Networks

Another approach is to trace the formal and informal networks which exist, to determine who is in a position to take the relevant decisions affecting the business and which individuals or groups can influence these decisions, together with an analysis of their relationships with the decision-makers and the pressures which they can bring to bear. This technique has been well demonstrated by the Tavistock Institute and other sociological research groups.[36]

The diagram in Figure 6 was developed to explain the "information and support networks" which are cultivated by senior administrators in local government.

3. Political Agenda

Also it is important to have an agenda of the social and political issues which are being debated in various political parties and action groups and which may become the subject of legislation or regulation in the next five to ten years.

[36]John Friend, et al, op. cit.

Figure 6   *Networks for Public Policy-Making*

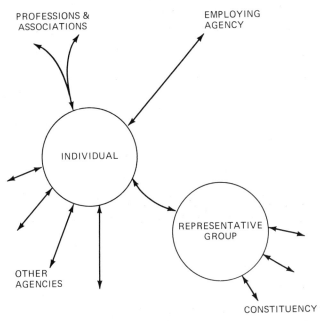

NETWORKS FOR PUBLIC POLICY-MAKING

PROFESSIONS & ASSOCIATIONS

EMPLOYING AGENCY

INDIVIDUAL

REPRESENTATIVE GROUP

OTHER AGENCIES

CONSTITUENCY

Source: J. K. Friend et al., *Public Planning: The Inter-Corporate Dimension.* (Tavistock 1974).

Figure 7   US Value-System Changes: 1969–1980 Forecast by General Electric

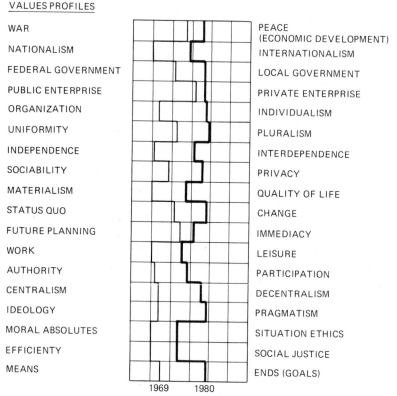

VALUES PROFILES

	1969	1980	
WAR			PEACE (ECONOMIC DEVELOPMENT)
NATIONALISM			INTERNATIONALISM
FEDERAL GOVERNMENT			LOCAL GOVERNMENT
PUBLIC ENTERPRISE			PRIVATE ENTERPRISE
ORGANIZATION			INDIVIDUALISM
UNIFORMITY			PLURALISM
INDEPENDENCE			INTERDEPENDENCE
SOCIABILITY			PRIVACY
MATERIALISM			QUALITY OF LIFE
STATUS QUO			CHANGE
FUTURE PLANNING			IMMEDIACY
WORK			LEISURE
AUTHORITY			PARTICIPATION
CENTRALISM			DECENTRALISM
IDEOLOGY			PRAGMATISM
MORAL ABSOLUTES			SITUATION ETHICS
EFFICIENTY			SOCIAL JUSTICE
MEANS			ENDS (GOALS)

Source: Ian H. Wilson, "Socio-Political Forecasting: A New Dimension to Strategic Planning," *Michigan Business Review,* July, 1974.

Typically, these issues are signalled well in advance. They are the subject of campaigns by pressure groups. They are the basis of proposals at Trade union conferences. They appear in party manifestos, are the subject of Royal Commissions and White Papers before they ever reach the statute book.

General Electric (U.S.A.) have made well-publicised studies of this kind analysing the demands of social pressure groups and attempting forecasts of sociological trends.[37] Figures 7 and 8 illustrate two approaches used by General Electric to forecast social changes. Figure 7 predicts changes in social values which are likely to occur in the U.S.A. during the 1970's. Figure 8 describes a method of arriving at an agenda of social issues. This involves listing the claims which interest groups are making on business and then cross-checking to deter-

[37]Earl B. Dunkel, William K. Reed and Ian H. Wilson, *The Business Environment of the Seventies—A Trend Analysis for Business Planning,* McGraw Hill, New York, 1970 and Ian H. Wilson "Forecasting Social and Political Trends" in Bernard Taylor and John Sparkes (Eds.) *Corporate Strategy and Planning,* Heinemann, London, 1977.

Figure 8 Analysing the Demands of Social Pressure Groups

SOCIAL PRESSURE GROUPS

DEMANDS ON THE FIRM	Consumer Protection	Ethnic Minorities	Environmental Protection	Equal Opportunity	Shareholders Rights	etc.
Marketing						
Production						
Personnel						
International						
etc.						

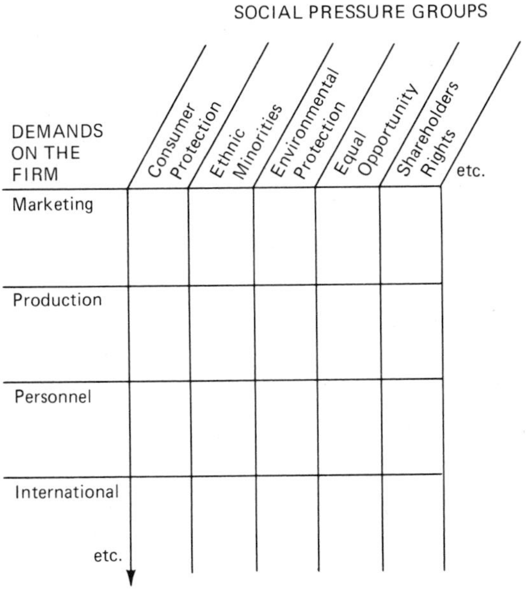

Source: Virgil B. Day, General Electric Company.

mine which of these demands are likely to increase over time because of the effect of various social trends such as increasing education or changes in population.

To quote Irving Shapiro, Chairman of the Board at E. I. Dupont:

"It is up to business to take the lead in focusing discussion on important questions before they become important issues."

4. Assessing Political Response

In relation to specific projects or products it is important to evaluate the likely response of social and political groups. This can be done conveniently by the use of some form of cross impact analysis e.g. by listing organisations or groups involved and estimating their likely reactions to a particular project, or alternatively, by looking at a political change e.g. a piece of legislation and evaluating its likely impact on various parts of the business.

Shell used a format for this purpose called a Societal Response Assessment Matrix.[38] (see Figure 9)

The purpose of the assessment is to examine the likely consequences of societal responses so that management can systematically adapt to them. "Constit-

[38]*Societal Response Profile Assessment Matrix,* Group Planning, Shell International Petroleum, London 1976.

Figure 9 Societal Response Assessment Matrix

CONCERNS / CONSTITUENTS	Economic					Societal				Involvement		
	Tax Revenues	Energy Security	Employment	Regional Development	Etc.	Safety	Regionalisation	Environmental Protection	Etc.	Information Disclosure	Consumer Relations	Etc.
Stakeholders												
Ministry of Energy	☐	☐	☐	☐	☐	☐	☐	☐	☐	☐	☐	☐
Shareholders	☐	☐	☐	☐	☐	☐	☐	☐	☐	☐	☐	☐
Employees	☐	☐	☐	☐	☐	☐	☐	☐	☐	☐	☐	☐
Etc.	☐	☐	☐	☐	☐	☐	☐	☐	☐	☐	☐	☐
Closely Involved Parties												
Bankers	☐	☐	☐	☐	☐	☐	☐	☐	☐	☐	☐	☐
Trade Unions	☐	☐	☐	☐	☐	☐	☐	☐	☐	☐	☐	☐
Customers	☐	☐	☐	☐	☐	☐	☐	☐	☐	☐	☐	☐
Etc.	☐	☐	☐	☐	☐	☐	☐	☐	☐	☐	☐	☐
Generally Involved Parties												
Environmentalists	☐	☐	☐	☐	☐	☐	☐	☐	☐	☐	☐	☐
Consumer Unions	☐	☐	☐	☐	☐	☐	☐	☐	☐	☐	☐	☐
Etc.	☐	☐	☐	☐	☐	☐	☐	☐	☐	☐	☐	☐

P. W. Beck, *Strategic Planning in the Royal Dutch Shell Group*, paper presented to the Institute of Management Science Conference on Corporate Strategic Planning, New Orleans, March 1977.

uents" include government departments, trade unions, etc. and their "concerns" cover areas such as tax, employment, safety, etc. The squares are coloured on a "traffic light" system to indicate the constituents' degree of concern. Then the matrix becomes a basis for discussing what action the company should take in relation to each issue and each group. The British Gas Corporation use an Environmental Impact Analysis as a form of check-list to describe and assess the potential effects of a new project on the surrounding environment: biological, aesthetic, land values, etc. (see Figure 10). Figure 11 illustrates the use of a Cross Impact Matrix to examine the consequences of political change on a business. For example we might ask what effect Spain's entry to the EEC might have on a Spanish automobile business. The same approach could be used to look at the likely effects of a change of regime in a developing country.

5. Organised Lobbying

Effective political action requires an organised pressure group. This means:

1. a permanent organisation with sufficient funds to appoint skilled professionals, not merely an ad hoc group hastily assembled to fight nationalisation or some other immediate threat;

2. an alliance of diverse and competitive interests representing an industry or a locality e.g. a chamber of commerce or an industry association rather than an individual firm;

3. the development of constructive and politically feasible proposals, in a form which politicians and officials can use instead of the more usual complaints and protests.[39]

Surveys suggest that businessmen tend to react to legislation in a negative way instead of anticipating an issue and putting forward their own proposals. Table 3 gives the results of a study of large businesses in the U.S.A. in the late sixties showing how the majority surveyed legislation but very few were prepared to participate in drafting new legislation. But, to quote Carl Desch, Senior Vice President of the First National City Bank:

"We have to worry about the three thousand bills that are introduced, not just the three hundred-odd that are passed."

As William May, Chairman of American Can says:

"Once the law is on the books, you have virtually lost the battle."

[39]Carol S. Greenwald, *Group Power Lobbying and Public Policy,* Praegar, New York, 1977.

Figure 10 Environmental Impact Analysis—British Gas Corporation Project Assessment

Section 1		Section 2		Section 3	
Checklist of Possible Products + Effects of Proposed Project	*Impact* ✕	*Description of Impact + Reference to Impact Statement (where relevant)*	*Assessment of Importance (+ or −)*	*Assessment of Effect &/or Comment on Promoter's Assessment*	*Assessment of Importance (+ or −)*
Biological a) flora b) fauna c) rare/unique Species & ecosystems					
Human activities + quality of life a) employment b) education c) recreation d) general life patterns e) health + safety					

Traffic
a) pedestrian
b) man-powered
c) animal
d) mechanical
   i) air
   ii) water
   iii) land, road and rail					

Infrastucture a) electricity b) water supplies c) sewerage d) telecommunications e) roads f) river & drainage					
Aesthetic/historic/ scientific a) land & sea scape b) urban landscape					

678

c) architectural features						
d) monuments						
e) visual impact						
i) near						
ii) far						
Land use/property values						
a) industrial						
b) mining/quarrying						
c) commercial						
d) residential						
e) farming						
f) forestry						
g) wilderness & open space						
Physical conditions						
a) earth						
i) surface						
ii) subsurface						
b) water						
i) quality						
ii) temperature						
iii) movement, etc.						
c) atmosphere						
i) climate						
ii) wind, etc.						
Waste products						
a) solid						
b) liquid						
c) gaseous + airborne						
d) smells						
e) noise						
Useful products						
a) solid						
b) liquid						
c) gaseous + airborne						
Effects on long term plans for land use						

Source: Environmental Data Services Report, September, 1979.

Figure 11   Cross Impact Matrix

EVENT / DIVISION	COMMON FISCAL POLICY	EMPLOYMENT POLICY	REGIONAL POLICY	INDUSTRIAL POLICY etc.
AXLES Purchasing Production Marketing Personnel Finance				
TRANSMISSIONS Purchasing Production Marketing Personnel Finance				
BRAKES Purchasing Production Marketing Personnel Finance etc.				

NOTE: IMPACT IS RANKED 1-5

Source: Robert Perrin, Stanford Research Institute.

In economic terms lobbying can be most cost-effective. For example, the strength of the agricultural lobby is well-known, both in the U.S.A. and in Europe. Carol Greenwald in her book on lobbying describes how U.S. dairymen's associations invested $600,000 to raise the milk price support subsidy in 1971 and received a 500% return on their investment.[40]

[40]Carol S. Greenwald, op. cit., p. 9.

Table 3   Corporate Political Activities: US Survey (1033 firms)

	%
Review legislative issues	98
Continuous or frequent review	63
Frequent presentations to government (mostly negative)	50
Proposals for new legislation	5

Source: The Role of Business in Public Affairs (Conference Board 1968).

6. Communications
Programmes

Management has the continuing task of marketing the company to the "stakeholders"—shareholders, financial institutions, dealers and distributors, suppliers and employees as well as the local community and various agencies of government.

Recent experience in Britain provides ample illustrations of this trend:

—the anti-nationalisation programmes of Tate and Lyle, the banks and the building industry;

—the employee communications campaigns of Chrysler U.K., British Airways and IBM. In 1976, for example, IBM launched a "two-way communications programme" in its European subsidiaries called *Dialogue 76* which involved 8,000 managers and resulted in a substantial rise in morale;[41]

—the regular use of opinion surveys and corporate image studies among employees, shareholders and various opinion-forming groups.

In most cases top management and the corporate planning team are closely involved in mounting these communications efforts and in certain cases, e.g. Chrysler U.K., the Corporate Plan has become the basis of a regular review of performance with employees.

7. Economic Impact Studies

The political process makes it possible for taxes to be raised and laws to be passed without any systematic attempt being made to assess their effects on business. Often the effect is disastrous. In recent years changes in Value Added Tax in the U.K. have crippled the boatbuilding and television tube industries and the taxation of stock appreciation did great damage to manufacturing companies before the taxation rules were amended. In the U.S.A., the Environment Protection Act has had a punitive effect, virtually outlawing a number of industries and handicapping others in international competition. And the field tests now required by the Food and Drug Administration have meant that only the largest firms can now afford to launch new drugs.

A most effective response to such legislation appears to be a well-publicised evaluation of the damage it is doing. Merrett and Sykes produced a most effective assessment of the British stock appreciation tax which led to its amend-

---

[41]Jacques Maisonrouge, "External Relations—The Challenge," *Chelwood Review*, B. A. T. Industries, 1978 No. 4.

Table 4   Analysing the Impact of Government Legislation

Type of Regulation	Appropriate	Questionable	Excessive
Environmental	42	2	19
Transportation	25	4	16
Health & Safety	12	1	9
Other	8	3	6
Total Regulatory Cost	87	10	50
%	59	7	34

Source: Business Week, April, 1977. Special Issue on Government Intervention.

ment. The British Food Manufacturers' Federation regularly surveys the effect of government price controls on the industry's cash flow and investment. Dow Chemicals have published widely their estimates of the inordinate cost of environmental protection.

Dow calculated (see Table 4) that government regulations covering environmental protection, transportation and health and safety etc. had cost them around $150 million in 1975 and $50 million of this was "excessive" i.e. the costs were incurred in meeting standards which were just not sensible. This kind of data is essential material for the public debate. To quote Robert Fegley, Communications Director of General Electric:

> "You can't beat somebody with nobody—and you can't beat something with nothing." [42]

8. Future Forecasts

A novel aspect of politics in recent years has been the growth of futures research as a background to the analysis of public policy. Nowadays, the public debate about major policy issues frequently entails the consideration of "alternative futures" for society. In Britain future government policies on Energy, Industry, Telecommunications and Education have become the subject of widespread public discussion. [43]

Certain States of the U.S.A., e.g. Hawaii and Iowa, have launched elaborate media campaigns to try to engage the public in debates about the future of their regions. And in the U.S.A. and in Western Europe, it is now common for

[42]"Government Intervention," *Business Week,* Special Issue, April 4, 1977.

[43]See for example: Raymond Williams, *Television Technology and Cultural Form,* Fontana, 1974.

governments to employ the services of Think Tanks and Futures Research Groups.[44]

Private institutes such as Hudson, Battelle and Stanford are widely used. Industry groups such as the Inter-Bank Research Organisation and the Chemical Industries Association are also engaged on Futures Studies.

It is essential that the point of view of business should be represented in these futures debates, by industries putting forward their visions of the future.

Indeed Theodore Levitt's injunction applies as much to industries as to individual companies:

"If you don't know where you're going, any road will lead you there."

Trade and professional associations have a growing responsibility in acting as a pressure group on behalf of their members. Their support is particularly important for the small businessman who cannot afford to do the necessary research and present his case on every political issue which may be important to his firm. Some industry associations are themselves too small to carry out this task and they will need to merge with other groups to set up the necessary organisation. Even in large associations, the work implies a re-orientation and the allocation of increased resources for research and external relations.[45]

9. Frequent Meetings with Government

In certain countries such as France and Sweden, close contacts between industrialists and civil servants are already established. But in others, such as Britain, relationships are less satisfactory. In some nationalised industries in Britain it is common practice—typically in June or July—for the top management team to review a limited number of key strategic issues with the relevant minister and his staff. This gives them an opportunity to influence government policy and to inform the politicians in advance what impact their policies may have on the industry. It also allows time for an interchange of views about the broad strategy for the business, before the preparation of detailed investment plans in the autumn.

[44]See: Congressional Research Service, *The States Look to the Future: A Survey of Tomorrow/2000/ Goals Organisations,* Library of Congress, Washington, D.C., 1975. Also: European Cultural Foundation, *Europe 2000: The Future Is Tomorrow,* Martinus Nijhoff, The Hague, 1972. Gunnar Hedlund and Lars Otterbeck, *The Multinational Corporation, The Nation State and The Trade Unions: A European Perspective,* Kent State University Press, Ohio, 1977. H. V. Perlmutter, F. R. Root and L. Plante, "Responses of U.S.—Based M.N.C.'s to Alternative Public Policy Futures" *Columbia Journal of World Business,* Fall, 1973.

[45]See, for example: Victor E. Line, *Interaction Between Government and Industry,* Industry Education and Research Foundation, London, 1970, p. 20.

Closer contacts with government could also prove helpful to the management of large private firms and it may become more common for businessmen to have regular discussions with government officials and politicians about industrial strategy, energy strategy, transportation policy etc.

CONCLUSION

In this paper I have suggested that in the context of a changing industrial environment we need to revise our ideas about Corporate Planning.

1. The Changed Political Environment

We must recognise that in recent years there has been a shift of power in society. At one time the autonomy of management was unquestioned. Now management decisions are regularly and successfully challenged by groups of employees, community interests and by numerous agencies of government.

Management is now faced by:

a. **Trade Unions** which have unprecedented political strength based on monopoly power, a close alliance with left-wing political parties and the proven ability of small groups of workers to bring modern society to a halt by industrial action.

b. **Pressure Groups** which are organised as never before to promote the cause of Consumer Protection, Conservation, Equal Opportunity for Women and Racial Equality.

c. **Political parties and government officials** which are committed to involvement in the management of industry in a way previously not contemplated except in times of war; through outright nationalisation, direct investment via government holding companies, the regulation of prices, wages and dividends and a whole spate of legislation affecting conditions of employment, industrial relations, industrial democracy, and programmes directed at the promotion and protection of specific industries and regions where jobs (and votes) are at stake.

2. Planning as a Political Process

In these changed circumstances it is unrealistic for management to regard Corporate Planning as a process which concerns management alone. They must find ways of involving and influencing the decision-processes of other interests and organisations who have the power to prevent their plans from being realised.

It is natural, too, that representatives of public authorities, groups of employees and community interests should wish to influence the decisions of businessmen regarding numbers of workers to be employed, conditions of work, levels of investment, location of factories, arrangements for pollution control etc.

Corporate Planning must be regarded not merely as a process internal to the company but also as a political and inter-organisational process. Firms in fact need to have a "foreign policy" towards other groups and organisations.

3. Sector and Regional Planning

If we are to solve the problems which face societies in Western Europe: regenerating manufacturing industry, meeting international competition, creating new jobs, finding secure sources of supply for food and raw materials, and controlling inflation, I believe we must have more effective industrial planning by sector and by region.

There is no alternative in many industries to a partnership between government and industry. Competition in certain industries—shipbuilding, steel, aerospace, even motor cars—takes the form of competition between alliances of major companies and national governments and there is no way in which an individual European company is going to compete successfully with a foreign company—in Russia, the U.S.A., Japan or the Third World—which has government backing.

However, to have effective industrial planning involves the creation of new institutions, new procedures and new relationships between government and industry. In Britain, the idea of industrial policy is debated in terms of political ideologies—as if the choice is between *either* a Free Market Economy *or* a state on the East European model. Instead of discussing political dogma we should follow the example of the Japanese, the Swedes and the French and get down to the practical task of developing the institutions we need to plan a new industrial structure. This will require the efforts of our best businessmen, civil servants and trade union leaders.

4. Employee Participation in Planning

One of the most remarkable developments in recent years is the demand of ordinary people—workers and citizens—for the right to participate in the decisions which affect them. And one of the greatest challenges to managers and administrators is to find a way to widen the planning process so as to engage the interest and mobilise the ideas and energies of large groups of employees and citizens.

From their point of view, on the shop-floor and in the neighbourhood, much of present-day planning is a charade—a confidence trick—a way of short-circuiting the democratic process. When managers and public officials talk about strategic plans, the man in the street is likely to ask "Whose plans?" "Whose objectives?." They are the ones who suffer the plans or receive the plans but they have no say in determining their own future. To quote Alvin Toffler: "Some people plan, others are planned upon." Present approaches to participation do not go far enough—organisation development programmes, works councils, autonomous work groups, all have the common feature that they concentrate on ways and means of achieving objectives and implementing plans which have been developed elsewhere.

Now, groups of workers are appearing who are producing their own Corporate Plans, and groups of citizens are coming forward with their own plans for new airports and new roads. If management do not find ways of including workers in the debate about the future of the enterprise, they may find their employees working with their unions and government agencies to achieve their own Alternative Corporate Plans.

5. Political Planning

To plan effectively in the 1980's requires new skills, new approaches, and new techniques which we might label collectively Political Planning or Legislative Planning. Some businesses—in the defence industries, in transportation and in energy—have traditionally had close contacts with government, and their managers have had to develop the necessary political contacts, an understanding of the world of government and the industrywide organisations which are required to lobby government effectively. In other industries the need for political activity is novel: the information systems, the relationships and the political organisation have yet to be developed.

In small and medium-size companies it is likely that the Chairman and the Board of Directors will be able to handle government and industry relations on an informal basis. In large companies, however, it will be necessary to appoint specialist staff to deal with "Public Affairs" or "External Affairs."

And we may see a wider use of formal techniques for analysing and forecasting the political environment and for planning and organising business activity in this area in a more constructive and systematic way.